enterprise

William B. GARTNER

Clemson University

with

Marlene G. BELLAMY

SOUTH-WESTERN
CENGAGE Learning

Australia • Brazil • Japan • Korea • Mexico • Singapore • Spain • United Kingdom • United States

SOUTH-WESTERN
CENGAGE Learning™

Enterprise

William B. Gartner with Marlene G. Bellamy

Vice President of Editorial, Business: Jack W. Calhoun

Editor-in-Chief: Melissa Acuna

Senior Acquisitions Editor: Michele Rhoades

Developmental Editor: Ohlinger Publishing Services

Editorial Assistant: Ruth Belanger

Marketing Manager: Nathan Anderson

Marketing Coordinator: Suellen Ruttkay

Senior Marketing Communications Manager: Jim Overly

Senior Content Project Manager: Kim Kusnerak

Media Editor: Rob Ellington

Frontlist Buyer, Manufacturing: Doug Wilke

Production Service: Integra Software Services Pvt. LTD

Compositor: Integra Software Services Pvt. LTD

Senior Art Director: Tippy McIntosh

Cover/Internal Designer: c miller design

Rights Account Manager—Text: Mollika Basu

Photography Manager: Robyn Young

Photo Researcher: Rachel Tisdale/Prepress

For product information and technology assistance, contact us at
Cengage Learning Customer & Sales Support, 1-800-354-9706

For permission to use material from this text or product, submit all requests online at **www.cengage.com/permissions**
Further permissions questions can be emailed to **permissionrequest@cengage.com**

Library of Congress Control Number: 2008939487

ISBN-13: 978-0-324-13085-0

ISBN-10: 0-324-13085-6

Student Edition:

ISBN-13: 978-0-324-78533-3

ISBN-10: 0-324-78533-X

South-Western Cengage Learning
5191 Natorp Boulevard
Mason, OH 45040
USA

Cengage Learning products are represented in Canada by Nelson Education, Ltd.

For your course and learning solutions, visit **www.cengage.com/southwestern.**

Purchase any of our products at your local college store or at our preferred online store **www.ichapters.com**

Printed in Canada
1 2 3 4 5 12 11 10 09 08

WBG—Dedication Haikus:

Luther Burbank was
A Baumgartner, my parents
Sought Rich Land vistas

Karl Vesper made real
Combinations, Schumpeter's
Theory visible

Connections Eames said
Were more important than things
Themselves, Stevens

Where are the maker's
Marks? Jerry Katz maps
Entrepreneurship

Get off your beach! Swim
In the big waves. Maryse and
Ellie beckon now.

MGB—

To my husband Don and my daughter Rebecca who supported my need to write
when the muse was with me, even if it meant well into the evening and on weekends,
and in memory of my Siamese cat Sabrina (and her successors Yofi and Shayna)
who provided a special brand of editorial oversight with her forays across
the keyboard.

Enterprise—(1) a willingness to take initiative;
(2) an organized, systematic, and purposeful activity;
(3) a project that is complicated and risky.

Enterpriser—one who undertakes an enterprise.

This book is about how to make things happen. We purposely use the word *enterprise* and *enterpriser* throughout the book, rather than words like *entrepreneur* and *manager* because we want to put you into a new mindset where you see yourself in the role of the enterpriser: someone who takes initiative to organize a project in situations with some complications and risk. When someone makes things happen, that is what they are doing—enterprising.

The phrase, "a willingness to take initiative" has many sides. We are all willing to take initiative in situations where we know we will immediately benefit from our actions. If you invested $100 in a U.S. series EE savings bond on September 31, 2008, you would receive $101.40 on October 1, 2009. That return is certain. The particular action of investing money has a specific future consequence. But, what about all of the other activities you could be involved in where the outcomes are much more uncertain and the outcomes much more unknowable? If you invested $100 in the creation of a new business, how much would you likely receive a year from now? It is probably difficult to know, for most new efforts, what the specific outcomes from particular actions are likely to be. So, under what conditions are you willing to take initiative?

You may be familiar with the phrase "Fools rush in where angels fear to tread." The challenge that we all face with situations where we can take initiative is in determining, to the best of our knowledge and abilities, whether our future actions will be foolish. Given that jobs and careers are unstable and short term, we are frequently put in situations where we have to make judgments about our future: Is this course of action a good one to take?

Enterprise focuses on skills to evaluate and actualize opportunities that will be best for *your* life. We are less likely to be foolish in our actions when we know who we are and what we want. We are less likely to be foolish in our actions if we can better determine whether certain opportunities are worthy of our time and effort. We are less likely to be foolish if we can better determine whether the opportunity is feasible, and we can risk being foolish when we know what the consequences of foolishness are. (As we know from Shakespeare, sometimes playing the part of the fool is the smart way to go.)

The process of getting things done cannot be done alone. It would be difficult to achieve anything without the involvement and assistance of other people and organizations. Think about how many activities you can do that don't involve resources, products, materials, or the interaction and involvement of other people. (We can think of only a few actions: singing and talking to yourself.) If you write something, for example, then you are probably using a pencil or pen and paper that have been made by someone else and shipped and delivered to a store, where you purchased them. Writing depends on other people for the materials to write with. Few of us make our own clothes, build our own houses, grow our own food, create our own entertainment, etc. We live primarily in an organizational world where our ability to make things happen requires that we understand how to create and develop enterprises to achieve our goals.

The abilities and skills to achieve our goals require that we learn about how to organize in a systematic and purposeful way the activities and efforts of others. When we create an enterprise we are concerned with how all of the various interactions among others—customers, employees, suppliers, government regulators, competitors—play out in a way that provides benefits for ourselves and others. An important paradox of the process of enterprising is that the more successful enterprisers are also those individuals who provide the most value and benefits to others. Enterprisers are involved in creating "win-win" situations.

Finally, the process of enterprising is complicated and risky. Even with thorough preparation and analysis, there are no certainties that a particular enterprise will be successful. Part of the skills and insights of successful enterprisers involves their willingness to judge and navigate the risks and uncertainties that are inherent in all future activities. When events don't turn out as planned, enterprisers have the resilience, fortitude, and adaptability to change. Failing is a part of the process of learning. There are no guarantees in the world of enterprise but that makes it all the more fun, interesting, and rewarding when events play out in your favor. The choice in the world of enterprise is to get into the game rather than watch from the sidelines.

Development of the Text

How many times have you heard these words: "The world is different now." "Times have changed." "I remember when, the way things used to be . . ." Well, the world *is* different. One just needs to watch the news or read the paper to see that "the way things used to be" is no longer. The world is more complicated. There is more competition. We live in a time when people vie for jobs and resources not only locally or nationally but also internationally. What people do in India or China or Botswana or Chile affects us in Detroit or San Antonio or Yakima or Red Rock. There is no denying that the ways people were successful in the past may not provide the same game plan for success in the future.

Few individuals are going to work in the same job for an entire career. At various points in our lives, we might work for a large company, be self-employed, expand self-employment into a business with employees, engage in independent consulting, start a business for another organization, or work in a smaller company. Indeed, we often have multiple jobs at the same time: working full time for a large company while we have a part-time business on the side or undertaking some consulting while we are working at starting our own business. In a world where everyone is likely to bounce from working in a small or a large business, to being an employee or an employer, to serving as a consultant or a client, we will need a new mindset plus new skills and knowledge to take advantage of these new and ever changing opportunities.

We decided to write *Enterprise* because "enterprise" is not a unique kind of personality, a special kind of job or role, or a unique lifestyle. It seemed to us that the word *entrepreneur* carries too much baggage about individuals who have a special set of personality characteristics or skills and abilities or achievements (e.g., Bill Gates, Richard Branson, and Mark Cuban) that then put them at a level of success few others believe they can achieve. Entrepreneurship seems to be all about business success rather than all about how people go about accomplishing things. And, it seemed to us that the word *manager* or *business owner* seemed to be words that are too passive. "To manage" seems to be more reactive, like tending sheep, rather than an activity that is pro-active and oriented toward risk taking and achievement.

So, we chose *enterprise* to constantly remind you that the mindset, skills, and abilities we offer in this textbook do require a different way of thinking. And, that becoming an "enterpriser"—someone who undertakes an enterprise—is a goal anyone can achieve. "To enterprise," then, is not a choice that only a few people will be making. In the future, we will all need to be enterprisers.

Approach of the Text

This textbook is organized into 20 chapters and 4 appendixes. *Enterprise* concerns itself with three levels of analyzing the situation you are in (i.e., by environment, person, and business) and introduces three levels of change (recognizing and developing opportunities, progress and growth, and transformation). Understanding how to enterprise involves navigating among the three levels of analysis and the three levels of change.

Three Levels of Analysis

By recognizing the three levels of analysis, students realize that their success in enterprise (business level) is dependent on their context (environment level) and their interests, goals, skills, and abilities (person level).

The Environment

A central theme of *Enterprise* is that enterprisers have to be attentive to what's going on internally and externally. Enterprises exist in a world and national economy, a political and regulatory system, a financial and banking system, an industry, and in a space where social networks and relationships among customers, suppliers, investors, and other community stakeholders matter. By addressing these environmental topics, students will be better prepared to make successful business decisions.

The Person

The textbook challenges students to explore their personal goals to see how their own lives mesh with their professional objectives. *Enterprise* focuses on developing enterprising ways of thinking and enterprising skills, rather than worrying whether a person has the right kind of motivations or the right personality to be an entrepreneur or small business owner. All individuals are enterprisers! Everyone, at some point in their lives, has to initiate, plan, and execute new ideas and projects.

Enterprise looks at four ways that entrepreneurs think about their situations and their approaches to solving problems that relate to enterprising success. Through self-assessments and other exercises, students are trained to take on an enterprising mindset. Four of these ways of thinking include the following:

- Attribution: How you explain the past

- Expectancies: How you explain the future

- Optimism: Expecting good things will happen

- Problem solving: Developing attitudes and skills to accomplish planned goals and deal with unforeseen issues

In terms of skills, enterprisers need the knowledge and capabilities to get what they want and to get the resources they need. *Enterprise* addresses skills involving personal planning and goal setting, networking, negotiation, and persuasion. Enterprise is a form of action. Students can learn these skills to actualize what is important to them.

The Business

At the level of the business, *Enterprise* focuses on the characteristics of enterprise success. The core feature of this discussion involves developing a business concept and exploring each enterprise's business model. The business concept is the enterprise's "story" that answers the 4Cs:

- Customer: Who is the customer?

- Consideration: What does the customer want?

- Connection: How is this consideration going to be provided?

- Commitment: Are you committed to this opportunity?

In developing the business model, we add a fifth C:

- Capital: Can you make money doing this?

The business model is the formula for how an enterprise makes money.

Three Levels of Change

Enterprise considers the life cycle of the person, business, and environment. Personal and business success is evolutionary; that is, the criteria for success that an individual and a business requires will change over time. Enterprise ownership, like any other job, should be considered as something temporary in everyone's work career. Being able to navigate through the transitions between startup, ownership and management, and divestment of an enterprise are critical skills. Individuals need capabilities to separate themselves from their enterprises. We all need skills at reaping the benefits of our present activities and freeing ourselves to undertake new challenges with new rewards. As economic and industry conditions change, enterprisers need skills to recognize how these environmental factors will impact their personal and business success.

Emergence: Recognizing and Developing Opportunities

This textbook shows that recognizing and developing opportunities are skills that can be used throughout the life of a person and a business. These skills can be used in a multitude of situations, not only for starting and developing a business. *Enterprise* suggests that recognizing and developing opportunities occurs in other business settings (corporations, governments, and nonprofits), as well as in personal projects, team projects, and other venues where goals are identified and realized. We devote the final chapter of the book to exploring social enterprise in all of its facets.

Newness: Progress and Growth

Enterprise covers topics involved in managing and growing enterprises, and offers examples and explores the skills for managing and monitoring personal goals and aspirations. One important perspective of *Enterprise* involves the affirmation of all kinds of enterprises as outcomes of an individual's choices and interests. We celebrate what are typically called lifestyle-type businesses: businesses that do not have rapid rates in sales or employee growth. All businesses are, in fact, lifestyle businesses: The growth of a business is determined, in part, by choices made by enterprisers, their skills and abilities, and environmental and industrial factors. Enterprisers must choose and be aware of the kind of enterprises that are appropriate for their goals, abilities, and skills and that fit the context of the industry and environment their enterprises will compete in. High growth enterprises are often inappropriate for many enterprisers and for many industries. Students should not be ashamed to choose a very small or low-growth business that supports their goals and interests. And, many small enterprises provide substantial financial rewards without the hassles of managing employees. Small can be beautiful!

Transformation

All individuals, environments, and businesses have a life cycle of initiation, growth, and, eventually, decline and/or change. All good things come to an end. Just as people age and their interests and goals change over time, an enterprise also ages and changes. *Enterprise* provides insights into how individuals evaluate the achievement of their goals for their lives and for their businesses. In this stage the enterpriser re-evaluates goals and priorities and celebrates past achievements as a way to transition the ownership and management of the business to others.

Organization of the Text

Part 1—An Enterprising Framework

The first five chapters of the book provide a basis for thinking about the nature of an enterprise in terms of context (person, business, and environment) and process (emergence, newness, and transformation). It is very important to see that context and process matters, particularly in how the kinds of businesses enterprisers develop significantly impact their own goals and aspirations. Each enterprise has its own needs and demands that are different from the needs and demands of their enterprisers. Recognizing what contextual factors are influencing the situations enterprisers are in is critical for reaching their own goals.

At the level of the person, we will also look at the wide variety and kinds of people who are likely to become enterprisers, and begin to lay out some of the ways enterprisers think about their situations so that they can make things happen. We also explore the essential skills enterprisers need: goal setting, persuasion, negotiation, and networking.

At the level of the business, students learn about the ways businesses are legally formed. These legal forms (sole-proprietorship, partnership, corporations, and not-for-profits) offer different paths for an enterpriser to develop a business. These legal forms both enable and limit the ways an enterprise can function and act in certain situations.

Finally, we look at the legal and regulatory environment that increasingly plays a significant role in how businesses operate.

Part 2—The Enterprising Process

This section of the book explores how opportunities are recognized, developed, and exploited through the process of creating opportunities, determining feasibility, and business planning. The creation of an opportunity intersects with the skills, knowledge, and interests of the enterpriser with an ever-changing environment. Enterprisers work to leverage their own skills and pay attention to the ways the environment changes. They also develop habits that can increase their luck. While many opportunities might prove to be worth pursuing, the process of feasibility analysis explores whether an opportunity is doable and whether it will make money. Finally, for those opportunities that are feasible, an enterpriser will enhance the likelihood of getting an enterprise started by developing a business plan. From our perspective, a business plan lays out the specific resources, tasks, and activities necessary to transform the opportunity into an ongoing business.

Part 3—Enterprising Strategies

A unique feature of this textbook is its focus on the many different ways enterprisers go about starting new enterprises. There is no one right way to develop a successful enterprise. We offer insights into eight major pathways that combine an enterpriser's personal capabilities and experiences, startup actions, enterprise strategies, and environmental characteristics into an *archetype* (a model or format) for enterprise success. Two of the major ways enterprisers develop businesses (purchasing an existing business and franchising) are explored in detail.

Part 4—The Enterprising Mind

Enterprise is fundamentally a book that focuses on creating successful individuals. This section of the book reemphasizes the importance of one's own values and goals, and it explores how these values are heavily influenced by the kinds of commitments we make and the kinds of stories we tell about ourselves to others. Individuals can readjust their thinking in significant ways to become more aware of the many possibilities and options in their future. Enterprisers need to be grounded in how they will satisfy the four different goals of a well-lived life: achievement, significance, legacy, and happiness.

Part 5—Progress, Growth, and Transformation

Once an enterprise has been created, it needs to be developed, sustained, and transformed over time. We focus on the identities of the enterprise and enterpriser by looking at how to develop and tell stories about their unique capabilities and attributes: the brand. An enterprise's (and enterpriser's) brand positions it to successfully compete among other businesses and individuals in the marketplace. Students learn techniques for marketing and promoting their brands as well as ways to sell the brand's capabilities and attributes to customers.

Enterprises are sustained and grow because they are successful at identifying and solving customer needs and problems. We explore how to engage customers, provide cost effective and profitable solutions, and adapt and respond to changing customer interests and desires over time. One of the ways to successfully grow an enterprise is through the imaginative use of resources that enterprisers have at hand: their own knowledge, skills, and efforts; their use of relationships (family, friends, acquaintances, and business colleagues); and their situation and location. We also look at how to acquire and gain control over resources owned by others.

Enterprisers learn that organization growth is only sustainable through the identification and development of the knowledge, skills, and talents of others, besides the enterprisers themselves. Students acquire skills to find and work with outsiders (such as mentors, advisors, consultants, and service providers) and insiders (such as employees and independent contractors) to meet customer needs and adapt to changing competitive conditions.

Financial success is the outcome of both doing the right things and doing things right. Enterprisers acquire techniques to monitor and control the operations of their enterprise as well as explore their own changing values and motivations for owning and operating their enterprises. Finally, enterprisers realize that not only will their enterprises change over time, but they will change too. Students will identify the signs that point to developing the "second half" of their lives, and acquire knowledge about how enterprises often go through transformations such as family enterprises, ESOPs (Employee Stock Ownership Plans), publicly held firms, sale, dissolution, and bankruptcy.

Part 6—Creating the Social Enterprise

Enterprises can be created that focus not solely on the values and interests of the enterprisers who created them but more on the values, needs, and interests of others: the social enterprise. The last chapter of *Enterprise* explores how individuals create enterprises for a social purpose (e.g., solving a social problem or market failure) that generates value for others while operating in a financially efficient and effective manner with the innovative capabilities of a privately owned business. Social enterprises, then, have:

- An *enterprise orientation:* They have a focus on customers—but more broadly defined than customers in Chapters 13 and 14.

- *Social aims:* The values of the organization focus on the community and the environment.

- *Social ownership:* Often social enterprises are owned, but more likely they are overseen, by members of the community. These members are accountable to a wider group of stakeholders concerned with having a social, environmental, or economic impact on others.

Students develop an awareness of the many different kinds of social enterprises that have successfully been created, the variety of business models used in social enterprises, and strategies for effectively operating social enterprises.

Chapter Structure

Each chapter includes these features to aid students in their mastery of the material:

1. Key Concepts—The chapter opens with an outline of its fundamental objectives.

2. Introduction—Offers some insights into key issues and problems the chapter will address.

3. Topics—Provides examples, description, and analysis of ideas and subjects critical for enterprising.

4. Enterprisers—Each chapter has a short case that requires students to make decisions by applying the topic material to actual small businesses. These cases are accompanied by videos that are available on the website.

5. Enterprising Ethics—These boxes focus on the ethical implications of the material and engage students by posing critical thinking questions that lead to good class discussions.

6. An Enterprising World—These short boxes show how even small businesses connect to the global marketplace; they also include several discussion questions.

7. Summary—Important highlights of the topics in each chapter are provided.

8. Review Questions—Questions specific to exploring the topic material in each chapter are offered to reemphasize critical ideas and issues.

9. Applying What You've Learned—A variety of exercises are provided for students to take the topic material and relate it to their own experiences and to the enterprise opportunities they might plan to develop.

10. Enterprisers on the Web—This section points to materials, exercises, and examples of topic ideas and issues that students can easily access through the Web as a way to expand their options for learning about enterprising.

Supplements

Instructor's Resource CD-ROM (ISBN 0-324-13086-4)

This CD provides instructors with "one-stop shopping" for various teaching resources, including the chapter PowerPoint slides, the Instructor's Manual, and the Computerized Test Bank.

PowerPoint Presentation Slides

Developed by Charlie T. Cook, University of West Alabama, in close coordination with the text authors, the slides provide a comprehensive review of each chapter in the book. Also available online at www.cengage.com/management/gartner.

Instructor's Manual

The instructor's manual for *Enterprise* was prepared by Mary E. Gorman, Ph.D., University of Cincinnati, and includes the following content:

- Key Concepts as described in the text.

- Chapter Outline of main headings with developed lecture notes and references to all exhibits.

- Developed Answers for the discussion questions that accompany the two box features, An Enterprising World and Enterprising Ethics.

- Developed Answers for the Enterprisers Video Case Studies discussion questions.

- Answers to Review Questions.

- Suggested Answers and Suggested Instructor Strategies for the activities presented in Applying What You've Learned.

- Suggested Instructor Strategies for the activities in Enterprisers on the Web.

Also available online at www.cengage.com/management/gartner.

Test Bank

The ExamView computerized testing system is an easy-to-use test-creation program that is compatible with Microsoft Windows and Macintosh and enables instructors to create printed tests, Internet tests, and LAN-based tests quickly. The QuickTest Wizard lets test generators assemble a test in minutes, using a step-by-step selection process.

Instructors can choose from over 1,000 questions in true/false, multiple choice, and short essay formats. The printed test bank can be downloaded at www.cengage.com/management/gartner.

Gartner Enterprise Product Support Website (www.cengage.com/management/gartner)

Instructors can go to this site to download the text supplements and glossary.

Enterprise Online (www.cengage.com/management/enterpriseonline)

Available with every new book via a bind-in card, this site offers broad instructional and student support, including:

- Interactive Quizzes—These quizzes (available for every chapter) offer students a quick check of their understanding of the chapter material.

- Complete Sample Business Plan—The Beau-Ties business plan is discussed in Chapter 8, *Business Plans and Planning*, and the entire plan can be viewed here.

- Small Business School Videos to accompany Enterprisers Case Studies—Small Business School, the series on PBS stations, is hosting the video materials for this book. At the special link provided, students are taken inside the largest video library in the world about small companies. On PBS since 1994, every episode delves inside the mind of an owner to discover why the business was started and what steps that owner had to take to turn an idea into profits. Owners from San Diego to Boston and from Miami to Seattle talk to the camera and tell their own story about what it takes to start, run, and grow a business. Watch, listen, and learn.

- Flashcards—Students can test their understanding of key terms.

WebTutor on WebCT and WebTutor on Blackboard

WebTutor on WebCT and WebTutor on Blackboard complement *Enterprise* by providing interactive reinforcements that help students grasp key concepts. WebTutor's online teaching and learning environment brings together content management, assessment, communication, and collaboration capabilities to enhance in-class instruction or deliver distance learning. For more information, including a demo, visit http://webtutor.cengage.com.

Final Remarks

"Before you can think out of the box, you have to start with a box."—Twyla Tharp

Chris Miller, of c miller design, who designed the cover of this book (as well as the format of the book's contents) did a very insightful job of capturing, in a visual way, the book's essential perspective. We think of *Enterprise* much like a tool-kit of knowledge, attitudes, skills, and actions that can enable others to engage in enterprise. The tool kit is the box that one starts with, and, after gaining the tools in the box, one is really ready for "out of the box" thinking. Second, the achievements we attain, begin, always, in smaller forms and sizes. We take the adage "Mighty oaks from little acorns grow," seriously. Whatever one hopes to achieve in life always begins small, like a seed, and then can flourish. On the cover, the little "enterprise" begins in the foreground of the larger ENTERPRISE that eventually emerges.

This book is a collaborative effort to develop a text that provides the latest knowledge and insights about enterprise in a style that is accessible, easy to read, and interesting. Thank you for using this text.

William B. Gartner
Arthur M. Spiro Professor of Entrepreneurial Leadership
Clemson University

Marlene Bellamy
Writeline Associates

Acknowledgments

The creation and development of this book has been an enterprise itself. There are so many people who have played a significant role in turning this book from an idea into a reality. We have had opportunities to work with many innovative and enthusiastic colleagues at various universities (University of Virginia, Georgetown University, San Francisco State University, the University of Southern California, and Clemson University) who have been so important to our development as teachers and writers. We are particularly indebted to Tom O'Malia and Bill Crookston at the University of Southern California for their insights and collaborative efforts to imbue inspiration and passion into the practice of entrepreneurship. Caron St. John at Clemson University has shown how to develop students into collaborative innovators and community entrepreneurs. At Cengage Learning, John Szilagyi played a significant role in convincing us of the value of developing a new approach toward a textbook that looks at entrepreneurship, management, and small business. Michele Rhoades has continued to provide a stable and constant route for the completion of this work through the ups and downs of the corporate landscape. Tippy McIntosh worked to insure that the look of *Enterprise* was consistent with the book's ideas and views. Monica Ohlinger (Ohlinger Publishing Services) was the glue that kept this project from falling apart. Without her constant encouragement, humorous cajoling, and focus on deadlines, this book would not have been completed.

For their helpful suggestions during the preparation of this book, we are especially grateful to the following individuals:

Robin Anderson, University of Portland

Marilyn Besich, MSU, Great Falls College of Technology

Dr. Dorothy S. Gleckner, Bergen Community College

Jack P. Doo, Jr., California State University, Stanislaus

Dr. Todd A. Finkle, Fitzgerald Institute for Entrepreneurial Studies, University of Akron

Barbara Frazier, Western Michigan University

Dr. Dorothy S. Gleckner, Bergen Community College

Mary E. Gorman, University of Cincinnati

Daniel R. Hogan, Jr., Loyola University in New Orleans

Norma Juma, University of Texas at Arlington

Karen G. Killinger, Salt Lake Community College

Richard Kimbrough, University of Nebraska, Lincoln

Antoinette (Toni) Knechtges, Eastern Michigan University

Donald L. Lester, Ph.D., Arkansas State University

Gideon D. Markman, Ph.D., Colorado State University

John V. Mullane, Middle Tennessee State University

Margo Reign, University of Delaware

William J. Rossi, University of Florida

Dr. Milton Silver, Ph.D., Le Bow College of Business, Drexel University

Marcene Sonneborn, Syracuse University

Kenneth R. Taurman, Jr., JD, Indiana University Southeast

Amy M. Tomas, Ph.D., University of Vermont

Dr. Robert Wyatt, Drury University

contents

William B. Gartner

William B. Gartner is the Arthur M. Spiro Professor of Entrepreneurial Leadership at Clemson University. He received all of his degrees (B.A., MBA, and Ph.D.) from the University of Washington. Prior to joining Clemson University, he was on the faculty at the University of Virginia, Georgetown University, San Francisco State University, and the University of Southern California. In 2005, he received the FSF-NUTEK Award, which is an international award for outstanding accomplishments in entrepreneurship and small business research that was instituted by the Swedish Foundation for Small Business Research (FSF) and the Swedish Business Development Agency (NUTEK). He is a research fellow at ESBRI—Entrepreneurship and Small Business Research Institute in Stockholm, Sweden, and on the Board of Advisors for IDEA—the International Danish Entrepreneurship Academy. Professor Gartner is one of the co-founders of the Entrepreneurship Research Consortium, which initiated, developed, and manages the Panel Study of Entrepreneurial Dynamics (PSED). The PSED is a longitudinal dataset on enterprisers in the process of starting businesses (http://www.psed.info). His research has been published in *Journal of Business Venturing, Entrepreneurship Theory and Practice,* the *Academy of Management Review, Journal of Management, Small Business Economics,* and the *Journal of Small Business Management,* and he has received funding from the Kauffman Foundation, Coleman Foundation, U.S. Department of Education, U.S. Small Business Administration, the Small Business Foundation of America, the *Los Angeles Times*, the Pacific Gas and Electric Company, the Corporate Design Foundation, and the National Endowment for the Arts. His research explores how enterprisers find and identify opportunities, recognize and solve startup problems, and undertake actions to successfully launch new businesses. He is also involved in developing methods, materials, and a scholarly community for the study of entrepreneurial narrative.

Marlene G. Bellamy

Marlene G. Bellamy formed Writeline Associates in 1990 after 13 years as an investment and corporate banker. She has applied her finance experience to the academic and corporate arenas, collaborating with authors and publishers on 15 major college and graduate-level business textbooks and related educational materials. Her contributions include chapters; special features such as chapter opening vignettes, practitioner and investor interviews, boxes, and case studies; and instructor's manuals for corporate finance, investing, marketing, management, introduction to business, and personal finance textbooks. She also provided corporate communication services in finance, marketing, and technology to units of Deloitte & Touche LLP, for whom she co-authored annual reports on the software industry, wrote and edited several technology-oriented newsletters, and prepared marketing communications materials. She lives in La Jolla, California, and received her B.A. from Smith College and MBA from Boston College.

ENTERPRISE

PART ONE

An Enterprising Framework

chapters

Enterprise: Creating a Framework for Success

KEY CONCEPTS

1. An enterprise is a business that is conceived and managed by independent, energetic individuals who systematically seek results that serve their personal and professional objectives. To enterprise is to take initiative in an organized way.

2. People take initiative in a variety of different contexts. While some individuals may work independently to accomplish specific goals, others may organize and coordinate their efforts with others who strive for a common goal. Organizations have proven to be important social entities that benefit all individuals involved.

3. The sum total of all human activity, individual and organizational, occurs in the context of the environment.

4. Change is the only constant in all human activity. Evolutionary theory can be used to explain how this change occurs.

Suppose your biggest love in life is surfing the waves in Southern California and hanging out with surfer friends on the beach. You enjoy good stories, simple food, and the beauty of nature. The last thing you want to do is cut your hair, put on a suit, and sit behind a desk from 9 to 5. Then suppose your parents, who have worked hard all of their lives in the restaurant business, keep nagging you to "Grow up and get a 'real job.'"

© Radius Images/Jupiter Images

This chapter features a case that describes how three brothers in this situation, Wing Lam, Ed Lee, and Mingo Lee, created Wahoo's Tacos, a restaurant chain that enables them to keep their love of surfing and to combine it with special abilities and insights they developed from early childhood. Enterprisers with an independent, energetic spirit, they followed their passion, created a unique small business, and grew it into a successful, fun enterprise.

Let's now look at the organizational world, where small businesses like Wahoo's play an important role, and learn how businesses interact with their environment.

1.0 An Organizational World

Organizations are so pervasive in our economy that it is nearly impossible to consider what the world would be like without them. An **organization** is simply an entity that involves people doing work for a purpose. Take a

Organization An entity that involves people doing work for a purpose.

moment and think about all of the organizations that you come in contact with during each day. How many organizations do you think you could identify? An organization was likely involved in building your house or apartment; making the sheets on the bed; manufacturing the carpet; providing the toothpaste; and growing, delivering, and selling the food you eat. Organizations provide the electricity for the lights. Organizations set up the traffic lights and stop signs to regulate traffic and enforce traffic laws. Organizations provide the entertainment you watch and the opportunity to watch or participate in a sport. From the moment you get up in the morning until you go to bed at night, you are in constant contact with products and services that are provided by organizations. Most of our day-to-day activities involve or are impacted by organizations.

To succeed in an organizational world, it is important to understand how to create, manage, own, and operate these organizations. This is the focus of *Enterprise*. Throughout this book, you will study the role of **enterprisers**, individuals who engage in activities that initiate and then direct an organization to serve their purposes. Enterprisers are involved in all aspects of the life of organizations, from starting businesses, managing and owning businesses, purchasing or inheriting businesses, and selling businesses. The ability to enterprise encompasses activities beyond the scope of what is typically considered as entrepreneurship.

Entrepreneurship is one form of enterprise. **Entrepreneurs** are individuals who are involved in the start-up of a business. This textbook looks beyond the process of business start-up to consider all of the ways that individuals can take initiative and be proactive in businesses. In fact, this book should be helpful in teaching you how to be successful in any business situation. A **business** is an organization that is started and operated for the purposes of its owners. Typically, a business is started and managed so that it provides a profit

for its owners. A **profit** is the money left over after all expenses are paid. This book explores the environment in which businesses operate and the stages of inception, growth, and transition most businesses pass through. In addition, this book provides you with the skills and knowledge you need to seize entrepreneurial opportunities and use businesses to your advantage.

When most people think about businesses in the United States, they often assume that most businesses are big corporations such as General Electric, Exxon, or Procter and Gamble. Yet, the reality is quite the opposite: *Nearly all businesses in the United States are small businesses!* According to the Small Business Administration, there are about 25 million businesses in the United States, of which about 19 million have no employees. Based on tax returns, the majority of these businesses— about 19 million, or 82 percent—had sales of less than $100,000. About 85 percent of these businesses employ fewer than 20 people, and most of these businesses are sole-proprietorships (owned by a single person). In fact, 99 percent of all businesses in the United States have fewer than 500 employees, which qualify them as small businesses.[1] Similarly, most European businesses are considered small. About 93 percent of all firms in Europe have fewer than nine employees.[2] Since most businesses are small businesses, it makes sense to understand how these organizations are successfully started and operated.

Large businesses have a dominant role in our economy, providing employment for over 50 percent of the U.S. workforce. In addition, of about 5 million corporations that operate in the United States, the largest 9 percent control about 97 percent of all corporate assets. In comparison, it might appear that the economic and employment impact of small businesses is relatively minor. In fact, small businesses represent a powerful economic force in the United States:

- Small businesses created a significant proportion—60 to 80 percent—of new jobs in the United States within the last decade. In fact, during recessions, small businesses create nearly all new jobs in the economy while large firms reduce their employment.

- Small businesses are a major source of innovation in technology and new product development in nearly all industries in the United States.

- Small businesses account for approximately one half of all private sector goods and services

---

Enterpriser   An individual who engages in activities to initiate and then direct an organization to serve his or her purposes.

Entrepreneur   An individual involved in the start-up of a business.

Business   An organization that is started and operated for the purposes of its owners.

Profit   The money left over after all expenses are paid.

produced in the United States. In terms of scale, American small businesses would rank as the third largest economy in the world, next to the United States' economy as a whole, and Japan.

- Small businesses provide an important pathway for social and economic advancement, especially for women, minorities, and immigrants.

- Small businesses play a leadership role in local neighborhood and community development. Studies have found that compared to large businesses, small businesses contribute at nearly twice the level of funding per employee to local community organizations.[3]

In addition, small firms form the seedbed for all growing firms in the United States. Every large firm was once a small business. While firms such as Microsoft, Yahoo!, Home Depot, and Cisco rank as large corporations today, each of these organizations began with a smart business idea pursued by a zealous entrepreneur. Exhibit 1.1 lists some of the largest high-growth U.S. corporations, when they were founded, and their 2005 revenues.

This chapter outlines the basic concepts of enterprise. We offer a process for leveraging your efforts toward business success. In addition, we offer a framework for thinking about businesses in the larger context of the nation and the world.

exhibit

1.1

Selected High-Growth Firms

Firm	Year Started	Fiscal Year 2007 Revenue ($ billions)
Amazon	1995	14.8
Amgen	1980	14.8
Apple Computer	1977	24.0
Cisco	1984	34.9
Dell Inc.	1984	61.1
eBay	1995	7.7
Genentech	1976	11.7
Google	1998	16.6
Home Depot	1978	77.3
Hewlett Packard	1939	104.3
Intel	1969	38.3
Microsoft	1976	51.1
Oracle	1977	18.0
Qualcomm	1985	8.9
Starbucks	1985	9.4
Texas Instruments	1930	13.8
Wal-Mart	1962	378.8
Yahoo!	1994	7.0

1.1 The Context of Enterprise: Levels of Business Activity

Take a minute to consider all of the businesses that are profiled in this book. These businesses engage in very different kinds of activities to achieve their goals. They operate in a variety of contexts—farms, factories, services, retail, and restaurants—in a variety of business formats. Think, for example, about all of the different kinds of restaurants that exist: fast-food, sit-down, fine-dining, ethnic. Businesses employ many different types of people with various skills and abilities in each business format. As a way to understand all of this variation in enterprise, this book looks at three major levels of activity: *persons, businesses,* and *environment,* as illustrated in Exhibit 1.2.

Persons

At the simplest level, a *person* can create and exchange goods and services with others. In this scenario, a single person undertakes all of the activities necessary to make a product or provide a service and then engages in exchanges with others. For example, if you were interested in selling music CDs, you could be involved in composing the music, playing all of the instruments and singing all of the lyrics, recording the CD, making copies of the CD, and selling each CD. Yet, engaging in all of these different activities is time consuming and complicated. Few individuals are gifted at doing a variety of tasks well, or find doing all of these tasks interesting and fun. But what if you are a highly talented guitarist and enjoy performing more than all of the other activities? Wouldn't it be more efficient and rewarding for you to focus on performing and delegate all other activities to other specialists?

This is not a new idea by any means. Adam Smith, in his 1776 book *The Wealth of Nations,* offered an example of individuals undertaking all of the tasks in manufacturing a specific product: pins. He described how one individual could manufacture 20 pins each day. Each person performed every aspect of pin manufacture: cutting the wire, pounding the tip of the wire to make a point, and flattening the rear of the wire to make the head of the pin. Once the pins were manufactured, each individual went out and sold these pins, using this money to purchase more wire to make more pins. Smith pointed out that when individuals combined their

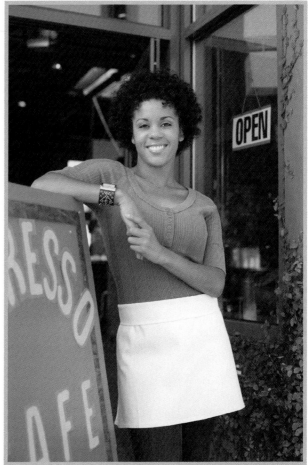
© Jupiter Images

efforts at pin making, they could dramatically increase the number of pins produced. By forming groups, each pin maker specialized in one activity, thereby increasing the efficiency of each person's actions. One person cut the wire, one person made pinpoints, and one person made pinheads. By combining their efforts and specializing in one activity, a group of ten pin makers increased their production of pins to 48,000 pins a day, or 4,800 pins for each person in the group. That is a significant increase in productivity!

The Business

Clearly, individuals who collectively organize and coordinate their efforts are significantly more efficient than individuals performing every task alone. Let's return to our original example of making and selling CDs. Assume that a group of individuals agrees to work together in the CD venture. The members divide the individual tasks of composing, performing, recording, manufacturing, and marketing the CDs among themselves based on their talents and interests. This group performs all of the functions of a business—an organization that is

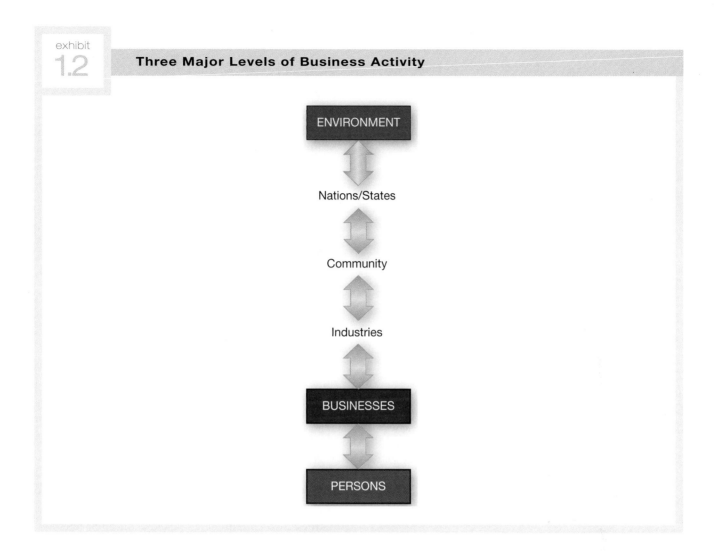

exhibit
1.2

Three Major Levels of Business Activity

started and operated for the purposes of its owners. Dividing all the functions of the business among the group results in a significant increase in productivity. Therefore, businesses exist because they can more effectively create goods and services than individuals working independently.

The Environment

The level of the **environment** is the entire context of activities that surrounds the operation of a business. There are so many different issues to consider when recognizing the environment that, at this point, this section will only highlight some of the environment's important features. All of the businesses that are involved in making and selling CDs are identified as an **industry**, a group of businesses producing similar products and services—in this case, the music-recording industry. An industry can be defined in many different ways. We could define the music industry as all of the people who

are paid to produce, perform, record, distribute, and sell CDs. Or we can narrow the definition of the industry to only those individuals and businesses that are paid to produce rock or classical music CDs. The collection of all industries is considered a **community**. For example, we think of all of the different industries involved in music as the music industry. This includes industries involved in making musical instruments and recording equipment, and companies involved in transporting and setting up the stage and equipment for musical performances, as well as service industries such as advertisers and concert promoters.

Environment   The entire context of activities that surrounds the operation of a business.

Industry   A group of businesses producing similar products and services.

Community   A collection of related industries.

The environment also consists of the *state* or *national* level, where all communities of organizations in a particular geographic area are regulated. At the state or national level, governments regulate and coordinate all of the business, economic, and social activities in a specified area. Finally, the environment consists of all the physical, social, economic, and political features of the world we inhabit. In creating, making, and selling CDs, we would need to consider the legal issues involved with the ownership of the music performed. With changes in technology, it is now possible to record and exchange songs performed by others over the Internet. Should each individual have the right to record music that was created by others for free? The intellectual property rights of music creators and performers are regulated by their respective nations. Compensation for the creators of intellectual property is a political decision that will have a significant impact on the growth and viability of particular industries, including the music industry.

These three levels of activity—individual, business, and environment—are the primary ways we will explore how enterprise occurs. While the focus of this book is on the business level as the primary form of enterprise, we always need to recognize our role at the individual level and the effect of the environment on business activity. In fact, we believe that one of the unique features of this book is its emphasis on individual-level issues for determining business success. Your success is as important as the success of the business you are involved in.

Emergence   The first stage of a business's life cycle: New venture formation.

1.2 The Process of Enterprise: An Evolutionary Perspective

One word summarizes the evolutionary perspective of business: *change*. All businesses will change over time. This change takes place in various forms—size, legal form, location, financial stability, ownership, management, and goods and services offered, to name just a few.

As shown in Exhibit 1.3, three processes foster change in businesses: emergence, newness, and transformation. The first process, **emergence**, involves great change as new businesses form and initiate new projects. These new businesses are the result of blind variations or intentional variations. A *blind variation* is a change that occurs by accident, chance, or luck. An *intentional variation* is the result of the conscious efforts of individuals or other businesses to create a new way to solve a perceived problem through business creation.

Most new businesses are likely to be a combination of blind and intentional variations. For example, the idea behind The Republic of Tea, a business that imports, manufactures, and distributes high quality teas and tea accessories, arose out of a chance meeting between two entrepreneurs who were flying home from a conference. As these two entrepreneurs talked about their likes and dislikes about the food service on airlines, they discovered that they both enjoyed drinking high quality teas and had problems finding sources for purchasing such teas. From that fortunate occurrence, they agreed on a plan to start a tea importing and sales business.

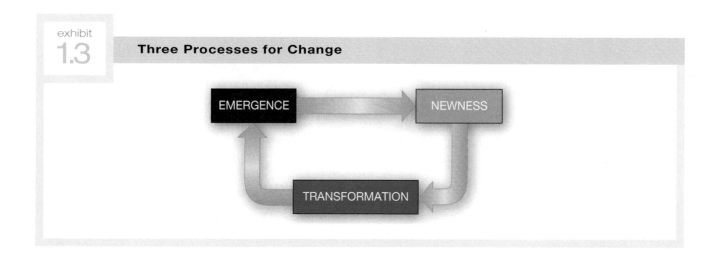

exhibit
1.3   **Three Processes for Change**

Once a business is successfully created, it then faces the problems of *newness,* the second phase of the evolutionary process. The process of newness involves developing and managing a fledgling business so that it survives and flourishes. This is a challenging stage, and statistics indicate the grim fact that few new businesses grow—most eventually fail. Academics have coined the term "the liability of newness" to describe findings that new businesses fail at higher rates than older and larger businesses. Not only do most new businesses fail, they also do not grow very large. Only 5 percent of all new businesses ever grow to larger than 20 employees. Much of the focus of this book is on the challenges of managing and growing a new and small firm.

According to the Small Business Administration (SBA), about 649,000 new businesses with employees were launched in 2006. Of those new firms, about 95 percent had less than 20 employees. In that same year, almost as many terminated operations—and again, 95 percent of those had less than 20 employees. Also, in 2006, another 336,000 people started firms that had no employees.[4]

Starting and stopping businesses is a normal part of the dynamics of a healthy economy. Businesses that close are not necessarily failures. About 60 percent become inactive, while others formally close. Many are sold or transferred to new owners.[5] Many were profitable over their lifetime; based on a recent study, about one-third of businesses were successful at the time they closed.[6]

According to studies of the survival rates of new business, which have been consistent over the past 50 years, most new and small firms fail. As shown in Exhibit 1.4, businesses are more likely to fail if they are small. After ten years, only 21 percent of businesses of all sizes have survived, while 62 percent of businesses that have hired five or more employees are still in existence.[7] Overall, ten years after start-up, nearly 80 percent of businesses had failed.[8] In sum, most businesses that are started do not last very long.

If a small business survives its early years, it may face more daunting challenges from changes in its economic, social, technological, and legal environments. To survive these inevitable upheavals, businesses must undergo a transformation to adapt to these changing circumstances.

With the growth of book "super-store" chains such as Barnes and Noble and the emergence of online booksellers such as Amazon.com, the number of small retail bookstores has significantly declined. To survive, small retail bookstores must transform themselves by offering other types of services and benefits besides carrying general books. For example, Hennesey and Ingalls, a

Newness   The stage in a business's life cycle that involves developing and managing a fledgling business so that it survives and flourishes.

Transformation   The transitions a business goes through during its life cycle to adapt to changing circumstances.

---

exhibit

1.4

Businesses Survival Rates

Years	Companies of All Sizes (%)	Companies That Hired 1–4 People (%)	Companies That Hired 5 or More People (%)
After 2 years	76	92	94
After 4 years	47	80	87
After 6 years	38	76	79
After 8 years	29	53	70
After 10 years	21	41	62

Source: *The State of Small Business: A Report of the President, 1997* (Washington, DC: U.S. Small Business Administration, 1997), p. 129.

bookstore in Santa Monica, California, has survived and prospered by catering to customers who want to browse among a comprehensive collection of books on the arts and architecture. This bookstore prides itself on having salespeople with a thorough knowledge of arts and architecture books who can assist customers in finding books that meet their interests and needs.

The Life Cycle of Enterprise

The three change processes we've just described correspond to the three broad stages of the life cycle of enterprise:

1. New venture formation (emergence)
2. Progress and growth (newness)
3. Transition and change (transformation)

New Venture Formation

New venture formation, the stage where the enterprise emerges, focuses on learning how to successfully start and initiate new ventures and then on combining the resources and competencies necessary to be successful. During this entrepreneurial stage, the enterpriser must recognize and discover opportunities, analyze feasibility, develop a business plan, and determine the best start-up path. This might be forming a completely new company, purchasing a franchise unit, or buying an existing business. We'll explore these topics in Part 2 of this book.

The skills required during this stage will prove valuable in many different contexts, not just in creating businesses. They are applicable in other settings such as corporations, government organizations, and nonprofits, as well as in personal projects, team projects, and other venues where goals need to be identified and realized.

Progress and Growth

Once an enterprise is launched, how do you ensure its ongoing success and overcome the liability of newness? During the progress and growth stage, the primary objective is to manage, monitor, and grow personal and professional achievements. In this book, you will explore the skills for managing and monitoring personal goals and aspirations, as well as the techniques and skills to operate an ongoing business. One important perspective

of *Enterprise* involves the affirmation of all kinds of businesses as outcomes of an individual's choices and interests and the environment in which the business competes. "Lifestyle" businesses, that is, businesses that do not have rapid rates of growth, are celebrated in this book. All businesses could be considered "lifestyle" businesses, because the growth of a business is partly determined by choices made by the business's entrepreneurs, the skills and abilities of these entrepreneurs, and environmental and industry factors. Entrepreneurs must be aware of the businesses that match their goals, abilities, and skills. It is important to learn when a business should stay small and when a business should grow. In any case, enabling a business to successfully operate, whether it is small or large, growing or stable, involves important enterprise skills.

It is possible for some businesses to enter a steady stage of maturity, where in essence the business could be put on autopilot, without a significant need to change. But this is not realistic for most businesses in today's fast-moving climate; they must keep adapting to survive.

Transition and Change

Just as individuals age and their interests and goals change over time, a business also ages and changes. Its transformation may be caused by changes in the environment or by the aging of an industry. For example, only a handful of businesses in the United States manufacture covered wagons, or horse-drawn carriages, or any other kinds of vehicles that require animals for locomotion. Yet, a few such businesses do exist and are very successful.

Thus, the final transition and change stage of the enterprise life cycle is characterized by the following actions:

- Enterprisers evaluate their personal and professional achievements. They celebrate their accomplishments with the expectation of moving on to new opportunities, or they take time to enjoy the benefits of their success.

- Enterprisers study the changes in the current environment and reevaluate their goals and priorities in light of environmental changes.

- Enterprisers make decisions about the future, such as selling a business, taking the business to the public through a stock offering, or transferring the management of the business to someone else. This is often a very difficult and emotional time. If the business has not been successful, the entrepreneur faces the trauma of bankruptcy or dissolution.

Life cycle of enterprise   The three stages of an enterprise's life: emergence, newness, and transformation.

AN ENTERPRISING WORLD

Entrepreneurship Goes Global

Most people think that the United States is the most enterprising country in the world. Well, it's not! By any number of measures of entrepreneurship, other countries have a higher percentage of people who are more enterprising.

Over the past seven years, a number of countries have participated in the Global Entrepreneurship Monitor, an ongoing study that measures entrepreneurial activities in a way that allows comparisons between countries. The 2005 report is based on data from 35 nations grouped into middle-income, high-growth and high-income, and low-growth categories according to per capita GDP and GDP growth rate.

One key measure of entrepreneurial activity is "early-stage entrepreneurial activity," the percentage of people who are involved in starting businesses and those who have started businesses within the past four years. In the most recent study, Venezuela scores 25 percent on this measure, which means that one out of every four people in that country are either starting a business or own a new business. Of the countries participating in this study, the United States ranks sixth, with an early-stage entrepreneurial activity rate of 12.4 percent—about half of Venezuela's rate. Exhibit 1.5 shows the early-stage entrepreneurial activity for each of the 35 countries.

As you look at this chart, you may wonder why some countries rank lower in terms of their enterprising activity than others. Countries like Hungary, Japan, Belgium, and Sweden ranked at the bottom, while Venezuela, Thailand, New Zealand, and Jamaica ranked near the top. For one thing, individuals have different motivations for starting businesses. The authors of the GEM report have identified two main reasons why enterprisers start new ventures:

- Opportunity: They see an opportunity to exploit by starting a business.

- Necessity: They start a business because they have no other choice. There are no jobs for them to take.

exhibit 1.5

Early-Stage Entrepreneurial Activity by Country

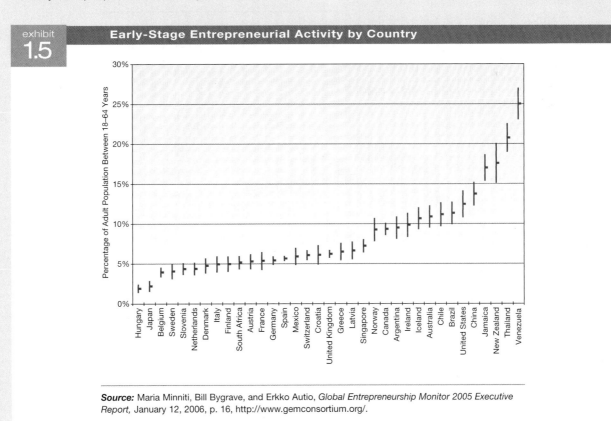

Source: Maria Minniti, Bill Bygrave, and Erkko Autio, *Global Entrepreneurship Monitor 2005 Executive Report,* January 12, 2006, p. 16, http://www.gemconsortium.org/.

(continued)

An Enterprising World (*continued*)

The ratio of opportunity- to necessity-based entrepreneurship also varies greatly around the world, as you can see in Exhibit 1.6. Countries such as New Zealand, Denmark, and the United States have very high ratios of opportunity enterprisers, which means that most entrepreneurs who are starting businesses see opportunities to exploit. In other countries—for example, France, Brazil, and South Africa—necessity enterprisers account for nearly 50 percent of all start-ups. In general, high-income countries exhibit a higher ratio of opportunity-driven to necessity-driven business owners than do middle-income countries.

Again, we might ask why countries differ significantly in the ratio of necessity to opportunity enterprisers. Why would France have such a high percentage of necessity entrepreneurs, while Belgium, its neighbor, has such a low percentage of necessity entrepreneurs? Both are in the high-income cluster. One reason for this difference involves the strict labor laws in France, which

make it difficult for companies to fire employees. Since companies cannot fire employees, they are often shy about hiring new employees, so many people in France cannot get jobs. Individuals in France, therefore, are more likely to turn to necessity enterprising.

Discussion Questions

1. What types of economic situations create a business environment that supports entrepreneurship?

2. What are some reasons that the ratio of necessity versus opportunity enterprisers differs so greatly from country to country?

3. In looking at Exhibits 1.5 and 1.6, do you think that necessity entrepreneurs seem to be important for promoting economic growth in certain kinds of countries?

Source: Maria Minniti, *Global Entrepreneurship Monitor 2005 Executive Report,* January 2, 2006, http://www.gemconsortium.org/.

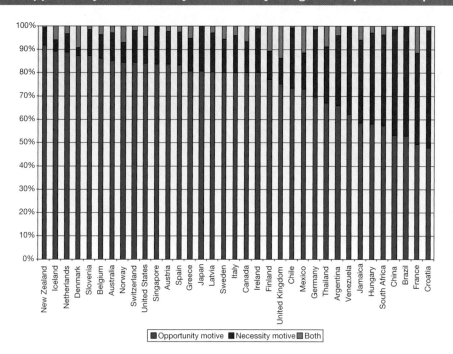

exhibit 1.6   Opportunity- to Necessity-Based Early-Stage Entrepreneurship

Source: Maria Minniti, Bill Bygrave, and Erkko Autio, *Global Entrepreneurship Monitor 2005 Executive Report,* January 12, 2006, p. 16, http://www.gemconsortium.org/.

Taking a Global Perspective

Change is occurring not only in how businesses compete against each other, but in many other ways as well. Now more than ever, companies are required to plan for business activities that extend beyond the United States' borders. In fact, part of the transformation process for a new business may include adapting its business model to accommodate the needs or utilize the resources of a new nation. Since 1990, 30 new nations have been recognized and offered membership in the United Nations. Not only do new nations emerge, but the demographic characteristics of existing nations change as well. Industrialized countries such as Japan and Italy are experiencing declining rates of population growth. The expected population change in Italy is from 58 million people in 2001 to 42 million people in 2050. Japan is expected to decline from 127 million people in 2001 to 101 million people in 2050. Other countries such as Brazil and India have populations that are very young and growing. In Brazil, 30 percent of the population is under the age of 15, and the country is expected to grow from 184 million people in 2005 to 260 million people in 2050. In India, 36 percent of the population is under the age of 15, and the country is expected to grow from 1.1 billion people in 2005 to 1.6 billion people in 2050.[9] Such changes in population will affect not only these nations but others who locate plants there and export goods to them.

Changes in population and economic conditions contribute to entrepreneurial activity in other countries as well as in the United States. In the An Enterprising World box, you'll discover which countries have the highest rates of early-stage entrepreneurial activity and why.

Evolving Industries

Industries are also changing. The invention of new technologies, such as the emergence of the Internet, drives the formation of new industries and companies. In the mid- to late 1990s, venture capitalists funded thousands of Internet businesses. Some, like Amazon.com, Yahoo!, and Google, were incredible success stories. The majority of the new Internet-related companies in the business-to-consumer sector, however, failed. Those that survived learned how to adapt the early business models to their advantage and to develop new ones as the new technology evolved. The Internet also forced companies and even whole industries to change their business models and to implement new ways of operating that take advantage of the Internet and electronic commerce (e-commerce).

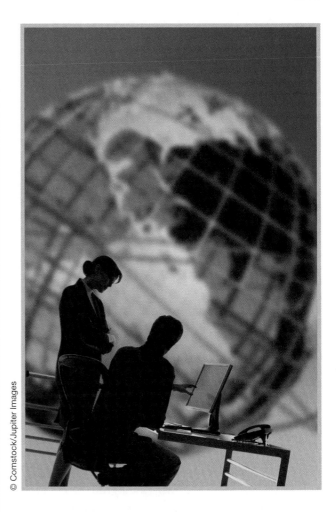

© Comstock/Jupiter Images

The success and failure rates of businesses in a particular industry are an indication of an industry's health. An industry is considered healthy when it rewards businesses that satisfy customer needs through innovation and lower prices. These businesses will experience growth through higher sales. Businesses that don't satisfy customer needs, on the other hand, will experience decreases in growth and sales. Keen enterprisers should be alert to industry changes to help them avoid some of the big mistakes made by dot-com businesses.

Individual tastes and preferences change, often in contradictory ways. Such changes may drive industry trends. For example, obesity has become a worldwide epidemic as the rate of obesity increases at an alarming rate. In the United States, as many as 65 percent of adults are either overweight or obese, 16 percent of children and adolescents ages 6 to 19 are overweight, and another 15 percent are at risk of becoming overweight.[10] At the same time, Americans consume huge amounts of snack foods, pushing snack food industry sales to almost $10 billion! Although there has been an increasing interest in healthier snack foods, sales of high-calorie nuts, corn chips, and potato chips have remained high.

And consumers appear to prefer flavored varieties that are higher in carbohydrates and salt.[11] Yet, the weight loss industry is booming as Americans spend billions on diet programs, foods, and supplements each year. Companies such as NutriSystem and Weight Watchers International report high revenue growth as consumers look for help in the fight against fat.[12]

If change is likely to occur in all aspects of our lives—individual, business, and environment—it makes sense to prepare ourselves for this inevitability.

1.3 Pursuing Personal Success

A fundamental premise of this book is that the pursuit of success in business should be a way to promote your success in life. We believe that you should give this personal success a higher priority than the success of the businesses and organizations in which you are involved. The focus of *Enterprise* is primarily on *you* and therefore it emphasizes the tradeoffs each person makes between personal and business priorities.

Being unaware of these tradeoffs may lead to decisions that do not benefit either the business or the individual. For example, an owner of a growing clothing retail business may decide to expand her business by renting and renovating space adjacent to her current store. She will require funds to pay for fixtures (such as clothes racks, wall racks, shelves, and display cases), additional space, and additional inventory (such as clothes and accessories). If the business does not have sufficient surplus funds to pay for this expansion, it will need to borrow money from lenders, such as banks, or take on additional investors. Many lenders require that the owner of the business cosign for a business loan. Cosigning obligates the owner to pay for the loan if the business cannot make the payments to the bank. If the expansion of the business does not generate enough profits from additional sales to pay back the loan, the owner of the business would have to pay this debt. Thus, the owner's decisions about expanding her business could place personal assets and savings at risk.

The idea of placing more value on your personal and professional aspirations may seem to be a selfish and self-centered perspective that appears to contradict other important values. Why should generous, kind, or altruistic people develop a self-serving attitude? How can persons who put themselves first work together in organizations? Wouldn't selfishness lead to everyone working alone? On the contrary, the pursuit of individual goals can actually benefit everyone else as well.

Know Thyself

This book is grounded in a philosophy of "self-actualization ethics," which emphasizes the unique value and importance of each person.[13] You are unique. No other person in the world is like you. Indeed, there has never been, nor will there ever be another person like you. You have certain qualities and abilities that no one else has. In the philosophy of "self-actualization ethics," it is each person's priority to realize his or her unique capabilities and gifts. In this philosophy, everyone benefits when each person pursues his or her unique capabilities. Much like Adam Smith's example of the pin makers, when each person strives for excellence on a particular set of tasks, and also coordinates those efforts with others, everyone achieves more. Each person's obligation, therefore, is to excel at his or her own unique capabilities.

To pursue this uniqueness, you must first discover your special abilities. Aspire to "Know thyself," taking the time and effort to discover your unique skills and abilities. For most of us, this is not an easy task. We may have some sense of our strengths and weaknesses in certain types of jobs. We may have accumulated enough experience to know the kinds of situations we enjoy and the kinds of people we like. Yet, we may be unclear about what we should be doing with our lives and how we might go about achieving our capabilities. We devote many parts of this book to exercises that will help you discover your values, goals, and capabilities. Self-knowledge makes it easier to make decisions and expend the time and energy to accomplish tasks.

Even when we have gained knowledge about our unique abilities and gifts, we still must undertake the responsibility to achieve these capabilities. Personal excellence takes time and energy. Fully utilizing your unique capabilities takes a lot of work. For example, a gifted athlete may be endowed with superb hand–eye coordination, nimbleness, and speed. But this talented athlete still needs training and practice to fully maximize his or her potential.

Changes in Disposition, Cognitions, and Actions

Just as a talented athlete needs training and practice, each of us should identify our unique abilities and gifts and develop them so we can reach our personal and professional goals. Each person is a composite set of dispositions, cognitions, and actions. Together, these characteristics may create a powerful foundation for building a rewarding and successful life.

A **disposition** is a set of personality characteristics that is likely to remain stable in nearly all situations, such as a person's temperament, character, or personality. If a person has a disposition toward eating sweets, we would assume that this person would enjoy sweets in most situations. Knowing about this "sweet tooth" allows us to make predictions about the kinds of foods that person might choose in most situations.

People vary on a number of personal dimensions, such as aggression, shyness, optimism, intelligence, sociability, self-control, and flexibility. These personal dimensions are characteristics that influence a person's behavior in all situations. For instance, a person with a shy disposition will find it more difficult than other people to be outgoing and is therefore less likely to meet and greet new people in social functions. That doesn't mean that shy people can't meet and greet new people; it simply means that it will be more difficult for them. Individual dispositions may constrain certain thoughts and actions, but they do not prevent them.

The psychologist and educator Howard Gardner suggests that people vary on different dimensions of their personality. These dimensions support various kinds of activities and occupations. Exhibit 1.7 briefly describes Gardner's **seven intelligences**. Gardner believes that

Disposition   A set of personality characteristics that generally remains stable in nearly all situations, such as a person's temperament, character, or personality.

Seven intelligences   The seven different types of intelligences that people may possess, as categorized by Howard Gardner: musical, bodily–kinesthetic, logical–mathematical, linguistic, spatial, interpersonal, and intrapersonal.

---

exhibit
1.7   **Howard Gardner's Seven Intelligences**

Musical Intelligence. The ability to perform and compose music. Some individuals have a natural ability to pick up a musical instrument and play it almost immediately, while others with a very low musical intelligence cannot carry a tune.

Bodily–Kinesthetic Intelligence. The ability to control one's body, which would be seen in an individual's movement, balance, agility, and grace. Individuals who excel in sports, such as Tiger Woods and LeBron James, display a natural sense of how their bodies should act in demanding physical situations.

Logical–Mathematical Intelligence. The ability to mentally process logical problems and equations.

Linguistic Intelligence. The ability to utilize language. A person's ability to construct and comprehend language will vary, but this trait is universal. Some people have exceptional abilities to learn many different languages and use language in creative ways—for example, gifted writers and public speakers like Barack Obama.

Spatial Intelligence. The ability to perceive and interpret objects in the physical world, as well as to abstractly comprehend and manipulate these objects mentally. Spatial intelligence is used to comprehend shapes and images in three dimensions.

Interpersonal Intelligence. The ability to interact with others, understand them, and interpret their behavior. Interpersonal intelligence is manifest in how people are able to discern the moods, temperaments, intentions, and motivations of others.

Intrapersonal Intelligence. The ability to understand and sense our "self," that is, who we are, what feelings we have, and why we are the way we are. A strong intrapersonal intelligence can lead to self-esteem and self-enhancement, and a strong character can help us solve internal problems. Others often do not recognize intrapersonal intelligence unless we show it as an emotion, such as anger or joy, or as something tangible, such as a painting or a poem.

Source: Adapted from Howard Gardner, *Frames of Mind: The Theory of Multiple Intelligences* (New York: Basic Books, 1983).

each individual has strengths and weaknesses across all seven intelligences and should recognize how to best use those unique capabilities. It is unlikely that any one individual will have exceptional talents in all seven intelligences. What Gardner suggests is that we should seek to discover our own unique profile of intelligences, and work toward enhancing and building them.

Your cognitions, thought processes that reveal what and how you think, significantly influence what you are likely to do. For example, psychologists have found that people who were diagnosed with depression were likely to experience "learned helplessness."[14] Learned helplessness is a condition where individuals evaluate negative events in their lives and think that the causes of these problems are enduring and pervasive personal defects. People with these attributes are likely to do nothing. They become helpless because they think that the characteristics of the situation cannot change. By not taking action to dispel their beliefs about a particular situation, they are unable to prove whether these attributions are correct. They

---

Cognition   Thought process that reveals what and how you think, significantly influencing what you are likely to do.

---

learn to be hopeless and then act helpless. Fortunately, we can modify our thinking process and learn to overcome this and other cognitions.

Finally, we want to behave and act in ways that support our personal values and goals. This book helps you develop behaviors that enhance the satisfaction you get from both your personal and professional endeavors. For example, you will learn about goal setting in Chapter 3. The activities involved in goal setting enable you to identify, set, and achieve goals for your own life. Goal setting is also key to business success and significantly improves the performance of employees in most business settings.

Enterprise provides a multitude of ways to increase your chances at personal and business success. These involve

- *Exploring your dispositions* to gain a realistic understanding of your inherent capabilities and the values and beliefs that motivate you.

- *Probing your thinking* to discover how your perceptions of your circumstances significantly influence the kinds of choices you consider.

- *Identifying new skills and behaviors* to increase ways to take control of your situations and influence your destiny.

1.4 ENTERPRISERS

Wahoo's Surfs Its Way to Success

Dressed in shorts and sandals and sporting a laid-back, surfer-bum attitude, Wing Lam, Ed Lee, and Mingo Lee may not look like successful entrepreneurs. But behind the casual demeanor lies plenty of business savvy. From Santa Ana, in Southern California surf country, the three Lam brothers run Wahoo's Fish Taco. Since opening their first restaurant in 1988, they have grown their company to over 30 locations in Southern California and Colorado, each generating more than $1 million in annual revenue. The company's plans call for selective growth in other areas as well.

How did the brothers turn a love of surfing and surfer food into such a success story? For one thing, they come from a family of restaurateurs. Their parents, refugees from communist China, opened one of Brazil's first Chinese restaurants. In 1975, the Lees and their three Brazilian-born sons immigrated to Southern California and opened Chinese restaurants on Balboa Island in

upscale Newport Beach and in Costa Mesa. When the senior Lees were ready to retire, they offered to turn the restaurants over to the boys.

"We had no desire to put on the white shirt, black pants, and the bow tie," recalls Wing Lam, who wanted to strike out in a different direction. With their parents pushing them to get "real jobs," the brothers looked for a way to earn a living and still have time to surf. Operating a restaurant was the logical choice. "All of us grew up in this type of business," explains Mingo Lee. "In Brazil, we lived on the third floor over our restaurant. From the day you were able to walk, you knew what was going on in the operation. We stood on Coke crates, peeling shrimp and washing dishes."

The Wahoo's concept grew out of the brothers' surfing trips to Baja California. They based their menu on the beach food they and their friends liked to eat. "Literally, the day before we opened, I actually sat in the kitchen and wrote things down, and tried a couple of things, and said, 'We're opening tomorrow,'" says Wing.

Although this would be risky for many other aspiring enterprisers, the brothers' boyhood experiences gave them an instinctual feel for the business. "When you cook all your life, you just know what goes with what," Mingo continues. After cooking up the first batches of beans, rice, and fish, they looked at each other and said, "Hey, that was okay!" The brothers also wanted to create a special feeling. "Sure the food's going to be good," says Mingo. "We felt confident in our menu, but we wanted people to walk in and actually experience something— sort of a getaway to our favorite spots down in Baja." They designed a place that would appeal to their own "Boarding Tribe"—surfers, snowboarders, and skateboarders—and have expanded to include all extreme sports enthusiasts.

The approach worked. Wahoo's reflects the brothers' personalities and Southern California lifestyle. Stroll into a Wahoo's restaurant, and you'll see happy customers digging into plates of fresh food, piled high and priced low. It's noisy, friendly, and even chaotic. The walls are plastered with real surf gear and posters from surfing, skateboard, and snowboard companies—a custom that began when employees from local surfing apparel manufacturers who ate at Wahoo's put up banners to mark their favorite booths. Wahoo's became the cool place to eat. "Instead of importing what's fashionable in New York, we're exporting our own culture," Wing says. Although just about all ages will find something good to eat at Wahoo's, its target customers are young men 18 to 24 years old, who eat out almost six times a week and are the biggest consumers of commercially prepared food in the United States, according to the National Restaurant Association.

"It looks easy on the outside," says Mingo, who is in charge of the finance area. But behind the casual and upbeat atmosphere of a Wahoo's eatery are a theme concept, carefully developed food preparation systems, and employee training programs. "Our parents gave us the tools by sending us to school, giving us the extra edge that they didn't have growing up," he says. Each brother has a business degree and speaks several languages.

They started small, originally planning on each brother running one store. As sole proprietors, they could keep operations simple and use their dad's "old school" methods. "You just keep everything between the ears," explains Mingo. "When you show up each morning, you put your inventory together. You just never have any paperwork in place."

This plan worked for those first three stores. As the Wahoo's concept gained acceptance and the fourth and fifth stores were coming on line, the brothers realized they needed better systems for growth. They set up administrative procedures, such as standard inventory sheets and computerized payroll. From there the brothers divided managerial responsibilities among themselves and added a fourth partner, Steve Karfaridis, who joined them in 1990 as director of operations.

Mingo is chief financial officer, handling all the finances and other corporate departments like human resources. "I am cheap to the core," he says. "I cut every corner that is not needed. I am concerned about the bottom line." Wing is in charge of marketing, including promotions and fundraisers, while Ed focuses on planning. "I handle the development of the restaurants," Ed explains. "I find real estate and make sure that it's within Mingo's budget, then build it out." Steve, an experienced restaurateur, serves as director of operations and implemented standardized methods and employee training programs that were critical to the chain's ability to grow. Keeping it simple was key. "We had created a training program that's based on single page modules," Steve says. Another company-wide practice is the ten-second rule. Ten seconds is the maximum amount of time a plate of food will wait in the pass-through or a customer will stand at the register before someone greets them. The company also prides itself on developing employees and promoting managers from within.

Part of the chain's unique quality comes from its marketing philosophy: "If you discount yourself, you cheapen the image that you have built all these years," explains Wing. "It's either full-price or it is free; there is nothing in-between. If we are going to give something, we give it with no strings attached."

From the beginning, Wahoo's gave away a lot of food at sporting events patronized by its core market groups. As Wahoo's helped other groups and stores promote themselves, they introduced potential customers to the great-tasting food the restaurants featured. Wing Lam believes that offering free food at community gatherings is cheaper and much more effective than relying on more traditional marketing methods. "Once they taste it, see it, smell it, and touch it, they connect it to you," he says. "Everyone wants to support a local business as opposed to a large corporate entity to which they are not attached. They see you being a part of the community and want to interact with you, support you because you are supporting the community. The giving comes back tenfold."

Discussion Questions

As you read the other sections of Chapter 1, keep in mind some of the insights and ideas of this story. The following questions will help you think about issues this chapter introduces:

1. What special abilities (or behaviors or instincts) did the founders of Wahoo's possess that were instrumental in their success as entrepreneurs?

2. How important is individual choice in determining an individual's success?

3. What environmental factors played a significant role in the early success of Wahoo's?

4. What kinds of actions did the founders of the business take to initiate the development of Wahoo's?

5. What obstacles should the founders of Wahoo's anticipate as they expand this business?

6. If you were thinking about starting a restaurant, how would you start this process?

Source: Adapted with permission from Small Business School, the series on PBS, at http://SmallBusinessSchool.com; Wahoo's Taco website, http://www.wahoos.com (June 12, 2008).

1.5 Business: The Organizational Imperative

Businesses are their own entities and need to be treated as if they are uniquely their own persons. The **organizational imperative** states that a business has its own needs and objectives that are separate from the needs and objectives of any of the business's other stakeholders.[15] For example, many high-technology firms need substantial amounts of funds from outside investors to grow and prosper. This financing supports research and product development, as well as the expansion of production facilities. When the founders of many high-technology firms raise capital from other investors, they often find themselves "fired" from their roles as managers of these new, larger firms. They may not have the substantial managerial expertise and background required to run the resulting high-growth business. Most successful high-growth technology firms need managers and leaders with experience at running and operating high-growth businesses. Therefore, it may not be in the best interest of the firm to have inexperienced managers in charge. Who, then, has the authority to make decisions about the needs and objectives of the business?

Determining who will make the decisions about a business's needs and objectives is based on the legal format of the business. In Chapter 4, we will explore all of the details that characterize various legal forms of businesses, such as sole proprietorships, partnerships, and corporations. The characteristics of these legal forms of business have many different implications for how the business will be managed and operated.

At this point, let's consider two major dimensions by which the interests of the business are determined. The *control dimension* involves determining who will manage the business. The person who manages the business makes decisions about the business's day-to-day operations. The *ownership dimension* involves determining who will share in the benefits of the business.

In most businesses, the individual who owns the business also controls the business. The goals and purposes of the business are determined by the *owner/manager* of the business. Sole proprietors are an example of a business where the manager is typically also the owner. When businesses need more capital to expand and grow, as in the high-technology example mentioned earlier, they require more people to invest in the business. Investors often ask for some ownership in the business as a way to insure that they gain benefits from the business's success. If a substantial number of people are owners of a business, their ability to control the day-to-day operations of the business become more limited. Think about the difficulty of operating a business if it had 10,000 owners who all wanted to run the business. Larger businesses usually separate the functions of ownership from the functions of control. Managers will make the day-to-day decisions about the needs and objectives of the business, while the shareholders will receive the benefits of ownership in the business through rising stock prices or dividends.

Organizational imperative   Concept that a business has its own needs and objectives separate from the needs and objectives of any of the business's other stakeholders.

Imagine, then, that a business can become of a size where it no longer needs its original founders or owners to survive and flourish. Few businesses that last longer than ten years keep their founding owners and managers. McDonald's no longer has the involvement of its original founders, the McDonald Brothers, or Ray Kroc, the person who took the McDonald Brothers' original concept and expanded it into an international company.

As these examples demonstrate, you are not your business—and the business is not you. While most entrepreneurs start businesses to support their own personal goals, it is very likely that as a business grows and matures, the goals of the business and the goals of its founder will change and diverge. It is important to be able to see when your personal goals and values no longer correspond to the needs and objectives of the business, and then, make appropriate choices to benefit both yourself and the business, if possible.

1.6 The Environment: No One Is an Island

No one is an island. We are all connected to each other. Our decisions affect a multitude of other people, and their concerns and issues will also affect our ability to make decisions. This requires an understanding of the *environment* in which enterprise occurs. As noted earlier, the environment includes the entire physical universe and all of its human and social activity. Simply put, the environment is everything that is not you. We have seen that human and social activity can be organized in many different ways. We all have different priorities, interests, and goals. All of the individuals, groups, communities, businesses, and governments in the environment have different and competing interests and concerns.

Balancing Stakeholder Interests

Suppose we want to use more electricity to power home appliances, TVs, and computers, and we decide to build more hydroelectric dams as a way to generate this electricity. A new dam will flood many square miles of land, displacing people living in towns and farms along the river. The flooded land will be lost for farming or any other activity. A new dam may disrupt the migratory patterns of fish in the river, so that fewer fish are able to survive. While some people will benefit

© John Zoiner/Workbook Stock/Jupiter Images

from the electricity the dam generates, other people will be harmed, and the physical and natural environment will also be changed. How can we acknowledge all of the different people and factors that comprise such a decision? A way to understand this constellation of cooperative and competing interests among other people and the physical and natural environment is through *stakeholder theory.*

Stakeholders are entities that have a legitimate interest in the processes and activities of a business. Exhibit 1.8 illustrates nine broad categories of stakeholders. To make effective decisions about you and your business, you must consider stakeholder theory, which recognizes the interests of every possible individual, group, or other entity that may have some connection to you and your business. Stakeholder theory has proven very valuable in helping us understand all of the forces that affect a business.

Stakeholder An entity that has a legitimate interest in the processes and activities of a business.

exhibit
1.8

Types of Stakeholders

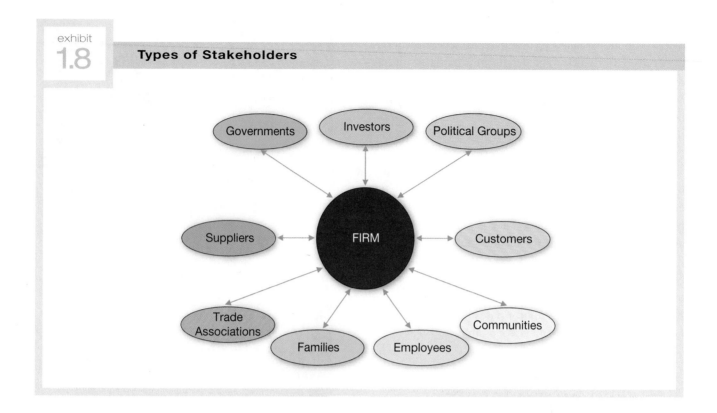

Stakeholder Theory in Action

To demonstrate the effects of these various stakeholders on the operations of a business, let's consider the ramifications of starting a pizza delivery business.

First, it is important to recognize the influence of your *family* on business decisions. Most entrepreneurs depend on their families to help them start and build their businesses so that families are often significantly involved in the decisions you'll make. Families typically provide both emotional and financial support for most budding entrepreneurs. Let's assume that your parents invested $25,000 in the business and also promised to help out on weekends. Tradeoffs between family needs and business needs will surface. For example, decisions to expand the pizza delivery business may mean that you have to use personal income to buy a larger pizza oven instead of spending for other personal needs. As a result, you may have to decide if cash generated by the business should pay for a larger pizza oven, purchase a new family car, or pay tuition for the children's schooling. How many hours should you devote to your business versus the number of hours spent with your family? Should the pizza delivery business be open until 2 AM to serve late-night customers? How many hours will you have available for your family if you work at the pizza delivery business until it closes? Should your

family members work for the business? And what salaries and benefits should your family members receive if they do work for the business? Balancing decisions involved with family and business are often the most difficult for entrepreneurs to make.

All firms will have *customers* who are concerned about the success and operation of the business. The decisions you make about the quality of your products and the level of the service you provide will influence them. For example, you may advertise that you will deliver pizzas to your customers within 30 minutes of receiving their telephone order, a great benefit to customers who want a hot pizza quickly. At the same time, this speedy delivery promise will involve other stakeholders. Your pizza truck drivers may have to speed along neighborhood streets. How will members of the community respond to seeing your pizza delivery trucks speeding along their streets? Will the *community* be angry about a 30-minute delivery guarantee that may make their streets less safe for their children? How should you balance the interests of your customers who want pizza delivered in 30 minutes with that of the members of the neighborhood who are not buying your pizzas but who want your delivery trucks to drive slowly and safely through their neighborhoods?

The community might form *political groups* who might protest and demonstrate at your pizza store to prevent you from delivering pizzas in 30 minutes. These political groups could initiate and promote legislation to make food delivery businesses illegal in their communities. Other stakeholders may also influence your ability to deliver pizzas within 30 minutes. The city *government* can pass a law preventing any business within the city limits to advertise and promise to guarantee food deliveries within 30 minutes. The government could monitor the safe-driving behaviors of your drivers by issuing speeding tickets if they drive too fast. In addition, the city will have an interest in knowing that your pizzas are safe to eat. The city will have regulations and inspectors to monitor the operation of your business by specifying health standards, licenses, and building and food safety codes. Without the proper licenses to operate your business, the city can prevent you from operating. You will need to ensure that your pizza business is located in an area that is zoned for businesses that can serve and deliver food.

Your pizza business will likely have *employees* who take phone orders, make the pizzas, and deliver pizzas. These employees have their own interests and concerns. For example, the pizza delivery drivers will be concerned about their safety when making deliveries and may not want to drive to certain locations to deliver pizzas—say, a city park—that are not houses or apartment buildings. Such delivery spots may be more likely to be places where drivers are often robbed and killed, particularly late at night. Should a driver be allowed to say, "I won't deliver a pizza to that location?" You will have to balance the concerns of your pizza drivers with the needs of some customers who want a pizza delivered to a park or street corner.

Your pizza business will also purchase food, boxes, and equipment from *suppliers*. These businesses hope that your company will be successful so that you will buy more supplies from them over time. As your business expands, they will benefit through increased sales. Your business also depends on the ability of your suppliers to provide quality materials on time and at reasonable prices. What if your pizza business uses real Italian mozzarella cheese as an important ingredient and your cheese supplier cannot acquire the cheese you want because of shipping problems from Italy to the United States? What would you say to your customers if you did not have the real Italian mozzarella cheese you advertise? Should you close your business until you have real Italian cheese? Should you try to find another source

of supply? Should you substitute Italian cheese with American cheese? What should you tell your customers, and should you price your pizzas differently because of this change?

As this pizza delivery business example illustrates, every business is connected in very complicated ways to multiple stakeholders who affect the business's success. Decisions that affect one group of stakeholders may have a profound effect on other stakeholders. Each group must be considered. More than likely, each group will make its views known. As an enterpriser, you have to be proactive in ascertaining the views and interests of all of the stakeholders that impact your business.

Ethical Behavior

Enterprisers make many types of business decisions in the course of a day. In addition to considering stakeholder needs, they must also take into account what they believe to be right and wrong. The owner of our pizza delivery business has choices in how to run the company and the standards he or she sets. These actions shape the ethics of the organization. Ethics refers to the standards of moral behavior used to determine whether something is right or wrong. Examples of unethical behavior include lying, unauthorized use of someone else's property, giving false impressions, bribing someone to get business, and failing to disclose information. Suppose our pizza delivery business owner doesn't tell customers that deliveries to addresses outside a five-mile zone carry an extra charge. This is unethical because it misleads customers about the total cost of their orders.

Managing businesses ethically has many benefits, including keeping customers loyal, attracting new customers, and retaining employees. Throughout this book, we will address ethical concerns that enterprisers face when starting and operating their businesses.

As we make transactions with other people, we can choose to act ethically so that everyone wins or act in ways that cause the enterpriser to win and the other party to lose. The Enterprising Ethics box presents a framework for evaluating such interactions.

Ethics A set of moral standards and values that helps individuals choose between right and wrong.

ENTERPRISING ETHICS

Who Benefits?

Our lives are a series of transactions between other people. These transactions occur whenever a person is involved with another person and represent experiences where there can be gains or losses between the two parties. When person A initiates an activity with person B, it has an effect on both A and B. We can diagram these transactions as a two-by-two matrix that shows gain or loss between party A and party B.

In our view, people who initiate an activity where both A and B win are *enterprisers.* They create situations where everyone gains. When you sell a product or provide a service, ideally the buyer of your product is better off because the transaction fills a need. You are also better off because you make money through the transaction.

A person who initiates an activity where he or she loses and the other person wins is a *saint:* Person A's actions result in a situation where A is worse off, but B is better off. For example, some people start businesses and sell products at prices below their costs to gain customers. While their customers benefit, the enterpriser eventually goes out of business. In this situation, others benefit while the enterpriser doesn't.

On the other side of the spectrum is the *bandit.* In this case, party A initiates an action where he or she gains but party B loses. Certainly, there are individuals who start businesses that eventually defraud others, where the business doesn't provide benefits to anyone

other than the owners. Only the owners win, while everyone else is worse off. We would hope that most of these people go to jail for such actions, but you can probably think of people who personally gained through their actions while others have not. The recent Enron, Tyco, WorldCom, and other corporate scandals are examples of such situations. Bandits can exist at small companies, too. Unscrupulous contractors with no credentials offer to fix a roof or driveway, take a sizable deposit, and don't return or do slipshod work. Get-rich-quick schemes also promise big profits. Unsuspecting customers pay for the materials, only to discover that the only one who gets rich quick is the promoter—who is clearly a bandit.

Finally, we have situations where A initiates an activity that ends up with losses for both A and B. In this case, A is *stupid.* People who cause accidents fall into this category. There are also individuals who initiate activities that they hope will be successful but which eventually fail. So not only does the initiator fail, but so do any others who are involved. Employees, customers, investors, and suppliers all are worse off, too.

While this framework may seem to be an oversimplification of interactions between people, it helps us think about the types of situations that might occur when people initiate new activities.

Discussion Questions

1. Give examples of enterprises that fit into these four quadrants.

2. Are people in other countries rewarded differently for being in each of these four quadrants? Are there some countries that expect people to act as saints rather than as enterprisers? Can you think of countries where people are more likely to act as bandits?

3. How would you characterize former Enron executives Kenneth Lay and Jeffrey Skilling: bandits or stupid?

4. What kinds of laws and regulations would you enact to promote more enterprisers versus bandits, saints, or stupid people?

Source: Carlo M. Cipolla, "The Basic Laws of Human Stupidity," *Whole Earth Review,* Spring 1987, pp. 2–7, http://www.mentalsoup.com/mentalsoup/index.html.

Summary

1. We live in a world where organizations have a profound effect on our day-to-day activities. To succeed in an organizational world, we need to understand how to create and control these organizations.

2. An organization is an activity-based system (work gets done) that is socially constructed (involves other people), goal directed (has a purpose), and is bounded (there is a distinction between members and non-members). There are many ways to compare and contrast the different types of organizations. For-profit versus not-for-profit organizations (differentiated by a purpose to make money) and private versus public organizations (differentiated by how membership is determined) are two ways that we can compare different types of organizations. A business is defined as an organization that is created for the purpose of generating value for its owners.

3. An enterpriser is one who undertakes an enterprise. To be enterprising is to be marked by an independent, energetic spirit and by a readiness to undertake or experiment.

4. A primary reason for focusing on small businesses is that most organizations are small. About 98 percent of all businesses in the United States have fewer than 100 employees. Small businesses create most of the new jobs in the economy. Small businesses are a significant source of innovations in technology and of new products, and are significant in the creation of new markets. Small businesses are a major pathway for the economic and social advancement of women, minorities, and immigrants.

5. Business activity occurs across three levels: person, business, and environment. At each level, there are forces that push for change. In an evolutionary perspective, change occurs through a cycle of emergence, newness, and transformation. In emergence, change occurs as persons, businesses, and forces in the environment seek variation. A variation is a difference in how things currently are. As enterprisers strive to develop new ways of doing things,

they face the problem of newness. Most new things fail. If a business survives its early years, then it is likely to face ongoing changes in the environment. Environmental change is inevitable as individual tastes and preferences change, new technologies are introduced, and social, demographic, environmental, and economic changes occur.

6. The three forces of change also apply to the life cycle of an enterprise. In the new venture formation stage, the focus is on starting and initiating new projects. During the progress and growth stage, the focus is on managing, monitoring, operating, and growing personal and business achievements. In the final stage, transition and change, the focus turns to reevaluating prior successes and achievements, recognizing changes in the environment and in personal goals and priorities, and making decisions about the future.

7. In an organizational world, it is important for all individuals to take an active role in their personal success. In "self-actualization ethics," every individual seeks to pursue his or her unique qualities and abilities. It is important to "know thyself" and seek an understanding of how one's disposition affects and is affected by one's way of thinking (cognitions) and actions.

8. The actions of individuals and businesses take place within the context of an environment. An environment involves everyone and everything that is not about you. Anyone affected by a specific business is a stakeholder of that business. Most businesses are likely to have investors, customers, communities, employees, trade associations, suppliers, governments, political groups, and family members of the owners of the business as stakeholders.

9. The organizational imperative states that a business has its own purpose and objectives, as well as its own needs and resource requirements that are separate from the goals, objectives, and needs of the owners and managers of the business. Two major dimensions by which the interests of a business are determined are control and ownership.

Review Questions

1. What is required in order to succeed in a world of organizations?

2. What is the difference between an "enterpriser" and an "entrepreneur?"

3. In what ways do small businesses contribute to the economy?

4. How might changes in one of the three levels of business activity (person, business,

environment) affect the other levels of business activity?

5. Study Exhibit 1.4. What reasons might explain why businesses with more employees are likely to survive at higher rates than businesses without employees?

6. Why would a philosophy of "placing yourself first," that is, self-actualization ethics, be of benefit to others?

7. Differentiate between disposition, cognition, and action and give examples of each.

8. What negative characteristics in attributing problems seem to lead to "learned helplessness?"

9. Identify and define Howard Gardner's seven intelligences.

10. Study Exhibit 1.8. Identify specific stakeholders for each category that would be affected by a business that manufactured bicycles.

11. Explain the concept of "organization imperative."

12. What are the two major dimensions by which the interests of a business are determined?

13. Where might opportunity recognition and development skills be utilized?

14. What characterizes the transition and change stage of an enterprise life cycle?

Applying What You've Learned

1. The first step in developing your future career plans is to examine your own life and goals. Here are some questions to get you started.

   (a) Do I have personal goals for my personal life?

   (b) Do I function efficiently and effectively?

   (c) Do I plan my daily schedule for maximum efficiency?

   (d) Have I set aside specific time each week to upgrade my knowledge and professional proficiency?

   (e) Do I work well with others?

   (f) Am I working to develop stronger leadership qualities?

   (g) Do I participate in community, civic, or church activities?

   (h) Do I have a positive attitude?

   (i) How well do I organize my work and home life?

   (j) Am I an asset to my community?

2. The primary activity for developing your own abilities and knowledge as an enterpriser is through networking. (This topic will be covered in more detail in Chapter 4.) Each week you should contact ten "strangers" (individuals with whom you have not had any previous personal contact) about aspects of enterprising that will be of benefit to you. These strangers can be entrepreneurs, experts, customers, or suppliers in an industry you are interested in; or venture enablers such as accountants, lawyers, and investors. Keep a log of these strangers. Provide a name and contact information (address, phone number, e-mail address) for each stranger. How did you get the name of this stranger? Why did you contact this stranger? What benefits were you hoping to offer this stranger? What benefits were you hoping this stranger would offer you? What other contacts was this stranger able to offer you to help you achieve your goals?

3. Review the descriptions of Howard Gardner's Seven Intelligences in Exhibit 1.7. Which of these are among your strengths? Weaknesses?

4. Choose a business in your area, such as a restaurant, grocery store, or gas station. Identify all of the different stakeholders that are affected by this business (e.g., customers, employees, and government). How does this business *succeed* with each stakeholder group? How similar, or different, are the measures of success for each stakeholder group?

5. Look around your house and choose an object that you use frequently (e.g., pen, pencil, and cup). How might this product be improved? Think about how you would go about the process of taking your ideas and developing them into a product that other people would buy. What would you need to make your idea become real?

Enterprisers on the Web

1. Go to the home page of Wahoo's Fish Tacos, http://www.wahoos.com, and use the information you find to answer the following questions:

   (a) What does the home page say about the style and priorities of this business?

   (b) Explore the Events, Photos, and Contests pages. How do these pages demonstrate the underlying marketing philosophy Wing Lam describes?

   (c) Read the latest news about Wahoo's on its News and Media page. What more can you learn about the reasons for Wahoo's success?

2. Using an online article database like Find Articles (http://www.findarticles.com) or InfoTrak, read what others are saying about this company. How do others perceive Wahoo's, and how does this compare to how Wahoo's sees itself?

3. Go to http://geography.miningco.com/science/geography/cs/worldpopulation/ and explore demographic changes in the population of the world and the United States. This site provides many different pathways to find demographic, social, and economic data on all regions and countries of the world. What kinds of changes are likely to occur in the world over the next 25 years? What kinds of changes are likely to occur in the United States over the next 25 years?

4. Go to *Inc.* magazine's website: http://www.inc.com/. Explore the various sections of this site. What kinds of resources are available for enterprisers?

5. Go to the GEM Consortium website, http://www.gemconsortium.org/, and explore the most recent version of the Global Entrepreneurship Monitor (GEM), which tracks entrepreneurial activity in dozens of countries throughout the world. Which countries appear to be engaged in more entrepreneurial activity, and what reasons does the report offer to explain these higher levels? Give several reasons why the United States is not the most entrepreneurial country.

6. Use one of the Internet directories (e.g., Yahoo!) to find a directory of businesses in your area. How many different kinds of businesses are identified in this directory? Why are there so many of the same kinds of businesses (restaurants, dry cleaners, retailers)? Are there any kinds of businesses that seem to be missing that might be successful in your area?

End Notes

1. "Frequently Asked Questions: Small Business Statistics and Research," *Small Business Administration, Office of Advocacy,* http://www.sba.gov (May 1, 2008).

2. Zoetermeer, *The European Observatory for SMEs: First Annual Report* (The Netherlands: European Network for SME Research and EIM Small Business Research and Consultancy, 1993).

3. *The Small Business Economy 2005: A Report to the President,* U.S. Small Business Administration (Washington, DC: Government Printing Office, 2005), p. 8.

4. "Frequently Asked Questions: Small Business Statistics and Research," *Small Business Administration, Office of Advocacy,* http://www.sba.gov (May 1, 2008).

5. William J. Dennis, *Business Starts and Stops* (Washington, DC: National Federation of Independent Business, 1999).

6. Brian Headd, "Redefining Business Success: Distinguishing between Closure and Failure," *Small Business Economics,* August 2003, pp. 51–61.

7. *The State of Small Business: A Report to the President,* U.S. Small Business Administration (Washington, DC: Government Printing Office, 1997).

8. William J. Dennis, *Business Starts and Stops* (Washington, DC: National Federation of Independent Business, 1999).

9. *2005 World Population Data Sheet,* Population Reference Bureau (Washington, DC: Population Reference Bureau, 2005), http://www.prb.org.

10. Eileen Marie Simoneau, "Get a Move on at Grandma's," *Orlando Sentinel,* March 12, 2006, p. J1; and Dixie E. Snider, "Obesity Statistics Still Grim," *Atlanta Journal-Constitution,* February 25, 2005, p. A15.

11. Greg Masters, "Peanuts or Pork Rinds?" *Retail Merchandiser,* July 2005, pp. 26–29.

12. Christopher Palmeri, "How NutriSystem Got Fat and Happy," *Business Week,* September 19, 2005, pp. 82–84; and Tatiana Serafin, "The Fat of the Land," *Forbes,* April 10, 2006, p. 104.

13. David L. Norton, *Personal Destinies: A Philosophy of Ethical Individualism* (Princeton, NJ: Princeton University Press, 1977).

14. Martin Seligman, *Learned Optimism* (New York: Pocket Books, 1998).

15. William G. Scott and David K. Hart, *Organizational America* (Boston: Houghton Mifflin Company, 1979).

Enterprisers

1. Entrepreneurship is a universal social and economic activity in the United States. Because being an enterpriser is more about *doing* than about *being*, nearly everyone has the same potential to become an enterpriser.

2. Enterprisers come from all backgrounds, ages, and experiences. Some characteristics (demographic and personal) can increase the likelihood of becoming an enterpriser. Although individuals can't change demographics—ethnicity, gender, and age—they do have some control over personal characteristics. Education, for example, is a primary driver of entrepreneurship.

3. Successful enterprisers are more likely to think differently from other individuals. They are more likely to view their situations optimistically, focus on ways to leverage their means (current resources and capabilities at hand) to come up with a variety of solutions (ends), and engage in accomplishing "small wins."

Suppose you are an African American male, the youngest of seven children, who grew up in a Texas ghetto. The biggest support in your life is your grandmother, who insists that you put God first, your family second, and everything else after that. Your father is a doorman who wants you to grow up to be a businessman. You start your first business venture as a child, mowing lawns for 50 cents. Its success encourages you to follow your entrepreneurial instincts and acquire those characteristics and dispositions that help you prosper.

This chapter introduces a case about how a determined young man from government housing, Albert Black, went to college on a football scholarship and built a successful business in spite of many setbacks while he still maintained the values his grandmother instilled in him. As you read this chapter, you will learn how you, too, can enhance your chances of becoming a successful enterpriser.

2.0 Enterprisers

"Am I an entrepreneur?" It's a common question that many people ask before they embark upon their journey as enterprisers. When we see successful people, we often wonder whether they have "something special" that makes them different from other people. Do enterprisers have personality characteristics that make them unique? We don't think so. In terms of their personalities, enterprisers are just like everyone else. Although you might suspect that most enterprisers are outgoing, sales-oriented people, in fact, all personality types are represented. Introverts who avoid risks at all costs are just as likely to be successful enterprisers, under the right circumstances, as extroverts and risk takers. Successful enterprisers find business situations that match their personal characteristics and skills.

This chapter explores a variety of dispositional and cognitive characteristics that determine whether enterprisers are different from other people. **Dispositional characteristics** are natural or acquired habits or characteristic tendencies in a person or thing. **Cognitive characteristics** are intellectual rather than physical—the ability to think, learn, and remember—and include mental

---

Dispositional characteristics A person's natural or acquired habits or characteristic tendencies.

Cognitive characteristics Intellectual rather than physical traits—the ability to think, learn, and remember. Examples include comprehension, reasoning, perception, decision making, planning, and learning.

processes such as comprehension, reasoning, perception, decision-making, planning, and learning. As you will discover, enterprisers are of all ages and come from all kinds of backgrounds and experiences. No personality characteristic prevents a person from becoming an entrepreneur. Certain characteristics, however, seem to increase the chance of becoming an enterpriser and achieving success.

For example, people who already earn a lot of money are more likely to start businesses than those who earn less. Knowing this fact doesn't prevent individuals who earn less money from becoming enterprisers. The statistics provide a sense of the *relative probabilities* of success for someone in a particular category. So when we talk about the following dispositional and cognitive characteristics, think of them as providing some individuals with a slight advantage at the starting line. Being rich is an advantage, but it doesn't guarantee future success—just as being poor doesn't prevent a person from becoming successful. You are likely to share some of the characteristics of successful enterprisers.

Our basic philosophy is that being an enterpriser is more about *doing* than about *being*. In Chapter 3, we cover some fundamental behaviors that you can practice to become a better enterpriser. Enterprising is not about *who you are;* it is about *what you do* with your life. Enterprising is a mindset and a way of acting.[1] Yet, we all worry about whether we have the "right stuff" to become an enterpriser.

As we discussed in Chapter 1, we think about individuals in terms of dispositions, cognitions, and actions. *Dispositions* are a person's characteristics, what a person has at hand at a particular moment in time. *Cognitions* are the way a person thinks, and *actions* are what a person does—behaviors.

We hope that by the end of this chapter you will agree that nearly all of us can become an enterpriser *if that is what we truly desire* and if we undertake the actions necessary to achieve this goal. As we mentioned earlier, learning about the dispositions and cognitive characteristics—for example, age, gender, marital status, and optimism—should offer encouragement by demonstrating that nearly everyone has the chance to become an enterpriser.

The Panel Study of Entrepreneurial Dynamics

Until recently we have had surprisingly little systematic evidence about the fundamental nature of the individuals involved in business start-up or the entrepreneurial process. The fall 2002 publication of an introduction and overview to the Panel Study of Entrepreneurial Dynamics (PSED) provides important research to substantially enhance our understanding of entrepreneurship.[2]

New business formation is one of the most important indicators of economic growth around the world. The self-sufficiency and independence that lead individuals to create new businesses significantly affect economic growth, innovation, and job creation. Entrepreneurs have played a major role in shaping the business environment in the United States. Of today's Fortune 200 corporations, about 97 percent had entrepreneurial beginnings. Think about the personal computer, Internet, and biotechnology industries. Many leading companies in these sectors didn't even exist 25 years ago! And it's not just technology firms. With Starbucks Coffee, Howard Schultz changed the way the world thinks about a cup of coffee, while Fred Smith's Federal Express revolutionized the small-package delivery system and gave us an alternative to the U.S. Postal Service. Schultz and Smith are two examples of how **nascent entrepreneurs,** individuals who undertake the efforts necessary to initiate and start new businesses, create new industries (overnight delivery) or change and restructure how businesses in established industries compete.

The PSED focused on four fundamental questions:

1. Who is involved in starting businesses in the United States?

2. How do they go about the process of starting firms?

3. Which of these business start-up efforts result in new firms?

4. Why are some of these business start-up efforts successful in creating new firms?

Through questionnaires and detailed interviews with 830 nascent entrepreneurs, the PSED gathered information about the type and sequence of start-up activities, the sources and kinds of resources nascent entrepreneurs used, work and career experience, social networks, perceptions of entrepreneurial climate, risk assessment, social skills assessment, competitive strategy, and future expectations.

The PSED is unique in several ways. By collecting information while entrepreneurs were starting their firms, the study gathered knowledge of their *current* expectations and thought processes rather than the reminiscences of entrepreneurs *after the fact*. Second, the PSED sample reflects a variety of attempts to get into business, not just of those individuals who successfully started firms. By following these start-up efforts over time, the PSED

Nascent entrepreneurs   Individuals who undertake the efforts necessary to initiate and start new businesses.

sample helps to differentiate characteristics of successful and failed efforts to create new businesses. Finally, the PSED included not only nascent entrepreneurs but also a comparison group. The PSED can be used to compare nascent entrepreneurs to the population of working-age adults across a wide variety of demographic, economic, social, and psychological factors.

Key Findings of the PSED Study

The results of the PSED indicate that all groups and types of individual are involved in the new business formation process. The highlights of the study include these findings:

- Entrepreneurial activity in the United States is widespread. Approximately 10.1 million adults in the United States are trying to start new businesses at any time, either as individuals or in teams.

- Men are twice as likely to start new businesses as women.

- Enterprisers span all adult age groups. Among the most active are young men aged 25–34; those over 65 are less likely to start businesses.

- African Americans are about 50 percent more likely to start a new business than whites.

- Education significantly predicts emergent entrepreneurship, particularly for African Americans and Hispanics.

- Those with higher incomes are more likely to be involved in starting a business.

- Where people live affects entrepreneurial activity. The presence of certain economic, demographic, and educational factors contribute to higher entrepreneurial activity in more urban areas.

Clearly, entrepreneurship is a universal social and economic activity in the United States.

2.1 The Demographics of Enterprisers

Americans devote a lot of energy to entrepreneurial activity.[3] Today, over 10 million adults in the United States are involved in new business creation. In fact, 6 percent of all U.S. adults over the age of 18 are trying to start new firms. Even though men and women are roughly equal in numbers in the population, men are almost twice as likely to start businesses as women. For men 18 years and older, the rate is 8 percent, almost twice the 4.5 percent rate for women 18 and older.

People like to work together when they try to start businesses. While over 40 percent of new businesses are formed as sole proprietorships, the average start-up team is about 1.8 people,[4] suggesting that nascent entrepreneurs are attempting to form well over 5 million new firms. Compare this to figures for marriages and births in the United States: According to the *Statistical Abstract of the United States: 2006,* there are about 2.2 million marriages and 4.1 million live births in the United States each year.[5] In short, the creation of a new firm is more widespread than the creation of a new household or the birth of a baby!

Age and Gender

Age and gender are correlated to whether individuals initiate efforts to start a new business. While men and women of all ages engage in the entrepreneurial process, this activity is more likely to occur in certain age groups. As Exhibit 2.1 shows, the highest prevalence rate for both

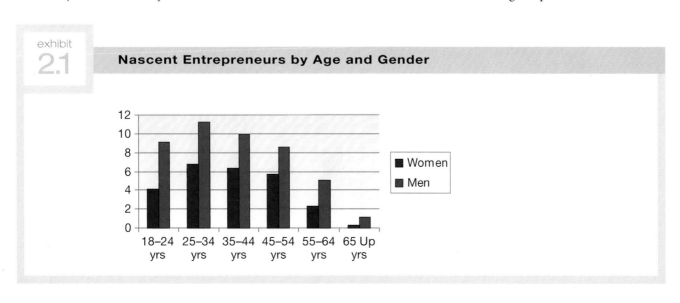

exhibit
2.1

Nascent Entrepreneurs by Age and Gender

men and women is among those 25–54 years old—the prime years for work success.

Ethnicity

Ethnic background influences the likelihood that individuals will start new businesses. Based strictly on numbers, there are more white entrepreneurs. As we see in Exhibit 2.2, however, the PSED estimates that the rate of business formation by African American men and women is about 50 percent higher than for whites, and for Hispanic men it is about 20 percent higher than for white men. Many people may find these findings surprising because earlier studies of minority enterprise indicated that blacks and Hispanics were less likely to be self-employed than whites.[6] However, both groups have always had strong traditions of business ownership.[7]

2.2 Personal Characteristics of Enterprisers

Demographic characteristics are those characteristics that one is basically "born with." You cannot change your ethnicity, gender, and age. Individuals do have some control over the following personal characteristics, however.

Education

Given the many educational programs available to prospective enterprisers, it comes as no surprise that schooling plays an influential role in the entrepreneurial process.

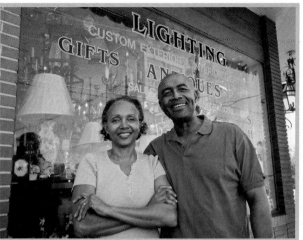

As Exhibit 2.3 confirms, individuals who finish high school and complete some additional education or training are more likely to try to start a new business venture. However, the impact varies substantially by ethnic group. Post–college graduation training significantly increases the likelihood of black men and women and Hispanic men becoming entrepreneurs.

You, the reader of this textbook, are likely to be a person who is getting a college degree. This places you in a category of people who are more likely to start businesses. Education is the one major factor that people can leverage to improve their chances of becoming a successful enterpriser.

Household Income

Like education, household income influences the likelihood that an individual will start a new business. The higher the household income, the greater a person's tendency to participate in start-up activities. Most

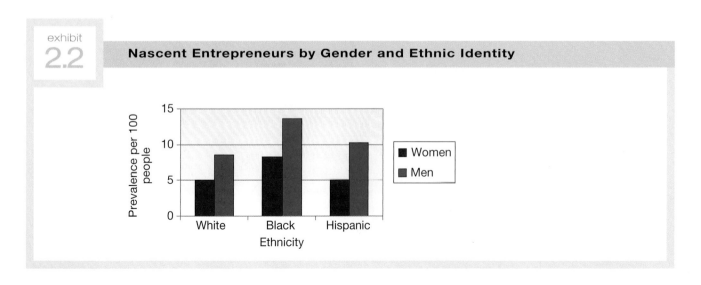

exhibit
2.2

Nascent Entrepreneurs by Gender and Ethnic Identity

Prevalence per 100 people

- ■ Women
- ■ Men

Ethnicity: White, Black, Hispanic

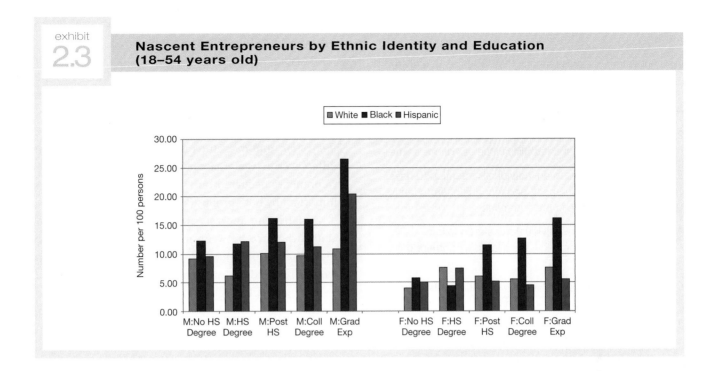

exhibit
2.3

Nascent Entrepreneurs by Ethnic Identity and Education (18–54 years old)

people can't easily change the amount of money they earn—at least in the short term. Yet, there is considerable evidence that household income is highly correlated with education. We can all position ourselves to achieve higher incomes by acquiring more education. *Education is, therefore, the primary driver of entrepreneurship.*

Marital Status and Household Characteristics

The PSED study also considered whether characteristics such as marital status, size of household, and age of children in the household have an impact on entrepreneurial activities:

- Marital status and the number of people living in a household have a small effect on whether individuals start new business.

- Respondents with children in the household are more likely to report being involved in a business start-up.

Labor Force Participation

Do people start new businesses out of desperation, because they have lost employment or cannot find a job? You might think so, but the PSED results do not support this popular belief. The rate of business start-ups for those 18 and older with full-time jobs is 8 percent, versus 7 percent for those working part time. In contrast, the rate is about

5 percent for those not currently working (such as the unemployed, students, and homemakers), and about 1 percent among those who are retired (5 percent among those retired but under 65 years old). Active participation in the workforce seems to have a positive impact on entrepreneurial activity, with little variation by gender or ethnic group.

Having a job provides a number of advantages for people considering starting a business. People with jobs are likely to be closer to potential customers, and therefore see new opportunities for products and services. People with jobs are more likely to have connections to suppliers, as well as have a deeper knowledge of how a particular industry works so that opportunities can be more easily identified and exploited.

2.3 Cognitive Characteristics: Career Reasons

Do enterprisers start businesses for different reasons from those individuals who have other kinds of careers? Do they think differently from others? As we mentioned earlier, many people believe that enterprisers are "different" from others, and that enterprisers have a greater desire for higher levels of financial success, autonomy, and independence. A recent study using the PSED compared nascent entrepreneurs to nonentrepreneurs on six career motives:[8]

1. Innovation involves reasons that describe an individual's intention to accomplish something new, such as developing an idea for a product and being innovative and on technology's cutting edge.

2. Independence describes an individual's desire for freedom, control, and flexibility in the use of one's time.

3. Recognition refers to an individual's intention to have status, approval, respect, and recognition from family, friends, and those in the community.

4. Roles describe an individual's desire to follow family traditions or follow the example of others one admires.

5. Financial success involves an individual's intention to earn more money and achieve financial security for himself or herself, spouse, and children.

6. Self-realization refers to the pursuit of self-directed goals—for example, challenging oneself, fulfilling a personal vision, leading and motivating others, and greatly influencing an organization.

More Alike than Different

The results of this study were surprising. As we see in Exhibit 2.4, there were no significant differences between nascent entrepreneurs and the comparison group on four of the scales—*innovation, independence, financial success,* and *self-realization*—but significant differences on two of the scales—*recognition* and *roles.* The analysis also showed that for all six reasons, the nascent entrepreneurs were likely to have *lower* scores than the nonentrepreneurs, overall.

In addition, all respondents (the nascent entrepreneurs and the nonentrepreneurs) were likely to rank the importance of the six reasons in the same order. *Independence* was the most important career reason, followed by *financial success, self-realization, recognition, innovation,* and *roles.* Interestingly, the more significant differences between nascent entrepreneurs and nonentrepreneurs occurred on scales that were rated as *less* important by both groups (such as *roles*).

Finally, the analysis showed a small but significant difference between men and women. Men had higher scores on *financial success* and *innovation* than women, regardless of their category. It is important to note that although the score women assigned to financial success was lower than that given by men, women still saw financial success as an important reason in career choice and equal in their ranking to self-realization.

Universal Values

The insights from this study suggest that for individuals in the United States, the desire for financial success, independence, self-realization, and innovation is universal. In fact, in studies of individuals from countries around the world, the reasons people give for why they work are surprisingly similar. An international research consortium, the Work Importance Study (WIS), analyzed data on the importance of work and or work values from 11 countries.[9]

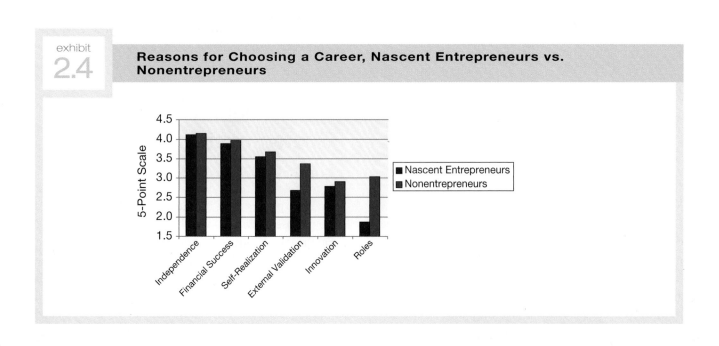

exhibit
2.4

Reasons for Choosing a Career, Nascent Entrepreneurs vs. Nonentrepreneurs

ENTERPRISING ETHICS

What Does a Kazaa Do, Anyway?

Imagine starting a company based on a product that you believed had a great future—even though you were not sure how people would use it! Niklas Zennström and Jan Friis did just that. Zennström, who earned business and computer science degrees at Uppsala University in Sweden, met Friis at Swedish telecom provider Tele2 in the 1990s. Tele2, the first Internet service provider in Sweden, now serves more than 30 million customers in 22 countries with fixed and mobile telephony, broadband, and cable television—successfully challenging the government monopolies.

These European technology entrepreneurs parlayed their prior telecommunications expertise into Kazaa, a company they developed around the commercialization of their proprietary peer-to-peer file-sharing software and launched in 2001. To date, the software has been downloaded onto more than 389 million computers worldwide. The original company was incorporated in the Netherlands.

Although Zennström thought the technology was promising, he admits he was not sure how people would use it. Some possibilities included sharing software and videos. "So we made it as open as possible and then we thought we'd see what people used it for," he says. "It was more a technical proof of concept that it was possible to transfer files between two end users rather than going through servers."

The software is free; all revenues come from advertisers who place ads on the Kazaa website. As users tried Kazaa software and liked it, it became the world's top download. Still, the partners did not expect the company to become so successful as a tool for music downloads. They attribute its popularity to the very user-friendly technology and interface, which was easier to use than rivals such as Napster.

An important difference between Kazaa and the now-defunct Napster was technology. Kazaa's peer-to-peer technology does not rely on central servers that are controlled by the company, as with Napster. Instead, users download the software to their own PCs, and the software automatically connects individual users to each other directly over the Internet—with no central management point. Kazaa provides the software but neither has control over how it is used nor knowledge of what users are doing when they are online. Kazaa and other file-sharing networks continue to maintain that their software has many legal uses and they should not be held accountable when users deploy the applications illegally.

This difference became important as the popularity of music- and movie-sharing services soared. Music publishers in many countries, including Australia and the United States, sued Kazaa and other file-sharing companies for copyright violations. After a Netherlands court ruled against Kazaa, Zennström quickly restructured the company, giving the software code to a company with operations on a British island known to be a tax haven and in Estonia, which has lax intellectual property regulations. They sold the Kazaa interface and the license for the file-sharing technology to Sharman Networks, a newly formed Australian company incorporated in Vanuatu, an island nation in the South Pacific. Because Vanuatu levies no taxes and does not release financial information about its companies, the companies are able to avoid regulation and legal challenges. However, major recording and movie studios soon sued Sharman Networks for copyright infringements.

Discussion Questions

1. How responsible are Nicholas Zennström and Jan Friis for the ways their creation is used? Should entrepreneurs care if others use their products or services in illegal ways? What steps could they take to prevent this from happening?

2. Why did Kazaa's acquirer, Sharman Networks, incorporate in Vanuatu? Discuss the ethical implications of incorporating in a country solely to avoid legal liability for the use of Kazaa's peer-to-peer file-sharing programs.

3. Visit the website for Kazaa, http://www.kazaa.com. What types of advisories are posted on the site? Do you think they protect Kazaa from legal action, and why?

4. Do a Web search to learn the outcome of the lawsuits against Sharman Networks/Kazaa. Summarize your findings and discuss whether you agree with the decisions.

Sources: Jane Black, "Napster's Sons: Singing a Different Tune?" *Business Week,* February 21, 2002, http://www.businessweek.com; Ted Bridis, "'Kazaa' Makers Settle Piracy Lawsuits," Associated Press, July 28, 2006, http://www.businessweek.com; "How Skype and Kazaa Changed the Net," BBC Click Online, June 17, 2005, http://news.bbc.co.uk; Kazaa website, http://www.kazaa.com (May 30, 2008); "Kazaa," http://en.wikipedia.org (July 30, 2006); Andy Reinhardt, "2005 Stars of Europe—Innovators: Niklas Zennström," *Business Week,* May 30, 2005, http://www.businessweek.com; and Todd Woody, "The Race to Kill Kazaa," *Wired,* February 2003, http://www.wired.com.

The study identified five factors and compared them cross-nationally:

- *Individualistic orientation* (autonomy, lifestyle, creativity, and personal development)

- *Orientation toward self-actualization* (ability utilization, altruism, and aesthetics)

- *Social orientation* (social relations, social interaction, variety, and working conditions)

- *Utilitarian orientation* (economics, advancement, prestige, and achievement)

- *Adventurous orientation* (risk, variety, and physical activity)

The findings indicated that the career value structures of individuals were surprisingly similar. In all the countries studied, the self-realization values (personal development, ability utilization, and achievement) are ranked highly, whereas people place little importance on risk taking and the desire for authority and prestige.[10]

Given these similarities, then, what differentiates enterprisers from others? Basically, enterprisers are less likely to care about how other people view their pursuit of success and do things themselves. They pursue financial success, independence, self-realization, and innovation on their own terms.

2.4 Cognitive Characteristics: Optimism

How we think about what happens to us, and how we think about what *will* happen to us, is vital for enabling us to take actions that can make a difference in our lives. Thinking optimistically involves viewing our past and future situations in a way that we don't get stuck and not take action when necessary. Living life successfully involves a certain level of risk taking. You will often be in situations where you need to take action, but you will not be sure whether your actions will result in the outcomes you intend. There is always a chance that your actions may turn out differently from what you intended.

Research on success has found that individuals who take action are more successful than those who don't, *even if those actions are not necessarily the best or the right*

© Comstock Images/Jupiter Images

actions. Much of this book is about learning the skills and abilities to determine the right actions to take. However, simply knowing what to do does not necessarily lead to action. You must still take action—and you should put yourself in the right frame of mind to take action.

Positive Thinking

People who are more likely to take action are probably also optimists. An **optimist** is a person who believes that good things will happen. It sounds simple: Just believe that your actions will result in good outcomes. But it is not always easy to adopt this mindset. We encounter situations where we feel discouraged and hopeless or *pessimistic,* that bad things will happen, no matter what we do. This section discusses how to think about our situations so that we become optimists and take actions that lead to good outcomes!

What characterizes an optimistic viewpoint? Individuals make three attributions about their experiences:[11]

- First, we make a judgment about whether the situation is *internal.* Is it about us or our efforts, or is the situation *external* to us? For example, if a person was involved in an automobile accident,

Optimist   A person who believes that good things will happen.

an internal attribution would be, "I caused the accident," while an external attribution would be, "A dog jumped in front of the car, and I swerved to avoid hitting the dog."

- Second, we determine whether the situation is *stable,* likely to exist for a while, or *variable.* "I caused the accident because I have poor vision," is a stable attribution. Poor vision isn't something that is quickly corrected. "I was answering the cell phone when the accident occurred," is temporary; it occurred only in that moment.

- The third type of attribution involves a judgment about whether the cause is *global* and will extend into other situations or is *specific* to the incident. "I always fail to pay attention," is a global attribution compared to, "I just didn't see the car come out of the driveway until it was too late," which is a specific attribution.

Consider a good situation you have recently experienced. For example, imagine that you just took an exam and received the highest grade in the class. An optimist offers internal/stable/global attributions for this situation, such as, "I always do well on multiple choice exams." This comment indicates that you consider your success to be because of you (an internal attribution) and that you believe you'll be successful in taking other exams in the future (a stable and global attribution). A pessimist will offer attributions that are the opposite of the optimist's—an external/temporary/specific attribution of the situation, such as, "The professor gave an easy test today." The pessimist doesn't attribute any of the success to himself or herself (an external attribution) and doesn't believe that this good event will last or have any significance for other situations (a temporary and specific event).

Optimists attribute external/temporary/specific causes to bad situations. For example, if an optimist gets a poor grade on an exam, the optimistic attribution would be, "The professor put questions on the exam on material that we didn't cover in class." The poor grade is due to an external situation that is also temporary and specific to this one exam. The pessimist will offer an internal/stable/ global attribution for a poor exam score, "I'm not very smart," which attributes the poor exam score to himself or herself and suggests that such poor performance on this one exam is likely to occur on other exams as well.

Believe in Yourself

The previous examples were for attributions that people make about their past, explanations for the causes of what happened to them. Individuals also offer their expectations for what they believe will occur in future situations. The same patterns hold true. An optimist will offer explanations about future situations indicating that he/she expects good things will occur. These good things will result from his/her own efforts (internal), will continue (stable), and will extend to other situations in his/her life (global). The pessimist, on the other hand, doesn't expect that his/her own efforts will help good things occur (external). Any good things that do happen will be short-lived (temporary) and apply only to that situation (specific).

Because optimists expect good things to happen, they are likely to put effort into achieving their expectations. Pessimists, who expect that bad things will happen, tend to give up too soon, thinking that their efforts will be for naught. Certainly, there are many situations where one should give up, but giving up is appropriate only when there are other goals that might be more attainable, achievable, or appropriate. *Giving up, and doing nothing, is not an option for an enterpriser.*

An optimistic way of thinking about our lives provides tremendous benefits, even in difficult situations. For example, in studies of students who are making the adjustment to college life, researchers found that students with higher levels of optimism were less stressed, less depressed, less lonely, and had more social support.[12] In studies of cancer patients, optimists were more likely to have less distress and were more likely to be able to cope with the difficulty of having cancer and undergoing treatment.[13] In work situations, optimists are likely to be more problem-focused than pessimists. Pessimists often avoid dealing with problems by escapism, overeating, and overdrinking.[14]

As Exhibit 2.5 (on page 38) clearly illustrates, researchers have found that optimists are more able to engage in the kinds of behaviors that enable them to cope with difficult situations. Optimists exhibit less stress in difficult times and accept the situations they are in. They are proactive in looking for solutions. Their pessimistic counterparts are likely to be in denial and not do anything to improve their lot.[15]

There are relatively few, if any, situations where it is better to be a pessimist. Indeed, researchers suggest that pessimistic thinking often cripples individuals from undertaking any action on important goals in their lives. When individuals are hobbled by thoughts that their actions will result in bad outcomes, they fall into a state of lethargy, where it seems impossible to do anything that might improve the situation. Believe that your efforts will lead to success, and your chances of success will increase!

exhibit
2.5

Coping Tendencies of Optimists and Pessimists

Optimists	Pessimists
Information seeking	Suppression of thoughts
Active coping and planning	Giving up
Positive framing	Self-distraction
Seeking benefit	Cognitive avoidance
Use of humor	Focus on distress
Acceptance	Overt denial

Source: M. F. Scheier, C. S. Carver, and A. W. Bridges, "Optimism, Pessimism, and Psychological Well Being," in E. C. Chang (Ed.), *Optimism, Pessimism: Implications for Theory Research and Practice* (Washington, DC: American Psychological Association, 2001), Exhibit 9.1, p. 204. Reprinted with permission of C. S. Carver.

2.5 Cognitive Characteristics: Ends and Means

We can approach problems in two ways: focusing on the ends or on the means. When we have a particular problem to solve, the *ends* of the problem are the characteristics of the problem itself. The *means* refer to the capabilities necessary to solve a particular problem. In most situations, we tend to focus on developing the means to satisfy particular ends.[16] The differences between ends and means may, at this point, seem rather trivial. However, these two approaches yield very different—but equally important—ways to accomplish our goals. Here is a simple example of the difference between ends and means.

Imagine a chef is assigned the task of cooking dinner. The task can be organized in two ways. In the first, the host or client picks out a menu in advance. All the chef needs to do is list the ingredients needed, shop for them, and then actually cook the meal. This is a process of focusing on ends. It begins with a given menu and concentrates on selecting effective ways to prepare that particular meal.

In the second case, the host asks the chef to look through the cupboards in the kitchen for possible ingredients and utensils and then cook a meal. Here, the chef has to imagine possible menus based on the given ingredients and utensils, select the menu, and then prepare

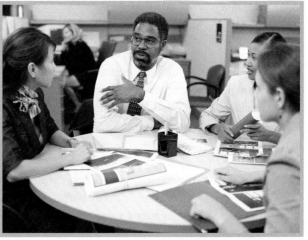

the meal. This is a process of focusing on means. *It begins with given ingredients and utensils and focuses on preparing one of many possible meals with them.*[17]

Ends

When we focus on *ends,* we *start* with the solution. Most problem solving uses this approach. Assume that you love dogs and are also artistic. Frustrated in your current job at a public relations firm, you decide you want to start a canine-themed business. From your experience with your own large dogs, you know that currently available dog collars and leashes don't do a good job of letting the handler control large dogs, and you choose to focus on designing attractive and effective products that solve this problem. As you develop your plans, you would perform certain steps to create your dog collar and leash business, including the following:

- Determine the resources necessary to make collars and leashes, such as the supplies, equipment, and employees to make and assemble them.

- Gather market information about the people who purchase collars and leashes and where they are likely to purchase them (such as pet stores).

- Make contacts with retail stores who might display your company's collars and leashes for customers to purchase.

We begin with a specific goal, or end: a collar and leash business. We then work out the means to achieve that goal.

When we start with ends, we use our creativity to generate the necessary means to achieve given ends. Indeed, we often hear of individuals who identify new means to solve particular ends. Our entrepreneur will need supplies (means)—for example, nylon webbing, buckles, and fasteners—for the collar and leash business, yet may have very little money to purchase these supplies. The creative enterpriser might convince a supplier to provide the necessary materials on credit or offer the supplier a partnership in the new business as a way to obtain the necessary materials to make the collars and leashes.

Means

Focusing on *means* takes a different approach to the situation. We begin with what we have at hand. Let's assume that the general problem is the same as before: controlling large dogs. What might we already have available to us that could control large dogs?

We might first consider our ability to train a large dog to obey our commands. Rather than starting a collar and leash company, we might consider using our dog-handling skills to open a training school for large dogs. We could take our dog to a park where dogs can run and play without leashes and demonstrate our abilities to control our dog without a leash. Other dog owners may notice our well-behaved dog and ask for tips on dog training. We could turn these queries into sales by suggesting that we will train their dogs for a fee.

We could also put up fliers announcing our dog-training classes. The training classes could grow into a substantial business. We might end up training other people to teach the classes and generate revenues from their activities. We might then decide to write a book on dog training as another possible way to help people control their dogs. We might consider conducting seminars on dog training or developing a television show or video about this topic.

By focusing on our *means*—what we have currently available to use—we can expand the many ways that our skills and abilities in controlling large dogs might develop into a business. These become the starting point for achievement.

Differences Between Ends and Means

Let's consider the ways these two approaches differ and how companies might apply them in developing a business strategy. Exhibit 2.6 (on page 40) summarizes the major differences between ends and means.

It is important to understand that efforts toward accomplishing a goal are likely to combine both ends and means. Few situations are likely to be pure forms of one or the other. These approaches are points of view about how individuals accomplish activities. Enterprisers should explore both and can be effective using either approach.

2.6 Exploring Ends and Means: Powell's Books versus Amazon.com

To more clearly illustrate the distinctions between means and ends, let's look at two Internet companies that represent these contrasting styles: Internet businesses Powells.com and Amazon.com. We'll start with the givens of each firm's situation and then compare each in terms of the categories in Exhibit 2.6.

Givens

In the Ends approach, the enterpriser starts with the desired effect (outcome). Amazon.com started operations in July 1995. The company's objective was to use the Internet to change the way people purchased books. Founder Jeff Bezos set about acquiring the resources necessary to start an online bookstore, including selling stock in his company. Bezos also formed an alliance with a major distributor of books to gain access to a nearly unlimited inventory of books that could be shipped to customers.

---

exhibit
2.6

Ends vs. Means

Ends versus Means

Categories	Focus on Ends	Focus on Means
Givens	End is a given	Means and capabilities are a given
Decision-making criteria	Choose between means to achieve a given effect	Choose between possible ends that can be created with given means
	Selection of means based on expected return	Selection of ends based on affordable loss or acceptable risk
	Outcome dependent: Choosing means is driven by the characteristics of the outcome that the decision makers wants to create and their knowledge of possible means	Actor dependent: Given specific means, choice of outcome is driven by characteristics of the actors and their ability to discover and use contingencies
Competencies employed	Exploiting knowledge	Exploiting contingencies
Nature of unknowns	Focus on the predictable aspects of an uncertain future	Focus on the controllable aspects of an unpredictable future
Underlying logic	To the extent we can predict the future, we can control it	To the extent we can control the future, we do not need to predict it
Outcomes	Market share in existing markets through competitive strategies	New markets created through alliances and other cooperative strategies

Source: Adapted from S. D. Sarasvathy, "Causation and Effectuation: Toward a Theoretical Shift from Economic Inevitability to Entrepreneurial Contingency," *Academy of Management Review* 26 no. 2 (2001), p. 251.

In the Means approach, the enterprise starts with current capabilities. Powell's Books is a used and new bookstore that began operations in Portland, Oregon, in 1971. The company's sales grew to the point where the store occupied an entire city block, and the company transformed itself into "Powell's City of Books." Powell's increased book sales by branching out into specialized types of books: technical books, travel books, and books for gardeners and cooks. The company's growth was evolutionary. As customers requested certain kinds of books, Powell's Books offered them. With a reputation for having a comprehensive stock of both used and new books, Powell's Books had customers from all over the world who used mail and phone orders to buy books without entering the Portland bookstore.

When companies like Amazon.com began to show that many book buyers were using the Internet to purchase books, Powell's Books decided to pursue this approach as well—but with a difference. Powell's Books'

primary effort built on current capabilities and involved the development of a computerized database to identify the books they already owned. In the past, its salespeople had to physically go into the book stacks and find out whether it had a new or used copy of a book in inventory. The decision to offer books on the Internet was, for Powell's Books, a decision about expending the effort to identify the resources they already owned.

Decision-making

In the Ends approach, the enterpriser chooses means based on the desired goals. Jeff Bezos' goal of creating the leading Internet bookseller required him to seek substantial resources to achieve his objective. In addition to selling equity to the public, he also raised two billion dollars by selling bonds that could, at a later date, be converted into stock if the price of Amazon stock continued to rise. With over four billion dollars to spend, Bezos could invest

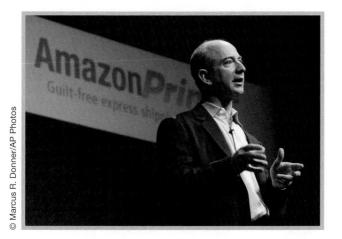

substantial resources to create an innovative and easy-to-use Internet site, build warehouses and distribution centers to distribute books, and buy a substantial amount of inventory to be able to ship books upon order.

In the Means approach, the enterpriser chooses possible effects given the capabilities and resources on hand. Powell's Books decided to sell books on the Internet as one of many possible ways they could sell books to customers. While Powell's Books was tentatively establishing an Internet presence, they were also opening other stores in the Portland area. Its investment in the website also involved upgrading the firm's inventory management system. Powell's Books made choices to expand based on enhancing current capabilities. The investment in building a website was a minor cost when compared to the cost of their overall operations. The risk of failing to sell books on the Internet would be an affordable risk for Powell's Books.

Competencies

In the Ends approach, the enterpriser exploits knowledge. Amazon.com was a pioneer in online retailing. One of its major innovations was "one-click" purchasing. The company spent millions of dollars to develop and patent a simple, convenient way to buy books at its Internet site. Customers could make a purchase without having to enter relevant customer information each time they visited the site. With "one-click," a database kept the customer's address, credit card information, and any other information that Amazon.com would need to complete the book sale. Initially, the "one-click" system was new knowledge that only Amazon.com could exploit and use.

In the Means approach, the enterpriser exploits contingencies. Powell's Books was an established bookseller, so it could pursue opportunities based on its existing capabilities. It already had a massive inventory of used

and new books to sell. Adding Internet sales was a natural extension of its current mail and phone order sales process. Powell's exploited its strength in various ways, such as expanding its downtown store, opening other stores in the area, and increasing nonlocal orders with the addition of capabilities for ordering books online. The means—books—were the same. How Powell's sold the books—the ends—changed as Powell's customers asked for different ways to purchase books.

Unknowns and Logic

In the Ends approach, the enterpriser seeks to predict the characteristics of an uncertain future, because if one can predict the future, one can control it. Amazon.com's focus has been to capture a growing share of all book sales by encouraging book buyers to purchase via the Internet. To predict its ability to achieve its desired market share, Amazon.com must estimate the number of people who will purchase books using the Internet and compare this to the number who purchase through other channels like bookstores and mail and phone sales. If Amazon.com improves the incentives—say, by offering free shipping, larger price discounts, or faster shipping—will more people purchase from Amazon.com instead of Powell's? Once the company has greater insight into the mindset of book buyers and knows how different incentives increase sales, it can adapt these incentives to cater to these buyers.

In the Means approach, the enterpriser seeks to control aspects of the unpredictable future, because if one can control the future, one does not have to predict it. Powell's Books attempts to control the various ways that a person might want to purchase a book. Certainly, in Portland, Oregon, a book purchaser can buy a book by driving to the downtown location, visiting one of the many branch stores, placing a phone order, buying through catalog mail order, or using the Internet. If Powell's Books provides a variety of options for purchasing books, Powell's is there no matter which option a customer chooses!

Outcomes

In the Ends approach, the enterpriser seeks to increase market share in existing markets. For this category, the roles of Powell's Books and Amazon.com are reversed. Powell's Books wants to increase its market share of new and used book sales, particularly in the Portland, Oregon, area.

In the Means approach, the enterpriser seeks new markets through alliances and other cooperative strategies. Amazon.com sought a variety of strategic alliances to pursue new opportunities. Any book owner can list used books for sale on the Amazon.com site. Amazon.com, which at no cost to itself essentially gains a vast number of potential partners, earns a percentage on each used book sale. Amazon.com has also greatly expanded its online offerings through strategic alliances. Site visitors can buy much more than books at Amazon.com. It has teamed up with a wide variety of companies, many of whom have their own e-commerce sites, to offer a wide variety of other products and services—from apparel to electronics, home furnishings, jewelry, sporting goods, magazine subscriptions, photo finishing, and more. Nordstrom, Macy's, Foot Locker, Sephora, Target, Office Depot, Cooking.com, eToys, TigerDirect, J&R Music, and Computer World are just a few of the retailers whose products customers can

buy through Amazon.com. The partners earn a percentage of the revenues from these jointly shared transactions. It's a win-win situation: Amazon attracts more visitors to its site because it offers so many products and can boast of having "the earth's largest selection," and the other merchants benefit from Amazon's online retailing expertise and huge customer base.

What is important to take away from these comparisons between ends and means is an appreciation that *enterprisers must explore both.* Enterprisers can be effective using either approach. Knowing which approach will be more appropriate for you will depend on your circumstances and on thoroughly knowing your own capabilities.

AN ENTERPRISING WORLD

A Swede, a Dane, and Technology Equal a Global Success Story

Swedish entrepreneur Niklas Zennström and his Danish partner Jan Friis, whom we met earlier, exemplify global entrepreneurship at its best. The founders of Kazaa, which was formed in the Netherlands, sold the company to Sharman Networks, an Australian company, in 2002, and quickly moved on to their second venture. Skype Technologies, an even more lucrative business, was incorporated in Luxembourg in 2003 and based in London and Tallinn, Estonia.

The technological foundation for both Kazaa and Skype is peer-to-peer networking of user computers. Kazaa users were able to share music and video files between computers. With Skype, the technology was adapted for telephone calls. By downloading Skype's free software, users can make free, high-quality calls to another Skype user who is also online—anywhere in the world—using an Internet connection and headsets or microphones plugged into their computers. Now available in 27 languages, Skype's customer base grew to more than 54 million users in its first two years and is currently expanding at a rate of about 150,000 users a day.

"Skype has blazed a new trail," says Ian Cox of Juniper Research Ltd. Not only does it advance Voice over Internet Protocol (VoIP) technology, but it also presents a very different business model. While the software and basic computer-to-computer phone service, video calls, chats, and some conference calls are free, Skype earns revenues from fee-based premium

features. SykpeOut lets Skype users call from PCs to landline and mobile phones worldwide, for rates averaging about $0.02 per minute. Voicemail costs $20 per year, and SkypeIn offers a phone number and voicemail for $30 per year. Personalized services such as ring tones cost $1.20 to $1.95. By partnering with hardware and software companies, Skype is able to offer new services and products, such as headphones and WiFi phones.

Even more interesting is its ability to grow without spending much money. Unlike traditional telecommunications providers, Skype has no investment in capital equipment or marketing. Its customers use their own computers and Internet connections to make calls and invite others to join. As more people join to use the free services, Skype has more opportunities to sell its premium services. As Zennström explains, "We want to make as little money as possible per user, [because] we don't have any cost per user, but we want a lot of them."

Skype's success in the VoIP sector attracted the attention of major new media companies such as Google, News Corp., Yahoo!, MSN, and AOL. In September 2005, Skype surprised everyone by accepting a $2.6 billion acquisition offer from eBay, which will also pay a $1.5 billion bonus if Skype meets financial performance goals. Why eBay? The two companies can help each other grow. eBay is the largest in the United States, while Skype has more presence internationally. Other synergies include a stronger link with eBay's

PayPal online payment unit and the ability of eBay users to speak to each other via Skype. A major plus for Zennström and Friis, however, was eBay's promise to let them continue to develop Skype to become the dominant Internet communications provider, for all media, internationally. "When Yahoo! and Microsoft buy companies, they typically disintegrate them," says Zennström.

The eBay-Skype partnership is working. By mid-2008, Skype had more than 310 million registered users who had made more than 100 billion minutes of free calls. It keeps offering improved usability and more features. Skype is available in 28 languages and is used in almost every country around the world.

While they continued to work at Skype, Zennström and Friis began developing their third project, code-named the "Venice Project," a global communications venture that builds on file-sharing software technologies—this time for distributing TV shows and other forms of video over the Web using peer-to-peer technology. In 2007, they launched Joost (http://www.joost.com), the results of their collaboration, to bring free TV to an international networked community. What makes Joost different is the ability of viewers to use Internet tools, such as instant messaging and channel chat, to share the TV experience.

Discussion Questions

1. What dispositional and cognitive characteristics do Zennström and Friis display, and how do these traits contribute to their success?

2. Is the story of Skype an example of ends or means? Explain your answer with specific examples. What does your answer tell you about Zennström and Friis?

3. Discuss the implications of Skype's business model and how it relates to means and ends.

4. How did Zennström and Friis use small wins to grow Skype?

Sources: "About Tele2," http://www.tele2.com, July 27, 2006; "How Skype and Kazaa Changed the Net," BBC Click Online, June 17, 2005, http://news.bbc.co.uk; Olga Kharif, "Skype Piles It On," *Business Week,* May 3, 2006, http://www.businessweek.com; "Q&A: Skype's Niklas Zennström," *Red Herring,* November 21, 2005, http://www.redherring.com; Andy Reinhardt, "2005 Stars of Europe—Innovators: Niklas Zennström," *Business Week,* May 30, 2005, http://www.businessweek.com; Steve Rosenbush, "Kazaa, Skype, and now 'The Venice Project,'" *Business Week,* July 24, 2006, http://www.businessweek.com; "Skype's 'Aha!' Experience," *Business Week,* September 19, 2005, http://www.businessweek.com; Joost website, http://www.joost.com (June 16, 2008).

2.7 Small Wins: The Building Blocks of Enterprise

Moving on from disposition and cognitions, then, we need to think about how to position ourselves for success. Based on where you are at this moment, it might seem that you can't do much to change anything in your life. That would indeed feel depressing! Yet, there is a strategy for moving forward: small wins.

Given your situation, if you wanted to become an enterpriser, what would you do? Where would you start the process? The tasks and activities involved in enterprising may seem daunting at the outset. Just look at all the chapters in this book—so much to learn and to do! Taking the first steps toward achieving a major goal may seem overwhelming, difficult, and complicated. Enterprising, with all it involves, is not easy.

Anything of significance, whether it's a new craft project such as building a bookcase or starting a new business venture, takes time to achieve. After all, Rome wasn't built in a day! Yet, we often fail to take this basic concept into account when we begin something new, forgetting that significant accomplishments rarely result from big actions. Rather, they emerge from a series of small activities.

Even gigantic organizations like Ford Motor Company started small. Henry Ford began his first effort in the automobile industry in 1896 while working full time for the Edison Illuminating Company. He devoted his evenings and nights to building his first car, the "quadracycle," which he completed in 1898. When this automobile was completed, he sold it for $200 and used the proceeds to invest in his first automobile company, the Detroit Automobile Company. This company was started in 1899 and failed in 1901. Undaunted, he started another automobile company, the Henry Ford Company, in 1901, and this company failed too! It was on his third try, when he started the Ford Motor Company in 1903, that he finally succeeded. We often forget that big companies start out small, and that enterprisers often fail before they learn how to succeed.

A Journey of a Thousand Miles Begins with a Single Step

Most accomplishments begin with the idea of small wins, which are achievable, tangible accomplishments that are within a person's capabilities and produce visible results.[18] A series of small wins creates a pattern of visible success that attracts supporters to your cause and deters possible competitors. Put into practice, the concept of small wins helps companies make steady progress toward improved performance. Actions that may initially appear to be rather simple and trivial often solve seemingly difficult and impossible problems.

For example, Greyhound of Canada was losing customers. When it asked customers why they were not riding its buses, they offered a variety of responses. Some preferred other means of transportation, and others complained of inconvenient bus routes, schedules, and bus terminals.

Although unable to identify an obvious solution that would bring back its customers, one senior vice president, John Munro, decided to take action—an action that seemed trivial but ultimately proved to be a small win that was successful. Munro decided that the restrooms in the bus terminals needed to be kept immaculately clean. To demonstrate Greyhound's commitment to cleanliness, Munro held black-tie dinners in the restrooms. Over 70 percent of the station managers began keeping their restrooms clean, and Greyhound hired janitorial services to bring the others into compliance. The result was an overall increase in customers, with a 10 percent increase in women customers.[19]

How could something as simple as clean restrooms increase the number of customers riding the bus? To customers, clean restrooms translated into safety and comfort. Customers felt that the company was being attentive to their needs. Greyhound of Canada did much more to attract new customers, but cleaning the restrooms was a start. And although it wasn't initially apparent that customers thought that clean restrooms were an important part of the bus riding experience, it was a small win that Greyhound of Canada could immediately achieve. Small wins, such as having clean restrooms, are how individuals and businesses begin the process of accomplishment.

Small wins   Achievable, tangible accomplishments that are within a person's capabilities and produce visible results.

© Creatas Images/Jupiter Images

Characteristics of Small Wins

From a psychological perspective, small wins reduce the stress and anxiety that individuals feel when faced with situations they perceive as overwhelmingly complicated and difficult. Under pressure, they are less able to apply the right skills to solve a problem and tend to respond less effectively.

The small wins approach helps them to see problems as being within the scope of their abilities and effort instead of impossible to solve. The result is a feeling of "I can do this," rather than tension and helplessness. Small wins, therefore, are very much about how we describe problems in the first place. With the small wins perspective, we define problems so that our efforts and capabilities matter—and thereby increase our ability to successfully resolve them.

The small wins concept is not the same as breaking down a large task into small steps. Small wins typically don't follow a linear progression from one step to the next. They do, however, move in the same general direction toward a goal.

Given the importance of small wins to achieving larger goals, we need to build them into our daily lives. We need to discover opportunities and then find ways to improve the situation through some action that is within our control. Although they are hard to design, small wins are easy to recognize from their five identifying characteristics.

Ability to Control Actions

When Mary T. Meagher won three gold medals in swimming at the 1984 Los Angeles Olympics, she ascribed her success not to practicing more than other swimmers but to two fundamental changes in her practice routine. First, she arrived at swimming practice on time, which gave her a sense that every minute of her training counted. Second, she made sure to do all her practice turns correctly, according to the competitive rules. This meant always touching the side of the pool with two hands, not sometimes touching with one hand. Within a year of implementing these two small changes, Meagher was the world record holder in the butterfly. As she points out, "People don't know how ordinary success is."[20]

Meagher could control her ability to arrive to practice on time. She could control whether she did her turns correctly during practice. Both activities were within her capabilities. Her small wins didn't involve doing more of the same thing but doing something differently. By simply controlling her own actions, she made a major change in the outcome.

Willingness to Take Action

Small wins include some action and the belief that our actions will make a difference. This optimistic view of our activities is what motivates us to proceed, even though we know that we have no guarantee of success. The alternative is doing nothing, which leads to neither success nor failure. Think of a small win as an experiment, where we can test our assumptions about the situations we face and discover whether our beliefs are valid or not. Often allies (as well as detractors) come to the forefront only when we take action.

To save the redwood trees, 23-year-old Julia Butterfly Hill, a preacher's daughter, climbed a redwood tree and lived in it for more than two years. Her action helped identify supporters such as various environmental groups, government bureaucrats, and wealthy donors, as well as opponents, including logging companies and loggers. By bringing together and mobilizing the supporters, she saved many hundreds of redwood trees.[21]

Hill had no guarantee that her actions would save any redwood trees, let alone the tree she was living in.

And she never expected her crusade to last two years. Each day brought its own problems and opportunities, which she faced with the same positive attitude that took her up the tree in the first place. She experienced a series of small wins by acting on her intentions.

Activities that Stand Alone

A small win is a completed outcome. Take the process of making "cold calls," calling strangers on the telephone to sell a product or service or arrange a meeting with a potential investor. Every cold call is a small win that stands alone. Each phone call results in a completed outcome: The person responding to the phone call hangs up, asks for more information, agrees to a meeting, or makes some other choice. It is a completed accomplishment—whether the call's outcome is a success or a failure. Individuals who make cold calls can learn from each attempt, using each phone call to explore what kinds of pitches are likely to result in a higher chance of a sale.

Communicating an Intent

Any action, no matter how small, signals likely future intentions. For example, at CNN, Ted Turner instituted a $100 fine for any CNN employee who used the word *foreign*. Turner felt that the word *foreign* did not make sense in a global economy, and that news knew no borders. Simply fining those individuals who used the word *foreign* sent a strong message that he wanted CNN staffers to think globally.[22]

Emphasis on Details

Small wins occur because people don't overlook the specifics of their own situations. All the examples mentioned above involve noticing things that others appeared to miss. When we pay close attention to the specifics of the situation at hand, we gain the intimate knowledge to discern the small ways we can make changes. Munro's knowledge of buses and bus terminals provided insight into what small things could be changed, such as bathrooms. Meagher's knowledge of swimming helped her to identify changes she might make in her swim practice. Hill's knowledge of redwood trees enabled her to live in one. Developing detailed knowledge of the situations we face provides a significant advantage, particularly if we are looking for those small ways to leverage a task into meaningful action.

Inherent in the small win perspective is a view of situations where the future is ambiguous, subject to interpretation and change, malleable, and within our grasp. Because the future is not predetermined, our actions can make a difference. Small wins provide options. They may appear to amount to little, but because they are in fact wins, they encourage us to keep taking positive action.[23]

When you consider all the activities necessary to successfully enterprise, remember to create small wins.

Choose activities that are within your knowledge and capabilities. Understand the details and intricacies of the situation. Seek accomplishments that can stand alone. Treat each action as an experiment, and then learn from it.

2.8 ENTERPRISERS

On Target Hits the Bull's-Eye

Albert Black is a self-proclaimed capitalist. The baby of seven children, Albert grew up in Dallas, Texas, in government-subsidized housing (Frasier Courts) and started his first business when he was just eight years old. Today, he is CEO of On Target Supplies and Logistics, which provides business services and logistics management for companies. In 2002 the company employed 117 people and had revenues of over $28 million. His customer list includes the who's who of Dallas: EDS, Texas Instruments, Southwestern Bell, Texas Utilities, NationsBank, and Lone Star Gas. On Target services large corporations throughout Texas, Oklahoma, Louisiana, Arkansas, and Missouri from its offices and warehouses in Dallas and other Texas locations. In 1998, the kid from the projects was named Ernst & Young's Entrepreneur of the Year. On Target is also on the Inner City 100 list and Black is recognized as a leading minority entrepreneur.

"For me, the roots of capitalism took place right here in Frasier Courts," Black recalls. "I remember going up to the office and renting a push mower, knocking on doors and cutting yards for 50 cents." His lawn service prospered to the extent that he incorporated it when he was 19. Black continued to own Best Friends Lawn Service until he sold it in 1985.

He credits his grandmother with instilling the character traits that have helped him reach success: treat people with compassion, always look out for the other fellow, do what you say you're going do, take care of others before you take care of yourself, tell the truth, love and expect to be loved, and put God first, your family second, and everything else somewhere after that. His mother also influenced him: "She didn't think that she should expect anything but the best from her children, and that drives the way we run On Target Supplies and Logistics now." "You may live in the ghetto, but you're not ghetto material," she would tell her children. "And I don't—I won't—stand for you acting that way."

Soon after his 1982 college graduation, he started On Target to provide businesses with custodial supplies and janitorial services. Black had to get a second job while he built the company's business, and for ten years worked from 5 PM to 1 AM. "I had a goal," he says. "Not only would I earn income, I would pick up a skill set, a management ability, a competency that I could bring into my company and make it work."

Black and his wife Gwyneith worked hard to start On Target, often spending 14–16 hours a day and using their own car to make deliveries. They tried many different ways to spread the word about On Target's services. When trade fairs, direct mail, and cold-calling didn't work, they came up with a novel approach that did.

On Target became involved in communities, providing leadership for nonprofit organizations in and around town. Volunteering for those nonprofits gave Black and his company the opportunity to network, gaining exposure and business connections, while also "doing good" for the city of Dallas by sharing skills.

This approach worked, and On Target's business began to grow. Within five years, however, Black realized that the market had changed, with large companies turning to outsourced janitorial services. He redefined On Target's services to focus on supply distribution and logistics services and acquired his first big corporate account, Lone Star Gas Company. "I think our ability to listen, to plan, to present, to perform, to review, and to adjust is what corporate clients need today more than any other time in their history," says Black. On Target demonstrated its flexibility and ability to add value for the customer. Normally products went from On Target's loading dock to Lone Star's. "We came in with a strategy to take it to desktop distribution, and for the same price," says Black. "That saved them time. It saved them money. It saved them inventory expense."

Black credits his education—a bachelor's degree from the University of Texas at Dallas and an MBA from Southern Methodist University—with giving him a better foundation for management and leadership. As a result, he has made continuing education a priority at On Target, which pays for employees to pursue the next highest educational degree in a business-focused area. "As a company, we're willing to pay for it. As a CEO or a leader, I'm willing to insist on it," Black asserts. "There's no written policy that employees must go to college and achieve a bachelor's degree or you will be fired, but I think everybody around here knows that when Albert's sitting down with you and gives you that old south Dallas smile and insists or suggests that you go to college, I think they get the message."

In addition to what Black calls traditional financial income, On Target promises employees two other important incomes: educational and psychological. The company does more than pay for college. "If you come to work with us, you will know how to run a business," Black says. "We have absolute open-book accounting. You would know every expense in this business. You will know every revenue stream. You will know all the cost of sales. You will know how to run a business in a couple of years. That's the educational income." Black then supports employees who want to start their own businesses in areas serving complementary parts of On Target's market. More than ten former employees have taken advantage of this program to take the entrepreneurial plunge themselves.

Psychological income means feeling good about what you're doing for the company. "An esprit de corps, the attitude that says, 'Together we can climb mountains and win battles'—that's what we offer people, that psychological income of making a contribution every day."

To Black, financial income is the least important of the three, although he recognizes that for some it is the most important. Even here, however, his employees have reason to be happy, because the company pays above-market wages. "We like to bring people in, and over the course of their career here give them above-the-industry average, and then so much above the industry average that their desire to leave is based on the first two—psychological and educational income—and not financial considerations."

Never content with the status quo, Black encourages his employees to keep learning. The company gives each employee 60 hours of training annually to develop a well-trained, highly motivated, and customer-service–oriented staff. "We have a great sense of security that our employees are trained on a greater level than that of our competitors," Black says.

"We have to continuously resharpen the saw, find new information, new strategies, new principles, new foundations to employ in our business," he explains. "If we don't do that, well, we can look to be fired as the leaders of our organizations. How do people fire us? They quit. I think leadership and the mandate on leadership is to get the job done. If it means an ultimate sacrifice of giving all of your time and energy, all of your hopes, dreams, aspirations, and prayers toward that endeavor, I think that's what we must do."

Black's efforts in Dallas and throughout Texas have corrected many misconceptions. "Myths about small business—that we cannot capitalize ourselves in order to finance growth; myths about minority businesses—that we can't put together the type of management team necessary to take advantage of market opportunity; myths about black people, African Americans, that we do not have the right stuff in order to take full advantage of the American free-enterprise system." "I've dispelled a lot of myths," he says. "I get a chance to hire people, improve infrastructure, pay taxes, provide leadership, and get rich along the way."

Discussion Questions

1. Does Albert Black fit the characteristics (demographic and cognitive) of an entrepreneur described in this chapter? If so, why? And, if not, why not?

2. Why is Albert Black successful?

3. Are there characteristics that all entrepreneurs must have in order to be successful? What evidence would you offer to support your viewpoint?

4. What advantages or disadvantages does a person's family background provide? Can these be gained in other ways?

5. Are there any "small wins" in how Albert Black has developed and managed his business?

Source: Adapted with permission from Small Business School, the series on PBS, at http://SmallBusinessSchool.com.

Summary

1. Enterprisers come from all backgrounds, ages, and experiences. No one specific personality characteristic will prevent a person from becoming an entrepreneur, although some dispositional and cognitive characteristics may provide a slight advantage to those considering entrepreneurship. In fact, enterprisers represent all personality types. Successful enterprisers find business situations that match their personal characteristics and skills.

2. Entrepreneurship is a universal social and economic activity in the United States and is an important indicator of economic growth around the world. Research from the Panel Study of Entrepreneurial Dynamics (PSED) enhances our understanding of entrepreneurship. It focuses on nascent entrepreneurs—individuals who initiate and start new businesses, create new industries, or change how businesses in established industries compete. According to the PSED, entrepreneurial activity in the United States is widespread. All groups and types of individual participate in the new business formation process, with about 10.1 million adults in the United States trying to start new businesses at any time, either as individuals or in teams.

3. If we look at the demographics of nascent entrepreneurs, we find that they span all adult age groups, with the highest activity among young men aged 25–34. Men are twice as likely to start new businesses as women. Black men and women are about 50 percent more likely to start a business than white men and women, with business formation by Hispanic men about 20 percent higher than for white men. Hispanic and white women have comparable rates of business formation, with both groups lagging considerably behind black women. Those with higher incomes are more likely to be involved in starting a business. Where people live affects entrepreneurial activity. The presence of certain economic, demographic, and educational factors contributes to higher entrepreneurial activity in more urban areas.

4. Education is an important predictor of entrepreneurial activity for all individuals, and one that individuals can use to their advantage. Those who finish high school and complete some additional education or training are more likely to try to start a new business venture. For white men and women, there is a slight increase of participation with higher levels of education. Education has a greater impact for blacks and Hispanics. Black men and women and Hispanic men reporting any post–college graduation training are two to three times more likely to be involved in a firm start-up.

5. In terms of other personal characteristics, marital status, size of household, and age of children in the household have a minimal impact on entrepreneurial activities. Contrary to popular belief, jobholders in all ethnic groups report a higher incidence of entrepreneurial activity than those who are unemployed. People with jobs have more opportunities to identify ideas for products and services, make connections to suppliers, and acquire industry knowledge.

6. Many career motives of nascent entrepreneurs and a comparison group of nonentrepreneurs are similar, particularly in four areas: innovation, independence, financial success, and self-realization. There were significant differences in only two areas: recognition and roles.

   In addition, all respondents tended to rank the six career reasons in the same order of importance. Independence was first, followed by financial success, self-realization, recognition, innovation, and roles. These findings hold true in other countries as well. Self-realization values (personal development, ability utilization, and achievement) are ranked highly, whereas people place little importance on risk taking and the desire for authority and prestige. Regardless of where they live, enterprisers are less likely to care about how other people view their pursuit of success and to pursue financial success, independence, self-realization, and innovation on their own terms.

7. Individuals who take action are more successful than those who don't. People who are more likely to take action are probably also optimists. You can put yourself in an optimistic mindset so that you will be more likely to take action. We make three judgments about a situation: is it internal or external to us, stable or variable, and global or specific? Optimists attribute external/temporary/specific causes to bad situations. The pessimist, on the other hand, will offer an internal/stable/global attribution. Optimists also expect good things will occur in the future from their own efforts (internal), will continue (stable), and will extend to other

situations in their lives (global). As a result, they are likely to put effort into achieving their expectations. Pessimists, who expect that bad things will happen, tend to give up too soon, thinking that their efforts will be wasted.

8. We can approach problems and accomplish activities in two ways. We can focus on the *ends*, starting with a specific goal and then generating the necessary solution. Most problem solving uses this approach. When we emphasize the *means* approach, we look at what we have currently available to use and make these the starting point for achievement. Then we use our skills and abilities to solve the problem. Few situations call for pure forms of means or ends approaches. Typically people combine both methods to accomplish a goal. Exhibit 2.6 summarizes the major differences in these approaches. It's important to know which approach is more appropriate in a particular situation.

9. Small wins—achievable, tangible accomplishments that are within a person's capabilities and produce visible results—occur because people pay close attention to the specifics of the situation at hand. We then notice the specifics of situations that others appeared to miss, discovering small ways we can make changes and leverage a task into meaningful action. Small wins reduce stress and anxiety by helping us to see problems as within our capabilities instead of as overwhelming. They provide options, and by creating the feeling that we can do this, encourage us to keep taking positive action. The five identifying characteristics of small wins are ability to control actions, willingness to take action, activities that stand alone, communicating an intent, and emphasis on details.

Review Questions

1. Approximately 6 percent of all U.S. adults are involved in starting businesses. Why aren't more (or less) people involved in starting a business?

2. At what age groups are people more likely to be involved in starting businesses? Why are they more likely to start businesses at that age?

3. Why are men more likely to start businesses than women? What factors might account for this difference?

4. Why would African Americans and Hispanics be more likely to start a business than whites?

5. How important is education for starting a business? Why?

6. Who is more likely to start a business: someone who is unemployed, working full time, or working part time?

7. Are the reasons that nascent entrepreneurs offer for starting businesses different than the reasons that other people give for their career choices?

8. Who is an optimist? What are the characteristics of optimistic thinking? Why is it important to think optimistically?

9. What are the differences between focusing on ends versus focusing on means? Provide some examples of how an enterpriser might start a business using an ends focus and some examples of how an enterpriser might instead take a means focus.

10. What is a small win? What are the characteristics of small wins? Why is it important to focus on small wins rather than on "big wins?"

Applying What You've Learned

1. What personal characteristics might help or hinder your ability to become an enterpriser?

2. Interview an entrepreneur to discover what personal characteristics and reasons are offered for starting a business. Use the following questions to guide your discussion:

-   What is the opportunity the entrepreneur decided to pursue?

-   What influenced the entrepreneur to identify and pursue this opportunity?

- How did the entrepreneur's background (family history, prior education, and work experience) affect the opportunity discovered?

- How did the entrepreneur evaluate the opportunity?

- What criteria did the entrepreneur use to determine whether to pursue the opportunity?

- What were the perceived risks of this opportunity and how did the entrepreneur expect to manage them?

3. Identify three experiences you recently had (e.g., got an exam back, had lunch, and went on a date). How did you think about those experiences in the attributional framework (internal/external, stable/variable, and global/specific)? Were your thoughts optimistic? If not, why not? Would it have been more helpful for you to think of these experiences in an optimistic perspective?

4. Think of a business that you would like to start. How would you start this business if you focused on means? How would you start this business if you focused on ends?

5. Kazaa, the subject of this chapter's Enterprising Ethics box, is a good example of the unforeseen consequences of entrepreneurial action when the focus is on means rather than ends. Identify the different ways that Kazaa focuses on means in the process of developing the company. What other outcomes (ends) might result from the Kazaa file-sharing software? Can you identify other types of businesses that could be created? Discuss whether these businesses would be legal or ethical.

6. Revisit the story of Skype in the Enterprising World box. If you were a consultant to Zennström and Friis, on what basis would you recommend that they evaluate the various acquisition offers? Which factors would influence you most? Or would you suggest that they keep the company independent, and why?

7. What small wins did you accomplish today? What small wins might you accomplish tomorrow? How might these small wins help you become an enterpriser?

Enterprisers on the Web

1. The Panel Study of Entrepreneurial Dynamics (PSED) is an ongoing research effort. Check out its website at http://www.psed.info for its recent research activities. In the Publications section, look through the annotated bibliography of research publications using the PSED data. Choose an article that is of interest to you and find it on the Web. What do the findings of this article tell you about people who are entrepreneurs? How are these people similar or different from other people?

2. Who is using the "small wins" strategy, and how? Type "small wins" into any Web search engine and select two examples, one of which involves enterprisers. Describe the situation and explain how others have modified the "small wins" strategy to fit their objectives and interests. When might a "big wins" strategy work better than "small wins?"

3. The Martin Seligman website http://www.authentichappiness.sas.upenn.edu has numerous resources for exploring the value of an optimistic mindset and other ways of thinking that are helpful for enterprising. (Registration is required for this website, but it is free.) After taking the optimism exam on this website, are you an optimist? Why do you think your score on the optimism exam turned out the way it did? What do you find are your core strengths and values? How might these strengths direct you?

4. The web business eBay (http://www.ebay.com), the leader in online auctions, is an example of a means-focused business. Visit the eBay website and determine how eBay uses the means of the online auction to sell products on the Web. Next, discuss the ways eBay has branched out from the original auction format. Has it been effective, and why? Finally, identify other websites that utilize the means of an online auction and discuss how well this works. (Hint: Think of any goods or services that you might want to purchase on the Web. Use a search engine to locate other sites where on-line auctions take place.)

End Notes

1. William B. Gartner, "Who Is an Entrepreneur? Is the Wrong Question," *American Journal of Small Business* 12 no. 4 (1988), pp. 11–32.

2. Paul D. Reynolds, Nancy M. Carter, William B. Gartner, Patricia G. Greene, and Larry W. Cox, "The Entrepreneur Next Door: Characteristics of Individuals Starting Companies in America" (Kansas City, MO: E. M. Kauffman Foundation, 2002).

3. Paul D. Reynolds, S. M. Camp, W. D. Bygrave, E. Autio, and M. Hay, *Global Entrepreneurship Monitor: 2001 Executive Report* (Kansas City, MO: Kauffman Center for Entrepreneurial Leadership, 2001).

4. M. Ruef, H. E. Aldrich, and Nancy M. Carter, "Don't Go to Strangers: Homophily, Strong Ties and Isolation in the Formation of Organizational Founding Teams" (Chicago: American Sociological Association National Meetings, 2002).

5. "Table 72: Live Births, Deaths, Marriages, and Divorces: 1950 to 2003," *Statistical Abstract of the United States: 2006*, 125th ed. (Washington, DC, 2005: U.S. Census Bureau, 2006), p. 64.

6. U.S. Department of Commerce, *The State of Small Business: A Report of the President* (Washington, DC: U.S. Government Printing Office, 1996).

7. J. S. Butler, *Entrepreneurship and Self Help Among Black Americans: A Reconsideration of Race and Economics* (Albany, NY: State University of New York Press, 1991); and P. G. Greene and J. S. Butler, "The Minority Community as a Natural Business Incubator," *Journal of Business Research* 36 no. 1 (1996), pp. 51–59.

8. Nancy M. Carter, William B. Gartner, K. G. Shaver, and E. J. Gatewood, "The Career Reasons of Nascent Entrepreneurs," *Journal of Business Venturing* 18 no. 1 (2003), pp. 13–40.

9. Donald E. Super, Branimir Sverko, and Charles M. Super (Eds), *Life Roles, Values and Careers: International Findings of the Work Importance Study* (San Francisco: Jossey-Bass, 1995).

10. Branimir Sverko and Donald E. Super, "The Findings of the Work Importance Study," in D. E. Super, B. Sverko, and C. M. Super (Eds), *Life Roles, Values and Careers: International Findings of the Work Importance Study* (San Francisco: Jossey-Bass, 1995), pp. 349–358.

11. Martin E. P. Seligman, *Learned Optimism* (New York: Pocket Books, 1998).

12. M. F. Scheier and C. S. Carver, "Effects of Optimism on Psychological and Physical Well-Being. Theoretical Overview and Empirical Update," *Cognitive Therapy and Research* 16 no. 2 (1992), pp. 201–228.

13. N. J. Christman, "Uncertainty and Adjustment During Radiotherapy," *Nursing Research* 39 no. 1 (1990), pp. 17–20, 47.

14. D. Strutton and J. Lumpkin, "Relationship between Optimism and Coping Strategies in the Work Environment," *Psychological Reports* 71 (1992), pp. 1179–1186.

15. M. F. Scheier, C. S. Carver, and A. W. Bridges, "Optimism, Pessimism, and Psychological Well Being," in E. C. Chang (Ed.), *Optimism & Pessimism: Implications for Theory, Research and Practice* (Washington, DC: American Psychological Association, 2001), pp. 189–216.

16. S. D. Sarasvathy, "Causation and Effectuation: Toward a Theoretical Shift from Economic Inevitability to Entrepreneurial Contingency," *Academy of Management Review* 26 no. 2 (2001), pp. 243–263.

17. Ibid., p. 245.

18. Karl E. Weick, "Small Wins: Redefining the Scale of Social Problems," *American Psychologist* 39 no. 1 (1984), pp. 40–49.

19. Thomas J. Peters, *Patterns of Winning and Losing: Effects on Approach and Avoidance by Friends and Enemies*, Unpublished doctoral dissertation, Stanford University, 1977.

20. Karl E. Weick, "Small Wins in Organizational Life," *Dividend* (Ann Arbor, MI: University of Michigan School of Business), 24 no. 1 (1993), pp. 2–6.

21. J. B. Hill, *The Legacy of Luna: The Story of a Tree, A Woman, and the Struggle to Save the Redwoods* (San Francisco: HarperSanFrancisco, 2000).

22. Weick, "Small Wins in Organizational Life."

23. Weick, "Small Wins: Redefining the Scale of Social Problems," p. 48.

Enterprising Fundamentals

KEY CONCEPTS

1. Achievement depends upon actions. These actions have two primary purposes: managing yourself and managing your situation.

2. Skills such as goal setting, time management, persuasion, negotiation, and networking are fundamental to future success, whether you are starting, operating, or selling a business.

3. Managing yourself starts with setting goals to determine direction, and then managing your time so that you can initiate the actions necessary to reach those goals. Enterprisers must also manage situations by interacting with others using persuasion and negotiation techniques. By building networks, enterprisers expand the range of interactions and gain competitive advantage.

Suppose, when you were in college, you were responsible for booking campus entertainment and dances. You quickly discovered the difference that proper lighting made in the overall staging of a performance. It didn't take long for you to realize that you had a knack for the complexities—and opportunities—involved in developing quality lighting packages that would become the industry standard.

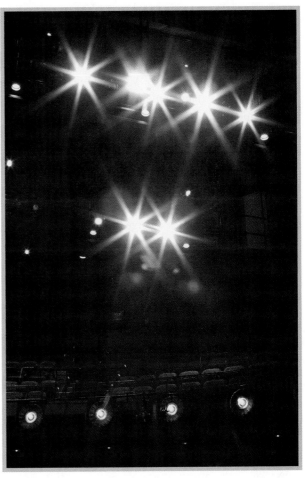

© Jupiter Images

This chapter presents the case of David and Janet Milly, who focused on their mission, "making money doing lights," set goals related to their mission, managed their time effectively, and used their networks to build a client base. They grew their company into a successful theatrical lighting company for top musical performers but remained committed to servicing the lighting needs of various small organizations in their own community.

In this chapter you will learn these and other practical personal skills you will need to manage yourself and your situation as you build an enterprise.

3.0 Essentials for Enterprisers

Enterprising involves action. Many people have the right attitudes, motivations, abilities, and skills, yet they don't undertake the necessary activities to achieve success. After watching an important sporting event, we have all played Monday morning quarterback—second-guessing the coach and players as to why and how they won or lost the game. Analysis helps us understand the factors that lead to success or failure. However, it is impossible to win a game by just watching! Only those who play get a chance to win (or lose). Many people can describe what should have happened or speculate on what should have been done. But knowing what to do without actually doing it results in nothing.

Enterprisers are doers. They act. They accomplish.

Achievement depends on your actions. Your actions can change your present circumstances, much like using a ship's rudder to change direction. Moving the rudder might not lead to a quick change in course, but soon the ship is sailing in a new direction. Even though it may appear that actions don't result in immediate changes, actions do pull you in certain directions, and you may soon find yourself on a different path.

This chapter provides you with a set of practical "action tools" and skills that will help you achieve success. It highlights the kinds of activities that everyone needs to undertake to be successful: goal setting, time management, persuasion, negotiation, and networking. These skills lay the groundwork for all enterprisers, whether they are starting, operating, or selling a business.

These enterprising fundamentals have a sound basis in the theories of organizational behavior. **Organizational behavior** is the study of people and how they act in organizations. Organizational behavior researchers tend to study people who work in large organizations, but their findings are relevant for enterprisers as well. We will introduce you to some of the academic theory that demonstrates why these skills are important to acquire and use, and then show how you, as an enterpriser, can apply them.

Enterprising fundamentals involve two kinds of skills: *Skills to manage yourself,* such as goal setting and time management, and *skills to manage your situation,* like persuasion, negotiation, and networking.

Organizational behavior   The study of people and how they act in organizations.

Managing Yourself

In organizational behavior terms, achievement is defined as a function of ability and effort. You need both ability (your skills and knowledge) *and* effort (the time devoted to the task at hand) to accomplish work.

$$\text{Work} = \text{Ability} \times \text{Effort}$$

In the absence of the other, neither ability nor effort is enough. Smart people who don't put in the effort won't succeed, and people who work hard but don't have the right skills and knowledge won't succeed.

One of the major reasons you are going to school is to acquire the skills and knowledge necessary to succeed in life. What we often underestimate in determining whether people will be successful is their dedication to putting in the necessary time and energy. We believe *the most critical factor for achieving your goals is the amount of time you have available.*

A number of years ago, John Sloboda, a researcher in England, interviewed over 250 music students attending prestigious academies in England to discover whether success as a musician was a function of ability or effort. He looked at how each student did on a national examination of musical ability. The results showed that a student's ranking on musical ability was highly related to the number of hours a student practiced. Students who scored the highest on the music examination were likely to practice eight times more than the lowest performing students. "People have this idea that there are those who learn better than others, can get further on less effort," Sloboda says. "On average, our data refuted that. Whether you're a dropout or at the best school, where you end up can be predicted by how much you practice."[1] Managing your time, therefore, is the best way for you to manage your life. If you don't have time to accomplish critical tasks in life, you won't achieve your goals.

Another way to look at the importance of time in managing your life is to consider your life as the "100,000 hour problem."[2] Think about what you want to accomplish in your life as a "job" and calculate the number of hours you have for this job over your lifetime. Assume that you begin working at age 20 and plan to retire when you are 70. If you work a 40-hour week, then you have 2,080 hours a year of work. With two weeks (80 hours) off per year for vacation, your work year is about 2,000 hours. If you work 50 years at 2,000 hours a year, you have 100,000 hours to accomplish what you want. That is your life!

When you think about it, 100,000 hours is not a lot of time. So to be an effective enterpriser, you must allocate the time to enterprise.

Managing Your Situation

Enterprisers, as we have defined them, involve other people. It is impossible to start or run a business without the involvement of others, whether they are employees, customers, or investors. In a new enterprise, it is a challenge to convince someone to purchase what may be an untested product or take a chance on your new service. You must be able to negotiate with suppliers for better prices, as well as payment terms that will enable your enterprise to grow. And, it is impossible to know everything about running a successful enterprise, so, you will need advice and mentoring from a variety of people that you can depend on. So, managing the involvement of others is critical to whether the enterprise will flourish or not. Your ability to build your enterprise will depend on leveraging the strengths of others.

In Exhibit 3.1, you might think of the five activities of goal setting, time management, persuasion, negotiation, and networking as a series of concentric circles. While each activity might be considered separate from the others, each activity is dependent on the other. At the center of your actions is goal setting. Without a clear sense of your goals, using your time wisely, and utilizing your network and your ability to persuade and negotiate with others are useless. And, time management skills will influence your ability to engage others in your enterprise. Negotiation depends on your skills and persuasion. And, networking depends on how skilled you are at using the other skills.

3.1 Goal Setting: The Key to Time Management

The phone is ringing as you walk into your office. Your sales manager tells you that he finally got an appointment with the CEO of the company you've been courting for weeks. Your assistant reminds you to call a new customer. Your calendar shows that you have a meeting with your accounts officer—at the same time you are supposed to meet with the CEO. It's only 8 AM, and it's clear that your day won't be going as planned. By 4:30 PM, you've also helped your purchasing manager with supplier problems, dashed off to do some errands, and interviewed a job applicant—but most of the items on your original to-do list remain undone.

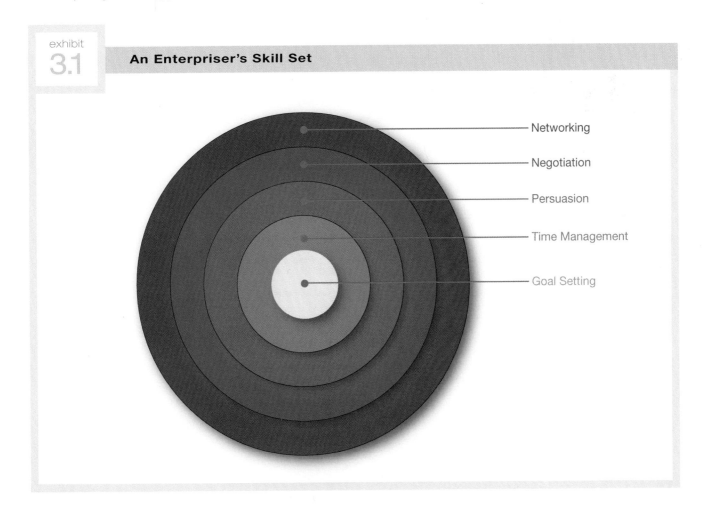

exhibit 3.1

An Enterpriser's Skill Set

Networking

Negotiation

Persuasion

Time Management

Goal Setting

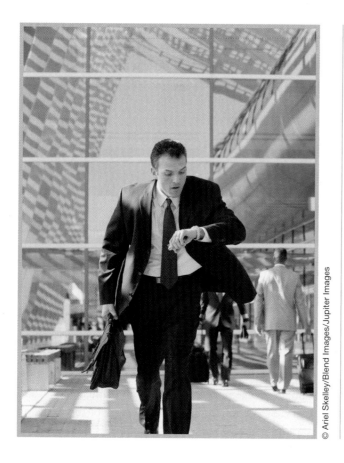

© Ariel Skelley/Blend Images/Jupiter Images

Sound familiar? We all have days like this, where carefully made plans get tossed aside to solve crises. Have too many of these days, however, and you will soon be extremely frustrated and feel like you will never achieve your goals.

Look at the matrix in Exhibit 3.2, which was developed by Stephen Covey in his book *First Things First*. He looks at two key issues: the importance of the problems one faces, and their urgency.

Most tasks we mentioned—and as Covey sees it, most of what we do in our day-to-day lives—fall into Quadrants 3 and 4, with a few in Quadrant 1. Quadrant 3 tasks are urgent and unimportant; activities that *other people* want but won't necessarily help us achieve our own goals. Quadrant 4 tasks, not urgent and unimportant, can end up taking most of our time. Many of these tasks involve short-term activities that steal valuable time from what should be our primary focus: achieving our long-term goals. Goal-setting activities are part of Quadrant 2, which Covey calls the Quadrant of Quality.[3]

Why Set Goals?

Formulating goals isn't easy, but the process is an essential component of personal and professional success. Goal

---

<table>
<tr><td>exhibit
3.2</td><td colspan="2">Types of Problems</td></tr>
</table>

	URGENT	NOT URGENT
IMPORTANT	**QUADRANT 1** Crises Pressing problems Deadline-driven projects	**QUADRANT 2** Preparation Prevention Values clarification Planning
UNIMPORTANT	**QUADRANT 3** Interruptions Some mail Some meetings Many popular activities	**QUADRANT 4** Trivia, busywork Some phone calls Time wasters Irrelevant mail Excessive TV

Source: Stephen R. Covey, A. Roger Merrill, and Rebecca R. Merrill, *First Things First* (New York: Simon & Schuster, 1995), p. 37.

setting involves specifying future objectives or accomplishments. Basically, it entails determining a direction for actions and indicating the amount or quality of work to be accomplished. When we develop our goals, we must also define our priorities and determine what is important.

Two broad findings emerge from laboratory and field research on goal setting:

1. People who set specific and more challenging goals achieve more than people who set no goals, or are asked to "do their best."

2. People who set specific and more challenging goals achieve more than people who set easy goals.[4]

In other words:

- Specific goals direct action better than vague or general goals.

- A difficult goal leads to better performance than easy or no goals, because people will try harder to achieve a more difficult goal.

- Effort is important for achievement.

- We all need to be challenged in order to achieve.

While these points may seem obvious, very often we neglect them in planning our lives.

To be useful, goals must have certain characteristics. They must be specific, results-focused, measurable, realistically attainable, relevant, and have a time frame for accomplishment. Suppose one of your goals is to earn more money. While this is an admirable goal, it is too vague to be useful. How much more money? Over what time period? Earning $300 more over the next three years meets this goal—but is that what you really meant?

A better goal would be, increase earnings by $2,000 in 12 months by getting a promotion. This goal statement is specific, measurable, and has a time period for completion—increase by $2,000 by getting a promotion within a year. It is results-focused and relevant—a promotion improves your career and your financial situation; and it is realistic—it is possible to accomplish this in a year.

Perhaps you are very ambitious and decide you want to start a new company within three months. This goal is specific and has a time frame. But is it realistically attainable? Not really. A goal that is beyond your reach—or too easily met—has little meaning. Well-designed goals challenge you, but are attainable with hard work. The basics of sound goal setting are summarized in Exhibit 3.3.

Rhonda Abrams, a small-business planning consultant, has two rules that capture the essence of goal setting:

1. You can't reach a goal you haven't set.

2. If you want something, you also have to "do" something.[5]

Never underestimate the importance of these two rules. A study by Harvard psychologists in the early 1980s looked at people who considered themselves happy. The shared characteristics of this group were not wealth, success, love, or health—however, they knew what they wanted, and they were taking steps to get it.[6]

From Wishes to Goals

We all have plans for the future, many things we want to achieve. Some are vague, like "I want to make lots of

---

exhibit
3.3

How to Set Effective Goals

1. Specify the general objective or tasks to be done.

2. Specify how the performance in question will be measured.

3. Specify the standard or target to be reached.

4. Specify the time span involved.

5. Prioritize goals.

6. Rate goals by difficulty and importance.

Source: Adapted from E. A. Locke and G. P. Latham, *Goal Setting* (Englewood Cliffs, NJ: Prentice-Hall, 1984), pp. 27–41.

money." These are dreams or wishes, not goals. They are not specific enough to qualify. We do, of course, have personal goals—buying a new car, starting a family, or learning a new hobby or skill—and business goals—meeting a sales quota or developing a new advertising campaign.

How can we move from wishes to goals, and then on to results? The first step is to sort out our true motivations and goals, those that are meaningful and relevant for *us,* not for others. Once we identify them, we can take the appropriate actions to accomplish our objectives. Rink Dickinson's goal was to create a company that would be an agent for social change by improving the lives of coffee growers. The Enterprising Ethics box tells how Equal Exchange fulfilled Dickinson's goal.

Setting Priorities

Because some goals are more important than others, *setting priorities* is the next step in the goal-setting process. This will help you find a balance between personal and professional goals and also manage your time more effectively.

ENTERPRISING ETHICS

Equal Exchange Plays Fair

When you buy coffee, tea, sugar, cocoa, or chocolate, you probably don't think about where the product was grown and by whom. Rink Dickinson, however, was concerned about the human rights of the poor coffee growers in Central America. He and two other managers at a New England food cooperative wanted to forge a closer connection between consumers and the farmers. The result was Equal Exchange, the oldest fair trade company in the United States.

Dickinson struggled to raise financing for his new venture. The company's unique business model combined a private, for-profit enterprise with a nonprofit mission. Most investors thought he was crazy. Why pay coffee growers a hefty premium rather than buy for the lowest price possible? Dickinson wanted his company not only to sell high-quality food products, but also to be an agent for social change, improving the lives of farmers and giving them more control over their economic futures.

Fairness to farmers was at the core of his strategy. By importing coffee directly from farmer cooperatives, he could streamline the conventional coffee supply chain. Cutting out middlemen freed up additional money to pay the farmers higher prices per pound while maintaining fair prices to consumers. This would support small farming communities and improve the lives of the farmers and their families. His vision went further and included promoting ecologically sustainable farming practices, educating consumers about fair trade issues, and structuring the company on democratic principles.

In 1986, he obtained $100,000 from like-minded investors to start Equal Exchange. In 1990, the company formalized its worker-owner cooperative structure, and in 1991 became part of the European Fair Trade network. Today the West Bridgewater, Massachusetts, company has 70 worker-owners—none of whom earn more than three times the lowest staff member's salary—and sells coffee, tea, cocoa mix, and other chocolate products from 30 farmer cooperatives in 15 countries. Equal Exchange's customers include about 2,000 restaurants, major supermarkets, natural food stores, consumer coops, cafes, universities, fair trade retailers, and places of worship. In 2005, it generated more than $20 million in revenues and earned a profit while remaining true to its founders' vision and values. It describes itself as a "self-sustaining but not wealth-accumulating enterprise," keeping its margins well below industry averages.

The mission of Equal Exchange is "to build long-term trade partnerships that are economically just and environmentally sound, to foster mutually beneficial relationships between farmers and consumers, and to demonstrate, through our success, the contribution of worker co-operatives and Fair Trade to a more equitable, democratic, and sustainable world." It was a pioneer in adopting fair trade—a voluntary program to create an alternative market for traditionally disadvantaged producers in developing countries, usually small-scale farmers—and has crusaded aggressively for its acceptance. Today more than 400 companies offer some fair trade coffee. The company's efforts have significantly benefited the growers and their communities by providing additional income for education, health care facilities, and other projects.

Dickinson's job is not yet done, however. He continues to raise the consciousness of consumers as

CHAPTER 3 ENTERPRISING FUNDAMENTALS

well as other businesses and is looking for other areas to apply fair trade standards, such as family farmers within the United States.

Discussion Questions

1. What goals led to the formation of Equal Exchange?

2. What kinds of companies and individuals might want to be involved in Equal Exchange? Why would they want to be involved?

3. Are there other ways that an enterprise could be founded that would meet the same goals as Equal Exchange? Who would most likely benefit if the company was designed solely as a for-profit enterprise?

4. What are the benefits to each party involved in organizing this company as a cooperative?

Sources: Sandy Coleman, "Grounds for Success," *Boston Globe,* February 26, 2006, http://www.boston.com; Equal Exchange website, http://www.equalexchange.com (September 20, 2006); and G. Jeffrey Macdonald, "How to Brew Justice," Time.com, December 11, 2005, http://www.time.com.

How do you set priorities among your goals? Start with what you love, not what you do well. This passion keeps you motivated to make the effort to reach your goals. To figure out what you want, you have to be willing to fantasize, to shut down the self-doubts that hold you back. For example, you may have an idea for a business, but that inner voice tells you that no one will like the product, you're not smart enough to run a company, you can't raise the money, and so on.[7] You give up before you investigate to see if your ideas are feasible. Take another look at Exhibit 3.2, focusing on Quadrant 2. How can you organize your life so that you have time for the goals that are priorities, so that you put first things first? According to Covey, you should start with the following steps:[8]

Step 1. Create a personal mission statement and connect with it. Ask yourself three questions: What is most important to me? What gives my life meaning? What do I want to be and do in my life? Then write a personal mission statement that sums up your answers and summarizes your long-term goals. It should define your values, principles, most important roles, relationships, and what matters most to you in life. Your mission statement should form the basis of your future goals and decisions, guiding you toward meeting your objectives. If you need help in formulating your mission statement, work through the Mission Formulator at the Franklin Covey website: http://www.franklincovey.com.

Step 2: State your short- and mid-term objectives. Start by identifying the many roles you have: entrepreneur, manager, employee, spouse, parent, son/daughter, student, hospital volunteer, community member, and so on. Include personal goals that enrich

you physically, socially, emotionally, mentally, and spiritually. This step increases your overall effectiveness and provides a foundation for success. Then choose one or two major (Quadrant 2) goals that you'd like to accomplish for each role. These should relate to your mission statement. Set a reasonable time frame to meet these goals.

Take a look at the Goal-Setting Worksheet in Exhibit 3.4, which lists the roles, goals, and action steps for Marianna Ravden, a 28-year-old marketing research analyst who wants to start a gift basket business. As you can see, Marianna's goals are more specific and make it easier for her to develop an action plan to reach her goals. Ranking the goals according to degree of priority is another important component of this worksheet. Filling it out offers one way to identify and set priorities for goals and then take the actions to achieve them. Take a moment to fill out your own goal-setting worksheet, which will become an important time management tool.

Managing Your Goals

Now that you've identified your goals, you need to prioritize them. Because you won't be able to accomplish all of your goals at once, you must choose one, most critical goal to accomplish. If you feel anxious that you have a number of equally important goals, consider these four different strategies to accomplish your goals:

- *Simultaneous goals:* If you have a number of goals, you may want to work on several at a time.

- *Sequential goals:* Change goals after working on one for a set time period.

exhibit
3.4

Goal-Setting Worksheet

NAME: MARIANNA RAVDEN   DATE: AUGUST 15, 2008

Role	Related Goals	Priority	Action Steps
Enterpriser	1. Find customers.	High	• Get directory of companies in local area.
			• Create a brochure of gift baskets.
			• Make up sample gift baskets.
			• Make appointments with corporate event planners and marketing representatives.
	2. Locate suppliers of unique foods and gift items.	High	
	3. Arrange for delivery helpers.	Low	
Mother	Take care of kids.	Very high	Morning wakeup.
	Keep up the household.		Meals
	Pay bills.		Transportation to school.
			Homework
			Fun
Spouse	Spend time with husband.	Very high	

- *Alternating goals:* Devote alternating blocks of time to different goals.

- *Multiple goals:* Design activities to combine two or three goals into the same situation.

Recognize that accomplishing your goals takes time, and that you won't satisfy all these goals immediately. Goal setting is an ongoing process. As you move through different life stages, your goals will change, as will your priorities. You will also face conflicts when determining priorities. But the more you clarify your goals, the easier it will be to manage them.

Getting Time on Your Side

Like many of us, Renée Madison, owner of a small computer consulting company, has a hectic life. On any day she might find herself developing or presenting proposals for new clients, meeting with employees to discuss scheduling and management of projects for current clients, and making troubleshooting visits. While she is juggling these tasks, she must field numerous phone calls and emails that interrupt her day. She also worries about finding the time to market her services to more clients so that she can grow her business and whether she'll be able to attend her son's soccer game after school.

While your specific activities and problem areas may be different, you can probably identify with Renée's concerns about using time efficiently, both at work and at home. Like her, you may find yourself moving from one crisis to another, sitting in unnecessary meetings, or getting bogged down in paperwork. At the end of each day, you are frustrated with what you *haven't* accomplished.

Learning and using time management techniques is one of the best gifts you can give yourself. It will pay off over and over again. As you gain control of your time, you will be more productive, reduce the stress in your life, enjoy work more, and balance work and personal time. Enterprisers in particular need to be excellent time managers, because there is no manager to monitor what they do. If you spend the day on low-priority activities, you will never be able to start or grow your business. See Appendix A for a discussion of some of the best practices in time management and how to incorporate them into your lifestyle.

3.2   Persuasion

Persuasion involves deliberately seeking attitude change through communication: using your personal influence to get someone to do or believe something. It is similar to negotiation and has the same objective: Helping other people meet *their* needs through involvement with *your* goals. Like negotiation, persuasion is based on creating "win-win" situations. However, persuasion is more subtle, because the other person probably doesn't realize that a negotiation is underway! It is proactive and requires you to have a clear idea of what you want, discover what the other person desires, and then figure out how to meet the other person's needs—and at the same time get what *you* want.

The Six Principles of Effective Persuasion

Some people are born persuaders. Not only do they naturally use charisma and eloquence to get others to do what they ask, they do it in a way that makes others eager to cooperate. But ask them what they do that is special, and they may not be able to tell you. Behavioral science studies, however, have identified six basic principles that appeal in predictable ways to fundamental human needs and desires.[9] Armed with this knowledge, you can apply these principles to become a skilled persuader.

The six principles of effective persuasion—liking, reciprocity, social proof, consistency, authority, and scarcity—are not mysterious or profound. Rather, they are common sense, obvious, and intuitive, explaining how people evaluate information and make decisions. Persuasion is all about attitudes and how you deal with others. Successful persuaders really pay attention to other persons. Exhibit 3.5 defines the six principles and illustrates how they can be applied in business settings.

Why are these six principles so powerful? Think about it. Isn't it easier to get a coworker's cooperation for a project when you've already become friends? Establishing

© Dmitriy Shironosov/Used under license from Shutterstock

areas of common interest creates goodwill that carries over to other areas. Praise also creates goodwill between people. Such positive comments make the other person like you and more willing to do what you ask at a future date. Praise can help you nurture good relationships and mend poor ones. When someone you like favors a product or idea, you are more likely to view it positively, too.

The six principles work best when you apply several at once. The combined effect is much more powerful. For example, during a seemingly casual conversation before a meeting, you can convey information about your areas of expertise and also ask questions that show your interest in the other person and gain valuable information to help establish similarities.

Persuasion is not the same as coercion. In fact, intimidating a person into agreement or being dishonest is counterproductive and manipulative. Unless the commitment feels voluntary, the other person will follow through begrudgingly, if at all. Persuasion is a mutually beneficial activity.[10]

In Exhibit 3.6 (on page 63) you'll find tips to increase your persuasiveness based on Dale Carnegie's famous book *How to Win Friends and Influence People*. These ideas are very basic, but you'd be surprised at how often people ignore them and act in ways that harm relationships.

Ready, Set, Persuade!

Have you ever made a presentation that you thought went perfectly, only to learn that your proposal wasn't

Persuasion   Deliberately seeking attitude change through communication—using your personal influence to get someone to do or believe something.

exhibit
3.5

The Six Principles of Persuasion

Principle	Definition	Application	Examples
Liking	People like those who like them.	Find *similarities* with others and offer *real praise*.	Create bonds, like a shared interest in a sport or hobby, with a recent hire during informal conversations. Use genuine praise to generate liking, even in a manager with whom you've had disagreements.
Reciprocity	People repay in kind.	Give what you want to receive; modeling a desired behavior makes others more likely to adopt it.	Lend a staff member to another manager who needs help to meet a deadline, and you're more likely to get help when you need it. Giving seasonal gifts increases the recipient's willingness to want to work with you.
Social Proof	People follow the lead of similar others.	Use peer power to persuade others.	Use testimonials from satisfied customers, especially those companies similar to your prospect. Convince an employee to support a new corporate initiative to get others to buy in.
Consistency	People align with their clear commitments.	Get others to make commitments that are active, public, and voluntary.	Ask an employee to confirm in a *written* memo a commitment to complete a project by a certain date.
Authority	People defer to experts.	Establish your expertise; it may not be as obvious as you think.	Find ways to work into conversation how you solved a problem similar to one the client faces or a particular skill you have mastered.
Scarcity	People want more of items that have limited availability.	Emphasize unique benefits and exclusive information.	Use limited-time, one-of-a-kind offers; share exclusive or advance information with key managers.

approved? You covered all the bases with well-organized data supporting your argument and delivered the report in a forceful yet pleasant manner. What went wrong?

Preparation Pays Off

In mastering effective persuasion techniques, you should not only incorporate the six principles of persuasion in your presentations and discussions but also give careful thought to the *receiver* of the message, as well as to content, context, and delivery. Who is the primary

decision maker, and how can you tailor your presentation to his or her style? Will you be in a casual setting or a formal meeting? Clearly, you wouldn't want to introduce a complex proposal during the social hour before a luncheon meeting. However, you could use this time to build rapport with someone you'll be meeting with next week to discuss a proposal.

The more you know about a person's values and needs, the better you can tailor your presentation to be consistent with what you've learned and persuade him

exhibit 3.6	**How to Become More Persuasive**

1. Become genuinely interested in other people.

2. Be friendly.

3. Make a good first impression: smile.

4. Remember that a person's name is to that person the sweetest and most important sound in any language.

5. Be a good listener. Encourage others to talk about themselves and let them do most of the talking.

6. Talk in terms of the other person's interests.

7. Make the other person feel important—and do it sincerely.

8. Be sympathetic with the other person's ideas and desires and try to see things from the other person's point of view.

9. Avoid criticism and complaints.

10. Show respect for the other person's opinions. Never say, "You're wrong."

11. Make the person happy about doing the thing you suggest.

Source: Adapted from Dale Carnegie, *How to Win Friends and Influence People,* Revised ed. (New York: Pocket Books, 1982).

or her to accept your point of view. If you are meeting with your boss or other company managers, you may have some clues to the decision maker's personality and "hot buttons." When you are dealing with a sales presentation to a potential client, you many not have the information you need. But listening carefully to the questions the person asks, asking good questions, and watching for other hints can help you respond appropriately.

Building Rapport

Developing *rapport* is essential to successful persuasion and relates to the first principle of persuasion, liking. When people have a high degree of rapport between them, they communicate more effectively. The other person understands clearly what you are thinking; both parties feel like they are on the same wavelength.[11]

You build rapport when you model the other person's gestures, movement, words, and mood, as well as show sincere concern and interest in the other person's needs. If you are talking to a calm, quiet person who speaks slowly, you should adapt to his or her tone. Nonverbal communication conveys your message as well, so use positive body language.

Questions are a good way to demonstrate your interest. Start with questions that discover values, and then follow up with related ones to define values and identify needs, and use that to incorporate mutual benefits into your presentation. Suppose you are the founder of a company that develops sales management software and will be making a presentation to a potential client. In your preliminary discussions with the client, you may have a conversation such as the one below:

Q: What is most important to you in buying software?

A: It should be easy to use.

Q: Why is this most important to you?

A: Our sales and marketing staff complain about our present systems and don't want to use them.

Q: What do you need most from your new software system?

A: Integration of marketing, sales, and inventory management systems.

Q: What do you require from the company that provides your software?

A: Good customer service.

Q: How do you define good customer service?

A: When we call for tech support, we get prompt answers to our problems.

You'll also ask about technical requirements, the hardware platform, price considerations, and similar needs.

With this key information—users of the product, environment in which it will be used, desired results, and problems with existing products—you can customize your presentation and demonstrate how your software's features address those issues. You will also be able to describe your company in a way that highlights its attention to customer service, offering examples of how it responds to customer calls.

Here are a few more points to help you make persuasive, win-win presentations:[12]

1. *Plan for a brief presentation, but also be ready to expand into a longer one.* The ability to explain your ideas briefly but clearly in less than a minute is a valuable skill. Some decision makers want the bottom line right away, while others want the supporting facts as well. Prepare several versions to cover all bases.

2. *State the objective concisely, early in the presentation.* Tell the other person why you wanted the meeting and how you can help meet his or her exact needs. For example, "I want to show you how your company can save about $20,000 with our inventory management software."

3. *Make your verbal and nonverbal communications agree.* Your tone of voice, body language, and overall style should be consistent and fit the situation. Don't forget to smile when discussing positive events. Know what your gestures say. Using a natural tone creates a warm environment.

4. *Listen attentively.* A good listener inspires confidence. Ask open-ended questions to get a better understanding of the other person, and allow plenty of time for the answer.

5. *Use client-centered thinking.* It's not enough to state the benefits of your proposal. You must answer the question, "What's in it for me?" for the other person. Do your employees care that you are adding a bond fund as a new investment option to the company's 401(k) plan? Probably not, until you explain that the bond fund offers an alternative to the stock offerings so that they can build more diversified-portfolios.

3.3 ENTERPRISERS

Theatrical Lighting Systems

Based in Huntsville, Alabama, with crews all over the country, Theatrical Lighting Systems (TLS) has a slogan: "We light the stars." Since 1981, David and Janet Milly's company has been creating lighting magic for performers like Tony Bennett, Lee Greenwood, Johnny Cash, and many others. Revenues come from lighting sales and rentals, and there's a division dedicated to the design and installation of permanent lighting systems that integrate both house and theatrical lighting.

"About 25 years ago, when I got into the business, entertainers would perform in a building and just flip the houselights on," says David Lilly. "Then people moved up to two or three lights for the performers, and they'd turn the houselights off. So the lighting business evolved from nothing to sophisticated half-million dollar lighting systems with computer controls and all that."

As performers discovered the benefits of good lighting, TLS began to grow. "If it's dark, people are looking around; they don't know what to look at," David explains. "You bring the light up—Boom!—that's what they focus their attention on, and it is the energy of a show. If the entertainer's moving around, the lights are moving around. If the entertainer is doing a slow ballad, the lights are a slow ballad. So lighting sets the mood and the tempo for the show and for the entertainer."

Because David understood lighting better than sound, he chose to specialize in lighting and not expand into other areas. "In the long run, it's paid off," he says. "Our mission statement, 'Making money doing lights,' keeps us focused."

Today the company has 30 employees and close to $5 million in revenues from three revenue streams: selling equipment to churches, schools, arenas, and nightclubs; consulting with architects to design light packages for permanent installation; and providing lighting packages for road shows with and without personnel. In 2002, TLS moved into a 57,000 sq ft. headquarters facility that is renovated to include administrative offices, a showroom, a demonstration room, a studio, and a repair lab. The new facility allows TLS to set up, test, and program multiple entertainment lighting systems simultaneously. In addition to this centralized hub for daily activities, the company has several branch sales offices.

Despite its growth and success, TLS remains committed to the small customers who were essential to establishing the business. If a local deejay, private party, small church, or little theater needs lighting, TLS is ready to help. "We've got what they need. We do the larger gigs—but we never forget the little guy," says David.

David's wife Janet has been his partner since the early days. At first she thought of TLS as just a small operation. After David took her to see several businesses which she considered large players in the industry, she discovered that they were not much larger than TLS. This helped the couple develop their vision for the company's future.

In the beginning, David and Janet did everything themselves, from operating the lights to managing the business. Once it started to grow, David recognized that he needed to concentrate on managing and hire others for the actual lighting projects. "Even though I felt that nobody could do it as well as I could, I had to force myself to send other people out," he says. "What I did best was run the business, and what the people I hired could do best was the lighting." Learning to delegate was one of the hardest lessons for him to learn, and he still finds that giving employees responsibility and authority is difficult, and that the people side of running his own company is the most challenging. "Selling the product, or stocking the product, or coming up with what to sell—that's the easy part," he explains. "Hiring the right people, keeping them pumped up all the time—that's the hardest part of being in business. That's a theme you're going to hear from me forever: Hire the right people, and you will be successful. You hire the wrong people, and you won't be."

Treating those people well is another part of the TLS formula for success. The Millys consider their employees part of their family. "When they get in trouble, they come to you," says Janet. "If they have a wreck, it affects your insurance. It's a constant thing. And, of course, we feel an obligation, also, to make sure that they can make a living and they can support their families. That's important to us."

David also acknowledges his own limitations and is willing to look outside the company for insight. When he was feeling frustrated with the company's growth, he hired a consultant to analyze the business practices that had evolved without much critical thinking. The consultant identified some inefficiencies—for example, too many people reported to David—and made several restructuring suggestions that David implemented.

He and Janet also recognize the value of networking. On the local scene, TLS belongs to the Huntsville/Madison County Chamber of Commerce, which David considers the best promoter of Huntsville and its community. "If a city is good to you, you've got to give something back," he says. He has also been active in the Entertainment Services and Technology Association, which has been instrumental in establishing standards for safety and self-regulation across the country. At trade shows, he and his colleagues share ideas about a variety of industry topics like leasing versus buying equipment and the latest information technology systems. "People who want to start businesses should study the competition," encourages David. "I learn so much from them. It's simpler to see what's been successful than to go out and make your own mistakes."

David has some important advice for would-be entrepreneurs. "Be sure you have a competitive spirit—or find something else to do. Business is definitely a competitive sport."

Discussion Questions

As you read the remainder of Chapter 3, you might want to keep in mind some of the insights and ideas in this case study. Answer the following questions that relate to the case study:

1. Evaluate the TLS mission statement, "Making money doing lights." What kinds of goals did David and Janet set for themselves and their business? Do they relate to the mission statement? Did these goals affect their ability to grow to a $5 million business?

2. What kinds of activities do David and Janet spend their time on? Which kinds of activities do you think might be the best use of their time?

3. How might TLS find new customers? Whom do the Millys know that might help them grow and manage their business?

4. How might TLS learn what other competitors are doing in the lighting industry?

5. How can the Millys expand their business without incurring additional risks? What risks does TLS face?

Sources: Adapted with permission from Small Business School, the series on PBS, at http://SmallBusinessSchool.com; and from material in the video "Invent an Industry from Theatrical Lighting", Small Business 2000, and on the TLS Inc. website, http://www.tlsinc.com.

3.4 Negotiation

When you hear the term *negotiation,* you may think first of executives working out a joint venture, labor unions negotiating with management, attorneys negotiating a pretrial settlement, or diplomats trying to bring about peace in the Middle East. However, negotiation is not just reserved for high-level situations or formal settings. We negotiate all the time, for minor as well as critical reasons. Asking for a raise, purchasing products from a supplier, deciding where to go on vacation, trying to get the best price on a new car—these, too, are negotiations. And regardless of the situation, the process is basically the same.

Negotiation involves two parties trying to reach a mutually acceptable solution to a problem or to accomplish something that neither party could do on its own. The goal is to satisfy both parties' interests and achieve a "win-win" situation where each party gains something it wants in exchange for making concessions and feels treated fairly. To be successful, therefore, negotiators must pay attention to their own goals and objectives and the other participants' goals and objectives.[13]

Negotiating Styles

How do people negotiate? Some approach negotiation as an adversarial process: what one side gives up, the other side gets, and vice versa. This negotiating style focuses on victory and fighting hard for one's position. While you may win, the cost may be high in terms of the future relationship with the other party. At the other end of the spectrum is the negotiator who makes concessions to avoid personal conflict; the goal here is reaching an agreement. Even though the outcome seems positive and fosters future relationships, this softer style often results in a less satisfactory agreement and makes it hard to separate the people from the negotiating process. The negotiator may feel exploited.

A better method, described in Roger Fisher's and William Ury's book *Getting to Yes,* is *principled negotiation* or *negotiation on the merits.*[14] This technique applies to most negotiation situations and produces mutually satisfactory results using a friendly rather than an adversarial approach. The key elements of this clear-cut negotiating style are the following:

Negotiation   Back-and-forth communication process by which two parties try to reach a mutually acceptable solution to a problem or to accomplish something that neither party could do on its own.

- **People:** *Keep the people and the problem separate.* Deal with emotions separately from the substantive issues. Be soft on the people and hard on the problem.

- **Interests:** *Focus on interests, not positions.* Interests define the problem; by identifying shared desires and concerns, the way to reconcile conflict becomes more apparent. When you think primarily in terms of gaining acceptance for your position, you lose sight of what you really want, instead of looking for mutual interests.

- **Options:** *Develop multiple possibilities before making any decisions.* It's tough to develop creative solutions when you are under pressure. Instead of quickly looking for one solution, look for many mutually acceptable alternatives and discuss which is best for all concerned.

- **Criteria:** *Base the result on an objective standard.* Discuss and choose fair standards acceptable to all parties—for example, precedent, moral standards, professional standards, market value, replacement cost, and competitive prices. Then you can negotiate the issues in terms of the search for an outside principle, instead of pressure from the other party.

To sum up, think of negotiation as problem solving rather than as driving a hard bargain or making trade-offs to get what you want. As Ronald Shapiro, James Dale, and Mark Jankowski explain in their book, *The Power of Nice,* the best way to get what *you* want is to help the *other* side get what it wants. If you first identify the needs of each party and clarify the interests of each side, the discussions proceed within a framework of mutual problem solving. The spirit of cooperation replaces a confrontational, winner-takes-all attitude.

Structuring the Negotiation

Each negotiation has three broad stages: analysis, planning, and proposing. The first two preparatory steps build a solid foundation for all successful negotiations and may, in fact, take longer than the actual discussion of the proposal. Within these stages you'll have other steps. For example, the face-to-face proposing includes stating your proposal, asking questions to clarify objectives and interests, generating options, and reaching an agreement.

Lack of adequate preparation is often the reason that people feel dissatisfied after negotiating. Exhibit 3.7 lists the seven elements of a successful negotiation that

exhibit 3.7	**Seven Steps to Negotiating Success**

1. **Know each party's interests and priorities.** Probe deeply and go beyond position to understand each party's needs, wants, and concerns. You are more likely to reach a successful outcome when you build on interests. Remember that money is not usually the priority.

2. **Create many options for solutions.** The first idea may not be the best. By exploring possible agreements or parts of an agreement and not getting stuck on one outcome, you increase the potential to maximize joint gains.

3. **Know the BATNA (best alternative to a negotiated agreement).** What happens if you can't reach an agreement? What is the other party's fallback position? Your objective is to find an agreement that is better than the BATNA.

4. **Legitimize your requests.** Using external standards or precedents when setting quantitative values provides the basis for a fair agreement and builds trust.

5. **Communicate efficiently, listen carefully, and deliver a clear message.** Good two-way communication helps reach agreement more quickly and clarifies the underlying assumptions. Know what you are listening for.

6. **Build a relationship with the other party.** Separating the people issues from the substantive issues will help to preserve and enhance the relationship.

7. **Don't commit until you've compared your options to your BATNA.** Know what issues to include in the agreement and the steps to take to reach an agreement.

Source: Adapted from Roger Fisher and Kris Frieswick, "Doctor YES," *CFO,* September 2001, http://www.findarticles.com; and Roger Fisher and Danny Ertel, *Getting Ready to Negotiate* (New York: Penguin Books, 1995), pp. 6–7, 14–16.

arise from the four key points of principled negotiation. These provide a useful framework to use throughout the negotiation preparation process by creating options, building relationships, and facilitating communication. Note that these points are similar to good persuasive techniques: to build relationships, establish areas of common interests, which promotes liking. Reciprocity is at the heart of the negotiating process: your goal is a mutually beneficial outcome. Good preparation, clear communication, understanding of the other party's interests, and rapport between parties improve the odds of success, whether you are persuading or negotiating.

The amount of time you spend on each element will depend on the complexity and importance of the situation you are negotiating.

Generating Options

Options are at the heart of principled negotiation.[15] Typically people get bogged down in particular positions and viewpoints. They think they have the one right answer—their own—and it is reasonable. Until they consider other ways to approach their situation, they remain stuck with opposing positions.

Here's an example of negotiating based on position, and how the situation can be turned around when options and interests enter the picture. You just had your annual performance review and have requested a $3,000 salary increase. Your boss tells you that isn't possible this year; he can only offer you $1,500. Naturally, you are upset by this low offer. This is a classic win-lose scenario: you win only if your boss loses, and vice versa. You each have stated your position, and now the bargaining begins. If you were to bargain from these fixed positions only, you might try to compromise at the midway point. Would either of you be really satisfied? Probably not.

Let's add some important interests. What do you really care about? Is it the money alone, or are you interested in professional growth, finishing your college degree, or perhaps moving to a different department within the company? Your manager's interests are to run a profitable department, work with talented employees who do high-level work, boost employee morale, and get promoted.

Look at these interests and assign priorities. If professional growth is really important, you can propose a number of options that address these interests, such as additional on-the-job training and company-paid educational benefits that give you additional skills, opportunity to work on a broader range of projects, and assistance in working toward a promotion to a position with even greater salary potential. These options keep the interests of your boss in mind: you become a more productive and competent employee and demonstrate to higher management how well your boss develops employees' abilities. The potential now exists for mutual gain.

As you develop options, resist the temptation to judge them. Brainstorm without trying to decide, so that you generate lots of ideas that can lead to other possible solutions. Then broaden your options. Don't look for the best answer, but rather to gather as many options from which you can eventually choose. Apply different types of thinking to the situation—both real world and theoretical—to analyze the problem and what can be done to solve it, as shown in Exhibit 3.8. Going down and up the steps and revisiting the theory behind a good option will help you come up with others.

> **BATNA (best alternative to a negotiated agreement)** What each party will do if the negotiation process fails to reach an acceptable agreement.

Consider the Alternative

Suppose your negotiation doesn't work and you decide to walk away without reaching agreement. What is your best alternative to a negotiated agreement, or BATNA?[16] Knowing your BATNA ahead of time, and making educated guesses about the other party's BATNA, sets a baseline for the negotiation. The BATNA becomes the standard against which you should evaluate any proposal. To succeed, *an acceptable agreement must be better than the BATNA.*

Many people plan to walk away if they don't get what they want. But the critical thing to consider is, "Walk away to *what?*" Exploring the BATNAs on each side helps the parties think through their options and often results in negotiators going back to the table to generate other solutions. If each side's BATNAs are worse than options in the negotiated agreement, then the parties are likely to continue negotiating. Your BATNA gives you more flexibility to investigate solutions, rather than reject them out of hand.

In addition, a strong BATNA can give you leverage to reach a deal. If your BATNA seems viable to the other party, your threat to stop negotiating is real. Going into a negotiation without a BATNA makes you vulnerable and unsure of when to stop negotiating. BATNAs will help you focus on your objectives and look into ways to meet them outside of the negotiation. The better your BATNA, the better your negotiated agreement has to be to top it. Your BATNA will also give you more confidence to negotiate.

---

exhibit
3.8

Four Steps to Create Broad Options

Step 4: Develop action ideas. These are specific steps that could address the problem at hand.

Step 3: List possible strategies/solutions. Think about what might be done, in theory, and develop broad ideas.

Step 2: Analyze the problem. Identify its symptoms and suggest causes. What's missing, and what may hinder resolution?

Step 1: What is the problem? Define the problem and its symptoms factually. Make sure you are solving the right problem!

Source: "Circle Chart: The Four Basic Steps in Inventing Options", from *Getting to Yes,* 2nd ed. by Roger Fisher, William Ury, and Bruce Patton. Copyright © 1981, 1991 by Roger Fisher and William Ury. Adapted and reprinted by permission of Houghton Mifflin Co. All rights reserved.

To develop your BATNA, ask yourself questions like,

- What are the alternatives that satisfy my interests if we cannot agree?

- What are the pluses and minuses of these alternatives?

- Which is my BATNA—the one I will really choose—and how can I improve it?

- What alternatives does the other side have, and what are the merits of each?

- Which looks best, and how can I lessen its attractiveness (make it harder to achieve, convince that it is unwise or costly, etc.)?

Clearly, we have only skimmed the surface of the negotiation process. There is much more to learn about effective communication, style, timing, structuring the discussion process, dealing with challenging situations and difficult people, and similar topics. But understanding how to set the stage for a negotiation by identifying interests, options, and alternatives will get you started on the path to negotiating success.

3.5   Networking

You've probably been networking all your life. When you ask friends to recommend a good restaurant, an auto mechanic, gym, or movie, you are networking. You also network in the workplace as you find out about job opportunities, learn what your competitor is doing, and gather resources you will need to start, run, and manage a business. As you go about your daily life, you interact with many different types of networks.

What Is a Network?

A person's **network** is the sum total of his or her relationships and involves all of the connections that a person has with other people. Exhibit 3.9 (on page 70) diagrams these relationships and connections among people who are involved with a local bicycle store. The bicycle store's owner is connected to suppliers and manufacturers who provide bicycles and bicycle accessories to the store. Some of these suppliers are connected to other bicycle manufacturers. Think about the different manufacturers and suppliers and how they both compete and work with each other, and how all of these relationships affect the bicycle store owner.

Consider also the people who visit the store to purchase bicycles and accessories. These customers interact with the store's owner and employees. As previous customers share their experiences with others, these word-of-mouth connections generate new customers. At the center of all of these relationships (manufacturers, suppliers, employees, customers) is the bicycle store's owner.

From its particular network of relationships, the bicycle store derives a competitive advantage over other bicycle shops that do not have such a network. Not every bicycle shop will have the same relationships to various manufacturers and suppliers of bicycles, or to particular customers. The unique connections between these parties (manufacturers, suppliers, bicycle customers) differentiate one bicycle shop from another.

Every situation has a unique social structure of relationships: Some individuals will trust others, some have obligations to others, and some are dependent on exchanges with others. The *structure* of these relationships provides advantages that can enable some people to be more successful than others.

Enterprisers use their networks to find opportunities and exploit them. The social scientist Ronald Burt calls gaps in the connections among people **structural holes**, and he suggests that *structural holes are where opportunities for success occur*. These opportunities include new institutions and projects that need leadership, funding initiatives looking for proposals, jobs in need of good candidates, or valuable items entering the market for which you know interested buyers.[17] An enterpriser connected to other people who know about these opportunities is in a better position to find and pursue them.

Opportunities occur in networks rich in structural holes—that is, *in situations where people are not connected to each other*. For example, farmers have apples to sell. There are buyers for these apples. The enterpriser fills the hole by making the connection between the farmers and the buyers. In most situations, individuals doing similar activities know each other; farmers are likely to know the other farmers and companies involved in the apple business. On the other hand, most farmers are unlikely to be connected to those who purchase and use their apples—and most apple purchasers will not be connected to the apple farmers.

Network   The total of a person's relationships and connections with other people.

Structural holes   Gaps in the connections among people, where opportunities for success occur.

exhibit
3.9

A Local Bicycle Store's Network

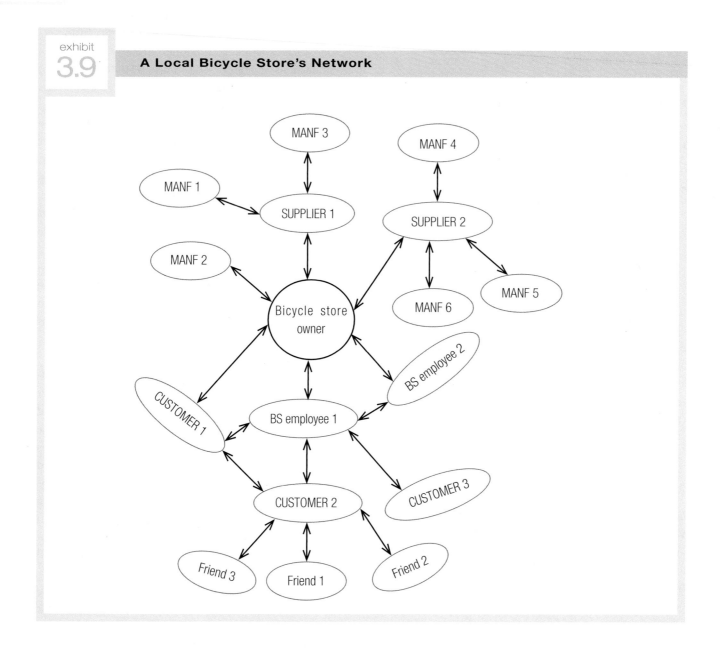

An opportunity exists in this structural hole between potential sellers—farmers with apples—and buyers. Think about all of the ways to fill this structural hole: farmer's markets, roadside produce stands, grocery stores, specialty food stores, apples on the Internet. The Enterprising World box explains how Brian Scudamore found an opportunity based on junk.

Advantages of Networking

Enterprisers who network gain a number of benefits. The first benefit involves *access,* or receiving a valuable piece of information and knowing who can use it.[18] For example, most job leads come from word of mouth. In fact, the Society for Human Resource Management found that 95 percent of all job applicants and personnel departments used networking and personal contacts to fill positions, and that both groups rated networking to be the most effective way to get a job.[19] Unless you are part of the network where a job opportunity is discussed, you won't be able to take advantage of the information and apply for the job.

The second benefit involves *timing,* that is, when a person might receive information that may have significant value. For example, suppose an enterpriser knew that a shopping center was going to be built in a particular area before others did. He or she could purchase land in the area at advantageous prices, well before most people knew about plans for the new facility.

AN ENTERPRISING WORLD

Junk Money

Have you ever noticed a business or service and asked yourself, "Why don't I do that, too?" Brian Scudamore, a college student in Vancouver, Canada, acted on his impulse after he noticed a junk-hauling truck. With an old truck and a clever name and slogan—"The Rubbish Boys: We'll Stash Your Trash in a Flash!"—he was in business. After several successful summers operating one truck, the young entrepreneur realized that many more people needed his services—and not just during the summer. By 1993, business was so good that he made The Rubbish Boys a full-time business and added two more trucks.

By 1996, the firm was generating $1 million in revenues, and Scudamore saw the potential to move into other markets in Canada and the United States. Under the new name 1-800-GOT-JUNK?, he decided to expand by selling franchises that would use the same name and operate with the business processes Scudamore developed. The idea caught on, and today 1-800-GOT-JUNK? is the world's largest junk removal service, with more than 270 franchises in the United States, Canada, Australia, and the United Kingdom. It ranked 292 on *Entrepreneur*'s 2006 Top Franchises list and 78 on its fastest-growing franchises list.

The business concept behind 1-800-GOT-JUNK? is very basic: Customers contact the company by phone or online at http://www.1800gotjunk.com to schedule pickups of nonhazardous items they no longer want and that may not qualify for municipal or other types of trash collection. The company offers 2-hour appointment windows and calls with an exact time shortly before arrival. Fully licensed, uniformed drivers evaluate the job on-site and present customers with a no-obligation price quote before beginning the job. Then they load the indicated items from the customer's site and even clean up after themselves. From furniture and appliances to truckloads of ceramic knick-knacks, mattresses, construction debris, and yard refuse—as long as two people can lift it, the company's trucks haul it to dumps, local charities, or recycling facilities. Prices are based on the volume items take in the truck and also include any dump or recycling fees.

Customers love and value the service: Through fall 2006, the company's trucks hauled away almost 800,000 tons of junk for more than 756,000 customers worldwide. Customers praise the company for saving them time and money and for the excellent customer service.

Despite the idea's simplicity, Scudamore was the first to develop the fragmented junk removal business into a recognized brand offering professional service. His idea appealed to franchisees because it wasn't a complex business, had low start-up costs, and demand was high. He also embraced technology to improve efficiency through JunkNet, a scheduling and operations management program.

Another key selling point was the commitment to a strategic vision and growth plan, which is clearly communicated to both headquarters employees and franchisees, who praise Scudamore's leadership and the quality of his management team. Employees at the headquarters are enthusiastic about the corporate culture Scudamore has created. They cite the company's passion for its vision and feel a strong sense of dedication to achieving that vision. They feel valued for their contributions, praising the supportive team environment, upbeat culture, responsive management, availability of flextime, generous profit sharing, and the excitement of being part of a rapidly growing company.

The future is bright for 1-800-GOT-JUNK? and Scudamore. Starbucks printed a quote from him on more than 10 million cups as part of its "The Way I See It" campaign. The company hauls away junk on the popular *Extreme Makeover: Home Edition* television series, and the company was named the best to work for in British Columbia in 2004 and 2005. Not bad for a guy who made it big with junk!

© Jeremy Hainsworth/AP Photos

(continued)

An Enterprising World (*continued*)

Discussion Questions

1. Why did Brian Scudamore choose the United States, the United Kingdom, and Australia to start his international expansion? Discuss the feasibility of starting and developing this business in other countries, citing specific examples.

2. What kinds of legal and environmental -regulations might prevent this business from succeeding in certain areas?

3. What goals did Scudamore set when starting and developing the 1-800-GOT-JUNK? concept? What additional goals did he use to guide the company's growth?

4. If you were Brian Scudamore, how would you manage your time during the early stages of the start-up process? What should be his priorities? List the kinds of activities he is likely to encounter and consider the amount of time he has to accomplish them. How will these activities and priorities change as the business grows?

5. How might you use the six principles of persuasion to recruit people to become franchisees for 1-800-GOT-JUNK?

6. What kind of network of people does Brian Scudamore need to develop and grow 1-800-GOT-JUNK? List the kinds of people that would be most helpful for developing this business. How might he go about finding and meeting these people?

Sources: "1-800-GOT-JUNK? Announces Massive Australian Franchise Expansion Plan," 1-800-GOT-JUNK? press release, March 31, 2006, http://www.1800gotjunk.com; 1-800-GOT-JUNK? website, http://www.1800gotjunk.com (September 17, 2006); Justin Martin, "From Cash to Trash," *Fortune Small Business*, November 2003, http://money.cnn.com/magazines/fsb/; Christina Occhipinti, "Life in the Dumps," *Westchester County Business Journal*, February 20, 2006, p. 19; and "Starbucks To Feature 1-800-GOT-JUNK? CEO on Coffee Cups across North America," 1-800-GOT-JUNK? press release, January 20, 2006, http://www.1800gotjunk.com.

Finally, enterprisers benefit from *referrals* they receive through a network. Being connected to other people who know about you provides legitimacy. Learning from a customer that the bicycle store's owner provides excellent service carries more weight than a newspaper ad for the store. Who would you more likely trust? The word of a friend, or an advertisement?

Clearly, when enterprisers have connections to people that others don't have, called "social asymmetry," they build relationships within and beyond the firm. These relationships form their *social capital*, which is just as important as the production-oriented, asset-based financial capital and human capital necessary to deliver goods or services. You build your social capital as you develop your networks because you

- Know people with "useful" information.

- Know people who are trustworthy (reliable information).

- Establish a large and diverse (nonredundant contacts) network.

The result of building up your social capital is new friends and associates and greater self-confidence. The more people you know, the more able you are to be in the center of a web of people with no connections to each other. Then you can fill the structural holes that exist, to everyone's benefit.

The Networking Process

Now that we know what a network is and the advantages networks bring, let's look at how to build your network and use it effectively. First, you must identify people to contact and figure out where to find those you don't already know. Then you need to approach them to share or acquire information.

Networking is the process of asking people you know (or could get to know through others) for information, advice, ideas, or help, as you plan and pursue your goals. It's a two-way street. First, you build up a wealth of contacts that help you find what *you* need. You share advice, ideas, leads, and resources with others—and, in turn, you receive information and assistance when you need it. Networking is a life skill you will use extensively for both personal and business reasons. The more you network, the higher your chances of success.

According to Susan RoAne, author of *How to Work a Room: The Secrets of Savvy Networking,* and *What Do I Say Next?,* networking is not a work style but a lifestyle

Networking   The process of asking people you know (or could get to know through others) for information, advice, ideas, or help, as you plan and pursue your goals.

that enhances our personal and professional lives. The best networkers are savvy and have common sense. They may not even realize they are networking. They're sharing themselves and their ideas. They may not have the biggest titles. What they do have is a huge contact base that they are willing to use to help someone else.[20]

Building Your Network

Think that you don't have a lot of networking contacts? Once you start making a list of potential resources, you may be surprised at how many people you do know! Include *everyone* who might be helpful, even if you are not sure. Use the categories listed in Exhibit 3.10 as a starting point, and sort your lists by group. Personal information management software can simplify the task of maintaining and organizing your lists.

To expand your circle of contacts, consider joining a networking club that covers your area of interest. For example, some specialize in job seekers, while others focus on small business owners. Alumni group gatherings often provide excellent networking opportunities. To find a professional organization in your field of interest, check out the Gateway to Associations at the American Society of Association Executives' website, http://www.asaenet.org (click on "Find Associations, People, and Businesses").

Work-related conferences and meetings are obvious places to network. However, remember that you have a networking opportunity any time you are in a room with a group of people. Certain events are better than others, but never miss a chance to add new people to your network. Regularly check local business periodicals for calendars of business and organizational events. Social and cultural events that may attract potential customers or people who you want to get to know also present networking possibilities.

Using Your Network

Now that you've begun developing your network and discovered the best places for networking, you are ready to use your network to your advantage. You must be proactive and

- *Feed the list.* Continually update, correct, and add as you make other contacts.

---

exhibit 3.10

Categories of Networking Contacts

Use this list to develop your own networking lists. Refine the categories to suit your personal needs.

- People in a position to influence
- People who know others
- Coworkers/former coworkers
- Clients/former clients
- Professionals: bankers, lawyers, accountants
- Colleagues and competitors
- Family/ex-family/extended family/friends
- Neighbors/former neighbors
- Former classmates
- Service providers, local merchants
- Associates from organizations: charities, religious organizations, clubs, civic groups
- Special interest groups: sports, community
- Trade associations and professional associations

- *Nurture your list.* Keep in touch; send articles of interest, birthday greetings, and such. Try to call those on your lists at least once a year to see how they're doing or what they might need. Communicate trust and mutual support.

- *Use the list.* Take advantage of all opportunities, formal and informal. Whenever you start something—a new marketing program, a career move, buying a house or car—think of your network. Tapping into those resources may save you money.[21]

Think of your list as a valuable reference tool. You can use it for many reasons, from recommending a garden service to a neighbor to finding an internship for a college student.

Never forget that *networking is a reciprocal process.* It involves using your resources and being a resource for others. We may have better contacts in some areas than others, and we are likely to know others who can fill in our gaps. Don't underestimate yourself; we all have a lot to offer. List your job responsibilities, job and general skills, and hobbies. Once you think about what you do well, you'll be more confident and better prepared to share your information.

Networking Basics

Networking is a win-win proposition. By developing relationships with people whom you don't know, you can provide an invaluable service by filling in structural holes. Like the bicycle store's owner and farmers in the prior section, you can be the link between groups of other people.

Look for ways to "exploit differences" among relationships. For example, if you have a friend who wants to rent a room in her house, and another friend is looking for a room to rent, you are "exploiting" the differences between these two friends by linking them together.

The fundamentals of networking are simple: Prepare, show up, and interact. Conversation is the key to making connections. The secret of conversation is to ask questions. The better your questions, the higher the quality of the information you receive. A brief conversation may lead to a relationship, which may then lead to new business.

Let's assume you are attending a meeting of high-technology business owners that will be on campus next week. To get the most out of your networking opportunity, *plan ahead.* Think about who will be at the meeting. If possible, get a list of registrants from the event sponsor. Decide who you'd like to meet and set up a few meetings ahead of time. Set goals so that you know what you want to accomplish. Make notes on the subjects you want to discuss and what you want to find out. This helps you to structure your discussions. Create interest with a clear, interesting self-introduction that you deliver with energy and confidence. Preparing it in advance helps to put you at ease and serves as an ice-breaker. Remember to make eye contact and use positive body language. Adapt the introduction to suit the event.

Focus on meeting new people. It's easy and more comfortable to head for familiar faces, but that approach won't yield the highest networking returns. Spend most of your time with people you don't know. As you talk to people, gain their interest with powerful questions. Look for ways to help. Instead of telling people what you do, share insights that help solve problems.

Don't be afraid to ask for information. It's a myth to think that people will know what you need and offer to help. Most people are happy to help when you ask. If you don't ask, the answer is always no! *How* you ask is just as important as asking. Remember the fundamentals of persuasion and incorporate those techniques when you request assistance. If you have established rapport, you are more likely to succeed. The best networkers ask in a way that lets people say yes—and gives them room to say no.

Networking may feel awkward at first, but the more you practice, the easier it gets. You'll learn to make the most of every networking opportunity. You should try to meet as many people as possible. By limiting the time you spend with each person, you can "work the room." Spending three minutes per person means you can make about 20 contacts in an hour. Chatting for ten minutes lowers that to six per hour. For large events, try to minimize the time per person, so you can talk to more people.

Good networkers establish trust with their contacts. They treat people with respect, courtesy, and integrity, using their resources appropriately. Reinforce the contacts you made by getting in touch afterwards. Always acknowledge the leads, ideas, information, and support you receive. If you promise to provide information, do so promptly. Follow up in a timely and appropriately persistent manner and you will build a solid network.[22] Exhibit 3.11 summarizes these key tips for networking success.

exhibit
3.11

Strategies for Networking Success

1. Plan ahead.
2. Set goals.
3. Develop a brief self-introduction.
4. Know how you can help.
5. Don't be afraid to ask.
6. Know how to ask.
7. Practice by doing.
8. Be aware of time.
9. Meet new people.
10. Follow up.
11. Establish trust.

Summary

1. Achievement requires action. Enterprisers leverage their abilities and their effort to get their goals accomplished: Work = Ability × Effort. Both ability and effort are required; one without the other is insufficient. To achieve their goals, enterprisers must manage themselves and others. Managing yourself begins with determining your goals and then allocating the time necessary to accomplish them. Enterprisers must also depend on the efforts, skills, and abilities of others in developing an enterprise. The fundamental tasks involved in managing others are persuasion, negotiation, and networking.

2. Many unimportant activities consume the majority of our time. To achieve our goals, we need to put our effort into tasks that are important, but not urgent. These tasks fall into Quadrant 2, which Steven Covey calls the Quadrant of Quality. We all need to be challenged in order to achieve. Those who set goals accomplish significantly more than people who don't. Those who set harder or more specific goals achieve more than people who set easy or vague goals.

3. Goals must be specific, results-focused, measurable, realistically attainable, relevant, and have a time frame. To create goals, you must identify your true values and the priorities for your life. Developing a personal mission statement helps you determine what is most important to you and what you want to do with your life.

4. Much of the hard work of goal setting is in making choices to prioritize one's goals. Ways to manage multiple goals include pursuing simultaneous goals by moonlighting between different goals; alternating between goals by devoting alternating blocks of time to different goals; choosing sequential goals, where goals are changed over a period of time; or engaging in actualizing multiple goals, where one combines two or three goals within the same set of activities.

5. Time management techniques increase productivity. Achieving one's goals requires a yearly, monthly, weekly, and daily plan of action. A weekly plan directs our efforts by linking the day-to-day activities to goals.

6. Persuasion involves efforts to change the attitudes and behaviors of others through communication. People are persuaded when they believe their own interests will be achieved. An enterpriser can use six principles to persuade others: *Liking:* people are persuaded by those who they feel are like them. *Reciprocity:* Those who give—get. People repay in kind. *Social proof:* Peer pressure will persuade others. *Consistency:* People often change their behaviors if they are asked to make commitments that are active, public, and voluntary. *Authority:*

We often defer to the judgment and knowledge of experts. *Scarcity:* People want things that are unique and exclusive. A persuasive individual understands the other person's values and needs and addresses these issues, creating win-win situations, where both parties see benefits in working together.

7. Negotiation involves two parties who are trying to reach a mutually acceptable solution to a problem or to accomplish something that neither party could do on its own. The best approach to negotiating is looking for win-win situations between the two parties. Successful negotiating involves four key elements: (1) Keeping the people and the problem separate; (2) focusing on interests rather than positions; (3) developing multiple options; and (4) basing the result on an objective standard.

8. Most negotiations involve seven steps: (1) Know each party's interests and priorities. (2) Create many options for solutions. (3) Know each party's BATNA. (4) Legitimize your requests. (5) Communicate efficiently. (6) Build a relationship with the other party. (7) Don't commit until you've compared your options to your BATNA.

9. The most critical aspect of the negotiating process is creating options. To develop options, (1) identify the problem to be solved; (2) analyze the problem for its specific symptoms and causes; (3) look for possible strategies/solutions; and (4) develop action ideas that might match the strategies/solutions. The alternative to a successful agreement is your BATNA. Reaching clarity about your BATNA can help you evaluate your options when negotiating.

10. A person's network is the sum total of his or her relationships, all the connections that a person has with other people. Enterprisers use their networks to find opportunities and exploit them. Opportunities occur in a network where there are no connections between some people (e.g., buyers) and others (e.g., suppliers). Enterprisers fill these "structural holes," those areas where there are no connections. Having a diverse network of relationships to other people provides a number of advantages. A network provides *access* to information that others might not have, *timing* benefits to those who gain information before others, and *referrals* that offer legitimacy (others can vouch for you). Enterprisers seek to build networks that involve people who have a lot of knowledge, are trustworthy, and diverse.

11. The networking process begins with the relationships your already have. Most people know more people than they realize. You can expand this base of contacts systematically by asking everyone for help in pursuing your goals. When asking for help you need to remember to return the favors given to you. Contacts with others need to be nurtured.

Review Questions

1. Why do you need both ability and effort to accomplish work? Do you agree with Sloboda's findings?

2. How do the five activities of managing yourself and others interrelate?

3. Differentiate between the four types of problems and give examples of each that you have experienced lately.

4. Why should you set goals? Define the characteristics of effective goals. Fill in Exhibit 3.4 with three goals you wish to accomplish in the next year and one you wish to achieve in five years.

5. What are the four techniques for managing goals? Apply them to develop a strategy to achieve the goals you listed in question 4.

6. Describe the six principles of persuasion. Give an example of how you would use each in a business and a personal setting.

7. Differentiate between persuasion and negotiation. How can you use elements of persuasion when you negotiate?

8. What are the four elements of principled negotiation? Why is this style so effective? Summarize the steps you'd take to prepare for a negotiation to buy a new car, using Exhibits 3.7 and 3.8 as guides.

9. What is the BATNA, and how can it help you become a more effective negotiator?

10. What is a personal network? Why is networking so essential to an enterpriser's success?

11. Describe the steps you'd take to expand your current network.

Applying What You've Learned[23]

1. Much of the work of goal setting involves figuring out what you want to do with your life. Begin by answering the following questions:

   (a) What is "meaningful work?"

   (b) What is the job from heaven and the job from hell?

   (c) Change the characteristics of the job from hell into that of the job from heaven.

   (d) Write scenarios about what the future job might look like.

   (e) Make a temporary permanent commitment to pursue the job from heaven.

2. What do you really want to accomplish in your life, and how can you overcome the blocks that get in your way? Use the questions below to learn the answers:

   (a) What are your escape dreams?

   (b) If you had all the freedom in the world, what would you do?

   (c) What would you do if you were bold? What would you do if you knew for sure you would succeed in making your dreams come true?

3. Write your own autobiography. Look back on your life 50 years from now. Write about what you accomplished, the places you went, and the people you met. What were your joys? What gave you the most pleasure doing? What will people remember you for?

4. Develop a plan to use each of the six -principles of persuasion to convince someone to

   (a) Purchase a specific type of car.

   (b) Take a course in a new area.

   (c) Go out on a date with a friend.

   (d) Invest in a new restaurant.

5. Divide the class into small groups. Have each person choose one of these situations and take turns role-playing these situations. The remaining group members should provide feedback on how persuasive the person was and how to improve the presentation.

6. Using the seven steps to negotiating success in Exhibit 3.7, demonstrate to your group how to use each step to negotiate in one of the following situations:

   (a) Pricing a new car.

   (b) Investing in a new restaurant.

   (c) Going out on a first date.

   (d) How does your negotiation strategy change if you are in a different role—the seller of a car versus the buyer of the car?

7. Who's in your network? Using the categories in Exhibit 3.10, list all your contacts, and consider how each of these contacts might be helpful for pursuing your goals.

8. Each day contact a person that you don't know, but who might be helpful in pursuing your goals. Call a stranger each day, Monday through Friday. Ask each person you know for the names and phone numbers of other helpful people. What did you learn from this activity?

9. Part of the networking process is getting used to meeting and talking with people that you don't know. Have everyone in the class meet and greet each other. Consider the class as a "networking event" and have the class mingle together, with each person introducing him/herself to others, individually. Have the class members talk to each other about their goals and what kinds of help they might need. By the end of the process, this group of students will make enough contacts to benefit many classmates.

Enterprisers on the Web

1. Develop your personal mission statement with the assistance of the Mission Formulator at the Franklin Covey website: http://www.franklincovey.com/missionbuilder/index.html. Did the results surprise you?

2. How well do you network? Take the quiz "What's Your Schmooze Quotient?" at http://www.susanroane.com/quiz.html. How well did you score? Develop a list of steps you can take to improve your networking ability.

3. Go to Mind Tools, http://www.mindtools.com/pages/main/newMN_HTE.htm, and look at their section on time management. Download the time management section, or read all of the articles online. Which time management activity did you find most helpful to pursue? In what areas of your life do you need to manage your time more effectively?

4. Virginia Tech has a website, http://www.ucc.vt.edu/lynch/TimeManagement.htm, that can help you better manage your role as a student. Go through the exercises in this website as a way to leverage your time and energy. Have you created a semester schedule? Assessed and planned your weekly schedule? Do you adjust your daily schedule? Have you evaluated where you invest your time each day? What kinds of tradeoffs do you need to make between the various activities that are important for you to be successful as an enterprising student?

5. The Persuasion Map at Read-Write-Think, http://www.readwritethink.org/materials/persuasion_map/, takes you through a set of questions and exercises to increase your ability to persuade. Choose a topic and person you want to persuade (e.g., going to a movie that you want to see, buying a car or a house) and see how this site can help you develop ways to convince others.

6. Your emotions and the emotions of those you are negotiating with are critical factors affecting your ability to negotiate. Go to Beyond Reason, http://www. beyond-reason.net/, and download their Emotions Preparation Tool workbook (found under Practical Negotiation Tools). Use the exercises in this workbook to consider how you would negotiate a house purchase, the sale of a restaurant, a divorce.

End Notes

1. Malcolm Gladwell, "Examined Life," *New Yorker,* December 17, 2001, p. 91.

2. Michael Warshaw, "Get a Life," *Fast Company,* June 1998, pp. 138–142.

3. Stephen R. Covey, A. Roger Merrill, and Rebecca R. Merrill, *First Things First* (New York: Simon & Schuster, 1995), p. 37.

4. G. P. Latham and T. W. Lee, "Goal Setting," in E. A. Locke (Ed.), *Generalizing from Laboratory to Field Settings* (Lexington, MA: Lexington Books, 1986), pp. 101–118; and E. A. Locke and G. P. Latham, *Goal Setting* (Englewood Cliffs, NJ: Prentice-Hall, 1984), pp. 27–41.

5. Rhonda Abrams, "Path to Success Begins with Action Plan," Gannett News Service, June 6, 2002, http://www.RhondaOnline.com.

6. Barbara Sher, *I Could Do Anything . . . If I Only Knew What It Was* (New York: Dell Publishing, 1994), pp. 2–6.

7. Ibid.

8. Covey, Merrill, and Merrill. *First Things First*, pp. 77–102; and Lori Ioannou, "Stephen Covey On Time Management," *FSB (Fortune Small Business)*, June 1, 2002, p. 73.

9. Robert B. Cialdini, "Harnessing the Science of Persuasion," *Harvard Business Review*, October 2001, p. 72–74.

10. Ibid., p. 79.

11. Section based on Kevin Hogan, *The Psychology of Persuasion* (Gretna, LA: Pelican Publishing Company, 1996), pp. 167–197.

12. Adapted from Robert Heller and Tim Hindle, "Communicating Clearly," *Essential Manager's Manual* (New York: DK Publishing, Inc., 1998), pp. 18–31; and Hogan, *The Psychology of Persuasion*, pp. 189–197.

13. Resources used to prepare this module include Heller and Hindle, "Negotiating Successfully," pp. 558–625; Roger Fisher and Danny Ertel, *Getting Ready to Negotiate* (New York: Penguin Books, 1995); Roger Fisher, William Ury, and Bruce Patton, *Getting to Yes*, 2nd ed. (New York: Penguin Books, 1991); Roy J. Lewicki, David M. Saunders, and John W. Minton, *Essentials of Negotiation* (New York: McGraw-Hill Irwin, 2000).

14. Fisher and Ury, *Getting to Yes*, pp. 3–14.

15. Section based on Fisher and Ertel, *Getting Ready to Negotiate*, pp. 21–44; and Fisher and Ury, *Getting to Yes*, pp. 56–80.

16. Section based on Fisher and Ertel, *Getting Ready to Negotiate*, pp. 45–60; Fisher and Ury, *Getting to Yes*, pp. 97–102; and James K. Sebenius, "Six Habits of Merely Effective Negotiators," *Harvard Business Review*, April 2001, pp. 93–94.

17. Ronald S. Burt, *Structural Holes: The Social Structure of Competition* (Cambridge, MA: Harvard University Press, 1992), p. 13.

18. Ibid.

19. "Study Reports Job Seekers, HR Depts. Rely on Personal Contacts," *Nation's Restaurant News*, April 23, 2001, http://www.findarticles.com.

20. Susan RoAne, "Create a Network of Colleagues, Cronies, Clients and Friends," Susan RoAne website, http://www.susanroane.com/articles/connect.html (June 13, 2002).

21. Haidee E. Allerton, "Personal Networking," *Training & Development*, October, 2000, http://www.findarticles.com.

22. Section based on Jeffrey Gitomer, "Networking Fundamentals That Work," *Business Journal*, January 21, 2000, http://www.findarticles.com; and Susan RoAne, "Nuances of Networking: A Savvy Approach for the Next Century," http://www.susanroane.com/articles/nuance.html (June 13, 2002).

23. Questions 1–4 from *I Could Do Anything if Only I Knew What It Was*, by Barbara Sher, Copyright © 1994 by Barbara Sher. Used by permission of Dell Publishing, a division of Random House.

ENTERPRISE

What Is an Enterprise?

KEY CONCEPTS

1. The choice of a business's legal entity affects how the business will be run, managed, and perceived in the world.

2. The three major legal forms for an enterprise are sole-proprietorship, partnership, and corporation. Other legal forms include limited liability companies, franchises, joint ventures, cooperatives, and not-for-profit organizations.

3. Each form has benefits and liabilities that can significantly affect how the enterprise is controlled and owned.

Suppose a high school guidance counselor suggests that you consider architecture as a profession because you get such good grades in both math and art. You go off to Europe to tour all of its major architectural sites and, as a result, you become convinced that studying architecture is right for you. But after graduation and several years as an associate at a large, prestigious firm in Los Angeles, you become disillusioned with the lack of creative flexibility you have at your firm. In your frustration, you begin to question the wisdom of your career choice.

© Creatas Images/Jupiter Images

This chapter describes the case of Ronald Altoon and Jim Porter, two innovative architects, who, with a third colleague, created a partnership that allowed all of them to use their individual talents to serve clients well and, consequently, grow a successful international firm. As you read this chapter, you will learn about the different organizational structures you can choose for your enterprise and the advantages and disadvantages of each form.

4.0 What Is an Enterprise?

As we mentioned in Chapter 1, an enterprise is created for the purposes of its owners. Individuals create enterprises for all kinds of reasons—to develop a new product, such as the Dyson "Cyclone" vacuum cleaner; to meet a customer need, such as a Web-design studio; or to serve the needs of the enterprise's owner, such as a fly fishing guide service. Two dimensions reveal the purposes of an enterprise's owners: *control,* designating who will manage the enterprise, and *ownership,* identifying who will share in the benefits of the enterprise.

The legal form of the enterprise determines how both control and ownership will be handled. Why focus on the legal form of the enterprise before looking at how an enterprise is actually started or how an enterprise would effectively be operated? While the legal form of an enterprise won't, intrinsically, determine whether the enterprise will be successful, choosing a particular legal form affects a variety of issues such as how the enterprise will be taxed and who will be responsible for its legal liabilities. Therefore, the legal form of the enterprise might be considered the "face" of the business—how it is seen by others, particularly others who are involved with regulating and taxing businesses.

The legal forms of an enterprise available to enterprisers who want to share in the benefits of their business are typically sole-proprietorship, partnership, and corporation. A number of other "hybrid" legal forms such as cooperatives and franchises have characteristics found in the three basic types. In addition, enterprises could be formed as "nonprofit" organizations, where individuals don't directly benefit from any surpluses the enterprise might generate but can still operate the business, as well as benefit through salaries and other forms of remuneration.

Although sole-proprietorships are the most popular legal form of business, they tend to remain small. Corporations, which only account for 10 percent of all businesses, generate about 84 percent of total sales and 64 percent of profits. Exhibit 4.1 compares the three basic legal forms in terms of numbers, sales, and profits.

The following are the major questions that we need to address when thinking about the legal form of enterprises are:

- Who will be in control of the enterprise?
- How will the benefits of the enterprise be shared and distributed?
- Who is liable for the actions of the enterprise?
- Who is responsible for any taxes the enterprise must pay?
- What are the differences in legal and administrative costs?
- What is the desired lifespan of the business?
- Will you need to raise capital from outside investors?
- How can owners of the business transfer their investment to others?

In Chapter 1, we discussed the contribution of the various types of businesses to the overall economy in the United States. One point to remember, though, is that all large businesses started, at some point, small. The choice to stay small or grow is one aspect of choosing the appropriate legal form. It is much easier, for example, to grow an enterprise that is formed as a corporation than it is to grow a sole-proprietorship or a partnership. This is not always the case, however. Kinko's started as a sole-proprietorship, and grew as founder Paul Orfelea formed separate partnerships with individuals at different locations around the United States. Before Kinko's was sold to a private investment banking company, Kinko's consisted of 450 separate partnerships. In 2004, FedEx acquired Kinko's, which currently operates as FedEx Kinko's Office and Print Centers and is part of the renamed FedEx Kinko's corporation.[1]

exhibit

4.1

Comparison of Forms of Business Organization

Firm	Number (%)	Sales (%)	Profits (%)
Sole-Proprietorships	72	4	14
Partnerships	9	12	22
Corporations	19	84	64

Source: Internal Revenue Service, as reported in Table 721, U.S. Bureau of the Census, *Statistical Abstract of the United States, 2008*, 127th ed. (Washington, DC: Government Printing Office, 2008), p. 487.

© Jacqueline Larma/AP Photos

Choosing the best form for a business is no easy task. Enterprisers should consult a lawyer before choosing the legal form of their organization. While an enterpriser may be well versed in many of the legal issues involved with each form of organization, qualified legal help can often spot potential problems in a partnership agreement or in articles of incorporation that can easily be overlooked by enterprisers using many of the forms that are available for partnership agreements or self-incorporation legal kits. Good lawyers are masters at spotting legal problems and issues that often have serious consequences to the business. Please seek legal advice.

4.1 The Sole-Proprietorship: A Solo Act

A sole-proprietorship can be best thought of as a one-person show: You are the enterprise! If you, as an individual, engage in business activities, you are acting as a sole-proprietorship. A **sole-proprietorship** is completely owned and operated by one individual.

Many sole-proprietors undertake business activities using a different name. For example, if the sole-proprietor's name is William Gartner, William could do business without using his own name by filing a *dba* (doing business as), typically with the city or county in which William resides. If William were running a flower store, he could file a *dba* for "Fast Delivery Flowers" and operate under that name (if no other business has registered that name as its business name).

Why Go the Solo Route?

Going it alone has many plusses:

- *It's easy to start.* By engaging in business activity, an individual is acting as a sole-proprietorship. Doing business would require a "business permit" granted by the city or county in which one resides. This permit is typically easy to obtain. There are also a few other licensing requirements and regulations applying to sole-proprietorships. For example, most cities and counties have zoning ordinances that require certain types of businesses to locate only in certain areas. There might also be health permits if the business is involved with food.

- *All benefits of the enterprise go to the owner.* Since the sole-proprietor is the enterprise, any income generated by the enterprise is the individual's income.

- *Complete control of the business.* Since the enterprise is the individual, the sole-proprietor is responsible for all of the enterprise's operations and does not have to answer to anyone else when making decisions. For example, the owner of a bakery can decide to open at 8:30 AM and close at 3 PM—even though bakeries typically open much earlier in the morning.

- *Fewer governmental regulations.* Other ways of organizing the business, such as partnerships and corporations, have more legal requirements and regulations to consider. Regardless of the legal form of business chosen, the firm will still be responsible for such legal and regulatory requirements as business permits, zoning permits, health and safety permits, and employee safeguards.

- *Taxed at the individual rate.* Since the sole-proprietor is the enterprise, all earnings of the business are taxed as income to the individual. For some individuals, this may mean a lower tax rate, compared to the tax rates if using other legal forms of business.

- *Easy to stop.* The sole-proprietor can end the business at any time without interference from others.

Sole-proprietorship   A business that is established, owned, operated, and often financed by one person.

© Didier Boutet/Brand X Pictures/Jupiter Images

Drawbacks to Going It Alone

On the flip side, there are also disadvantages to the sole-proprietorship form of enterprise.

- *Unlimited liability.* Since the enterprise is the individual, the activities of the enterprise can put all assets of the sole-proprietorship at risk. If the business fails, the liabilities of the business are the exclusive responsibility of the sole-proprietor, whose assets can be used to make up any claims against the business. Note that many business risks, such as a restaurant customer getting food poisoning or a defective enterprise product harming a customer, can be managed by purchasing insurance for these risks.

- *Business losses are considered the individual's losses.* Since the enterprise is the individual, any losses generated by the enterprise become the losses of the individual.

Partnership   An association of two or more persons who agree to operate a business together for profit.

General partnership   All individuals share in the profits and the management responsibilities of the business, as well as any liabilities that the business might generate.

Limited partnership   There are two types of partners: general partners, who share in profits, management responsibilities, and all liabilities; and limited partners, who do not share in the management of the business.

In summary, for some kinds of businesses, such as consulting practices and other kinds of service businesses (which depend on the expertise and skills of just one individual), sole-proprietorships are often the best way to operate. For businesses that depend on the skills and abilities of more than one person, it is usually better to organize as a partnership or corporation. Luckily, it is very easy for an individual to change from a sole-proprietorship into another legal business form.

4.2 Partnerships: Teaming Up

A **partnership** involves two or more individuals who agree to operate a business together for a profit. Suppose Fast Delivery Flowers is very successful and William Gartner wants to expand to another location or add related gift products. Rather than bear all the risk himself, he could bring in a partner to share the workload and also make an investment in the business.

In all cases, a partnership should involve a signed written agreement between the partners. It is possible to have a partnership based on an oral commitment between individuals, but when there is conflict between partners, such a commitment can be interpreted in different ways.

A partnership agreement will typically specify the partnership's name, the purpose of the business, the financial contributions of each partner, the management responsibilities of each partner, the salaries and profit percentages that each partner will receive, as well as agreements about how to resolve partnership disputes, the process for dissolving the partnership, and distributing any partnership assets.

There are two types of partnerships: general and limited. All individuals involved in a **general partnership** share in the profits and the management responsibilities of the business, as well as any liabilities that the business might generate. In a **limited partnership**, there are two types of partners: general partners, who share in profits, management responsibilities, and all liabilities; and limited partners, who do not share in the management of the business. The liability of limited partners in the business is limited to their investment, but they will share some portion of the profits and losses of the business. Limited partners typically are investors: individuals who are willing to invest in a business and share in the profits, but who are not interested in managing the day-to-day operations of the business.

Advantages of Sharing the Load

Partnerships offer several advantages:

- *Ease of formation.* Much like a sole-proprietorship, a partnership between individuals is easy to form. The legal regulations involving partnerships are not complicated; however, most partnerships involve contracts between the partners that can be expensive and difficult to create and to have all of the partners agree.

- *Fewer government regulations.* Again, much like sole-proprietorships, partnerships involve little government regulatory requirements. The state government registers and regulates most partnerships.

- *Taxation of profits at the individual rate.* Like sole-proprietorships, the profits of the business are directly passed through to the partners of the business, so there is no specific income tax on partnerships. The partners, themselves, are personally responsible for paying income taxes on their portion of the profits or losses generated by the partnership.

Problems with Partnerships

Even though having one or more partners can serve a business well, there is also a downside:

- *Unlimited liability.* All general partners are responsible for the actions of any of the partners in the partnership. For example, Thomas Jefferson was involved in a business partnership where his partner took on debts in the name of the partnership and promptly squandered all of the money. Jefferson was obligated to pay these debts, and, the only way he could generate enough funds was to sell all his books to the U.S. government. (This collection of books became the basis for the Library of Congress.) In many states, the laws for partnerships have been modified so that individuals can form limited liability partnerships (LLPs) that limit the liability of each partner to their own actions in the business.

- *Partnership conflicts.* All enterprises change over time, and the interests of the partners in an enterprise change as well. While business partners may begin their partnership with similar goals, these goals can diverge. Consider two individuals who form a partnership out of college. Both are single and put an equal amount of time and money into the partnership with the expectation that both will work equally hard, to insure that the business grows and is profitable. After five years, one of the partners gets married and decides to have a family. This partner wants to work fewer hours and use more of the profits of the partnership for his own personal use (e.g., buy a house, take more vacations), instead of investing his portion of the profits back into the business. The other partner sees new opportunities for the growth of the business and wants both partners to invest most of their profits to develop these new opportunities. How can such a dilemma be resolved when the goals of these two partners diverge? Partnerships have high rates of failure over time because of difficulties in resolving differences among partners.

Finding a Partner

Most people form partnerships with people whom they already know—trusted friends and family members, rather than "strangers." Yet partnerships formed between close friends and family are often the most difficult partnerships to manage and keep alive over a period of time. In this chapter's Enterprising Ethics box you'll meet two friends who ran into problems when they became business partners and founded an Internet company.

In a business, partners need to talk candidly about problems and point out ways that the other partner may need to change. Individuals who have been in supportive relationships with friends and family members often find it very difficult to be in situations where there is conflict—and all partnerships will experience conflicts. How partners recognize and resolve these conflicts is a key aspect of whether their partnership will survive. Exhibit 4.2 provides a list of possible questions to ask a prospective partner. We will explore many of these questions in later chapters of this book when we look at various ways that enterprises can transform their businesses.

4.3 Corporations: Structured for Growth

Assume that after operating Fast Delivery Flowers for three years, William Gartner and his partner want to expand even further and open additional locations in neighboring states. Bringing in more partners could be a cumbersome process, so instead they choose to form a

exhibit
4.2

Picking the Perfect Partner

Here are some questions for potential partners to ask themselves and each other:

1. What are you looking for in a partner?

2. What do you bring to a partnership?

3. Why are you willing to begin an enterprise with partners? What advantages do you see to such an arrangement? What disadvantages do you see to such an arrangement?

4. How will important decisions in the business be made? If one partner wants to invest the profits of the enterprise while the other partner wants to pay these profits to the partners as salaries, how will this conflict be resolved?

5. How will conflicts among the partners be resolved? Remember, in any enterprise, there must be someone who is ultimately in charge, and who can make the final decision for the business. Unresolved decisions in an enterprise will cause a business to flounder.

6. How can partners leave the enterprise, whether for personal reasons or due to conflicts that cannot be resolved? How will each partner's share of the business be valued? If the partnership's assets are tied up in inventory, plant and equipment, how will a partner who wants to leave be paid?

7. Finally, since many partnerships are begun between spouses or "significant others," both partners should ask themselves whether they really want to be with this partner 24 hours a day, sharing not only the partnership of the enterprise, but the family partnership as well.

ENTERPRISING ETHICS

Why govWorks *Didn't* Work

The concept for govWorks was simple: provide a way for individuals to pay parking tickets, register cars, and transact other routine local government business online. The company would make its money from fees. Childhood buddies Kaleil Tuzman and Tom Herman estimated that the potential market for their services was $450 billion. So with dollar signs in their eyes but little actual experience running a company, they convinced two other friends to join them. Pooling their resources, they came up with $200,000 in start-up funds. In 1999, they began working on the technology for the website. As investor interest grew, they successfully raised $60 million from leading venture capital funds.

With lots of money available to bring their vision to life, the founders quickly staffed up to develop the software for the site. As the site began to take shape, govWorks looked further afield and, like many other dot-coms, took a bigger-is-better mentality. The potential to make millions from tapping the power of the Internet got in the way of sound business practices. Before it had fully developed its primary concept, it formed a joint venture with Cotesa Holding, Ltd., to take the idea into Latin America and also acquired several companies, including Jobs-in-Government, a business that posted government positions. Soon it had 250 employees to pay—and little revenue, because municipal governments weren't signing on for govWorks' electronic payment services.

govWorks then decided to offer its software to local governments on a fee basis, cooperating with the municipalities' existing online strategies instead of competing with them. It was too late, however, because rival EzGov got the jump on govWorks and had already launched a site based on this business model. govWorks laid off 60 employees in April 2000. As more competitors entered the market, even offering free bill payment, govWorks had to cut its prices. Costs continued to far outpace revenues, expected financing was withdrawn, and additional layoffs reduced the staff to 60 by November 2000. The company struggled for a few more months, but by early 2001, govWorks had joined the ranks of dot-com has-beens. It "starred" in *Startup.com*, a documentary film that tells the story of the company's founders, their friendship, and govWork's brief but turbulent history. govWorks also earned the tenth slot on CNet's Top 10 list of failed dot-coms.

At first glance, Tuzman and Herman seemed like ideal partners with complementary capabilities. Tuzman, a former investment banker, was the consummate salesman, while Herman brought the technical expertise. Over the course of the following 18 months, the pair's friendship was tested to its limits by the challenges of running a fast-growing Internet company. They differed on critical management issues, such as the right direction in which to take the company. Eventually Tuzman, who was CEO, forced COO Herman to leave the company. Herman felt that Tuzman made him the scapegoat and was protecting himself. Despite his anger at being dismissed over these disagreements and asking for financial compensation for his original investment, Herman later said, "I did (and do) agree with his belief that you need *one* CEO who makes these decisions. When the CEO makes the decision, the rest of the company needs to get on board and make it happen."

What went wrong? According to Tom Herman, the basic business concept was sound—and has been executed successfully by other companies. The major mistake was trying to market directly to consumers rather than partnering with government agencies. govWorks also grew too quickly, without an organizational structure or consistent operational plan. It added staff without organizing them effectively or having clear job descriptions. It tried to go in too many directions at once. The founders were blinded by their early successes in raising funding and lost sight of their original business concept, chasing instead after Internet riches. Their egos got in the way of good sense. To make matters worse, the venture capital investors had their own ideas of how the company should be run.

Despite their troubles, Herman and Tuzman remained friends and continue to work together on several other business ventures. "There was no benefit to me, to Kaleil, or to any third party for us to be negative or not get along," says Herman.

Discussion Questions

1. If possible, view the movie *Startup.com* for more background. What lessons in entrepreneurship did you learn?

2. What were the expectations of the two partners in terms of how the company would evolve and what role each founder would take? What went wrong between them, and how could they have prevented their problems?

3. Is it ethical to make promises to investors and potential employees about the growth expectations of govWorks.com? Do you think, for example, that new employees were aware of the risk of this new venture? What responsibilities do the founders of the business have to their new employees when the business takes a downturn and they must lay off most of the staff?

4. How do venture capital companies "manage" the possible failure of their investments? Do they have a right to ask the founders to leave the venture?

5. How did Tuzman and Herman preserve their friendship despite the failure of govWorks? Suggest reasons that the pair has continued to work together on subsequent ventures.

Sources: Kent German, "Top 10 Dot-Com Flops," *CNet*, July 28, 2005, http://cnet.com; Anni Layne, "Close Encounters of the Dotcom," *Fast Company*, May 2001, http://www.FastCompany.com; Ryan Naraine, "Anatomy of a Distressed Dot-com: govWorks," January 12, 2001, http://www.atnewyork.com; Online Q&A with Thomas J. Herman, Co-founder, govWorks.com, WashingtonPost.com, July 18, 2001, http://www. publicdatasystems.com/wash_post_071801.htm.

corporation and raise money for the company's growth by selling equity to investors.

A **corporation** is a legal entity that is separate from its owners. A corporation is considered to be, legally, much like a person. A corporation can own property, borrow money, and can sue and be sued by other individuals and corporations. The corporation, rather than its owners, is

Corporation   A legal entity with an existence and life separate from its owners who are not personally liable for the entity's debts. A corporation is chartered by the state in which it is formed and can own property, enter into contracts, sue and be sued, and engage in business operations under the terms of its charter.

liable for its debts and actions and is a taxable entity. The laws of the state where the corporation is chartered govern how the corporation can act and how it is structured.

Many people are under the mistaken impression that because a corporation is solely liable for any debts, the owners of a corporation can have the corporation borrow money or lease cars and equipment and then be personally immune from any liabilities if the corporation can't make loan or lease payments. Most lenders are unlikely to lend money to a corporation unless there are guarantees that any loans will be paid back. To insure this, many banks and lenders require that the owners of the corporation personally guarantee any of the corporation's loans or leases.

Corporations have three organizational components: stockholders, directors, and officers.

- Stockholders or **shareholders** own the corporation through shares of stock. This ownership provides them with certain rights. While stockholders don't participate in management of the firm (unless they are also officers), they may share in the corporation's profits by receiving dividends, and they can sell or transfer their shares. Stockholders can attend annual meetings, elect the board of directors, and vote on matters that affect the corporation, in accordance with its charter and bylaws. Each share of stock generally carries one vote.

- A **board of directors**, elected by the stockholders, is responsible for the overall management of the corporation. The directors set major corporate goals and policies, hire corporate officers, and oversee the firm's operations and finances. Small firms may have as few as three directors, whereas large corporations usually have 15 to 25.

Stockholders   The owners of a corporation who hold shares of stock that provide certain rights; also known as *shareholders.*

Board of directors   A group of people elected by the stockholders to handle the overall management of a corporation, such as setting corporate goals and policies, hiring corporate officers, and overseeing the firm's operations and finances.

Officers   In a corporation, these individuals are hired by the board and responsible for achieving corporate goals and policies. They include top management such as the president and chief executive officer (CEO), vice-presidents, treasurer, and secretary.

Corporate boards usually have both corporate executives and outside directors (not employed by the organization), chosen for their professional and personal expertise. Outside directors often bring a fresh view to the corporation's activities because they are independent of the firm.

- The **officers** of a corporation, hired by the board, are responsible for achieving corporate goals and policies. These include top management such as the president and chief executive officer (CEO), vice-presidents, treasurer, and secretary. Officers may also serve on the board and own stock.

Enterprisers involved in small corporations are likely to have overlapping roles among the three groups. For example, the firm's owners (stockholders) may also be the corporation's officers and board members. Since the role of the board is to create policy and procedures to guide the corporation's officers who implement the goals of the corporation, many enterprisers will seek to find independent outside directors to provide a different perspective on the operations of the business. When enterprisers play all three roles in the company (owner, director, and officer), it is very hard to see the big picture when the day-to-day operating of a company often consumes all of the enterpriser's time and energy. Since the management of an enterprise will be covered in subsequent chapters in this book, we will look at the critical role of the board of directors in the growth and development of an enterprise.

Board of Directors

As a *fiduciary agent* of the corporation, a member of the Board of Directors has a legal responsibility to the stockholders of the corporation for the operations of the corporation. A growing body of laws and regulations makes directors personally responsible for the actions of the corporation. For example, stockholders can sue a director if the chief financial officer was found to misstate earnings, or an employee was found to have embezzled substantial amounts of money from the corporation and the board had not set into place a control system to closely monitor these employees' behaviors. Since a board member might be personally sued and liable for a corporation's actions, most outside board members require the enterprise to pay for liability insurance that covers any legal fees, possible fines, or monetary judgments. Members of a board of directors may even face criminal charges for the actions of a corporation.

Given the increasing personal liability that an individual can have as a board member, fewer individuals are likely to accept opportunities to serve on boards without considerable benefits. While some individuals will serve on a board of directors for nonfinancial reasons, most people have so many competing demands for their time that some form of compensation is necessary if you want them to pay attention to the affairs of your business. Such compensation varies. Some corporations pay their board members to attend each meeting, while others pay with stock or provide stock options.

There are a number of advantages to having board members who are not family, friends, or employees of the corporation. These outside board members often bring different, more objective views of the corporation's operations and strategies, as well as insights into how other companies are managed and operated. They also can provide helpful business contacts, such as lawyers, accountants, consultants, and prospective employees and investors, as well as contacts with suppliers and customers.

It should be noted that some enterprisers have a *board of advisors* to supplement the corporation's legally mandated board of directors. This group provides advice to the owner of a corporation. These individuals are not legally involved in the direction and operations of the corporation; rather, they offer insights and recommendations only to the owner. A board of advisors can avoid the personal legal liability, since its members are not fiduciary agents of the corporation.

The Incorporation Process

Creating a corporation involves more steps than the other forms of business we've discussed thus far. Each state sets its own registration procedures, fees, taxes, and laws regulating corporations. A firm doesn't have to incorporate in its home state; in fact, it may be advantageous to incorporate elsewhere. For example, Delaware's pro-corporate policies make it a popular state of incorporation for many companies, including about half the Fortune 500. Nevada is another corporation-friendly state.

Incorporating a company involves these main steps:

- Choosing the company's name.

- Writing the articles of incorporation (also called a charter or certificate of incorporation in some states).

- Filing the articles of incorporation at the appropriate state office, usually the secretary of state's office.

- Paying required fees and taxes.

- Holding an organizational meeting.

- Adopting bylaws, electing directors, and passing the first operating resolutions.

Exhibit 4.3 describes the components of the articles of incorporation.

Most states now have websites from which you can download the necessary forms to incorporate. For

---

exhibit 4.3

Articles of Incorporation

A company's articles of incorporation are prepared on a form authorized or supplied by the state of incorporation. Articles of incorporation usually include the following key items:

- Name of the corporation

- The company's purpose/type of business

- Types of stock and number of shares of each type to issue

- Life of the corporation (usually "perpetual," meaning with no time limit)

- Initial capital investment by stockholder

- Methods for transferring share of stock

- Address of the corporate office

- Names and addresses of the first board of directors

- Name and addresses of the incorporators

- Other public information the incorporators wish to include

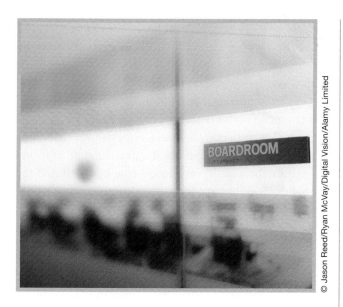

example, following this link will take you to the form for the state of Oregon: http://www.filinginoregon.com/forms/business.htm.

Types of Corporations

The two most common corporate forms are the C and S corporations. C **corporations** are the "basic" or conventional type of corporation. Small businesses have another option to achieve liability protection, the S corporation.

The S **corporation** also has stockholders, directors, and officers but receives special tax treatment from the Internal Revenue Service (IRS). By electing S corporation status, an enterprise's taxation is similar to a sole-proprietorship or partnership rather than the corporation paying corporate income taxes. Profits or losses pass directly to the stockholders and are taxed as personal income of the shareholders, thereby avoiding double taxation of corporate profits (once to the corporation and again to the shareholders). As with C corporations, the owners of an S corporation are not personally liable for the corporation's debts. The tax

C corporation   A conventional or basic corporate form of organization.

S corporation   A hybrid entity that is organized like a corporation, with stockholders, directors, and officers, but taxed like a partnership, with income and losses flowing through to the stockholders and taxed as their personal income.

advantages and the liability protection are the major benefits of S corporations.

To qualify as an S corporation, the company must

- Be an eligible entity (a domestic corporation, a partnership, or a single-member or multiple-member limited liability company).

- Have fewer than 100 shareholders.

- Limit shareholders to individuals who are U.S. citizens or residents; no corporate shareholders are allowed.

- Have only one class of stock.

- Allocate profits and losses to shareholders proportionate to each one's interest in the business.

- Use the calendar year as its fiscal year.

Most states recognize S corporations and give them the same tax treatment as the federal government. S corporation stockholders would include their shares of the profit or loss when they file state income taxes. However, there are some exceptions, so it's important to check with the state income tax agency in any states where the S corporation will do business to ask about the tax treatment before choosing this type of corporation.

The Corporate Advantage

Why go through all the formalities to form a corporation rather than choose a sole-proprietorship or partnership? There are several major reasons:

- *Stockholders are not liable for corporate debts.* This is perhaps the most important advantage corporations offer. The corporation is a legal entity that exists separately from its owners. If a corporation runs out of money, its creditors can go after the company's assets to repay the debt. The maximum the shareholders of a corporation can lose is their investment in company stock.

- *Credibility and stability.* Customers and vendors may perceive a corporation as more credible and long-lived than a sole-proprietorship or partnership. The corporate form implies a strong commitment to the business venture.

- *Tax advantages.* Corporations can reduce taxable income by deducting operating expenses and employee benefits such as insurance, travel, and qualified retirement plans. Tax rates may be lower than for other business forms.

- *Perpetual life.* A corporation has an unlimited life. Its existence is not tied to any particular person, so that the illness or death of an officer or stockholder does not end the corporation.

- *Greater access to capital.* A corporation can raise funding in several ways including selling stock and creating new types of stock with different voting or profit characteristics. The separation between personal and business liability makes it easier to attract investors. Bank loans are more available to corporations as well. Access to capital is necessary for growth.

- *Ease of ownership transfer.* The ownership of the corporation is easily transferred through the sale of stock and doesn't disrupt business operations.

- *Ability to be anonymous.* Unlike a sole-proprietorship or partnership, the owners of a corporation can have anonymity if they wish.

- *Management advantages.* Corporations have a broad base of management where all decisions are made by the board of directors, not shareholders. It's also easier for corporations, because of the advantages listed above, to attract and retain talented employees.

Drawbacks to Incorporating

Not everything about the corporate form is an advantage:

- *More difficult and costly to form.* As we've seen, setting up and operating a corporation is more complex than a sole-proprietorship or partnership. Not only are there more forms to file, but initial formation fees, filing fees, and annual state fees can run to thousands of dollars. These costs are partially offset by lower insurance costs.

- *More formalities and regulations.* Corporations must hold regular meetings of the board of directors and shareholders and keep written corporate minutes. They are also subject to numerous state and federal laws.

- *Double taxation.* Not only do corporations pay federal and state taxes on profits, but currently any profits distributed to stockholders are also taxed as personal income. (Congress is evaluating proposals to eliminate taxation at the personal level.)

Exhibit 4.4 summarizes the key characteristics of the three major legal forms of business organization.

4.4 Specialized Organizational Forms

While most new businesses choose one of the three dominant forms of business organization, several other options are worth considering: the limited liability company (LLC), professional corporations and professional LLCs, franchising, joint ventures, and cooperatives.

The Limited Liability Company (LLC)

A relatively new form of business is becoming more popular with enterprisers. The **limited liability company** (LLC) is a structure created for tax purposes. It combines the advantages of a corporation with the tax advantages of a partnership or S corporation. An LLC can also be a sole-proprietorship, a partnership, a C corporation, or an S corporation depending on the particular circumstances.

Like corporations, LLCs are separate legal entities that protect personal assets from business liabilities. Members are not personally liable for the debts of the LLC. However, LLCs don't issue stock but are owned by individuals such as company managers. LLCs are easier to form and have fewer restrictions than corporations. They are owned by members, who hold membership interests. Like partnerships and S corporations, any profits or losses pass to the owners and are taxed as personal income, thus avoiding double taxation.

The LLC's flexibility and simplicity make it attractive to many business owners. An LLC has no required structure (board of directors and corporate officers) or corporate formalities such as minutes or resolutions. It can distribute income as it chooses, rather than to all shareholders. Unlike the S corporation, the number or type of members is not restricted in the LLC. Transfer of ownership, however, is harder for LLCs than for corporations. The LLC must be terminated if a member dies or becomes bankrupt.

All states recognize the LLC, although actual regulations may vary. Establishing a LLC requires filing Articles of Organization with the appropriate state agency and paying any fees.

Limited liability company (LLC)   A hybrid organization that offers the same liability protection as a corporation but may be taxed as either a partnership or a corporation.

exhibit
4.4

Comparison of Major Forms of Business Organization

	Sole-Proprietorship	Partnership	Corporation
Profits and Losses	Owner receives all profits *and* bears all losses.	Partners share profits and losses.	Limited liability protects owners from losing more than they invest.
Ease and Cost of Formation	Easy; low organizational costs.	Easy; relatively low organizational costs.	Complex to form; more expensive to incorporate.
Liability	Unlimited liability; proprietor's total wealth can be taken to pay business debts.	Owners have unlimited liability; may have to cover debts of other, less financially sound partners.	Limited liability.
Taxation	Company's income taxed as personal income of proprietor.	Partnership income taxed as personal income of partners.	Receives certain tax advantages. But double taxation: both corporate profits and dividends paid to owners are taxed.
Access to Financial Resources	Ability to raise funds limited to owner's resources.	Fund-raising ability is enhanced by multiple owners.	Greater access to financial resources allows growth.
Management Responsibilities and Skills	Proprietor has all responsibilities; may have limited skills and management expertise.	More expertise and managerial skill available.	Can attract employees with specialized skills.
Life Span/ Continuity	Easy to terminate; also, business terminates if owner dies.	Dissolves or must reorganize when partner dies.	Perpetual life; difficult to terminate.
Transfer of Ownership		Difficult to transfer ownership, liquidate, or terminate.	Easy to transfer ownership through sale of stock.
Growth Potential	Limited to owner's abilities and resources.	Limitations on growth.	Can achieve large size due to marketability of stock (ownership).
Employees and Benefits	Limited long-range opportunities and benefits for employees.	Opportunity to become partner; more limited benefits than corporations.	Greater opportunities for advancement; offers more benefits.
Other Factors	Owner has sole control over company. Can maintain secrecy.	Potential for conflicts between partners.	Subject to more government regulation; financial reporting requirements make operations public.

Professional Corporations or LLCs

Professional service providers such as physicians, attorneys, accountants, architects, or consultants may set up professional corporations (PCs) or professional limited liability companies (PLLCs). States often require that certain types of professionals form professional or regular corporations to operate. The definition of professional services varies from state to state. In most cases, professions that require a license must set up their practices as PCs or PLLCs. They require the approval of the appropriate state licensing agency in addition to the filing of standard documents. In some states, professionals can choose whether to incorporate as a PC or a C or an S corporation.

Franchising

If you want to go into business for yourself but don't want to start a totally new company, franchising may be for you. Franchising has become an important way for enterprisers to start and grow businesses. In this chapter, we offer just a brief introduction. Chapter 11, "New Venture Creation Pathways: Franchising," provides a more detailed discussion of the franchise process as a route to business ownership.

Franchising is a form of business organization that involves a specific relationship between a **franchisor** who supplies the business concept and/or product and a **franchisee** who operates a franchise business unit. It includes a licensed trademark, a specific marketing plan, and a fee from the franchisee to the franchisor for the right to sell the franchisor's product or services in a specific territory.

Starting a franchise requires the same amount of work as starting an independent venture. However, the franchisor provides guidance on the operations, marketing, and management of the business—important contacts and knowledge to help you build your business. Most franchisees form corporations to own the assets of the franchise and are licensed to operate the franchisor's business system. They chose this "packaged" route to business ownership because they believe that using the franchisor's brand and systems will minimize the risks that start-ups face and enable them to be more successful than when going out on their own. A recent Gallup Poll of franchisees found that more than 94 percent considered themselves successful and that over 75 percent would buy their franchise again if they had to do it over.

The operations of a franchise are governed by a **franchise license agreement**, which specifies the rights and obligations of the franchisor and franchisee. It grants the franchisee the right to use the franchisor's business name, trademark, and logo. This contract includes provisions outlining how the franchisee will operate the franchise, the services provided by the franchisor, and the financial terms of the arrangement. For example, it may require the franchisee to maintain designated inventory levels, buy a standard equipment package, sustain sales and service levels, and participate in franchisor advertising and promotional programs. The franchisor generally provides a proven company name, symbols, operating procedures, managerial and accounting procedures, and price discounts for supplies, as well as assistance with financing, site selection, construction, management development, and manager and employee training.

Why Buy a Franchise?

The franchise alternative can provide a quicker route to business ownership with the following advantages:

- *Proven product with nationally recognized name.* Rather than start a small business with one local unit, a franchisee becomes part of a chain of locations with a recognized name and brand identity. You don't have to reinvent the wheel, because the business comes with a proven track record, standard goods and services, and national advertising. Because customers are already familiar with the company and its products, the franchisee has a lower risk and improved likelihood for success. Franchisees also benefit from the combined strength of the franchisee group, achieving economies of scale in purchasing materials, supplies, and services such as advertising.

- *Marketing support.* The franchisor provides national and local advertising programs to promote the business. Such pooled advertising has broader reach than possible for most independent business owners. In addition, the brand is already established and carries greater clout.

- *Standardized operating concept and procedures.* The franchisor provides an established operating format and procedures for running the franchise, including operations, management, and accounting. This also contributes to reduced risk.

- *Management training and assistance.* In essence, the franchisor serves as a management consultant for the franchisee. The franchisor has already

Franchising   A form of business ownership involving a contractual arrangement where a parent business (the *franchisor*) provides an investor (the *franchisee*) with the rights to sell products or services in exchange for fees and/or royalty payments.

Franchisor   Parent company that owns and controls the rights to offer the franchise's product concept to the *franchisee*.

Franchisee   The individual or company that owns one or more franchises and sells goods or services in accordance with the terms set by the *franchisor*.

Franchise license agreement   The principal legal document that defines the terms of the relationship between the franchisor and franchisee, including the license to use the franchisor's brand for a specified time period, payment terms, and operating restrictions.

developed a successful format for its business and transfers it to the franchisee. Initial training programs and manuals cover how to start and operate the business, and ongoing programs to train managers and employees. The franchisees themselves are another valuable resource for support and ideas.

- *Financial assistance.* A proven concept with brand identity is easier to finance than a new small business. Most franchisors offer financing advice to their franchisees, such as financial management, lender referrals, and assistance with loan applications. Many franchisors offer payment plans, loans for real estate and equipment, and short-term credit to buy supplies.

- *Expansion opportunities.* Franchisees who succeed with one unit and enjoy being part of the larger franchise network often acquire additional units.

Disadvantages of a Franchisee

As attractive as franchising sounds, it is not for everyone. Its disadvantages include:

- *Loss of control and operating flexibility.* The franchisee gives up operating freedom in exchange for the franchisor's proven system. You must be willing to take direction from the franchisor in all

> **Joint venture**   An alliance between two or more companies to pursue a specific project for a specified time period.

areas, including design for facilities, operating guidelines, and other standardized procedures. You may have to buy supplies from the franchisor or its approved suppliers—even if you can find a less expensive source elsewhere. The franchise agreement is a binding contract that may be difficult to end if you have problems.

- *High start-up and ongoing costs.* Franchising comes with a price that may be higher than starting an independent business. Costs will vary depending on the industry; a fast food franchise, for example, will have a much higher start-up cost for equipment than a business services franchise. Franchisees pay a front-end franchise fee and ongoing fees and/or royalties, typically tied to a percentage of sales. These cut into franchisee profits, as do contributions to national and local advertising programs.

- *Success tied to the larger franchise organization.* Your reputation is tied to that of the overall franchise network. Even though you are doing an exemplary job running your own unit, problems with other franchisees or with the franchisor could adversely affect your business.

Joint Ventures

A **joint venture** brings together two or more entities in a relationship for a mutually beneficial business purpose, usually for a specified time period. Typically, each participant contributes assets and shares risks. The parties to a joint venture can be individuals, groups of individuals, companies, or corporations.

AN ENTERPRISING WORLD

Cutting the Rug in Nepal

The idea for Stephanie Odegard's carpet company began with a Peace Corps assignment in Fiji. The former department store buyer worked with native artisans, showing them how to adapt their crafts for Western tastes. She continued this work at the United Nations and the World Bank, serving as a consultant to craftspeople in developing nations. A business trip to Nepal introduced her to the beautiful rugs produced by Tibetan refugees, who left their homeland

after China annexed Tibet in 1959 and during Mao's oppressive Cultural Revolution in the late 1960s and 1970s.

In 1987, she started Odegard Rare and Custom Carpets. She had a dual mission for this business: developing a profitable business to showcase high-quality, handwoven Nepalese carpets and at the same time improving the lives of the native craftspeople. A quote from Mahatma Gandhi, which she had seen many years before in an Indian railroad station, provided the inspiration to create a socially conscious business. It encourages a person who has doubts to "ask yourself if the step you contemplate [will] lead to comfort for the hungry and spiritually starving millions."

Odegard first developed contemporary interpretations of ancient and traditional Asian textile designs that would suit American clients more than traditional tribal patterns. Odegard also increased the knots per square inch to produce more luxurious carpets and developed dyes for more modern colors. She created her designs in New York and contracted the production to four locally owned factories in Nepal.

The rugs were a difficult sell at first, and the company almost went bankrupt in 1993. Then, Odegard discovered that interior designers and architects were the best market for her expensive and unique products. Business took off, and today Odegard, Inc., is one of the major Tibetan rug importers in the United States, generating about $10 million in sales each year. Its rugs grace the floors of museums, luxury hotels, and celebrity homes. Recently she added home accessories, jewelry, and shawls through the Stephanie Odegard Collections.

Doing business with Nepali factories was challenging. Handmade rugs are very labor-intensive, and these factories employ more than 10,000 workers. Of particular concern to Odegard were the working conditions in these and other rug factories. By raising awareness of Tibetan and Nepalese carpets in the design community, she was able to command high prices. In return, she paid her weavers fair wages, rather than exploiting them. She also opposed using children to make the rugs. Factory owners claimed that the children worked faster and did better work—for lower wages. Odegard became a major supporter of the Rugmark Foundation, which works to end child labor in India, Pakistan, and

Nepal and provide children with educational opportunities. All her rugs carry the Rugmark label to indicate that no child labor was used to make the rug, and she serves on Rugmark's board. Odegard and her company have won numerous awards for both her exceptional products and her philanthropic activities, among them a 2001 award from the Peace Corps for promoting international economic development, respecting cultural diversity, and creating a model workplace for employees.

All her decisions continue to be guided by the Gandhi quote. As she explains, "I think, 'Is it going to benefit my business, which benefits many people?' The idea that each of us can raise the standards in this world and conduct business on a meaningful level has made a big difference in my life."

Discussion Questions

1. What special challenges did Stephanie Odegard face when forming a company that imports all its products from a developing country? What form of business organization should Odegard use, and why?

2. Should Odegard consider forming a partnership with her factory owners? If so, what different types of laws might apply to an international venture such as this one? How might the risks and rewards of the carpet factory be allocated between the partners?

3. Suggest other organizational structures that might work for this enterprise.

4. How has Odegard been able to combine social responsibility and business success?

Sources: "Giants of Design: Stephanie Odegard," *House Beautiful*, June 2004, http://www.odegardinc.com; Nancy Hass, "Good Weaves Meet Good Deeds," *New York Times*, September 25, 2002, http://www.nytimes.com; Odegard website, http://www.odegardinc.com (March 27, 2008).

Participants form joint ventures for various reasons, including access to new markets, products, or technology. Two companies may join forces to take on a project that is too large for one of them to handle alone. Both large and small companies can benefit from joint ventures. Often a small company will join a larger company in the same industry to gain broader product distribution and marketing. Joint ventures are subject to state laws and are treated like partnerships for income tax purposes. They may also be structured as corporations and governed accordingly.

Joint ventures are also popular with companies that want to enter overseas markets. Some countries require a joint venture with a local, well-established company to do business within their borders. In other cases, it makes good business sense. For example, a joint venture with a company based in another country provides local relationships, customers, and knowledge of business regulations. The company that wants to enter the foreign market brings products or new technologies not currently available in that country. The Enterprising World box describes a business that has partnered with Nepalese rug factories.

Cooperatives

Yet another business form, the **cooperative**, belongs to and operates for its members—the people who have organized it—to provide themselves with goods and services they need. Cooperatives share some features with corporations, such as operating as a legal entity, limited liability, an unlimited life span, an elected board of directors, and an administrative staff. The member-owners share in the management and control of the organization and meet regularly. The elected directors hire managers to run the cooperative to serve the members' interests. Members buy shares in the cooperative to provide capital for a strong and efficient operation. They also pay annual fees and share in any profits, which are distributed to members in proportion to their contributions. Cooperatives do not retain any profits and are therefore not taxed.

Cooperatives operate in almost all sectors of the economy and offer just about any good or service—for example, business services, child care, credit services, equipment, food and food services, health care, housing, insurance, legal and professional services, and product marketing. Over 120 million people are members of 48,000 U.S. cooperatives. Cooperatives can take one of several forms:

- **Seller, or producer-owned, cooperatives:** Popular in agriculture and small businesses, members jointly support market development, national advertising, and other business activities. Agricultural and artisan cooperatives focus on processing and marketing goods and providing credit, equipment, and production supplies. Retailers and small businesses organize cooperatives to provide supplies or common services. Some familiar agricultural cooperatives are Sunkist (citrus products), Land O'Lakes (dairy products), Ocean Spray (cranberries and juices), Blue Diamond (nuts), and Farmland Industries (feed, fertilizer, petroleum, and grain).

- **Buyer cooperatives:** These may be consumer-owned or business cooperatives. They combine members' purchasing power to buy goods or services in volume, at lower prices. For small businesses, cooperatives also improve efficiency and strengthen their competitive position. Food cooperatives, credit unions, health maintenance organizations, mutual insurance companies, hardware and other consumer goods retailers, and rural electric cooperatives are examples of buyer cooperatives. Ace Hardware is one of the largest cooperatives in the United States.

- **Worker-owned cooperatives:** These are employee-owned and controlled businesses. Found in many industries, worker cooperatives include employee-owned food stores, processing companies, restaurants, taxicab companies, sewing companies, timber processors, and light and heavy industries.[2]

4.5 Not-for-Profit Organizations

In some circumstances, an enterpriser might consider choosing a legal form of business that involves a not-for-profit tax status, which is described in the U.S. Internal Revenue Code (IRC) as a 501 (c) organization. A **not-for-profit organization** is defined as an organization that is exempt from most state and federal income taxes, and has a purpose that will be of benefit to others. In addition, the individuals responsible for operating the not-for-profit organization cannot substantially benefit from the organization, though they can take salaries and be reimbursed for their expenses. Under the IRC there are many different kinds of 501 (c) organizations such as: 501 (c) (3) charitable organizations,

---

Cooperatives   Legal entities typically formed by people with similar interests, such as customers or suppliers, to reduce costs and gain economic power. A cooperative has limited liability, an unlimited life span, an elected board of directors, and an administrative staff; all profits are distributed to the member-owners in proportion to their contributions.

Seller (producer-owned) cooperatives Individual producers who join together to compete more effectively with large producers. Members jointly support market development, national advertising, and other business activities.

Buyer cooperatives   Consumer-owned or business cooperatives that combine members' purchasing power to buy goods or services in volume, at lower prices.

Worker-owned cooperatives   Employee-owned and controlled businesses.

Not-for-profit organization   An organization that is exempt from most state and federal income taxes and has a purpose that will benefit others.

501 (c) (4) civic leagues and social welfare organizations, 501 (c) (7) social clubs, and 501 (c) 19 veterans' organizations. It should also be noted that there are other kinds of not-for-profit organizations under the IRC, such as 501 (d) religious associations, 501 (e) cooperative hospital service associations, and 501 (f) cooperative educational associations.

In this section, we will focus on 501 (c) (3) organizations, which are charitable organizations that focus on such activities as: "the relief of the poor, the distressed, or the underprivileged; advancement of religion; advancement of education or science; erection or maintenance of public buildings, monuments, or works; lessening the burdens of government; lessening of neighborhood tensions; elimination of prejudice and discrimination; defense of human and civil rights secured by law; and combating community deterioration and juvenile delinquency."[3] A 501 (c) (3) organization could be an amateur baseball league, a literary magazine, a school or day-care center, a soup kitchen, a church, or any variety of organizations whose primary purpose is to benefit others.

Not-for-Profit Advantages

Why would you decide to start an enterprise as a not-for-profit organization? There are several advantages:

- *Ability to receive contributions and gifts from others, the value of which can be deducted as a charitable contribution on personal income tax statements.* For example, if you are interested in starting an organization that would help young single mothers graduate from high school, it is unlikely that these women could afford to pay the full costs of your services. A not-for-profit organization could solicit donations from others (which are tax deductible to them) that could be used to pay the expenses of these educational programs. The government, in essence, is willing to provide a tax subsidy to enterprisers who are willing to start and operate organizations that help others.

    To receive money from other foundations, or from many government agencies in the form of grants or donations, most organizations have to be not for-profit organizations. For example, some foundations give grants for educational activities, but these grants must be given to other nonprofit organizations, rather than to individuals or for-profit businesses.

- *Exemption from federal and state income taxes.* Any revenues raised and profits earned by the non-for-profit organization can be devoted to charitable purposes, rather than to paying a percentage for taxes—as long as the organization's activities are related to the purpose of the organization.

- *Limited liability.* By organizing as a not-for-profit corporation, members of the organization obtain the same kinds of personal liability protections granted to for-profit corporations.

- *Other financial benefits.* Not-for-profit organizations also gain special postage rates as well as exemptions from certain property taxes on real estate and other property that is owned.

The difference between "related" and "unrelated" activities can be confusing. To clarify these, the IRS has designated some activities non-taxable, even if they aren't related to the nonprofit's purpose. Here's a quick rundown of the activities that aren't taxed:

- Activities in which nearly all the work is done by volunteers.

- Activities carried on primarily for the benefit of members, students, patients, officers, or employees (such as a hospital gift shop for patients or employees).

- Sales of merchandise that has been mostly donated to the nonprofit (such as a thrift store).

- Rental or exchange of mailing lists of donors or members.

- Distribution of items worth less than $5 as incentives for donating money (such as stamps or preprinted mailing labels).[4]

Not-for-Profit Disadvantages

As with all forms of business organization, not-for-profit organizations have some disadvantages. These include rules that limit their activities:

- *No contributions to political campaigns.* Nonprofit corporations with a 501(c) (3) tax exemption (the most common) may not participate in political campaigns or contribute money to them. Doing so may result in revocation of their nonprofit status and assessment of a special excise tax against the organization and its managers.

- *Limitations on lobbying activities.* Tax-exempt 501(c) (3) nonprofits that influence legislation to any "substantial degree" may lose their nonprofit status. The IRS does permit tax-exempt nonprofits to spend a limited amount on political activities.

- *No distributions of profits to members, officers, or directors.* By definition, a nonprofit corporation cannot be organized to financially benefit its members, officers, or directors. However, it may pay reasonable salaries and expense reimbursements.

- *Payment of taxes on income from "unrelated activities."* A nonprofit organization sometimes earns income from activities that aren't directly related to its nonprofit purpose—for example, the administrator of a nonprofit medical clinic may collect a consulting fee for advising other nonprofits. Any such income over $1,000, even if the group uses it to fund its tax-exempt activities, is subject to corporate income taxes on such unrelated income.

- *Prohibition on earning substantial profits from unrelated activities.* Spending too much time on unrelated activities or generating "substantial" income from them may jeopardize the group's nonprofit status. It's advisable to consult a lawyer or tax expert with experience in nonprofit law before engaging in such activities.

- *Dissolution of a nonprofit corporation requires distribution of its assets to another tax-exempt group.* Since tax-exempt organizations and their assets have no owners, they can never be sold. To disband the organization, its directors must donate its assets to another nonprofit group. This also means that once property goes into a nonprofit corporation, it cannot later be distributed to a member or director.

A good resource for more information on not-for-profit organizations is Nolo.com, http://www.nolo.com.

4.6 ENTERPRISERS

A Well-Designed Partnership

In 1984, Ronald Altoon and Jim Porter left a large architectural firm to start their own business. Since Altoon + Porter opened its doors, it has designed and put into construction projects worth over $3.5 billion in 24 countries. The firm now has seven partners and employs more than 50 people. In addition to the Los Angeles headquarters, offices in Amsterdam and Hong Kong provide the firm's planning, urban design, architecture, interior architecture, and graphic design to a global clientele.

The pair traveled different routes before deciding to form their own firm. A high school guidance counselor suggested the career to Altoon because he was good in math and art. Even though architecture history and art history were his favorite classes in architecture school, he tried to transfer out three times. To find out if this was the right career for him, he bought a cheap ticket to Europe and, with a friend, visited every important architectural landmark in Europe. "I came back so charged up that I knew this is what I wanted to be a part of," he says.

After three years at a very large, prominent architectural firm in downtown Los Angeles, Altoon discovered that a large firm, as good as it was, did not satisfy his needs as an individual. He then switched to a much smaller firm, staying a year until he outgrew it. Next he went to work for Frank Gehry, a famous and innovative architect. "In three and a half years there, I probably got the equivalent of six years' worth of experience," Altoon recalls. "It was an extraordinary time, with very bright and capable people." He met his future partner, Jim Porter, in Gehry's office.

Porter's interest in drawing, creating spaces, and the building process started when he was a child. However, he came from a musical family and worked full time in that field for a while until his dad, also a musician, urged him to learn an "honest profession." That led him back to his original creative pursuits and architecture. He, too, joined Gehry's firm, where he met Altoon. Eighteen months later, Porter left Gehry to join a large commercial firm. He invited Altoon to head up the design department of their six-office, 115-person firm.

Over time the friends became leaders of that firm, serving on the management committee and board and becoming stockholders. Although they managed the firm for a year, they were unable to gain financial and business control. "We thought, 'Hey, there's actually more risk to staying here and taking on all of this baggage, as opposed to going into business for ourselves,'" says Porter. "We've never looked back."

With another colleague from the larger firm, they formed a partnership—a structure common to many architectural firms. "We set up a three-legged stool, in effect, that had strengths in all key areas of the practice: the business, the design, and the technical aspects," says Jim. They were determined to avoid a major difficulty they observed in other small architecture firms. "They are so focused on the design issue, they can't focus at the same time on the management or the technical issues of projects," Altoon explains.

Instead of structuring the firm on a departmental basis or as studios under one partner, Altoon and Porter combined the best of both into a matrix management system. Every partner has an area of expertise. One partner is responsible for the legal, accounting, insurance, and contracts for all projects. Altoon is the partner in charge of design, while others handle project management or technical services. This system has served the firm well. "Instead of each project getting the eyes of one partner, they get the eyes of all partners, who all have a vested interest in every project," Altoon says. The partners assign the employees best suited to a particular project, client, or venue.

Unlike many architects, Ronald Altoon and Jim Porter left their egos at the door and focused on the customer. They built their architectural firm using product power, not star power. Their attention to project management and technical details, as well as design, paid off. Personal relationships and high-quality work also contributed to the firm's rapid growth. Revenues tripled in each of its first three years. "I would say most of our business comes to us by referral," Altoon says. "The best way to get business is to serve your clients well, have them come back, and have them refer you to other people. We are also very active across the board in the partnership, in industry organizations. We've been involved in the Urban Land Institute, the International Council of Shopping Centers, and the American Institute of Architects."

In the firm's seventh year, Altoon began feeling dissatisfied with the firm's emphasis on retail projects. He missed the institutional and public projects he had done at other firms but didn't see that there was room for this type of work at Altoon + Porter. He tendered his resignation—but with a seven-year timeframe. "Because it took us seven years together to build the firm, I figured I owed them seven years out the door," Altoon says. "So I said, 'If we're not there in seven years, I want you to know right now that I'm going to go do something else.'" The firm was able to accommodate his wishes, and 20 years later it is still going strong.

The partners recognize the advantages of working as a team. "I'm the one that tends to be willing to take whatever risks we need to take," says Altoon. "I can't do that unless I have partners that keep everything in balance." He also focuses on leadership creation: "We have to breed leaders in our firm. It's not just leaders of projects, or how we conduct our practice, but it's creating leaders in the greater community."

As the partnership moves ahead, it faces new challenges. "I'd like to see us have a bigger impact," says Porter. "I think there's enough talent here in this pool of partners and senior people that we should be able to produce more work at this same quality level."

Discussion Questions

1. Why is the partnership form of business organization popular with professional services firms like Altoon + Porter?

2. How might this partnership be structured in a different way? Are there other legal forms of business that architects can choose?

3. How would this partnership go about attracting new partners to the firm? What should the partnership look for in attracting someone to become a partner? At the other end, how should partners who wish to leave be compensated for their prior contributions?

4. As the needs of the partners in the partnership change, how should differences among the partners be resolved?

Sources: Adapted with permission from Small Business School, the series on PBS, at http://SmallBusinessSchool.com; Altoon + Porter website, http://www.altoonporter.com (April 2, 2008).

Summary

1. Choosing the appropriate legal form of business for an enterprise determines how both control and ownership will be handled, how the enterprise will be taxed, who will be responsible for its legal liabilities, and how it will be managed and perceived by those who interact with it, from employees, customers, and suppliers to regulators and taxing entities.

2. Sole-proprietorships are easy and inexpensive to form. The owner has the rights to all profits and exerts control over the business. These businesses have low levels of government regulation, no special taxes, and are easy to dissolve. On the other hand, the owner has unlimited liability for debts, personally absorbs all business losses, and must make a large time commitment to the business to be economically successful. It may be hard to raise capital and attract employees.

3. Partnerships can take one of two forms: a general partnership, where the partners co-own the assets, share the profits, and are each individually liable for all debts and contracts of the partnership; or a limited partnership controlled by one or more general partners with unlimited liability and limited partners. Financial partners, whose liability is limited to their investment, are not involved in the firm's operations. Partnerships enjoy ease of formation, availability of capital, diversity of managerial expertise, greater flexibility to respond to changing business conditions, and relative freedom from government control. Unlimited liability for general partners, potential for conflict between partners, limited life, sharing of profits, and difficulty leaving the partnership are among the disadvantages.

4. The organizational structure of a corporation, a legal entity chartered by a state, includes stockholders who own the corporation, a board of directors elected by the stockholders to govern the firm, and officers responsible for implementing the board's goals and policies. Stockholders can sell or transfer their shares, and are entitled to receive profits in the form of dividends. The major advantage of corporations is limited liability. Others include ease of transferring ownership, stable business life, and ability to attract financing. Corporations, however, are subject to double taxation of profits, more costly and complex to form, and subject to many government restrictions.

5. The S corporation offers special tax status. It is organized like a corporation but taxed like a partnership, with income and losses flowing through to the stockholders and taxed as their personal income. Another organizational alternative is the limited liability company (LLC). It provides limited liability for its owners but also is taxed like a partnership or a corporation, making it attractive to many small firms.

6. Franchising involves an agreement between a franchisor, who supplies a business concept and goods or services, and a franchisee, an individual or company that buys the right to sell the franchisor's products in a specific area. A franchise provides an established business concept, use of a recognized brand name, a proven product, operating methods, management training and assistance, and financial assistance. Franchises can be costly to start and restrict operating freedom because the franchisee must conform to the franchisor's standard procedures.

7. Two or more companies can form a joint venture to undertake a special project. They can structure joint ventures through partnerships or special purpose corporations. Companies can reduce the risk of new enterprises by using joint ventures to pool management expertise, technology, products, and financial and operational resources.

8. Cooperatives are collectively owned by individuals or businesses with similar interests that combine to achieve more economic power. Cooperatives distribute all profits to their members. Three types of cooperatives are buyer, seller, and worker-owned.

9. A not-for-profit organization is one whose primary purpose is to benefit others rather than make a profit. It is exempt from most state and federal income taxes. In addition, the individuals responsible for operating the not-for-profit organization cannot substantially benefit from the organization. Gifts and contributions to these organizations are deductible from the donors' personal income taxes. Not-for-profit corporations enjoy the same personal liability protections that are granted to for-profit corporations. They also gain special postage rates as well as exemptions from certain property taxes. To qualify for these advantages, not-for-profit organizations must follow certain restrictions. For example, they should not contribute to political campaigns and are limited in their lobbying activities.

Review Questions

1. Summarize the advantages of forming and operating a sole-proprietorship. What types of business are well suited for this legal form?

2. How do partnerships compare with sole-proprietorships in the following areas: ease of formation and termination, ownership transfer, taxation, growth potential, and owner's liability?

3. Differentiate between general and limited partnerships.

4. What are the benefits and drawbacks of incorporating? Describe the corporate structure.

5. Why are S corporations and limited liability companies (LLCs) attractive to enterprisers?

6. Explain why franchising is an increasingly popular route to business ownership. Who are the key parties in a franchise relationship?

7. Describe why enterprisers should be familiar with joint ventures and cooperatives.

8. Under what circumstances might an enterpriser choose to form a not-for-profit corporation, and why?

Applying What You've Learned

1. A good friend plans to start a computer training and consulting business. While she has considerable technical experience, she lacks business knowledge and has asked you for advice on how to choose a legal form for the business. What information would you need to help her decide? Tell her the pros and cons of at least two possible alternatives.

2. Your friend's computer consultancy has been very successful, and she wants to take in a partner to expand the business. She has several possible candidates. What are the key characteristics she should look for in a potential partner? Develop a list of questions for her to use in her interviews.

3. Your uncle has decided to form a partnership with his daughter in a retail and wholesale bakery business. His daughter will be running the business full time, and he sees his role as an investor (he will be contributing 90 percent of the funds to start and operate the bakery) and will offer her advice from time to time. She has five years' experience as a bread and pastry chef at an upscale restaurant; he has 25 years' experience running a deli and sandwich shop. He has asked you for your advice about what the benefits and liabilities of a partnership would be. What legal form of business would you suggest he consider? Why?

4. A neighbor has owned and operated a very successful hamburger stand for the past ten years. Her business has recently gained significant notoriety after a food reviewer from the city newspaper rated her hamburgers as the "best in the state." Since this review, the hamburger stand has had customers waiting in long lines. She has been approached by a number of wealthy individuals who would like to see her expand her business to other locations around the city and state. Some other people have approached her to consider franchising her business. She is worried that other locations will not have the same quality since she won't be able to manage these locations' day-to-day operations. Which of the legal forms of business might best help her expand her business and insure that she can maintain the quality of her hamburgers, and why would you recommend this form?

5. The elementary school in your neighborhood is so bad that many of the parents are thinking of starting an alternative school for their children. They have identified a number of the top-ranked teachers in the school district who have all agreed to teach at this new alternative school if a location can be found and money can be raised to insure that they are paid for the first year of teaching. Each parent is willing to put up $5,000 to fund the new school. What would be the advantages and disadvantages to each parent if the school were organized as a for-profit corporation, versus organizing the school as a nonprofit corporation?

Enterprisers on the Web

1. There are many different businesses on the Web that promise to do much of the legal activities necessary for incorporating a business. Use a search engines such as Yahoo! or Google and type "incorporation" to find many of these companies. What specific services do these companies offer and for what price? What are the pros and cons of using one of these services to incorporate rather than using a lawyer?

2. Nearly all city and county governments have information on their websites about the process and the legal forms necessary to file for a business license. Search the Web to find out what your city or county requires you to do in order to start a business and summarize the requirements to get a business license.

3. Every state has information on the process and the forms required to incorporate a business. Search the Web to find out what your state requires you to do to incorporate your business. Choose another state, such as Nevada or Delaware, which is known as a good place to incorporate. Compare the two states and explain which one you would choose to incorporate your business.

4. The following sites provide a wealth of information on the benefits and problems with franchising. The International Franchise Association (IFA) is the trade association that works to promote and regulate franchising in ways that benefit all franchisors and franchisees (http://www.franchise.org). The IFA site has seven readings that provide a good overview of franchising issues. Please be sure to cover the last two readings: "Most Frequently Asked Questions About Franchising" and "Self-Evaluation: Is Franchising for You?" The Federal Trade Commission is the government agency responsible for monitoring and regulating franchises (http://www.ftc.gov). The FTC site provides links to many resources on franchising, as well as details on the legal responsibilities of franchisors and franchisees. What kinds of problems should a prospective franchisee look for when considering a franchise? What kinds of *scams* are typical in the franchise industry?

5. Besides the IFA, *Entrepreneur* magazine is a good source for information on franchising. *Entrepreneur* magazine conducts a number of surveys of the franchise industry and they seek to ascertain new franchising trends and issues. Browse its Franchise Zone site (http://www. entrepreneur. com/franchises/index.html), which includes lots of advice on choosing and starting a franchise and databases such as the Franchise 500, Top New Franchises, and Fast-Growing Franchises, and more. What features do you find most useful and why? Compare this site to the IFA site. Which would you prefer to use, and why?

6. Using *Entrepreneur* (http://www. entrepreneur. com/franchises/index.html) and/or the IFA site (http://www.franchise.org), go to the "Franchise Mall" and search franchises by category. Find five franchise opportunities that are of interest to you and explain why. Both sites will provide links to the franchise businesses you will be exploring. Using the resources at these two sites and the franchisor sites, answer the following questions about these five franchise opportunities

    (a) What kinds of resources are necessary to participate in these five franchise opportunities?

    (b) What are the up-front costs involved with pursuing each franchise? What are the ongoing costs for each franchise?

    (c) What are the capabilities of the entrepreneurs these franchises seek?

    (d) What are the advantages that each franchise promotes?

    (e) What are the advantages of a franchisor that is small and new, versus a franchisor that is large and established?

    (f) What kinds of help and support does each franchisor offer?

    (g) Of the five franchises analyzed, which franchise seems to be better than the others? Why? Summarize your findings in report form and submit it to your instructor.

End Notes

1. "FedEx Kinko's," *Wikipedia,* http://www.en.wikipedia. org (September 21, 2006); FedEx Kinko's Website, http://www.fedex.com (September 22, 2006).

2. Cooperative section based on material from the National Cooperative Business Association Website, http://www.ncba. coop.

3. "Exemption Requirements," *Internal Revenue Service,* http:// www.irs.gov/charities/index.html (September 28, 2006).

4. "Tax Concerns When Your Nonprofit Corporation Earns Money," *Nolo.com,* http://www.nolo.com (September 29, 2006).

The Legal and Regulatory Environment of Business

KEY CONCEPTS

1. Businesses cannot operate without recognizing the importance of the regulatory and legal environment. Enterprisers who do not obey the law could face serious civil and criminal penalties. Ignorance of the law is not a legal defense.

2. A complex body of laws and regulations governs most business behavior. These laws and regulations occur at the federal, state, and local levels. An enterpriser should consult a lawyer for help navigating through all of the laws and regulations that might face the new endeavor.

3. Obeying the law is not the same thing as good ethical conduct—although one is not likely to have good ethical conduct unless one obeys the laws.

Suppose you worked in a hospital long enough to know all about caring for geriatric patients. You know that this market is growing quickly, so it should be profitable. Even more important, you are confident that you can start a small business that will provide medical care that could make a difference in the lives of older Americans. But then suppose that no bank will loan you enough money to get started.

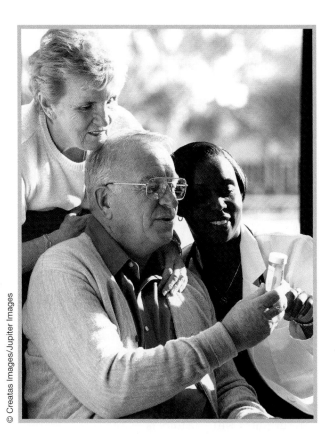

© Creatas Images/Jupiter Images

This chapter showcases JoAnn Corn, a former hospital administrator, who had both the vision and the determination to enter the fast-developing health care industry with a variety of services ranging from in-home nursing care to trips abroad tailored for an aging population. As you read this chapter, you will learn about the many different types of regulation and legal issues that she had to consider when starting and operating this type of business.

5.0 Laws and Regulations: A Framework for Order

One of the ways that stakeholders connect to your enterprise is through our system of laws and regulations. We focus on the legal and regulatory environment of business early in the book because enterprisers need to understand the legal system to avoid problems in developing and operating their businesses. Enterprisers may violate some law or regulation unintentionally. However, ignorance of the law is not a reasonable defense. We are responsible for obeying laws—even if we didn't know that these laws existed.

Even something as simple as using your own name as the name of your business could create legal problems. For example, if your last name is "McDonald," you cannot use your name for your business because the McDonald's Corporation owns that name for a variety of businesses.

The issue of zoning and permits is another legal issue confronting an enterpriser. Most cities have regulations that allow certain kinds of activities in an area, while barring others. For example, an enterpriser could not convert a home into a manufacturing center. Cities often enact zoning laws to protect an enterpriser's neighbors from the noise and traffic that might occur with a home-based business.

Conflicts arise from misunderstandings, unmet expectations, unfair competitive practices, and many other sources. Even though you should hire a lawyer to help you navigate through the laws that affect your business venture, you also should familiarize yourself with the regulations that affect your business so that you understand your rights as a consumer and as an enterpriser, and avoid disputes with customers and suppliers.

What are the most common types of legal problems that an enterpriser might encounter? A recent survey of Inc. 500 companies revealed that about 50 percent have disputes with customers, while supplier problems affected 24 percent. Other categories included patent litigation (15 percent), fraud (8 percent), product liability (4 percent), and employee injury (2 percent).[1]

This chapter provides a brief introduction to the basic structure of the legal environment and the types of legal issues that every enterprise is likely to encounter. After an overview of the regulatory environment in which businesses operate, we describe the fundamental concepts of business law, including torts, agency, property, and sales law. Then we examine in greater detail such key areas as naming, licensing/permits, and

Law   A statute enacted and enforced to establish rules of conduct for a society.

Business law   Regulations that provide a standardized environment to conduct commercial dealings.

contracts, emphasizing issues that impact the start-up and growth phases. Finally, we briefly describe the court system and alternative dispute resolution methods.

The Purpose of Laws and Regulations

Laws are statutes enacted and enforced to establish rules of conduct for a society. We may take some of these laws for granted. We trust that health professionals are properly licensed, that only registered voters can vote, and that food and drug products meet Food and Drug Administration (FDA) standards. Without laws to impose a sense of order, we'd live in chaos and disorder rather than in a smoothly functioning society. Over time, the system and the laws change in response to the economic, political, and social environment. Enterprisers must stay informed about legislation that affects their businesses.

The legal system also regulates how we conduct business. For instance, a person may purchase a cell phone and agree to a one-year plan that provides a certain number of minutes as talk time for a monthly fee. If the person uses more minutes in a month, the cell phone contract should include how much the additional minutes will cost. If the cell phone malfunctions, the contract should include provisions for returning the phone and getting credit for days the cell phone was not in service. The contract should also provide ways to resolve conflicts that arise.

This simple example illustrates how a contract between the customer and the service provider facilitates business transactions. The legal system includes laws for contracts that define how each party to a transaction will act and specify what will occur if one of the parties does not live up to the agreement. Contract law is one area of **business law**, the regulations that provide a standardized environment in which to conduct commercial dealings. We'll look at the key areas of business law later in this chapter.

5.1 The Regulatory Environment

Suppose you decide to form a company to develop a weight-loss pill you will make from plants growing in your backyard. Of course, you want to advertise that people who took these pills achieved significant weight loss. Before you move ahead with production and distribution, however, you discover that your business could be subject to numerous regulatory agencies:

- The FDA would be concerned about the medical value of your pills.

- The Federal Trade Commission (FTC) would carefully scrutinize your weight-loss claims to determine whether they were false or deceptive.

- If the pills were considered a type of food, state and local health boards would inspect your place of operation to see if it meets certain standards of cleanliness.

- Local zoning regulations could limit your ability to make the product in your home.

- If you hire employees, you must comply with employment and tax regulations.

- If you decide to sell stock, you must follow the Securities and Exchange Commission's regulations.

As an enterpriser, you will be subject to a host of government regulations in the normal course of business. Government regulation has another side for enterprisers: More regulation means higher compliance costs. The burden on small companies can be quite heavy in terms of costs and time. For example, the Small Business Administration estimates that compared to larger firms, firms with fewer than 20 employees spend 60 percent more per employee to comply with federal regulations and about twice as much on tax compliance.

Government Regulation and Administrative Agencies

The federal government has the authority to regulate businesses and business practices, and strives to find the best balance between regulation and allowing free enterprise to determine business practices. State and local governments may also enact laws that regulate businesses. The primary purpose of government regulation is to prevent improper conduct by one business against another. Among the many areas to which government regulations apply are production, distribution, financing, pricing, competitive practices, trade, and interstate transportation.

Administrative agencies, organizations created by governments to develop, implement, and enforce regulations pertinent to a specialized area, exist at all levels. Some well-known federal agencies are the FTC, the FDA, the Internal Revenue Service, and the Securities and Exchange Commission. State agencies include public utility commissions and professional licensing boards,

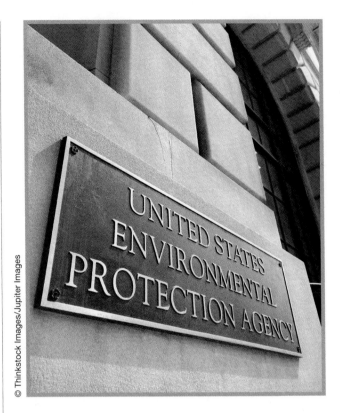

© Thinkstock Images/Jupiter Images

while local governments have zoning boards and planning commissions.

Today's agencies deal with everything from securities regulations to employment practices, exports and imports, and environmental protection. They have legislative, executive, and judicial responsibilities. They make rules, implement policies, investigate possible violations, conduct hearings pertaining to alleged violations, and impose penalties when infractions occur. Exhibit 5.1 lists many of the agencies that regulate business activities and protect consumers.

Laws Regulating Competition and Pricing

One of the first major regulatory concerns facing the federal government was preventing unfair practices that restricted competition between businesses. In the late 1800s, large firms (trusts) were able to monopolize certain industries, including oil, railroads, steel, sugar, and tobacco. The trusts' size and power allowed them to control trade, push smaller firms out of business, and then set high prices.

Administrative agencies   Organizations created by all levels of government to develop, implement, and enforce regulations pertinent to a specialized area.

exhibit
5.1

Major Federal Agencies That Regulate Businesses

Agency	Major Responsibilities
Consumer Product Safety Commission (CPSC)	Establishes and enforces consumer product safety standards under the Consumer Products Safety Act; protects consumers from unreasonable risk of injury from products through product recalls.
Environmental Protection Agency (EPA)	Establishes and enforces standards for environmental protection, including air quality and water purity; conducts research on harmful effects of pollution; works to prevent pollution of environment by various offenders.
Equal Employment Opportunity Commission (EEOC)	Prevents discrimination in employment practices; investigates and resolves claims of discrimination in employment.
Federal Aviation Agency (FAA)	Regulates the airline industry.
Federal Communications Commission (FCC)	Regulates the communication industry's interstate commerce, including television and radio.
Federal Energy Regulatory Commission (FERC)	Regulates natural gas sales and pricing, pipelines, wholesale gas and electric rates, and importing/exporting of gas and electricity.
Federal Trade Commission (FTC)	Regulates broad range of business practices including those involving fair competition, false advertising, mail fraud, misleading pricing, and packaging and labeling issues.
Food and Drug Administration (FDA)	Regulates sale and distribution of food and drug products; protects against unsafe, misbranded, or adulterated products.
Surface Transportation Board (STB)	Regulates interstate rail, truck, bus, and shipping companies with regard to rates and finances.
National Labor Relations Board (NLRB)	Administers the National Labor Relations Act by conducting elections to determine whether or not employees want union representation, and by investigating and remedying unfair labor practices by employers and unions.
Occupational Safety and Health Administration (OSHA)	Develops and oversees policies that promote safety and health at work.
Securities and Exchange Commission (SEC)	Regulates the securities industry, including trading and preventing fraud.

Congress took steps to regulate the competitive environment by passing the Sherman Anti-Trust Act in 1890. This act prohibits monopolies and any contracts, mergers, or conspiracies in restraint of trade through practices that control prices and exclude competitors. These include price fixing, agreements between competitors to divide markets, and boycotts in restraint of trade.

To strengthen its trust-busting efforts and correct vaguely worded clauses in the Sherman Act, Congress passed the Clayton Act in 1914. The Clayton Act more specifically defined and made illegal a number of business activities that reduced competition:

- *Price discrimination:* offering different prices to customers who are buying on the same terms.
- *Exclusive dealing:* preventing a customer from buying goods from a competitor.
- *Tying contracts:* requiring a customer to purchase unwanted products to get the one they need.
- *Interlocking directorates:* placing board members on boards of competing firms.
- *Community of interests:* buying large blocks of stock of a competing firm with the intent to reduce competition.

That same year Congress passed the Federal Trade Commission Act, creating the Federal Trade Commission (FTC) and giving it the authority to define and monitor unfair trade practices that curtail competition and take action against offenders. In 1938, an amendment to the FTC Act placed regulation of advertising under the FTC's control. The five-member FTC is one of the most powerful government agencies, with broad powers to enforce laws relating to fair business practices.

Subsequent congressional acts amended the Clayton Act to further promote fair prices and encourage competition:

- The Robinson-Patman Act of 1936 prevents a supplier from charging lower prices to customers who buy in large volume, unless they offer the same terms to all customers or can prove that such quantity discounts result in lower production and sales costs. It was passed so that large chain stores could not use their purchasing power to gain discounted prices based on quantity.

- The Celler-Kefauver Act of 1950, also called the Antimerger Act, prohibits companies from acquiring a company by purchasing its assets if the resulting merger or acquisition restricts trade. It also extended antitrust regulation to any merger that lessens competition, not just those in the same industry that create a monopoly, and gave the FTC and the Department of Justice the power to approve all mergers.

Consumer Protection Regulations

In addition to laws regulating the competitive environment, Congress has passed numerous regulations that protect consumers from adverse actions by businesses. Before starting any business, an enterpriser should become familiar with the laws that apply to that industry, as well as employment regulations.

Consumerism, a social movement that emphasizes strengthening buyer rights and powers with regard to sellers, has become an important driver of consumer protection legislation. Buyers should be able to

- Refuse to buy a product.

- Assume that products on the market are safe.

- Expect that the seller will fairly represent its products.

- Obtain sufficient information about products.

Sellers also have rights and powers. They may

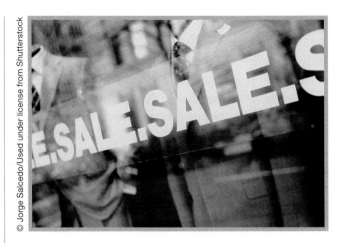

© Jorge Salcedo/Used under license from Shutterstock

- Introduce any type of product as long as it is not harmful or, if it is considered hazardous, provide appropriate warnings.

- Set prices at any level as long as similar classes of buyers receive the same price, in accordance with price discrimination laws.

- Promote the product in ways that do not interfere with fair competition.

- Develop any advertising messages, as long as they are not misleading or deceptive.

- Offer buying incentives.

Consumer protection legislation covers a broad range of issues, including product labeling, product safety, consumer credit practices, and persons with disabilities. Exhibit 5.2 summarizes key consumer protections laws.

Employment Laws

Employment practices are also subject to federal regulation. These laws protect job applicants and employees from discrimination in hiring, training, job placement, promotions, and compensation. Other laws cover payment of wages, pensions, and employee safety. Exhibit 5.3 lists the most important employment and labor laws.

These are just a few of the many different regulations that may apply to your business. Educating yourself about them in the early stages of your business development plan can prevent problems with suppliers, customers, employers, stockholders, and competitors. The websites listed in Exhibit 5.4 can help you research the many laws and regulations that apply to your business.

Consumerism   A social movement that emphasizes strengthening buyer rights and powers with regard to sellers.

5.2 Basics of Business Law

In addition to government regulation, businesses must comply with many business laws in the course of their daily operations. Laws that apply to business activities fall into several major categories, including contracts, torts, property, agency, bankruptcy, and intellectual property. Contracts, which are an important part of any business's activities, are covered in greater detail later in the chapter.

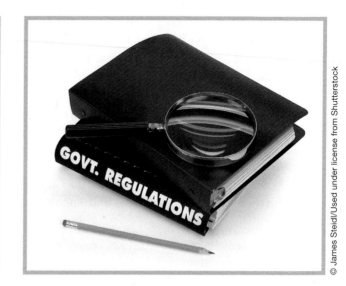

© James Steidl/Used under license from Shutterstock

exhibit
5.2

Consumer Protection Legislation

Law	Date Passed	Description
Fair Credit Reporting Act	1971	Gives consumers access to their credit reports if those reports are a reason for the denial of credit.
Magnuson-Moss Warranty Act	1975	Requires that warranties be written in easy-to-understand language, instead of legalese, and disclose all terms.
Nutrition Labeling and Education Act	1990	Mandates that food products regulated by the FDA must have labels providing accurate nutritional information.

exhibit
5.3

Employment-Related Legislation

Law	Date Passed	Description
Social Security Act	1935	Establishes Social Security Administration and provides retirement income and health care for seniors.
Fair Labor Standards Act	1938	Sets minimum wage levels and overtime pay.
Equal Pay Act	1963	Prohibits pay differentials based on gender.
Civil Rights Act	1964	Prohibits employment discrimination based on race, color, religion, gender, or national origin.
Age Discrimination Act	1967	Protects workers who are over 40 years old.
Occupational Safety and Health Act (OSHA)	1970	Protects worker safety.
Pension Reform Act	1974	Sets minimum requirements for private pensions.
Americans with Disabilities Act	1990	Prohibits discrimination based on mental or physical disabilities.

exhibit 5.4	**Web Resources for Laws and Regulations**

FindLaw (**http://www.findlaw.com**): One of the best overall sites to begin a search for information on laws and regulations.

Legal Information Institute (**http://www.law.cornell.edu/topics/index.htm**): Offers a series of "Law About" pages with brief summaries of law topics with links to key primary source material and other Internet and offline resources.

U.S. Code (**http://www.law.cornell.edu/uscode**): A searchable version of the U.S. Code.

LawGuru (**http://www.lawguru.com**): A good site for researching legal issues.

Nolo.com (**http://www.nolo.com**): A legal information site whose goal is to make the law more understandable for lay people; includes a law dictionary, legal encyclopedia, and articles on a variety of personal and business legal topics.

Torts

A **tort** is a civil (noncriminal) act that injures a person or property and does not arise from a breach of contract. The injured party has the right to sue the wrongdoer for monetary damages as compensation. Types of torts include physical injury, emotional distress, fraud, defamation of character, sexual harassment, and medical malpractice. For example, if a florist's delivery van is involved in an accident and the driver is at fault, an injured person could sue the driver and the company for damages. A company that violates zoning regulations would also be subject to tort law.

If the wrongdoer is convicted in court, he or she will be required to pay **compensatory damages** to the victim for actual loss and for suffering. Severe wrongdoing may result in the award of **punitive damages**, monetary payments that punish the wrongdoer and deter others by imposing fines that greatly exceed the actual losses. A well-known tort case is *Stella Liebeck* v. *McDonald's Corporation*. Liebeck, an elderly woman, suffered third-degree burns after spilling very hot coffee from McDonald's on her lap. She asked McDonald's to pay $20,000 to cover her two years of medical treatments. When the company offered $800, Liebeck sued and received $2.9 million dollars, of which $2.7 million represented punitive damages. As in many such cases, upon appeal the total award was reduced to just $640,000.[2]

Although most torts do not involve crimes, in some cases an act may be both a tort and a crime. If someone assaulted and injured you, that person could be tried in criminal court for violating a public law that prohibits assault as well as having to pay compensatory damages.

Types of Torts

Torts can be intentional or unintentional. Negligence and product liability are two categories of unintentional torts.

Intentional torts occur when the wrongdoer deliberately undertakes an action that could injure another party. Examples of intentional torts include making false statements to harm someone's reputation. When the offense is written or aired publicly on radio or television, it is called *libel*. *Slander* refers to oral statements. If you owned a café and spread false stories about getting food poisoning after eating at a competitor's restaurant, the competitor could sue you for slander. Other examples of intentional torts are trespassing, assault, and invasion of privacy.

Most tort cases fall into the negligence category. **Negligence** occurs when the defendant does not use a reasonable amount of care to protect others from injury.

Tort   Civil (noncriminal) act that injures a person or property and does not arise from a breach of contract.

Compensatory damages   Monetary award to repay the victim for actual loss and suffering.

Punitive damages   Monetary payments that greatly exceed actual losses; intended to punish the wrongdoer.

Intentional tort   Deliberate action that could injure another party.

Negligence   Failure to use a reasonable amount of care to protect others from injury.

The earlier example of the auto accident involving the florist's driver would be considered negligence if the injured party claimed the driver was driving recklessly. The vague definition of negligence has resulted in different interpretations of the term and made this area of tort law controversial.

Product Liability

A related area of tort law is **product liability,** which holds manufacturers and sellers responsible for injuries caused by defects in their products. Product liability claims can include negligence or strict liability, which are torts, or misrepresentation or breach of warranty, which come under contract law. Product liability suits can be based on one of three types of defect:

- *Design defects:* Flaws intrinsic to the product and are there before the item is manufactured.

- *Manufacturing defects:* Defects that arise during manufacturing or construction; may affect a limited number of items but not all.

- *Marketing defects:* Defects arising from improper instructions and warnings about possible dangers related to the product.

Strict liability extends the concept of product liability. A manufacturer or seller can be held liable for *any* defects in a product, even if these parties have exercised reasonable care in designing, making, and selling the product.

Product liability lawsuits are costly and can drag on for many years with appeals. Automobile manufacturers are frequently the defendants in product liability suits.

Product liability   Concept which holds manufacturers and sellers responsible for injuries caused by defects in their products.

Strict liability   Type of liability that holds a manufacturer or seller liable for any defects in a product, even if these parties have exercised reasonable care in designing, making, and selling the product.

Statutory law   Law written by legislative bodies (the U.S. Congress, state legislatures, and local governments); incorporation and bankruptcy laws are examples of statutory laws.

Uniform Commercial Code (UCC)   Set of business laws that provide a standard way for businesses to operate.

Ford Motor Co. was held liable for injuries resulting in a child's paralysis and ordered to pay $33 million in compensatory damages. A defective latch on a rear fold-down seat was blamed for the injury.[3] Another case dragged on for 11 years. Lee Raskin sued Ford Motor Co. claiming that defects in her 1988 Ford Escort driver's seat and restraint systems made injuries sustained during a 1992 accident worse. In the first trial, the court dismissed her claim as without merit. Upon appeal, this decision was overturned in her favor. In 2003, 11 years later, the Pennsylvania Supreme Court upheld the original verdict in Ford's favor, and Raskin's lawyer was considering yet another appeal.[4]

Other recent examples of product defects include the following:

- In 2007, Mattel recalled millions of toys made in China that were contaminated with lead paint and represented choking hazards.[5]

- Baxter International Inc. recalled the blood thinner Heparin in early 2008 because a fake ingredient was believed to have caused an allergic reaction that may have resulted in 19 deaths.[6]

- The U.S. Department of Agriculture announced a recall of 143 million pounds of beef (the largest recall in its history) produced by Hallmark/Westland Meat Packing in February 2008. The slaughterhouse was accused of inhumane treatment and slaughtering sick animals, which is not allowed by law because of the risk of the animals having mad cow disease.[7]

Because product liability cases fall under state jurisdiction, laws can vary by state. In an effort to standardize regulation, the Department of Commerce developed a Model Uniform Products Liability Act (MUPLA) for voluntary use by the states.

The UCC, Sales Law, and Warranties

Most sales transactions fall under state jurisdiction. Prior to 1952, each state had its own laws regulating business practices, making it difficult for companies to do business across state lines. To facilitate interstate commerce, all states except Louisiana adopted as **statutory law** the **Uniform Commercial Code (UCC),** which establishes a standard set of laws that apply to business transactions. (Louisiana has enacted portions of the UCC.) The UCC includes 13 articles that govern many areas of commercial law. One of the most important to enterprisers is

Article 2, which controls all aspects of the sale, whether between merchants and consumers or business-to-business transactions.

Article 2 establishes laws for the sale of most goods and services, with the exception of leases (covered in Article 2a), secured transactions (regulated by Article 9), investment securities, personal services, and real estate. Among the provisions are rules for transfer of ownership from seller to buyer, buyer and seller rights, making offers, inspecting goods, delivery, transfer of ownership, and warranties. All transactions in excess of $500 must have a written sales agreement. Article 2 also includes guidelines to resolve problems arising from sales.[8]

Warranties, the sellers' promise to stand behind their products after the sale, are also covered by Article 2. These can take several forms. **Express warranties** are statements by the seller that the buyer can interpret as fact, such as indications of quality and performance. The following are examples of express warranties that give the buyer specific information about product performance or features:

- A written 90-day warranty that comes with a factory-refurbished copy machine.

- An ad for a digital camera that describes the camera as "3.2 megapixels, 3x optical zoom".

- A sample photo from a demonstration model of a color printer.

- A salesperson's claim that a copy machine can handle your office workload of 4,000 copies a month.

Express warranties can be either full or limited. *Full warranties* require that during the warranty period the seller must replace or repair a defective product, within a reasonable time, at no charge to the buyer—regardless of whether the buyer registers the product. A *limited warranty* offers less protection. For example, restrictions imposed by limited warranties include coverage only for parts or repairs, charging handling fees for the repair, refunding only a portion of the item's cost, requiring the buyer to return a registration card to be valid, and eliminating certain types of repairs from the warranty.

Under the Magnuson-Moss Warranty Act, express warranties for consumer goods valued at more than $10 must clearly state whether they are full or limited. The Act also states that a warranty must clearly describe what it covers, the remedies offered in the case of a defective product, the length of the warranty period, and contact information for customer service.

Implied warranties are unwritten but specified by law. They grant certain protections to the buyer: the title to the goods is valid, the merchandise will perform as advertised, and the item will serve its intended purpose.

Clearly, enterprisers who produce goods or provide services should be aware of the laws regarding warranties. Even if they do not offer an express warranty, they are bound by the implied warranties mentioned above. Under implied warranties, sellers can be held liable for as long as four years after the sale.

Agency Law

Agency law deals with certain contractual relationships. **Agency** refers to a situation where one party, the *agent*, agrees to represent and act on behalf of another party, the *principal*. Enterprisers may use agents to rent or buy office space, obtain property or health insurance, hire accountants and consultants, or make investments. A firm that outsources some of its operations will also enter into agency relationships.

Each party has certain responsibilities in an agency relationship. For example, the principal must compensate the agent according to the contract between the parties, reimburse the agent for related business expenses, and be cooperative. The principal is held liable for an agent's actions on his or her behalf. Usually the principal transfers authority to the agent using formal document called a *power of attorney*. The agent's obligations include loyalty to the principal, performance of the agreed-upon tasks, accountability, and notification.

Express warranties Indications by the seller that the buyer can interpret as fact, such as descriptions of an item, promises of quality and performance, or samples of products; written warranties must indicate whether they are full or limited.

Implied warranties Unwritten warranties specified by law that grant certain protections to the buyer, including warranties of title, merchantability (merchandise will perform as advertised), and fitness for a particular purpose (the item will serve its intended purpose).

Agency Situation where one party, the agent, agrees to represent and act on behalf of another party, the principal.

Property Law

As an enterpriser you are likely to own property, whether it's office equipment or real estate, and should understand your rights regarding that property. The law defines property as anything of value that one can own and the rights that go with that ownership. Property is a very broad category and is typically divided into three major categories:

- **Real property:** Land and anything permanently attached to it.

- **Personal property:** All property other than real property.

- **Intellectual property:** Property arising from a person's creative activities.

Personal property can also be *tangible*, anything having physical existence, or *intangible*, existing through written documentation that grants legal rights. Merchandise for sale, cars, books, and appliances are examples of tangible property, while bank accounts, stock certificates, insurance policies, and trademarks are types of intangible property. We will discuss rights with regard to tangible property in this section and consider intellectual property, which includes copyrights, patents, and trademarks, in the following section.

Many business transactions involve the transfer of property ownership. The law requires written documents for all transfers of real estate. If Wahoo's Tacos buys a site to build a new restaurant, the current owner will give Wahoo's a deed that transfers title, or the right of ownership, to the property. Wahoo's may also be able to arrange for temporary use of a site or an existing restaurant through a **lease,** a written agreement that transfers real estate or other tangible assets to the user for a specified time period in exchange for payment of rent.

Property law dictates when ownership of personal property transfers to the buyer. Such determination is based on the form of payment. Title passes immediately upon payment in full—for example, writing a check for the entire amount to buy a new computer for your office. For goods purchased using installment payments, title transfers when the buyer takes possession of the items because the buyer has agreed, usually in writing, to make the payments. If you arrange to buy a new copier by paying $59 per month for three years, you receive title to the machine when it is installed in your office.

Intellectual Property

Enterprisers are creative people likely to come up with inventions, distinctive corporate logos and product packaging, and computer programs as they build their companies. These examples of intellectual property are assets that need special legal protection to prevent unauthorized copying. Rights to intellectual property are secured in one of three ways: patents, copyrights, and trademarks. If you don't protect your creative endeavors, anyone can steal your ideas.

Copyrights

Copyrights protect authors of written material by giving them exclusive rights to publish, perform, copy, or sell an original work. The copyright period extends for the life of the author plus 70 years. Copyrights apply to any written work, as well as to computer software, artworks, photographs, architectural designs, musical compositions, plays, and video and audio productions. It is important to understand that the copyright doesn't protect the idea but rather the form in which the idea is expressed.

Claiming a copyright is easy: You automatically have one for any original work you create. Just place the copyright symbol "©" or the word *copyright* on your work, along with the year and your name. To formalize a copyright, however, you should register your copyright with the Copyright Office, along with a copy of the work.

Patents

A **patent** is a legal right granted to an inventor that gives the owner exclusive rights to make, use, or sell a product

---

Real property   Land and anything permanently attached to it.

Personal property   All property other than real property.

Intellectual property   Property arising from a person's creative activities.

Deed   Written document that transfers ownership of real property from one party to another.

Lease   Written agreement that temporarily transfers interest in real estate or other tangible assets to the user for a specified time period.

Copyright   Gives the creator of an original work the exclusive rights to publish, perform, copy, or sell the work.

Patent   Exclusive right to make, use, or sell the product or process for 20 years from the date the patent application was filed.

or process for 20 years from the date the patent application was filed. To qualify for a patent, an invention must be new, useful, and not obvious to an ordinary person. Inventions can be machines, products, or methods. Improvements to inventions also qualify for patent protection.

Patenting an invention is a time-consuming and expensive process. It requires the inventor to file a lengthy application with the United States Patent and Trademark Office. It may take two years for the office to review an application and approve a patent. Because patent law is a specialized area, consult a patent attorney before beginning the process.

Trademarks

Another important area of intellectual property law that enterprisers may overlook is trademarks, or commercial identifiers. These are the words, names, slogans, packaging, colors, or symbols that identify a company and its goods. *Service marks* are similar to trademarks but apply to a company's services rather than products. For example, most legal company names are protected, as are brand names. General Motors' company name and its many brands—Chevrolet, Buick, Cadillac, GMC—are protected by trademark law. So are symbols, such as the Apple Computer apple and McDonald's Golden Arches. Slogans, such as "Northwestern Mutual, the Quiet Company" and UPS's "What can Brown do for you?" are also considered registered service marks.

A recognizable brand or company symbol is a valuable asset and marketing tool. Trademarks serve as advertisements and also indicate standards of quality to consumers. The Patent and Trademark Office reviews applications for trademarks and grants exclusive rights to a brand name or symbol for an initial period of 20 years. The trademark can be renewed indefinitely as long as the owner continues to protect the exclusive use of the trademark. If you look closely at advertisements, you will see the symbols "®" and "™". These symbols show that a company has registered its rights to use the slogan. Financial institutions and telecommunications companies will place "SM" after their slogans.

Within a local service area, a small business may establish rights to a trademark simply by using it. However, before going into new market areas, businesses should perform a trademark search to be sure the trademark is not in use and register the trademark to prevent others from using it. Enterprisers should also consider the message that the brand name or trademark they use sends to consumers. The Enterprising Ethics box describes a situation where a consumer sued a company because he believed its trademark was misleading.

Bankruptcy Law

Despite an enterpriser's best intentions, he or she may get into financial difficulties and be unable to meet the firm's financial obligations to its creditors. When a company's assets are inadequate to pay its debt, it is insolvent and may decide to file for bankruptcy. Bankruptcy is a legal procedure that helps debtors restructure their financial obligations and equitably distribute assets to creditors, thereby resolving their debts. Bankruptcy proceedings are governed by the Bankruptcy Reform Act and heard in U.S. Bankruptcy Courts, which are a specialized type of District Court.

Bankruptcy can be *voluntary*, where the debtor files the petition of bankruptcy, or *involuntary*, when initiated by the creditors. Certain actions may trigger an involuntary bankruptcy, such as not paying principal or interest when due, hiding or transferring property to defraud creditors, or providing a written statement of not being able to pay debts.

Debtors have three ways to resolve a bankruptcy filing. Chapters 7 and 11 of the Bankruptcy Reform Act apply to businesses or individuals and generally have a court-appointed trustee who supervises the proceedings and protects creditor interests, while Chapter 13 is for individuals only:

- *Chapter 7, Liquidation:* Can be voluntary or involuntary. All nonexempt business assets are sold, and the proceeds are distributed to the creditors in accordance with the Act, and the business goes out of existence. Exhibit 5.5 shows the basic steps in a Chapter 7 filing. This is the most common form of bankruptcy.

Trademark   Words, names, slogans, packaging, colors, or symbols that identify a company and its goods and services.

Bankruptcy   Situation where an individual or business cannot meet financial obligations and seeks legal protection to repay or restructure debts.

ENTERPRISING ETHICS

What's in a Name?

Can you rely on a brand name or trademark to describe a product? Paul Bass, a Miami, Florida, lawyer, believes that consumers should be able to make that assumption. He purchased vitamin E bearing the "Nature Made" trademark thinking it was derived from natural sources but then discovered that—product name notwithstanding—it was a *synthetic* form of the vitamin. Bass promptly sued Pharmavite, the California-based manufacturer, for deceptive advertising under the Florida Deceptive Trade Practices Act. Because the Lanham Act, a federal law, regulates the rights to use a trademark, the case was subsequently sent to federal court.

Nature Made is one of the leading brands of vitamins and supplements in the United States. Its products include a wide range of vitamins, minerals, supplements, and herbal products. On the Frequently Asked Questions (FAQ) page of its website, Pharmavite claims that

Nature Made® and Nature's Resource® product lines are made to strict quality standards of purity, potency, and release. Most all products are produced without artificial colors or preservatives. The few products that do contain artificial colors will state this in the ingredient listing on the label.

The company also says that:

All Nature Made® products meet or exceed strict quality standards of the U.S. Food and Drug Administration and the United States Pharmacopoeia (USP). We guarantee the potency of all labeled ingredients as long as the product has been properly stored and is within its shelf life.

Nowhere does it state that its products are totally natural. Why does this matter to Paul Bass? In many cases the natural and synthetic versions of vitamins are identical. This does not hold true for vitamin E, however. Natural vitamin E is derived from vegetable oils and called d-alpha-tocopherol; the synthetic form is chemically derived and called dl-alpha-tocopherol. Why does this matter? According to some research studies, the body absorbs and retains natural vitamin E better than the synthetic one. The Nature Made FAQ claims that some studies show "both natural and synthetic forms of vitamin E to be absorbed equally well, while other studies show that the natural form is slightly better absorbed in the body."

Discussion Questions

1. Who should regulate the claims made by companies about the characteristics of their products, particularly when a product might have medical or nutritional value?

2. Is it reasonable for a buyer of a product named Nature Made to assume that the product is 100 percent natural?

3. Does the fine print on the package describing the source of the vitamin as "synthetic" resolve any complaints buyers of the product might have?

4. Should individuals have the right to sue for damages for the purchase of a product that is less than $25.00 in value? What harm has Mr. Bass really suffered?

Sources: Nature Made website, http://www.naturemade.com (October 31, 2006); Pharmavite website, http://www.pharmavite.com (October 31, 2006); "When Is a Trademark Deceptive Advertising?" *The Nutritional and Dietary Supplement Law Blog,* June 18, 2006, http://nutrisuplaw.com/.

- *Chapter 11, Reorganization:* Can be voluntary or involuntary. Allows a company to reorganize (reduce costs and restructure operations), continue operating, and propose a plan to repay a portion of debts. Companies have time to reduce costs. If the court approves the reorganization plan, the remainder is written off and the company makes a fresh start.

- *Chapter 13, Adjustment:* Voluntary only. Similar to Chapter 11, individuals (including small business owners) with regular income can file in court a plan to repay all or a portion of the debts over a three- to five-year period. If the repayment plan is approved, the debt is considered fully discharged. The debtor does not lose any assets.

exhibit
5.5

Bankruptcy Proceedings under Chapter 7

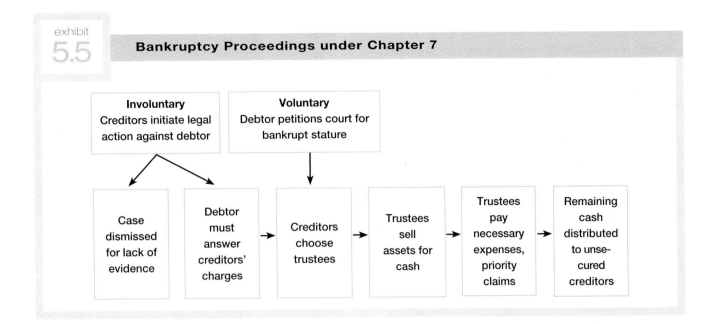

5.3 Legal Issues at Start-up

While the primary emphasis during the start-up of a business is preparing to provide goods or services that benefit other people, there are a number of legal issues that an enterprise should consider at this time. This section will cover two critical issues: naming the business and obtaining the proper licenses and permits.

What's in a Name?

Selecting a name for your business is not as easy as it may seem. For example, someone could already legally own your name for business purposes. Anyone with the last name "Dell" would be unable to name an electronics business "Dell's." Common words such as "apple" have been trademarked to identify electronic products made by the Apple Computer Corporation, while Apple Records has trademarked the name for music products.

Coming up with a name that other enterprises have not claimed can take a significant amount of time and money. In fact, there are businesses that specialize in identifying unique business names. Some companies pay firms hundreds of thousands of dollars to come up with company and product names that are novel, memorable, and can be legally protected.

Protecting Your Name

With the rise of electronic commerce, local businesses can more easily have a global presence by selling through a website. Even if you don't intend to sell online, you might have an informational website. The addition of an online presence brings businesses into direct or indirect competition with firms that may be half a world away. Without a unique name, potential customers in the next state may have problems finding your site.

In general, the wider the reach of your business—the more customers and the broader the geographic coverage your business is likely to have—the more important it is to have a business name that can be protected. As a general guideline, if you intend to use your own name for a small business or one-person service business and will operate only in a local market, you can probably use the name without running into trademark problems. Otherwise, you should research your proposed name carefully.

Why should you put so much effort into selecting and protecting your business name? If you invested resources in advertising a business name that already belongs legally to another company, you could be sued and have to pay damages for infringing on its name. Devote time and money to choosing a business name that you will be able to legally protect as your business grows in the future.

The Selection Process

The first step in the business and product name selection process is considering where you expect your new venture to go in the future. Any enterprise who anticipates that the business may become larger than a sole-proprietorship should plan to get a trademark or service mark for the business. As you learned earlier, you can protect your exclusive rights to use your trade or service mark by registering it (your unique name or symbol).

Enforcement of your trade or service mark is your responsibility. If others use your trademark, you must inform them that they are infringing on your mark and that they should stop. If they continue, you will need to go to court and seek an injunction. Legal action is expensive, as it will surely require a lawyer.

An easy way to begin creating a trade or service mark is to check the federal government's trademark database, Trademark Electronic Search Service (TESS), to determine whether other businesses are using your proposed name, and the kinds of goods or services to which their marks apply. (You'll find TESS at the U.S. Patent and Trademark Office website, http://www.uspto.gov.) Conflicts could occur if your proposed name is a synonym, a phonetic equivalent, an alternative spelling, or an already registered name or mark.

In addition, you should also search the yellow pages (locally and nationally), the Internet, newspapers, industry trade journals, and magazines to discover whether any business might be using a name that you are considering. In most cases, the first user of a name will have rights to that name, even if it isn't registered.

As we discussed in Chapter 4, state law may specify some aspects of the name you might select for your business. Obviously, you cannot use "Inc." or "LLC" in the name of your business unless your business was actually incorporated or formed as a limited liability corporation and registered with your state. Each state has laws about the use of names for corporations, so be sure to check with the state office to see if other corporations have rights to use your proposed name in your state. State laws also specify words that you can't use in your corporate name at all or unless you are a certain type of business.

Many businesses often conduct business under an assumed or fictitious name. For example, a partnership may not want to name the business for all of the partners (e.g., Van Gogh, Monet, Manet, and Matisse) and use a name such as "The French Painters" for the business. In many states, sole-proprietors and partnerships are required to register their assumed or fictitious names with a local city or county office. In addition, these names are often published in the local newspaper's public notice section, listing which individuals and partnerships are "doing business as" (DBA) under a particular name. Some states require a DBA filing to open a business bank account or to conduct any contractual or legal matters using the business name. If a corporation or LLC is doing business using a different name than the one on file with the state, it must complete an assumed or fictitious name registration.

Licenses and Permits

Nearly every start-up enterprise needs licenses and permits from various federal, state, and local governments. Permits and licenses are required for two primary reasons: (1) to generate revenues for various government agencies and (2) to protect the public for various health, safety, and aesthetic reasons. Without the proper permits and licenses, you could be prevented from operating your business and may have to pay fines and penalties. Suppose, for example, that an enterpriser puts a large neon sign above the entrance to a retail store. If that business location is in a zone that does not permit neon signs, the local government could require the enterpriser to take down the neon sign, pay damages, or even close the business.

Obtaining the necessary licenses and permits can be a significant hurdle for enterprisers. For example, if you were thinking about starting a restaurant, you would have to obtain a multitude of different licenses and permits to establish your business, including

- A zoning permit from the city or county approving that your location is zoned for restaurants, with sufficient parking for the restaurant's capacity.

- Health department permits to serve food and licenses indicating that your kitchen and food storage areas are sanitary and will keep food safe and at the right temperatures.

- Licenses from the city, county, and state to serve alcohol.

Because you will have employees, you will also need to register with the federal, state, county, and city governments and make payments for employee taxes, social security benefits, and state unemployment benefits.

It may be tricky to find out which licenses and permits your enterprise requires and file the applications. Contact a local government business development agency in your area to get help determining which licenses and permits your business will need. Ignorance of the law is not a reasonable defense. Don't assume that you can start your enterprise or take actions on building, hiring employees, or making any sales without notifying the proper government authorities. You may want to have a lawyer or a business development agency help you fill out the necessary documents.

Federal Licenses and Permits

Many of the employee- and tax-related permissions and regulations occur at the federal level. For example, if your business

- Hires an employee or uses an independent contractor, you should consider applying for an employer identification number (Form SS-4).

- Has employees, you will need to withhold income tax and Social Security taxes from paychecks, and pay this money (along with your employer contribution for Social Security tax) to the federal government.

- Hires independent contractors, you will need to file IRS Form 1099 for each.

- Will be an S corporation, you must file Form 2553 (Election by a Small Business Corporation).

- Exports goods or services, it may need to obtain export licenses from a government agency.

Various federal government agencies regulate specialized business activities: the SEC regulates investment advisors; the Federal Motor Carrier Safety Administration, moving and trucking companies; and the Food and Drug Administration, drug manufacturing. If your business reaches a certain number of employees, you may need to comply with the federal Occupational Safety and Health Act (OSHA), which requires certain safety provisions and may decide to inspect your premises.

Exporting is another area that involves a host of complex regulations and government agencies, both at home and abroad.[9] Lists of approved products for export, tariffs, export licenses, and antiboycott regulations are just some of the regulatory issues you will encounter in the United States. Exhibit 5.6 lists some of the government agencies that regulate exporting. In addition, each country where you sell has its own import laws to consider. Trade barriers such as restrictions on the ports of entry and issues regarding compliance with the more than 250 trade agreements between the United States and other nations further complicate the exporting process. The Enterprising World box provides additional information on export regulations and the penalties for violating them.

State Licenses and Permits

Nearly all states require licenses for certain occupations such as accountants, architects, auto mechanics, barbers, building contractors, cosmetologists, dentists, doctors, insurance agents, lawyers, pharmacists, and real estate agents. The list of regulated occupations varies from state to state, so an enterpriser should check to find out which occupations may require a license. The requirements

---

exhibit
5.6

Agencies That Regulate or License Exports

U.S. Department of State regulates exports of defense articles and defense services.

U.S. Department of Commerce, Bureau of Industry and Security (BIS) implements and enforces the Export Administration Regulations (EAR) that regulate exports of most dual-use commercial items—items that have both a commercial application and a potential for weapons of mass destruction, conventional arms, or terrorist end-use. Dual-use items range from the surprisingly mundane—chemicals used in ballpoint pens that could also be used in weapons—to sophisticated technologies and equipment. (More specialized exports fall under the jurisdiction of other U.S. government agencies.)

Nuclear Regulatory Commission licenses nuclear material and equipment.

U.S. Department of Agriculture monitors the export of animal and plant products.

Department of the Interior controls the export of endangered fish and wildlife species.

Food and Drug Administration licenses medical devices and drugs.

Bureau of Customs and Border Protection and Bureau of Immigration and Customs Enforcement ensure that all goods entering and exiting the United States are in accordance with all U.S. laws and regulations.

AN ENTERPRISING WORLD

The Dangers of Exports

You might think that selling your goods or services in foreign countries is a simple matter of finding a buyer who wants your products. You must decide which items are good candidates to export, where to sell these goods, how to price them for foreign markets, what payment methods to use for exporting, and how to get them to consumers. You must also comply with many more government regulations: export laws in the United States and import laws in the countries where you plan to sell. Without a thorough understanding of U.S. export laws, enterprisers might unknowingly violate one of the regulations. In addition to losing export privileges, possible administrative or criminal penalties include fines ranging from $11,000 to $1 million per violation and prison sentences.

First, an enterpriser should determine whether the item to be exported requires a license. Although most export transactions do not require specific approval or licenses from the U.S. government, certain product categories call for special licensing. These include sophisticated and high-technology products, such as software and hardware, and technical information, and products with defense, strategic, weapons development, proliferation, or law enforcement applications. The need for a license is based on such factors as the item's technical characteristics, destination, end-user, and end-use. Once a company receives a license, it must comply with the specific terms of that license. (The Bureau of Industry and Security website, http://www.bis.doc.gov, provides detailed information to help companies comply with export control regulations.)

In 2000, Roper Scientific, Inc., exported night vision cameras to South Korea, Japan, Italy, and other countries without obtaining the proper licenses or retaining required export control documents. Roper also made false statements on a Shipper's Export Declaration. The company, which voluntarily self-disclosed the violations and cooperated fully with the BIS investigation, paid a $422,000 administrative penalty. In 2003, Worldwide Sports & Recreation, which does business as Bushnell Corporation, was convicted for illegally exporting Night Ranger™ night vision devices to Japan and 14 other countries, from 1995 to 1997, without BIS export licenses. Bushnell's sentence in the criminal case

was $650,000 in fines and five years' probation. The company also had to pay $223,000 in administrative penalties and was given a one-year suspended denial of export privileges.

Even exporting ordinary items that are not usually subject to export controls can cause problems, as it did for 3-G Mermet Corporation. The company ran afoul of special export controls and authorizations for exports to countries declared to be "state sponsors of terrorism" when it tried to send window shade fabric through its French parent company to Iran without authorization from the Department of the Treasury's Office of Foreign Assets Control (OFAC). 3-G Mermet paid a $17,500 administrative penalty and agreed to set up an export management system.

Transshipment, or using an intermediary country to bypass U.S. export regulations, was the downfall of Ebara International Corporation and its founder and former CEO Everett Hylton. Ebara sold special pumps to Iran by first selling them to a French company. Hylton also falsified documents. The company received a harsh criminal penalty—a $6.3 million fine—and Hylton was fined $10,000 and sentenced to three years' probation. He also had to pay a $99,000 administrative penalty.

Discussion Questions

1. How could the export of sunglasses become a violation of U.S. exporting laws?

2. How would you make sure that the products or services you were exporting did not violate U.S. export laws?

3. How might other countries go about avoiding compliance with these U.S. export laws?

4. Should the U.S. government have the right to prevent subsidiaries of U.S. companies that are operating in other countries from having the opportunity to export products or services made in those countries?

Sources: Bureau of Industry and Security website, http://www.bis. doc.gov (November 1, 2006); *Don't Let This Happen to You!: An Introduction to U.S. Export Control Law*, Bureau of Industry and Security, May 2007, http://www.bis.doc.gov; and International Trade Association website, http://trade.gov (November 1, 2006).

for a license may also vary. For example, some states require that an individual must have a law degree and have passed the state bar exam in order to get a license to practice law. Some states—California is one—only require that an individual pass the state bar exam. Some occupations, such as architecture and real estate, often require individuals to work with a licensed practitioner for a number of years before becoming eligible for a license. Many licenses are of a limited duration, so that individuals might need to show continued improvement in their skills (through courses or seminars).

Nearly all states require businesses to register with a state agency. Your enterprise is likely to need a state tax identification number. Most retail businesses are likely to need a state tax license and submit sale taxes that are collected in a timely manner (quarterly or monthly). If your business has employees, there will be a state agency that requires your enterprise to pay state unemployment taxes and worker's compensation insurance. If one of your employees is injured while working for you, your business will need worker's compensation insurance to pay for his or her medical bills and lost wages. Some businesses will also need specific state licenses to sell items such as alcohol, food, and gasoline. Finally, your business may need state environmental permits if your business emits anything into the air or water or the business uses potentially dangerous chemicals and materials. Dry-cleaning businesses, which use chemicals for cleaning, are likely to need such permits.

Local Permits and Licenses

Local authorities also have numerous rules an enterpriser must follow. In many areas, your business will need a city or county business license, even if your business is a sole-proprietorship. Many states, cities, and counties share taxpayer information with the federal government, so that income reported on a taxpayer's federal tax return on Schedule C (business income) can be matched with state, county, and city business tax records to see whether local taxes have been paid. There are often significant financial penalties for individuals who fail to pay local taxes on income reported on their federal income tax statements. Some cities and counties require businesses to pay taxes on property, such as furniture and equipment, and on inventory, as well as taxes on gross sales or on net income from the business.

If you will be selling food, it is likely that you will need licenses and permits from the health department. They will certify your food preparation areas, such as counters, food storage refrigerators, and cooking equipment. Your business may need sinks and dishwashing areas of a certain size and need to be completely free of any pests. Many localities require a "Certificate of Occupancy" that indicates your business location is safe and has properly working doors and windows, exit signs, and emergency lighting. This certificate is often granted through the local fire department.

Most local governments will require permits for any construction. Permits are typically required for electrical, plumbing, heating and ventilating work, and may require an inspector to certify that the work is done correctly. Check to see which building codes may be enforced *before* signing a lease or buying property. For example, if you purchase an older two-story building, you may find that you must install an elevator to meet the requirements of the Americans with Disabilities Act to accommodate employees or customers who cannot use the stairs. Doorways and hallways in older buildings may also be too small to meet current building code requirements. An experienced building contractor can help determine whether significant changes may be necessary to bring a work area up to code.

Finally, the location for your business must be zoned for the appropriate kind of business usage, such as retail, light manufacturing, or commercial. If customers will come to your establishment, your business may need to provide off-street parking. Some commercial areas may have limits on the number of certain kinds of businesses allowed, such as restaurants, gas stations, and liquor stores. An area zoned as a historical district may require that the outside signs, paint color, and changes to the building's façade be approved by a city department. In some cities it may be illegal to operate certain kinds of home-based businesses.

While the number of permits and licenses that may be required for you to start your business may seem overwhelming, there are a number of ways you can get help and assistance. Most local chambers of commerce have ample experience with helping newer and smaller businesses identify the necessary permits and licenses for your area. In addition, contact the trade association for your type of business for insights into laws and regulations governing your type of business. Finally, ask owners of businesses similar to yours for referrals for lawyers with whom they have worked on licensing and permits.

5.4 Contracts

John sees an advertisement that says "Earn $10,000 a week as a court reporter." John calls and talks to a person who says that his court reporting business is so busy that he needs to hire outside contractors to process all of the transcripts. These contractors can earn up to $10,000 a week processing transcripts using special software that costs $2,500. John asks the business owner to send him a contract before he sends any money. The contract states that the $2,500 is for the purchase of the software only. John calls the owner and asks, "If I send you the money, what guarantee do I have that I will get $10,000 a week in business?" The owner says "Well, as I said, I've got more than enough work here. Once you buy the software, you'll be getting business from me." So John buys the software—but he never receives any work from the owner of the court reporting business. John decides to go to court and sue to get his money back. Does John have a chance of winning this dispute?

Enterprisers use contracts for many types of business transactions, from buying and selling goods and services to hiring employees. Because contract law is complex, we will summarize the basic requirements for a binding contract and the remedies if the promises made in the contract are not upheld. Before entering into any contracts, however, enterprisers should consult an attorney to make sure that the contract meets all conditions for enforceability.

A **contract** is a legally enforceable agreement between two or more parties with regard to the performance of a specific action. Contracts can be express or implied. *Express contracts* spell out the terms in words, in writing or orally—for example, a boutique owner giving a jewelry designer a written purchase order for 100 necklaces that states the price of each style and the date of delivery. *Implied contracts* are derived from the actions of the parties and inferred by law. When you use the phone or electricity in your home or business, you have an implied contract with the utility company: the company will provide you with the service and you promise to pay the bill.

> **Contract**   A legally enforceable agreement between two or more parties with regard to the performance of a specific action.
>
> **Consideration**   The exchange of something of value; must be present to have a valid contract.

Requirements of a Valid Contract

To be valid, a contract must contain the following six essential elements:

- *Agreement:* One party must make a clear oral or written offer to enter into an agreement with another party, and the receiving party must indicate clearly that he or she has accepted that offer. The offer must be specific, firm, and communicated clearly so that the parties understand what is to take place under the terms of the contract. A discussion of a job and the possible price does not constitute a contract because the offer is still tentative and subject to further negotiation.

- *Consent:* Both parties must agree voluntarily to the terms of the contract and must communicate their agreement. If pressure, fraud, unintentional misrepresentation, or honest mistakes are involved, the contract is not valid.

- *Consideration:* To be valid, a contract must involve **consideration**, the exchange of something of value.

- *Contractual capacity:* The parties to the contract must be legally able to enter into contracts. The law prohibits minors (in most states, those under 18), drug and alcohol addicts, convicts, and the mentally incompetent from entering into contracts.

- *Legality:* The contract's purpose must be legal for it to be enforceable. A contract to remodel a facility without bringing it up to required building codes would not be valid because to do so intentionally is illegal.

- *Proper form:* Contracts do not have to be written to be valid. A phone order is considered a valid contract. Some states require written contracts for the sale of goods costing more than $500, the sale of real estate, terms that cannot be fulfilled in one year, and promises to pay the debts of another party. To prevent later misunderstandings of contract terms, it is a good idea to get most contracts in writing.

In the example of the court reporting transcript business, John signed a written contract indicating that he was purchasing "computer software only" for $2,500. The written contract would take precedence over any verbal agreements that might have been offered by the court reporting transcript business owner. So based on contract law, John would not have a good case.

Consideration is one of the most important elements of a valid contract and differentiates it from a gift. For example, suppose you hire Painter Brothers to repaint your office and agree to pay $650 plus the cost of materials. Because they did such a great job and finished three days earlier than expected, you tell the workmen that you are so pleased and will include a $125 bonus for them. Are you legally bound to pay the bonus? Under the terms of the contract, Painter Brothers is entitled to receive consideration—$650 plus reimbursement for materials—in exchange for their painting services (your consideration). You did not receive any additional consideration for the bonus payment, so you are not obligated by law to make that payment. Similarly, if you offer to help a friend install a new computer, at no cost, and your friend accepts your generous offer, you do not have a binding contract. Your friend did not give you any consideration in exchange for your time and efforts.

A few other points with regard to contracts are worth remembering:

- Written contracts are a good idea even if not required by state law. These do not have to be formal or lengthy as long as they clearly spell out the terms of performance.

- Unless the contract includes a specific expiration date, the offer remains valid for a reasonable time. What's reasonable depends on the type of business and the facts of the situation. For example, perishable items obviously require prompt acceptance. To avoid possible misunderstanding, your offer should state a deadline for acceptance. You should also accept or reject an offer promptly.

- The person making the offer has the right to rescind it at any time prior to acceptance. If you are still considering an offer to paint your office for $650 and Painter Brothers decides that it really needs $700, it can revoke the offer because no contract exists until acceptance.

- No contract exists until the parties reach an agreement. For example, when you called Painter Brothers, they stated a price of $750 to paint your office. You responded that you can only pay $575. So far, no contract exists because you are still in negotiations. When you accept a counteroffer of $650 and communicate this to Painter Brothers, you have a valid contract, even though you haven't signed a formal document.

- You can't break a contract if you later decide you made a mistake, such as agreeing to pay too much for a used car. If you enter into a valid contract, you are probably bound to pay the agreed-upon amount, unless the courts decide that under the doctrines of fraud or misrepresentation the price is grossly unfair.

- If you sign a contract based on a false statement by the offering party, you have grounds to break the contract. This holds true even if the other person does not intentionally misrepresent the item or service. Suppose you buy a copier because the salesperson tells you that he thinks it is capable of making 5,000 copies a month. Once you have it on site, it continually breaks down—although your monthly copying volume is only 4,000 copies. You have legal grounds to cancel the contract and return the copier.

- You can rescind a contract if you discover you have misunderstood it. For example, you call a seller who advertised a computer and printer for sale. She names a price, which you assume is for both items. However, she assumed it was for the computer only. Although you had an honest understanding of what the price included and both acted in good faith, you could cancel the contract. (As noted earlier, however, if you agree to a price for an item, you can't get out of the contract if you later discover that you overpaid.)

Exhibit 5.7 provides a checklist of the clauses a typical contract would include. You may want to develop a basic contract and use attachments to describe the performance requirements. This allows you to tailor the contract to each transaction without having to write a totally new document.

Be sure to check the laws in your state, which may require specific clauses for certain types of contracts. You can often find sample contract forms applicable to your line of work that include such clauses. The legal sources on the Web (Exhibit 5.2) provide sample contract forms. If possible, choose wording that is easy to understand. For more complex transactions, consult a lawyer who can review your contract to make sure that it accomplishes your objectives and protects you.

Breach of Contract

In most cases, the parties fulfill their obligations under the terms of the contract (this is called *performance*)

exhibit
5.7

Summary of Contract Clauses

The following list summarizes the key clauses you may want to include when writing a contract. You don't need all of them to have a valid contract, and the actual clauses will vary depending on the type of transaction.

- Names and addresses of the parties.

- Dates when each party signs the contract to provide evidence that the parties entered into an agreement.

- Preamble ("recitals"), a brief background description of the parties.

- Description of the agreement between the parties. This may be supplemented by attachments or exhibits that provide a more thorough description and clarify the project. Referring to the attachment in the contract makes it part of the contract.

- Delivery date.

- Length of contract period.

- Price.

- Payment terms: in full, installments, interim payments tied to performance.

- Warranties.

- Conditions for termination.

- Penalties for nonperformance.

- Dispute resolution procedures.

and the contract expires. Sometimes the parties come to a mutual agreement to end the contract. If one party does not perform as required, however, a **breach of contract** occurs. For example, suppose you hired Painter Brothers to paint a newly leased clothing store before you move in, and the contract specifies a completion date that allows you several days to move your inventory to the new location and set it up before the lease expires. Unfortunately, moving day arrives and the painters have not yet started. Under contract law, you have several remedies:

- Cancel the contract, thereby ending your obligation to make any payments to Painter Brothers.

- Sue for damages. If you and Painter Brothers cannot work out terms, even with the assistance of your lawyers, you may have to go to court. Damages can take several forms. You can have Painter Brothers honor their contract to paint and compensate you for lost sales (which you must be able to prove with some degree of certainty). You could hire another painter who could do the job more quickly but at a higher cost and sue Painter Brothers for the extra cost.

Some contracts include clauses covering *liquidated damages,* which spell out the monetary damages owed in the case of a breach of contract. In this example, you might indicate that Painter Brothers would owe you a set amount for each day beyond the contract's stated completion date. Because timing is critical to your opening the store in its new location, including a liquidated damages clause in your contract is a good business decision.

Breach of contract   When one party does not perform as required under the contract terms.

5.5 Resolving Disputes

When disagreements arise, individuals, enterprises, and governments have several options for dispute resolution. They can use the court system or other alternative processes such as mediation or arbitration.

The Court System

Disputes that call for a trial are initiated and resolved through the court system. The court system, or **judiciary** branch of our government, is responsible for interpreting the law and resolving disputes. The United States has a multilevel (federal, state, and local) court system to accomplish these objectives. The appropriate court for a particular case depends on the type of case and where it arises. For example, a zoning dispute between a city and a business would come under the jurisdiction of a state or local court. A newspaper that believes its constitutional right to freedom of the press has been violated would bring the case to a federal court.

The federal court system deals with issues that involve violations of federal law (criminal cases), civil cases that involve disputes with the U.S. federal government, conflicts between individuals or enterprises residing in different states involving damages of $75,000 or more, and cases that involve issues with the U.S. Constitution or federal laws and treaties. These include disputes regarding patents, bankruptcy, taxes, immigration, postal matters, international trade, U.S. claims, Indian tribes, and military appeals.

Civil courts handle cases between individuals or businesses, such as fraud, personal injury, product liability, unfair competition, and slander or libel. Criminal cases involve violations of a public law and might deal with burglary, theft, forgery, and income tax fraud.

Alternative Dispute Resolution

In many situations, a trial is not the best way to settle a dispute. Trials take a long time, and they are also expensive. The parties involved may instead choose a nonjudicial procedure such as arbitration or mediation. Another reason that businesses and individuals like settling disputes out of court is privacy. In most cases, the testimony and settlements can be kept confidential rather than become a matter of public record. **Alternative dispute resolution (ADR)** refers to a method of resolution that takes place outside a courtroom. The two most common out-of-court methods are arbitration and mediation.

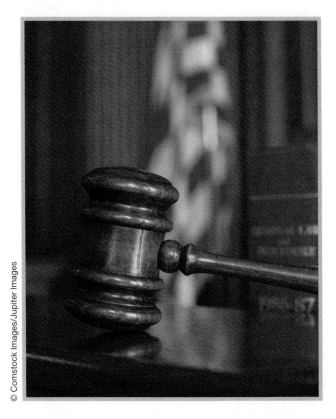

© Comstock Images/Jupiter Images

Arbitration is a method of ADR in which an impartial third party (the arbitrator or arbitration panel) hears the evidence and makes a ruling. Often the chosen arbitrator has expertise specific to the industry. Because the procedures for arbitration, such as rules for presenting evidence, are less formal than those used for trials, cases are often settled more quickly and at lower cost.

Arbitration may be binding—the parties must abide by the arbitrator's decision—or nonbinding, where the arbitrator recommends a decision but the parties are not obligated to follow it. Settlements reached through binding arbitration are not subject to appeal unless

Judiciary   Branch of government that interprets and applies the law to resolve disputes for individuals, enterprises, and government. It uses a multilevel court system to accomplish these objectives.

Alternative dispute resolution (ADR)   Nonjudicial method of resolving disputes.

Arbitration   Out-of-court method of dispute resolution whereby an impartial third party (the arbitrator or arbitration panel) hears the evidence and makes a ruling.

one party can prove fraud or corruption. Contracts, such as those between financial institutions or health care providers and customers, often include clauses requiring mandatory arbitration in the event of a dispute. Arbitration is often used to settle workplace disputes between employees and employers, such as allegations of discrimination.

In **mediation**, the parties work together, with the assistance of a trained mediator, to arrive at a mutually agreeable solution. The mediator facilitates the process by helping the parties establish procedures to follow and negotiate a settlement. While the mediator may make recommendations, the parties are under no obligation to accept them. Mediation is more flexible than arbitration and focuses on getting the parties to compromise where necessary to resolve the dispute.

Other options for out-of-court settlements include:

- *Med–Arb:* This hybrid method allows an arbitrator to act as a mediator. In this role, the third party will also attempt to bring about compromise to settle a dispute.

- *Reference to a Third Person:* The parties to a dispute may agree to have disputes decided by a designated third party. Often such a provision is included in a contract. For example, insurance companies that cannot agree on the amount of a loss often turn to independent appraisers to arrive at the settlement amount.

5.6 Business Ethics and the Law

You've recently opened a restaurant serving Cajun food on a street adjacent to a residential community. In keeping with the restaurant's theme, you feature live New Orleans-style jazz music Thursday through Saturday evenings. You have all the required permits but you have heard that your neighbors object to the music. What would you do?

Mediation   Less formal dispute resolution process that uses a neutral third party (the mediator) to help the parties negotiate a mutually agreeable solution.

Business ethics   Application of moral standards and values to business situations.

Or perhaps you have just started a consulting business and are bidding on a project. It calls for more in-house resources than you have on your staff, but you know you can hire independent contractors to fill the gaps. Is it okay to present your proposal as if you already have the necessary expertise and personnel?

No laws prevent you from offering entertainment at your restaurant, but should you? Are you lying if you imply in your project bid that your firm is larger than it actually is? These are examples of ethical dilemmas that enterprisers frequently face as they interact with customers, suppliers, employees, creditors, investors or competitors. *Ethics* refers to moral standards and values that help individuals choose between right and wrong. Similarly, **business ethics** applies moral standards to business situations.

Both personal and business ethics derive from various sources, including the law and customary practices. Suppose you sell a used laptop computer and include the phrase "As Is" on the sales contract. If the hard drive fails two days later, you have no legal obligation to repair the laptop. However, your personal code of ethical conduct and fairness may prompt you to fix it anyway.

Ethical guidelines help us decide what to do when we know that an action is legal but question whether we should go ahead and do it. You have the legal right to have live music in your restaurant—but do you want to annoy the neighbors who could then keep patrons away? On ethical grounds you'd want to consider the best interests of the community. You might hold a community meeting and discuss your plans with residents to find out if they do object. You could also agree to control the music's level after a certain hour and provide a way for community residents to register complaints if problems arise.

Many questions of ethical practices involve more weighty issues than restaurant music, of course. Lying about a company's profits, manipulating accounting rules, sexual harassment, employment discrimination, withholding important product information, running misleading advertisements, conflicts of interest, and similar behaviors are examples of unethical business conduct.

Benefits of Ethical Conduct

Enterprisers who follow and encourage ethical personal and business practices build trust with stakeholders and set the values for others to follow. Developing a good reputation can provide a competitive advantage and, in the long run, lead to higher profits. In fact, numerous studies demonstrate that companies with strong value systems are more likely to succeed and survive. Those whose ethical lapses come to light—Enron and Tyco are two notable examples—must struggle to overcome their bad reputations and rebuild trust with stakeholders.

When companies do not act ethically, the government may step in to prevent further breaches. The result is more regulation and higher compliance costs. As noted earlier in the chapter, many laws and regulations arose in response to business abuses—for example, consumer safety regulations and product labeling laws.

However, the "right" course of action is not always easy to determine. The interests of one stakeholder group can conflict with another's. Reducing prices on your product could win you more customers but could lower earnings, which would harm your investors. Balancing these competing interests requires looking at a potential action from a variety of viewpoints. Other questions that can help you analyze a situation include the following:

- Have you correctly identified the problem and those affected by it?

- Would the proposed action injure anyone?

- Can you discuss your decision with those affected by it?

- Would you be comfortable telling other people close to you, both at work or at home, about the planned action?

- Could you justify your decision in a public forum?[10]

Many businesses adopt formal, written codes of ethical conduct to guide managers and employees. The code describes the firm's expectations and policies in terms of conduct toward other employees, customers, and vendors. Typically, a code of ethics will address such issues as honesty and integrity, respect in interpersonal dealings, product quality, trust, responsibility, fair disclosure, and confidentiality. It may specifically prohibit certain actions, such as engaging in transactions for personal gain, conflicts of interest, taking or giving bribes, and abuse or misuse of company property. While it is impossible to cover every situation, the guidelines in a company's code convey an overall attitude toward ethical conduct and create an environment that supports it.

Resolving Ethical Dilemmas

Let's return to the ethical dilemma posed at the beginning of the section: whether to play jazz at your restaurant. The questions posed earlier are one starting point. Several other models offer different frameworks for analysis:

- *The Three-Question Test:* Asking yourself the following three questions is a quick way to get a handle on your problem: Is it legal? Is it balanced? How does it make me feel? Many major corporations recommend this test to their employees. Clearly, if the proposed action violates a law, you need go no further, as compliance with the law takes precedence. Balance refers to fairness and asks you to consider your decision from other viewpoints. The final question personalizes the issue by asking you to examine your conscience.

- *Front-Page-of-the-Newspaper Test:* How would you feel if a reporter published an objective story about your decision on the front page of your local newspaper?

- The Wall Street Journal *Model:* This is another three-question test. Does the conduct comply with the law? What does the decision contribute to the company's stakeholders? What are the consequences of the decision?[11]

Applying the various tests to the music issue, we see that it is legal to play music at your restaurant as long as you comply with any local laws that require it to stop at a certain hour. In terms of balance, you should consider the views of your neighbors and discuss your plans with them. If you were indeed considerate of the community's interests, you would have no problem reading about the entertainment in the paper. On the other hand, if you did not consult with the residents and simply decided to play loud music anyway because it was legal to do so, you would not pass the balance or consequences tests. Nor would you be happy to read about the angry citizens in the newspaper story!

5.7 ENTERPRISERS

A Healthy Regard for the Law

Denver-based Health Care Resources Group (HRG) is riding the wave of the health care future. Specializing in providing home health care—with "home" meaning the house you owned for years, a long-term care facility, or a retirement center—the company is well positioned to serve an aging population that wants to remain as independent as possible. HRG's 250 part-time and 100 full-time employees can help the firm's clients stay in their own homes or receive additional care in a long-term care facility. Its health care providers deliver oxygen and other physician-directed procedures to the patients, wherever they live.

JoAnn Corn, the company's founder, is a former hospital administrator who understood that the demand for temporary and home health nursing care was growing and could be profitable. "I knew there was a marketplace and I knew the people," JoAnn recalls. The first company she started was too small. "If you had a bad month or if the money didn't come in, the clients didn't pay in time, you were in a bad predicament."

She then formed a company with only Medicare clients, and the two businesses balanced each other. "Maybe the private company didn't do so well one month, but the Medicare company would pick up," she explains. The third business provided oxygen for clients and was started in response to client needs. Instead of referring them to Lincare, a large national provider, Corn could go to one of her own businesses. This led her to wonder, "Why can't we eventually get one-stop shopping, where any home care need that they have can come from us?"

Her next venture was in long-term care such as nursing homes. "Let's staff the retirement centers and the assisted living sections of the retirement centers," she thought. After that came a school to provide more advanced training for her employees. "We're dealing with sick people. You need quality. You need knowledge. You need a certain type of individual working for you. So we started the school and we became certified." HRG's school now teaches aides for other long-term care facilities and is a separate business process center.

Recognizing that people with health problems have a difficult time traveling, Corn acquired a travel agency. "We'll take 15 or 20 clients that have either respiratory problems or are diabetic and are afraid to leave the country because of the health care in other countries," she says. A physician who is familiar with the travelers' medical history accompanies them. "A lot of people with

health conditions love to travel, but they don't want to take the chance of going overseas. They just need us to put the trips together."

Like most start-up businesses, Corn's young companies were stretched for cash and she had to come up with some creative strategies to manage cash flow. She didn't yet have enough of a history to obtain bank financing. Being in the health care industry made it even more difficult, however, because the payment cycle often involved reimbursement from insurance companies and Medicare. "I always offered a discount for payment in advance," says Corn. "But some customers would make us wait, 60, 70, 80 days." This strained the company's finances, especially when the Internal Revenue Service's payroll taxes were due every two weeks. Sometimes Corn delayed paying these taxes to have the cash for other expenses, knowing that she'd have to pay additional penalties.

To get the quality personnel she needed to grow the company, she recruited employees from big, national health care companies. "They train their people well," she says. However, the bureaucratic mindset at a larger firm often makes people unhappy, so Corn offers more flexible hours that attracts workers.

Discussion Questions

1. What federal, state, and local regulations did JoAnn Corn have to consider when starting HRG's various business units? List the many different types of agencies and laws that would have jurisdiction over her companies.

2. What form of business organization would you suggest that Corn use for her company? What advantages does it offer? Should she avoid any particular form, and why?

3. A home health care business involves hiring people to work in people's homes. Who is liable when a home health care worker is injured at another person's home? If a home health care worker steals from a patient? What might a home health care company do to prevent the possibility that some of their home health care workers would steal from clients?

4. Who would be responsible if a home health care company failed to deliver oxygen and a patient died?

5. What are the legal and ethical implications of not paying payroll taxes on time? Should a business ever put itself in the position of violating the law in order to continue to operate?

Source: Adapted with permission from Small Business School, the series on PBS, and at http://SmallBusinessSchool.com.

Summary

1. Businesses cannot operate without recognizing the importance of the regulatory and legal environment. Laws establish rules of conduct for a society, including the way it transacts business. Enterprisers should become familiar with the many federal, state, and local laws that apply to their actions before starting a business. Ignorance of the law does not provide a valid excuse for breaking that law. Enterprisers should consult a lawyer for advice on the laws that pertain to their business. Doing so will avoid conflicts arising from improperly drafted contracts, misunderstandings, unmet expectations, unfair competitive practices, and many other sources.

2. Government regulation of businesses, whether at the federal, state, or local level, is designed to set standards of fair conduct for all businesses to follow. It covers all aspects of business. Government regulations take the form of laws passed by Congress or state legislatures and rulings from administrative agencies, organizations created by governments, to develop, implement, and enforce regulations in a specialized area. These agencies deal with both economic and social matters. The Federal Trade Commission, the Food and Drug Administration, the Internal Revenue Service, and the Securities and Exchange Commission are among the many federal agencies, while public utilities commissions and licensing boards are examples of state agencies. Agencies have broad powers to make rules, apply congressional policies, investigate and conduct hearings pertaining to alleged violations, and set penalties when companies break rules.

3. Early federal regulatory legislation focused on competitive practices. The Sherman Anti-Trust Act, passed in 1890, promotes competition by preventing monopolies, mergers, or other actions that restrain trades. The Clayton Antitrust Act clarified regulation regarding price discrimination, exclusive dealing, tying contracts, and other areas, and the Federal Trade Commission Act created the Federal Trade Commission to oversee business practices. The Robinson Patman Act of 1936 also regulates prices. More recently, the emphasis has shifted to consumer protection regulation that deals with rights of buyers and sellers, including such issues as product safety, warranties, product labeling, and consumer credit. Many employment practices also fall under federal regulations, which prohibit discrimination in hiring, promoting, and compensation; set minimum wages and private pension requirements; and regulate workplace safety.

4. Business law is a specialized field that creates the standards for commercial transactions. It includes contracts, torts, sales, property, agency, bankruptcy, and intellectual property. Torts deal with civil acts that injure a person or property. Torts may be intentional or unintentional or result from negligence. If found at fault, the wrongdoer may be required to pay damages to the victim. Product liability is another area of tort law.

5. The Uniform Commercial Code (UCC) establishes a standard set of laws that apply to business transactions. Article 2 of the UCC governs business to business transactions or those between merchants and consumers, including warranties, which describe what the seller will do if the product is defective or performs improperly. Express warranties are specific statements that the buyer can interpret as fact and can be full or limited. Implied warranties, while unwritten and unspecific, convey certain protections under the law.

6. Agency law deals with situations where a principal hires another party to act as agent on the principal's behalf. It defines the responsibilities of both parties.

7. The law governs property transactions involving real property, personal property, and intellectual property. Intellectual property law protects your recorded work through copyright, invention by means of a patent, and business name or unique identifier with a trademark.

8. A business that cannot pay its debts may have to file for bankruptcy protection. The firm's creditors can also initiate bankruptcy proceedings in certain situations. Under Chapter 7 of the Bankruptcy Reform Act, liquidations, the unencumbered assets of the business are sold and the proceeds used to repay creditors. The business no longer exists. With Chapter 11, a company reorganizes and continues to operate while repaying a portion of its debts according to a plan filed with the court. Chapter 13 is similar to Chapter 11 but applies to individuals, not businesses.

9. An enterprise should be aware of legal issues that affect business start-ups. You could be sued if you choose a name that another company has already legally claimed. The more customers and the

broader the geographic coverage your business is likely to have, the more important it is to have a business name that can be protected by trademark. In addition, an enterpriser should find out what licenses and permits are required for the type of business he or she plans to operate.

10. Contracts, legally enforceable agreements between the parties with regard to performance of a specific action, are an essential part of doing business. Valid contracts must include agreement, consent, consideration, contractual capacity, legality, and proper form. Contracts can be written or oral. If one party to the contract fails to perform, the other party can sue for breach of contract and either cancel the contract or sue for damages.

11. Disputes that require a trial are initiated and resolved through the court system. Both the federal and state court systems include trial courts, appellate courts, and a supreme court.

Civil lawsuits usually start with the filing of a complaint by the party who initiates the dispute process (the plaintiff). In criminal cases, the prosecutor initiates the process. The defendant is the party who must respond to the lawsuit. Formal procedures govern the investigation process and the trial itself. Arbitration and mediation offer nonjudicial means to resolve disputes that can save time and money.

12. Enterprisers who follow and encourage ethical personal and business practices build trust with stakeholders and set the values for others to follow. Developing a good reputation can provide a competitive advantage and lead to higher profits. A written code of ethics describes a firm's expectations of employees in dealing with other employees, customers, and suppliers. The three-question test, the front-page-of-the-newspaper test, and *The Wall Street Journal* model are among the models enterprisers can use to resolve ethical dilemmas.

Review Questions

1. What is a law, and why should enterprisers understand the legal and regulatory environment within which they operate? List several business-related circumstances that require knowledge of legal issues.

2. Explain the role of administrative agencies in regulating businesses. Give examples of three federal and two state agencies and their areas of responsibility.

3. Why were competitive practices a major concern for the federal government in the late 1800s? How do the provisions of the Sherman, Clayton, and Robinson Patman Acts prevent abuses?

4. Define consumerism and describe three key laws that protect consumers.

5. Which employment practices fall under federal jurisdiction, and how are they regulated?

6. What is business law, and what types of transactions does it cover?

7. Differentiate between intentional and unintentional torts. List several specific examples of each. What are the two categories of penalties that may be imposed on a business found guilty of wrongdoing in a tort case?

8. How does the UCC facilitate interstate commerce? What are the principal areas covered by Article 2 of the UCC?

9. How do express warranties differ from implied warranties?

10. Define the three categories of property and discuss the types of laws that apply to each. How do copyrights, patents, and trademarks protect intellectual property rights?

11. Explain the differences between Chapter 7, Chapter 11, and Chapter 13 bankruptcy filings.

12. Describe the types of legal issues an enterpriser should consider when starting a new company.

13. What is a contract, and what six elements must a valid contract contain? What remedies do you have in the case of a breach of contract?

14. How are conflicts resolved through the court system? Describe the two most popular alternative dispute resolution processes an enterpriser can use.

15. What are the benefits of operating a business ethically? If you were a business owner, would you develop a written code of ethics, and why?

Applying What You've Learned

1. Imagine that you were thinking of starting the following three kinds of businesses: a pizza delivery business, a biotechnology firm that would eventually manufacture and sell drugs to cure cancer, and a web page–design business.

    (a) What kinds of federal, state and local agencies are likely to regulate each of these businesses?

    (b) What kinds of laws would each business be subject to?

    (c) What should be the first legal steps that each business should take?

    (d) What kinds of legal liabilities might each business face?

2. Look through the last week of a major newspaper (e.g., *The Wall Street Journal, USA Today,* or *The New York Times*) and identify companies that are facing legal issues. What are some of these issues? What kinds of actions were these businesses alleged to have undertaken that have gotten them into trouble? What could they have done to avoid these legal issues?

3. Look through the last week of a major newspaper (e.g., *The Wall Street Journal, USA Today,* or *The New York Times*) and identify companies that are in bankruptcy. Which kinds of bankruptcy are these firms in? What steps are these firms taking to get out of bankruptcy? What steps are their creditors taking to get their money back?

4. Pick a business that you would like to start.

    (a) What legal issues will this business face at the federal, state, and local level?

    (b) Interview the owners of two businesses similar to the one that you would like to start about the legal and regulatory issues that they face. How do they respond to these issues? How do they use lawyers to help them with their legal needs, and how much do these lawyers charge for their services?

5. Using the format guidelines for contracts outlined in Exhibit 5.6, write a contract about the course you are using this book for, including

- Names and addresses of the parties.
- Dates that each party signs the contract. Evidence that the parties entered into an agreement.
- Preamble ("recitals"). Brief description providing background on the parties.
- Description of the agreement between parties. This may be supplemented by attachments or exhibits that provide a more thorough description and clarify the project. Referring to the attachment in the contract makes it part of the contract.
- Delivery date.
- Length of contract period.
- Price.
- Payment terms: in full, installments, interim payments tied to performance.
- Warranties.
- Conditions for termination.
- Penalties for nonperformance.
- Dispute resolution procedures.

Use your course syllabus, college catalogue, and other materials provided by your school as resources for writing your contract. How much of the contract for your course is currently "implied," "verbally agreed to," or written out?

6. Find a small claims court in your area. When it is in session, observe the kinds of legal disputes that are adjudicated. What kinds of disputes seem to take up the majority of the court's time? How are disputes resolved in favor of one party versus another?

7. Look in the newspaper for current disputes between businesses or between a business and its employees or customers. Select one and use it to answer the following questions:

    (a) What are the major issues involved in this dispute, and why do the two parties disagree?

    (b) Why are these parties willing to go to court to resolve their differences?

(c) Would you recommend an alternative dispute resolution process, and why?

(d) If you were mediating this dispute, what additional information would you need in order to resolve this dispute fairly?

(e) How would you resolve this dispute?

8. Describe the types of ethical issues an enterpriser might face in the following areas: human resources, marketing, financing, and production. Are these issues different than those facing larger companies, and why?

Enterprisers on the Web

1. Think of a name for the kind of business you would like to start. Search the Web to find out what other businesses are using this name. What kinds of legal steps have these businesses undertaken to protect this name? Have these businesses trademarked their name?

2. Using any one of the major search engines, find federal, state, and local governments that would likely regulate the kind of business you are considering starting. What kinds of forms are you required to fill out? How much are the fees?

3. Find the major trade association for the business you are interested in starting. Identify the kinds of legal issues that the trade association is concerned with. Are these legal issues at the federal, state or local levels? What is the trade association doing about these legal issues?

4. Search the Web for corporate codes of ethics and find several examples. How do they differ, and how are they similar? Does the company's industry make a difference in the content of the code?

5. One of the best sites for online business ethics resources is the University of Illinois Web-Miner Business Ethics site, http://www.web-miner.com/busethics#top. Divide the class into small groups. Have each group go to the Case Studies section and select one case that interests them. After identifying the key ethical issues in the case, the group should analyze the dilemma using the questions and models presented in the text and prepare a brief report for the class that includes a recommended course of action.

End Notes

1. "Brief Profiles of 2003 Inc. 500 Companies," *Inc.*, October 15, 2003, http://www.inc.com.

2. "McDonald's Coffee Case," *Wikipedia*, April 29, 2004, http://en.wikipedia.org/wiki/McDonald%27s_coffee_case.

3. Beth Warren, "Ford Must Pay for Girl's Injury," *The Atlanta Journal-Constitution*, March 3, 2004, p. B1.

4. Eric Freedman, "Court Upholds Verdict for Ford in Defect Suit," *Automotive News*, December 22, 2003, p. 18.

5. David Barboza and Louise Story, "Mattel Issues New Recall of Toys Made in China," *New York Times*, August 14, 2007, http://www.nytimes.com/2007/08/14/business/15toys-web.html?_r=1&oref=slogin (June 12, 2008).

6. Catherine Larkin, "Baxter, FDA Link Bad Heparin to Fake China Ingredient (Update5)," Bloomberg.com, March 5, 2008, http://www.bloomberg.com/apps/news?pid=20601087&sid=ajsqo.CubTAM&refer=home (June 12, 2008).

7. Victoria Kim and Mitchell Landsberg, "Huge beef recall issued," *Los Angeles Times*, February 18, 2008, http://www.latimes.com/news/local/la-me-beef18feb18,0,5385542,print.story (June 12, 2008).

8. "Sales Law: An Overview," *Legal Information Institute*, May 4, 2004, http://www.law.cornell.edu/topics/sales.html.

9. Bureau of Industry and Security website, http://www.bis.doc.gov (October 31, 2006); "Export Basics," *Export.gov*, http://www.export.gov (November 2, 2006); International Trade Administration website, http://www.ita.doc.gov (November 1, 2006); and International Trade Association website, http://trade.gov (November 1, 2006).

10. Ivan Fox, David P. Twomey, and Marianne Moody, *Anderson's Business Law & the Regulatory Environment: Principles & Cases*, 14th ed. (Cincinnati, OH: West Legal Studies in Business, Thomson Learning, 2001), pp. 28–30, 44.

11. Ibid. pp. 43–45.

PART TWO

The Enterprising Process

Discovering Opportunities

KEY CONCEPTS

1. Business opportunities are favorable events involving customers, consideration, connection, and commitment that have the potential to become a successful business. Recognizing opportunities requires understanding the context in which the "4 Cs" of an opportunity might prove viable. Successful businesses are based on business opportunities that are different from existing businesses.

2. Opportunities occur because the environment is constantly changing. Enterprisers leverage their background and skills to discover opportunities from sources that others might overlook, such as unexpected occurrences, incongruities, process needs, changes in industry and market, demographics, perception, and new knowledge. They pay attention to environmental trends and know-how to enhance their luck.

3. The challenge of identifying a viable opportunity to pursue involves factors such as leveraging your experience, increasing mindfulness, and making your own luck. In addition, enterprisers must evaluate the fit between an opportunity and their personal goals.

Suppose you love fabrics and colors—sewing them and wearing them—but your nursing job forces you to wear the same drab uniform every day. Out of frustration, you start to sew more appealing scrubs for your own wear. Much to your surprise, your coworkers want your designs, too, and two years later word has spread about your great products. Then suppose your husband introduces you to a businessperson with apparel manufacturing experience.

© Photodisc/Alamy Limited

This chapter presents the case of Sue Callaway, a San Diego nurse, and her husband and partners who turned a sideline home business into a major company that changed the look of uniform clothing for millions of health care workers. She recognized a great idea and took the necessary steps to convert it from an opportunity to a business concept and then to a successful enterprise.

6.0 What Is an Opportunity?

Where do enterprisers find opportunities for successful businesses? Are entrepreneurs just lucky individuals who stumble upon an idea for a successful business? Successful enterprisers are more aware of their surroundings. They understand the context in which an opportunity might prove viable and systematically seek opportunities. Enterprisers then use a variety of techniques to evaluate the related environmental and industry factors to identify opportunities that are worth further study. In other words, by their actions they create what others may call luck.

Because environments and industries change, savvy entrepreneurs need to think ahead and consider how environmental changes might affect present opportunities. The purpose of this chapter is to help you recognize the many different paths for finding opportunities. We will explore ways to increase your awareness of environmental characteristics that will affect these opportunities, as well as help you understand how environments might change over time and give rise to new opportunities. Then we'll explain how to turn an opportunity into a successful business by developing a business model that includes a sound business concept and a viable financial plan. As a result, you'll have the tools to make your own luck.

More than Ideas

We define opportunities in a unique way. Opportunities are not just ideas, but also take into account four features of a situation: customers, consideration, connection, and commitment:

- **Customers:** Who will buy an enterpriser's good or services?

- **Consideration (see Chapter 5):** Do the enterpriser's specific goods or services provide significant value to the customer?

- **Connection:** How will an enterpriser identify and reach specific customers? This is often called the channel of distribution.

- **Commitment:** Is the enterpriser committed to the idea and willing to execute it to create an actual business? People bring their own unique interests to a situation. Few people seem to be able to create successful businesses solely on whether

Customers   Those who buy an enterpriser's goods or services.

Connection   How enterprisers will identify and reach specific customers.

Commitment   The enterpriser's dedication to the idea and willingness to implement it.

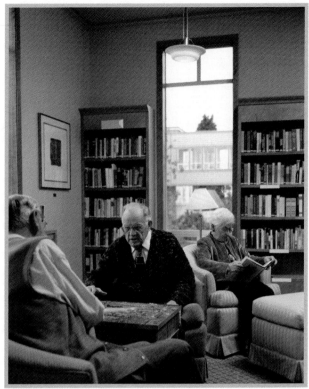

© Keith Brofsky/Photodisc/Getty Images

the business will make a lot of money. Nearly all enterprisers start and build businesses because their businesses reflect their own passions and values.

For example, a chain of adult day care centers might be a great idea for a business. As the population ages, demand may increase for a place for elderly people to go for daytime supervision. While this might seem to be a great idea, does it meet the test of these 4 Cs? Exhibit 6.1 presents the 4 Cs for this opportunity.

Opportunity recognition, then, is about paying attention to your own situation and seeing your own life as a set of favorable events that you can turn into a successful business. An enterpriser's primary activity is recognizing a situation as a "favorable event" and evaluating its business potential using the 4 Cs.

It's Not Just Luck

Enterprisers are often seen as lucky people. In fact, studies suggest that entrepreneurs make their own luck because they devote substantially more effort to scanning the environment than individuals in other occupations. Scanning the environment typically represents the amount of time entrepreneurs spend reading newspapers and popular and trade magazines and also talking with other people, including strangers. Entrepreneurs are

---

exhibit
6.1

The 4 Cs of an Opportunity: Adult Day Care Centers

- **Customers:** In this case, the most likely customers are the relatives who serve as caretakers for the elderly person. These are the people who would pay to have someone else look after their loved one during the day.

- **Consideration:** The price of using the adult day care center must offer an advantage or benefit to the person who pays the fee. Having someone else supervise and monitor an older person at an adult day care center might be an important benefit to a spouse or sibling who is exhausted from giving 24-hour care.

- **Connection:** An adult day care center would have to find customers who would find this service of value and also have the money to pay for this service. Finding customers can often be expensive and time consuming. This opportunity could be implemented at a specific location, where older individuals are picked up from their homes and taken to the care center, or by individual caretakers who go to the older person's home and provide one-to-one services.

- **Commitment:** Not everyone is likely to be interested in adult day care, even though the adult day care business might prove to be very profitable. An enterpriser who had problems finding good care for an aging parent might be more motivated to implement this idea and have the passion and commitment to make it work.

---

prolific gatherers of information; they pay attention to their surroundings and they ask questions.

Opportunities come from a variety of sources. As you might expect, most opportunities arise from previous work experiences. The business environment offers chances to make connections among the various individuals necessary to transform ideas into viable businesses: customers, suppliers, employees, and investors. As they work, enterprisers navigate among these networks of individuals. They find opportunities because markets are inefficient: people do not have the same information nor do they have the same relationships. Entrepreneurs can exploit these gaps in knowledge and connections among people.

Enterprisers also understand that changing environments create both challenges and opportunities. For example, health care businesses are likely to be affected by changes in government regulations and reimbursement policies as well as by changes in technology. Failure to recognize and plan for possible changes in health care regulation could prove to be extremely harmful to a new medical care company.

The development of an opportunity requires a lot of hard work and effort—dedicated commitment. Such commitment is the result of choosing an opportunity that is aligned with the entrepreneur's goals and interests. Opportunities that don't match the entrepreneur's interests and goals will not be sufficiently exploited.

Later in the chapter we'll provide a series of exercises that help you explore your personal goals and interests, so that you can screen out those opportunities that can't meet your personal criteria.

One last point: The initial process of enterprising involves *variation*. Starting an enterprise that will be successful involves doing something different from other businesses that exist. Because each enterpriser brings unique skills and experiences to the situation, the enterprise he or she creates will be distinct from one another enterpriser might develop. The resulting business can provide a unique set of benefits to customers.

6.1 The Business Concept

Ideas are not opportunities. Opportunities don't exist unless they include the four constructs defined earlier—customers, connections, consideration, and commitment. What most people call opportunities are really just ideas. So each of the following does not qualify yet as an opportunity: the Internet (a connection), doughnuts (a product with a set of considerations or benefits), elderly people (a general description of a customer), or "I love pets" (a commitment to one's passion). An idea becomes an opportunity, or business concept, when it covers all four elements.

Understanding this key concept is fundamental to opportunity recognition. We may start with one aspect of the opportunity (business concept), such as "I love pets," and then we begin to think of customers, ways to connect to those customers, what benefits those customers are likely to want, and how committed we are to following through and obtaining funding. Once we have all four, the opportunity can become a reality.

The ability to come up with business concepts is more of a projective and creative process rather than an analytical process. The process involves looking for new ways that differences in the 4 Cs can be combined. Overall, this means asking, "What if?" What if people didn't buy their books at a bookstore? Consider all the different ways that books can be sold. You might first think of selling books on the Internet, like Amazon.com or bn.com. Yet, one of the fastest growing distribution channels for books has been discount merchandisers such as WalMart and Costco. We will explore this process further when we look at how to develop a concept grid.

Telling the Story

The business concept forms half of the business model, while the other part is about numbers, or profitability. (We will address feasibility analysis and profitability in the following chapter.)

A **business concept** is the story that an enterpriser tells about the kind of opportunity he or she wants to develop. The story has to talk about the four characteristics of **opportunities**: customers, consideration, connection, and commitment. The way to evaluate a business concept is to ask:

- Does this story hold up?

- Does it make sense?

- Do the four characteristics of the story fit together?

For example, suppose you are thinking about starting a hamburger delivery service. Many food items, such as pizza and Chinese food, are home delivered so perhaps people would like hamburgers delivered as well. The business concept is home delivery of hamburgers. The customers are people who want home delivery; their

benefit (consideration) is that they don't have to leave home to get a hamburger; the connection is through your delivery service; and you are interested in pursuing this business because you are interested in food.

What you would do next is explore whether the hamburger delivery service holds up as a story. Is a delivered hamburger something that people really want (does it offer the customer significant consideration or value?). Do enough people want such a service? Is home delivery of hamburgers a reasonable way for people to enjoy hamburgers? This issue involves exploring the different ways that people are connected to getting hamburgers, such as drive-through windows, sit-down restaurants, hamburger chains such as McDonald's and Wendy's, homemade hamburgers, and hamburgers in the frozen food section in the grocery store. Each connection has advantages and disadvantages, and each connection delivers certain considerations to the customer.

Once you have convinced yourself that the story seems reasonable, you need to consider the final part of the business model: Does it make money? The numbers are based on assumptions about how the four business concept characteristics work together.

An interesting business concept may not work because of the numbers. Take the online home grocery business. The business concept for companies like Home Grocer, Webvan, and Peapod involved people placing online grocery orders that would be selected and packed at an automated warehouse and delivered to customers' doorsteps. The enterprisers believed that this type of service wouldn't be significantly more expensive than going to the grocery store because the business would make it up in volume. What they didn't include in the financial equation was the time element, a key factor that increased the cost of operating a home grocery delivery business.

Think about how we shop for groceries: we drive to the store and spend half an hour or longer going up and down the aisles selecting products. We discount this time at the store (we don't pay ourselves to do this activity)—but we aren't necessarily willing to pay someone else to take the time to do this for us.

The Internet grocery store was a great business concept: customers valued home delivery of items if the cost was the same as going to the grocery store themselves. However, once the additional labor cost of selecting, packing, and delivering the groceries was included, the business simply didn't work at the prices the service charged. So a great story does not always translate into a viable business financially.

Opportunity or business concept   Favorable events involving customers, consideration, connection, and commitment (the 4 Cs) that have the potential to become a successful business.

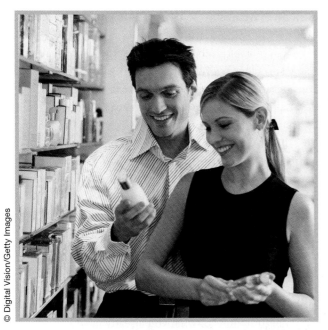

Some people enjoy shopping for certain items, so an online model would not appeal to them.

© Digital Vision/Getty Images

Peapod, one of the surviving online grocers, has succeeded by paying attention to its customers and the environment and adapting its business concept accordingly. Peapod's first business concept was to use personal shoppers to fill orders at local supermarkets that would give Peapod a 6 percent discount. However, Peapod discovered that the cost to fill a $100 order was $40! So Peapod changed its business concept to use centralized distribution centers to fulfill orders.[1] Peapod's concept changed again when it became a subsidiary of Royal Ahold, a major international grocer, in 2000. It now uses a "clicks and bricks" concept and partners with Ahold's U.S. supermarket chains, including Stop & Shop and Giant Food. Certain parts of its business concept remained constant, such as its commitment to quality, customer service, the proprietary Stay Fresh delivery system, state-of-the-art order-fulfillment technology, and proprietary transportation routing system.[2]

Enterprisers should focus on both customers and consideration. They need to identify a group of people with needs that the enterprise can fulfill. At some fundamental level, the concept development process starts when someone asks, "What causes you pain?" If finding a cure for your pain is important and another person can provide it, you have the beginning of a business concept that might be worth pursuing.

The Business Concept Grid

A good way to visualize the business concept is a grid that demonstrates the relationship between the 4 Cs. These variables are interdependently manipulated to develop a coherent story about the nature of an opportunity. As Exhibit 6.2 illustrates, the grid is a table with the 4 Cs across the top.

Let's use "chocolate" as the basic idea from which we want to generate concepts (opportunities). First, we would think about the many different categories of customers who would be interested in buying chocolate and place them in column one. Next we would think

---

exhibit 6.2

The Business Concept Grid

Customer	Connection	Consideration	Commitment
Kids	Grocery stores Candy stores		
	Movie theaters	(1) Can't go out to other places and buy while movie is showing.	Loves movie theaters.
		(2) Extra treat besides the movie as special occasion.	Enjoys selling. Likes candy.
		(3) Must be able to eat it in the dark.	
	Ice cream stores Vending machines Halloween		

about all of the ways that chocolate products could be connected to each customer—for example, all the different places an enterpriser might provide opportunities for kids to buy chocolate—and list them in the customer column as in Exhibit 6.1(page 137).

For each customer and connection, we then identify all of the ways that we can provide consideration for that option. For example, let's take kids as the customer, and movie theaters as the connection for providing chocolate.

Given this particular connection, it probably makes sense that chocolate products sold in movie theaters tend to be larger than the sizes sold in other places, and the kinds of chocolate products are often less "messy" (e.g., M&Ms), rather than something like a hot fudge sundae that would be difficult to eat while watching a movie.

Finally, enterprisers have to think about whether the particular configuration of customer, connection, and consideration is appealing for them to pursue. In this example, are you excited about selling candy to children? How do you feel about working to increase candy purchases in movie theaters? If you aren't really passionate about this concept, then you probably shouldn't pursue it—even though it might prove to be very profitable.

One of the major ways for enterprisers to succeed is to think about new ways to connect to customers. For example, Dell sells computers directly to customers through the Internet and through mail order, rather than through retail stores. Customers can order exactly what they want, and the computer is "made to order" for them. This is different from a customer going to a retail store (different connection) and buying what the retailer has on the shelves of the store.

We can start the concept grid in any area. For example, we might start with the connection "movie theater," and consider the types of customers who might be attracted to a movie theater: kids, adults, couples on dates, movie buffs, and so on. Then, we could think about the various considerations that each group of customers would want from their movie experience. For example, what kids might want from their movie experience could be very different from what a movie buff might want. Not only would the movies be different, but also the kinds of seats and snacks a movie buff might prefer could be different from what we'd offer for kids. An enterpriser might be passionate about serving some kinds of customers and not others. An enterpriser who is a film buff may show classic movies, art films, and foreign films more often than mainstream titles. Another enterpriser may target the family market. Each

customer, then, has different ways to connect to certain kinds of considerations.

The concept grid provides a visual way of realizing that each category of the concept (customer, connection, consideration, commitment) can be a starting point for developing a viable concept. For many enterprisers, their concept will begin with their passion. Starting with a love of fishing, for example, an enterpriser could think of numerous opportunities that might involve fishing (a commercial fishing boat, offering fishing tours, creating fishing supplies (like lures), a fishing school, etc.).

Enterprisers can work at leveraging their ideas into concepts through effectuation. Begin with what you have (the customers you already know, the connections you already have, the considerations that you can already provide, and the commitments you want to pursue), and look to discover a business concept that might work from combinations of what you already have.

6.2 Sources of Opportunity (the Environment)

Now that we know what opportunities are, how do we find them? We should start with the big picture view—the environment—and then take a closer look at how an opportunity fits with an individual's personality, needs, and talents. The environment includes not only the business environment—a company or an industry—but also the broader social, intellectual, economic, political, regulatory, and global environments.

This section introduces you to several approaches to environmental analysis. First, we'll examine Peter Drucker's strategies for what he calls "systematic innovation." Then we'll consider trend analysis and describe several resources for this important phase of opportunity recognition.

Disciplined Innovation

Because the world is changing every day, a constant stream of new opportunities emerges through changes in the environment. Management expert Peter Drucker believes that innovation is more than inspiration or luck. It takes a different type of hard work—knowing instead of doing. "Above all, innovation is work rather than genius . . . hard, focused, purposeful work," he writes. "If diligence, persistence, and commitment are lacking, talent, ingenuity, and knowledge are of no avail."[3] His classic 1985 book *Innovation and Entrepreneurship* describes seven sources of opportunities that he considers essential to successful systematic innovation:[4]

1. *Unexpected Occurrences:* Individuals capitalize on unexpected successes or see things that don't work and realize that this "failure" indicates some other kind of opportunity. For example, IBM originally thought the science sector would be the primary users of computers. The company quickly switched its focus when initial demand for computers came from businesses that needed to automate payroll calculations for payroll. This unexpected success led to IBM's leadership role in the computer industry. The Ford Motor Company learned through the failure of the Edsel that buyers bought cars because of their identification with a lifestyle, and because of this insight, the company designed the Mustang.

2. *Incongruities:* Incongruities occur when expectations and results don't match. Logically we would expect that companies and industries that grow and become more efficient would in turn earn higher profits. In some cases, the reverse might be true because of incongruities between reality and the basic assumptions about how success in the industry occurs.

   For example, during the first part of the 20th century, the shipping industry was in decline despite the introduction of faster and more fuel-efficient ships to transport cargo. Yet fewer goods were being shipped. The problem lay not in the time a ship was at sea, but rather on the number of days a ship was in port. The opportunity recognition centered on finding ways to speed up loading and unloading cargo to reduce the number of days that ships were in port. Once the industry converted to container ships and roll-on and roll-off ships, the shipping sector grew and returned to profitability. A more recent incongruity involves the Internet grocery business. Knowing that many consumers hate to go to the grocery shop—in one study they ranked it next to last on a list of favorite household tasks—companies like Webvan, Peapod, and Home Grocer were sure that their online supermarket services would attract lots of customers. To their dismay, they discovered that their early assumptions based on such studies were wrong. Shoppers weren't willing to pay more for the convenience and the time they saved.

3. *Process Needs:* Another source of opportunity is identifying changes in how things work. One reason for growth in the pharmaceutical industry is the use of drugs, rather than surgery or other treatment methods, to combat disease. For example, rather than have patients with depression see a psychiatrist weekly, doctors can treat many cases of depression with drugs, thereby reducing costs to the patient, as well as providing opportunities for more individuals with depression to be treated through drugs, rather than through the high expense of psychotherapy. The process needs provided the opportunity.

4. *Industry and Market Changes:* Often changes in laws and regulations have a significant impact on opportunities available for new companies to pursue. Changes in industry structure also create opportunity. The breakup of the nationwide monopoly held by AT&T brought significant opportunities to the telecommunications industry. Thousands of new companies took advantage of these available opportunities, installing telephones, telephone systems, and pay phones, and selling alternative local and long-distance services. The deregulation of the airline industry enabled firms like Southwest Airlines, JetBlue, Ryanair, and easyJet to take advantage of underserved markets by requiring lower airfares, typically at underused airports and in places where demand for air transportation has been hindered by high prices.

5. *Demographic Changes:* The number and age of a population is predictable, so that understanding trends becomes a source of opportunity. The United States went through a baby boom after World War II through 1960, and then couples had fewer children from 1960 until 1980. The greater number of births during the baby boom has a predictable influence on what will occur in the economy over time. As the average age of the population increases, opportunities arise to provide services for the growing number of people over the age of 65. Also, it is important to recognize that everyone who will be in the workforce in 2020 has already been born! The "market" in the United States in 2020, therefore, is already "fixed" unless there is a significant influx of immigrants.

6. *Changes in Perception:* What people value and find important change over time. The fashion industry is an obvious example of how tastes in clothing change constantly. As the population of the United States ages, our perception of what "old age" means also changes. We now expect to live healthy and active lives into our 70s and 80s, continuing to play tennis, ski, or mountain climb. As a result, our perception of health is changing as well.

7. *New Knowledge:* Regardless of the field, the hardest and most complicated way to pursue innovation is through new knowledge. The innovations that come

Systematic innovation   As defined by Peter Drucker, a purposeful and organized search for and analysis of changes and the opportunities these changes create.

from discoveries in science, technology, education, and sociology take more time to develop and carry greater risk than most other factors. This concept has been documented over time, as the following quote from Nicolo Machiavelli's *The Prince,* written in 1505, proves:

> And it ought to be remembered that there is nothing more difficult to take in hand, more perilous to conduct, or more uncertain in its success, than to take the lead in the introduction of a new order of things. Because the innovator has for enemies all those who have done well under the old conditions, and lukewarm (indifferent, uninterested) defenders in those who may do well under the new.

More recently, Hillary Johnson, writing in *Inc.,* expresses a similar view in an article about her father, a visionary entrepreneur who never quite made it, despite a series of innovative ideas:

> The world does not welcome innovators or artists, though not out of malice. The problem is a structural glitch. The world is set up to function as smoothly as it can, and it doesn't recognize the difference between innovation and disaster: Either one throws a wrench into the system. Trying to make the world really better is as much a crime against society as trying to make it worse. Only small incremental improvements are rewarded and applauded.... Some people believe that good ideas always rise to the top. They're wrong. Good ideas occasionally rise, but just as many sink into oblivion. Success in the technology industry in particular, has always depended on having the right product at the right time, not necessarily on having the best product ... Living with a frustrated inventor for 40 years has taught me something I didn't learn even from the cold war, and that is simply this: The scariest thing about the future is that the future isn't necessary.[5]

Trendsetters

Paying attention to how trends affect our lives, both personally and professionally, is an important way to identify potential opportunities for new businesses. Successful enterprisers tend to be more aware of trends in the environment than others. They track them on an ongoing basis and know when important changes occur.

Sources for trends are plentiful. Many magazines, from business periodicals like *Fortune* and *Business Week* to general news magazines like *Time* and *Newsweek,* feature articles on trends. *Red Herring* (http://www.redherring.com), a technology magazine, is a good source for trends relating to the intersection of technology, business, government, globalization, and investing.

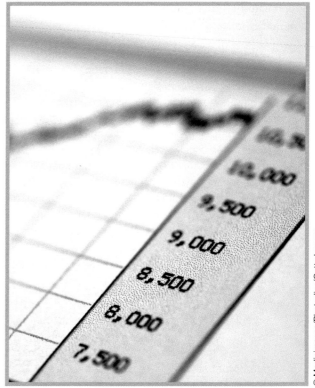

© Medioimages/Photodisc/Getty Images

In recent years, *Red Herring's* trends have covered a wide range of industries, including telecommunications, semiconductors, nanotechnology, biotechnology, venture capital, and broadband.

Several recent books document the broad changes occurring in the world. Peter Schwartz, cofounder and chairman of the Global Business Network (GBN), is a noted futurist and business strategist. GBN's website, http://www.gbn.org/, provides valuable insights about how to think about the future and which environmental factors are likely to be important. In his book *Inevitable Surprises*, he describes major trends that he believes are inevitable—but also predicts surprise twists that can create opportunities:

1. *An aging world.* In 1950, the average age at death was around 60; in 2003, it was around 77. People are likely to live and to be productive a lot longer. If people retire in their 60s and live to their 90s, they would spend nearly one-third of their lives not working. No society can afford to support this. The surprise twist: what if people don't stay healthier as they age? How do we afford significantly rising health care costs?

2. *The great flood of people.* While the average age in the United States is getting higher, this is not the case in many other parts of the world. An influx of immigrants will tend to make the country younger,

more Latino, and less educated in the short term. China will face the "one child problem," and because families have tended to have boys rather than girls, there will be a significant shortage of marriage-able women over the next 20 years. Europe will have to face its own immigration issues, as many more nonnationals cross borders to work and live because of the open border policies of European Union nations. The surprise twist is that Europe will face the same challenges as the United States in creating a cohesive society because many of these countries (i.e., Germany, France, Sweden) are based on a particular cultural heritage (i.e., German, French, Swedish).

3. *Return of the long boom.* Schwartz believes that technology contributes to rising rates of productivity, which improve everyone's standard of living. He believes there will be a sustainable "long boom" in prosperity. The surprise twist: Every country needs to invest in infrastructure (airports, power grids, highways, hospitals, public safety, etc.) in order for society, as a whole, to benefit.

4. *The new world order.* Can the United States, as the only superpower, work with other nations to make the world a safer place? Schwartz believes that it cannot make the world safe by going it alone. The surprise twist, then, is that U.S. strength will come through increasing commitments to cooperation among other nations.

5. *The forces of destabilization.* Will terrorism continue to rise? Will the forces that lead to terrorism, such as radical religious views, not only in the Middle East but also in South East Asia and Africa, lead to continual wars and conflict? The surprise twist: If prosperity and freedom continue to grow across the world, many of the forces that spawn terrorism and discouragement (i.e., poverty, lack of opportunity) will diminish.

6. *Benefits of science.* Schwartz sees the continuing importance of biotechnology, computers, and all other applications of science leading to significant benefits to all people in the world. The surprise twist: Every new technology brings possibilities for benefits as well as harm. For instance, the ability to manipulate atoms has led to nuclear power plants for electricity (supplying France with 70 percent of its electricity) as well as the material to make nuclear bombs.

7. *The challenge of dealing with the environment.* Will choices be made to improve the air, water, and land around the world, or not? These are political choices more than just economic choices. The surprise twist is that as the economic well-being of citizens rises in any country, their interest in improving the environmental standards of their air, water, and land also increases.

© Carlos Sanchez Pereyra/Used under license from Shutterstock

James Canton, CEO and chairman of the Institute for Global Futures, published *The Extreme Future*, a book describing the major trends that present strategic challenges for the world's leaders over the next 5–20 years. He believes that every individual, organization, and country should be aware of and prepare for these top-ten trends, many of which echo Schwartz's earlier predictions:

1. *Energy:* The need to solve the current energy crisis and to understand energy's pivotal role in business and society.

2. *Innovation industries:* The global economy will be driven by innovation in such fields as nano-, bio-, neuro-, and information technologies.

3. *The changing workforce:* Diversity and multiculturalism will characterize the workforce of the future. A shortage of talented workers will create competition to hire and retain the best employees.

4. *Medical advances:* Biotech and genomic research are helping us stay healthy longer.

5. *Weird science:* Ongoing advances in technology will change our lives, culture, and economy. Nations and

businesses that invest in future science will profit in economic growth.

6. *Reducing security risks:* Protecting ourselves from threats to our physical well-being and also to our identities has moved to the fore.

7. *Globalization:* Both opportunities and risks will increase from open global trade. China and India will gain in economic importance. Cultures and ideas will clash.

8. *The changing climate:* Global warming and pollution are changing the ecosystems. These, along with threats to biodiversity, present challenges as well as new business opportunities.

9. *Protecting individual rights:* Individuals and society must find a way to balance personal freedom, privacy, and security.

10. *America's relationship with China:* These two countries could have the greatest impact on the world's future.[6]

Economic trends are critical components of many of the trends we've discussed so far. Successful enterprisers also follow what's happening in the economy. Exhibit 6.3 lists a number of valuable websites that provide helpful information on a diverse group of economic indicators, including some more unusual ones.

As our discussion of trends demonstrates, change is guaranteed. Anyone who is looking at the future can see that some kinds of changes (demographic changes, for example) will happen. Along with change come opportunities.

6.3 Finding Opportunities (You and the Environment)

The secret for identifying an opportunity involves leveraging your own experience (background and skills) by (1) paying attention and (2) enhancing one's luck. As we will see, experience provides both pluses and minuses to an individual's ability to notice and exploit an opportunity.

exhibit
6.3

Tracking Economic and Demographic Trends

These websites will link you to a wealth of economic surveys, statistics, and other information that will help you identify trends.

Indicator/Source	Link	Description
Business Roundtable's CEO Economic Outlook	http://www.businessroundtable.org	Conducts quarterly CEO Economic Outlook surveys that ask about expectations for the short-term economic outlook.
Bureau of Labor Statistics	http://www.bls.gov	A good place to find statistics on inflation and consumer spending, job growth and unemployment, earnings, productivity, business costs, and demographics.
U. S. Census Bureau	http://www.census.gov	Statistics and analysis on people, households, and businesses.
BizStats.com	http://bizstats.com	Links to a variety of business and industry statistics.
MBA Mortgage Applications Survey	http://www.mortgagebankers.org	Weekly mortgage applications survey predicts trends in home sales; economic outlook and forecasts on market environment.
Consumer Outlook	http://www.pollingreport.com/consumer.htm	Reports the results of several consumer confidence surveys, including ABCNews/Money Consumer Comfort Index, Conference Board, AP/Ipsos Consumer Attitudes and Spending by Household (CASH) Index, Gallup surveys, and others.

Experience

The way to look at experience is to see it in light of the 4 Cs: customers, connection, consideration, and commitment. Experience involves building up your capital, or resources, with regard to the 4 Cs. For example, if you have experience as a restaurant waiter, you are likely to have some knowledge of what menu selections and drinks interest customers who come to that restaurant. You have some sense of how much the restaurant's patrons are willing to pay for a meal and those special occasions when customers are likely to splurge on a meal. So as a waiter, you would have some sense of both customers and consideration (what kinds of benefits customers enjoy: food, service, atmosphere), and you would have some sense of whether you actually enjoyed the restaurant business (your sense of your own commitment). What you might not have knowledge of as a waiter would be the connections—for example, the details of how the food is prepared, how the restaurant is actually operated, and who the best suppliers for food are.

What we find is that enterprisers work to gather up information across the 4 Cs to identify an opportunity worth pursuing. What entrepreneurs do differently is to maximize their unique capabilities and skills to generate benefits to a specific set of customers. Entrepreneurs use their experience as a starting point for identifying an opportunity and then for gathering the resources necessary to pursue that opportunity. It is rare that an enterpriser has all of the background experiences that are likely to enable him or her to completely see all aspects of the 4 Cs in an opportunity.

It is important to realize that all enterprisers "begin where they are." We emphasized this point in Chapter 3 when we talked about effectuation. With regard to experience and its influence on recognizing opportunities, people don't see opportunities outside of the boundaries of their own experiences, that is, their "prior knowledge."

A good example of this involves a research study that looked at individuals who applied for rights to license a specific technology invented at the Massachusetts Institute of Technology (MIT).[7] This technology is three-dimensional printing (3DP), which was invented by four MIT faculty members and doctoral students and patented in the United States on December 8, 1989. According to the patent documents, 3DP involves:

> a process for making a component by depositing a first layer of a fluent porous material, such as a powder, in a confined region and then depositing a binder material to selected regions of the layer of powder material to produce a layer of bonded powder material at the selected regions. Such steps are repeated in a selected number of times to produce successive layers of selected regions of bonded powder material so as to form a desired component. The un-bonded powder material is then removed . . . (US Patent #,204,055).

Having read the description of this patent idea, what kinds of customers do you think might be interested in this idea? In what ways could this idea be made into a product or service that customers would consider buying? What value would this product or service have for these customers? And, finally, can you think of a combination of customers, connections, and considerations involving this idea that you would be committed to pursuing?

The MIT Technology Licensing Office widely circulated the 3DP idea in scientific magazines and the popular press to encourage entrepreneurs to notice this idea and come up with ways to exploit it. MIT was willing to give individuals or companies exclusive rights to use the 3DP technology if they could show how they might exploit it in a particular application. Of the thousands, if not millions, of individuals who might have noticed this idea, only eight groups devoted significant effort to getting a license to use the 3DP idea to exploit an opportunity. Four of these efforts resulted in successful companies, while the other four failed. Exhibit 6.4 provides information about the companies, the opportunities, and the current status of these efforts.

Exploring the experiences and backgrounds of the entrepreneurs involved in these eight efforts reveals several key insights:

- *The range of opportunities that could be generated from the 3DP process is not obvious to everyone.* When you read the patent description, did you come up with the list of eight opportunities listed in Exhibit 6.4? In fact, each enterpriser who came up with a specific opportunity to exploit the 3DP process was surprised to find out that other enterprisers had come up with other ways to use the 3DP technology. "I certainly never thought that someone would make pills with the 3DP process," said Walter Bornhorst of Z Corp. What, then, led each enterpriser to see a specific opportunity in 3DP technology that no other enterprisers saw?

- *The opportunity that each enterpriser noticed was driven by his or her prior industry experience.*

exhibit
6.4

Entrepreneurial Opportunities for 3DP

Company	Opportunity	Forecast Market Size, Year 5	Forecast Sales, Year 5	Forecast Operating Earnings	Current Status
Z Corp	Machine to make rapid 3-D prototypes for industrial and architectural design	$100 million	$10 million	$2 million	Privately owned and funded by founders
Therics	Pharmaceutical delivery systems	$9 billion	$2 million	–$7.5 million	Privately owned and funded by venture capital
Specific Surface Corporation	Ceramic filters for power generation	$800 million	$31.5 million	$13 million	Privately owned and funded by venture capital
Soligen	Direct shell production casting to make ceramic mold from CAD model	$20 billion	$50 million	$8.5 million	Public company
3D Partners	Provide 3-D models to clients	$10 million	Never done	Never done	Abandoned; found market too small
3D Orthopedics	Custom orthopedic devices for medical and dental markets	Never done	Never done	Never done	Abandoned; not funded by venture capital
3D Imaging	3-D models for surgeons to reduce error	Never done	Never done	Never done	Abandoned; lost $50,000 business plan competition
Conferences	Retail chain to make 3-D sculptures of people	Never done	Never done	Never done	Abandoned; technology inappropriate for intended use

Source: Reprinted by permission, Shane, Scott, "Prior Knowledge and the Discovery of Entrepreneurial Opportunities," *Organizational Science* 11 no. 4, July/August. Copyright 2002, the Institute for Operations Research and the Management Sciences (INFORMS), 7240 Parkway Drive, Suite 310, Hanover, MD 21076 USA.

Industry experience is "code" for knowledge of the 4 Cs. For example, Z Corp., which focused on applying 3DP to make three dimensional prototypes, was developed by individuals with industrial design experience who were working in a company concerned with quickly creating three dimensional prototypes. They had knowledge of customers, they had an understanding of the kinds of prototypes that customers wanted, and they were able to see how the 3DP process could serve as the connection between what these customers wanted and their specific considerations. The enterpriser for Therics had 25 years of prior experience in pharmaceutical manufacturing, product development, and regulatory approval. When he learned about 3DP technology, he could apply it to the manufacture of drugs.

- *In all eight cases, the enterprisers saw the 3DP process in relationship to solving a particular customer problem.* These enterprisers had a particular set of considerations in mind that helped them notice how an idea such as 3DP could solve these customer problems. They *recognized* the opportunity but were not searching for it. So a good way to look for an opportunity is to begin with customer problems.

- *Individuals don't explore ideas in unfamiliar areas.* For example, if we don't have experience and knowledge of biotechnology, we aren't likely to think about how an idea might become an opportunity in that area. Even the entrepreneurs who looked at the use of 3DP in orthopedics didn't broaden their approach to other medical applications. The environmental factors discussed earlier in this chapter, for example, are ideas that will broadly influence our lives. But turning these factors into opportunities requires an understanding of the specifics of the 4 Cs: Who are your customers? What do they want (consideration)? How will these needs be met (connections)? Do you want to do this (commitment)?

As the 3DP story clearly illustrates, experience is a constraint that has a major impact on opportunity recognition. It is critical to the types of connections we make among the 4 Cs. In addition, we are less likely to recognize opportunities that are outside the realm of our prior experiences. Broadening our horizons by creating varied experiences will maximize the chances of discovering business opportunities.

At the same time, developing experience-based business concepts brings other challenges. One of the most critical is ownership of opportunities that an enterpriser discovers while employed by someone else. Most companies have conflict of interest clauses in their corporate codes of conduct that cover this situation, as the Enterprising Ethics box explains.

ENTERPRISING ETHICS

Whose Opportunity Is It?

As a talented research scientist at a mid-size biotechnology company specializing in drugs to treat cancer, you are known for your creative approaches to research. Working in your lab after-hours, you believe that you have discovered a new diagnostic test for multiple sclerosis, a neurological disease. Because this type of product is outside the scope of the company's mission, you plan to start your own company to market the tests. Do you own your idea, and are you within your legal rights to develop it on your own?

Or perhaps you are a financial advisor at a major brokerage firm and believe that your firm is not serving women clients well, especially those who find themselves responsible for their own investments after a divorce or death of a partner. You want to start a specialized advisory firm for these women and begin compiling a list of your current employer's female clients. Have you violated the company's code of ethics?

These are just a few examples of the complexities surrounding intellectual property (IP) and potential conflicts of interest. Conflicts of interest arise when the private interests of an employee or director interfere with those of the company in any material way. They affect both employees with ideas for a new product or service and employers who want to protect their company's IP.

While you may think IP is limited to technological discoveries, computer source code, patents, and copyrighted designs, it also includes trade secrets, business plans, marketing strategies, sales leads, price lists, lists of customers, lists of suppliers, and similar items. Trade secrets refer to proprietary knowledge—formulas, patterns, designs, software, special equipment, or processes—used in one's business that provide a competitive advantage and thus have independent economic value.

Most companies today have codes of ethics with very specific clauses concerning actual or perceived conflicts of interest and related matters. They require that employees and directors and their immediate families avoid any conflicts of interest and disclose potential conflicts of interest. Typically, the language is very broad and prohibits employees and directors from engaging in any activities that conflict with the company's business, may negatively impact the company's reputation, or prevent accomplishing assigned job responsibilities. Examples of prohibited activities include

- Receiving compensation in any form from another company or accepting personal loans, gifts, fees, favors, or other material benefits from such a company.

- Using opportunities discovered while using the company's property (including intellectual property) or the company's property for personal gain.

(continued)

Enterprising Ethics (*continued*)

- Using information gained through a person's position at the company, about the company, a competitor, supplier, or customer, for personal gain.

- Insider trading (using nonpublic information for personal financial benefit or sharing that information with others who may use it as the basis for making stock trades).

- Owning equity in a company with whom the employing company has a business relationship (customer or supplier) or that competes with the employing company.

- Participating in joint ventures or similar business arrangements.

- Simultaneous employment with another company or any activities that advance another company's interests, such as marketing competitive products.

In many cases, a company will allow certain activities that have been presented to and approved by the company's audit committee or other governance group.

Discussion Questions

1. How would you react if you were the CEO at the biotechnology firm and learn that your employee is starting a side business with an idea developed in your laboratories? Do you have the right to approve whether your employee pursues the opportunity to develop the diagnostic test—and should you have this right?

2. What criteria would you use to evaluate whether an employee's opportunity is in conflict with the organization? Are employees who are mindful of the opportunities around them penalized by conflict of interest policies?

3. What kinds of experience does an employee receive from an organization, and should the organization benefit from any opportunities derived from that experience?

4. Should all employees be subject to conflict of interest policies, or only employees who are more likely to discover opportunities closely tied to the company's current products, services, and customers?

Sources: "Business Conduct and Ethics," Chevron website, http://www.chevron.com/investor/corporate_governance/biz_conduct.asp (November 30, 2006); "Code of Ethics," NTL Incorporated website, http://investors.ntl.com (November 29, 2006); Peter Fiske, "Opportunities: Intellectual Property, Part 1," *Science Careers*, November 10, 2006, http://sciencecareers.sciencemag.org; "Genentech Good Operating Principles," Genentech website, http://www.gene.com/gene/ir/governance/ggop.jsp (November 29, 2006).

Paying Attention

Ellen J. Langer's work on mindfulness provides a good description of mindfulness. She writes:

> A mindful approach to any activity has three characteristics: the continuous creation of new categories, openness to new information, and an implicit awareness of more than one perspective.[8]

The concept of **mindfulness** revolves around certain psychological states that are really different versions of the same thing: (1) openness to novelty; (2) alertness to distinction; (3) sensitivity to different contexts; (4) implicit, if not explicit, awareness of multiple perspectives; and (5) orientation in the present.[9]

What are the strategies for increasing mindfulness, and why would mindfulness lead to discovering opportunities?

Mindfulness   As defined by Ellen J. Langer, an awareness of the present moment that includes openness to new information and multiple perspectives.

As we've defined an aspect of opportunity recognition, we have to be able to spot things that are "different." Instead, we often become habitual in our thinking, and, we lose our ability to notice anything that is different in our situation. We can learn to be more mindful:

- *Vary the way you do things.* When you do something different, pay attention—in the moment—to how these differences change the situation. For example, many people get their best ideas when they travel because traveling puts them in entirely new situations. We need to vary how we do things, and then pay attention to what is new and different in the current situation.

- *Increase the novelty in the situation.* Look for a situation's unique features. What is different about this situation? Focus on and pay attention to differences rather than assuming that every situation is the same as every other situation.

- *View situations from different perspectives.* Become more mindful by looking at situations from other stakeholders' perspectives, for example, your customers or employees. Ask yourself these questions: How would customers or suppliers look at the product? What are their needs and interests? Their perspective may be totally different from yours.

- *Turn work into play.* If it is fun and enjoyable, one pays more attention to engaging in the activity. Most entrepreneurs consider their "job" to be about fun, rather than about "work."

- *Draw distinctions.* When we look for differences, we find that we must pay attention to the specifics of the context. By being open to thinking about distinctions, we find ourselves seeing new things that wouldn't be apparent to us otherwise.

Veteran entrepreneur Norm Brodsky is a good example of mindfulness at work. He has repeatedly gone into competitive markets that others considered saturated and built successful companies. About 25 years ago, in the early days of computer usage, he started a messenger business but was having difficulty getting customers, even though he courted law firms, advertising agencies, and others that made many deliveries and passed their costs to their clients. Taking a different perspective—the customer's—he discovered that cost was not the primary concern and identified a problem he could solve. In discussions with an office manager who was a potential customer, the office manager indicated a need for receiving invoices by each client served. This change in the billing process would make the office manager's life much easier and save administrative time. Other messenger firms provided only aggregate billing information, and it took many hours to assign costs to the client. Brodsky hired a programmer and figured out how to provide invoices that grouped pickups and deliveries by client. This feature gave him the jump on his competitors and was a key factor in the company's success.[10]

Two additional ways to increase mindfulness are to think about levels of analysis that occur and to talk about scope. A problem that you may think is an issue about the individual might really be about the group or society. Asking yourself, "Is it above or below what is happening in the situation?" will help to identify the correct level.

Mindfulness is less about getting right answers than about opening yourself up to new and different ideas and situations. As Langer says,

How can we know if we do not ask? Why should we ask if we are certain we know? All answers come out of the question. If we pay attention to our questions, we increase the power of mindful learning.[11]

Paying attention isn't necessarily about achieving a particular outcome; rather, it is about exploring the world and understanding your experience. Particularly in the process of concept development, many different alternatives could satisfy a customer's needs. The more ways you can discover through mindfulness and paying attention, the more opportunities you will find.

Making Your Own Luck

Making your own luck is very similar to the process of becoming mindful. In an experiment to uncover how lucky people act in different ways from unlucky people, researchers asked people to count photographs as they paged through a newspaper. The researchers had placed a half-page announcement on the third page of the newspaper that said: "Stop counting. There are 43 photographs in this newspaper." The lucky would notice the ad and stop counting, while the unlucky would just continue looking for photographs. In this experiment, the researchers were testing participants' ability to notice things outside of the assigned task.

They discovered several important differences between lucky and unlucky people.

- Lucky people are open to new experiences. Unlucky people are stuck in routines, and they don't pay attention.

- Lucky people are less focused. They are willing to experience different situations and do not have a specific goal in mind. They are open to different outcomes and expect success.

- Lucky people reframe experiences so that they see them as valuable outcomes. If something goes "wrong," they consider it a learning experience rather than a failure.

(For more information about the Luck Project, visit its website: http://www.luckfactor.co.uk.)

Among the ways to create better luck for yourself are the following:

1. *Maximize chance opportunities.* This is a way of saying, "get out in the world, meet people you don't normally meet, and see what happens."

2. *Listen to your lucky hunches.* Pay attention to your intuitions and don't readily discount them.

3. *Expect good fortune.* Expectations become self-fulfilling prophecies. People who keep luck journals, writing down lucky things that happen to them, notice that over time, more lucky things happen in their lives.

4. *Turn bad luck into good.* Lucky people reimagine situations where bad things happened and realize that things could have been worse. Then they move on and take control of the situation.

Making your own luck is similar to some of the strategies we discussed in Chapter 4 that focused on optimism and small wins. If you expect good things to happen to you, they do. If you continue to take actions to make your life better, it gets better. Opportunities occur to those who expect to find opportunities.

6.4 Enterprisers and Opportunities (Evaluation of Personal Fit)

Not every opportunity is worth doing. Enterprisers need to take time to evaluate whether the opportunities they consider meet their own needs. This process is often very difficult. An enterpriser's initial commitment to an opportunity can change as the enterpriser gains more experience.

Take, for example, a business student who was also a wonderful baker. By all accounts she made a fantastic peach pie, one of the best anyone had ever tasted. Everyone who had a bite of her peach pies said the same thing: "You should sell these peach pies!" So she did. She began baking pies at home and took samples to various restaurants and gourmet shops around town. Everyone who tasted her peach pies said, "How many of these pies can I get?" Soon she was baking 50 peach pies a day and had orders for many more.

She quickly moved from making peach pies at home to renting a licensed kitchen with an industrial oven. Within about three months, as the business grew, she realized she had less and less interest in wanting to bake pies as a business. While she enjoyed making one or two peach pies for herself and for her friends on the weekends, it was less fun to get up at 4 AM to begin mixing ingredients for hundreds of pies, bake them, and get them delivered. Then she had to insure that all of her clients paid their bills. As the fresh peach season came to an end, it became more and more difficult to find enough fresh peaches (or even high quality frozen peaches).

While her friends might be forgiving if one of her pies might have a blemish on top, or look slightly crooked, the restaurants and gourmet shops wanted only perfect-looking pies. After about six months, she decided to quit making pies and to work for a company that sold baking supplies to bakers. She found that she enjoyed being around other bakers, but she didn't want to have a business as a baker. What lessons can we learn from her experience?

First, find entrepreneurs who you would like to emulate. Spend time talking with them about their businesses, what they like—and don't like—about their day-to-day lives. Interviewing entrepreneurs gives you a good sense of the start-up process. You might find that some industries have really "awful" entrepreneurs and people working in them—entrepreneurs who don't return phone calls or respond to emails and are mad and unhappy when they are interviewed. This is often a good sign that getting into that kind of business will not be fun! If the people in the industry are unhappy, the odds are high that if you get into that kind of business, you will be unhappy too.

Besides finding lots of mentors and examples of entrepreneurs in the kinds of businesses that interest you, you should consider doing an internship (paid or unpaid) to get experience with the day-to-day realities of the business that interests you. Another student loved kayaking and thought it would be great to have a kayaking store. He was able to get an internship at a major outdoor adventure store that specialized in selling kayaks. He found that his time was occupied with the details of running a retail store, and he wasn't spending any time kayaking. In selling to customers, he found he was impatient to be outside kayaking and didn't particularly like talking about kayaking.

When the personal fit is there, success can follow. In the Enterprising World box, we'll meet Lionel Poilâne, whose passion for bread and vision of a bakery with global reach helped him capitalize on opportunities and earn the title of the most famous baker in Paris.

It is important to ask yourself a number of questions about whether a particular opportunity, will be worth pursuing. These include broad-based questions that address major lifestyle issues you might ask when devising a life plan. Exhibit 6.5 lists some ideas to get you started.

exhibit
6.5

How to Achieve a Balanced Life

As you evaluate the 4Cs of a potential business opportunity, ask yourself the following questions. Use them for an annual check-up as well, to make sure that the business continues to meet your personal goals.

1. Does the business reflect my core values and what is truly important to me? Does it reflect my dreams?

2. Does the business allow me to spend enough time with my spouse and children? How will it affect my relationship with my partner?

3. When do I want to retire, and what is my exit plan at that point? Do I want to sell the business or scale back? What type of succession planning do I need to accomplish these goals?

4. What are my financial goals for the business? How much capital do I need to start and grow the company?

5. What are my personal financial goals, both now and in retirement, and can the business support them?

6. Do I have enough time for my friends? Time for my interests and hobbies?

7. Is my work fun?

8. Where do I want to live, and how does this opportunity fit with that plan?

9. Does the business allow me to maintain my health?

10. Does the business allow me to make a contribution to society and my community? Is this important to me?

Source: *Inc.:* The Magazine for Growing Companies by Staff. Copyright 2004 by Mansueto Ventures LLC. Reproduced with permission of Mansueto Ventures LLC in the format Textbook via Copyright Clearance Center.

AN ENTERPRISING WORLD

Breadwinners

How about a nice fresh loaf of bread, from the most famous bakery in Paris—without stepping on a plane? Thanks to the innovative thinking of the late Lionel Poilâne, you can order Poilâne Bakery's signature loaves or other select bakery products from its website (http://www.Poilâne.com) and have them delivered to your door via FedEx.

Lionel Poilâne began his baking career—albeit reluctantly—at age 14 as an apprentice at his father Pierre's bakery established in 1932. However, his vision went beyond "a bakery in which my horizon was an oven." Even as a young man, he wanted to "bring the world into my business." He turned the most humble of foods—bread—into a branded item that was the foundation for a £15 million business. At the same time he was building the bakery's reputation and expanding its business, he maintained Pierre's traditional baking techniques and ingredients. Poilâne's breads contain only natural ingredients—stone-ground flour, water, salt, and

natural starter (for leavening)—and are still baked by hand in wood-fired ovens. The result is not the typical French baguette but a large, hearty round loaf with dense texture that weighs about four pounds.

Lionel embraced a special creative philosophy that he termed "retro-innovation." "I'm neither a traditionalist nor a progressive: I try to create a culture using the best of tradition and the best of new technology," he said. He immersed himself in the history of bread, interviewing old French bakers to learn their techniques and refining his father's methods to produce old-fashioned, Norman-style dark bread based on an ancient regional recipe. Although the coarse bread had fallen into disfavor after World War II because of its association with deprivation, it became popular again in the 1970s.

As demand increased, Poilâne maintained quality by building a large, modern factory with 24 wood-fired ovens in the Paris suburbs rather than opening stores

(continued)

An Enterprising World (*continued*)

© Jacques Brinon/AP Photo

in multiple locations. He and his wife Irena, an interior architect, designed the building and its special clay and brick wood-fired ovens that replicate a 16th-century French design. True to his philosophy of retro-innovation, he was able to combine the local with the global, traditional methods and modern techniques. The bread is made by hand, but this modern eco-bakery uses solar power and burns waste wood in its ovens.

As the Poilâne Bakery's reputation spread, requests for his bread came from beyond Paris. He opened a bakery in London because it was close enough to visit on a day trip. To fulfill orders, he turned to FedEx for next-day delivery to stores, restaurants, and individuals in other countries. He also added other bakery products selectively—some other types of bread, brioches, tartelettes, pains au chocolat, and a special cookie—but preferred to focus on his basic loaf. "If you start to make

too many things, that's extension," he said. "My motto is, Do things with intention, not with extension."

Tragically, Lionel and Irena died in a helicopter crash on November 1, 2002. Immediately their daughter Apollonia, then just 18, took over the family business. She managed it from her dorm room at Harvard University until she graduated in 2007, traveling back to Paris every six weeks or so. "In my heart I always knew that I would take over the company and carry on the tradition," she says.

Today Poilâne produces about 7,000 loaves per day and ships about 20 percent of them to 40 countries. "The quantities may sound industrial, but the process is artisanal," says Apollonia, who has inherited her father's reverence for bread. "Bread is not just wheat, leaven, salt, and water; it is about language and culture, peace and revolution; its symbolism is central to literature and especially religion," she says. "For me, bread's relation to everyday life is what makes it thrilling."

Discussion Questions

1. What are the opportunities that Lionel Poilâne was able to discover and exploit? How can Apollonia build on this foundation?

2. What external factors led to the discovery and development of the opportunities pursued by Lionel Poilâne?

3. Why was Lionel Poilâne able to identify and pursue this opportunity while others were not?

4. What other types of businesses might be able to replicate the kinds of opportunities that Lionel Poilâne has been able to exploit?

Sources: Amanda Friedman, "Legendary Baker Poilâne Leaves Legacy of Passion for Bread," *Nation's Restaurant News*, January 13, 2003, p. 68; Tina Isaac, "Born Bread," *Evening Standard* (London, UK), June 16, 2006, p. 21; Gregory Katz, "Her Daily Bread," *American Way* magazine, July 15, 2005, p. 34; Paul Levy, "Obituary: Lionel Poilâne," *Independent* (London, UK), November 2, 2002, p. 22; John Lichfield, "Flour Power," *Independent* (London, UK), November 5, 2002, p. 4.5; Ron Lieber, "Give Us This Day Our Global Bread," *Fast Company*, February 2001, pp. 158+; Poilâne Bakery website http://www.Poilâne.com (April 25, 2008); and Alison Arnett, "Bread Is the Staff of Her Life," *Boston Globe*, January 17, 2007, http://www.boston.com.

6.5 ENTERPRISERS

S.C.R.U.B.S.

Sue Callaway, a nurse in the neonatal intensive care unit at Children's Hospital and Health Center in San Diego, was tired of wearing the same thing to work every day. Since she was a child, Callaway had loved sewing. So she made

herself scrubs from a pastel print. "Everyone wondered where I got them and wanted them, too," she recalls. She started Callaway Casuals in her bedroom, recruiting neighbors and friends to help make the scrubs.

At first, S.C.R.U.B.S—Simply Comfortable Really Unique Basic Scrubs—was a sideline for Callaway, who continued her nursing career. Within two years, however, she had 600 customers. As order volume grew, Sue's husband, Rocky Cook, convinced her to turn her hobby into a business. He introduced her to Steve Epstein, a businessman with apparel manufacturing experience. "She pulled all these little cute tops out of her bag, and I was fascinated by them," says Epstein. "I saw it and a little bell went off in my head and said, 'This is a good idea.'"

In 1992, Callaway, Epstein, and their spouses pooled savings and loans from family and friends to form S.C.R.U.B.S. in the Southern California town of Santee, near San Diego. S.C.R.U.B.S. grew from a home-based business to 150 employees who handle sales, customer service, and some manufacturing functions. Callaway outsourced the sewing to another small company just a few miles away.

Callaway's scrubs became popular very quickly because they are made of 100 percent cotton and come in unusual colors and prints. At one time, institutional scrubs came only in white, green, or pale blue, and contained polyester. With some imagination, Callaway changed the look and feel of clothing for millions of health care workers.

Epstein helped Callaway make the transition from essentially a one-person operation to a thriving corporation. With his industry experience, he had the vision to see the potential for a sizable business based on the large number of health care workers. Callaway first targeted RNs and then expanded to include other health care workers, from dentists to veterinarians and physicians. "Sue's scrubs are unique and fill a need for something fun in a somber business like health care," he says.

Callaway and Cook decided to partner with Epstein and his wife Ida. "We bring four different pieces to the puzzle," Cook explains. "Sue is, in her creative way and also her personable way, the driving force behind it all. Steve is the real business mind. He brought with him computer systems, fabric knowledge, and garment industry knowledge. Ida is a personnel specialist."

To finance the start-up, the two couples tapped personal resources. They borrowed from friends and family, maxed out all their credit cards, and even sold vehicles that were paid off and leased vehicles to get the cash.

Two events converged to make the timing perfect for Callaway's success. New research showed that germs are not transported on clothing but on the hands. Therefore, uniforms don't have to be laundered at extremely high temperatures, which would fade bright colors quickly. Second, with an eye to cost cutting, hospitals began to allow health care personnel to choose their own uniforms. For years, hospitals had provided scrubs, which purchasing agents bought in solid colors in a cheaper cotton-polyester blend, which had a longer life.

Nurses also wanted more stylish uniforms that fit their personalities and lightened the atmosphere in a hospital. "It's a very difficult job, very stressful," says Cook. "If you can lighten the mood, it helps, not only for the infants that they work with and their parents, but older adult patients as well. It really starts a conversation, changes their day."

S.C.R.U.B.S. began as a mail-order catalog business, which suited a product with a highly targeted audience. As it grew, Callaway hired Kathy Murphy, who had direct mail marketing expertise. "I know before I mail what my break-even is on the catalog, and the break-even takes into account the cost of producing the catalog and mailing it, the cost of fulfilling the order, the cost of the building that we're in, and everybody's salary," says Murphy. She has a pretty good idea of the expected order rate before she mails catalogs and uses that to determine the number of catalogs in a particular mailing. "If I think it's a really strong list, I might mail 10,000. If I'm trying something new, like creative teachers—you know, teachers who teach kindergarten kids how to paint. I think they would love our scrubs, but it's really not our core market—I might only mail 5,000."

A good mail-order company needs three elements to succeed: a unique product, a good price, and good customer service. S.C.R.U.B.S. has all three. "It has very sound fundamentals," says Epstein. "We are extremely quality conscious. We don't take any shortcuts when it comes to quality. We are very customer service conscious, to the excess probably. We provide guarantees to the customer that make the purchase totally non-risk to them." One of the frustrations for customers buying from a catalog is not knowing if they will like the product. To solve that problem, S.C.R.U.B.S. developed a mailing envelope that also serves as a postage paid return envelope. The customer writes "exchange" or "refund only," reseals it, and drops it in the mailbox.

"A really small business owner might say, 'I cannot afford to give my customers $3 worth of postage if they don't like this.' You have to look past that," Callaway explains. "That customer will order 10 times more in the year maybe, or in the lifetime. Then you've got a true customer and you will make money on the customer."

S.C.R.U.B.S. was a good idea at the perfect time from a person who knew she needed help to grow. And grow S.C.R.U.B.S. did—from 11,000 catalogs mailed to 18 million in five years. What's on the horizon? "Quite a bit larger company," says Epstein. While continuing to grow the catalog business, the company opened several retail stores to capture another market segment—those who prefer to walk in and try on the clothing before buying.

For Callaway, S.C.R.U.B.S. is not just about the money. One of her greatest joys is to walk into a hospital and have a nurse say to her, "I love my scrubs." Making people happy and bringing color into their lives bring her great satisfaction. "You have to choose something that you really love, that you really enjoy doing. You'll wake up thinking it, go to bed thinking it. You'll need to spend a lot of hours, long hours every day. But that won't matter, because you'll love doing it."

Adds Cook, "It's just not a business for us that started because, 'Wow, there's a niche, maybe we can make a buck.' It's more of a, 'Wow, there's a business where we might be able to do something that we enjoy, that's good for someone and that creates a living.'"

Note: Sometimes bigger is not better. Since this case was taped for the PBS series *Small Business School*, Sue and her partner opened too many retail stores too fast and found themselves in big trouble. S.C.R.U.B.S. was bought by SmartPractice in July of 2000 and has restructured; Sue is still involved.

Discussion Questions

1. What other kinds of business concepts might Sue Callaway have recognized as a nurse in a hospital?

2. Why did Sue Callaway recognize S.C.R.U.B.S. as an opportunity versus other possible opportunities? What roles did environment, experience, and mindfulness play?

3. What is the business concept for S.C.R.U.B.S.? Demonstrate how it meets the 4 Cs test.

4. What other business concepts might S.C.R.U.B.S. pursue?

5. Why would Callaway and Cook decide to take on a business partner? How might they have been able to pursue their vision for getting into business without a partner?

Sources: Adapted with permission from Small Business School, the series on PBS, and at http://SmallBusinessSchool.com; also based on Sherry Chiger, "S.C.R.U.B.S—Crossing the Catalog Retail Line," *Catalog Age*, January 1998; and at Carla Goodman, "Medical Garb With A Smile—S.C.R.U.B.S. Grows to $16 Million-a-Year Business," *Nation's Business*, May 1999, both downloaded from http://www.findarticles.com.

Summary

1. A business idea becomes an opportunity when an enterpriser recognizes that a particular situation includes the 4 Cs: customers, consideration, connection, and commitment. Each element is essential to business success.

2. Enterprisers pay more attention to their environment and devote substantially more effort to gathering information, both from reading business and general periodicals and meeting other people.

3. Opportunities come from a variety of sources. Previous work experiences and changes in the business environments are among the most popular sources. Because each enterpriser brings different skills and experiences to the situation, the business that results will provide a unique set of benefits to customers.

4. An enterpriser can start exploring a business opportunity with any one of the 4 Cs and then move on to the others. Developing the idea into a viable business concept is a creative process that involves answering these key questions: Does this story hold up? Does it make sense? Do the 4 Cs of the story fit together? The business concept grid helps enterprisers visualize the relationship among the 4 Cs. Even if the customer, consideration, and connection elements are present, the opportunity is not likely to succeed without commitment. An enterpriser must therefore choose an opportunity that matches his or her goals and interests.

5. Peter Drucker's "systematic innovation" is a useful approach to environmental analysis. He believes that innovation is not just luck but requires discipline and hard work: knowing, not just doing. Drucker identifies seven sources of opportunity: unexpected-occurrences, incongruities, process needs, changes in industry and market, demographic changes, changes in perception, and new knowledge.

6. Following trends is another good way to identify business-opportunities. Many magazines report on trends, including *Red Herring,* which focuses on technologically based trends. Futurist Peter Schwartz also reports on trends. Analyzing current trends such as an aging population, obesity as a health issue, the impact of biotechnology, and economic trends and finding ways to respond to the changes helps enterprisers discover problems that need solving.

7. Enterprisers are not necessarily more creative than other people. However, they are better at leveraging their experience (background and skills). Sometimes experience can be a disadvantage, because it makes it harder to recognize opportunities that fall outside the enterpriser's field of experience.

8. Enterprisers can increase mindfulness (a form of paying attention) by being open to novelty, varying the way they do things, looking for differences, and viewing situations from multiple perspectives.

9. Enterprisers can make their own luck when they are open to new experiences and different outcomes. They reframe experiences, and even failures, to learn from them.

10. Successful enterprisers evaluate the fit between an opportunity and their personal goals before proceeding. Talking to other entrepreneurs in a particular field provides needed information, as well as potential mentors, to determine how well a business concept works for you.

Review Questions

1. Differentiate between a business idea and an opportunity. When does a business idea become an opportunity?

2. What are the 4 Cs? Define each briefly and explain how it contributes to business success.

3. A friend tells you that successful enterprisers are just luckier than other people. Based on information in the chapter, tell your friend why you disagree.

4. What is a business concept? Suggest several ways to develop business concepts. How can you evaluate a potential business concept?

5. How does the business concept grid help an enterpriser use the 4 Cs and show the relationship between them?

6. What does Peter Drucker mean by-"systematic innovation?" What are his seven sources of opportunities, and how do they apply to environmental-analysis?

7. Why is trend analysis a good way to find business opportunities? Where can you learn about current trends?

8. Discuss the pros and cons of leveraging your experience to identify business opportunities. How does using your experience relate to the 4 Cs?

9. Explain how mindfulness helps to discover opportunities. What strategies can you use to improve mindfulness? Include some specific examples in your answers.

10. What characteristics make some people appear luckier than others? Describe several ways to increase your luck.

11. Identify several strategies to evaluate the fit between a business opportunity and the enterpriser's personal goals. Develop a list of questions that would help you analyze a new business you might wish to pursue.

Applying What You've Learned

1. Read three of the following articles from *Inc.*:

   - "Educating Octavia": http://www.inc.com/magazine/19890601/5677.html

   - "Cookie Monsters": http://www.inc.com/magazine/19890201/5528.html

   - "The Next Big Thing": http://www.inc.com/magazine/19900701/5242.html

   - "Made in the U.S.A.": http://www.inc.com/magazine/19890101/5492.html

   - "Seeing Red": http://www.inc.com/magazine/19890501/5636.html

Develop a spreadsheet that compares and contrasts the three start-up companies in the articles you selected across the following categories:

(a) *Search Process*—What kind of search process did each entrepreneur use to find the idea for this business?

(b) *Industry Experience*—Did the entrepreneurs in each case have industry experience similar to the opportunity they pursued?

(c) *Time*—How much time did it take each entrepreneur to develop the idea into a business?

(d) *Change*—Was there a significant change in the business opportunity over time?

2. Choose one of the companies you selected in Question 1 and answer the following questions based on the article and additional information you can find online:

(a) How important are previous industry and work experience to discovering opportunities?

(b) When are industry and work experience likely to be important? Why?

(c) What are the characteristics of industries where previous experience is less likely to be a factor in discovering opportunities?

(d) What seem to be the characteristics of industries that have good opportunities to pursue?

(e) What are the characteristics of a good opportunity?

(f) Are the characteristics of an opportunity idiosyncratic, that is, are the characteristics of an opportunity based on the unique characteristics of the entrepreneurs who might discover them? Are you likely to spot the same opportunities as your classmates? Why, why not?

3. Develop a business concept grid for either a business you would like to start or one of the three companies you chose in Question 1.

4. The following two articles provide different viewpoints about the opportunity recognition process.

- "Where Really Bad Ideas Come From": http://www.inc.com/magazine/19981015/1114.html

- "Where Great Ideas Come From": http://www.inc.com/magazine/19980401/908.html

After reading these articles, answer the following questions.

(a) How are the sources of "bad" ideas different from sources of "good" ideas?

(b) What makes a bad idea? How does this compare to a good idea?

(c) What are the characteristics of good opportunities?

5. Evaluate the personal fit of the business concept you chose for Question 3. Use the questions in Exhibit 6.5 and any others you need to determine how feasible it would be for you to pursue this opportunity. Share your findings with the class.

6. Networking is a primary activity for identifying and developing your own opportunities. You can accomplish a "small win" by contacting "strangers" (individuals with whom you have not have any previous personal contact) about aspects of entrepreneurship that will benefit you. Contact three strangers about any aspect of entrepreneurship that is of benefit to you. These strangers can be entrepreneurs; experts, customers, suppliers in an industry that interests you; and venture enablers such as accountants, lawyers, and investors.

(a) Keep a log of these strangers. Provide a name and contact information (address, phone number, email) for each stranger.

(b) How did you get the name of this stranger? Why did you contact this stranger?

(c) What benefits were you hoping to offer this stranger? What benefits were you hoping this stranger would offer you?

(d) What other contacts was this stranger able to offer you to help you achieve your goals?

Enterprisers on the Web

1. A primary resource for business ideas is the U.S. Patent Office. Perform a search for patents by word, choosing an area of interest to you such as *toys*. Using the first two URLs in the list below, compile a list of many different ideas, as well as the names and addresses of individuals who have patented these ideas. Then look at a few of the other suggested sites for more

ideas. After scanning these sites, consider what factors, besides the idea, will affect whether an opportunity can be developed into a successful-business.

- USPTO Web Patent Database: http://www. uspto.gov/patft/index.html
U.S. Patent Office database on patented inventions since 1976

- IBM Patent Search Database—The IBM Intellectual Property Network: http://www. patents.ibm.com/
A user-friendly process for exploring patents and ideas

- National Inventors Hall of Fame: http://www. invent.org/
Examples of successful inventors and assistance for finding and protecting ideas

- Inventor's Net: http://www.geocities.com/ CapeCanaveral/3861/
No-profit organization listing inventions as opportunities

- Institute of Inventors: http://members.aol.com/ mikinvent/
A United Kingdom site devoted to inventions that could be developed into businesses

2. Using several of the resources suggested in Entrepreneur.com's article, "Finding the Perfect Business Idea," http://www.entrepreneur.com/ article/0,4621,304276,00.html, pick three ideas that interest you. How well does each meet the 4 Cs test? Evaluate them for personal fit using the questions in Exhibit 6.5.

3. Using three of the sites listed in Exhibit 6.2, prepare a brief overview of current economic trends.

4. Visit the Red Herring website, http://www. redherring.com. What are the top trends for the current year, and how do they compare to the ones in the chapter? (Registration, if required, is free.)

End Notes

1. Paul Farris, with assistance from Richard R. Johnson, Lauren Killgallon, and Kimberly Lockhart, "Case Study: Online Grocery: How the Internet Is Changing the Grocery Industry" (Charlottesville, VA: University of Virginia Darden School Foundation, 2002).

2. "Peapod, Inc. Opens 6th Market," Peapod, Inc., press release, March 17, 2004, http://www.peapod.com, and material from the "About Peapod" section of the corporate website, http:// www.peapod.com (July 16, 2004).

3. Peter F. Drucker, Innovation and Entrepreneurship (New York: HarperCollins Publishers, 1985).

4. Ibid.

5. Hillary Johnson, "If at First You Don't Succeed," Inc., July 2003, p. 102.

6. Adapted from James Canton, The Extreme Future (New York: Dutton, 2006), p. 2; and "The Top Ten Trends of the Extreme Future," Global Futurist website, http://globalfuturist.com (January 3, 2006).

7. Discussion based on Scott Shane, "Prior Knowledge and the Discovery of Entrepreneurial Opportunities," Organization Science, July/August 2000, pp. 448–469.

8. Ellen J. Langer, The Power of Mindful Learning (Cambridge, MA: Perseus Publishing, 1997), p. 4.

9. Ibid.

10. Norm Brodsky, "The Path to the Top," Inc., February 2003, pp. 44–45.

11. Langer, The Power of Mindful Learning, p. 139.

Feasibility

1. Feasibility analysis involves determining whether a business concept will actually work—that is, make money or satisfy the goals and interests of the enterpriser. It starts with an analysis of four key areas of a business model: revenue sources, cost drivers and cost structure, investment size, and critical success factors. Analyses of your market and sales and distribution strategy will provide knowledge about your customers, competitors, suppliers, substitutes for your product/service, and barriers to entry. A value analysis identifies the specific benefits that your customers perceive as important to them and demonstrates how well your products meet these customer needs.

2. Probably the most important factor in determining whether a new enterprise can start and grow is the commitment of the individuals involved. As you develop a detailed description of your customers, competition, and industry, and the way in which your enterprise will operate, you must seriously consider whether this kind of business meets your personal needs and goals.

3. Finally, a feasibility analysis will help you broadly identify the capital (human, financial, and social) that you will need to start, operate, and grow your venture. Imagine all of the resources your business will need. This is taking a "grand tour" of your business. Often the easiest way to conduct a grand tour is to observe your competitors and make a detailed analysis of all financial, human, and social resources they seem to require to operate.

Suppose you major in Greek and Latin as an undergraduate, complete a law degree, and, after a few years in a law firm, discover you have some entrepreneurial interests. With some like-minded friends, you start a new mail-order catalog featuring high quality children's products. You don't have any knowledge or skills about this business, but you are willing to learn, you have plenty of determination to succeed, and you are willing to put as much work into the business as it requires. Your idea takes off, and you are so successful that one day, Robert Redford knocks on your door.

© UPI Photo/Monika Graff/Landov Media

In Chapter 7's case, we'll meet Harry Rosenthal, who developed Redford's business concept into the Sundance Catalog, a feasible business model that since 1989 has offered customers unique items that showcase and support the talents of American craftspeople.

7.0 Feasibility: Is This Project Doable?

Let's say that you were considering the following business concept: a delivery-only Mexican food business. Basically, you hope to become the Domino's Pizza of Mexican food. You know that there are many people who order pizza and Chinese food for delivery in your neighborhood, and a number of pizza and Chinese restaurants seem to be doing a brisk business in delivering food.

Is this concept worth pursuing? To answer this question, you will need to ask many more, among them:

- What do you have to know about your customers, their needs, and the business of preparing and delivering Mexican food?

- Might this concept be viable in other neighborhoods besides yours?

- What is the potential for this business?

- How much money do you think such a business might make?

Feasibility involves revising the business concept to test whether the business you are considering is "doable" and worth pursuing. The feasibility process is about answering the question, "Under what conditions will I go forward?" This process requires both discovery and adaptation: Will this business concept actually work? Will it make money, or satisfy the goals and interests of the enterpriser, and what aspects of the 4 Cs (customers, consideration, connection, commitment) must you change to improve the business concept and enhance success? We now add a fifth C to our analysis: capital. What are the capital resources—financial, human, and social—needed to make this business feasible? We'll discuss capital in greater detail later in this chapter.

It is important to realize that only under very rare circumstances does an enterpriser's initial business concept become the blueprint for the actual business. The entire process we describe in Chapters 6, 7, and 8 is extremely iterative. Enterprisers constantly change their original ideas as they gain more information through the concept development, feasibility, and business planning stages.

Appendix B provides a detailed framework to help you prepare a thorough feasibility study for your proposed business concept.

Feasibility   Process of revising the business concept to test whether a business is worth pursuing and under which conditions.

Business model   A plan that shows how all of the different major aspects of a business work together to generate a profit.

7.1 The Business Model: How Will This Concept Make Money?

Every business operates on a **business model** that describes how the major aspects of that business—customer, consideration, connection, commitment—work together to generate a profit. Business models focus on the decisions a company makes to determine whether a particular way of doing business is profitable. A particular business is worth pursuing if it makes money—that is, the cost of providing a service or product to a customer is less than the income the customer provides. Even then, there are situations where a business concept could be profitable, but the enterpriser decides the returns and rewards of engaging in that kind of business are insufficient to proceed.

Some businesses use the same business model, while others don't. This is really a key idea in the feasibility process. Enterprisers now begin to move from just considering their own business model, to thinking about how their business model could be successful vis-à-vis other businesses and about those other business models.

No single formula works for all businesses in an industry. For example, thousands of businesses sell personal computers. How can so many businesses successfully compete and survive? There are a number of different business models in the personal computer industry. Some manufacture and sell directly to the end-user, like Dell. Others sell through third-party retailers. Yet others focus on specific types of customers.

A computer business focusing on doctors' offices would have a different configuration of customers, considerations, connections, and commitments than a computer business that focused on home computer users, insurance agents, or small retail stores. A doctor's office has specialized needs, such as a billing system for various types of insurance companies, a patient tracking system, and a system for keeping track of medical supplies. The factors that contribute to the profitability of a business that sells computers to medical offices will be different from one that sells computers to home computer users. Understanding these differences shows how various businesses in the same industry can succeed and presents an important lesson for enterprisers: individuals can be successful in many different ways, even within the same industry.

© Icholakov/Dreamstime LLC

Understanding the Business Model

How do we determine the kind of business model for a proposed business? We do that through business model analysis. In developing a business concept, we begin to answer, very specifically, these three questions:

1. Who is the customer?

2. What does the customer want? (consideration)

3. How is this consideration going to be provided? (connection)

In developing a business model, we add a fourth question:

4. Can you make money doing this?

In developing a business model, the enterpriser works through a framework to consider how money is made for a particular concept considered. In the rest of the chapter, we demonstrate how one such framework can help an enterpriser analyze and refine a business model.[1]

Basically, we examine four key areas to determine how a business makes money:

- *Revenue sources:* All the revenue streams a particular business model will produce, and the source, size, significance, and growth potential of each.

- *Cost drivers:* The cost structure of a business model (fixed, variable, recurring, etc.), relative importance, and how it may change over time.

- *Investment size:* Amount and timing of investment to produce positive cash flow, including cash required for startup and working capital.

- *Critical success factors (CSFs):* Elements that have the greatest impact on the company's becoming profitable.

Let's look at each of these factors and the trade-offs they involve. Exhibit 7.1 (page 162) is a summary of the

questions an enterpriser should ask about each area to fully understand how it affects the business.

Revenue Sources

First, an enterpriser must consider where the many different sources of revenue from customers are coming from. These fall into four broad categories:

- *Single stream:* one main revenue source

- *Multiple streams:* significant revenues from several products or services

- *Interdependent:* Sale of related products to generate revenues from other products

- *Loss leader:* several revenue sources, but not all are equally profitable, and some may actually incur a loss while promoting sales of other, more profitable, items or services

Remember the concept grid in Chapter 6 involving selling candy at a movie theater (see page 139)? Let's use the movie theater as an example of how a business may have different sources of revenue (see Exhibit 7.2 on page 163).

Therefore, when you are thinking about the revenues your business concept will generate, you need to ask yourself these two questions:

1. What kinds of revenue streams will my business have?

2. If one is a loss leader revenue stream, how will other revenue streams cover the losses?

The second consideration centers on which of these revenue streams the business actually captures. Identifying all the various revenue streams in the business is developing a **revenue model** for the business. Businesses can generate revenue in five ways: subscription membership, volume- or unit-based pricing, advertising sales, licensing fees, and transaction fees.

Let's say that you were planning to open a DVD rental business in your local neighborhood. You will need to think about how quickly you will generate revenues and from what sources, including

Revenue model All the revenue streams a business will generate from sources such as subscriptions/memberships, volume- or unit-based pricing, advertising sales, licensing fees, and transaction fees.

exhibit
7.1

Key Questions for Business Model Analysis

Sources of Revenue

1. What kind of revenue stream does this model produce?

2. If a loss leader revenue stream, how will losses be covered by other revenue streams?

Revenue Model

1. Do I have a single or hybrid revenue model?

2. How quickly will revenues increase?

3. How long does it take to collect cash following a sale?

Cost Drivers

1. What are the cost drivers of the business model?

2. How much volume can be supported with the fixed cost base?

3. Are the primary cost drivers expected to change over time?

Cost Structure

1. What are the largest cost centers for the business model?

2. What is the relative size and importance of each cost center?

3. Do any of the cost centers deliver a strategic cost advantage?

Investment Size

1. What is the maximum financing the business needs, and when is the cash needed?

2. When does positive cash flow occur?

3. When will the company reach cash breakeven?

Critical Success Factors (CSFs)

1. What are the CSFs of this business model?

2. How do these affect revenues and costs and cash?

3. What happens if any of these CSFs change?

Source: The business model analysis presented in this chapter is based on a Harvard Business School teaching note: Richard G. Hammermesh, Paul W. Marshall, and Taz Pirmohamed, "Note on Business Model Analysis for the Entrepreneur" (Boston: Harvard Business School Pubhlishing, 2002).

- *Selling memberships:* This membership fee could be a one-time fee that gives customers the right to rent DVDs on an individual basis or a monthly membership fee that allows customers to rent an unlimited number of DVDs each month, which would then be your major revenue source.

- *Charging a rental fee per DVD (volume- or unit-based revenue stream):* The more DVDs that a customer rents, the more revenue you earn.

- *Selling ads:* You could offer free DVDs if customers were willing to watch DVDs that had ten minutes of advertising at the beginning. Advertisers could then pay your business a fee to place ads on your DVDs.

- *Licensing:* You could license your successful business model to other enterprisers.

- *Earning transaction fees:* You might set up an area where customers could sell used DVDs on a consignment basis and take a fee for each one sold.

exhibit
7.2

Revenue Sources for a Movie Theater

Category	Revenue Source
Single stream	Sale of movie tickets only.
Multiple streams	Sales of movie tickets, snacks; revenue from video game machines.
Interdependent	The multiple revenue streams are interdependent; if more people buy tickets, snack sales will be higher.
Loss leader	Paying 100 percent of ticket revenues to a movie studio during a movie's first two weeks because the revenues generated from selling snacks will make up for the expense of showing the movie; the movie is the loss leader.

When you are thinking about your business concept, ask yourself these three questions:

1. Do I have a single or hybrid revenue model?

2. How quickly will revenues increase?

3. How long does it take to collect cash following a sale?

Using the DVD store as an example, you would have a single revenue model if you generated revenues only from renting DVDs. You would have a hybrid model if you charged a membership fee to join and a rental fee for each DVD.

Internet-Based Revenue Models

The Internet and electronic commerce (e-commerce) have opened up new avenues for enterprisers to launch businesses and to expand existing businesses by providing additional revenue sources. At the same time, the Internet requires companies and even entire industries to rethink their business models. Just a decade ago, for example, most retailers operated with a very simple business model and limited revenue streams. They sold products to their customers at a physical location or through catalogs, with orders placed by mail or phone. As the Internet's popularity and sophistication grew, retailers created informational websites. Soon they recognized the power of bringing the store to the consumer electronically and developed merchant business models such as online storefronts, either to supplement traditional stores or as their primary sales channel. These models include the following:

- Virtual merchants, who sell a variety of goods and services from many different manufacturers only through the Internet (Amazon.com, Overstock.com).

- Catalog merchants, who reach customers through traditional media, such as a mail-order catalogue or telemarketing, and also have websites for online browsing and ordering (Avon, Lillian Vernon).

- Clicks-and-mortar companies, with both physical locations and a Web presence (Powells Books (powellsbooks.com), Macy's (macys.com), Target (target.com), etc.).

- Bit vendors who sell and distribute digitally based products, including software and music, through the Web (iTunes.com, eBooks.com, and Symantec).

- Direct merchants who sell the majority of the products they manufacture through the Internet (Dell Computer).

The ability to network with other retailers led to more revenue options and business models, such as paid advertising with clickable links to other sites and subscription models. General portal websites such as Yahoo.com, Google.com, and MySpace.com entice users to use their sites as their first stop on the Web. Advertisers who seek large numbers of Internet participants may pay the portal to post text- or graphical-based advertisements, either on the home page or on specialized pages such as Yahoo's Finance, Entertainment, Autos, or Travel pages. Classified ad sites such as Monster.com for job listings and Craigslist.com for a broad array of goods and services are just two of the many sites in this category. Subscription models provide information that users pay for on a monthly or annual basis. *The Wall Street Journal's* online edition, www.WSJ.com, is one of the most successful content subscription sites. Networking sites such as Classmates.com offer access to other individuals who share the same interests or experiences. It offers some free services, but others are available only to subscribers. This two-tiered approach is often used by financial sites as well. Affiliate models generate revenues through referral fees and commissions when a user clicks through to the affiliated merchant. For example, an online parenting community that has a book review section may establish an affiliate relationship with Barnes and Noble (www.bn.com) and will receive a percentage of all purchases made when members link to bn.com from the site.

More complex models emerged once these early models demonstrated their success. Companies can also choose from several different types of market-making (brokerage) and community models, as summarized in Exhibit 7.3. Community models generate revenue through advertising on their sites, user fees, or payments for specialized content.[2]

Companies also combine models. A merchant or subscription business may also incorporate the advertising model. The Power to the People box (page 166) describes how Threadless.com and its sister companies at skinnyCorp combine community and virtual merchant models.

As you will see in the next section, you will have a number of costs associated with starting your business that will need to be covered. Generating sales and collecting cash will therefore become very important in order to pay these expenses.

Cost Drivers and Cost Structure

Now that you understand the sources of revenue for your business, you must identify the costs of providing goods and services to the enterprise's customers. It is very important to recognize that the kinds of cost drivers and cost structures of the enterprise might not be directly linked to the revenue model of the business.

Fixed costs   Costs that do not vary with sales volume, such as rent.

Variable costs   Costs that vary directly and proportionally with sales such as raw materials and shipping costs.

Semi-variable costs   Costs that change, but not in direct relationship to sales volume.

Nonrecurring costs   Fixed costs that occur only once during the life of a business.

For example, the development of a computer game is a fixed cost, and the cost structures for the computer game are primarily payroll centered (paying programmers and designers to create the computer game) and facilities costs (the space/rent and computers to house these people and help them develop the game). There will also be minimal costs to print disks or deliver the game over the Internet. So in this business model, the majority of costs are fixed while the revenue model is likely to be volume based and therefore variable. Whether the company sells one game or ten million games, the costs are nearly the same. A game company, then, hopes to score big with a game that will sell millions of units. Once the company covers its fixed costs (reaches a breakeven point) nearly all additional revenues flow to the bottom line as profits.

A business can incur four types of costs:

- Fixed
- Semi-variable
- Variable
- Nonrecurring

Fixed costs are constant and not tied to the volume of goods or services produced. For example, if you were thinking of opening a restaurant, the fixed portion of your expenses would be the equipment and building. You would have these costs whether you served one customer or thousands. **Variable costs** change in relationship to your sales volume. In a restaurant, your variable costs would be the costs of the food and drink served. Every meal ordered would be composed of specific ingredients that you could specifically "cost out"—that is, you could determine the exact cost of the meat, vegetables, and other food products that go into that meal. **Semi-variable costs** change depending on certain levels of revenue generated. For example, the cost of a waiter in a restaurant is a semi-variable cost. Each waiter can serve only so many tables during a specific time period, so at times when the restaurant is crowded, such as noon to 2 PM, you would need more waiters. If you know that one waiter can handle 10 tables and your typical lunch crowd fills 12 tables, you would need two waiters, even though you have the capacity to serve 20 tables. **Nonrecurring costs** are often fixed costs that occur only once during the life of a business. For example, the purchase of your kitchen equipment—the stove, range, freezer, and cooler—is likely to be both a fixed cost and a nonrecurring cost.

exhibit
7.3

Second-Generation Web Revenue Sources

Business Model	Forms of Model Implementation	Description	Examples
Market-Making (Brokerage)			
	Auction	Website where sellers list products on which buyers place bids. Auction site host receives a fee from the seller once an auction has been completed.	eBay
	Marketplace exchange	Electronic exchanges for business to consumer (B2C) or business to business (B2B) markets that facilitate buying and selling. Exchange host receives a fee for facilitating these transactions.	Travelocity (B2C) offers flights, hotels, and rental cars from numerous vendors; ChemConnect (B2B) is an industry-based exchange.
	Buy/Sell fulfillment	Website that takes orders to buy or sell products at a specific price and receives a fee or commission from the seller for completing the transaction.	CarsDirect.com
	Demand fulfillment	Online matching site where buyers make a firm bid for a product or service. If a seller meets the buyer's price, the buyer is obligated to complete the transaction.	Priceline.com
	Virtual mall	Online hosting service for other merchants; host's revenue may come from site set-up, listing fees for products or services, and transaction fees for products and services sold.	
	Transaction broker	A third-party intermediary.	
Community			
	Social networks	Websites where users can meet others who might share some common interest.	Facebook.com, Myspace.com, Friendster.com
	Open source	Develops products or services (typically software) that other users may modify, enhance, and support.	Red Hat
	Open content	Based on community generated content, where users can modify current content that is posted.	Wikipedia
	Blogs	Web logs or online journals where individuals or companies post information; blogs that create substantial traffic sell advertisements or generate revenue through specific links to other sites.	TechCrunch.com (posts about new Internet products and companies); BeautyAddict.com (cosmetics); Gizmodo.com (cutting-edge consumer electronics and gadgets)

POWER TO THE PEOPLE

Threadless.com

Imagine a T-shirt company that in just six years generated estimated revenues of $25 million and profits of $7 million—without a design, sales, or marketing staff. You'd be describing Threadless.com, brainchild of Jake Nickell and Jacob DeHart. The "two Jakes," as they are often called, were studying design—Nickell at the Illinois Institute of Art in Chicago and DeHart at Purdue University—when they met at an Art Institute of Chicago design course in 1999. Both had submitted designs for a T-shirt competition, which Nickell won. Nickell then decided to try the idea out on a larger scale.

With each contributing $500, the pair launched Threadless.com. The premise was simple: people submit T-shirt designs for posting on the Threadless.com website (http://www.threadless.com). The community votes for a week, and Threadless produces the highest-scoring shirts and sells them at the site. "In the beginning, we wanted to create an outlet for designers," explains Nickell. "It turned into this great business, and now we've extended the model to ties, music, cocktails. … In 10 years, who knows where we might be?"

The idea caught on quickly, although for the first two years the founders took no salary and supported themselves with full-time jobs in Web development. Today Threadless has more than 400,000 registered users and is growing at about 20,000 new members each month. More than 150 designs pour in from around the world every day, with 90 chosen for the weekly contest. Community members vote on a one-to-five scale. The top five to seven designs become part of Threadless' inventory, with most shirts selling for about $15 to $17 each. Threadless orders print runs of 500 to 1,500 of each design from its screen-printing company. By year-end 2006, the company was selling about 80,000 shirts a month.

The winning designers receive a $1,500 cash award, plus $500 in Threadless merchandise credit. Customers who refer new buyers or send in pictures of themselves modeling Threadless shirts earn points toward store credit.

Threadless follows four basic rules. "We let the community create the content," explains DeHart. "We let the community build itself—no advertising. We let the community help with the business; we add features based on user feedback. And we reward members of the community for participating."

The high level of customer involvement is unique and keeps costs low, as does outsourcing the T-shirt production. Nickell and DeHart developed the company's order fulfillment software in-house. Profit margins run about 30 percent. "Most of the energy comes from how fast the product line is changing," says Nickell. "There's something for users to do every day—see which new designs are out, score the latest submissions, post a blog entry. It's just a very active community."

skinnyCorp currently employs about 20 people, mostly to fill orders. It operates on the basis that work should be fun, and the two Jakes are committed to the idea that having fun is more important than growth or maximizing profits. For example, they turned down offers from several major retailers to carry Threadless shirts. "We want to keep things simple and about the community," says Nickell.

Experts praise Nickell and DeHart. "It's a brilliant application of participatory culture," says Ted Byfield, associate chair of the communication, design, and technology department at Parsons. The New School for Design. Adds Harvard Business School professor Karim Lakhani, "They've recognized that knowledge and innovation reside outside the firm. People spend gazillions of dollars trying to figure out what demand is going to be. These guys have said, 'We're not even gonna try—let the community decide.'"

Threadless.com's success led the two Jakes to form a parent company, skinnyCorp, and experiment with other community-based concepts:

- 15 Megs of Fame: A music site where emerging underground musicians can post sound tracks. Visitors can listen to the music, download free audio clips, and post comments.

- Naked & Angry: Creates high quality clothing from fabric patterns submitted and chosen by the brand's audience.

- ExtraTasty: An interactive drink site with inventive bar recipes.

Another site, OMG Clothing, allowed people to submit just slogans rather than designs. It was recently merged into Threadless. In response to member demand, Threadless now offers a women's style shirt, children's sizes, sweatshirts, and hoodies for some designs.

In late 2006, skinnyCorp entered into a deal with Insight Partners, a venture capital firm, to provide funding for future expansion into other types of merchandise. However, the community remains fundamental to skinnyCorp's activities. "We don't make any moves without consulting the community."

Discussion Questions

1. Describe Threadless.com's unique business model. Why do you think it has been so successful and also profitable? Suggest other types of products that could use this model and some which could not use it effectively and explain why.

2. Who are the customers for Threadless.com? What are the benefits that different kinds of customers receive from Threadless.com? How does Threadless.com go about making money by providing these various benefits?

3. What are the cost drivers for Threadless.com and skinnyCorp? How do these cost drivers compare to a retail store selling T-shirts?

4. How has the commitment of the founders changed over the life of Threadless.com? Could the founders have predicted at the beginning of this venture how it would have evolved?

Sources: Based on Brandon Copple, "40 under 40 2006: Jake Nickell and Jacob DeHart," *Chicago Business*, October 18, 2006, http://www.chicagobusiness.com; Darren Dahl, "Nice Threads," *Southwest Airlines Spirit*, December 2006, p. 8694; Jeff Howe, "Amateurs Rank," *Print*, November/December 2006, pp. 298–300; skinnyCorp website, http://www.skinnycorp.com (December 22, 2006); Brad Spirrison, "skinnyCorp to Purchase New Threads with Venture Deal," *Chicago Sun-Times*, December 11, 2006, p. 60; and William C. Taylor, "To Charge Up Customers, Put Customers in Charge," *New York Times*, June 18, 2006. p. BU5 (L).

The *cost drivers*—anything that affects total costs—in your business model focus on the timing of those costs and the relationship of costs to changes in revenues. As with revenue streams, you must ask several key questions about the cost drivers of your business model:

1. What are the cost drivers of the business model?

2. How much volume can be supported with the fixed cost base?

3. Are the primary cost drivers expected to change over time?

The *cost structure* of your business model explores the kinds of costs your business might have. There are five broad categories of costs:

- *Direct:* Cost for individuals who are actually providing a service or producing a good for the customer.

- *Indirect (support):* Cost of individuals not directly involved in providing a good or service, but help the organization provide the service or goods.

- *Inventory:* Cost of material necessary to provide a good or service.

- *Space/Rent:* Costs to buy or rent facilities to house the business.

- *Marketing/Advertising:* Costs to attract, acquire, and retain customers.

A computer consultant working with a client or a worker on an automobile engine assembly line would be a direct cost. Members of the accounting, purchasing, and human resources departments in an organization are support costs. Steel would be an inventory cost in the manufacturing of an automobile body; pepperoni would be an inventory cost for a pizza restaurant. All businesses need a location and must make rent or mortgage payments. Some businesses, such as a restaurant, may need more space than a computer consulting business; the computer consultant might be able to operate the business out of her or his home or car. Finally, most businesses will incur marketing and advertising costs. For example, a mail-order catalog business is likely to have a significant cost for mailing catalogs and for advertising to bring the company's catalog to potential customers' attention.

Each business, then, will have a different cost structure. The three primary questions to ask about the business model for your concept are

1. What are the largest cost centers for the business model?

2. What is the relative size and importance of each cost center?

3. Do any of the cost centers deliver a strategic cost advantage?

Investment Size

Some enterprises need more resources than others. For example, the costs to build a 100-seat, sit-down, gourmet restaurant might be $5 million, while the cost to build a mobile hot dog stand might be less than $5,000. And that $5,000 hot dog stand might generate more profits (revenues minus costs) than the $5 million restaurant. Now you must make an estimate for the investment necessary to support your business concept and its configuration of customers, connections, and considerations. This requires asking the following three questions:

1. What is the maximum financing the business needs, and when is the cash needed?

2. When does positive cash flow occur?

3. When will the company reach cash breakeven?

For example, let's assume that the total investment to open the hot dog stand and operate it for six months is $8,000. You would first need to buy the stand for $5,000 and obtain needed permits and licenses to operate a food stand in the desired location. Then, you will have to purchase supplies such as a cash-box, paper goods, fuel for cooking, and inventory—hot dogs, buns, condiments, and beverages. You may want to print flyers to advertise your stand. And if you don't want to be tied to the stand during all the hours it is open, you will have to pay someone to staff the stand in your absence. Exhibit 7.4 summarizes the investment needs for this business venture and the timeline for the cash infusions.

At this point, you may not have the financial skills necessary to make accurate estimates of these costs. Don't worry. We will explore these issues in great detail in later chapters. For now, you should be aware of all the

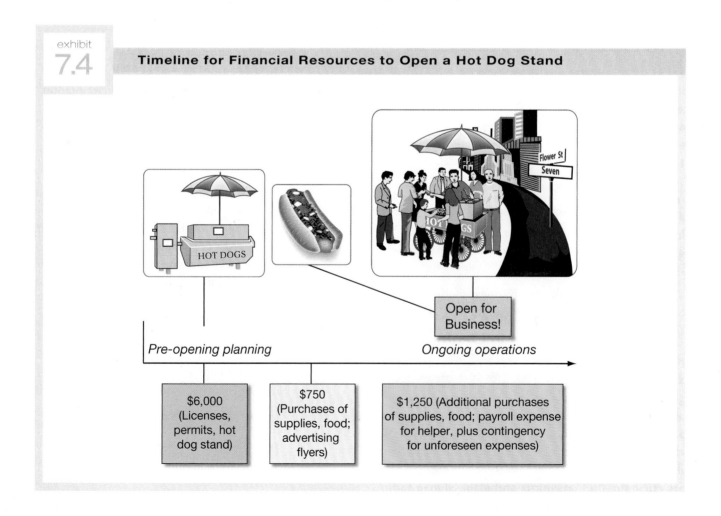

exhibit
7.4

Timeline for Financial Resources to Open a Hot Dog Stand

Pre-opening planning

Ongoing operations

Open for Business!

$6,000 (Licenses, permits, hot dog stand)

$750 (Purchases of supplies, food; advertising flyers)

$1,250 (Additional purchases of supplies, food; payroll expense for helper, plus contingency for unforeseen expenses) costs involved with providing your products or services to your customers. It is very important for you to explore how other enterprises develop estimates of their revenues, costs, and investment requirements.

Critical Success Factors

Critical success factors (CSFs) are operational functions or competencies that a company must have in order for it to be profitable. Each business will have a set of critical success factors that are necessary for the business to be successful. For instance, a CSF in a high-end restaurant is a chef who can create wonderful innovative and delicious dishes, night after night, and in peak demand situations like the dinner hours of 7 PM to 9 PM. A chef who can make wonderful meals may be unable to manage a kitchen staff of eight assistants who need to serve 50 such wonderful meals an hour. Without this ability to deliver all the meals patrons order, a high-end restaurant could not charge high prices and bring in enough customers to make the business work.

A critical success factor might also be a piece of equipment (a restaurant needs a fully-equipped kitchen), a location (successful gas stations are typically located on streets with a lot of traffic and easy in and out access), or special knowledge (a patent or knowledge about how to make a particular product). The three major questions to ask about your CSFs are:

1. What are the CSFs of this business model?

2. How do these affect revenues, costs, and cash?

3. What happens if any of these changes?

You shouldn't be discouraged if you can't provide answers to all of the questions posed in the business model analysis. The rest of this chapter and the next provide a framework for getting answers to these issues and for helping you begin to take the actions necessary to take your ideas and make them real—and profitable to you!

7.2 Customers: Market Analysis

Most enterprisers will be developing businesses in markets where an identifiable base of customers *and* competitors serving those customers already exists. Most new businesses offer new products and services to an established group of customers who have unmet or insufficiently met needs. Determining sales forecasts for markets and customers that don't yet exist is a quick way to create an unviable business. To survive, all businesses need *identifiable* customers who will buy their products. If your business depends on developing a base of customers over a long period of time, consider whether you will have sufficient resources to undertake this process.

In addition, all businesses have identifiable competitors. Therefore, another important component of a market analysis is understanding your competition. Once you know who your customers and competitors are, you can describe the characteristics of the market you wish to enter. Then, you should perform research using industry studies and interview industry experts who can validate forecasts for future changes in the growth of the market.

Who Will Buy?

Finding customers involves identifying specific individuals who require specific considerations through specific connections. The concept grid helps you answer a critical question: Under what conditions will customers buy?

You can learn about your customers in two ways: primary and secondary research. *Primary research* is what you learn first-hand from specific individuals such as potential and existing customers, experts who study your market, and suppliers and distributors to competitors in your market. The goal of primary research is understanding what will be necessary to sell to specific customers. Many individuals (potential customers) will often tell you that you have a good idea. What you want to discover from your primary research is whether they will *actually buy* from you. You want to get beyond compliments to contracts.

Secondary research is what you learn from others—for example, learning about your market and how your competitors already serve the customers you hope to attract. You can often find this type of information in articles and research materials at the library and on the Internet.

In testing for customers, you want to get individuals to engage in "phantom sales," to sign prospective purchase orders that indicate their willingness to buy if such a product or service was available to them. Many businesses are started because a potential customer was willing to give an enterpriser money up-front to develop a product or provide a service that the customer wanted.

Critical success factors (CSFs)   Operational functions or competencies that a company requires to be profitable.

How sure are you that customers will actually give you money for the product or service you want to provide? Ideally, they will give you money up-front, because they are committed to you and your business concept. An acceptable test is being able to answer the question, "How sure are you that customers will buy?"

Who Is Your Competition?

Individuals who plan to sell a new product or service often believe that they have no competition and that their new company will be wildly successful because no other competitor offers a similar product or service. WRONG! *All products and services have competition. All products and services have substitutes.* What entrepreneurs create are businesses that offer products and services that offer *advantages* over other competitors. It is rare that a business can create a product or service that customers will immediately purchase without comparing it to other products or services already on the market. If you cannot identify your competition or substitutes, you need to devote substantial efforts to this task.

The intellectual framework that many enterprisers have used for exploring the competitive dynamics of their industry is Michael E. Porter's *Competitive Strategy*, published in 1980 by the Free Press. This book uses information from industrial economics to specify a set of rules that govern whether a particular company can/will be successful in a particular industry. One of the primary tenets of this book is that the profitability of a business is often determined by the characteristics of its industry. For example, nearly all companies in the pharmaceutical industry are very profitable, while companies that are in industries such as farming and coal mining are less likely to be very profitable. What are some of the factors that determine whether an industry will be profitable? How might a business take advantage of the structure of its industry to develop a "sustainable competitive advantage?"

What Drives Industry Competition?

Porter describes five forces that drive industry competition: direct competitors, barriers to entry, substitute products/services, the power of suppliers, and the power of customers. These are shown in Exhibit 7.5.

exhibit
7.5
Five Forces of Industry Competition

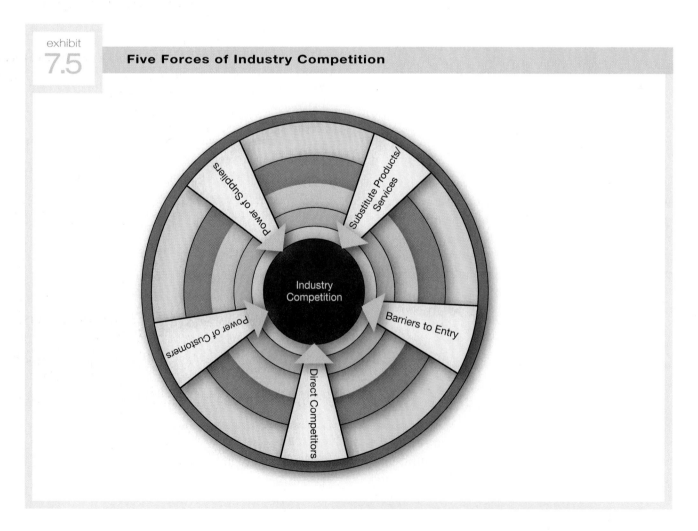

Your direct competitors are your *rivals*. The degree of rivalry in your industry varies. Industries that are more competitive (have lower overall profitability—i.e., lower margins) are likely to be composed of firms that have the following characteristics:

- Numerous or equally balanced competitors

- Slow industry growth

- High fixed costs

- Lack of differentiation or switching costs

- Capacity augmented in large increments

- Diverse competitors, where each company seems to be playing by different rules of the game

- High strategic stakes

- High exit barriers such as high fixed costs to exit, specialized assets, emotional barriers, government and social restrictions, and strategic interrelationships

Barriers to entry refers to ways to keep possible new competitors out of your industry. High barriers to entry should lead to high profits. As shown in Exhibit 7.5, barriers to entry might include economies of scale, product/service differentiation, capital requirements, switching costs, access to distribution channels, government policy, cost disadvantages independent of scale (such as proprietary technologies or products), location, and "the learning curve."

Substitute products or services perform the same function as the products/services in your industry. For example, a new boat, a ski vacation in Colorado, or a home computer might all be considered as substitutes for a home audio/video entertainment system; all provide a form of recreation. Substitute products/services can become a major factor in determining the profitability of an industry if the price/performance ratio changes between your product/services and the substitutes. For example, could airfares decline to the point where the costs of a ski vacation are substantially less than they are now? Could the cost of boats decline? How will the functions, price, and capabilities of home computers affect sales of home audio/video entertainment systems? If the value of your product/services is perceived to decline relative to other substitutes, your industry will become less profitable.

Customer power is the ability to drive prices lower, insist on higher quality and service, and create bidding wars among various competitors. Customers are powerful if:

- Purchases are perceived as "standard" or undifferentiated.

- There are few switching costs.

- If customers can integrate backward (do what you do, such as buy direct from the manufacturer or rep, and service and install the products themselves).

- If the industry's products/services are unimportant to the buyer.

Supplier power occurs if vendors can unilaterally raise prices or reduce quality. A supplier group is powerful if:

- The supplier group is more concentrated than the industry it sells to.

- It does not have to contend with other substitutes to sell to your industry.

- Your industry is not an important customer to them.

- The supplier's product is a critical input for the success of your industry.

- The supplier's products have switching costs.

- The supplier group can forward integrate (do what you do, set up their own retail stores).

At this point, the details of the dynamics of an industry can seem overwhelming. There are so many different industry considerations that can affect how a firm can be successful. Exhibit 7.6 shows all of the competitive forces that affect your purchase of this textbook. You may have purchased this book from the college bookstore. The bookstore was one of a number of competitors that had an opportunity to sell you this book. Maybe another bookstore around your campus sells textbooks. These bookstores are direct competitors of each other. They have a physical location for you to go and purchase books for your classes. They likely purchase books from a book wholesaler, or from the book manufacturer at the same discount. Their competitive advantage is likely to be their closeness to your college, so it is convenient for you to drop by their stores, and, their ability to get information from professors about what books will need to be ordered for upcoming classes. So the local college bookstores are likely to have the books you want at a convenient location for you to purchase.

Yet, you have alternatives to purchasing your books from the local bookstore. You could use the Internet and see whether you could purchase the book, perhaps at a lower price, from a company like Amazon.com, or you

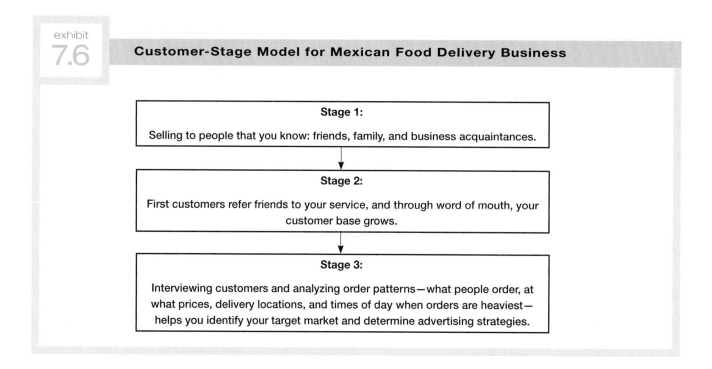

exhibit
7.6

Customer-Stage Model for Mexican Food Delivery Business

> **Stage 1:**
>
> Selling to people that you know: friends, family, and business acquaintances.

> **Stage 2:**
>
> First customers refer friends to your service, and through word of mouth, your customer base grows.

> **Stage 3:**
>
> Interviewing customers and analyzing order patterns—what people order, at what prices, delivery locations, and times of day when orders are heaviest—helps you identify your target market and determine advertising strategies.

could search eBay and see whether there were individuals who had your book for sale, or you could talk to your friends and find out whether there might be someone who took the class already and wanted to sell you the used book. Indeed, you can substitute any one of these options for the campus bookstore to obtain the book you need.

Now let's broaden our discussion to include all the textbook publishers who publish business books for the college market. You are likely to have many options for purchasing books on the topic of enterprise. One aspect of purchasing a college textbook is its selection by the professor. In doing so, the professor creates a monopoly for that particular book for his or her students.

As a supplier of textbooks, a textbook publisher would like to generate incentives to insure that college instructors are more likely to select and require its book for a class. The publisher might provide the teacher with additional materials (teaching manual, slides, Internet support, a help line, and other added value for students and teachers) that help to use the book more effectively. The costs to develop these additional materials can often be expensive, and the price of a new textbook can be very high to cover these costs.

Once students use a book for a class, they have the option of selling their used books to others. A textbook publisher would get no revenue from this sale to help cover the costs of developing ancillary materials that helped convince a professor to select the book for the course. This creates yet another dilemma for the publisher—over time, the number of used textbooks

increases, and sales of these used textbooks compete with sales of the manufacturer's new textbooks.

You can begin to see, then, how the competitive dynamics of book publishers, book distributors, bookstores, and book buyers can get complicated. These differences and dynamics are what create opportunities for enterprisers to pursue. For example, a number of new enterprises sell used textbooks on the Internet, thereby enabling buyers to avoid the price mark-up that a retail bookstore might require. Some enterprisers act as a clearing house for students who want to sell books, while others buy review copies of new textbooks from college professors and then sell these books to bookstores or online.

Enterprisers might also consider better ways to distribute and sell the information that textbooks provide. For example, an enterprise might sell "electronic textbooks" that students purchase and read online. These could be customized to follow a professor's syllabus by reordering chapters or only including those chapters that the instructor wishes to cover. Indeed, a textbook company might sell textbooks both as "hard copies," or as electronic versions.

While new entrants are always trying to spot opportunities to exploit an industry, it is likely that companies who are already players in that industry (your rivals, suppliers, customers, and substitutes for your specific products/services) are also thinking of new ways to meet their customer's needs. How, then, are you likely to compete?

Competitive Strategies

To have a competitive strategy, an enterpriser must find or create a position that he or she can defend and maintain. The primary measure of a successful competitive strategy is your company's ability to generate profits. Porter defines two basic generic competitive strategies:

1. *Low cost:* Sell the most for less (economies of scale) to become the industry's low cost producer. Strategies to achieve this objective require finding all possible cost advantages such as economies of scale, proprietary technology, and preferential access to raw materials.

2. *Differentiation:* Have a unique product/service customer niche that other companies will have difficulty duplicating or acquiring. Such uniqueness commands a higher price.

When you consider the college textbook industry, you can see how different businesses pursue these two different strategies of low cost (eBay, Amazon.com) or differentiation (your local bookstore). As you consider your business concept and model, you need to think about whether there will be enough customers for your enterprise to generate income to both pay expenses and provide you with some income, as well. Is the potential size of the market large enough for you to make the kind of profit that you would like?

For example, if you decided at the end of the semester to sell only your own used textbooks on eBay, the revenue you received would unlikely be enough to consider living on these proceeds. To expand the idea and begin an enterprise selling used college textbooks, you would need to consider where to get a supply of used books as well as where you might find potential buyers for these books, whether you could purchase enough books at a price lower than you could sell the books to others, *and* if you could cover all of the costs of coordinating this effort, mailing the books, keeping track of the process, and so forth.

The underlying issues that an entrepreneur must explore when considering market size and competition include such questions as:

- Is the market large enough (are there enough customers) for your business to earn the kind of profits to warrant investment?

- How are you different (better) than your competitors?

- What do you do better than other competitors?

- What will it take for a competitor to gain that same competitive advantage as your business?

An ability to thoroughly describe the characteristics of the industry that your company will be competing in, as well as the details about the competitors in this industry, will help convince others about the thoughtfulness and thoroughness of your preparation to start your company. Naïve entrepreneurs often underestimate the power of competitors and companies offering substitutes to change and adapt their products and services to meet the competitive threats of new entrants. They also underestimate the loyalty of customers to established companies, goods, and services.

One way to consider the value of conducting a thorough industry analysis is to view the descriptions of competitors and substitutes as background for celebrating the benefits of your company's products and services. The more detail you can provide about other products and services on the market, the more information you have available to make valid and insightful comparisons with your company's offerings.

Often entrepreneurs fail to admit that their competition is formidable and offers products and services that provide many benefits to customers. They should be honest when they describe their competitors and substitutes. Smart entrepreneurs recognize their competitors' strengths as well as weaknesses. An established company that has been in business for a while is doing something right. Understanding why your competitors are successful can help you generate a more effective competitive strategy for your company. For example, your firm may decide to target a different customer base or offer benefits that other companies cannot provide.

Once you have completed your market analysis, you should be able to analyze the business models of each competitor. How does each competitor specify customers, connections, and consideration? Where are the similarities between competitors and your business model? Where are the differences in each of the business concepts that competitors in the industry have, or don't?

7.3 Connections: Sales and Distribution Analysis

Now let's turn our focus in the feasibility process to "how:"

- How will specific customers be identified?

- How will specific customers be targeted?

- How will these customers be attracted to purchase products/services?

You must identify the specific activities the business will undertake to generate sales. To know whether your business concept is feasible, you should be able to "walk through" the entire process—from identifying customers to collecting the cash from the purchase to providing ongoing service (if the purchase requires it). Details, details, details! The success of the business will depend on how these details are executed.

Selling to Your Customers

A *stage model* is likely to be the most viable way for describing the activities involved in identifying, targeting, and attracting customers. The model for customer acquisition has three stages:

- Stage 1: How will you identify and sell to the first customer group?

- Stage 2: How do you identify and sell to the second and third customer groups?

- Stage 3: How will you use the information from Stages 1 and 2 to identify additional customers?

As customers accumulate, they will likely reflect a pattern of similar characteristics and emerge as a "target market." These specific target markets form the business's total market.

Exhibit 7.6 (page 172) shows possible stages for the Mexican food delivery business discussed at the beginning of the chapter.

Some specific details of the feasibility process involve making determinations about advertising and promotion. If sufficient effort has been undertaken in the section on identifying customers, you will have completed numerous personal interviews of potential customers. These interviews will provide you with the information you need to describe how they are alerted to new products and services and how they are likely to be reached through advertising and promotion. Some products and services will need to be sold through personal selling (e.g., medical supplies and pharmaceuticals), while other products might require an advertising campaign (e.g., groceries and soft drinks). Your customers will tell you how they buy.

Reaching Your Customers

It is also likely that the purchase process involves a channel of distribution from your business to a final customer. You will need to describe how the business's products and services will reach your final customer and how you will sell to each link in this distribution process:

- Can you sell directly to the end-user, or does your product/service require an intermediary, such as a wholesaler, or a value added reseller to reach your final customer?

- If your business sells directly, will you use an internal sales force or manufacturer's representatives?

- How will you hire, train, and reward your sales force?

- How will you select manufacturers' representatives or other kinds of intermediaries and provide them with sales support and training?

- What kinds of incentives will these intermediaries need to sell and service your products or services?

- How will you support these intermediaries to insure they can accomplish the sales goals your have specified?

As described in industry analysis, you will have already compiled detailed information on the pricing policies of your competitors (price, terms, credit policy, service, and warranty policies). This data will help you differentiate your business from others. In addition, you will be able to offer reasons why the industry prices products at certain levels and why the margins for certain products and services are as they are.

For businesses that are selling products to customers through a retail channel, you will describe the details of your merchandising strategy:

- How will products be sold in retail environments?

- Will the product require packaging?

- How will the product be displayed by retailers?

- What kinds of incentives might be required for retailers to actively sell your products?

Finally, you need to step back and look at the big picture. Be sure that the tactics involved in identifying and selling to customers make sense as a whole. For example, if you identify a certain customer type, are the methods for attracting these customers consistent with the places these customers purchase products and services? Do these customers require service and warranties that are covered in the price of the product offered?

The sales and distribution analysis of your feasibility study provides some of the strongest evidence about an entrepreneur's understanding of how the business will be successful. This section offers concrete information about the entire process of generating sales. Knowing that the possible market for a product/service may have a potential for sales in the millions of dollars is important, but showing how sales will specifically be achieved is critical.

Being able to demonstrate that you have detailed knowledge of the entire sales process is a significant undertaking. Yet, describing all of the details of identifying, targeting, attracting, and selling to customers insures that sales to customers will likely occur. An in-depth and comprehensive description of all of the details of the selling process is a significant indicator that the business will be viable and successful.

While we will cover marketing and selling in a later chapter of this book, an enterpriser who is developing a feasibility study must consider *how,* specifically, to sell the product or service to a particular customer. It is one thing to know that there is a market, but it is often difficult to get specific customers to purchase your products or services. Therefore, you should consider the specific process of selling to the customers you have identified in your feasibility study. Here are five parts to the selling process that you should consider:

1. *Contact:* Basically, there needs to be contact made between the buyer and the seller. A buyer receives a phone call, is greeted at the door to a restaurant, is asked: "Can I help you?" from a clerk at a store, etc. How will this contact between you and the customer occur?

2. *Identifying the need:* Why is the customer interested in buying? Ask open-ended questions to get to the buyers' sense of what they want—"What are the problems your restaurant is facing in terms of your produce needs?"

3. *Solution:* Given your needs, these are our products or services that can solve them.

4. *Benefits:* These are the benefits of the products and services we have that can meet your needs.

5. *Closing:* The buyer purchases your product or service by offering you an approval and a commitment to buy. "Can I wrap those jeans for you now?"

Your enterprise will be successful only if you can get customers to complete a purchase: You provide them with goods or services, and they provide you with money. Remember, a market, no matter how large, doesn't give you money. *Customers* pay for goods and services.

7.4 Consideration: Value Analysis

Why will individuals want to purchase your products or services? Why are they interested in buying from you? The answers to these questions involve *value analysis.* Many enterprisers start businesses based on their love of a product or service that they, themselves, would be interested in having or using. Indeed, many product ideas originate with the creator's personal need for that product. When Monica Ramirez, a former model and beauty pageant winner from Peru, couldn't find cosmetics from existing companies in tones that were appropriate for Hispanic women's skin tones, she started her own company. Zalia Cosmetics features products with more yellow and golden tones, rather than the pink-based formulations of mainstream cosmetics companies.[3] The first product of Brian Le Gette and Ron Wilson's company, 180°s, was an ear warmer that wrapped around the back of the head instead of the top. The idea came to Wilson as he was walking across his snowy college campus: What could keep his ears warm yet not have him looking like a dork? From there he and Le Gette developed other innovative products that they wanted to use, such as running gloves with a retractable windproof "hood" for cold weather use and sunglasses whose sidepieces pivot to prevent lens scratching and breakage.[4]

If everyone else is like you, and you came up with an idea for a new product or service, then it would be likely that everyone else would buy it. But we know that we are all different, that we all have different wants and needs. Enterprisers must identify those individuals who want what they have to offer. If those potential customers do not exist, then, the enterprisers must modify their products and services so that they can sell enough to make a profit.

In assessing the value of a business concept, ask three major questions:

1. What are the benefits that you will provide your customers?

2. What are the benefits that your competitors provide your customers?

3. What is the "value chain" between you and your customers?

Benefits

In general, there are three broad reasons that individuals buy something that they don't already have: it's better, faster, and/or cheaper. *Better* means that the product or service has benefits that other competitors don't offer. For example, mobile phone companies are always touting new features to attract customers, such as more minutes for your monthly fee, better service area coverage, better games and Internet access. Many customers want *faster*, that is, they want something *now*. For example, Barnes and Noble has a service that will deliver books to individuals the same day that they are ordered if they are in stock at a local store. That is fast. Software companies may offer product downloads, again providing immediate delivery.

Finally, if buyers are going to compare products or services and their benefits are nearly equal, most people will choose the cheaper offering. Enterprisers who can compete with other companies by selling the same products or services for less can be very successful. In fact, this is often the way that many enterprisers in services compete. An enterpriser often doesn't have the same level of expenses that a big corporation might have. Take consulting as an example. A big corporation would have to pay for an expensive suite of offices and lots of staff, whereas an enterpriser may operate from a home office and not have rent or staff costs. But the enterpriser's skills as a consultant could be better than what bigger companies offer, allowing the sole practitioner to compete on price and still earn a significant profit.

Another technique to evaluate the specific needs of a customer is to consider the customers biggest "pain." No one wants to be in pain; we want to avoid it. Customers who have a "pain" in their needs have a problem they want solved *now* and are likely to pay more to have this pain go away. Ask your potential customers, "What is your biggest pain? What keeps you awake at night? What do you need solved now?" Finding how to relieve their pains will provide a significant benefit to them—and help you develop more ideas to modify your products and services to generate sales.

While is it important to identify the specific needs of a customer, it is worth thinking about what these customers are likely to value. What lies behind the needs? What goals serve as the basis for those needs? Exhibit 7.7 lists a number of possible values that drive needs.

For example, some products don't sell because buyers have to change their ways of doing things. And, some products—Microsoft Word is one—continue to sell because people don't want to change the way they do things (inertia). They prefer to stick with products and services that might not really meet their needs. The cost of making the switch may be too high, as we discussed in the competition section earlier in the chapter.

© PhotoLink/Photodisc/Getty Images

Your Competitors' Benefits

How does your competition provide benefits to your customers? If you have identified the business concepts and business models of your competitors using the process suggested in the previous section of this chapter, you already have a good idea of the answers to this question. You know about the specific customers, connections, and considerations that each of your competitors is focused on. Now you can take this information and create a grid that identifies your potential competitors and describes how each competitor meets specific customer considerations. This grid provides insights on what kinds of benefits and features each customer considers important. You would do such a grid for each customer group that you think you might be pursuing.

For example, let's go back to the concept of delivering Mexican food. You would begin with a grid that would identify all of your possible competitors who deliver food, not just any direct competitors (those that deliver only Mexican food). You would list all of the pizza, Chinese, and Thai food delivery businesses, or any other restaurants that have delivery service in the first column. Exhibit 7.8 shows a partially completed competitive grid. Across the top of the row, identify what particular customers look for in making their purchases from these restaurants, such as timeliness (how fast it takes to get an order), price, food quality, menu variety, and customer service. As you interview customers who purchase delivered food in your prospective delivery area, you'd ask from whom do they order, and why, filling in the grid as you learn about each restaurant.

The competitive matrix can show you that buyers often buy from a variety of competitors, depending on their values at that particular moment. Sometimes a customer might want to buy on price and timeliness; at

exhibit
7.7

What Customers Value

1. Prosperity—People want to increase their wealth, so products or services that either save them money or help them make more money address this value.

2. Accomplishment—Can your product or service help people meet their goals and achieve what they want? For example, a service that helps a person learn a language is a service that enables people to accomplish something.

3. Security—Improves their sense that they won't come into any harm. Some people buy products because they fear if they don't, then they might not succeed. A salesperson could say "well your competitor has three of these machines" and a buyer might buy because to NOT have one of these machines could be a mistake.

4. Freedom—Increase one's options by purchasing something (e.g., often, a value associated with buying a car—the freedom of the road, cars allow you to get away).

5. Happiness—Ask the question, how could I make your life happier? It can lead to product or service ideas from your customers.

6. Pleasure—A product or service will enable people to have more fun.

7. Self-respect—Things that make people feel good about themselves.

8. Friendship—Often, purchasing over time occurs because relationships are developed between buyers and enterprisers. This may be a very important aspect of why some buyers buy from certain providers. We buy from people we like and who we think share mutual interests.

9. Understanding—We buy if we think the sellers are listening to our needs. Listening is the beginning of understanding. The most important aspect of selling a product or service, actually, is listening. What do my customers want from me?

10. Convenience—Some people will buy if the product or service makes their lives easier.

11. Consistency—People stay in a certain direction, and feel right about that direction.

12. Inclusion—People want to be liked by other people, and be part of the fashion "in crowd." Follow the latest trends in fashion—but don't forget to put away your Ugg Boots when stilettos heels replace them!

13. Excitement—Not being bored or doing something new is important for some buyers.

14. Getting what one thinks one deserves—Often, luxury products are sold because they appeal to the sense that buyers are purchasing something that they've earned, and because of their achievements, they now deserve a new watch, or jewelry, or a new car. Hotels are now marking this value. You deserve to get away and be pampered at our hotel!

15. Feeling important—We all want to be treated special. Restaurants where the host knows our name when we enter the door, or a bar that lets us past the velvet rope are all signs that we are important. In some ways, the VISA Signature card, which is being marketed now, is about feeling special and unique.

16. Knowledge—Things that help a buyer learn more.

other times, quality of the food and variety may be more important. You are trying to see where your concept will fit among all of the other competing business concepts. How similar are you on price, timeliness, quality, and variety? The competitive grid also shows whether you are too much of a significant outlier in the marketplace.

For example, if you decided that your Mexican food delivery service was going to offer delivery for $50 gourmet meals, your competitive matrix is likely to show that few, if any competitors are providing delivered food at that price point. Whether or not there is a market for meals in that category is a different question entirely!

exhibit
7.8

Competitive Benefit Grid

Restaurant	Timeliness	Price	Food Quality	Menu Variety	Customer Service
Domino's	Delivery in 30 minutes	$10–$25	Good	Pizza, soft drinks, chicken wings, bread sticks	Fast, takes credit cards
Pizza Hut			Good		Fast, takes credit cards
Papa John's			Good; Fresh ingredients		Fast, takes credit cards
Best Neighborhood Pizza	Delivery in 30–45 minutes				Cash only
New York Pizza			NY style pizza, good quality		
Tasty Thai	Delivery in 30–45 minutes				
Cheerful Chinese	Delivery in 25–45 minutes				
Sushi to Go	Delivery in 45–60 minutes	Minimum order for free delivery $15			
Taste of India	Delivery in 30–45 minutes				

The Value Chain

Every product or service begins with inputs that are processed and then delivered to a customer. How the product or service goes from inputs to the customer is its **value chain.** In a value chain analysis, one is looking for where the "value" is actually added to the product.

For example, let's say that you want to start a data systems company that develops and sells point-of-purchase sales terminals and the related computer inventory systems to small jewelry stores. The business concept for your enterprise centers on the jewelry stores' desire to manage their inventory better. They want to immediately see what jewelry items are selling, whether they should order more of the best sellers, and

to identify and mark down poorly selling items. The value chain for such your jewelry data system business would include such things as the cost of the computer components, software costs, installation, and debugging. The value chain for this project might look like the table in Exhibit 7.9.

With this information, we can identify the costs of the system and determine where the value is. As you can see, the value chain for selling a computer inventory system has most of the value added in the installation and debugging of the system. Many businesses look similar to the above example, particularly in services. Often, a company might price hardware and software, initially, at close to their costs, knowing that they will make their money by providing installation and services later on.

Another example might be in automobile sales and services. An automobile dealer might sell a car at "cost" and not generate much revenue in the value chain by selling

Value chain   The process by which a product or service moves from inputs to the final customer.

ENTERPRISE

exhibit
7.9

Value Chain for Jewelry Data Systems

Item	Cost	You Charge	Value Added
Hardware	$5,000	$6,000	$1,000
Software Costs	$10,000	$12,000	$2,000
Installation and Debugging	$5,000	$17,000	$12,000
TOTAL	$20,000	$35,000	$15,000

the car. Instead, the dealer may make money servicing the car, especially if the car can only be under warranty if it is serviced where it is sold. This strategy might not work if a customer could still keep the car under warranty and go to a dealer that has lower service and repair costs.

Mapping out the value chain provides you with insights into your costs and where the biggest spreads are between costs and revenues. It is at these points that enterprisers can often find opportunities to pursue. You should also develop a map for your competitors.

Certainly, one of the best examples of how this has occurred in many industries has been using the Internet to sell directly to customers without the use of middlemen such as wholesalers and retailers. For example, if Amazon sells books directly to customers in the value chain, then, the retailer markup, which is typically 40 percent of the wholesale cost of the book, goes to Amazon rather than through the value chain of the retailer. Amazon can keep this value added (if it sells books at the retail listed price), or provide books at a lower price and split the value between itself and its customers.

In computers and computer software, it seems that most of the value added has been in the computer chip (Intel) or in the computer software (Microsoft), and less in other components of the system (disk drives, the case, or other parts of the hardware).

7.5 Commitment: Personal Analysis

Now that we have analyzed the customers, consideration, and connections, we turn to the fourth C, commitment. Are you sure YOU want to pursue this business concept? An enterpriser might have a great business concept, but

developing that concept into a viable business may not be an enjoyable prospect for that particular person. Or perhaps the concept calls for specific talents and skills.

For example, an enterpriser might come up with a business concept that requires efforts at direct sales and significant amounts of cold calling on customers to generate sales. Cold-calling and talking to people might not be significant strengths of the enterpriser. In this case, the enterpriser has two options: choose not to pursue the concept or find people with these strengths to participate in the business.

Talking It Up

The best way to learn about the personal commitment required to start and run a particular type of business is to talk to entrepreneurs who are already in your chosen industry. Asking them lots of questions about the business you are considering will reveal key information about their lifestyle. Only then can you see how well your proposed business venture fits with your personal goals.

For example, if you want to spend time with family and friends and find that the enterprisers in the business you enjoy spend 18 hours a day, 7 days a week at work, it is unlikely you'll have sufficient time for friends and family. You will have to decide if you want to make this trade-off.

Please note that the startup of a business, and the effort that the startup of a business takes, may require substantially more time at the beginning, than as the business matures. Make sure to ask other enterprisers how much time it took them to start their businesses versus how much time it currently takes to operate and manage their businesses. Then ask yourself if you are willing to devote the necessary time for each phase.

You could have a very good idea but not be willing to dedicate enough time to implement it. Some businesses are easy to start and hard to operate (many restaurants are this way), and many businesses, such as technology companies, are hard to start but easier to operate.

Signature Strengths

In the book *Authentic Happiness* and at his website (http://www.authentichappiness.com), Martin Seligman suggests that you will be happier if your work revolves around your signature strengths. A **signature strength** is one that you are more likely to use frequently. It makes you feel good when you use it, and so you want to discover ways to use this strength even more often. Some examples of signature strengths are curiosity/interest in the world, love of learning, integrity/genuineness/honesty, and perseverance/industry/diligence.

To know whether a strength is a signature strength, ask yourself, "When I use this strength, does it invigorate me or not?" If this activity provides you with more joy and enthusiasm, then it is likely to be one of your signature strengths. Take the time to identify your personal signature strengths and consider them when you evaluate a particular business concept. If the business does not help you focus on your signature strengths, you are less likely to be happy pursuing that activity. You can go to the Authentic Happiness website (http://www. authentichappiness.sas.upenn.edu) to learn more about signature strengths.

Signature strength   A strength that you are more likely to use frequently, feel good about using, and want to use more often.

Answering Tough Questions

As you evaluate a business concept from the perspective of personal commitment, ask yourself the following questions:

- Do you have the talents for the business or know where to find people who do?

- What are your aspirations and how well does this business fit them?

- Where do you see this business in five years, and can you picture yourself running it?

- Do the activities and time commitment required for your proposed enterprise match the kind of lifestyle that you want?

These questions seem simple to answer, but when you begin to write down your responses, you may find that your personal goals and aspirations will not likely be an exact fit with the needs and requirements of starting and running the enterprise you've mapped out in the feasibility study. As you have more information about your intended enterprise, ask yourself, "Is this really what I want to do?" If you find that with each hour and day you devote to your enterprise that you find less and less enjoyment from it, you should seriously consider doing something else, or working to modify your business concept and business model to design an enterprise that will meet your needs.

We are sure you have heard the expression, "If there is a will, there is a way." The development of an enterprise will invariably have days of successes and disappointments, and days when you will need to adapt and change because what you thought would work doesn't. Enterprisers who really love what they are doing will have the enthusiasm and energy to push through the many difficulties that will occur in the startup process.

7.6 ENTERPRISERS

Bringing Home the Sundance Concept

When you hear the name "Sundance," you probably think first of Robert Redford's independent film festival. But Sundance is also a 6,000 acre site in the Provo Canyon area of Utah that Redford bought to protect it and also to provide a place for artists to develop their craft. Redford funded his enterprise with earnings from one of his first big hits, *Butch Cassidy and the Sundance Kid.* Because Redford couldn't get a loan from a bank, he found inves-tors who shared his vision. What started 30 years ago is today a premier place to visit, a venue for filmmakers, and a mail-order catalog company.

Redford brought Harry Rosenthal, CEO of the catalog, into the organization because of Rosenthal's success in his own catalog business. As Rosenthal tells it, he was an unlikely entrepreneur. "[At college] I majored in Greek and Latin literature, perfect background for mail order," he says jokingly. "It's so perfect that I went to law school. There's not a lot else you can do with a

Greek and Latin major." After a few years as a lawyer, he and some friends who shared his entrepreneurial spirit started a mail-order catalog called Right Start, featuring high quality products and educational toys for babies and young children. "We all quit our jobs, knocked on doors, raised money," he says. "We thought that we had the range of skills necessary to start up and succeed at a business that we knew nothing about."

In fact, they succeeded in the mail order business in spite of their lack of knowledge. They found that their skills were not as applicable as they'd anticipated. Rather, their success was based on the ability to work very hard, react very quickly, and fly by the seat of their pants. "The first thing you learn, I think, when you start a new business in an area where you're inexperienced is that you really don't know anything," says Rosenthal. "The sooner you learn that, the faster you begin succeeding. It's when you think you know things that you don't know that you run into trouble."

Once Right Start was on the road to success, Rosenthal left the company to pursue other opportunities. A mutual acquaintance who was Robert Redford's lawyer knew that Sundance was considering adding a mail-order catalog and brought Rosenthal and Sundance together. He was skeptical at first about the Sundance team's concept and discouraged them. However, Sundance was persistent and asked Rosenthal to consult and write a business plan. He agreed after clarifying that Sundance understood what the business entailed. He also recommended that they have someone on the startup team who was passionate about the business: "Someone who is going to get up in the morning and go to bed at night living and breathing that business. It helps if that person has experience, but it's more important, in a lot of cases, to have the drive and the dedication." Rosenthal offered to use his industry contacts to help Sundance find such a person but had no interest in filling that role himself.

Pleased with Rosenthal's business plan, in 1989 Sundance formed the catalog company, obtained financing, and then asked Rosenthal to head the company. After carefully considering the attractive business opportunity and the lifestyle changes, it would entail to move him and his family from Southern California to Utah, he decided to join Sundance.

While both Right Start and Sundance were new catalog companies, there was a major difference: Sundance already had name recognition and the Robert Redford connection. "Redford stands for many things— support of the environment, support of the arts—that are meaningful to people in America," explains Rosenthal. This name recognition made it easier for the made it easier for the Sundance Catalog to become profitable. "Most catalog companies take four to five years to begin turning a profit," says Rosenthal. "We did it much faster than that." One reason was the merchandising expertise of Brent Beck, who was running Sundance's very successful General Store. The store's offerings reflected the Sundance area and appealed to the vacationers who stayed at the lodge. When they wore their apparel purchases at home, friends wanted to buy similar items and began calling the store to request mail orders. The Sundance Catalog filled that need very well—and also provided a means for Redford to fund the artistic and environmental disciplines that he supports.

What makes the catalog's products so marketable? All the items convey the special sense of Sundance, blending environmental responsibility, creativity, craftsmanship, support of the arts, and responsible business. "That's what Bob [Redford] lives for, what he's passionate about, and so that's the vision of this catalog," says Beck. Many items are unique and created by local artisans such as scented glass objects and sculptures based on scrap iron. Textures are important. The products reflect their Western heritage and the Sundance lifestyle.

Sundance had a big advantage in Redford's fame, but that only goes so far. In the catalog business, repeat purchases by customers are the key to profitability and success. "A spokesperson, a famous name, or a famous brand gets people to try your product or service once," says Rosenthal. "If you deliver a good quality product or service at a good price and people are satisfied with the experience they have, then they will come back. If they don't have a good experience, you won't have a successful business." In addition, Sundance tries to exceed, not just meet, customer expectations and involves customers with the community's goals—protection of the environment, the promotion of the arts—so that they feel that they are making a contribution with each purchase. This sets Sundance apart from other catalog companies. "If you're thinking of starting up anything from a corner drugstore to a software company, somebody else has tried it at least in some way; maybe not exactly the idea that you have, but in some way," says Rosenthal.

He offers prospective enterprisers the following advice: First, learn about the business—the target market, competition, and business operations. "Think about what people are doing that is similar to what you're doing, and find out all you can about them," he says.

"Find out how they make their money, what works and what doesn't work." "Step number two," he says, "is to prepare a rigorous business plan that spells out capital needs." "Most businesses start out undercapitalized," he says.

"Optimism rules among entrepreneurs," Rosenthal warns. "Whatever it is, it's going to take longer and it's going to cost more. So be really rigorous in your business plan. Figure out how much capital you're really going to need, then add to it. And usually the early years of a company involve losses."

Next, be prepared for what Rosenthal says might be "five years of the most abject misery" before you succeed. If your capital runs out, you could have a few really rough years before you finally turn the corner. "Don't get discouraged," he says. "When you're new at something, you make mistakes. You'll think, 'How did I ever get into this? When am I going to come out? When is it finally going to turn the corner?' Most new businesses go through that. It's better to understand that you have problems to overcome than to live in a fool's paradise and wake up one day with a train wreck."

In the long run, the Sundance catalog's success was built on the quality products it carried—unique items that celebrate American crafts. Its product lines now include apparel, accessories, home décor, furniture, and gift items. Robert Redford continues to write a special message for each edition of the company's catalogs, and customers can also buy from the company's website. In June 2007, the Salt Lake City-based lifestyle retailer opened a flagship retail store in Denver, Colorado, and announced a national expansion plan to open another 20 stores though 2011. "I couldn't be more pleased that this venture will go beyond residing online and in catalogs and now make a home for itself in communities," said Redford.

Note: In 2004, Robert Redford and Bruce Willard, who was CEO of the Sundance Catalog at that time, sold the profitable company to two private equity firms. Redford retained a minority share.

Discussion Questions

1. What is the business concept for the Sundance catalog?

2. Discuss the business model for the Sundance catalog, including customers, revenue sources, cost drivers and cost structure, investment size, and critical success factors using the questions in Exhibit 7.1 (page 162).

3. Outline a plan to guide Rosenthal's analysis of the market for the Sundance catalog, using Exhibit 7.5 (page 170) as a guide.

4. Prepare a competitive benefit grid for Rosenthal to use in his value analysis. How does Sundance plan to differentiate itself from its competitors?

5. How does Rosenthal's advice to Sundance and then to enterprisers in general relate to the 5 Cs?

6. Go to the Sundance catalog site, http://www.sundancecatalog.com. How well has Sundance realized its business concept? What contributes to its feasibility?

Sources: Adapted with permission from the transcript of the show "More than a Catalog," Small Business School, the series on PBS, and at http://SmallBusinessSchool.com; Paul Miller, "Sundance Catalog Sold," *Multichannel Merchant,* July 9, 2004, http://multichannelmerchant.com; "The Sundance Catalog Story" and "Sundance Community," Sundance Catalog website, http://www.sundancecatalog.com (February 28, 2006); and "Sundance Catalog Flagship Retail Store Opens for Business in Denver," *PR Newswire,* June 20, 2007, http://www.prnewswire.com.

7.7   Capital: The Fifth C

The final part of the feasibility process involves identifying all the resources that you will need in order to make your enterprise a reality. We call this the fifth C—Capital. Every enterprise consists of three different kinds of capital:

- *Human capital:* Your expertise, your knowledge, and the expertise and knowledge of your partners and employees.

- *Financial capital:* The specific resources, such as land, building, equipment, machines, desks, supplies, and inventory necessary to start and operate the business.

- *Social capital:* The network of relationships that you and your enterprise need for the business to succeed.

In accounting, there is a concept called *good will* that puts a value on the intangible elements of the business. These intangible parts of the business often consist of such social capital as the reputation the business has developed with customers and suppliers, the value of a strong brand, the network of advisors the business has created, the use of helpful suppliers that may be willing to extend the business longer credit terms, and buyers that provide helpful suggestions for improving your products and services. Often the inclusion of these intangibles will give a business a significantly higher value than the financial resources of the business would suggest.

The key questions to ask as you begin to examine your capital requirements are:

- What financial, human, and social capital do I need to provide customers with the considerations I've identified?

- When will these capital requirements be needed?

The Grand Tour

To answer these questions, you need to take a "grand tour" through your business concept and literally or figuratively walk around your business. As you identify everything that has to happen for the business to become real and when it has to happen, you will also discover all of the financial, human, and social requirements of your business.

Let's take, as an example, the printed T-shirt business. Your business concept involves silk-screening T-shirts and selling them at special events. In the imaginary tour, you will think about everything that your T-shirt business requires to operate. Exhibit 7.10 presents some key questions you'd want to answer.

---

exhibit 7.10

"Grand Tour" Questions for a T-Shirt Business

Human Capital:

What knowledge and skills do you bring, and what do you need to find in partners/employees?

Who will design your shirts?

How many employees will you need?

What skills should these employees have?

Who will handle the marketing, sales, financial management, and operation (management of the making of the T-shirts), as well as distribution of the T-shirts?

Social Capital:

Who are your customers?

How will you contact them (mail, personal contacts, door to door, on the phone, etc.)?

Once contacted, how long will it take to make a sale?

Who are the best suppliers?

What relationships do you already have with potential investors, customers and vendors?

How can you leverage these relationships?

Financial Capital:

Where will your facility be located?

What kind of equipment do you need to silk screen T-shirts (a printer, drying racks, boxes for the shirts)?

Where will you purchase your T-shirts, inks, and stencils?

How much will supplies, equipment, rent, utilities, labor for help, etc., cost you?

When will you need all of these items?

What sources of financing do you already have?

How much additional funding do you need?

Enterprisers can be creative in looking for ways to cut down on the specific costs for getting into business. (We will return to this later in the financing chapter of this book.) For example, in the T-shirt business, you might find that a silkscreen machine might cost $1,000, but that you could buy one used for $500, or you could rent someone else's machine for $1 per shirt.

You can learn nearly everything you need to know about how to start and successfully operate your enterprise from someone else. You need to find mentors, experts, customers, suppliers, and even competitors who can help teach you. Your competitors are actually the best place to start acquiring information about the capital needs of your business. A good way to find enterprisers who might be willing to help you is to go to another city or state where your contacts (enterprisers) won't be in direct competition to you. What kinds of resources do your competitors use to operate their businesses? How big are their facilities, what kinds of equipment do they have, how many people do they employ and at what levels or expertise, and how much are employees paid?

For example, if your concept is to start a restaurant, go in and be a customer, and watch everything that is happening. How many people are working? How were you greeted? How many tables does the restaurant have for the number of workers? What is the quality of the dishes and silverware? What is the look and quality of the menus? How big is the restaurant, how big is the kitchen? How many chefs and cooks are in the kitchen? Pay attention to everything you see. Everything you note becomes part of the information you need to complete your "grand tour" of your potential enterprise.

A trade show is another excellent resource to include as you identify your capital requirements. Attending a show in your industry provides the opportunity to see what large numbers of potential competitors are doing, the products your suppliers are likely to provide, and to meet many buyers of the products and services you might be offering.

Your goal at this stage in the feasibility process is to develop a preliminary estimate of all the possible costs of doing business. This includes more than the obvious financial costs, such as equipment and rent, but also the social and human costs of operating the business.

Your restaurant will need a talented chef. Your T-shirt business calls for a creative designer. Perhaps your enterprise requires computer experts with PhDs. You have to be able to evaluate how good your experts are at their jobs regardless of the type of specialized skills they have. If your customers are CEOs of Fortune 500 companies, you'll need to know how to gain access to these individuals to make sales.

How do you develop social capital? Make it a habit to contact at least one person every day who can help you learn more about being a successful enterpriser. We call this the "one-a-day" rule. You will build a contact list of people who might help you learn. As you call individuals on that list who will offer you some important insights about your enterprise, you can ask for names of others who might help you. For every person you contact, think about how you might be able to help the person in return or think about how you might help some other enterpriser. As you ask others for advice and assistance, you must also return the favors to other enterprisers.

Taking Stock

With this final process of identifying resources, we've gathered enough information to really begin to answer the primary feasibility question we posed at the beginning of the chapter: Under what conditions would you go forward with this enterprise?

Review what you have discovered thus far about your customers, competitors, the industry, how your enterprise will operate, the requirements the enterprise will make on you (your commitment), and the resources you will need to start and operate your enterprise over time. You should have a good sense of whether making the commitment to take the next steps and actually start your business is the right decision—or not.

You might, at this point, realize that your business concept and model isn't as feasible as you originally thought. First, congratulations! Feel good that you aren't going to invest more time, effort, and resources in something that won't work. Second, you might take the information you've gained at this point and consider how to reconfigure this business concept and model so that it might be feasible.

An important characteristic of success in the feasibility process is an ability to change and adapt your business concept and model to incorporate the new information you learn. Your customers and competitors can give you many clues about what kinds of changes might be needed to make your enterprise feasible. There is no shame in abandoning a business concept that you find unfeasible. Plenty of other opportunities await you. The time and effort you have put into the feasibility process has improved your skills at learning from customers, exploring the strengths and weaknesses of your competitors, and finding experts and mentors to help you succeed. As we talked about in Chapter 4, stopping effort on an idea that won't work gives you the time to pursue ideas that will.

Summary

1. The feasibility process involves testing the business concept to determine whether the business is worth pursuing, both in terms of making a profit and satisfying the enterpriser's personal goals. After completing an analysis, an enterpriser should know the conditions required to move ahead with the business. Discovery and adaptation are essential components of feasibility, because the enterpriser must adapt aspects of the 5 Cs—customers, consideration, connection, commitment, and capital—to improve the business concept. Enterprisers constantly change their original ideas as they gain more information through the concept development, feasibility, and business planning stages.

2. The business model focuses on the decisions a company makes to determine whether a particular way of doing business is profitable. No single formula works for all businesses, even those within the same industry. Business model analysis examines four areas to determine the profit potential of a business concept: revenue sources, cost drivers, investment size, and critical success factors.

3. Enterprisers must identify the many different revenue sources for a particular business model, such as single streams, multiple streams from several products or services, interdependent (related) streams, and loss leaders. Revenues can be generated by subscription memberships, volume- or unit-based pricing, advertising sales, licensing fees, or transaction fees. The Internet has created additional types of revenue models, including several Web-based online merchant, advertising, and subscription models. Market-making (brokerage) and community models have become popular as the Web has developed.

4. Once enterprisers understand the revenue sources for a business concept, they can determine the costs associated with it—for example, fixed, variable, and recurring costs—their relative importance, and how the cost mix may change over time. Cost drivers affect total costs and can change over time. Five cost categories make up the cost structure of a business: direct payroll, payroll support, inventory, facility costs, and marketing and advertising. Knowing the size and importance of each cost center is a key part of this component of business model analysis.

5. An analysis of investment size will show the enterpriser the amount and timing of the required funding to start and operate a particular business concept.

6. Critical success factors (CSFs) are the elements that contribute the most to a company's profitability. These operational functions or competencies vary according to the type of business and may include specialized equipment and employee talents. Enterprisers should know how each CSF affects revenues, costs, and cash flow.

7. Market analysis uses primary and secondary research to help enterprisers identify customers for the business's goods or services. Because all goods and services have competition and substitutes, enterprisers must carefully explore the competitive environment that the proposed business will face. Understanding the competitive dynamics and characteristics of an industry and offering distinct benefits compared to the competition enhances a business's chances for success. Forces that drive industry competition are degree of rivalry, barriers to entry, threat of substitute products/services, the power of suppliers, and the power of customers. Low cost and differentiation are the two basic competitive strategies an enterpriser can choose.

8. Sales and distribution analysis focuses on how to make connections and provides critical information about the entire process of generating sales. This includes identifying and attracting customers so that they buy the company's products or services, making advertising and promotional decisions, and determining the appropriate distribution channels to get your goods or services to the end-user. The five parts of the selling process are contact, need identification, solution to those needs, product benefits, and closing the sale.

9. By performing value analysis, enterprisers gain insights into the benefits the potential business offers customers, how those benefits compare to competitors' products, and the value chain that links the business and its customers. Products that are better, faster, or less expensive provide a competitive advantage. Knowing what customers value and need will help the enterpriser refine the business concept further. Preparing a competitive benefit grid can aid in this part of the feasibility analysis. Charting the value chain shows where the business adds value and where the biggest spreads between costs and revenues occur.

10. The best idea in the world won't become a successful business without the personal commitment on the part of the enterpriser. This requires

looking carefully at whether the enterpriser's own aspirations and lifestyle considerations match the type of business.

11. Capital resources are the final component of feasibility analysis. In addition to financial capital, a business needs human capital (expertise, knowledge, skills) and social capital (networks of relationships). The enterpriser must identify not only the sources for each type of capital, but also the timing. Investigating the competition is a good way to learn about the capital requirements for a business prior to preparing cost estimates.

Review Questions

1. Explain the purpose and general framework of the feasibility process.

2. What is a business model? Discuss the four main areas of business model analysis.

3. Describe the different types of revenue streams a business can generate and how they relate to the revenue model.

4. How do the Web-based revenue models described in the chapter generate revenues? What types of cost structures, investment requirements, and critical success factors comprise these business models?

5. Define the four types of costs a business can incur and the five cost categories that make up a firm's cost structure. What should an enterpriser know about these cost centers when developing a business model?

6. How does investment size and timing affect a business model?

7. What are CSFs? List several CSFs for a business model for a new line of exercise clothing.

8. Differentiate between primary and secondary customer research and give examples of techniques used to gather data for each.

9. Describe the five drivers of industry competition and apply them to the analysis of a new chain of stores that sells teen-oriented furniture and accessories. What competitive strategy would you use for this business and why?

10. What would be involved in the sales and distribution analysis for the teen furnishings stores?

11. Why is value analysis such an important part of determining feasibility? Choose five types of values from the list in Exhibit 7.6 (page 172) that would apply to the teen furnishings stores and explain the reasoning for your choices. Chart the value chain for the concept.

12. Which Web-based businesses have disrupted past models of the value chain for particular types of goods and services? Can you also name Web businesses that have tried in specific industries and have failed? What are the characteristics of successful disruption of the value chain through a Web-based business?

13. You want to start a company that makes dolls with ethnic features for Hispanic, Asian, and multiracial markets. Discuss how you would analyze your competitors' benefits and develop a plan to gather the information.

14. How does personal commitment relate to feasibility analysis? How can you discover if you have enough commitment to pursue a business concept that seems interesting?

15. What is a signature strength? Pick three strengths from Exhibit 7.9 (page 179) that apply to you and explain how they would be used in a business.

16. Define the three types of capital and give examples of the capital requirements for the ethnic doll company.

Applying What You've Learned

1. Select a business concept that interests you. Begin applying the "one-a-day" rule to develop the knowledge and resources you need for your business concept. Prepare a strategy to identify and contact such people. What types of people do you need to include? What resources can you use to find specific names to contact? What questions do you want to ask, and what can you provide in return?

2. It takes at least five interviews with enterprisers who have founded businesses very similar to the kind of business you want to start to gain a true

sense of how a particular business is started and operated. Talk to two such enterprisers. Discuss how their businesses are similar and different. Can you come up with a similar "formula" for success for these enterprisers and their businesses?

3. Spend the equivalent of an entire day observing a major competitor. Then prepare a summary of your observations that answers such questions as, How does the company do business? What kinds of customers does your competitor have? How do employees dress? How does the staff interact with customers? If your enterprise is a store, shop at the store and see how you are treated as a customer. If your enterprise is a service business, see how your competitor responds to customers who ask them for help. Identify at least five things that your competitor is doing right and five that the business is doing wrong. For each mistake, explain what you would do differently.

4. Ask yourself, how will my competitors change their behaviors once they see how successful my business is? Identify five ways that they might change the way they operate their business once you become one of their competitors. What steps can you take to counter their actions?

5. Identify the major trade associations and trade group meetings for your industry. Which appear to be the best for your particular business concept? If you can, become a member of your industry's trade association, and attend any trade shows that your industry trade association puts on. Prepare the questions you'd ask your competitors and your prospective suppliers.

6. Identify at least five people who are known as experts in your industry. These people might be reporters who write for trade journals, suppliers, or consultants. Ask them for their insights and advice about industry trends, the strengths and weaknesses of your competitors, and any "rules of thumb" for starting and operating your business.

Enterprisers on the Web

1. Visit Martin Seligman's Authentic Happiness website: (http://www.authentichappiness.com). Take the VIA signature strengths survey (you'll have to register first). Did the results surprise you, or were the results in line with what you already knew? Do your strengths match the kinds of skills and attitudes needed to make your business concept successful? Compare your findings with your classmates.

2. Browse through the success story archives of the Service Corps of Retired Executives (SCORE) at http://www.score.org. Pick one service company and one product story. For each, describe the following:

   - revenue streams

   - investment size

   - critical success factors

   - value chain

   - enterpriser's personal commitment

   - enterpriser's signature strengths

3. Go to a business website like http://www. ceoexpress.com and search for information on the industry you are considering. Information to look for could be in annual reports of publicly held companies, so you could use the Security and Exchange Commissions website, EDGAR, http://www.sec.gov/edgar/searchedgar/webusers.htm, which provides information that all publicly held companies must file quarterly with the government about their operations.

4. Go to the U.S. Census Bureau site at http://www.census.gov/statab/www/, to find information on the demographics of customers in your area. The Census Bureau has detailed information on your state, over 5,000 data items on each country, and data of cities with a population of more than 25,000 people.

5. If you are going to be making products or your business needs specific parts or products, you can identify suppliers and other manufacturers who might be your competitors at http://www.thomasregister.com/. Look for products that are similar to the kind of product you might be offering, and get information on these products from companies that will likely have websites with information about them.

6. An easy way to find information about business organizations in your type of enterprise is to use http://dir.yahoo.com/economy/organizations/professional/. Identify all of the professional and

trade associations that might be able to provide you with information on your industry and on your competitors.

7. Go to http://www.inc.com and search for articles about innovative and growing businesses in your industry. Can you find any businesses in your industry that are part of the Inc. 500 fastest privately held growing businesses? Can you find any businesses in your industry that are part of the Inc. 100 publicly held fastest growing businesses? If a company is a publicly held business, you can use EDGAR to get more information about its operations such as names of all of the top management team and a listing of their salaries. Once you have identified fast growing businesses, use any of the web search engines to locate these businesses. Write up profiles on each. Why are they successful? What kinds of customers do they focus on? What kinds of benefits do they provide? What channels do they use? Finally, how might you successfully compete against each of these fast growing businesses?

End Notes

1. The business model analysis presented in this chapter is based on a Harvard Business School teaching note: Richard G. Hammermesh, Paul W. Marshall, and Taz Pirmohamed, "Note on Business Model Analysis for the Entrepreneur" (Boston: Harvard Business School Publishing, 2002).

2. Michael Rappa, "Business Models on the Web," *Managing The Digital Enterprise*, http://digitalenterprise.org/index.html.

3. Zalia Cosmetics website, http://www.zalia.com (December 3, 2004).

4. 180's website, http://www.180's.com (December 3, 2004).

ENTERPRISE

Business Plans and Planning

KEY CONCEPTS

1. While many enterprisers start successful businesses without writing business plans, the chances of successfully starting a business increase by 250 percent for those who do write a plan. Just as a sports team benefits from practicing and preparing a game plan that provides a strategy for competition, a business plan provides practice before actually starting a business. It enables you to build your business on paper and record the actions—past, present, and future—you are taking to make your business a reality.

2. A business plan should demonstrate that you and your partners have the requisite skills to make the business a success, demonstrate that you understand the competitive environment in which your business will operate, explain the need for and benefits of the goods or services you plan to offer, and encourage others to get involved in your business. It should include an action plan that identifies risks and suggests strategies to minimize them. Specific forecasts based on experience—your own and what you learn from others—are another key preparatory step.

3. Most business plans have three main parts: a one- to two-page executive summary with highlights, a body describing the enterprise and its major issues, and an appendix with supporting documents. Business plans are dynamic documents. As you gain knowledge about your industry and experience in running your business, you should revise your plan to reflect this additional information.

You have a flair for designing products that are not only attractive but also practical. As your reputation for using good design to solve problems in unique ways spreads, many new clients want your services. You have a vision of building a company that integrates art and the social sciences with industrial design. Your employees will come from many disciplines and have few constraints placed on their creative efforts. The early years are tough, but soon your creations are winning awards at the Industrial Design Excellence Awards competition.

In this chapter, you'll meet Sohrab Voussoughi, founder of Ziba Designs, and learn how he turned his dream into reality. More than 20 years after starting his company, he is still passionate about his work. With a thoughtfully conceived business plan, you can also live your dream.

8.0 Business Plans: Why Bother?

If you have talked with other enterprisers about business plans, you probably discovered that most enterprisers did not write a business plan before starting their businesses. Yet, recent research on new venture business planning suggests that those enterprisers who write business plans are 250 percent more likely to successfully start a business.[1] While a business plan does not guarantee a new successful business (because most new businesses fail), business planning does increase your chances of success.

We want you to think about business plans and business planning in a very different way—in the same way that a team practices and a coach creates a game plan. In sports, teams not only practice before playing the game, they also have a *game plan* before competing against a specific opponent. This game plan identifies the opponent's specific strengths and weaknesses and maps out specific ways to defeat the other team. In professional football, many coaches study videos of their opponents over and over to spot weaknesses in their opponents' games. Coaches then develop a set of plays for both offense and defense to counteract each opponent's strengths and weaknesses. Some coaches, for example, have a list of plays that will be run at the beginning of the game that will be undertaken no matter what, as a way of getting their team into the game. Coaches then adjust their team's efforts once they see how their opponents respond. That is what business plans and planning are really about: practicing before playing the real game and developing a set of specific activities that can help you defeat your competition.

If you have played competitive sports, you probably spent many hours in practices before actually competing against opponents. These practices gave your team more experience to help it win. If your opponent didn't practice, your team had an advantage—and a greater chance of winning.

If both teams practiced before their games, practice alone might not lead to success. That is why, in some circumstances, enterprisers who write business plans find those plans don't help them to win. Perhaps their competitors have much more experience and knowledge (another type of practice) about competing in their industry. They have already played the game and have developed a set of actions that have helped them be successful against other competitors. In these situations writing a business plan is a necessary, but not sufficient condition for becoming successful. You need to practice, but practicing doesn't necessarily mean that you will defeat your opponent. So, why write a business plan?

A business plan and the planning process can be like practicing before playing the real game. You can try out different ways to compete against a team as you practice. You can simulate whether certain actions might work and improve the odds of winning. Just as in sports, writing a business plan serves the same purpose as practice sessions and provides an advantage in situations where your competitors are less prepared. As the competition in your industry becomes more sophisticated, you will find that your competitors are practicing and developing plans to defeat your business.

Business plan   A written plan for a business that documents an enterpriser's past, present, and future actions and helps identify the right actions for success. Shows where you are going and where you have been.

We recognize that writing a business plan is not the same thing as actually taking the actions required to start a business and operate it. At some point, every enterpriser has to show up and play the game—that is, actually start and operate the business. In many industries, that will be enough for enterprisers to succeed, and writing a business plan wouldn't necessarily help them be more successful. Why not just show up and not bother with writing a business plan?

If you think you can win at the game of enterprise without practicing or having a game plan, then don't write a business plan! Play the game of enterprise and see what happens. Or, take time now to practice how to be successful in your business, and identify those activities (have a game plan) that might lead your enterprise toward success.

We believe it is better to be prepared to be successful, rather than hope that circumstances will turn in your favor. As we said in Chapter 5, you can make your own luck, and becoming lucky involves preparation. You need to be ready for the changes in circumstances that occur while playing the game of enterprise. The best way to be ready is to engage in planning and in writing a business plan.

This chapter will show you how to "practice" being successful in the start-up and operation of your business, and to have a game plan of tactics for successfully competing in your industry.

8.1 The Feasibility Study versus the Business Plan

How is writing a business plan different from undertaking a feasibility study? In many ways they are similar. However, a business plan goes beyond the feasibility study and identifies the specific tactics and actions for enterprise success. The feasibility study collects sufficient information about a specific opportunity to determine whether you should go forward and convert your opportunity into an ongoing business. The **business plan** is a way to record your successes and failures while you practice for success at making your business a reality. And, for those enterprisers who just take action to start a business and then realize that they need a business plan, the business plan identifies what they have already accomplished. Indeed, for whatever stage of the start-up process you are in, the business plan is documentation of your actions: past, present, and future. The business plan is not the business. The underlying purpose of a business plan is to help you take the right kinds of actions for success. Your feasibility study has already helped you identify the strategy and goals for success. The business plan will specify the tactics you'll use to take concrete actions that will make your business a reality.

Two other major reasons for writing a business plan might convince you to engage in this effort. Writing a business plan helps you to

- *Get a better understanding of why your business is going to be successful.* That is, you write a business plan for yourself to become more efficient and effective. When you write down what you know about your business, you can see what you know and don't know. Writing a business plan can help you spot the flaws in your strategy and tactics for becoming successful. When you put your "game plan" on paper, you see your business. As you may recall, part of the enterprising process is creating a vision, that is, seeing what the future of your business will be like. Writing a business plan gives your vision much more clarity.

- *Engage others in your efforts.* Many enterprisers write business plans to raise money to start and grow their business. However, raising money should not be the sole purpose of writing a business plan. Money is just one of several types of capital that you will need to start your enterprise. As a document that talks about your actions (past, present, and future), the business plan can help others see where you are going and where you have been. You are more likely to get money, hire people, lock in suppliers, and get customer orders when you have something (a business plan) that you can show, rather than just talk about. The problem with writing a business plan solely for the purposes of raising money is that many enterprisers make promises to prospective investors that are not based on reality. If you write a business plan based on what you think investors want to hear, you put yourself in the position of having to deliver on issues that they think are important rather than on issues that the business must focus on.

Business plans serve as both a reality check for the enterpriser and an invitation for others to join the enterprisers' efforts. When you develop your business plan, you show others how you will implement your game plan, which helps them see what role they might play in helping you win the game. As such, the business plan is written to answer four fundamental questions:

1. *Why you?* Your response should demonstrate that *you* have the knowledge, skills, and abilities to make your opportunity become a reality. What accomplishments have you and your partners achieved that provide the basis for the future success of your enterprise? Can you successfully achieve the game plan you have mapped out?

2. *Whom do you hurt?* No enterpriser starts a business that doesn't involve *competitors* in some form. In all likelihood, your success will come at the expense of someone else. Who will lose when you win? Who are these competitors? How will your entry into the market affect them? What will these competitors do in response to your entry? How will their responses affect you? Your game plan is not only about your team. It must also recognize the other teams against whom you will compete.

3. *Why now?* Is there a proven *need* for the products/services that your enterprise offers? How does your enterprise go about meeting the needs of specific customers? Why are your products/services better than those offered by your competition? What are the facts that indicate your enterprise will be successful? If you follow professional sports teams, you have probably seen situations where a team has "peaked" before the playoffs—that is, as they come up against more competitive teams, they find that they have spent their time and energy too soon and don't have the necessary attitude and effort to triumph. Your enterprise could find itself in the same position. You might be offering products or services that customers are not ready to purchase now, but might be interested in later. Can your enterprise survive the wait?

4. *Why me?* This question focuses on issues that *others* considering involvement in your effort will ask. Why should they get involved? What skills, knowledge, abilities, or resources do they provide that are necessary for your venture's success? If they do get involved, what is in it for them? Investors who provide money will want to know when they will get their money back—plus some sense of likely future earnings. Prospective employees will want to know how viable the enterprise is so that they will likely get a salary, stock options, or other forms of payment. Suppliers will want to know whether they should extend credit to your business and if your business will be an important source of their future sales growth. Your game plan provides each player (investors, employees, suppliers, customers) with an understanding of how they fit into your winning formula for enterprise success.

Answering these four questions provides you with the material to convince yourself and others to take action to successfully start and operate your business. We will explore how to answer these questions in more detail later when we survey the format for writing a business plan. Before we explore a format for a business plan, however, we want you to create action plans that methodically identify what you and your partners will need to accomplish.

8.2 Developing Action Plans

Action plans are a way to identify the primary risks facing your enterprise and the specific actions you will take to address these risks. An action plan helps you identify the right actions—the effective and efficient efforts—that will actually make a difference in the success of your enterprise. Effective actions solve important problems facing your enterprise, and efficient actions mean that you expend the least amount of effort to get the best results. You don't want to waste your time and energy on issues that may seem important, but are actually trivial for the success of your enterprise.[2]

Creating an action plan is a three-step process, where you (1) identify risks, (2) develop a response strategy, and (3) control and monitor the risks and responses. Exhibit 8.1 summarizes the action plan–preparation process.

> **Risk**   A situation that causes concern and/or uncertainty and could therefore result in negative outcomes.

In the first step of the action plan, you should list all of the risks you identified in your feasibility study: business concept risks, business model risks, and business feasibility risks. What were the risks inherent in your business concept? What kinds of customer, consideration, connection, and commitment risks do you face? What are the risks in your business model? What risks might prevent your enterprise from making money or generating the capital necessary to accomplish your enterprise's objectives?

What do we mean by risk? A risk has a condition and a consequence. A condition is a statement that describes a situation that is causing concern and/or uncertainty. A consequence is a statement that describes the possible negative outcomes that may be caused by this condition. Here is an example of a customer risk for a software company that has a product designed for manufacturing companies. The *condition* is that customers require any new production software they purchase provide demonstrated cost savings of 25 percent in the first year of use. The following are three *consequences* of this condition:

1.   Unless we can show cost savings, customer won't buy.

2.   This is a new software product and we don't have any customer history with it.

3.   Another product we produced has shown cost savings of 50 percent after two years of use.

We would then begin to identify likely outcomes of this risk. In our example, we would ask how likely it is

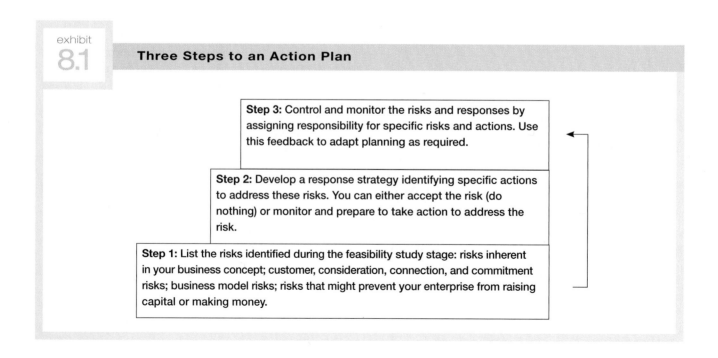

exhibit
8.1

Three Steps to an Action Plan

Step 3: Control and monitor the risks and responses by assigning responsibility for specific risks and actions. Use this feedback to adapt planning as required.

Step 2: Develop a response strategy identifying specific actions to address these risks. You can either accept the risk (do nothing) or monitor and prepare to take action to address the risk.

Step 1: List the risks identified during the feasibility study stage: risks inherent in your business concept; customer, consideration, connection, and commitment risks; business model risks; risks that might prevent your enterprise from raising capital or making money.

that the customer won't buy without a "lead user," the customer won't buy without a "money-back guarantee," or the customer won't buy without some other condition.

By listing risks in such a detailed way, you can move to Step 2 and develop a response strategy that identifies specific actions you might take to deal with those particular risks. You can either accept the risk (do nothing) or take actions to reduce or eliminate the risk. In our software example, actions to address your customer risks are offering a money-back guarantee that the software will work or partnering with someone who meets the customer's criteria. Taking action should increase your odds of success.

Finally, an enterprise needs to control and monitor these risks and responses. This third step involves assigning responsibility for specific risks and actions and indicating when reports on risks and actions need to occur. This process of identifying risks, developing responses, and controlling and monitoring them is time consuming and difficult. In the next section, we offer a way of breaking down these broad goals into specific tasks.

The Structure of Work

Your abilities and efforts should focus on specific tasks to achieve specific goals. Broadly, the goal of your business planning effort is to start and operate a successful enterprise. In looking at the structure of this work effort, ask yourself, "What tasks are necessary to complete the project?" By analyzing the specific tasks, your action plan can be broken down into smaller tasks or projects. For example, these projects include marketing, selling, finding resources to make your product or provide your service, finding employees, and so forth. Creating a feasibility study has already helped you identify the major groups of tasks you need to accomplish. As you move to the business planning process, you divide these larger groups of tasks, such as marketing, into specific projects that you can actually make sense of and accomplish. You begin to see what you need to do to be successful. "Marketing," for example, becomes a series of specific efforts and actions.

Continuing with the software company example, we have a specific project—selling software to manufacturing companies. We have identified the risks inherent in this effort and ways that we might respond to these risks. We now ask, "What are the specific tasks required?"

In answering this question we also identify the sequence of specific tasks, specify how groups of tasks are related to each other, outline a schedule for completing these tasks, indicate the resources required to complete these tasks, and then determine a budget. By putting effort into identifying tasks for each project required to reach the broad goals of starting and operating your enterprise, you can monitor the progress of your efforts and create a more accurate sense of the costs and time it will take to achieve your goals. In addition, task identification will help others see what needs to be accomplished. Marketing, selling, financing, hiring, and other required functions are no longer broad generalities. They become activities that others can see, grasp, and undertake. Rather than say, "Go out and sell" to an employee, you will establish the specific set of actions necessary to undertake the process of selling.

In thinking about the tasks required for selling, for example, you should consider what these tasks will achieve: What are the major deliverables? The sum of your deliverables equals a particular project, and the sum of a set of tasks would equal a particular deliverable. Exhibit 8.2 illustrates the relationship between these project steps.

For example, a major deliverable in selling would be to identify customers. Some of the tasks to achieve this deliverable would be identifying target industries for the manufacturing software, listing manufacturers in these industries, and getting phone numbers and names of individuals at each company who can authorize purchases of software. Another deliverable would be the sales presentation your salesforce uses, which incorporates the results of the "identify customers" deliverable. In fact, there might be many more tasks that need to be accomplished to complete the deliverable of "identifying customers." It is not easy to break down even such a simple activity as "identifying customers" without undertaking a significant amount of work to determine how much work you must actually do. Exhibit 8.3 offers several suggestions for constructing a set of tasks.

Determining the tasks for a deliverable such as identifying customers is often easier for enterprisers who have engaged in this kind of effort before. For example, a salesperson who has sold software to manufacturing companies is much more likely to know how to identify customers. If you do not have experience in accomplishing specific tasks for a particular project, you need to find individuals with the requisite expertise to help you, such as mentors, other enterprisers in your industry, and industry experts.

Determining specific actions that you and others need to take to accomplish your goals is critical. Your game plan should show how members of your team

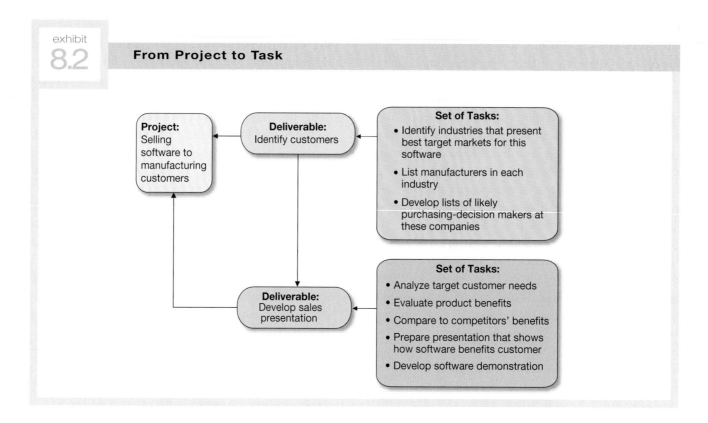

exhibit
8.2

From Project to Task

exhibit
8.3

Five Tips for Successful Task Construction

1. 8/80 rule: Tasks should be no smaller than 8 hours or no larger than 80 hours.

2. Tasks should be no longer than the time between reporting periods, for example, reported each week, or every other week. (At that meeting, one would report whether the task is "Complete" or "Not Complete.")

3. Smaller tasks are easier to estimate.

4. Smaller tasks are easier to assign.

5. Smaller tasks are easier to track.

would accomplish their roles to help your enterprise win. For example, a game plan for a professional football team would show what each person would do for each particular play: which team members would block specific opponents, who would catch the ball on a pass play, and how a receiver would get "open" (away from a defender) to catch the ball. You could compare a professional team's game plan specifying each person's role and actions with an informal game among friends where the only game plan might be "run as fast as you can down the field, and I'll throw the ball to you." Wouldn't everyone

involved in your enterprise feel more confident if they knew exactly what they would be doing?

Finally, an important part of specifying tasks for each project involves determining when a task is actually accomplished. How will you know when a task is complete? How will you know when a person on your team has done his or her job? Think about how you will define *success* in completing a specific set of tasks and deliverables. For example, in achieving the deliverable "identifying customers," you should consider how long it will take to identify manufacturing companies and the people in these companies who would be your buyers, and you should have some idea of how many specific companies and buyers you think are necessary to identify. Is identifying ten buyers a satisfactory completion of this task—or do you need to identify 25 buyers, or just one? It would be valuable to ask others for their feedback on what indicators work best for various tasks and to construct checklists that use these indicators to show completion of specific actions.

Specifying tasks and actions might seem to take a lot of effort, and you may wonder how exploring the minutiae of the enterprise will contribute to your successful goal achievement. Devoting adequate time to these small activities pays off. For example, preparing customer lists and telephone numbers of important contacts is a tedious task; but you cannot make a software sale unless you have specific customers to sell to! The success of your enterprise will actually be determined by how well you accomplish each of these small tasks.

The Critical Path

As you identify deliverables and tasks for each project, you will begin to understand how particular tasks and projects relate to each other. For example, if one of your projects for selling software involves demonstrating the software, this project is dependent on having software to demonstrate. As you discover which projects are related to each other and which projects must be completed before you can undertake other projects, you determine the critical path for your enterprise.

The critical path in the start-up of your enterprise involves thinking through the key milestones that need to be achieved. A milestone is a major project that has been accomplished. Each project will involve specifying tasks to be achieved, the people who will complete these tasks, the resources necessary for these individuals to accomplish their tasks, and the length of time you estimate for completing these tasks. Identifying resources will require you to make estimates of the equipment, materials, or other kinds of capital necessary to finish a project. We will look at how you go about making these estimates in the next section.

In generating a critical path, you begin by creating an initial schedule of all major projects necessary for the development of your enterprise. You then estimate the time it will take to accomplish each major project. As you list tasks that need to be completed on a month-to-month basis, you will see which tasks are more critical than others. For example, before you can demonstrate your

software, you must develop the software, and to develop the software, you need to hire programmers to write the software. Once the programmers are hired, they need a certain amount of time to create the software.

Knowing which tasks and projects are critical, you can focus your efforts and resources on them. Otherwise, you could spend time on projects that are not crucial for your business. For example, if developing software is the most important project on your critical path, it is less important to hire sales people and develop a marketing program, particularly if software development might take a year to complete. Hiring salespeople who have nothing to sell could drain your enterprise of limited resources and negatively affect employee morale.

Forecasting Future Effort

Generating estimates of time, effort, and resources necessary to accomplish a project in the future is no easy task. "Guesstimates" are usually wrong, and usually not in your favor. When you try to pad your estimates (that is, add an arbitrary factor such as an additional 25 percent), you don't do much better. A better method for forecasting an action plan is using your personal experience or someone else's. For nearly all start-up efforts, you can find previous similar start-up efforts. If you have experience in sales, you are likely to make better judgments about the time and effort to achieve your sales goal. You can benefit from the expertise of others by asking the right questions when you interview entrepreneurs in your industry, and then applying their experiences as you generate your action plan estimates.

Whatever you plan to undertake, someone else has probably done something similar. Learn from their successes and failures! Find similar efforts to the one you are undertaking and modify your game plan based on what they have done. You don't have to create a business that is totally unique. Such a unique business actually doesn't exist.

For example, if no company has previously sold the kind of software to manufacturing companies that you plan to sell, you can still learn from companies that have sold products or services to your particular customers. You can learn how long it took to sell their products and

Critical path The activities required to complete a project and the order in which they must be completed to keep a project on track.

services. You can learn what kind of sales pitch helped sell their products. You can also learn from companies that have developed a different type of software. You can learn the length of time they needed to develop and debug similar software. Even though other businesses might not be "exactly" like your business, their experiences can serve as benchmarks to determine whether the tasks you have specified can reasonably be accomplished with the people and resources you have identified.

Many novice enterprisers ignore this important step of learning from others. Big mistake! Even if your product is unique, you can benefit from looking at other companies that have sold unique products. When enterprisers say, "I am unique" they are often indicating, "I am ignorant."

With the information you learn from your competitors, you are better prepared to develop good forecasts. You can estimate the number of people you should hire, the amount of time these employees will need for specific tasks, and the equipment, facilities, and materials they will require to produce the item or service.

Forecasting, therefore, is about using the past to help predict the future. The more you know about how others have been successful in the past, the more likely you will be to accurately identify what to do in the future. Again, ignorance of the past experiences of others is your worst enemy when you are trying to forecast.

In practice, though, things don't go the way you plan. Even with all the time and effort you devote to learning from others what will be necessary to achieve your goals, your forecasts are likely to be inaccurate. As you actually play the game of business, you will find that your competitors may not respond in the ways that you predicted in your game plan. The opposing team is likely to respond to your actions and revise their efforts and activities. This does not mean that you should not make forecasts. It means that a forecast is your best understanding of what you think is likely to occur. You will need to revise your forecasts as you go forward. You don't throw out the game plan because a particular play doesn't achieve the objectives you planned. Great coaches revise their game plan as the game develops.

Revising your forecasts is a dynamic process that involves actively reestimating tasks and resources as you learn from your own experiences. As you go forward with creating your enterprise, you will likely change task assignments (e.g., put more resources into software development rather than sales), add or subtract from levels of people and equipment you originally estimated, and change your criteria for determining a successful

outcome. For example, you might find that the manufacturing software you planned to sell to appliance manufacturers is not appropriate for their needs and might be better suited to automobile part manufacturers. The goal of identifying buyers in the appliance industry will need to be revised to reflect your new objective of identifying buyers in the automobile part industry.

The challenge in forecasting is to be as specific as possible when making estimates of what needs to be done and when. Broad general estimates likely mean that you will not have the necessary people and resources to achieve your goals, and that you may not know what is required for success.

It is better to recognize and attempt to manage the risks your enterprise will likely face. This is not easy. We tend to minimize risks that we have not faced before. We often see this in a highly ranked team that does not take an unranked competitor seriously. The highly ranked team doesn't devote the time and effort to prepare for what they expect to be an easy game, and then find, during the actual game, the unranked opponent is tough to defeat.

The process of planning is, then, the struggle to identify what you don't know, and to realize that what you don't know is likely to significantly impact your business. The process of identifying the risks in your business and specifying actions to take is a very humbling experience. All enterprisers find that there are often significant gaps in what they know, and they discover that there will always be room for learning more about their enterprises.

8.3 Writing the Business Plan

There are knowns,
Known unknowns,
And unknown unknowns.
> —Anonymous

As we indicated at the beginning of the chapter, you write a business plan for yourself and for others. When writing a business plan for yourself, think of the process as an effort to collect all information you know about your business in one place. We suggest that you get a three-ring binder (or binders) to house the information you collect about your business. Three-ring binders are ideal because you can update sections of your business plan as you gain more knowledge about your situation. You will then use this information to answer the questions outlined in the "Business Plan Format" section.

As you compile this information, you will see the gaps in your knowledge. For example, if your expertise is sales, you might find that your marketing and sales section is very detailed, while the finance section is missing a lot of information. These gaps provide clues to potential blind spots in developing the enterprise, and you will know to focus more attention on these particular sections.

As the quote at the beginning of this section suggests, your task in business planning is to identify the "knowns" (what you know) the "known unknowns" (what you know you don't know), and attempt to minimize the "unknown unknowns" (issues that you don't know might have an impact on your enterprise). The business plan format that we outline in section 8.5 may force you to address those aspects of your enterprise about which you really have little knowledge. Significant problems that confront many businesses are more likely to come from the "unknown unknowns." Ignorance is rarely good protection for problems that are likely to confront your business.

Filling in the Gaps: A Business Plan for Your Own Use

The development of a business plan for your own use requires that you be completely honest with yourself in terms of what you actually know or don't know. The difficulty that many enterprisers face often comes from assuming that unanswered questions are likely to be unimportant to the enterprise's subsequent success. Clearly, you will never know everything that might be important to being successful in the particular business you choose to pursue. There will always be gaps in your knowledge. Recognizing that such gaps exist—and assuming that your lack of knowledge in a particular area might create significant risks to the business—will help you develop strategies to reduce those risks and undertake the right actions in developing and operating your enterprise.

Here are a few issues that often cause enterprisers trouble when writing their business plans:

- *Making unrealistic projections:* As we mentioned earlier, it is difficult to generate accurate forecasts, particularly sales forecasts. Many enterprisers are tempted to make sales projections that fulfill other requirements for business success—for example, sales forecasts that create financial statements that show the business will make money sooner, rather than later—rather than specifying realistic sales goals that are achievable.

- *Underestimating time:* Most enterprisers assume that activities take less time than they actually do. For example, we have met enterprisers who thought that customers would purchase their product after the first sales call, and then found out that most customers took 18 months to evaluate their products and decide to purchase. If you didn't budget for an 18-month lag between the first sales call and the actual sale, your enterprise would probably run out of money paying salaries and expenses before you collect the cash from the first sale.

- *Failing to understand the competitive landscape:* Many enterprisers think that their competition will be only those businesses that sell exactly the same products or services. They forget that most buyers are likely to consider a wider range of alternatives. For example, if your enterprise is selling bottled juices, your competition is not only businesses that sell bottled juices, but also all those businesses that sell other beverages such as milk, bottled water, and soft drinks. Competitors selling other types of drinks will have a significant influence on the prices you charge for juice. Many of these competitors, such as soft drink companies, are likely to determine how much visibility your product has in a grocery store or whether your product can even be sold in certain stores or outlets.

- *Insufficient due diligence:* A thorough investigation of investors, partners, potential employees, customers, and suppliers, called **due diligence,** is an essential part of the start-up process. Many enterprisers do not check references or confirm the details of a person's resume. They hire people assuming they are trustworthy, only to discover later that these employees are dishonest. After an employee has stolen from the company, the enterpriser learns that this person has a history of theft. Due diligence is also required to explore

Due diligence   The process of thoroughly investigating all parties who will be involved in your business, including investors, partners, potential employees, customers, and suppliers.

how prospective investors have worked with other companies. Did other enterprisers who worked with an investor have enjoyable and satisfying experiences, or was dealing with the investor difficult?

As your enterprise goes through the process of start-up, it is tempting to hire the first person that walks through the door (because you need help "right now"), or take money from the first person that offers to invest (because you are short of cash). Please perform your due diligence and investigate the previous experience of any person you plan to be involved with. You should also investigate the reliability of your suppliers, and you need to get confirmations that materials can be delivered at a particular price and time. You don't want to be caught in a situation where you have promised your customers that you can deliver your product at a particular time, and then find out that the parts you need to manufacture your product are out of stock, or cost much more than you assumed.

Know Your Audience: Gearing a Plan to Other Readers

You will also write business plans for other people to read. Please consider who they are and why they are reading your plan. Then tailor the plan to those specific readers: employees, customers, investors, or suppliers, for example. Although you will base this business plan on the information in your personal business plan, you should not share your personal business plan with them. For example, if you were sharing your business plan with your customers, you would probably not share information on your markups for materials and labor, nor would you likely share all of the information you have obtained on your competitors (such as your competitors' strengths) that might entice your customers to buy from them. You may not need to share with prospective investors the specifics of your operations to provide your goods or services to customers. It is important, therefore, to clearly understand your readers before you send them a business plan and write your business plan accordingly. No single business plan can meet the needs of the various types of people who will be involved in your enterprise.

Here are a few issues that enterprisers should consider when writing a business plan for others:

- *A business plan is like an invitation to a dance, but it is not the dance itself.* The purpose of sharing your business plan with others is to help you engage them, in some form, in your enterprise. For example, a business plan written for a prospective investor is an opportunity to begin a dialog about the investor's relationship with you. When you involve an investor, you are not only asking for money, you are also asking the investor for his or her personal involvement in your business: advice, questions, phone calls, concerns. A business plan is just one of many ways to present your vision of your enterprise. A business plan is not the last word you will offer, but the first of many chances to convey your knowledge.

- *The business plan is a reflection of the enterpriser.* A business plan may be the first impression an outsider has of you. It is important to present a document that does not have spelling and grammatical errors. The plan should be easy to read, legible, and well designed. If the business plan looks like a mess, outsiders are likely to think that the enterpriser is also a mess.

- *Write in words that your reader can understand.* For example, engineers and scientists tend to use technical terms that only other engineers and scientists would understand. If the business plan is being written for investors who are not scientists, enterprisers need to help these readers understand the scientific aspects of the enterprise, but without the scientific jargon.

- *When presenting financial information, it is not quantity, but quality.* A business plan is not about the numbers; rather, it is about the *logic* of the numbers. It is easy to get caught up in the creation of financial spreadsheets that offer thousands and thousands of numbers and ten-year projections, quickly padding a business plan with pages and pages of financial data. Offering many spreadsheets is not as convincing to an outsider as identifying how you arrived at your estimates for such broad categories as sales, cost of goods sold, expenses, and the timing of the acquisition of necessary assets. The financial information you provide is, therefore, a numerical summary of the logic of your business model. The primary purpose of your financial statements is to describe how the business will make money.

- *Finally, never make promises that you can't keep.* A business plan creates expectations. If your plan promises too much and you don't meet these goals, you will find yourself with many unhappy and disappointed investors, employees, and so on. It is better to underpromise in your business plan and overdeliver in how the business actually does, than vice versa.

A Special Plan Worth Having

A traditional business plan provides the game plan for your business venture and forces you to analyze all the aspects of your proposed venture: product, customers, competition, operations, and financing. There is another important aspect to running a business, however, that requires consideration. In the aftermath of ethical and financial lapses at Enron, Tyco, Adelphia, and other corporations, there has been an increased emphasis on ethical conduct and developing formal ethical codes that define acceptable behavior for executives, board members, and employees. These documents set forth the ethical foundations on which your company is based. They provide standards to guide stakeholder actions and a framework for appropriate behavior. For example, in Chapter 6, we learned that most company codes of ethics include specific clauses about conflicts of interest.

The process of developing a code of ethics is in itself a learning experience. Just as writing a business plan requires you to confront all the issues of forming and running your enterprise, your code of ethics asks you to reconsider your mission, corporate values, and your relationship to your business environment and the larger society. The Enterprising Ethics box offers advice for preparing this important document.

ENTERPRISING
ETHICS

Developing an Ethics Plan

As they develop business plans to guide the formation of their new companies, enterprisers also should give careful thought to the underlying corporate values and codes of conduct that they want as a foundation for ethical behavior. A formal code of ethics prepared early in the company's life defines the values and ethical responsibilities an enterpriser wants to own and communicates those expectations to anyone who becomes involved with the company. This includes shareholders, employees, customers, suppliers, and local/national community. The code of ethics serves as a management tool as well, providing guidelines for managing workplace ethics. Companies with well-crafted and effectively implemented codes of ethics are more likely to avoid ethical conflicts and dilemmas.

While every organization's code of ethics should be unique, the basic steps to develop the plan are similar. Senior management must set the tone and commit publicly to the business ethics policy. Because values and ethics are related to corporate governance, the board should also support this initiative. Involving employees and external stakeholders in the writing of the code is critical, so that it reflects their needs as well as management's and increases buy-in. A code should not be formulated and decreed by the company's board or human resources or legal departments. The best codes include topics that matter to employees. Reading examples of other codes can be very helpful in providing a framework and ideas to jump-start the development of your code, although it's essential to take the time to customize the content to your company.

Before beginning to write a code of ethics, it's important to consider some general questions:

- What is the code's purpose—to inspire or to regulate behavior? Do you want the code to guide people or to set out requirements?

- Will your ethics document include some sort of enforcement? If so, what kind?

- Who will develop your code?

- How will you identify the needs of your organization?

- What steps will you take to publicize and implement the code?

- How will you incorporate the values set forth in the code into organizational policies and practices?

- What procedures will you use to enforce the code?

- How often will you revisit the code and revise it?

The first phase in code preparation is identifying and articulating the company's key values and behaviors. Some guidelines for this difficult and critical process follow:

1. *Review all values related to laws and regulations.* Your organization should already be in compliance with them. Values that support these laws should be part of your code.

(continued)

2. *Identify values important to your product, service, and industry or profession.* These may include product safety, confidentiality, fair pricing, community involvement, and others.

3. *Interview employees to identify values related to current workplace issues.* These might include avoiding discrimination in the workplace (age, race, gender, sexual orientation), inappropriate dress, prohibiting drug and alcoholic beverage usage on the premises, accepting personal gifts from stakeholders, and avoiding conflicts of interest. Also include values that promote desired behaviors such as teamwork, honesty, and respect, and any other issues that might have ethical repercussions for your company.

4. *Take into account ethical values relevant to stake-holders.* For example, the communities where you locate plants may consider concern for the environment an important value.

5. *Review the values developed in the preceding steps and select those with the highest priority for your company.* These might include the six ethical values named by Josephson Institute of Ethics: trustworthiness, respect, responsibility, caring, justice and fairness, and civic responsibility.

After completing the value identification process, it's time to actually write the code of ethics. Many ethics codes have two parts. The first is typically an inspirational section summarizing the organization's ideals. The second section lists the guidelines for ethical behavior, often by priority for the company. These might be classified by stakeholder group or by topic, such as compliance with law, work environment, acceptance of gifts, conflicts of interest, insider trading, and use of company assets.

The best codes include examples of behavior associated with key corporate values. A code cannot cover every type of ethical dilemma. It can, however, offer guidelines on how to resolve most ethical dilemmas. The wording should also make it clear that the code applies to all employees. In addition to defining values and ethical behavior, the code should include a procedure for employees to discuss or report ethics-related questions.

Before finalizing and implementing the code, key executives and your legal advisors should review the document carefully. It is helpful to test the code with a few representative groups. The code can then be revised to incorporate feedback from these reviewers.

The implementation of the code must go beyond merely announcing it and distributing printed copies to all employees. The code should be a dynamic document that becomes an integral part of the way the company does business. Many companies hold special sessions to explain the code when it is first introduced and include it in new employee orientation sessions. In addition, a company's code of ethics should be reviewed annually and updated as new situations arise.

Discussion Questions

1. Why should an enterprise have a code of ethics? What are the key issues to consider when developing an ethics plan for an enterprise?

2. Outline a process for developing a code of ethics for your enterprise.

3. What kinds of ethical dilemmas might an ethics plan identify and solve as an enterprise develops and grows?

4. Using the information provided, the resources suggested below, and other online resources, write a code of ethics for your enterprise.

Suggested resources: Carter McNamara, *Complete Guide to Ethics Management: An Ethics Toolkit for Managers,* http://www.managementhelp.org/ethics/ethxgde.htm; Chris MacDonald, "Creating a Code of Ethics for Your Organization," *EthicsWeb.ca,* http://www.ethicsweb.ca/codes.

Sources: Adapted from Chris MacDonald, "Creating a Code of Ethics for Your Organization," *EthicsWeb.ca,* http://www.ethicsweb.ca/codes (January 3, 2007); Chris MacDonald, "Considerations For Writing A Code Of Ethics," in Gene Marks Ed., *Streetwise Small Business Book of Lists* (Cincinnati, OH: Adams Media, 2006); "Codes of Ethics," *Institute of Business Ethics,* http://www.ibe.org.uk/codesofconduct.html (January 6, 2007); and Carter McNamara, *Complete Guide to Ethics Management: An Ethics Toolkit for Managers,* http://www.managementhelp.org/ethics/ethxgde.htm (January 4, 2007).

8.4 ENTERPRISERS

Integrating Design and Function at Ziba Designs

Did you ever wonder where all the gadgets and gizmos we use every day originate? Many come from Ziba Designs, an internationally known industrial design firm with a reputation for creative excellence. Headquartered in Portland, Oregon, with offices in Tokyo, Taipei, Boston, and San Jose, the company is a wonderful mix of personalities and nationalities. Sohrab Vossoughi, who is originally from Iran, started Ziba in 1984 as a brand consultancy with expertise in product development. His goal was to solve business problems with great design. "Ziba means beautiful in Farsi, the language of Persians," Vossoughi explains. "I wanted a name that was easy to say, easy to spell and at the same time has a meaning."

From humble beginnings—Ziba's first big product was the Cleret Bathroom Squeegee—the company has grown to 120 employees and over $12 million in revenues. Its client list includes Intel, Hewlett Packard, McDonald's, FedEx, Procter & Gamble, Rubbermaid, Nike, Microsoft, Ford, and Whirlpool. "Design is a continuum," Vossoughi explains. "It never ends; once you do something, you know it can be done better." He also believes that design should reflect the integration of many disciplines and hires not just industrial designers but also employees with experience in art and the social sciences. Clearly, his strategic design vision is working. In 2001, Ziba became the first firm in the world to win four Gold Awards in the annual Industrial Design Excellence Awards competition. Ziba also holds the record for the most awards per employee.

According to Bob Marchant, a friend, mentor, and customer to Ziba's founder Sohrab Voussoughi, Ziba is one of the world's top five design firms. "They have created products for leading global brands all over the world, and their products have been consistently successful," Marchant says. He believes that Ziba's focus on economics is a primary factor in its success. "Their designers understand that it does no good for a product to win an award but not make a profit for the client who is actually bringing it to the marketplace. It is not enough for the form to be interesting or exciting—or for the form to generate market acceptance. It's important for the form to be profitable, for somebody to be able to make it and for it to work reliably."

From the beginning, Vossoughi refused to place limits on what can or cannot be done. By asking many "What if?" questions, he encouraged his employees to challenge the norm. "We are our own worst competitors," he says. "We are like athletes; we try to beat our own time. We do our best for our clients, and we deliver way beyond what we promised."

The early years were difficult. "For the first six months, I didn't take a single dime out of the business," Vossoughi recalls. "We had our savings; we got rid of the house, we lived with one car, we did everything. There is a saying back home in Persia that says, 'For one year you eat bread and water—then you can eat bread and butter for the next ten years.'" His sacrifice paid off as his vision became a reality and won him the *Business Week* "Entrepreneur of the Year" award in 1992.

As a service business offering creative design capabilities, Ziba's "product" is not easily explained. Each project is unique. For example, Ziba developed the Cleret Squeegee in response to a request for a nice-looking and efficient squeegee to clean glass shower doors. The resulting design was so popular that the design client had revenues of $16 million in its second year—just from this one product! Its design was so impressive that the squeegee appears in the Smithsonian Museum's permanent collection and was sold at the Museum of Modern Art's store.

Ziba also helped Coleman, best known for camping gear, use the strength of its brand name to break into the home market. The design team developed the Safe Keep smoke detector product line with a unique feature: an easy way to turn off the monitor in the case of a false alarm. Ziba's award-winning design was simple: a broom button allows the homeowner turn off the alarm with the push of a stick. Coleman quickly went from no presence in this market to 40 percent market share.

"This is what design should be about—defining a problem and moving a business forward," says Vossoughi. "It's all about creating the right product for the market. We design not for the manufacturer, not for the designer, but for the user. We get into people's minds. We want to understand the user's latent needs."

This dedication to integrated user-focused design and the innate understanding of human nature are major contributors to the company's ongoing success. Among Ziba's other innovative products are the Clorox ReadyMop, the Polycom conference phone, outpatient care furniture for Herman Miller's health care furniture systems, and the Stair Assist Bar and Guide Rail System to help people climb stairs without bulky in-home elevators. Ziba also worked with a Portland bank to redesign a more friendly branch atmosphere and with FedEx to create its new look, from logo to courier uniforms.

Vossoughi remains passionate about the work Ziba does. "I didn't start the business because of money; I started because I loved what I was doing," he says. "I can use my creativity and my talent for different things. I can't wait to get up in the morning and come to work. It's still fun. I love challenge. Everything that happens, every obstacle that comes up at Ziba, I look at as a challenge and a problem to solve. And that is our business—we are problem solvers."

Discussion Questions

1. How would a business plan for a service business like Ziba differ from a business that manufactured and sold products? What are the particular challenges in preparing Ziba's business plan?

2. How might Vossoughi's personal goals for the business be different from or similar to the goals of the business? What entrepreneurial characteristics does he possess or lack?

3. Assume that you are Sohrab Voussoughi and you get in an elevator with the CEO of a company that manufactures household products. What would be your elevator pitch to this CEO if you were asked, "What do you do?" (See page 261 for a description of the elevator speech.)

4. If you owned Ziba Designs, what would be the critical issues and questions that you would focus on in writing a business plan for yourself? Could this business be sold to someone else? If so, what aspects of this business would make it valuable to others?

Sources: Adapted with permission from the video "Possibility School," Small Business School, the series on PBS, and at http://SmallBusinessSchool.com; Mary Bellotti, "Design from A to Ziba," *Portland Tribune*, August 16, 2002, http://www.ziba.com; Joan'C. Hamilton, "Coleman's No-Nuisance Lifesavers," *Business Week*, June 2, 1997, http://www.ziba.com; and Leigh Buchanan, "Innovation: How the Creative Stay Creative," *Inc.*, June 2008, http://www.inc.com.

8.5 The Business Plan Format

A business plan should follow a format that makes the most sense for the type of business you are planning to pursue and its stage of development. For example, a business plan for a company that is making a new product will likely have a greater emphasis on the stage of the product's development—for example, is the product at the idea or prototype stage? Is there a version that can be manufactured, or is the product already being manufactured? A business plan for a janitorial services business, on the other hand, will have very little about product development and more of a focus on finding customers and the process for consistently delivering janitorial services.

We are not saying that each business plan is unique and that you will not be able to find good examples of business plans from similar businesses. Rather, you must pay attention to the specifics of *your* business—and not be seduced into filling in the blanks of a business plan workbook, business plan computer program, or just substituting your information into a preexisting business plan.

A number of websites provide assistance for developing business plans; some offer business plan outlines. Exhibit 8.4 lists several sites where you can learn more about the format and structure of a business plan.

Your business plan is the story of your enterprise. When you write a business plan in your own words, describing your understanding of the most important issues facing the business, your readers will perceive you as "authentic." Most people who read business plans can quickly tell whether your plan was written from your own personal knowledge and experience or whether it seems to follow someone else's format. Remember, other people—investors, customers, employees, partners—will get involved in your enterprise because of *you*. If your plan does not have your "voice," if it does not reflect your thoughts and concerns and hopes, then other people will quickly see the plan as a "fake" and not representative of your vision for the business. Would you be willing to get involved in a business where the business plan seemed to be nothing like the enterpriser who supposedly wrote the plan?

Appendix C provides a generic format for a business plan. This format is merely a guide to prompt you to think through the critical issues in developing and growing your enterprise. No business plan will follow this format exactly or address all of the questions in this outline comprehensively and thoroughly. The format identifies the important questions and issues you should address—even though you are unable to provide answers to some questions in your plan. If you ignore any of these questions, you might find that these "unknown unknowns" have a significant impact on the success of your business.

exhibit
8.4

Business Plan Websites

Name	URL	Description
The Business Plan: Road Map to Success	http://www.sba.gov/starting/indexbusplans.html	Small Business Administration business plan tutorial and outline
Business Plan Components	http://www.quicken.com/small_business/cch/tools/?topic=4&subtopic=0&article=buspln_m#article	Business Plans on Quicken.com
Creating an Effective Business Plan	http://home3.americanexpress.com/smallbusiness/resources/starting/biz_plan/	Business Plans on Americanexpress.com
Business Planning Tools	http://wsj.miniplan.com/	The Wall Street Journal StartupJournal.com's MiniPlan that guides you through the basics of creating a business plan
Business Plan Software and Sample Business Plans	http://www.bplans.com	Guidelines to write a plan and several sample plans

Finally, you should visualize the format of your business plan as a pyramid with three parts, as shown in Exhibit 8.5: (1) Executive Summary, (2) Body of the business plan, and (3) Supporting Materials. The top of your business plan pyramid is the Executive Summary, a one-to two-page summary of your entire business plan. The Body of the business plan should be about 20 pages long. This section provides the reader with a narrative of

exhibit
8.5

The Business Plan Pyramid

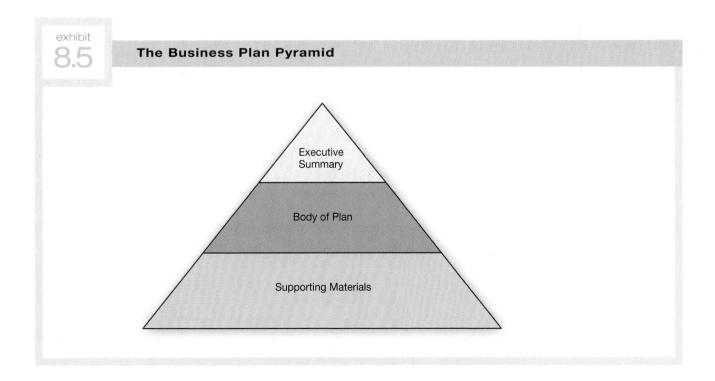

the major issues of your enterprise. In this section you, the writer, tell the story of your enterprise. The Supporting Materials section offers evidence for the statements made in the Body of your business plan. For example, when you discuss the size of your market and the types of customers your enterprise focuses on in the plan's Body, the Supporting Materials section will provide information that shows how you determined size of market, how you went about identifying customers, and so forth.

The pyramid structure for a business plan recognizes that few people will want to know all of the details of your proposed business at one sitting. Each section of the business plan demands a greater commitment from the reader to delve into your business. Most readers will stop after the Executive Summary. Few will want to make the plunge into the Body and Supporting Materials, and it will be those few individuals who really want to be involved.

Executive Summary: The Elevator Speech

The Executive Summary is your "elevator speech" about your business. It represents the essence of your plan, what you would tell an important investor whom you happen to meet as you get into an elevator and says, "Tell me about your business." You have just two to three minutes of that investor's undivided attention to make your best pitch. You want the investor to say at the end of your pitch, "WOW! Tell me more."

The Executive Summary is your invitation to the readers of your plan to get interested enough in the highlights to read more. Attention spans are shorter and shorter. With most TV and radio commercials taking 30 seconds or less, we are conditioned to ignore most messages quickly unless they really engage us. The Executive Summary is like a commercial for your business plan. If the Executive Summary does not engage your readers immediately, you will lose their interest.

You can also think of the Executive Summary as the first impression you will likely make for many prospective investors, employees, partners, etc. Most people make decisions based on those all-important first impressions, even if they only last a few seconds. Many enterprisers put almost as much time into writing the Executive Summary as they do into the rest of the plan.

The Executive Summary is, therefore, written *after* the rest of your business plan. It distills the essentials of your business down to a sound bite of one to two pages, just like a TV advertisement tries to get you to stop and watch rather than change the channel.

Imagine yourself presenting your executive summary to a group of potential investors.

Body of the Business Plan: The Full Tour

The main section, or body, of the business plan will provide the reader with a 20-page tour of the critical issues involved in your business. This tour should describe your business, analyze your market (customers and competitors), explain your value proposition and distribution strategy, discuss management's qualifications, explain how the business will be organized and why, provide an overview of operations, and present a financial plan. Your feasibility study will provide much of the necessary information for the plan's body. Appendix C provides a more complete description of the plan body.

Marketing Analysis: Who Are Our Customers?

As we discussed in Chapter 7, the identification of customers for the business is probably the most important business planning activity. The customer section of the business plan provides evidence as well as the logic you used to make sales estimates and supports the sales forecasts in the financial statements. The reliability and validity of the sales forecast depends on a thorough understanding of your customers and the reasons they will purchase your products or services. In an ideal situation, you would want commitments from customers to purchase products (purchase orders) as evidence of demand.

Interviewing actual customers is very important for describing the reasons that customers buy, as well as the selling cycle (the time from first customer contact to receipt of payment). The activities involved in moving from first customer, to second customer, to tens, and then hundreds of customers are another important consideration when estimating sales for the business.

As with all of the sections of the business plan, the evidence and logic you offer to convince your reader about the reliability and validity of your findings is very important. What facts will convince the reader that your estimates of the number of customers who will purchase your products or services are accurate? What facts are missing? Why are those facts missing?

Your business will have a number of different customer groups besides the people who buy your products and services. We categorize customer groups into two types:

- Primary customers—those people who buy your products and services.

- Secondary customers—those people who have some interest in the operation of your business.

In evaluating your primary and secondary customers, you should seek the answers to questions like those summarized in Exhibit 8.6.

To demonstrate that you thoroughly understand your customer base, you should summarize the results of your extensive interviews with potential customers and provide more complete documentation in the plan appendix. Such in-depth interviews will offer reasons why customers want to purchase your products or services, as well information about their sensitivity to price, quality, and other benefits. Offering more evidence increases the likelihood that your sales estimates are realistic and that your plan is the basis of a successful enterprise. Also, if your business depends on growing a base of customers over a long period of time, consider whether you will have sufficient resources to engage in this process.

Marketing Analysis: Who Are Our Competitors?

Do you think your product is totally new and appeals to a new market? This is probably not the case. Most entrepreneurs will develop businesses in established markets, with competitors who serve an identifiable base of customers. Often, new products and services are offered to an established group of customers who have unmet or insufficiently met needs, not customers who don't yet exist.

All products and services have both identifiable competition and substitutes. What entrepreneurs create are businesses that offer products and services that provide some advantages over what their competitors offer. Most customers will not immediately purchase your products or services but will first compare them to others already on the market. Identifying your competition or substitutes will show you how to position your goods or services relative to your competitors. This analysis will help you focus on the benefits of your company's products and services as well as help you identify weaknesses and problems your products/services may face in the marketplace.

You have many options when it comes to situating your business among various competitors and substitutes. Methodically describing the characteristics of your industry as well as the details about your competitors will help you convince others of the feasibility of your business concept. Trade associations provide a good way

---

exhibit

8.6   **Understanding Your Customers**

Primary Customers (Buyers of your goods or services)	Secondary Customers (Others interested in your business)
Who are your primary customers?	Who are your secondary customers (What other groups of people affect your business)?
What do your primary customer groups value?	What do your secondary customer groups value?
What value do you provide to each of these primary customer groups?	Do the strengths of the business match what each secondary customer group values? Why or why not?
Do the strengths of the business match what primary customer group values? Why or why not?	What other groups of customers should this business be serving? Why? What are the strengths of the business that would benefit these customers?

to gain a better understanding of the industry in which you will operate. Most markets of sufficient size have organizations that cater to the needs of businesses that serve certain types of customers. These groups often publish magazines and newsletters that offer insights into changes in the industry, lists of companies in the industry, and advertisements from suppliers offering products and services to the industry. Trade associations also provide information on changes in government regulation, plus ideas about possible trends occurring in the industry. Assume that the kind of business you are starting will be part of an industry with a trade association—and then locate it. If you cannot find a trade association, then you probably have not devoted enough effort to exploring the characteristics of your industry.

Armed with a thorough knowledge of your competition, you can now apply Michael Porter's competitive dynamics framework (explained in Chapter 7, page 172) to describe your competitive environment and set forth your competitive strategy. Your business plan will provide details about the five forces that drive industry competition: direct competitors, the threat of new entrants, substitute products/services, the power of suppliers, and the power of customers.

The competitive strategy you develop defines (or creates) a position that you can defend and maintain. The primary measure of a successful competitive strategy is your company's ability to generate profits. The underlying issues that an entrepreneur considers with regard to market size and competition are reviewed in Exhibit 8.7.

The competitive environment is dynamic, and your competitors will adapt their products and services to meet threats from new entrants. Naïve entrepreneurs often underestimate the loyalty of customers to established companies, goods, and services. Many potential customers may complain about your competitors'products or services, but these complaints may not be sufficient for them to switch to your company. Assume that your potential customers will use your company's products and services to force your competitors to offer them better deals. Don't be a naïve entrepreneur!

Smart enterprisers recognize their competitors' strengths. An established company has typically been in business because it is doing something right for its customers. Accurately describing why your competitors are successful can help you generate arguments for how your company can successfully compete. For example, your company may sell to different customers or offer significant product benefits that other companies cannot provide.

Marketing Strategy: How Will We Deliver Value to Our Customers?

Now the business plan shifts from "what" to "how:"

- How will you identify specific customers?

- How will you target these customers?

- How will you attract these customers to purchase your products/services?

- How will you get your products to the end-user?

This section, therefore, focuses on the activities the business will undertake to generate sales. It will lead the reader of the business plan through the entire sales cycle, from identifying customers to collecting the cash from the purchase to providing ongoing service if required.

---

exhibit
8.7

Questions for Developing a Competitive Strategy

1. Is the market large enough (are there enough customers) for your business to earn the kinds of profits to warrant investment?

2. How are you different (better) than your competitors?

3. What do you do better than other competitors (your strengths)?

4. What are your weaknesses relative to your competition?

5. What will it take for a competitor to gain that same competitive advantage as your business?

Details, details, details—but the success of the business will depend on how you execute the sales details.

The stage model you developed as part of your feasibility analysis (see Chapter 7, p. 172) forms the basis for your description of sales activities. Recall that you began by describing how you would identify and sell to the first customer and then move on to subsequent customers. As customers accumulate, they will likely reflect a pattern of similar characteristics so that patterns of similar customers define your target markets. These specific target markets combine into larger customer groups that form the business's total market. A strong business plan depicts each customer in detail and describes all of the activities involved in the sales process. The action plan you developed for selling your product or service will serve as the basis of this section of the plan.

You will also address your advertising and promotion strategies. The numerous personal interviews with potential customers provide you with information about how these people discover new products and services, which advertising and promotion strategies work best, and how they buy. Does your product require personal selling, like medical supplies and pharmaceuticals, or is it better suited to an advertising campaign, like groceries and soft drinks?

The purchase process also involves a channel of distribution from your business to a final customer. Your plan must describe how the business's products or services will reach your final customer and how you will sell to each link in this value chain. For example, if your product/service requires an intermediary, such as a wholesaler or a value-added reseller, to reach your final customer, you should explain how you would satisfy these intermediaries. What kinds of incentives will these intermediaries need to sell and service your products and services? How will these intermediaries be supported to insure they can accomplish the sales goals you have specified?

Mapping out the value chain for a single transaction for your product or service is a good way to visualize the many steps. Indicate the cost at each stage of the process, from raw materials to finished product purchased by your customer. This clearly identifies the "added value" at each stage and the revenue for each unit, as well as estimates of the fixed costs associated with producing your product or providing your service. How might the fixed or variable costs change if certain key issues in your business change? For example, if you are manufacturing a product that requires an expensive piece of machinery, the portion of your fixed costs to be allocated to each product produced will be significantly different if you are making 100 items versus 1 million items. You should begin to estimate at what level of sales (by number of items or by sales volume) you will break even. We will cover how to estimate breakeven in a later chapter.

If your business will depend on an internal sales force, the business plan will describe your plans to hire, train, and reward these individuals. If you prefer to use manufacturers' representatives or other intermediaries, your plan will describe how you will select these companies and provide sales support and training to insure that they will actively sell and service your products.

The plan's prior discussion of the business's industry, including information on your competitor's pricing policies (price, terms, credit policy, service, and warranty), will help you set your own policies and differentiate your business from others. In addition, you will be able to offer reasons for why the industry prices products at certain levels and why the margins for certain products and services are as they are.

Will your business sell its products to customers through retail channels? If so, you will now describe the details of your merchandising strategy, such as:

- How will products be sold in retail environments?

- Will the product require packaging?

- How will the product be displayed by retailers?

- What kinds of incentives might be required for retailers to actively sell your products?

Finally, be sure that your strategies to identify and sell to customers make sense as a whole. For example, if you identify a certain customer type for your product, the methods for attracting that customer must be consistent with the places this customer purchases products and services. Do these customers require service and warranties that are covered in the price of the product offered? Some products may need to be demonstrated to certain customers before they will purchase. For example, some individuals will want to hold, see, and use a laptop computer before purchasing it. You would need retail outlets where these customers could do this. In comparison, you might find that some buyers of laptops are willing to purchase their computers on the Internet, with no more than a photograph and a written description of the product listed. You will need to identify which customer group you are pursuing and specify how your sales efforts will meet their specific needs.

The "Sales Goals" section of the business plan provides some of the strongest evidence about the entrepreneur's understanding of how the business will be successful. It offers concrete information about the entire process of generating sales. Knowing that the possible market for a product/service may have a potential in the millions is important, but showing how sales will specifically be achieved is critical. Demonstrating to a reader that you have detailed knowledge of the entire sales process—identifying, targeting, attracting, and selling to customers—becomes a significant indicator that the business will be viable and successful. The action plan that you developed for generating sales will help you highlight the critical selling tasks to be accomplished.

Implementation: Management and Organization

The next two sections focus on implementation: who will manage the firm and the activities they will perform. These detailed sections on management and organization, operations, and execution can be very difficult to write, requiring an imagination and significant due diligence to describe the operations of the business in a concrete way.

An entrepreneur who assumes that he or she can learn how to operate the business as it emerges will have some costly lessons. A start-up can face critical problems that can easily overwhelm a fledgling firm. What if your suppliers are late with a critical parts delivery? What if your equipment breaks down? Perhaps your employees turn out to be less skilled or incompetent at selling to your customers or providing good service. What will happen if your customers don't pay on time? This section of the plan will indicate to the reader that you are prepared for success and know what to do when things go wrong.

The "Management and Organization" section of the business plan identifies the key managerial and organizational skills necessary to run the business and links these skill sets to positions within the organization. In addition, the plan should identify which individuals who are a part of the start-up team have these necessary skills. If the existing management team lacks some of the necessary skills, the plan explains how additional critical personnel will be hired to fill in any gaps. Organization charts of duties and responsibilities should not only cover the present situation but also show how the business may change as it grows over the next few years.

There are many ways to organize a business to successfully compete. Some businesses organize by function, with a department in charge of marketing, human resources, finance, production, and so on. Others structure along product line, type of customer, or geographic region. Companies vary in their degree of centralization and how

You may have to interview and hire critical personnel to get your enterprise up and running.

© Endostock/Dreamstime LLC

rigidly they define their overall structure. In addition, companies can have a clearly defined chain of command with many levels of managers, or adopt a flatter structure with fewer layers. The particular configuration of resources and capabilities you select will depend on the type of business and its needs.

Few start-ups will have a team of individuals who have all of the necessary skills to successfully operate the business. Be honest about weaknesses in the skills and abilities of the current management team. Show how you will counteract these weaknesses by hiring employees, consultants, or advisors. Provide descriptions of critical outside board members, advisors, consultants, lawyers, and accountants. Describe how these individuals are involved in the management of the business and provide information on how you will compensate these individuals. Enterprisers who use experts and advisors wisely show others that they have a sound understanding of what it takes to manage the business successfully.

Implementation: Operations and Execution

The "Operations" section of the business plan provides a detailed description of the activities necessary to run the day-to-day operations of the business. The issues to consider vary depending on whether the firm makes and sells products or is a service business.

For manufacturing firms, the plan's "Operations" section describes the entire manufacturing process from the purchase of raw materials to the sales and service of the product in the field. The reader should feel as if he or she is walking through the factory. The enterpriser should identify critical problems that might occur in the manufacturing process and offer solutions for these issues. An often-ignored issue in managing a business is determining cash flow needs. The "Operations" section will identify suppliers and their capabilities, the payment terms specified by suppliers for parts and raw materials, and the likely time the business will need to collect cash from customers. This section should also list important machinery and equipment necessary to manufacture the products and the facilities required to house these machines and store raw materials, work in process, and finished good inventories. Repair and maintenance procedures and alternative methods of production in the case of critical machinery downtime are also important to include.

A service business will provide a detailed description of how it will provide services. This includes identifying the individuals responsible for providing services to customers and describing all the tasks necessary to insure customer satisfaction. How will service personnel be managed from initial customer contact through payment? How will quality control be handled? What kinds of support systems and equipment will service personnel need to complete their assignments?

For all businesses, the plan should outline the accounting and control systems necessary to operate the business. After reviewing this section, the reader should know:

- Who will be responsible for managing the company's assets and cash?

- How will cash accounts be monitored to prevent fraud and malfeasance?

- How will inventory and supplies be managed?

- What business licenses and permits are required to operate the business?

- Will the location of the business need to be inspected?

- What kinds of measurement systems will the business implement to insure that the business is successful?

- What key metrics will monitor the business' critical success factors?

- What are the key indicators that the business is on the path to success? What are the key indicators that the business is failing?

- What remedial activities will the enterprise implement if the business appears to be failing?

The "Execution" section of the business plan will indicate all of the critical milestones in the life the organization. These are the issues you addressed when you created the action plan described earlier in this chapter and developed the critical path for the business:

- When will essential employees be hired?

- When will a building and offices be rented or purchased?

- When will machinery be purchased and installed?

- When will training for key manufacturing and service tasks occur?

A timeline will help you identify the critical events that are necessary for business success and the correct sequence of these events. For example, the manufacture of a product will require that you install and test your machinery, order raw materials, and accept delivery before you begin production.

It is well worth your effort to prepare contingency plans for likely problem situations you may encounter. Possible "what if" scenarios include the following:

- What will happen if a key part necessary for the manufacture of your product is not delivered on time? Will you manage this problem by having a substantial inventory of this product, or will you have alternative sources of supply?

- What if a critical machine breaks down?

- What happens if renovations to your plant and offices take longer than anticipated?

- What if critical permits and licenses are delayed?

- What will occur if a key employee quits?

- Will your business have the resources, skills, and capabilities to weather unforeseen problems?

Start-ups tend to follow Murphy's Law: Anything that can go wrong, will. Are you prepared? Showing your readers that you have considered problems in advance indicates an ability to cover all your bases.

Many enterprisers are big-picture visionaries: good at seeing and selling the possibility of success and opportunity. The ability to grasp the specific details necessary to achieve these opportunities often requires a different mindset and skills. The successful development and growth of a business will require attention to these details. If the "Management and Organization," "Operations," and "Execution" sections of the business plan are well thought out, the ideas and vision of the business will come to life. The readers of the plan should be able to see how all of the aspects of the enterprise connect and how the enterprise will operate successfully. Invariably, as the business develops and grows, unforeseen problems and issues will arise, including those that were not considered in the business plan. The entrepreneur who demonstrates an ability to solve problems identified in the business plan will be better prepared to solve unforeseen issues and circumstances as they occur.

Financial Plan: How Will We Measure the Results?

The "Financial Plan" section of the business plan looks to be the most daunting aspect of the planning process. There is a strong temptation to create financial documents and reports by using formulas with estimations of growth rates. For example, it is easy to create a series of scenarios with good, better, and best estimations for sales and expenses, where "good" might be a 5 percent growth rate, "better" is a 15 percent growth rate, and "best" is a 50 percent growth rate. "Good, better, best" says that you don't have an accurate estimate of sales that you believe you can achieve. "Good, better, best" says to many readers that you are guessing. It is far better to struggle through the logic involved in generating each number rather than taking the easy route.

A good strategy for completing the financial statements is to start at the end. Begin by identifying all of the specific financing needs of the business and their timing. For example, list the cash outlays for salaries, rent, purchases of raw materials, machines, and all other expenses and capital investments and indicate when these cash outlays will occur. In addition, show when you will receive cash inflows from investments, loans, and the collection of cash sales and accounts receivables. These figures form the basis of your cash flow statement. The cash flow statement serves as the fundamental operating document for the day-to-day management of the business. Without cash, the business will be unable to meet its financial obligations.

For each figure listed in the financial statements, provide a footnote for how you arrived at this figure. For example, if equipment was purchased for cash, reference the "Operations" section of the business plan that describes this equipment. The business plan appendix will include documents describing this equipment—price, where the equipment will be purchased, maintenance agreements, and any other important technical data. For sales and expense estimates on the income statement, reference the marketing sections of the business plan that describe how you generated sales forecasts and support your forecasts with materials in the appendix, such as purchase orders from prospective customers and marketing research reports. For your own benefit, you want to know which figures in the financial statements are solid and which are guesses. The goal is to derive financial estimations that you can substantiate with evidence and logic.

Information on key industry ratios and standards will serve as a benchmark for the performance of your business. You will want to know whether the financial values you are specifying in your business plan are reasonable compared to other firms. For example, is the gross margin for your business similar to other competitors? Are the expenses in your business similar to other competitors'? Is your business more or less efficient than other businesses? If the financial standards of your business are significantly different from those of other businesses, you will need to offer reasons for these differences.

The Risk Management Association is one of the major sources of performance standards and publishes financial ratios by industry type and firm size. Most libraries and banks have copies of RMA materials. Most trade associations have information on the financial performance of firms in their industries. This information is often accessible to association members on websites. Other resources for generating industry standards are the *U.S. Industry and Trade Outlook*, published by NTIS, and the Small Business Advancement National Center, (http://www.sbaer.uca.edu), where you'll find 33 small business industry profiles.

If the business plan relates to an existing business, you should provide actual historical financial statements for the last two to five years. This information will show readers how the business has operated successfully (or not) in the past and why. You should include extensive footnotes to these financial statements that explain the rationale for these numbers.

You will be generating prospective financial statements for two to five years—a sufficient period to be able to determine at what point the firm will generate positive cash flow as well as satisfy its cash flow needs. The date when positive cash flow occurs is a very important milestone, and your financial estimates should continue for at least two years beyond that date. Important financial statements to include are income statements, balance sheets, cash flow statements, sources and uses of funds, and a list of all capital equipment and the dates and prices of purchase. Prepare statements showing monthly figures for the first year and quarterly figures for subsequent years.

Numbers that cannot be supported through evidence or logic should be referenced as "guesses." Don't pretend to know information. If you have problems generating specific numbers for parts of the financial plan, you probably have not done sufficient research on previous business plan sections.

Appendix (Supporting Documents)

The Appendix will provide information that supports the claims in the body of your business plan for such key issues in your enterprise as estimating sales, costing out your product or service, and demonstrating the competence and capabilities of yourself and your management team. The Appendix will include resumes of your management team and key advisors. You should also consider including such documentation as

(a)   market analysis data and market research studies

(b)   action plans for sales and distribution

(c)   product specifications and photos

(d)   action plans for production, operations, and service

(e)   letters of reference

(f)   census and demographic data

(g)   contracts

(h)   letters of commitment from customers, suppliers, and lenders

(i)   buy/sell agreements among partners

A reader who delves into the Appendix will be looking for detailed evidence of how you arrived at critical numbers (e.g., sales, costs, product development process). You have to show that you have facts to back up your claims.

8.6   The Final Product

Congratulations! If you have persevered in completing the business plan in sufficient detail, you have built a business on paper. This business plan provides you with a good indication of how the business will operate and the critical issues that will determine its success or failure. It creates a road map that depicts where you will meet with success, as well as encounter difficulties.

Reading an actual business plan is perhaps the best way to understand the value of preparing your own plan. We have provided the business plan for Beau-Ties, Inc., on our website, www.cengage.com/management/enterpriseonline. As you read it, you will see how a team of enterprisers presented its plan for a company that manufactures and sells bow ties. Let's take a quick tour of the plan so that you will be familiar with it and can answer the questions posed later in the chapter.

- **Executive Summary:** These enterprisers have done a good job of presenting the highlights of their business in just one page. They pique the reader's interest by mentioning the undeveloped competitive structure of the industry, low initial investment, integrated merchandising program, and high growth rate and potential profitability of the men's fashion accessory sector of the men's apparel industry.

- **Body of the Plan:** In the "Business Description" section the principals clearly and concisely present an overview of the business concept and why they believe it can succeed. By stating their specific goals, the principals demonstrate their understanding of their business venture's market and how they intend to achieve these objectives. The product description includes not only the features of the bow ties themselves, but also the merchandising program and support services that make their concept unique. The product matrix and product design matrix exhibits highlight these characteristics. A discussion of the men's fashion accessory industry, including statistics and results of interviews with retailers, follows. A table comparing other companies in this market to Beau-Ties supports the analysis of the competitive environment. The "Marketing Analysis/Strategy" section describes the two target customer groups and how Beau-Ties will market its product to each category. It also identifies the unique benefits the company's marketing and promotional strategy offers.

The next part of the business plan's body is devoted to the management team and operations. In addition to biographies of the principals, other equity participants, and consultants, this section outlines the overall company operating structure (three functional areas). The "Financials" section opens with the anticipated financial needs, proposed sources of funding, and expected rate of return for investors. It then summarizes the profitability (picture presented) in the detailed financial statements and refers readers to the exhibits for the statements themselves and the assumptions used to develop them.

- **Exhibits:** The 14 exhibits provide evidence that substantiates the claims made in the plan narrative. They cover product design, market data, marketing research, marketing strategy, qualifications of the management team, financial reports, and assumptions in the financial statements.

This business plan reflects the principals' understanding of their business at one particular moment in time: now. As they move forward, the business will change, and the knowledge and experience they gain in developing and operating Beau-Ties will require them to modify this business plan. The business plan enables them to see how the business *should* operate and helps them determine whether their assumptions are accurate.

Your business plan will help you be conscious and thoughtful, so that you do not manage your business moment to moment. It should be a useful, dynamic document. To keep it that way, you should revise it regularly—on a quarterly, semi-annual, or annual basis. Look upon these modifications as opportunities to reconsider why and how your business is successful. A reevaluation of your business plan will help you see whether your assumptions about your business are accurate, and whether new metrics and measures are needed. Typically, as your business grows, your priorities change—and so do those of your customers, suppliers, and employees.

Remember, if you don't have a road map and plan for your business, any route will get you there. Having a business plan will help you achieve the goals you set for yourself. Keeping your business plan updated will help you reexamine your goals and priorities.

Summary

1. A business plan serves as a game plan for your business. It provides an opportunity to practice operating your business and gives you experiences that provide an advantage over your competition.

2. Your business plan records the actions—past, present, and future—you are taking to make your business a reality. It goes beyond the feasibility study and identifies the specific tactics and actions for enterprise success. As you write a business plan, you will be able to visualize your business and gain a better understanding of what it will take to make it successful. It will show you what you know and what you need to know, as well as point out the flaws in your strategy. In addition to serving as a reality check, the business plan also becomes a valuable tool to engage others in your efforts.

3. A business plan should answer four key questions: Why you? Whom do you hurt? Why now? Why me? Your responses should demonstrate that you and your partners have the requisite skills to make the business a success and that you understand the competitive environment in which your business will operate, explain the need for and benefits of the goods or services you plan to offer, and encourage others to get involved in your business.

4. An action plan serves as preparation for writing a business plan. The three steps of an action plan are (1) identify risks, (2) develop a response strategy, and (3) control and monitor the risks and responses. Developing an action plan includes breaking each project down into deliverables and specific tasks necessary to accomplish your goals. The sequence of actions is another key component. Knowing how tasks relate to each other allows you to develop a critical path that shows the schedule of important milestones, the order to follow, and tasks to reach them.

5. Forecasting the future starts with understanding the past. The more specific you can be, the more useful your forecasts. Learning from others is an excellent way to improve your knowledge of the industry and business. Experience, either yours or someone else's, will help you develop meaningful forecasts of the time, people, equipment, facilities, and funding you need to start your business. Your forecasts should be dynamic. You will revise

them in response to changes in your business environment. It's also important to identify gaps in your knowledge base so that you can fill them.

6. You should write the first business plan for yourself. As you prepare it, you will become aware of your knowledge gaps and can develop strategies to address them. Pitfalls to avoid include making unrealistic projections, underestimating the time it takes to accomplish various tasks, failing to understand the competitive landscape, and performing inadequate due diligence.

7. Your personal business plan forms the basis for the business plans you write to attract others to participate in your enterprise. You should customize these plans to the readers' interests and to your purpose in sharing it, choosing the appropriate language for your audience. The plans you write for others serve as introductions to your business and should encourage them to find out more. They should be a true reflection of you as an enterpriser and focus on the quality of the information, not the quantity.

8. The business plan format should take into account the type of business and where it is in its life cycle. While each business plan will be different, most plans share certain characteristics and contain three main parts: the one- to two-page executive summary, the 20-page body of the business plan with a narrative that describes the enterprise and its major issues, and a section with supporting materials that provide evidence for the business facts you've described.

9. The Executive Summary provides the highlights of your business plan and invites the reader to delve into the body of the plan. Even though it is the shortest section, it is extremely important to your success and serves as the first impression readers get of you and your proposed business venture. While it comes first, you write it after you have prepared the rest of the report.

10. The body of the plan serves as a tour of your proposed business venture. It should describe your business, analyze your market (customers and competitors), explain your value proposition and distribution strategy, discuss management's qualifications, explain how the business will be organized and why, provide an overview of operations, and present a financial plan. Your narrative should address not only the management's perspective but also stakeholder issues.

11. Marketing analysis starts with the identification of customers, probably the most important business planning activity. In addition to primary customers—those people who buy your products and services—enterprisers should also identify the business's secondary customers, those people who have an interest in the operation of your business. Marketing analysis also includes understanding your competition and substitutes for your products or services.

12. Once you have analyzed your market, you can focus on how you will attract customers and distribute your goods and services to the ultimate user. This includes understanding your sales cycles, developing appropriate advertising and promotion strategies, setting pricing and credit policies, and selecting distribution channels. A value chain map can help identify the steps required to accomplish these objectives and demonstrate how they work together.

13. The next sections of the plan's body present the implementation program for the business. The "Management" section of the business plan describes the executive team and the capabilities they bring to the business, as well as the outside consultants and professional advisors (attorneys, accountants). This section should also include an organization chart that shows the overall business structure and who will be responsible for key functional departments. After reviewing the "Operations" section, a reader should have a clear picture of the firm's daily activities and how the firm will produce its goods or services. This section should also address potential problems and offer solutions. The "Execution Plan" summarizes all the important activities you identified in other parts of the plan and plots them on a timeline of critical milestones. The timeline demonstrates that your activities are internally consistent and coordinated with the financial projections.

14. The "Financial Plan" includes both actual historical financial statements for an existing business and projected financial information for the next two to five years. It is important to explain the assumptions you use to develop the projected statements and indicate how the financial statements compare to industry benchmarks. This section also identifies the financing needs and their timing, as well as possible sources.

15. The Appendix contains documents that support the assumptions on which you based the plan's marketing analysis, action plans, product specifications, and financial statements. Presenting the facts that back up your claims lends credibility to your plan.

Review Questions

1. What is a business plan and why do many enterprisers start businesses without writing one? List several reasons for writing such a plan and describe the benefits of doing so.

2. Describe the four questions a business plan should answer and explain the objective for each.

3. Discuss the three steps required to prepare an action plan and the importance of each step.

4. What is a critical path and why should you identify it for the business you want to start?

5. Describe several steps enterprisers can take to increase the accuracy of their projections.

6. Differentiate between the business plan an enterpriser writes for his or her own use and the plans that are written for others. What are the key issues to consider for each type of business plan?

7. Name the three major parts of a business plan and what each should include. Why should you write the executive summary last?

8. Summarize the key points in the business description.

9. What two broad topics are the focus of the marketing analysis section? Describe the types of information this section should include.

10. How does marketing strategy differ from marketing analysis? What are the major issues that this section addresses?

11. Describe the information you'd include in the "Management" section of a plan for a new business.

12. Why is it important to provide a detailed operations summary and execution plan in the business plan and what should these sections cover?

13. What are the drawbacks to developing a "good, better, best" financial plan? How should an enterpriser prepare financial information?

14. What is the objective of the Appendix and why should the supporting documents go here rather than in the plan's body?

Applying What You've Learned

1. Differentiate between a feasibility study and a business plan. When are business plans necessary, and when are they not?

2. Consider how the content of a business plan might differ based on the interests of the reader. What would an investor be looking for in a business plan that a potential employee might not? What would a potential supplier be looking for in a business plan that a customer might not?

Read the Beau-Ties business plan provided on our website, www.cengage.com/management/enterpriseonline, before answering the following questions.

3. You are one of the founders of Beau-Ties. You want to prepare a business plan before proceeding any further, but your partners don't think it is necessary. How would you convince them to write a plan, and why?

4. For whom do you think the Beau-Ties business plan was written, the founders or other readers,

and why? How well does the plan address the issues presented in section 8.3, "Writing the Business Plan?" Explain your answer.

5. Develop a critical path chart for Beau-Ties. Include the rationale for the milestones you've chosen.

6. Write the "elevator speech" for Beau-Ties. Divide the class into teams of two to four members, with half playing the role of company founder and half taking the part of a potential investor. Make the presentation to the investor(s). Get feedback and revise the speech as needed. Pick several groups to present their final speeches to the class for more feedback.

7. Analyze the sections of the Beau-Ties business plan as follows:

    (a) *Executive Summary and Business Description.* How well do they answer the questions posed in the chapter's discussions of these sections?

(b) *Marketing analysis and strategies.* How well do the enterprisers identify potential customers, competition, demand, and potential market size for the company?

(c) *Management.* Is the Beau-Ties management team qualified to turn this business plan into a viable business, and why?

(d) *Operations and execution plan.* Does it enable the company to meet its stated objectives?

(e) *Financial plan and the assumptions.* Do they seem reasonable for the business as described in the plan?

(f) *Exhibits.* Are the documents included as exhibits sufficient to support the business plan? What additional material would you like to see in this section?

In your opinion, does the Beau-Ties business plan make a good case, and why?

Enterprisers on the Web

1. An enterpriser can buy software designed specifically for writing business plans. Using an Internet search engine such as Google, Yahoo, Excite, or Lycos, select three such programs.

   (a) Compare their features.

   (b) See if you can find user reviews to determine how well the programs live up to their claims.

   (c) Based on your analysis, which seems to be the best, and why?

   (d) Now, read the *Inc.* article "Garbage In, Garbage Out," which discusses advantages and disadvantages of using one of these programs to write a business plan (http://www.inc.com/-magazine/19960801/1764.html). Summarize the article's arguments and compare them to your research. Do you agree and why? (While the article is old and some of the software mentioned may no longer be available, the basic information is still valid.)

2. Using resources such as the sites listed below, locate three companies in an industry (or industries) in which you might like to start a business. (You can also find annual reports at companies' websites.) How does each company describe itself? What are the goals and objectives of the companies? How do they describe their customers and competitors? How do they describe their competitive advantage?

   CEOEXPRESS at http://ceoexpress.com/

   Public Register's Annual Report Service at http://www.annualreportservice.com/

   Hoovers Online at http://www.hoovers.com/

3. Using a general search engine such as Google, Yahoo, Excite, Askjeeves, Altavista, or hotbot), search for trade associations that cater to the industry in which you'd like to start your business.

   (a) What services and publications does this trade association offer?

   (b) How often does the trade association meet for trade shows?

   (c) What are the dues for belonging to the trade association?

4. Now search for industry reports on your chosen industry. Who is publishing these reports? Why do they make this information available to others (e.g., they are consultants to this industry, they do mergers and acquisitions for companies in this industry, they sell stock in businesses in this industry)? Which appear to be the most valuable and why?

5. Using the industry resources you've identified thus far, answer the following questions:

   (a) What companies are identified in this industry? Why are these companies identified rather than others? What constitutes the characteristics of these companies that would put them in this industry?

   (b) What trends in this industry are likely to occur in the next five years?

   (c) What do industry experts predict is the likely growth rate of this industry in the next five years?

End Notes

1. Frédéric Delmar and Scott Shane, "Does Business Planning Facilitate the Development of New Ventures?" *Strategic Management Journal,* December 2003, pp. 1165–1185; and Jon Liao and William B. Gartner, "The Effects of Pre-Venture Plan Timing and Perceived Environmental Uncertainty on the Persistence of Emerging Firms," *Small Business Economics,* August 2006, pp. 23–40.

2. This section is based on material in Eric Verzuh, *The Fast Forward MBA in Project Management* (New York: John Wiley and Sons, Inc., 1999).

PART THREE

Enterprising Strategies

Pathways to Enterprise Creation

KEY CONCEPTS

1. Enterprisers can start businesses in many different ways. Pursuing opportunities involves a wide range of new venture strategies, situations, and behaviors. We all have different interests, skills, knowledge, and abilities. It is important to discover our strengths and to use them to choose the most appropriate route to entrepreneurship.

2. The use of a typology to describe new venture pathways focuses attention on the differences among enterprisers rather than on the supposed differences between enterprisers and "others."

   We can group similar businesses into eight -archetypes, each of which suggests different start-up strategies and behaviors that enterprisers can apply to their start-up situations. The eight pathways to enterprise creation are:

   1. Type 1—Escaping to Something New
   2. Type 2—Putting the Deal Together
   3. Type 3—Using Prior Skills & Contacts (Professionals)
   4. Type 4—Purchasing a Firm
   5. Type 5—Leveraging Expertise
   6. Type 6—Aggressive Service
   7. Type 7—Pursuing the Unique Idea
   8. Type 8—Methodical Organizing

3. In addition to describing the archetype profiles, it is helpful to analyze them using 19 factors that cover environment, business, person, and start-up process. These archetypes can serve as broad guides for getting into business. However, your own start-up pathway is likely to be a blend of several of the eight archetypes.

Suppose as you travel to other cultures, you see how women use plant-based products for skin care. Working in a plastic surgeon's office and then as an aesthetician, you continue to increase your knowledge about natural skin care. Because you live in Colorado, you are especially interested in the healing properties of local plants and start mixing ingredients on your stove. Once you develop a formula that works, you start a home-based company to make your first product, Cowgirl Cream.

The case study in this chapter tells the story of Cowgirl Enterprises' founder Donna Baase, and follows the growth of her natural beauty products company. You'll learn about her particular path to success, and the chapter describes seven other pathways to entrepreneurial creation. Which one will you choose?

9.0 What Kind of Enterprise Are You Starting?

Just as there are no average or typical kinds of enterprises, there is no one "right" way to start a business. As we discussed in Chapter 1, enterprisers can start and successfully operate many different types of enterprises. For example, you'd start a pizza restaurant in a different way than you would a biotechnology company. A business consulting company will be started in a different way than a company that intends to make and sell ice cream. In this chapter we'll explore the different ways that enterprisers can start their businesses. You'll learn to pinpoint and focus on the specific issues for the kind of business you want to form.

To accomplish this, we group similar types of businesses into broad categories called archetypes. An **archetype** is a model or prototype from which similar things can be made. In this case, we refer to a model for an ideal business in a particular group. The archetype does not describe each individual enterprise in the group but rather the best representation of a typical business in that group. As we delve more deeply into the archetypes presented in this chapter, you will get a better sense of how the ideal type for each group is both

Archetype   A model or prototype from which similar things can be made.

similar to and different from the examples we use to describe actual businesses in these groups. You might also consider each archetype as a particular pathway and set of directions to use when setting off on the journey of enterprise creation.

This chapter describes eight broad archetypes for starting enterprises, as listed in Exhibit 9.1.[1] The profile for each archetype includes the three major levels of analysis we identified in Chapter 1 (individual, enterprise, environment) plus the start-up process for that type of enterprise. Each archetype, therefore, answers four questions:

1. What kinds of individuals are likely to start this kind of enterprise?

2. What does this kind of enterprise look like and how does it compete?

3. In what kind of industry and environment does this enterprise compete?

4. What does the enterpriser do to start this kind of enterprise?

For these four questions, we identify 19 specific issues to help categorize the wide array of different enterprises as shown in Exhibit 9.2. An archetype will not differ from the other seven types on all 19 characteristics. The *pattern* of responses to the 19 questions is what may differ. Exhibit 9.3 illustrates the significant similarities and differences among the archetypes across the 19 questions.

9.1 Eight Pathways to Enterprise Creation

Each archetype represents an ideal pathway that enterprisers use for getting into business. Think of these archetypes as templates for the kinds of people, firms, environments, and start-up activities that are most likely to be associated with each other. Our research shows that certain types of individuals are more likely to start particular kinds of firms in specific industries, using distinct kinds of activities to start these businesses. For example, the start-up of some businesses, such as accounting, law, and veterinary practices, requires those enterprisers to have specific skills and abilities. In addition, they also are more likely to have established a network of potential customers to whom they can provide their services. It is this cross-level combination of characteristics at the individual, organizational, and environmental levels that provides us with some important insights into the firm start-up process.

Now let's look at the characteristics of each archetype and at an example of an enterpriser who started this form of business.

Type 1: Escaping to Something New

Individuals who start enterprises often seek to escape from their previous jobs—jobs that, from their

---

exhibit
9.1

Eight Archetypes for New Business Ventures

Type	Name
1	Escaping to Something New
2	Putting the Deal Together
3	Using Prior Skills & Contacts (Professionals)
4	Purchasing a Firm
5	Leveraging Expertise
6	Aggressive Service
7	Pursuing the Unique Idea
8	Methodical Organizing

Source: William B. Gartner, Terence R. Mitchell, and Karl H. Vesper, "A Taxonomy of New Business Ventures," *Journal of Business Venturing,* May 1989, pp. 169–186.

exhibit
9.2

19 Questions for Business Archetypes

Individual Level

1. Did the enterpriser's previous work experiences provide opportunities for advancement? (great to none)

2. Are the enterpriser's previous work experiences similar to the work required in the new enterprise? (similar to unrelated)

3. What was the enterpriser's interest in starting a business? (always interested to never interested)

4. Did the enterpriser see much chance that the new venture would fail? (0% to 95% chance of failure)

Enterprise Level

5. Did the enterprise have any partners when it was started? (yes or no)

6. When did the enterprise begin to offer its products/services compared to its competitors? (First to after all of the others)

7. What is the quality of the enterprise's goods/services compared to its competitors? (lower to higher)

8. How similar are the enterprise's goods/services compared to its competitors? (different to same)

9. How flexible is the enterprise to adapting its goods/services compared to its competitors? (much lower to much higher)

Environmental Level

10. How complex are the technology and skills required to manufacture products or deliver services in this industry? (simple to complex)

11. How important are contacts with suppliers in this industry? (important to not important)

12. Do customers need a lot of expertise to purchase goods/services in the enterprise's industry? (high to none)

Startup Process

How much time did the enterpriser spend (a lot to none) on the following:

13. Convincing customers to buy the enterprise's products/services?

14. Seeking advice from lawyers, consultants, bankers and friends?

15. Seeking resources (loans, equity, suppliers, etc.) to start the enterprise?

16. Advertising, issuing press releases, sending out brochures?

17. Manufacturing the product or providing the service?

18. Was the enterprise purchased or is it a franchise? (yes or no)

19. At the beginning of the startup process, how much time did the enterpriser devote to starting the new enterprise? (full time to part time)

Source: William B. Gartner, Terence R. Mitchell, and Karl H. Vesper, "A Taxonomy of New Business Ventures," *Journal of Business Venturing,* May 1989, pp. 173–174.

exhibit
9.3

Profiles of New Business Ventures

	Type							
	1	2	3	4	5	6	7	8
	Escaping to Something New	Putting the Deal Together	Rollover Skills/ Contacts	Purchasing a Firm	Leveraging Expertise	Aggressive Service	Pursuing the Unique Idea	Methodical Organizing
Individual Characteristics								
Opportunities for advancement in previous work	Low	NS	NS	NS	NS	NS	High	High
Similarity of previous work to work in new venture	Low	High	High	NS	High	High	Low	Low
Previous interest in starting a company	NS	NS	NS	NS	Low	High	High	NS
Perception of risk of new venture failure	NS	Low	NS	Low	Low	NS	NS	High
Organizational Characteristics								
Active partners involved in operations	Likely	No	No	No	Yes	No	Likely	Likely
Product/service pioneer	NS	NS	NS	NS	NS	NS	Yes	NS
Relative quality of products/ services	NS	NS	NS	NS	High	High	High	High
Relative similarity of products/ services	NS	Unique	Similar	Similar	Unique	NS	Unique	NS
Relative flexibility to adapt to customer's needs	NS	NS	NS	High	High	High	NS	NS
Environmental Characteristics								
Technology	Simple	NS	Complex	NS	Complex	Complex	Simple	NS

Importance of contacts	NS	High	NS	NS	NS	High	NS	NS
Customer expertise in product purchasing	Low	Low	Low	Low	High	High	High	High
Process Characteristics (How much did you spend?)								
Selling	NS	NS	Low	NS	High	High	Low	High
Seeking advice	NS	Low	Low	NS	NS	High	High	High
Seeking resources	NS	NS	Low	High	NS	NS	High	High
Advertising	NS	NS	NS	NS	NS	NS	NS	NS
Manufacturing/ delivery service	NS	NS	NS	High	High	NS	High	High
Purchase firm	NS	NS	NS	Yes	NS	NS	NS	NS
Time commitment at start-up	NS	Part-time	Full-time	NS	NS	Full-time	Part-time	NS

NS, not a significant differentiating variable for this gestalt.

Source: William B. Gartner, Terence R. Mitchell, and Karl H. Vesper, "A Taxonomy of New Business Ventures," *Journal of Business Venturing,* May 1989, pp. 176–177.

perspective, offer few rewards in terms of salary, challenging work, and promotion opportunities. The new venture is in a different industry and represents a different type of work from the enterpriser's previous job. The enterpriser begins the enterprise part time and eventually works up to a full-time commitment, meeting capital requirements through savings and loans from family and friends. The majority of the enterpriser's time is devoted to finding a location for the business and in making sales.

This is an enterpriser oriented toward the general, or average, consumer. This type of firm enters an established market and offers goods or services similar to its competitors. The goods are not technically complicated (e.g., pets, furniture, clothes), yet the industry is very competitive because of the many other firms offering similar products or services.

Janice Myers (all names disguised) and her sister, a speech therapist, took this pathway to start their pet store. Both women had become dissatisfied with their jobs. After spending several months discussing business ownership, they convinced themselves that they had the skills and resources to proceed. After taking classes on how to start a business at the local university and the Small Business Administration, the sisters spent about three months preparing to open their business. They did a market location study, found a building in a good area of town, signed a lease, and began renovating the interior. They used personal funds to finance the business.

During this time, they went to other pet stores in their area and asked for advice. One owner allowed them to look at her books and introduced them to the right suppliers. The two sisters also ran this person's store for a couple of days to better understand how to operate this kind of business.

Why were these enterprisers successful in getting into business? The sisters attribute their success to their enjoyment of running a pet store, which is apparent to their customers. The sisters have established a good reputation around town for their knowledge of pets and for the service they provide. Although most of the products the sisters sell are available at lower prices at other places, their customers prefer to shop at this store because of the advice and good service the sisters provide.

Type 2: Putting the Deal Together

Enterprisers in this group assemble the different aspects of the business (suppliers, wholesale and retail channels, customers) into a "deal" designed to ensure success for each participant. Two types of enterprises make up this group. The first is the real estate developer. This enterpriser's experience putting deals together for other firms forms the basis for the business start-up. The other type of enterprise is the novelty firm start-up, where an enterpriser comes up with an idea for a product, finds a manufacturer to make the product, makes sales calls to wholesalers and retailers, and generates primary demand for the product. The novelty firm coordinates the different functions of the business among the various parties (manufacturer, wholesaler, retailer, etc.). For both types of firms, a good contact network—knowing the right kinds of people—is a critical factor. The real estate developer needs to know the landowners, the builders, and the investors for projects. The novelty enterpriser has to know purchasing agents in key stores.

John Bosworth is a good example of a Type 2 deal maker. Using his experience developing houses for the elderly with the state housing authority, he started a real estate development company to assist other businesses in obtaining state contracts to build housing for the elderly. His firm puts deals together: arranging financing from the state to build housing, getting an architect to draw up plans for the buildings, finding a builder willing to construct the units for a given price, and locating the land. Mr. Bosworth's actions, beyond his deal-making activities, involved incorporating and investing some money in renting an office. The work he was able to get came from contacts he had from his previous work.

Type 3: Using Prior Skills and Contacts (Professionals)

Professional start-ups are formed by enterprisers who held positions in which they used technical skills and expertise similar to those required in the new business. These enterprisers did not have a long-term desire to start a business and only began to pursue the pathway of enterprise creation after discovering that job advancement and career and salary growth were blocked. They view starting a business as a risky effort. Rather than searching for capital, these enterprisers use their own money. Because the enterprisers bring industry expertise and contacts to the table, they spend very little time studying the industry or learning the technical requirements of the job. They sell to their previous customer contact base rather than devote energy to marketing or advertising. These enterprisers quit their jobs to work full time in their new business. Examples include enterprises that depend on the enterpriser's professional expertise, such as CPA firms, consultants, personnel agencies, and advertising firms. In many respects, these enterprises offer a generic service that other firms also offer. The new enterprise competes by offering better service than others.

An example of this archetype is April Burke, who started a management compensation consulting business—the same kind of work she had performed for another company for the previous six years. She believed she could provide higher quality service on her own. She first contacted a lawyer to help her incorporate her business. Then she contacted some of her previous clients to offer her services. Developing a reputation for good work was very important because most of her clients (human resource departments in large corporations) knew one another. Ms. Burke also wrote articles in trade journals to build a strong reputation in her industry.

Type 4: Purchasing a Business or Acquiring a Franchise

Both purchasing a business and acquiring a franchis are significant pathways for becoming an enterpriser.

Because so many enterprisers use these two pathways to start their businesses, we will devote a chapter to each method. For now, we will outline the characteristics of enterprisers who are more likely to pursue these two routes.

Three types of firms fall into this category of new business venture: the purchased firm, a firm that is family owned or started with family assistance, and the franchise. All three types offer products and services of the same kind and quality as their competitors. These firms compete by adapting to the changing needs of their customers. The types of goods and services offered are not complex, and the entrepreneur's work background is typically similar to the venture acquired. Although enterprisers who follow this path had opportunities for advancement and growth in their previous jobs, they had long-term goals of owning a business. These enterprisers perceive the new enterprise as low risk.

With both purchasing and franchising, enterprisers must find capital to fund the business acquisition or purchase the franchise. Much of the owners' time is devoted to financial planning. Enterprisers who follow this path make a full-time commitment upon purchase or start-up of the franchise. In purchasing an ongoing concern, they view it as a turnaround situation and hope to run it more profitably than the previous owners. With an acquisition of either an independent company or a franchise, enterprisers spend a great deal of time evaluating the business' goods or services and becoming very familiar with the different aspects of the business.

A good example of a Type 4 start-up enterpriser is Lance Vermont, who purchased a bike shop. Lance describes himself as a bike person, and from childhood he dreamt of owning a bike shop. After retiring from the military, he decided to go to college. While at college he found a bike shop and bought out the owner. Why did he buy an existing business rather than start his own? He recognized that the college town could support only one bike shop. Since buying the firm, Lance has quadrupled its sales. His success is based on four factors:

(a) His enthusiasm for biking.

(b) Providing better service than other bike shops in the general area.

(c) Taking courses to learn how to operate a business, including marketing, for which he did a study of bike purchasing patterns for his area.

(d) Absence of competition; although some department and discount stores sell bikes, he has the only store that services bikes and handles 99 percent of the repair market.

Type 5: Leveraging Expertise

These enterprisers are experts, among the best in their technical field. Past work experiences provided a great deal of opportunity for growth, and the enterprisers had little previous interest in starting a business. But when an opportunity presents itself (usually an idea for a new product or for the modification of an old product that their present employer declines to pursue), they feel that pursuing such an opportunity presents little risk. Even though the business is in an established market, it offers very different products/services, of higher quality, than its competition. These enterprisers typically seek the help of partners to start the business.

The industry environment is usually characterized by high technical change and complexity. The firm is highly flexible in adapting to customer needs, because the enterprisers' expertise keeps them keenly aware of changes in the industry. Customers are purchasing agents or committees who analyze the business' products/services before purchase, making sales strategy a major focus of the business. Other firms pose a low competitive threat since the experts' products/services have special features that attract customers.

A good example of a Type 5 enterpriser is Virginia Albertson. She and several partners quit their jobs to start a business that installs a special type of inventory tracking software on PCs. Her previous work involved writing software for the same type of application, but for larger computers. As PCs became more powerful, she and her four partners saw an opportunity to start a business using the Intel/Windows platform. The enterprise is nationally known as the best supplier and installer of this type of inventory tracking software. Most of their clients are Fortune 500 corporations.

AN ENTERPRISING WORLD

Baidu Searches for China's Market

With more than 210 million Internet users, the second largest online market, China attracts many companies eager for a share of its riches. Unlike other countries, however, where Google and Yahoo! fight for the lead, China has its own search giant: Baidu. Often called the Chinese Google, Baidu is the brainchild of Robin Li, who studied computer science in the United States after graduating from Beijing University. Tiring of academia once he completed his master's degree, Li joined *The Wall Street Journal's* online edition in its formative years. Intrigued by the problems involved in sorting information, he moved to InfoSeek, a search engine. By 1998, however, many firms, Infoseek and Yahoo among them, were shifting their focus from search as a business to content-driven business models.

Li believed passionately that search had a strong future. He left Infoseek, raised $1.2 million in funding from U.S. venture capital firms, and returned to China. In 2000, he and partner Eric Xu, a former Xerox employee, started Baidu as a uniquely Chinese search company.

Later that year the pair raised an additional $10 million in venture capital.

The name Baidu, inspired by an ancient Chinese poem, means hundreds of times and represents the "persistent search for the ideal." Li and Xu chose the name to reinforce the company's Chinese heritage, positioning it as a local company that understands China, the Chinese, the Chinese language, and the regulatory environment. "We think search is not just about technology," explains Li, who owns 22 percent of Baidu. "It's also about language. It's also about culture." Designing a search engine that can deal with the complexities and nuances of the Chinese language was a major challenge, and one at which Baidu excelled.

Although Baidu mimicked Google's simple look, it let advertisers pay to rank higher in search results—a major cultural difference between China and the United States. The Chinese see paid results as demonstrating an advertiser's confidence in its products, whereas Americans believe that paid search compromises objectivity. "If an advertiser wants to pay a lot of money, that probably says something," Li says. "The best measure for this is our growth pattern. If users keep coming back to our service, we're doing the right thing."

Baidu often reminds users of its Chinese ownership, playing up a historical distrust of outsiders. It runs ads showing locals saying to foreigners, "You don't understand us, you don't understand us." According to Dick Wei, a JPMorgan Chase China Internet analyst, "Google is still perceived as a foreign search engine, so Chinese prefer to use Baidu when searching for anything about China. They only use Google for foreign information. Also, the relevancy of search results from Baidu is better than Google's results in China, which has helped Baidu win market share."

Understanding the Chinese business and regulatory environments gives Baidu a significant advantage over its foreign competitors. Government censorship is a particularly difficult area for companies such as Google. They are subject to strict rules and censorship, which conflict with their usual ways of conducting business. Baidu chose to let government censors oversee its site, thereby winning government support.

These reasons propelled Baidu to the top of the Chinese search market, despite its Western rivals' more sophisticated technology and management expertise. Baidu excels in Mandarin-language searches and commands more than 62 percent of the market. In the growing online ad market, Baidu was the choice of 60 percent of new advertisers, versus Google at 13.5 percent. This translates into stellar financial performance. Baidu has been profitable since 2004, and in June 2008 had a market value in excess of $11 billion. Its market dominance continues to grow at the expense of Google.

Today Baidu offers more than search, with news links, MP3 music and image searches, message boards, a wiki encyclopedia (with content provided by users), a social networking service, maps, and more. Its Post Bar feature combines online message boards and social networking. Recently it added phonetic search so that a user can enter Chinese keywords using the English alphabet. Major U.S. companies, such as Viacom and Microsoft, acknowledge Baidu's leadership in China and are forming strategic alliances to gain entry to the Chinese market. Viacom teamed with Baidu to distribute television shows and music videos through a new MTV channel at Baidu's site.

Baidu continues to expand. In late 2007 Baidu introduced Baidu TV, mobile search, and in 2008 entered Japan's search market. "Our proven strength in non-English-language search, the high Internet penetration in Japan, [and] similarities between the Chinese and Japanese languages make this market an ideal next step," Mr. Li said.

Discussion Questions

1. Using the 19 factors as a way to evaluate the Baidu story, what new venture pathway seems to best fit?

2. Which aspects of Robin Li's prior experience were helpful in starting Baidu?

3. How has emphasizing its Chinese heritage given Baidu an advantage over its competition?

4. What steps might non-Chinese Internet companies take to gain market share in China?

Sources: Based on "The Baidu Story," Baidu.com website, http://www.baidu.com (June 3, 2008); "Baidu.com, Inc." *Hoover's Company Records*, June 1, 2008, downloaded from ProQuest database January 10, 2007; Andrew Batson, "Viacom Forges Online-Video Deal with China's Baidu to Boost MTV," *Wall Street Journal*, October 18, 2006, p. A19; David Barboza, "The Rise of Baidu (That's Chinese for Google)," *New York Times*, September 17, 2006, pp. 3.1, 3.7; David Greising, "Baidu vs. Google," *Chicago Tribune*, December 3, 2006, p. 1; Normandy Madden, "Baidu," *Advertising Age*, March 17, 2008, p. 58; Normandy Madden, "Google Is Clearly King of search-Except in China," *Advertising Age*, January 22, 2007, p. 18; and "Microsoft Teams Up with Baidu to Deliver Paid Search Listings in China," Baidu press release, December 14, 2006, http://www.baidu.com (January 11, 2007).

Type 6: The Aggressive Service Enterprise

Compared to the Type 3 enterprise (professionals), the Type 6 enterprise is a very intense service-oriented firm. Type 6 businesses are usually consulting firms dedicated to a very specialized area such as technology transfer or certain types of executive recruiting. The enterpriser's involvement level is very high; a great deal of time is spent identifying and selling to customers, advertising, and scanning for new opportunities. Little time is spent searching for resources, because start-up costs are low or the enterpriser knows people who will contribute the necessary resources. Individuals who form Type 6 firms have always wanted to start a business to build on previous work or educational training. The environment requires that these enterprisers have specific professional or technical expertise. The products/services are offered to a very narrow range of customers with very specific needs. Knowing the right people in this industry is very important for making sales or for gaining access to those who influence which firms have the opportunity to make sales. The firm enters a marketplace which is relatively new. The firm's products/services are somewhat better and different from those of other ventures.

Jefferson Smith's investment banking company is a good example of a Type 6 start-up. Before going into business for himself, he had been an investment banker at three different Wall Street firms. A very aggressive and outgoing person, he was always meeting new people and contacts who provided opportunities for investment banking deals.

To start his company, he filed papers of incorporation, found an office, talked with many people in the investment banking business about his new firm, and expanded his contact base using his present contacts to make others. He also developed an innovative way to provide investment banking services, which he marketed to his clients. He sought out new markets in areas of the United States that lacked the services he provided, and he sold his products/services in those areas.

Type 7: Pursuing the Unique Idea

This type of enterprise is created to pursue an idea for a new product or service. These products/services are of high quality but not technically sophisticated or difficult to manufacture. The business is flexible in changing its products to meet customer needs. Since this is the first business in the marketplace to offer this item or service, there is some uncertainty as to whether customers can be found. The work in this new business is different from the enterpriser's work in a previous job, which offered opportunities for growth and advancement. However, the enterpriser has always wanted to start and own a business and is constantly alert for new opportunities. The enterpriser doesn't know if it's possible to acquire the resources required to begin the business and to deliver the products/services with the desired high quality. Therefore, the new venture seems risky.

Franklin Boots worked in advertising and in his spare time developed his own innovative product ideas. One business that he started involved replacement collar stays, since he often needed them for his own shirts. His idea incorporated a unique package for these collar stays. Using the yellow pages, he called manufacturers of collar stays and purchased some. He then devoted a great deal of time to developing his package and label. He went on the road to generate orders, selling his product through manufacturers' representatives. Because this was a very small and unique market, he had no competitors.

Many enterprisers, however, aren't sure what steps to take to bring a product idea to reality. They may look to consultants who specialize in commercializing ideas. The Enterprising Ethics box explains how Big Idea Group (BIG) acts as an idea broker for inventors and the ethical implications of doing so.

Type 8: Methodical Organizing

This type of firm takes form slowly during the start-up period. The enterpriser devotes a great deal of time to all of the aspects of the enterprise—planning, marketing, production, and finance—and has to learn the entire business from the ground up. The enterpriser's previous work experience provides excellent opportunities for job growth and salary increase, yet this person has a high desire to own a business. The new business is seen as risky since it is in an area where the enterpriser has little previous experience or expertise. The enterpriser's use of planning, both in acquiring skills and performing the tasks required for the new venture, reflect the methodical aspects of this path to business creation.

The firm's products/services are similar to those of other firms, but the firm has some new twist, either by having a slightly different way to manufacture the product or provide the service, or by selling to a slightly different type of customer. This is a very competitive environment. Customers require highly technical and competent products/services, and there are many firms trying to meet these demands. The enterpriser frequently deals with middlemen—retailers or purchasing agents—to reach customers and spends considerable time and money on advertising. Initially the enterpriser makes a part-time commitment to get the venture on its feet and earns money elsewhere to keep it afloat.

Lindsey Price started a company that manufactured collapsible baby strollers. She had a BA in English Literature, an MBA in finance and marketing, and work experience in marketing with a large food conglomerate. She quickly became dissatisfied with the corporate lifestyle. She decided to start a business in an industry meeting the following criteria:

(a) small industry

(b) not capital intensive

(c) history of a low rate of innovation

(d) little credit extension required of manufacturers to retailers

(e) weak competitors

She identified several industries that met these criteria before choosing the children's furniture industry. She conducted focus groups to learn which children's furniture products were the most unsatisfactory to consumers. Because the baby stroller was most often mentioned, Lindsey designed a collapsible baby stroller that folded into a very small size. It was the first of its type on the market. She sought out major retailers to carry this stroller. The business devoted a great deal of time to meeting the needs of the large retailers by doing things such as creating specialized packaging. Lindsey's goal was to saturate the market with her unique stroller design before other competitors entered. She contracted with another company for the initial production of the stroller. The business plan estimated sales per year and she had calculated breakeven at a certain number of units per month. Within a year, sales per month were three times breakeven, and she took over manufacture of the stroller.

ENTERPRISING ETHICS

Making Money from Other People's Ideas

For many enterprisers, coming up with an exciting idea is not the difficult part. Figuring out what to do next presents a major challenge, however. Is the idea as good as it seems? Is there a large-enough market for it to build a profitable business? How should the product be priced, packaged, and sold? Is financing available to develop the business concept?

Michael Collins, a former inventor, knows just how frustrating this process can be. He started Kid Galaxy, a toy company that produced Bendos, action figures that could be posed. From his own experience he saw a need for a company to work with independent inventors who needed help commercializing promising ideas. Often innovators do not have the skills or interest to become entrepreneurs and build a company, Collins believes. These inventors are better off licensing their ideas to another company.

In 2000 he formed Big Idea Group (BIG), a Manchester, New Hampshire, company that matches inventors with companies that can manufacture and market these consumer products (http://www.bigideagroup.net). In addition to representing inventors, BIG offers corporations access to its network of more than 8,000 inventors with marketable concepts. To date BIG has helped inventors develop and market more than 50 products, including toys, cosmetics, luggage, pet products, office supplies, crafts, kitchenware, housewares, tools, and storage and organization products. The company's major corporate clients include Avon, Gillette, Fortune Brands, Staples, Sunbeam, Target, and Toys "R" Us.

Ideas come to BIG in several ways. Inventors submit them directly to BIG by mail or phone, or in person at BIG Roadshows throughout the United States. At Roadshows, inventors present their ideas privately to a panel of industry experts. BIG also conducts Idea Hunts on behalf of corporate sponsors looking for marketable ideas in a specific industry. BIG evaluates ideas at no charge and offers advice to inventors. Its Entry Agreement includes confidentiality protection for inventors. BIG then conducts additional research and responds to inventors in about a month. "Innovators can lose objectivity when it comes to their ideas," Collins says. "My job is to guide them through the process. I ask them a series of questions, and based on the viability of their idea, help them decide what to do with it."

BIG evaluates ideas for appeal, originality, market potential, competitive environment, and compliance with safety standards. When BIG finds an idea it likes, it offers to become the inventor's agent, again at no charge. The inventor signs an agreement that gives BIG either the right to represent the idea for 180 days, or the right to commercialize or sublicense the idea. Its revenues come from royalties and advances from companies that license the idea, and they split this revenue 50–50 with the inventor. Because BIG provides most of its services for free, it is very selective in the ideas it chooses to represent: Only 1 to 3 percent of submissions become agented deals.

Discussion Questions

1. What kind of enterprise start-up pathway is BIG? What benefits does it provide to inventors?

2. How does BIG deal with the ethical issues related to ownership of an idea with business potential?

3. How does BIG develop trust between the inventors and the clients that BIG represents?

4. As a successful entrepreneur, you've been asked to participate on BIG's Roadshow panel when it comes to your area. You receive no payment for serving on the panel and helping BIG spot marketable ideas. Would you participate, and why?

Sources: BIG Idea Group website, http://www.bigideagroup.net (June 5, 2008); D.C. Denison, "BIG Founders Aim To Be the Fathers of Invention," *Boston Globe,* April 28, 2002, p. C.2; and "Making It: Michael Collins," *Business NH,* August 2006, p. 46; and Gwendolyn Bounds, "You Have a Great Idea. Now What?" *Wall Street Journal,* May 9, 2005, pp. R1-R3.

9.2 What Kind of Enterpriser Are You?

As we indicated at the beginning of the chapter, exploring these eight types of business creation pathways helps enterprisers recognize the various ways to craft strategies for success. Now let's look at the differences and similarities among these pathways in greater detail. We'll compare the pathways using each of the 19 variables shown in Exhibit 9.2 (p. 223), dividing them into the four categories of individual, organization, environment, and process, as in the exhibit. In the following section, we will compare some of the archetypes as a whole to other pathways. For each category we describe, we will also provide some examples of enterprisers that seem to fit the characteristics of that category. Note that each example is in some respects unique—and that no example will fit each of the types exactly.

We believe that by making comparisons among the 19 variables and the 8 types, you will begin to realize that many kinds of businesses require a specific type of person. If you were thinking of starting an enterprise that sold real estate, it would quickly become obvious to you that you would need to devote time to obtaining a real estate license. But as we've shown in the descriptions of the eight archetypes, certain kinds of businesses—especially Type 3 (professional) businesses like real estate brokerages—require more than specific skills and knowledge. Enterprisers who start real estate brokerage businesses need an established base of contacts in the community, both buyers and sellers of houses, and a reputation for being successful at helping customers buy or sell their homes. Knowing how important it is to have skills, knowledge, contacts, and many years of work experience in the real estate industry will enable you to evaluate your skills and abilities and match them to start-up pathways that will result in a successful venture.

For example, a number of our students were interested in starting a financial planning and investing business catering to wealthy individuals. When they interviewed enterprisers who started businesses in this field, they learned that nearly everyone had first worked a minimum of five and as many as ten years in a firm that provided just these financial planning and investing services. Most of these enterprisers acquired the specific knowledge and skills necessary for this business by meeting the standards for a Certified Financial Planner's designation, developing a track record of successful investing, and establishing a network of clients who would be willing to use their services. It would be naïve for students to believe they could start a firm engaged in financial planning and investing without first putting the necessary pieces of the puzzle (skills and knowledge, certification, reputation, contacts) in place. Starting this kind of firm, therefore, would entail a five-to ten-year effort before an enterpriser could actually engage in the activities of start-up.

Exploring these archetypes in more detail will help you answer the question: What kind of enterpriser are you? It will also help you identify the kinds of skills and abilities, connections, and experiences in other firms that you might need to start the kind of business that interests you. Recognizing the variety of different ways that people start firms will help you see that everyone can become an enterpriser. There is an enterprise that is more likely to be the right kind of business for you. By better knowing yourself as well as seeing the many different ways that enterprisers start businesses, you will be better prepared to position yourself to take advantage of the opportunities that come your way.

These archetypes can serve as broad guides for getting into business and provide clues about the factors (individual, firm, environment, process) necessary to start a business. However, your own start-up pathway is likely to be a blend of some of these.

Individual Level

The variables that come into play at the individual level include opportunities for advancement at prior jobs, similarity of previous work experience to the new venture, interest in starting a business, and risk of the new venture. The variables of job advancement and similarity of work are often directly correlated. When enterprisers saw that opportunities for job advancement were low, the likelihood that they would seek opportunities in areas where they had previous work experience was also low. For example, enterprisers in Type 1 (Escape to Something New) indicated that their current jobs offered little opportunity for advancement, challenging work, or salary increases. These enterprisers saw their current careers in these jobs as a dead end and sought higher levels of job satisfaction through entrepreneurship. Conversely, when job advancement was high, the odds of enterprisers starting businesses in the same industry were also high.

A good example of an enterpriser who typifies these variables of limited job advancement coupled with business ventures in new areas is Jerry Dawson, who started a waterbed store. Jerry was 20 years old, going to college, and working at a grocery store. He decided to take some entrepreneurship courses, and through this education grew confident he could start a business. He had grown dissatisfied working for other people because he felt they were less competent than he was. He began the start-up process by searching for a retail business to start. He first thought of stereos but discovered the market was saturated with stores. He decided on waterbeds when a friend asked him about the waterbed he was currently using. Jerry decided to interview waterbed storeowners. From these interviews he learned about an excellent waterbed manufactured locally. The manufacturer, a very important contact, put him in touch with accessory suppliers. Jerry then sought out a good location, negotiated a lease, named his business, and read a lot of books about starting a business. He used his own capital, which he raised by selling most of his personal possessions, and also borrowed money from his family.

The first few months of business were slow. Jerry had never been a salesman and it took time to learn how to communicate with prospective buyers. Slowly the business began to grow. He worked long hours and spent the initial earnings of the business paying for advertisements in a local "penny savings" newspaper. He persuaded a local finance company to make consumer loans to his customers.

In contrast, the second and by far larger group of enterprisers was satisfied with their present jobs and careers. The professionals in Type 2 (Deal Makers), Type 3 (Using Prior Skills & Contacts), Type 5 (Experts), and Type 6 (Aggressive Service) were all involved in jobs that they found very satisfying. However, they found some aspect of their previous jobs limiting. For example, they would have liked more responsibility, a wider range of work experiences, and freedom to pursue their own ideas. For these professionals, starting a business was a part of the same career pathway. The work they performed in their new businesses was very similar to the work in their previous jobs.

Ann Champion, an enterpriser in the Aggressive Service category, started a company that published specialty books. This company identifies a specific audience and then develops a book to sell to that market. It handles all phases of the process—writing, publishing, and distributing the books. Ann worked part time on several books that she and a partner had published while she was working full time as a financial controller. Her part-time experience provided her with the skills to become a book publisher full time. With sales from two previously published books, she quit her job and devoted her efforts to the publishing venture. Since the company does most of the publishing functions, its overhead is low and the books are of consistent quality. The publishing industry is very competitive, but Ann's publishing company is successful because it carefully targets books to markets where sales are likely.

It should be noted that the correlation between job advancement and similarity of work is not always so direct. Enterprisers in Type 7 (Pursuing the Unique Idea) and Type 8 (Methodical Organizing) were the most highly satisfied with their jobs, yet they usually started firms in unrelated work areas. Why? These two categories of enterpriser found better opportunities for advancement and success than their current jobs could offer.

Most enterprisers indicated they had frequently thought about starting a business. The only type that had less previous business start-up interest was the experts in Type 5. Experts usually had interesting jobs in firms where their expertise was highly valued. They had little interest in starting a company until their career paths were blocked.

For example, Virginia Albertson's new venture in writing software for PCs (described earlier in Type 5) was created when her former company did not want to pursue the PC marketplace and stayed with software for mainframe computers. Robert Jones is another example of an expert who enjoyed his current job yet found he could have more freedom by starting his own company. Robert is involved in international technology transfer. His company puts together joint ventures and represents U.S. corporations in China. Mr. Jones had many years' research experience in high technology areas, as well as seven years' technology transfer experience in China, working for an R&D company. The R&D company constrained his freedom to try new projects. While pursuing his MBA at night school, he began to consider starting his own company. He quit his job to develop new projects through his own company. He found a good lawyer to work with him, since technology transfer involves contracts and securities. He also found a partner with seasoned business experience for managing the company. He then went to previous clients and sold them on his new projects.

The perception of risk was not a differentiating factor. Most enterprisers perceived a moderate level of risk in pursuing their businesses, except that Type 2 (Deal Makers), Type 4 (Purchase/Franchise), and Type 5 (Expert) perceived lower levels of risk, while Type 8 (Methodical Organizing) perceived higher levels of risk. Some enterprisers saw lower levels of risk because their new ventures would use their previous experience, skills, and contacts (Deal Makers and Experts), or the business itself was successful before its purchase or its franchise acquisition (Type 4). One of the reasons why enterprisers in Type 8 (Methodical Organizing) perceived a higher level of risk than other types of enterprisers was that the Methodical Organizers were entering industries where they lacked experience and knowledge. The focus on business planning for Type 8 is a way for these enterprisers to identify and respond to these unknown risks.

Enterprise Level

At the enterprise level, the variables to consider include the existence of partners; comparison with competitors with regard to the timing of product introductions and quality and unique characteristics of goods and services; and flexibility of the new enterprise in adapting its offerings in response to competitors' products.

The enterprises most likely to have partners were Type 1 (Escaping to Something New), Type 5 (Experts), Type 7 (Unique Idea), and Type 8 (Methodical Start-up). The Type 1 and Type 8 enterprisers, who left their previous jobs for new and unfamiliar ventures, often took partners to provide the necessary expertise and moral support. Enterprisers in Type 5 (Leveraging Expertise) were in highly complex industries where each partner contributed a share of the needed knowledge and skills necessary for the business's success.

An example of Type 1 partnership start-up is Jennifer Rose. She started a fresh fish wholesaling business with her father, who lost his job after 26 years with a wholesale frozen fish company. As part of his termination package, he agreed to not work for any other frozen fish company. Jennifer, who was working in the marketing department of a large corporation, decided to start the wholesale fresh fish company with her dad. The initial product was fresh perch that they sold in the Midwest, where that fish is the most popular. Jennifer's father purchased fresh perch from his previous employer. He then called on his old frozen fish customers in the Midwest and convinced them to sell fresh perch. Once orders were placed, the fish was sent via air freight to the buyers. The partners located more suppliers of fresh fish, paying them as quickly as possible to insure supply in the future. Jennifer felt that her venture was successful because they placed a high priority on excellent customer service, always had access to fresh fish, and provided a full line of fresh fish to customers.

The types of start-ups where partnerships were least likely to occur were Type 2 (Deal Markers) and Type 6 (Aggressive Service Firms). In these firms, contacts with suppliers and customers were extremely important, which suggests that the network of personal relationships developed by these enterprisers is a critical success factor. While another person with as many contacts might be a good partner, he or she would have been more likely to start his/her own venture.

The product/market newness variable measures the entry position of the new venture. Businesses in Type 7 (Unique Idea) were first to offer their products in the market. Next in terms of perceived newness were firms that were purchased (Type 4). Enterprisers in this category often talked about purchasing a business with the idea of turning the business around by orienting the purchased firm's current products/services to a new market. Alisa Showers, for example, purchased a small newspaper publishing company that was printing two bi-weekly papers in a large metropolitan area. She had operated these two papers for an owner who lived 2,000 miles away. After months of negotiation, Alisa purchased the fixed assets of the company. Alisa chose to purchase the two newspapers rather than start new publications because she felt that it would take her four years to reach the same base of readers that the two purchased newspapers had. With the existing reader base, she could pursue new advertisers who would be interested in selling their products/services to her readers.

At the other end of the product/market newness scale are businesses in Type 1 (Escape to Something New), Type 5 (Experts), and Type 8 (Methodical Start-ups). Type 1 consists of retail firms and restaurants that offered the same products as their competitors. Type 5 firms (Experts) generally modified an existing product for an already established market familiar to the expert. For example, a Type 5 enterpriser started a company in which he substituted an all-electronic temperature control system technology for an electromechanical technology and offered these advanced products to his old customers. Enterprisers in Type 8 firms (Methodical Organizing) followed systematic start-up procedures to enter established markets where they could imitate or learn from existing firms. For example, one enterpriser visited other microfilming services before setting up his own firm in this field.

Almost by definition, enterprisers in Type 7 (Unique Idea) perceived their firms as offering different products/services from their competitors. Founders of Type 2 firms (Deal Makers) also believed they offered different products/services compared to competitors, because they considered each deal to be unique. Deal Makers were also the only type of firm to rank the quality of their products/services similar to their competition. Either these enterprisers found the quality of deal making difficult to ascertain, or they did not compete on the basis of quality. All other types of firms regarded their products/services as higher in quality than their competitors.

Finally, the enterprisers in all eight types rated their firms as being more flexible than their competitors. The Experts (Type 5) rated their firms as the most flexible. Since firms in the Expert category provided products/services that were often designed to the specifications of a narrow range of customers, flexibility would be an important characteristic of these firms.

Environmental Level

At the environmental level, we can compare pathways to new business ventures on the basis of complexity of technology and skills required to manufacture products or deliver services in this industry, importance of contacts with suppliers in the industry, and customer expertise as the key environmental variables.

The variable technological complexity and change differentiated the high technology businesses (Type 3—Using Prior Skills & Contacts, Type 5—Experts, and Type 6—Aggressive Service) from low technology firms (Type 1—Escape to Something New, Type 2—Deal Makers, Type 4—Purchase/Franchise, and Type 7—Unique Idea). This comes as no surprise; as we stated earlier, high technology firms were likely to be started by enterprisers with previous experience in high technology industries.

Intensity of competition proved to be highly correlated to customer contacts. In other words, firms that placed a high value on contacts with suppliers and customers were perceived to be in the most competitive environments. Enterprisers identified the customer contact variable as the one best way to separate the Type 3 firms (Using Prior Skills & Contacts) from the Type 6 firms (Aggressive Service). Both types of firms are service firms. The Type 6 firm places a higher priority on making and maintaining contacts, while the firms in Type 3 relied more heavily on their reputations to draw new customers.

There is a high correlation between customer expertise and degree of technology in each type, except for Type 7 (Unique Idea). Type 7 enterprisers sold low technology products, but some uniqueness of the design caused the products to appeal to a narrow range of customers (expert customers). For example, Bill Sanders started a part-time business manufacturing and selling baby towels that incorporated a unique design his mother had created and made as gifts for friends. Recognizing that this product was a marketable item that no one else was selling, he bought some material and had his mother and a friend construct prototypes of the baby towel. He designed a package and took the product to stores, where buyers reacted positively to his design. Then he contracted with a clothing manufacturer to produce the baby towels.

Start-Up Process

The variables in Exhibit 9.2 that relate to the start-up process describe the time allocated to selling and promoting the product or service, seeking advice and resources, producing the item, and purchasing a business or franchise versus starting a totally new business. Another key factor is whether the enterpriser made a full-or part-time commitment to the new venture.

Two of the eight types of start-up pathways were defined, primarily, in terms of the behaviors of the enterprisers. The enterprisers in Type 8 (Methodical Organizing) performed more of the seven behaviors listed in this section than enterprisers in any of the other seven types. Enterprisers in Type 8 felt that they were entering complex industries with little or no previous experience, and therefore, believed they had the double burden of learning the business as they started it. The primary characteristic of Type 4 (Purchase/Franchise) was also largely identified by a specific behavior—purchase or franchise.

Enterprisers in Type 7 (Unique Product/Market) spent the least amount of time marketing/selling. They believed that their idea so perfectly fit a product/market niche. They either did not feel a need to convince customers to buy the product or felt that it would be impossible to convince unwilling customers to buy their products. A good example of this conundrum involved a Type 7 firm that manufactured a unique silk-screened fabric that was sold to a limited number of high fashion clothing designers.

On the other hand, enterprisers in Type 6 (Aggressive Service) spent significantly more time marketing/selling than did the professionals in Type 3. This characteristic, along with the importance of contacts factor previously discussed, further differentiated these two groups of enterprisers who possessed expertise. Taking both of these variables into account, we can conclude that marketing/selling behaviors were a key route to establishing contacts with customers.

The amount of time devoted to resource acquisition varied among the eight pathways. Enterprisers who purchased firms (Type 4) spend a great deal of time seeking resources. Acquiring resources was also important to enterprisers in Type 2 (Deal Makers) and Type 7 (Unique Idea). Frequently, a crucial part of the Deal Maker's transaction involved lining up resources (from insurance companies, banks, builders, landowners).

9.3 ENTERPRISERS

Cowgirl Enterprises Rides to Success

What do you think of when you hear the term *cowgirl*? Like Donna Baase, at first you might picture somebody in boots on a horse. But Donna realized that the term conveys much more and chose to name her natural beauty products company Cowgirl Enterprises. "To me, it has to do with independence, resourcefulness, staying in the saddle, taking the reins, making use of the natural resources around us," she explains. "I meet cowgirls of all walks of life. It's about really driving your own life."

Started in Boulder, Colorado, in 1994, Cowgirl Enterprises offers customers a full line of unique natural skincare products based on healing desert botanicals. Its products, which soothe and nourish dry, weather-stressed skin, have been praised by a wide customer base, including climbers to Mt. Everest, scientists in Antarctica, women's track teams, New York City firemen, and everyday cowgirls and cowboys.

Donna's interest in plants and their healing properties started when she was a child and her family had a garden. "I grew up with a lot of beauty around me. My mother was very inspiring and we had a lot of flowers," she recalls. In the early '70s, she traveled extensively. In India and South America, she noticed how women incorporated plants into their beauty routines and for medicine. "I watched women comb coconut oil into their hair, and pretty soon we were doing that, too," she says. "This period of travel profoundly influenced my outlook on beauty, health and how plants are the source of medicine, cosmetics and well-being and became the seed for the Cowgirl products."

She returned to the United States and for eight years worked for a plastic surgeon in Miami, who became her mentor. "I probably was the first paramedical makeup

© Bananastock/Jupiter Images

artist in Miami in the early '70s, using makeup to alleviate bad medical conditions, such as bad burns or terrible scarring from accidents," she says. "I learned how the body healed." When she and her family moved to Boulder, she continued working in skincare as a licensed aesthetician. She also took advantage of Boulder's extensive network of people in alternative therapies and studied skincare, herbalism, and aromatherapy. "Then I started teaching classes in how to make your own cosmetics—for example, how to take some yogurt and egg yolk, mix in a couple of drops of lavender, and you have a mask," she says. "It is really using food for the skin."

Donna recognized the historical roots of what she was doing and wanted to continue this tradition in the modern world. "The whole skin-care industry and beauty business started in the kitchen," she explains. "After women made their candles, their soaps, their cough syrups and put up their preserves for the winter, they might have some time left over to take chamomile and infuse it in some olive oil. Here in Colorado, they would have found horsetail (or bottle brush) and infused that to make a salve for wound healing. You could take aloe vera and sunflower oil and you might add a little bit of the lavender from your garden, and then you have a beautiful, natural oil for the skin."

The idea for the natural beauty products company came when Donna's family was driving home after a vacation in Oregon. "I started asking myself, 'What the heck did people put on their skin?' I wondered what native people, the indigenous women, the pioneer women, cowgirls riding those horses, did to protect their skin in the bleak winters and also those rough summers," she remembers. "I also thought about the plants that grow in the West, and how they really heal the skin. And a light bulb went off in my head—Cowgirl Cream!"

Donna mixed the first batch of Cowgirl Cream in her kitchen and operated as a home-based business for about six months. As it grew, Donna realized that she couldn't run the business out of her house, with employees working at her kitchen table. "Between the packing boxes and peanut bags, my house was just being taken over." The move to her present location was a big step. "It felt frightening because it was a commitment to pay the rent," Donna says. "But as soon as we got here, business increased."

The idea for Donna's next product after the cream was the Ranch Hand Cream, which she developed after a friend brought her an olive oil and beeswax bar from

Italy. "This is brilliant," Donna thought. "Every product for hand and body care, hand creams particularly, comes in pump bottles, as liquid or lotion. I came up with a formula for a solid cake to heal chapped hands. Beeswax is difficult and messy to work with; if you spill it, it immediately dries. So you need a place where you can really be sloppy with beeswax—not your kitchen!" Donna also realized that she needed outside resources to make the product and others she wanted to create, such as a cleanser to go with Cowgirl Cream.

Donna consulted with Ben Fuchs, a pharmacist and owner of the Rocky Mountain Natural Laboratories, which produces her liquid products. "I develop a very strong personal bond with all my customers," Fuchs says. "I learned what Donna needed, not just as a businesswoman, but also from a personal standpoint, so I could provide the best service. I love my customers, working with creative people." Donna arranged for Ben's company to help her craft her products and then manufacture and bottle them, paying him on a fee basis.

Next Donna developed a three-channel distribution strategy: independent sales reps, contacts from trade shows, and cold-calling. She began by selling her products at local Boulder natural product stores and their branches around the Denver area. Then she expanded to Santa Fe, another good market for natural products. "I had really terrific sales reps that took our product line on the road. We sent press releases, and I made presentations when I went on the road locally. Then we started getting into the gift market. We found a showroom down at the Denver Merchandise Mart selling Western apparel and accessories and they agreed to carry the products. Sales came in right away, and suddenly we were in the gift market—a whole new world. They didn't even know how great the ingredients were until later. They just thought they were adorable little boxes. And they liked the name." Gift stores at spas also began carrying Cowgirl products.

The company's third product was an herbal rub for sore muscles. "We called it the Trail Boss Bar because on a trail ride the boss would have the medicine kit. The same concept applies to Ranch Hand Cream. It has a beeswax base and sunflower oil, but we added to that some wonderful herbal ingredients that are known to promote circulation and wound healing. It's not greasy, it doesn't have a heavy aroma, and it brings warmth and circulation."

Customers love Donna's products. "They want pure products and they want the natural ingredients," says Jennifer Biller, a sales rep. "Donna doesn't use any fillers or synthetic chemicals. It's all natural and very concentrated." As one storeowner commented, "We're fortunate to carry Cowgirl products because we have a customer demand for it. Especially living here in Boulder, where it is very dry and women need it. At first, they're attracted to the packaging, it's beautiful. They give it as gifts or take it home. But once they try it, they're back for more."

Cowgirl Enterprises also uses direct mail to keep its name in front of customers. "We use direct mail to let our customers know about new promotions," says Kendra Harris, Trail Boss (operations manager). "Every six to eight weeks, we put together a program and design postcards to send to our retail accounts and our mail-order customers. We've learned that our customers really like seeing product photographs rather than line drawings, and they buy more. It costs more but it's definitely worth it. We use inventory codes and our software tracks order sources, and we can see which marketing programs are producing results."

Running a small business brings a special set of challenges, such as finding sources of labor. "I would also say that some of the difficulties come from sales," Kendra says. "We don't have a solid distribution network set up yet. We're in the process of doing that and that takes a lot of work for a small company." Donna has been creative in tapping unusual labor pools, such as using inmates in the Boulder County Jail to package products.

Currently Cowgirl Enterprises makes seven items: Cowgirl Cream, Extreme Cream, Trail Boss Bar, Ranch Hand Cream, Cowgirl Lip Balm, Desert Recovery Serum, and Round Up Gel. The company first sold through retailers but began selling online in 1999. Growth has been slow but steady.

However, Donna does not want to run a manufacturing plant. Instead, she built a virtual corporation that operates with a minimal number of full-and part-time employees and four business alliances. She outsources the manufacturing, with one lab making the liquid products and two other companies producing the bars and lip balm. And, of course, jail prisoners do packaging. This concept represents a new way to run a business: do what you do best, then find others to do the rest. Forming alliances is efficient and saves you from burdening yourself with infrastructure and overhead. For now, Donna is glad to have teams of people who don't work for her, but with her, as well as consultants to advise her.

For example, Cathy Price, also a customer, is Donna's insurance adviser. "One of the main concerns in cosmetics is the pollution exposure. . . . That's a real concern when you're the insurer. The other real high-risk end of cosmetics is how it can possibly hurt a customer. . . . The beauty of Donna's product is it's all natural ingredients."

Despite the small size of Cowgirl Enterprises, Donna wants everyone involved to enjoy working there and to have fun. "I often will walk in and say, 'Hey, what do you think of this?' I want everyone's opinion. It's important that we all buy the Cowgirl way, to see this through my filter in a sense." Her employees agree. "Donna has great ideas and she believes in herself," says Paula Gardner, who handles customer service. "We all believe in her. We believe in the product. And we've seen the success because she's motivated, she has tenacity, she just keeps on going." At the same time, Donna allows room for self-expression. "But ultimately, I have to be the one leading it," she says. "That's kind of where I am. Just be me. And just hold the reins."

Discussion Questions

1. In which of the eight archetypes does Cowgirl Enterprises fall? Could it fall into more than one? Briefly explain your answer. Are there other ways that Donna could have started Cowgirl Enterprises? How would her background, skills, activities, and competitive strategy be different if she were to choose another pathway?

2. As best possible, use the information in the case to answer the 19 questions in the Exhibit 9.2 as they apply to Cowgirl Enterprises. Create a table that summarizes your answers. Compare your table to your classmates' and discuss any differences.

3. Based on the table you created in question 2, select the archetype that most closely resembles Cowgirl Enterprises. Does it match the one you chose in question 1? Why or why not?

4. Discuss the advantages and disadvantages of operating Cowgirl Enterprises as a virtual corporation. Do you agree with Donna's decision to use this form? When should she consider bringing more operations in-house? What questions could she ask to help her choose if and how to accomplish this?

Sources: Adapted with permission from the video "Staying in the Saddle: Cowgirl Enterprises," Small Business School, the series on PBS, and at http://SmallBusinessSchool.com; "About Cowgirl Enterprises," Cowgirl Enterprises website, http://www.cowgirlenterprises.com (January 10, 2007); and Nettie Hartsock, "Interview with Donna Baase," *iBizInterviews.com,* January 2001, http://www.ibizinterviews.com/donnab1.htm.

The unique idea/market (Type 7) was frequently all that the enterpriser had, so that the process of acquiring resources to realize the idea was a high priority. For example, two women who decided to open the first cookie store in their city (their unique idea) indicated that the acquisition of sufficient resources (a store, oven, supplies) was critical for their idea to succeed.

As we would expect, service-oriented firms (Type 3—Professionals and Type 6—Aggressive Service Firms) are less capital intensive and spend little or no time seeking resources. The Experts (Type 5) also spent little time seeking resources, because these firms were the most likely to have partners who invested in the new venture. Experts are recognized as the best in their field, and, as discussed earlier, these experts were developing products that were perceived to have a high probability of success, making it easier to find investors for such ventures.

The time commitment to the new venture varied across types. Enterprisers in both service-oriented categories (Professionals and Aggressive Service) quit their jobs and devoted all their time to their new ventures. Since these enterprisers frequently tapped customers from their previous jobs, a definite break with the old employer would be an important factor. On the other hand, Deal Makers (Type 2) typically began their businesses part time. The part-time group was, for example, largely composed of real estate brokers. The nature of the real estate industry makes it possible for them to arrange deals on the side. The other group of Type 2 ventures, novelty firms, are similar to firms in Type 7 (Unique Idea). Both types of enterpriser based the start-up on a novel idea and worked at the new firm on a part-time basis. The new concept took some time to develop and catch on, and enterprisers worked full time at something else until they were ready to give all their attention to the new business.

The enterprisers who purchased or franchised firms spent the most time involved in the manufacturing/operational aspects of starting their businesses. We surmise that these enterprisers devoted more time to manufacturing and operations so that they could understand how the firms they purchased/franchised actually operated. The enterprisers who devoted the least amount of time to manufacturing and operations were Type 1 (Escaping to Something New) firms. These firms were more likely to be focused in the retail industry.

9.4 Finding the Best Pathway for You

As this chapter explains, nearly all enterprises that people start will follow one of the eight pathways we've described. Now that we have a fuller understanding of the eight pathways and their defining characteristics, we can use it to make better enterprising decisions.

Let's go back and look over the 19 questions that differentiate the eight archetypes, listed in Exhibit 9.2 on page 223. These questions will help you figure out how to approach the development of your potential enterprise.

We believe that the primary issue for most enterprisers is the choice to start a particular kind of enterprise that will satisfy their own interests. The individual-level questions are the first questions to ask yourself: Will you use your previous work experience, and will you be satisfied starting an enterprise based on this work experience? If you like the kind of work you are doing and the industry you are currently in, the next critical issue you need to address involves whether you want to continue working for your current employer. If you don't see opportunities for advancement in your current position, and you don't seem to get much satisfaction from working for your current employer, you might be in the position to take your current skills and apply them in your own enterprise, serving your current customers or customers similar to your current customers.

A decision tree can help you visualize your own route to enterprise formation. Exhibit 9.4 illustrates a sample decision tree based on the answer to one of the questions on individual characteristics: Do you want to use your prior work experience in your new venture? If you answer "yes," then you might consider whether you are satisfied with your work and have opportunities for advancement in your current position. A "yes" answer may mean that you don't have a strong desire to start a new business. If you are not happy at your present job yet want to use the same skills and contacts, you would begin exploring Types 2, 3, 5, and 6 (based on the profiles in Exhibit 9.3, pages 224–225). You'd proceed by asking yourself some of the other questions posed in Exhibit 9.2 and could create another decision tree to guide you.

Suppose you want to try something different. Then you might follow the lower path on the decision tree. As Exhibit 9.4 shows, your options include Types 1, 4, 7, and 8. You might consider customer expertise as the next factor to consider in narrowing your search. If you want to sell goods or services that do not require customer expertise in purchasing, you'd investigate Types 1 and 4. If your interests lie with products that call for educated customers, you'd move toward Types 7 and 8.

If you are reading this book because you are serious about enterprising, you should explore another very important question: Is your current situation—job or school—leading you toward what you want to do in the future? Are the skills and knowledge you are acquiring creating more satisfaction in your life?

For example, let's say that you are studying accounting and expect to become a CPA. However, you may discover that you really have difficulty handling the many details and number-crunching that accounting requires. As you worked as an intern in an accounting firm, you got a taste of the profession. Now you can ask yourself more specific questions, such as whether you like auditing and if you can work the long hours that are often necessary around tax time. Do you like working with individuals at firms that need accounting help? If you don't like accounting now, it is unlikely that your experience in an accounting firm would help you start an accounting business and enjoy running it.

As you have seen in the description of the eight pathways, some require that you have previous work experience involving the acquisition of knowledge and skills as well as connections to clients who are likely to become your customers. One of the challenges, then, that you face is choosing jobs in areas that provide you with satisfaction with doing that kind of job (e.g., accounting, real estate sales or investing, information technology consulting) so that you gain the necessary skills, knowledge and contacts. Pathways 3 (Professionals), 5 (Leveraging Expertise), and 6 (Aggressive Service) are all based on individuals who have first gained experience in an area they truly enjoy, so that they pursue opportunities to develop enterprises that use those skills.

Pathway 4 (Purchase) typically involves enterprisers who seek to purchase a business in an industry that they are already familiar with and enjoy—even though the profile of Type 4 shows that this characteristic is not significant. Enterprisers who don't have industry experience may miss the problems and flaws in an established business that could lead to failure. As we will see in the next chapter on purchasing a business, enterprisers often seek to purchase a business in an industry where they have experience. They know how to exploit new opportunities at an established business, increasing the odds of success.

exhibit
9.4

Choosing a Path

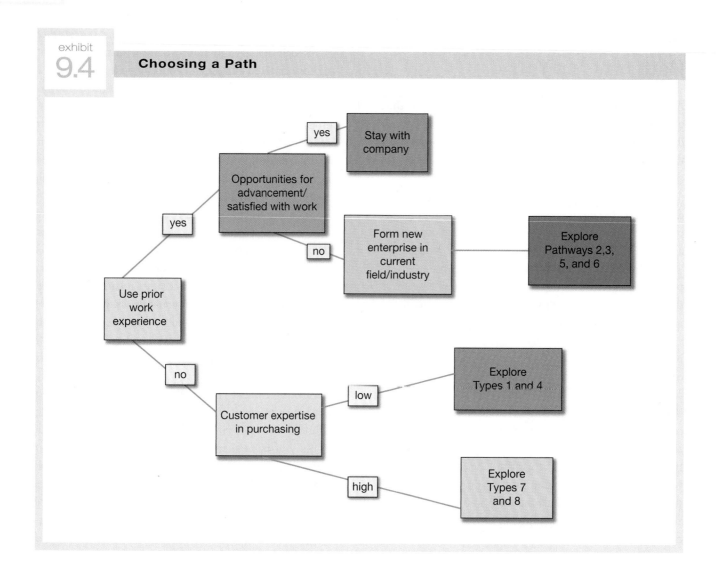

Summary

1. Enterprisers can start their businesses in many different ways. Pursuing opportunities involves a wide range of new venture strategies, situations, and behaviors. We group similar types of businesses into eight broad archetypes for starting enterprises. The eight pathways to enterprise creation are the following: Type 1—Escaping to Something New; Type 2—Putting the Deal Together; Type 3—Using Prior Skills & Contacts (Professionals); Type 4—Purchasing a Firm; Type 5—Leveraging Expertise; Type 6—Aggressive Service; Type 7—Pursuing the Unique Idea; and Type 8—Methodical Organizing. These eight pathways present a repertoire of different start-up strategies and behaviors.

2. The profile for each archetype includes four levels of analysis: individual, enterprise, environment, and start-up process. These categories are further

divided into 19 factors, as shown in Exhibit 9.2. The profiles (summarized in Exhibit 9.3) describe the types of individuals who are likely to start this kind of enterprise, what the business looks like, how it competes, the industry environment, and the start-up process. By understanding the differences and similarities between archetypes, an enterpriser can choose the best route to business ownership.

3. Enterprisers who choose Type 1 (Escape to Something New) have limited opportunities for advancement in their current jobs and are dissatisfied with their jobs. They generally gravitate to industries different from their prior work experience and may begin with a part-time commitment to the business. Competition is high because these businesses operate in established markets, offering low-technology products that target the general consumer. Funding for these firms comes form

the enterprisers themselves, along with loans from family and friends.

4. Type 2 (Putting the Deal Together) enterprisers assemble the different aspects of the business (suppliers, wholesale and retail channels, customers). Typically they have experience in their chosen field. Real estate developers and novelty firms that outsource the manufacturing and distribution of the enterpriser's product idea are the two businesses that fall into Type 2. Both types of firms depend on good contact networks. Unlike Type 1 businesses, the services or products of Type 2 firms are unique.

5. Professionals who decide to go into business for themselves create Type 3 (Using Prior Skills & Contacts) companies. Because they stay in a familiar industry, they draw on the technical skills, expertise, and contacts acquired in previous positions. Like Type 1 enterprisers, they use their own money to finance the firm. Examples include CPA firms, attorneys, consultants, personnel agencies, and advertising firms. Type 3 firms differentiate themselves from the competition by offering better service.

6. Type 4 (Purchasing a Business or Acquiring a Franchise) is a popular route to entrepreneurship, especially for those who like the industry where they work but want to own a business. Firms in this archetype offer low-tech products and services similar to their competitors and differentiate themselves by adapting to the changing needs of their customers. Financial issues take up a lot of the owners' time. Enterprisers who buy existing businesses hope to improve it and increase profits.

7. Experts with technical knowledge form Type 5 businesses when they identify a new product opportunity in their industry. They often team up with partners to start the business. The industry environment is typically characterized by high technical change and complexity, and successful Type 5 firms are flexible in adapting products to customer needs.

8. Type 6, or Aggressive Service, enterprises are service-oriented firms such as specialized consulting firms. The enterpriser builds on prior work experience or training and is intensely involved in all phases of operations, such as business development, advertising, and product offerings. Start-up costs for these knowledge-based companies are low. The enterpriser's networks are an important resource.

9. Certain enterprisers start Type 7 companies to pursue new ideas for low tech but high quality goods or services in different industries. Since this is the first business in the marketplace to offer this item or service, there is some uncertainty as to whether customers can be found, making these ventures seem risky.

10. The Type 8 firm, Methodical Organizing, starts up slowly as the enterpriser spends considerable time learning about all aspects of the enterprise—planning, marketing, production and finance. Enterprisers who chose this category typically have a long-standing desire to own a business and look to a new industry rather than continuing in the same one. The firm's products/services are similar to those of other firms but with some new twist to make it stand out in a very competitive environment.

11. Comparing pathways to new businesses in terms of the 19 variables helps enterprisers determine the best fit for their individual needs. For example, many kinds of businesses require a specific type of person, experience, or skill set. Certain patterns emerge, such as the high correlation between limited opportunities for advancement in a current job and starting a business in a different industry. Enterprisers in the Deal Maker, Professional, Expert, and, Aggressive Service categories generally continue to build on experience and stay in the same industry. Types 1, 5, 7, and 8 are more likely to have partners than the other four archetypes; unique products characterize Types 2, 5, and 7. Exhibit 9.3 summarizes the similarities and differences across all 19 factors.

12. Looking across the whole archetype gives enterprisers a more complete picture of which types are best for them. Some archetypes seem quite similar, such as Type 3 (Professionals) and Type 6 (Aggressive Service).

Review Questions

1. How does grouping enterprises into broad categories help enterprisers choose a pathway to new business formation?

2. Why should enterprisers analyze businesses on four different levels—individual, enterprise, environment, and start-up process?

3. Describe the key characteristics of Type 1—Escaping to Something New.

4. Which two types of companies comprise Type 2—Putting the Deal Together? Why are they grouped together?

5. Compare and contrast the major characteristics of Type 3, Using Prior Skills & Contacts (Professionals), and Type 5, Leveraging Expertise. How does Type 6, Aggressive Service, compare?

6. Explain, using the 19 factors in Exhibit 9.2, why Type 4, Purchasing a Firm or Franchise, is such a popular pathway.

7. What types of products would you find at a Type 7 firm? Differentiate between the enterprise characteristics of Type 7 and Type 1.

8. Which archetype is most similar to Type 8—Methodical Organizing? Which form differs most from this pathway? Explain your answers.

9. Explain how you can apply your understanding of the eight archetypes to choose a pathway to entrepreneurship.

Applying What You've Learned

1. Review the eight pathways to new business formation and choose the one that appeals to you most. Explain your reasons and why you think this is most suitable. What is your second choice? Describe one or more businesses that you might start for each of these archetypes.

2. Which of the 19 variables in Exhibit 9.2 were the most important in making your choices in question 1, and why?

3. After leaving Laser Diagnostic Technologies, a company he founded, Andre Dreher was looking for a new business opportunity. Recognizing the potential of applying wavefront-guided technology to improve visual acuity, he obtained commercial rights from the company that developed it and formed Opthonix, a vision care company, in 2000. Dreher arranged for financing from several leading venture capital firms. Ophthonix's patented high definition vision technology is the first fully customized form of vision correction and uses the Z-View™ Aberrometer to measure the patient's eyes for both low and high order aberrations. The Z-View then generates a fully customized prescription that is used to produce customized eyeglasses and contact lenses that optimize vision. In 2004 Ophthonix entered into a strategic alliance with Optical Connection, a San Jose company. Optical Connection will use wavefront-guided technology to produce contact lenses for distribution by Ophthonix.[2]

   (a) Which archetype best describes Ophthonix? Explain why you selected this pathway, including the most significant of the 19 variables.

   (b) Compare your answer with your classmates' and discuss the different selections. Does a different archetype seem more appropriate?

4. Robert Warfield (not his real name) started an executive-search consulting firm. Rather than following the traditional "headhunting" process (finding an individual to fill a job and receiving a fee based on the placed person's salary), he chose to work with a company's upper management to develop a strategy for executive recruitment and compensation. Mr. Warfield has many years' experience as a recruiter in government and private industry and worked hard to develop a strong base of individuals on whom he could call in the future. Once he started his company, he let his network know he was available for executive search consulting. This led to several contracts and an expanding client base. Mr. Warfield is well regarded as a qualified specialist who can solve management's personnel problems, and his firm has a solid track record of success.[3]

   (a) Evaluate this company on the 19 variables and assign it to an archetype.

   (b) Compare your answer with your classmates' and discuss the different selections. Does a different archetype seem more appropriate?

   (c) You instructor will now give you the classifications assigned by a computer model and the entrepreneur himself. How do these compare with your selection?

   (Note: Both were Type 8, Methodical Organizing.)

5. Marilyn Brooks and four partners started a company that developed a process to print on mylar. One of her partners had developed the special technology. Although they worked as a team, each partner was responsible for a functional area in which he or she had expertise: marketing development, art, production, innovation, and general marketing. The first market they identified was labels for lawn mowers, because the metal labels then in use were not attractive, and paper labels fell off. Mylar labels looked better, were more durable, and cost the same as metal labels. The partner in charge of general marketing negotiated a deal with a lawn mower manufacturer. After this first success, the company expanded into other areas.[4]

    (a) Evaluate this company on the 19 variables and assign it to an archetype.

    (b) Compare your answer with your classmates' and discuss the different selections. Does a different archetype seem more appropriate?

    (c) You instructor will now give you the classifications assigned by a computer model and the entrepreneur himself. How do these compare with your selection? (Note: Both were Type 5, The Expert.)

Enterprisers on the Web

1. Visit the archive of success stories at the Service Corps of Retired Executives (SCORE) website, http://www.score.org/success_story_archive.html. Select two companies in different industry groups.

    (a) Summarize the enterprisers' start-up stories.

    (b) Evaluate these companies on the 19 variables and assign each to an archetype.

    (c) Discuss your answer with classmates. How well do these firms fit into the pathways?

2. *The Wall Street Journal's* http://www. StartupJournal.com lists many businesses and franchises for sale. Go to the Startup Journal's home page, http://www.startup journal.com, and navigate to the businesses for sale page. Fill in the form with your preferences as to industry and location. Review the list of businesses and choose one that interests you. What qualifications do you have to operate this type of company? What would you need to do to make this venture feasible?

3. Select the pathway that seems best for you. Then choose an industry of interest and search the Web for businesses that fall into this industry and archetype. Pick two and summarize the characteristics that place them in the archetype.

4. Go to the *Inc.* website and look for the current listing of the Inc. 500 (the 500 privately held companies with the highest growth in sales): http://www.inc.com/resources/inc500/2006. Select 5 of the top 25 fastest growing companies.

    (a) Which of the eight pathways to success do these companies follow?

    (b) Are there some pathways that are not likely to result in high growth firms?

5. *Entrepreneur's* website features stories of successful start-ups at http://www.entrepreneur.com/startingabusiness/successstories/index.html. Select 5 success stories that interest you and identify the pathway that each followed. Are the pathways to success for companies profiled by *Entrepreneur* different from the Inc. 500 companies? How are they similar or different? Why?

End Notes

1. This chapter is based on William B. Gartner, Terence R. Mitchell, and Karl H. Vesper, "A Taxonomy of New Business Ventures," *Journal of Business Venturing,* May 1989, pp. 169–186.

2. Based on information from Ophthonix' website, http://www.ophthonix.com (March 29, 2005).

3. William Baum Gartner, *An Empirical Model of the Business Startup and Eight Entrepreneurial Archetypes,* Ph.D. dissertation, Graduate School of Business Administration, University of Washington, 1982, p. 209.

4. Ibid., p. 203.

Purchasing a Business

KEY CONCEPTS

1. Purchasing a business is one of the most popular ways to become an enterpriser, and buying an existing firm can be a faster and more cost-effective route to business ownership than a start-up. Before making a business purchase, however, enterprisers must perform a thorough analysis of the business, from business model to market environment, operations, and financial feasibility. This due diligence process is similar to evaluating a new venture, except that it applies to a going concern. The objective is the same: to determine if the enterpriser can successfully operate the business and earn an appropriate return on the investment of time and money.

2. A business's value is ultimately what a buyer is willing to pay for it and depends upon many factors. The value of an ongoing business should be based on the business's ability to generate earnings. Enterprisers can choose from different valuation techniques, such as asset-based (book value, replacement value, and liquidation value), market-based, earnings formulas, and cash flow methods. Each has advantages and disadvantages.

3. The terms negotiated between the buyer and seller can be as important as the price for the business. These include whether the buyer acquires only the assets or the entire business and the payment terms, each of which carries different tax implications for the parties. Often sellers provide financing for the purchase; they may also take a portion of the payment in future payments of either a percentage of profits, a noncompete fee, or an employment contract. Enterprisers should consult both an accountant and an attorney during the extensive due diligence process.

Suppose you are laid off from your position in sales and marketing of food products. Although you have many years' experience in this field, you have a desire to innovate that hasn't been satisfied working for large corporations. You and your wife, who also has a marketing background, want more time for your family. Rather than look for another job, you decide to buy a company.

In this chapter, you'll meet Paul and Vickie Scharfman, who bought the Heim Cheese Company in 1991 after in-depth research into the cheese industry and due diligence into the company's operations. They focused on niche markets such as underserved ethnic groups, developing natural cheeses for Hispanic, Middle Eastern, and Indian consumers. By following the Scharfmans' example, you can learn how to assess an ongoing business, apply valuation techniques, and negotiate satisfactory terms to buy a business.

10.0 Make or Buy?

As we indicated in Chapter 9, purchasing a business or a franchise (Type 4) is one of the eight pathways to business ownership—and a major way for enterprisers to go into business. Why is this pathway such a popular route? Stop and think for a minute about all the different types of businesses in your area. Any of them might be for sale at some point. That opens up a lot of options! Many enterprisers have found that buying an existing business is a simpler and faster way to get into business than creating one. In some cases it may even be less expensive than starting from scratch. While buying a business with a track record does not guarantee future success, the enterpriser begins with fewer unknowns and less risk. Although there are many similarities between buying an independent business and a franchise outlet, we'll look at each option separately. We'll focus on purchasing a business in this chapter and the franchising process in Chapter 11.

Deciding whether to purchase a business rather than start a new one is similar to buying a home. Prospective homeowners have two choices: build a new house or buy an existing home. They will find more existing houses on the market than new or to-be-built houses. If they were interested in living in a particular area, they might only find existing homes available. In the same way, enterprisers may discover that it is easier to purchase a business in a particular industry sector than to create one.

We can also look at the purchase versus start-up decision as a make or buy decision. Just as some companies decide to make all the component parts of a product, enterprisers who choose an independent start-up are essentially making their own businesses. They do everything themselves: identify an opportunity, develop a product or service from this opportunity, find customers, determine channels of distribution, develop a marketing plan, acquire resources to execute their plan, and operate the business. Or, like other companies who outsource all or part of the manufacturing process, they could find a business that has all the desired attributes and purchase it.

In evaluating a potential business purchase, enterprisers must explore what makes a successful business. Before deciding to buy a business, they have to ask a critical question: "Can this business be successful?" Answering it requires delving into the fundamentals we discussed in earlier chapters: the business model, feasibility, and the business plan. Only by getting a complete picture of the business and how it operates—the customers, competitors, operations, employees, products/services—will they be able to determine its future profitability. The due diligence process is quite extensive and includes many of the same issues involved in a start-up, along with some new ones. For example, is the business priced fairly, and what is the basis for the valuation? What is the reputation of the current owners? The more thorough the research, the fewer surprises later.

Industry studies show that most enterprisers who begin exploring the purchase option search about 18 months for a business to buy and fewer than 10 percent actually complete the purchase. In the rest of the chapter, we'll help you determine whether the purchase route is right for you, and if so, how to increase the odds of success.

10.1 Why Buy a Business?

Enterprisers buy businesses for many reasons, including the speed with which they can get into business for themselves and economic factors. Here are several motives they often cite for choosing the purchase option:

1. *Buying a proven business concept.* A business that is already profitable has proven that it works, and there is less uncertainty about whether it will be successful. The business may have significant market share, and if not, the enterpriser can develop a plan to increase it. The odds are in the enterpriser's favor, although of course it depends on a number of factors such as customer loyalty, employee retention, and the response of competing firms. Overall, buying an established business should mean less risk to a purchaser compared to a start-up situation.

2. *Getting into business for yourself more quickly.* The business is already established and operating, which makes it easier to finance. Your business has name recognition, trained employees, a vendor network, and an established base of customers already buying your products or services, all of which take a great deal of time to develop. Operating procedures are in place as well.

3. *Purchasing is often less expensive than a start-up.* Marketing and sales costs for an existing business should be lower than for a new venture. When an enterpriser buys a business, the client list is usually one of the intangible assets. For example, many professionals such as dentists, doctors, and accountants often buy established practices. While clients may prefer the old dentist/doctor/accountant, the new owner of the business gets the opportunity to develop a new relationship with these clients, who are already in the habit of visiting that office. Buying the firm's fixed assets also saves money. Operating costs should be lower than in a start-up situation.

4. *Generating positive cash.* By purchasing a going concern, the enterpriser acquires inventory and receivables, as well as assets. These produce immediate cash flow when the business sells the products in inventory and collects the receivables owed.

5. *Improving an undervalued business.* Enterprisers often find businesses that need changes and improvements for sale at a good price. With some effort and skill, enterprisers can implement these changes and make the business more valuable. This is similar to buying a rundown house, fixing it up, and then selling it for a profit. For example, you might come across a house for $150,000 that you can renovate for $50,000 in materials and your time, and then sell it for $275,000. Likewise, some enterprisers are actually in the business of buying businesses, turning them around, and then selling them for a higher price.

6. *Counseling from the seller.* Because sellers often finance part of the business purchase price, they have a keen interest in the new owner's success. They will share their knowledge to help the new owner get off to a good start.

In addition, it may make more sense to purchase rather than start certain types of businesses. Service businesses, for instance, fall into this category because they bring established clients. Buying businesses situated in a prime location or with a dominant position in a particular market makes sense—if the purchasing rights to the location or market are included as well. Later in this chapter, we will look at the various parts of a business that one might consider purchasing rather than creating.

Buyer Beware

Of course, buying a business has its risks, too:

1. *Obtaining large initial financial outlay.* The selling price of a going concern reflects the investment the current owner has made to build the business. The cost may be higher than starting from scratch when financing needs occur over a longer time period. Closing costs, transfer fees, and other costs can drive the financial outlay even higher.

2. *Setting the right price.* Determining whether the seller's asking price is fair can be difficult. The valuation process has many variables, and there are different methods of valuing a business. However, the future earning power of the business should be your primary focus, as we will discuss later in this chapter.

3. *Discovering problems after the fact.* Owners who want to present their businesses favorably may hide or fail to disclose problems that could reduce the value of a business. For example, the balance sheet may include accounts receivable that cannot be collected. The business may have credit problems with its banks and vendors. The business may have had negative publicity. A new competitor may be entering the market. The city might be considering new taxes or zoning regulations. The main product may be at the end of its life cycle. These are just a few possible pitfalls that could await the new owner. Being extremely thorough when performing your due diligence and researching every aspect of the business is the best way to protect yourself. We suggest you review the feasibility study questions in Chapter 7 as a format for evaluating any business you might plan to purchase.

4. *Underestimating the commitment required to operate the business.* In their eagerness to buy a firm, enterprisers may not consider carefully the realities of running a particular type of business—and the commitment it will take in both time and money. As a result, they may find themselves spending long hours dealing with unexpected problems or facing a financial crisis because they didn't provide adequate working capital.

5. *Verifying the seller's claims.* Some business owners may overstate their company's advantages and downplay the negatives. It is up to you to get all the information you can, from objective sources when possible, before buying. If the owner brags about extra income that was not reported to the IRS and wants to include it when valuing the business, watch out! Not only is there no way to determine the accuracy of such cash income, but this practice is illegal. An owner who tells you about cheating the government may be stretching the truth in other areas as well.

Should You Buy?

In addition to understanding the pros and cons of a business purchase, an enterpriser must also consider personal motivation and goals. Because buying a business requires a major financial commitment, you should take your time to make sure it makes sense for you. Exhibit 10.1 provides a list of questions to get you thinking about the many issues that are involved. For example, you may want to own a company to supplement your current job rather than replace it. Knowing that ahead of time will help you focus your search on businesses that you can run part time. Also note that the primary issues involved with buying a business are similar to issues one would face in starting a business. The viability of the business concept (Chapter 6), the feasibility of the business model (Chapter 7), and the implementation and ongoing operations of the business (Chapter 8) will need the same level of diligence before you buy. You'll need to understand the industry you are considering, which means going to trade shows, industry association meetings, site visits to similar businesses, and interviewing business owners. When you evaluate management, you'll want to consider whether a poorly managed company offers an opportunity to turn around the business.

Use these questions to make some basic decisions about (1) whether to purchase a business and (2) the type of business to seek. Try not to limit yourself in these early stages. You may think you want to own a party-planning business until you learn that you will be working most weekends and have to sacrifice important family time. Rather than give up, think about what interested you in this type of business and see if there are other ways to follow your passion. For example, you might want to start with corporate events that take place mostly during the week.

Then you can go more deeply into the overall feasibility, examining the business model, market environment, value proposition, and capital considerations. In the final analysis, only you can decide if a business purchase meets your personal goals and is a good fit for your particular situation.

10.2 Business for Sale

Before you buy a business, you should find out as much as possible about the owner's motives for selling. Knowing the circumstances behind the sale is critical information for your evaluation of the enterprise's future profit potential. If, for example, the owner has neglected

---

exhibit
10.1

First Questions to Ask Before Buying a Business

1. What are your primary reasons for taking the purchase route to business ownership? Keep them in mind as you look at various businesses.

2. Are you buying a business as a full-time or a part-time endeavor? What are your income expectations?

3. Would you prefer to buy a business in your current industry or go into a new field?

4. What appeals to you about a particular industry? How well have you researched this field?

5. Why does this particular business opportunity excite you? Would you feel proud to own this type of business?

6. Why is the owner selling this business?

7. What skills and experience do you bring to the business? Do you need to hire people to provide expertise in specific areas?

8. Can you identify ways to improve the business to make it more successful?

9. Will you need partners to help you finance or operate the business successfully? If so, do you want to work with partners or would you prefer solo ownership?

10. Does the business make sense financially? What factors indicate the potential of revenue and earnings growth?

11. On what are the valuation and price based? Do they seem reasonable?

12. How easily will it be for you to obtain the financing you'll need to buy the business?

13. How well has the business been managed? Do you want to keep many of the current managers or employees?

14. Does it make sense to buy rather than start this type of business?

---

the business for a while, you may be able to implement immediate changes that quickly increase revenues. An owner who wants to cash out and move to another venture may hand over a thriving business that is still growing rapidly—or that has reached its mature stage.

People decide to sell businesses for many reasons. The owner may want to move on to a new venture, be ready to retire, or be in poor health and decide that he or she no longer wants to operate the business. If no family members or employees are interested in taking over the company, the owner may have no choice but to sell.

Life Cycle Issues

As we described in Chapter 1, every enterprise has its own life cycle that is often tied to the life cycle of the enterpriser. As enterprisers get older, their interests and abilities to successfully operate a business may diminish. Let's face it—most people, enterprisers included, after a certain age, aren't that interested in having a full-time job

and working long hours each day. Operating a successful business takes considerable time and energy. At some point, it becomes too much for many business owners, and they decide to sell their businesses. Also, if an owner dies, the business may owe significant estate taxes upon transfer to family members. The heirs may need to sell the business to pay taxes.

In many situations, an enterpriser's family might be interested in taking over the business. The enterpriser may groom a relative to own and manage the business. This doesn't always occur, however. Family members may have other career opportunities they wish to pursue. For example, an enterpriser might own a café at which his or her children worked as they grew up. As both the café and the owner mature, the kids might decide that they have had enough of the restaurant business and its particular problems and challenges. The same circumstances can apply to the café's employees, who may not have either the inclination or the financial resources to buy the business.

Working in a business where the owner is likely to sell the business can be an excellent way to acquire a business. Many enterprisers have joined businesses with an understanding, often through a written contract, that the enterpriser will take over the business from the owner at a specified price and time. This is certainly a very viable strategy when no family members or other employees are interested in running the business.

Even if family members might want to take over the business, the current owner might decide that it would be better for a nonfamily member to own the business, and pay the current owner and family. A family member might not have the necessary resources to purchase the business, or the business might be split into so many ownership shares among a family that it would make more sense (for the benefit of the business) if an outsider purchased all of the family's interests for a fair price.

Also, family members often end up disagreeing about how the business should be run, which can lead to disastrous results. A good example of this is the Haft family in Washington, D.C., which at one point owned a very large drug store chain, as well as Crown Books, one of the first discount book chains. Father and son disagreed about how to run these businesses; the mother sided with the son, and the father sued both the mother and the son for control of these businesses. Legal disputes took so much of the family's time that no one was minding the store—literally—and these businesses subsequently went into bankruptcy. These enterprisers might have survived if the family had sold them to an outsider to manage.

New Interests

Starting a business doesn't mean that the enterpriser will always want to run that type of business. Enterprisers thrive on challenges, so it is not unusual for them to lose interest after running a business for a while. They may become bored with doing the same thing day after day, whether it is making pizzas, selling hardware, or developing a new compound to fight disease. Or they may discover a different opportunity that seems more appealing.

Many enterprisers want to move on to something else, and they actually plan on selling their businesses as a part of their enterprising strategy. A good example of a serial entrepreneur is Terry Allen, author of *No Cash, No Fear,* who has probably started over 50 businesses. He quickly recognized that he had a talent for starting profitable businesses but was not very good at running them. So he always looked for exit strategies, such as selling the business to employees or to an outsider, freeing him to move on to the next start-up opportunity.

Management Problems

Some owners don't have the managerial, financial, and operational capabilities to run businesses. For example, most businesses need enterprisers who can understand financial statements and manage the cash in the business. Some individuals just can't figure out how cash flows through the firm and how their actions affect profitability. Sometimes they hit on a formula for success. But as the competition changes and they try to adapt to changing customer needs and competitive pressures, the formula no longer works. The enterpriser is clueless about what changes to make in the business model to ensure success.

Poor Businesses

And, finally, there are some businesses that are dogs—poor choices, literally and figuratively! They will not be successful no matter what a new owner does. The reason may be changing customer needs. Take, for example, a small appliance repair business. It is probably cheaper to purchase a new coffee maker for $20 at the local discount store than to fix a broken one. In fact, it could be *more* expensive to repair it! The same holds true for audio equipment, computers, and electronics. Because people prefer to buy new rather than repair, owning a repair business might just not be feasible, no matter what the enterpriser does to make the business a success.

Ethical considerations also have a bearing on the decision to buy a business. The basic issue is one of information asymmetries between the buyer and the seller. The owner usually knows more about the nature of the business for sale than the prospective buyer and also has other types of information about the business that the buyer doesn't. Typically, we say "buyers beware" and place most of the risk on the buyer to do as much due diligence as possible. But is it ethical for a seller to withhold information that might significantly affect the purchase price of a business, its operations, or its potential growth in the future? The Enterprising Ethics box presents some ethical dilemmas a seller might face.

ENTERPRISING ETHICS

Buyer Beware—The Ethics of Selling a Business

For the past 30 years, you have enjoyed owning and operating a upscale clothing store in an affluent suburb. You started with women's clothes and expanded into juniors at the request of your customers. When the adjacent store became available, you leased that space as well. You enlarged the original store to include more lines of women's clothing and used the new space to begin selling high-quality children's apparel as well.

Over the past year, managing the store and its ten employees has become increasingly stressful for you. You are open seven days a week from 10 AM until 6 PM, and until 8 PM on Thursday. The long days are taking a toll on your health. It might be time to sell the business, retire, and finally have time to travel. As you begin to prepare sales materials for potential buyers, you discover several matters that could be troublesome for a new owner.

The business is conveniently located on a busy street with a high volume of pedestrian and vehicle traffic and plenty of parking. Last month, however, you received a notice that the city is planning to widen the road in front of your business. Construction will take at least a year, and access to your business and the parking lot is likely to be affected by this.

Even though you have employees to help you at the store, you have been its primary manager. Of your ten staff members, two are long-term employees whom you can trust to open and close the store and oversee other employees in your absence. Two others are also trustworthy, dependable, and good with customers. You are not so sure about the other six and suspect that one or two might be stealing from the business—an easy thing to do because about one-third of your sales are for cash. However, you don't have concrete proof of this.

© Volker Kreinacke/istockphoto.com

One of the reasons for your store's success is its exclusive right to sell a prestigious designer's clothes. No other store in a 20-mile radius is allowed to sell this clothing line. Nor does the designer sell on the Web, believing that a strong retail network with trained sales representatives helps customers coordinate clothing and accessories. Last week, the designer's representative told you that the designer was considering constructing his or her own boutiques to showcase the fashions. Your store derives 25 percent of its revenue from this designer's products, and because the line has a high markup, it accounts for about 40 percent of your profits. You also sell many accessories, such as scarves, jewelry, and belts that compliment the designer items and will likely lose sales for these products as well. You might be looking at a 50 percent reduction in sales, and an even greater reduction in the profits.

Discussion Questions

1. In your opinion, how much information should a seller disclose to a prospective buyer about the business for sale? What general guidelines would you suggest?

2. Do you have an obligation to tell a prospective buyer about the following, or should you assume that the buyer will find out through due diligence?

   a. The city's plans to widen the road.

   b. The rumor concerning the opening of designer boutiques that would compete with your store.

   What are the implications of your decision? What could you include in the seller's agreement to protect yourself from lawsuits if there are significant changes arising from either of these situations?

3. A buyer indicates that he plans to keep the current employees after purchasing the store. What, if anything, should you say about your employees to him, and why? Should you express your concerns about the two employees you suspect may be stealing, even though you aren't sure about this? Could you be sued by these employees if they were let go by the new owner?

4. Another option is to sell the business "as is," so that as the seller you are not responsible or liable for any changes in the performance of the business after the sale. Do you think this would be ethical? Why or why not?

10.3 Finding Businesses for Sale

Once you decide to buy a business, you have to find the right one. You can consult a professional whose expertise is buying and selling companies or go it alone by reading classified ads in newspapers and magazines or attending business opportunity trade shows.

Professionals who specialize in business purchases fall into several categories. Those involved in buying and selling large businesses (like Fortune 1,000 businesses) are called investment bankers. They have the capital and connections to broker billion-dollar transactions. For the smaller deals that account for most of the business purchase activity in the United States, an enterpriser would look for a *business broker*. Merger and acquisition specialists concentrate on the middle range between these extremes.

Business Brokers

Business brokers are similar to real estate agents. They act as agents for sellers of businesses, listing businesses for sale. In that role, they may also be a consultant to the seller of the business, providing advice and expertise about valuing the business and presenting the business to prospective buyers. Business brokers often qualify potential buyers for sellers, screening buyers to ensure they have the financial resources and requisite expertise to complete a purchase.

There are many different kinds of business brokers. Brokers often focus on a particular business segment, such as:

- Certain types of businesses (doctor's offices, restaurants, service businesses and retail stores).

- Specific size categories (e.g., businesses priced under $100,000, or over $1 million).

- A geographic region (city, county, state, or region).

Finding a business broker is easy; just search for "business broker" using any major Internet search engine, and it'll generate a long list of sites offering businesses for sale. State business broker associations and the yellow pages of your local phone book are additional resources. Membership in the International Business Brokers Association (IBBA), a nonprofit organization that promotes professionalism in the buying and selling of businesses, is an important credential for a broker to have. The IBBA offers educational courses and a certification program. In addition to a member database

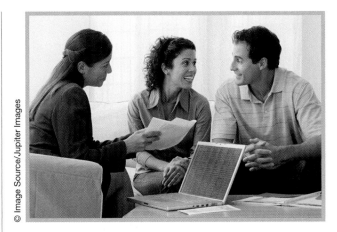

© Image Source/Jupiter Images

searchable by geography, it lists over 3,000 businesses for sale that can be searched by geographic location, firm and industry type, and purchase price. Another site is the World M&A Network, which lists businesses by industry and type.

Browsing several broker-sponsored "business for sale" sites is a good way for prospective enterprisers to learn what kinds of businesses are sold, reasons that owners of businesses sell them, and the terms business owners offer a prospective purchaser. While the formats of these listings vary from site to site, most include similar information. They provide a quick overview of many different types of businesses, along with asking price and financial highlights such as gross revenue and **cash flow**, the cash generated by the business after subtracting taxes and adding back noncash expenses such as depreciation. The representative listings in Exhibit 10.2 are typical of what you will find.

Typically, a business broker will enter into an agreement with the seller to list the business for sale. The agreement usually includes:

- What is offered for sale (assets such as equipment, inventory, facilities, patents; stock).

- Initial offering price and terms (e.g., 100 percent cash payment; seller financing offered).

- Broker's commission rate: These vary but typically a business broker would receive 10–15 percent of the sales price up to a certain amount (often $1 million), and a sliding scale commission on the sales price above $1 million, such as 5 percent. The seller pays the broker's-commission.

Cash flow   Cash generated by the business after subtracting taxes and adding back noncash expenses such as depreciation.

exhibit
10.2

Business for Sale Listings

While hypothetical, the following listings are based on actual business for sale ads from a variety of sources.

Children's Gymnastics & Activity Center

Offers full range of gymnastics, tumbling & trampoline classes, as well as Day Camps, Parties, Special Events, and Indoor Rock Climbing option. Great business with low down payment, and seller financing possible to qualified buyer. Established 1980.

Industry:	Educational
Industry Segment:	Other Educational
Geography:	United States/Midwest
Asking Price:	$650,000
Gross Revenue/Trend:	$955,188/Increasing
Cash Flow:	$180,648
Cash Flow Type:	Seller's Discretionary Earnings
Value of Equipment:	$184,000 (Included in asking price)
Seller Financing:	Negotiable
Mgmt. Training/Support:	Owner will train
Reason for Selling:	Retiring and pursuing other interests
Facilities:	23,450 sf with option for another 5,800 sf for Indoor Rock Climbing. Owner offers favorable long-term lease.
Market Outlook/Competition:	Excellent; business has set high barrier to entry for similar businesses, and has room to expand.

Bagel Shop

Beautiful, well-equipped bagel shop serving breakfast (60%) and lunch (40%) in a comfortable 60-seat dining area. Bagels represent about 70% of the business. Located in an extremely busy, upscale shopping center in Orange County, CA, with many high traffic tenants, including Long's Drugs. Business is being run semi-absentee; a full-time, hands-on owner could certainly build upon the current operation.

Asking Price:	$130,000
Industry:	Food & Beverage: Coffee, Cafe, Dessert
Reason for Selling:	Other business interests
Year Established:	1991
# of Employees:	7
Yearly Revenues:	$300,000
Yearly Cash Flow:	$54,000

Additional Details:
- The property is leased.
- The owner is willing to train/assist the new owner.
- The owner is not willing to work for the new owner.
- This is not a franchise opportunity.
- This is not a distressed business or bankruptcy situation.

Energy Conservation Project Management

East Coast Energy Conservation Project Management business with excellent growth potential. Home-based business; can be relocated anywhere in the country; the best sites are Atlanta, Baltimore, Florida, and North Carolina. National client base of big box companies and department stores; projects require travel to all parts of the country and typically take 2 days to 3 weeks. Current project contracts, mostly in eastern United States, extend through next year, with solid project pipeline. Sales will exceed $1 million. The usual project will last 3 days to 3 weeks.

Industry:	Professional Services
Industry Segment:	Consulting
Asking Price:	$210,000
Gross Revenue:	$672,400
Cash Flow:	$121,000
Value of Equipment:	$5,000 (Included in Asking Price)
Seller Financing:	Seller will provide financing, with $60K down
Year Established:	1993
Number of Employees:	6 full time
Home Based:	Yes
Mgmt. Training/Support:	Seller will provide training
Reason For Selling:	Other Interests
Facilities:	Home Based

© Jupiter Images

- Financing fee if a broker arranges financing for the buyer. This can range from 2.5 to 5 percent of the financing amount.

- Length of time the broker has exclusive rights to sell the business.

Other Resources

In addition to searching the Internet and contacting business brokers, several other avenues can help enterprisers locate businesses for sale:

- *Realtors.* Some real estate brokerage companies selling commercial properties also sell businesses that are "attached" to the property. Many kinds of retail firms fit this category. A realtor tries to find a buyer to buy the business and the location that goes with it, or buy the location and get the business as well.

- *People knowledgeable about an industry.* These would include anyone in the deal flow, such as supply chain contacts (suppliers and customers), competitors, and industry associations. Tapping into these and similar networks often turns up good leads.

- *Business owners.* Enterprisers can ask owners of businesses they like whether they would consider selling. This direct route often works, as we will see.

- *Business valuation seminars.* Attending a seminar designed to help business owners value their companies is a good way to meet enterprisers who want to sell their businesses.

- *"Business wanted" ads.* Placing an ad that summarizes the type of business you want to buy brings sellers to you. You may also hear from owners who have not yet decided to sell but are interested in exploring their options.

10.4 Valuation: What Is a Business Worth?

Finding a business to buy is just the first step. Next, an enterpriser must analyze the business and value it based on what it will earn. A business's value is ultimately what a buyer is willing to pay for it and depends upon a lot of factors: how long it's been in operation, how many employees, quality of physical assets (i.e., equipment, facilities, supplies, and inventory), market considerations, customer base and loyalty, and earning potential. You want to buy a business that you believe has all the necessary parts to operate successfully, both hard assets and goodwill. Goodwill represents intangibles, such as the value of the business's reputation and similar factors that come with a going concern, and can be difficult to ascertain.

Buying a business is similar to purchasing any asset that will generate some rate of return. If you purchased a $10,000 bond, you would expect the bond to pay you interest every year and return your principle when you sold the bond. It's the same for a business. When you buy a business for $10,000, you expect a return for your investment and the time and effort you spend working in the business. Otherwise, you'd be better off, financially, working for a salary elsewhere and looking for a separate investment that would generate money. (Of course, there are other reasons to be in business, but we believe that enterprisers should also make money doing what they love.)

The critical factor in determining a particular value for a business is earnings, or potential earnings—not the business's physical assets. As we explain the various valuation methods that enterprisers might apply to a particular business, please keep in mind that the *ultimate value of buying an ongoing business must be based on the business's ability to generate earnings.*

As we have covered in Chapters 6, 7, and 8, valuing a business begins with considering:

- The value of the opportunity.

- The enterprise's business model.

- The future feasibility of the enterprise.

- The specific ways the business operates—the business plan.

In purchasing a business, enterprisers should undertake the same types of analysis they would go through to start a business. Therefore, you should use the frameworks we provided in those chapters as guides for evaluating businesses you seek to purchase. We will refer to many of the same topics regarding the business model, feasibility, and business plan (customers, intensity of competitors, channels, benefits, etc.) at the end of this chapter, when we look at the nonfinancial issues that constitute the real value of purchasing a business.

The financial aspects of a business are, in many respects, a summary of the success (or failure) of the business over time. The financial figures represent the business—but they are not the business itself. Because the financial characteristics of the business reflect the critical success factors in the way the business operates, we have waited to introduce many of the financial aspects of the enterprising process until you were familiar with nonfinancial factors.

Some enterprisers hire a professional appraiser to do a formal business valuation, especially if they are interested in a large or complex business. However, enterprisers should always perform their own valuation analysis and not rely on the broker or the seller to give you the numbers. It's the best way to understand a business, get a frame of reference before proceeding, and avoid overpaying. Exhibit 10.3 lists some of the financial and legal documentation an enterpriser should request prior to beginning the valuation process.

There are many different valuation formulas, and some are more applicable to certain types of businesses. It's a good idea to calculate value using several methods to get a feel for a price range. Because valuation is a very complex topic, with whole books devoted to it, we will provide an overview of four popular bases of valuation: assets, market, earnings, and cash flow. Even if you choose to hire a professional to appraise a business for you, this basic knowledge will help you understand the benefits and limitations of each technique and be able to ask the right questions.

Asset-Based Valuations

Asset-based valuation approaches begin with placing a value on the business's assets. This category has several variations, with some using replacement or market value rather than book (depreciated) value. In addition to buildings, land, and equipment, these assets include improvements to leased space and all inventory (raw materials, parts, work-in-progress, and finished goods). For example, in valuing a printing company, you'd look at the buildings, presses and copiers, as well as ink, paper, and other supplies in inventory. Intangible assets include goodwill, logos, trademarks, and patents. Exhibit 10.4 briefly describes the four categories of asset-based valuations.

While these methods are relatively easy to calculate, they take a narrow look at a business, focusing on assets alone. They assign no value to the business's ability to use those assets to generate revenues. While modifying the asset values to either current market or replacement value provides a better estimate than book value, they are not as helpful as other valuation methods we discuss in the next section.

Asset-based valuation   Determination of a business's value based on the company's assets.

exhibit

10.3

Financial and Legal Documents to Request when Purchasing a Business

- All financial statements for the past five years
- Income tax statements for the past five years
- List of equipment and the depreciation schedule
- List of Accounts Receivables and their age (when they were due)
- List of Accounts Payables and their age (when they were due)
- Inventory list
- Any leases (rental agreements, equipment leases, automobile leases)
- Any contracts (customer, supplier, employment, loan agreements, labor contracts, royalty agreements, franchise agreements)
- List of partners and stockholders (indicating percentage of business owned and/or amount of stock held)
- Compensation for owners of the business (salaries and perks)
- Insurance documents
- Legal documents (articles of incorporation, partnership agreement)
- Copies of licenses and other documents pertaining to government regulations
- Tax payments for federal, state, and local governments

exhibit

10.4

Asset-Based Valuation Methods

1. **Book value:** The value according to the business' current financial statements, as shown on the balance sheet (financial statement listing assets and liabilities).

2. **Modified book value:** The asset values adjusted to their actual, or current, values.

3. **Replacement value:** The amount required to replace, at current market rates, the assets the business owns.

4. **Liquidation value:** The value of the assets if the business needed to be sold immediately. The liquidation value is likely to be much lower than the replacement value of these assets. This is not an especially useful figure, as why sell a business for the same amount you would receive for liquidating it?

Market-Based Valuations

Essentially, **market-based valuations** are determined by what other people will pay for this business or similar businesses. Industry valuation and multiplier formula valuations are two categories of market-based valuation.

Market-based valuation Valuation method that looks at process paid for comparable firms. Industry valuation and multiplier formula valuations are two categories of market-based valuation.

In a perfect world, a business would be sold for its **fair market value,** or the price that a business would command from a knowledgeable buyer and seller with the relevant information about the business and willingness to undertake the transaction. In some respects, one doesn't know the fair market value of a business until it is actually sold. So we have a catch-22: we can't determine fair market value until the business is sold, and the actual selling price of the business is the fair market value!

Market value includes a number of factors, and each may be viewed differently by various sellers and buyers. The value of a business, then, often lies in the eyes of the beholder:

1. *Different estimates of future earnings.* As we mentioned earlier, a good valuation technique must account for the future earnings of the business. The challenge for a buyer purchasing a business is estimating accurately the actual earnings for the business at some future date. Different buyers will no doubt have different earnings estimates for the same business. How could that be? One buyer might have 25 years of sales experience in the same industry and project rapid revenue growth based on the addition of revenues from many new clients. Another buyer might lack the industry experience and include only current clients in the earnings estimates.

2. *Risk perception.* Given that each buyer brings different skills, experience, and industry knowledge, the perceived risk of the enterprise to achieve estimated earnings levels will vary. A buyer with less experience in a particular business might view the purchase as more of a risk and therefore would likely pay less for something that might not achieve the earnings objectives. The buyer with considerable experience operating the same kind of business expects to meet the revenue and earnings goals and may be willing to pay more.

3. *Tax considerations.* Any sale of a business is likely to involve paying taxes to federal, state, and local governments. How a sale is structured can result in widely varying tax rates for both the seller and the

buyer of a business. We will discuss tax implications later when we look at how deals are structured. Clearly, the payment or avoidance of taxes can be a significant factor in whether a business is sold or not.

4. *Buyer synergies.* A buyer who has businesses in a similar industry may want to add another complimentary business. For example, a business that manufactures furniture might purchase a chain of furniture retail stores to provide a direct channel of distribution to the final customer. The retail furniture business might be more valuable to a furniture manufacturer than to someone who doesn't own any related businesses.

A number of sources provide valuation guidelines to help an enterpriser determine what a particular type of business might be worth. For example, *Inc.* magazine publishes a valuation matrix that enterprisers can download from its website (http://www.inc.com/valuation). It lists different types of businesses and median revenue, sales price, and a price range. Multiple factors determine the price for each type of business—total assets, liabilities, and earnings. In early 2007, for example, a lawn and garden services business had median annual revenues of $250,000 and a median sale price of $165,000, while a gasoline service station will have median revenues of $1,800,000 and a median sale price of $341,000.[1]

Earnings Valuations

Even though asset-based, market-based, and industry valuation techniques have some merit, the primary way to value a business is by exploring the past, current and future earnings of the business. Assets are meaningless if they don't generate earnings! As we have indicated in the chapters on the business model and feasibility, it is important to understand not only how much the business earns but also how the business creates these earnings. In addition, earnings will reflect the contribution of intangibles such as goodwill.

Cash Flow Valuations

Cash flow valuations are perhaps the most realistic approach to determining a business's value. After all, the future cash flows the business will generate are the basis of its financial success. As we will see in later chapters, it is better to operate a business that has more cash flow than one that has low cash flow—even if its income statement shows higher profits.

This method, also called **discounted cash flow** (DCF), is more difficult to calculate. It requires an estimate of future cash flow and then applies a **discount rate** that represents the buyer's expected cost of capital (the interest rate

---

Fair market value   The price that a business would command from a knowledgeable buyer and a seller with the relevant information about the business and willingness to undertake the transaction.

Discounted cash flow (DCF)   Valuation technique that finds the present value of a future cash flow stream at a specified discount rate.

Discount rate   A rate that represents the buyer's expected cost of capital (the interest rate for a loan to buy the company), as well as the desired return on investment and an adjustment for inflation.

for a loan to buy the company) as well as the desired return on investment. The resulting calculation provides the current value of the future cash flow stream.

10.5 Structuring the Deal

Structuring the purchase is often more art than science and requires considerable negotiating between the parties, whose preferences may be quite different. In fact, the purchase terms can be just as important as the price of the business.

It's important to note that the *face value,* or listed purchase price for a business, is often quite different from the *cash value* of the deal. Let's say that a buyer offered $1 million to purchase a firm that manufactured plastic garden equipment. The $1 million represents the face value of the purchase. Rarely are businesses sold for an all cash price at the time of transaction. Many sellers offer the buyer a loan to purchase the business or let the buyer pay for the business over time.

Let's now look at some of the decisions that affect the structure of a business purchase transaction.

What Are You Buying?

One of the first decisions an enterpriser makes when structuring a purchase transaction is whether to buy the entire business or only its assets. Usually buying the whole business is structured as a *stock sale* and includes the assets, liabilities, and owner's equity. The new owner is liable for any debts of the business. An *asset sale* is just what it implies: the buyer acquires only the business's assets. In this case, the seller must settle any outstanding debts. With an asset sale, the new owner avoids being saddled with unknown liabilities. The purchaser could choose to assume specific debts, such as a lease or mortgage on the facilities, if the terms were advantageous.

Tax considerations play a major role in the decision of what to buy, and the interests of buyer and seller may conflict. A seller usually prefers a stock sale, which would be taxed at lower capital gain rates. With an asset sale, any amount the seller receives for the assets that exceeds the book value on the balance sheet would be taxed at higher than ordinary income tax rates. A buyer, however, would prefer an asset sale because the purchase price of the assets becomes the value that the buyer can then list on the business's balance sheet. A higher asset valuation would mean that the buyer could likely deduct higher amounts of depreciation expenses, which would minimize the business's future tax liabilities.

Arranging Financing

While sellers would most likely prefer to sell their businesses for all cash, most buyers will not have the necessary funds to pay the full price up-front. To finance the purchase, the enterpriser must obtain financing from a bank or other lender, an investor group, or the seller. Regardless of the funding source, incurring debt to buy the business increases its risk by adding a high priority fixed obligation—the loan payment.

The availability of bank financing will depend on the type of business, the enterpriser's creditworthiness and experience, collateral offered, and similar factors. Banks prefer to make loans for specific asset purchases. For example, a loan for a delivery truck to the new owner of a furniture delivery service would be easier to obtain than one to cover rent and salaries for a tutoring company. The bank would take the truck as collateral (security) for the loan. If the delivery company fails to make its payments, the bank can repossess the truck. If the tutoring business fails to attract students and can't generate the revenues it projected, the bank has no other source of loan repayment.

Many sellers offer the buyer a note to help finance a portion of the business purchase. The buyer repays the note over a specified length of time at a specified interest rate. The seller often becomes the lender, rather than an outside lender such as a bank, for various reasons:

- Many small businesses have such poor financial records that other lenders (such as a bank) are unsure of what these businesses can actually earn.

- Privately held corporations often report income and expenses in a way that the financial statements show little profit. For example, the owner of the business can pay high salaries to themselves and their family, which is a business expense that would lower net income.

- If accurate financial statements are generated for the business, the owner could be subject to an IRS audit if the figures are significantly different than those submitted earlier.

- Many buyers purchase businesses that they have less experience in operating, putting the business at a higher risk—a risk that many outsider lenders are unwilling to take.

Like a bank note, a note from the seller will include an interest rate that provides an acceptable return—typically, a rate based on current market conditions. Taking a note for part of the purchase price of a business puts the seller in a risky position. What if the buyer cannot make payments to the seller at some point in the future? Most sellers are advised to include covenants in the purchase contract that require the buyer to limit salaries and other expenses so that the payment of the note is a priority. If the buyer cannot make payments, most sellers often specify that the business's assets or all of the business's stock must be put up as collateral for the loan. Should the loan go into default, the seller regains ownership of the business—not really what someone who is selling a business wants!

Many sellers may be willing to accept stock in the buyer's new company as partial payment for the value of the business. The new stock is a tax-free exchange of stock. In the U.S. tax system, the exchange of old shares of the selling company for new shares in the buying company are not taxed until they are sold. This can be an important tax advantage to a seller. Again, the seller has to believe that the buyer will grow the business in such a way that the shares in the buyer's business have more value than the shares in the old business.

Earn-outs

With an **earn-out**, the seller takes part of the payment as a certain amount of the future earnings of the business over a period of time. For example, a seller might want an earn-out of 50 percent of the profits of the business over a period of five years. The seller and buyer would determine what might be reasonable expenses to be charged, so that the business would generate profits. In an earn-out, the seller shares in the future risk of the business and the buyer's ability to generate earnings. Such a deal might occur because the buyer is uncertain about the business's ability to generate a specific level of cash payment over time (to make fixed

payments of principal and interest on a note). In nearly all earn-out agreements, the seller manages part of the risk of this arrangement by keeping ownership of the business until the buyer has met the terms of the earn-out agreement.

Noncompete Agreements and Employment Contracts

Buyers often want sellers to agree to a **noncompete agreement** that prohibits the seller from engaging in a similar kind of business for a set time period within the geographic area in which the purchased business competes. There may be an annual payment to the seller for this agreement. Besides noncompete agreements, many buyers ask sellers to take employment contracts as part of the price of the business. An employment contract is another tax-deductible expense to the business.

Once again, tax considerations come into play. Sellers prefer receiving cash for the business, which is taxed at the lower capital gains rate. Payments for a noncompete agreement or employment contract are taxed as current income to the seller. The buyer, on the other hand, likes these options because such payouts are expenses to the business that lower taxable income.

As these examples show, a business purchase transaction can be very complex and can take many different forms. The buyer and seller may have conflicts arising from competing interests. Deals are often limited only by the imagination of the buyer and sellers involved in the agreement. With so many complexities and tax implications in the purchase of a business, we advise you to involve a lawyer, an accountant, and a business appraiser in the process.

10.6 Other Considerations

As this chapter demonstrates, buying a business is a multifaceted process that includes both financial and non-financial considerations. Your analysis includes the same issues you'd consider if you were planning to start a business—the topics we discussed in Chapters 6 through 9. Here, though, we are performing the analysis on an ongoing business. For example, instead of looking at the financing required to start a company, the enterpriser would evaluate financial feasibility based on the purchase price and the terms of the deal. The bottom line is the same: Given everything the enterpriser now knows about the business, can he or she operate it successfully in the future and earn an adequate return on the investment of time and money?

Earn-out   Payment strategy that gives the seller of a business a certain amount of the future earnings of the business over a specified time period.

Noncompete agreement   Agreement prohibiting the seller from entering into a similar kind of business for a set time period within the geographic area in which the purchased business competes.

The primary concern for a prospective purchaser involves determining whether the business model is sound and will generate future earnings. Begin by asking yourself the four broad questions we posed in Chapter 7:

1. Who is the customer?

2. What does the customer want? (consideration)

3. How is this consideration going to be provided? (connection)

4. Can you make money doing this?

When investigating the purchase of a business, a savvy enterpriser should interview customers of the business to explore whether these customers are satisfied with the business's goods and services. If these customers are unhappy, the business may have a lower value because dissatisfied customers might go to competitors. Understanding the market environment is also important. Is the industry undergoing significant changes that could have an impact on current connections? For example, the desirability of buying a retail children's clothing store would change if a new Babies-R-Us store was under construction nearby, or if more people chose to buy children's clothes online. Attending industry meetings and talking to other business owners will provide valuable insights. The prospective purchaser needs to have a clear sense of how

the business makes money, and what key factors determine whether the business will generate profits.

As mentioned earlier, professionals should help you with your due diligence. An accountant can audit the financial characteristics of the business, while an attorney should review a number of other issues, as Exhibit 10.5 demonstrates.

Like those who choose to start businesses from scratch, business buyers must perform extensive due diligence before buying any business. It is very easy to overlook critical success factors that might be necessary for the business to be successful such as key employees, knowledge of how the business works, and knowledge of how to sell to prospective customers. Another important question to ask is whether the business is a good fit for your experience, skills, and personal goals. Paying proper attention to all the key factors will increase the likelihood that an enterpriser will be successful in both acquiring a business at a fair price and achieving desired operational and financial objectives in the future.

Whereas buying a business in the United States is a complex process, purchasing one in a foreign country is even more complicated. The Enterprising World box introduces you to the many issues you'd encounter if you wanted to own a business in France.

---

exhibit 10.5

Accounting and Legal Issues to Examine

An audit would explore such issues as

- Collectability and age of accounts receivable
- Age, condition, and value of inventory
- Age, condition, and value of equipment and physical plant
- Unknown liabilities
- Credit problems
- Tax payments

On the legal front, an attorney can review

- Compliance with local zoning and environmental regulations
- Validity of all required licenses and similar documents
- Current leases and contracts
- Insurance policies
- Existing and pending lawsuits against the business

AN ENTERPRISING WORLD

Working and Living Outside the United States

Like many Americans, you love to travel and have spent many happy vacations hiking and bicycling in Europe. You often daydream about moving overseas to live and work. Now you may be able to make your dream a reality, because an uncle has left you a generous bequest—enough for the down payment on a business venture in France, your favorite country. After browsing the business for sale listings, you discover what could be the perfect solution: A recently established cycle tour company and large farmhouse in Normandy. While the business is new, it is operational and has already developed a brand identity. Unexpected family health issues make it difficult for the founding owner, who lives in London, to spend enough time in France operating the company.

The business can be run from a home office, and the five-bedroom farmhouse has been renovated with modern kitchen and bathrooms. In addition to the main house, the property also has an adjacent building suitable for six more bedrooms and a gym equipped for cycle training. You and your spouse could live there and also develop a small inn to house your cycle tour participants.

Intrigued by the possibility of combining your passion for cycling with a business venture, you research the issues involved in buying a business in another country. Right away, you realize that the French business and legal environment is quite different from what you've experienced in the United States. First, the legal system in France is based on the Napoleonic Code, or civil law, rather than the common law system used in the United States and the United Kingdom. The public sector is large and bureaucratic, with many levels to negotiate. Public law covers municipal and tax law, and there are also private laws that govern commercial and corporate aspects of the transaction from construction and sale and purchase agreements to mortgages. You will be subject to French income tax regulations, which will also vary from U.S. tax laws.

The usual forms of business organization are unfamiliar to you and include:

- Enterprise individuelle (E.I.)—a one-person business

- Entreprise Unipersonnelle à Responsabilité Limitée (E.U.R.L.)—a private limited company under sole ownership

- Société à Responsabilité Limitée (S.A.R.L.)—a limited liability company

In addition, the law divides small businesses into three categories based on the main activity: Artisan (craftsmen) with no more than ten employees; Libéral, generally professionals such as physicians, attorneys, or consultants; and Commerçant (tradesmen).

Property sales procedures are different as well. For example, in France you are expected to sign a binding preliminary contract of sale prior to performing the various legal and other searches. In the United States typically you conduct your searches before signing any sales contract.

These are just a few issues you encounter in a quick search for information on buying a business in France. You wonder what else you need to know before proceeding further.

Discussion Questions

1. Prepare a list of questions you would want to ask before purchasing this business, including those relating to the business and its operations as well as the problems you might encounter in trying to purchase a French business. How would owning your own business in France be different from working for an employer based in France?

   Now, use a Web search engine to find information to answer the following questions:

2. What regulations apply to non–European Union persons purchasing a business in a European Union country like France? What are the visa, residency, and work permit requirements for a non–European Union citizen to work in France?

3. Because your bicycle business is seasonal, you plan to live part of the year in France, and part of the year in the United States, how would your tax liability for each country be determined?

4. Let's assume that the bicycle tour/inn business you purchased tripled in value over a five-year period, and, now you have decided to sell the property. What kinds of problems might you encounter selling a business in France? What tax liabilities would you face in France and the United States?

Sources: *Businesses for Sale*, http://www.businessesforsale.com (February 6, 2007); "Buying a Business in France," *Christie + Co.*, http://www.christie.com/christie/index.asp (February 3, 2007); and "Running *a Gite* Business in France," *FrenchEntrée.com*, http://www.frenchentree.com (February 6, 2007).

10.7 ENTERPRISERS

The Small Cheese

In a state known for cheese, Specialty Cheese Company is somewhat unique. Based in Lowell, Wisconsin, the company makes over 35 varieties of cheese that cater to diverse ethnic populations. From its four cheese plants, among the oldest and smallest in the United States, 110 employees, including ten Wisconsin-licensed cheese makers, produce both traditional and innovative award-winning products.

Owners Vicki and Paul Scharfman were newcomers to small business. Both have MBAs in marketing and many years' experience in big corporations and nonprofit organizations. Until he was laid off in January 1991, Paul had been the sales and marketing manager for the Louis Kampf Seafood subsidiary of Oscar Mayer, and before that he'd been a marketing manager for Oscar Mayer, Kraft, and General Foods. "An outplacement counselor gave me a battery of tests," he says. "None of them were terribly useful, but in total they helped me identify something that I could really believe in. I learned that I like to start things, to initiate, to innovate, to get going." He

© Polka Dot Images/Jupiter Images

and Vickie also liked living in the Madison, Wisconsin, area and wanted to find a better balance between work and family life. Putting those factors together with Paul's skills in food marketing, the Scharfmans began looking for a company to purchase.

The Heim Cheese Company, Wisconsin's oldest continuously running cheese factory, appeared to meet the Scharfmans' needs. Before buying it, however, the enterprising couple used their marketing backgrounds to extensively research the cheese industry. "I identified a company that fit my desires; they wanted to sell out, needed equity, needed marketing help," Paul recalls. "And I went to that firm and said, 'So what do you do well? What can I build on?' Well, I could say what they didn't do well—sales were dropping. The big question was, what do they do well?"

Heim already made very good cheese, including a Cuban cheese. That became the starting point for the Scharfmans' research. They analyzed census data and conducted extensive consumer research to identify underserved but high-growth niche markets, the largest of which was the Hispanic market.

Then they went directly to the potential customer and interviewed former residents of Mexico and South America. By asking what they liked and didn't like about the cheeses available in American grocery stores, the Scharfmans learned that Hispanic cheeses look, cook, and taste different from American or European cheeses. Hispanics found cooking with American cheese very frustrating because it melts when heated, whereas Hispanic cheese becomes soft and creamy but holds its shape.

Several months and many thousands of dollars later, they confirmed that there was an as yet untapped market for ethnic cheeses for Hispanic customers from several areas, including the Caribbean and Latin America. Paul recognized that the current producers weren't offering the variety that the market was asking for, and customer service was inadequate.

With these facts in hand, the Scharfmans bought Fred Heim's cheese company in 1991 and renamed it Specialty Cheese. Instead of going head to head with the large food companies like Kraft, they focused on natural cheeses for selected ethnic markets. "We make good cheese in small batches," says Paul. "But our most important ingredient is information."

They started the La Vaca Rica (The Rich Cow) line with what became their biggest seller: Queso Blanco.

"I bought a bunch of cheeses from Houston, Los Angeles, New York, and Miami, and brought them back to my cheese makers," explains Paul. "They were good enough to figure out how to make them." This fresh white cheese was an instant hit in major cities with large Hispanic populations.

Paul understood that he had inherited a valuable resource: talented employees. What the Scharfmans brought to the table was marketing flair, an understanding of how markets change, and how to tailor the products. "You guys make the cheese," Paul told the cheese makers. "My job is to represent the consumer, be it a housewife, an individual, a chef, a restaurant owner, and find out what the consumer needs."

As Paul explains, "The gist of it is simple: ask. People love talking. Ask them about something that they care about, and they will tell you more than you want to know. If you want to become a manufacturer of golf balls, start by asking people who play golf a lot about the product. It's free. You can do it." The Scharfmans conducted focus groups where people could see and taste the test products. From that they learned how to change their cheeses to improve marketability.

"The products that we inherited from the previous owner were on target, but they were maybe the wrong shape or the wrong color or the wrong name," says Vicki. They took slightly different versions of the products to the focus groups, until they began to get "Ahas."

From that base, the Scharfmans looked for other unique markets to which their master cheese makers could apply their skills. "We asked, 'Which cultures eat cheese,'" says Vicki. To find the answer, they hired someone to go through census data to learn the major languages people speak at home in this country. The result of that research was two additional product lines: The Rich Cow brand Middle Eastern cheeses and Bharatma brand Indian cheeses.

In a departure from its fresh cheese products, the company developed a new line called Just the Cheese™ Crunchy Baked Cheese™. The innovative, all-natural 100 percent cheese-baked cheese snacks have a potato chip-like crunch—"sort of a cheese and cracker combination all in one," Paul says. The first attempts to market Just the Cheese met with lackluster response. "It failed miserably," Scharfman says. "The world wasn't waiting for another gourmet snack."

However, the product's introduction in 1997 coincided with the growing popularity of low carbohydrate diets. A Wisconsin doctor told the Scharfmans that there was indeed a market for no-carbohydrate, high calcium Crunchy Baked Cheese—as a diet food. A tie-in with the Atkins Diet helped the product, which comes in white cheddar, garlic and herb, sour cream and onion, jalapeno, and nacho flavors. "On the Atkins Diet you can't have anything crunchy or salty—no chips, crackers, or pretzels. We have invented the salty snack category for people on this diet," Paul says. Customers from all over the world flocked to the Specialty Cheese website to order cases of the crunchy cheese chips, which now account for about 15 percent of the company's sales.

"We do niches," Paul says. "One set of niches is the ethnic market. By luck, we ended up in the diet niche with patented products." Although many of the company's market niches are small, the market research the Scharfmans performed helped them choose ones with potential that are strong and steady. Today's consumers are increasingly willing to express their desires about food products and have a strong interest in ethnic foods. They believe in "tribal marketing," a term Paul developed to describe marketing efforts geared toward different ethnic groups who have unmet product needs.

As Vicki explains, "There are many people who go out and say, 'I have God's gift to the product world. I have this fabulous invention. Everyone's going to love it. I'm going to make a mint. I'm gonna sell a gazillion of them.' They go out and they make this wonderful product, and it sits there and nothing happens. They can't understand why people aren't buying it. That is the backwards approach to marketing." Instead, she advises enterprisers to start with qualitative research to find out what your consumer wants and needs and what they are not getting from the current offerings in the marketplace. "Go out and tailor your dream to what they want," she says. "That's the fit that sells product."

Discussion Questions

1. What were the advantages to the Scharfmans of buying Heim Cheese rather than starting a new cheese company from scratch? The disadvantages? How well did the Heim Cheese Company fit with the Scharfman's personal goals? Suggest several reasons that Fred Heim might be selling his company.

2. What are the critical success factors for successfully running a cheese business? What skills and abilities and resources do the new owners bring to this business? What critical success factors don't they possess, and how will they insure that the business continues to have them?

3. What valuation technique would you recommend that the Scharfmans use to set a value for the Heim Cheese Company, and why?

4. You are helping the Scharfmans prepare a proposal for financing to buy Heim Cheese Company. Prepare an executive summary that describes the company's business model, marketing strategy, and other key points. What are some ways that they can structure a financial package to purchase the company? Suggest a number of ways they might be able to secure financing beyond their own resources.

Sources: Adapted with permission from "Meet the MBAs of Marketing Who Turned Around the Oldest Cheese Factory in Wisconsin," Small Business School, the series on PBS, and at http://SmallBusinessSchool.com; Carole Ashkinaze, "Spies Like Us," *Businessweek Online*, June 16, 2000, http://www.businessweek.com/-smallbiz/0006/ma3685105.htm; Kate Sander, "Specialty Cheese Co. Stands Ready to Expand Market for Its 'Diet' Cheese," *Cheese Market News*, February 11, 2000, http://www.cheesemarketnews.com; Specialty Cheese Company website, http://www.specialcheese.com (June 10, 2008); *The Specialty Cheese Market* (Lincoln, Nebraska: Food Processing Center, Institute of Agriculture and Natural Resources, University of Nebraska, Lincoln, October 2001), http://foodsci.unl.edu and Linda Spice, "Cheese, Hispanic Style," *Milwaukee Journal Sentinel*, June 27, 2004, http://www.jsonline.com.

Summary

1. Purchasing a business or a franchise (Type 4) is one of the eight pathways to business ownership—and a major way for enterprisers to go into business. Before making such a purchase, enterprisers must thoroughly analyze the business model, feasibility, and business plan.

2. Enterprisers choose to buy a going concern rather than start a business for several reasons. Buying a proven business concept lowers risk because the enterpriser has more knowledge of the firm's operations, market, and customer base. The speed with which they can get into business appeals to many enterprisers. An established business has a track record and may be easier to finance. It may cost less to purchase and operate a business than to start one from scratch, and the enterprise may already be producing a positive cash flow. The potential to improve an undervalued business is a factor for some enterprisers, who have a clear vision of changes they can make to increase profitability.

3. Drawbacks to buying a business include raising the financing, which can often be quite a large amount, and setting the right price. Sometimes sellers are overly optimistic when they describe their company and may also fail to disclose problems prior to the purchase. An enterpriser may discover that operating the new business requires more time or money than originally expected. Thorough analysis prior to entering into a purchase contract can avoid unpleasant surprises after the fact.

4. Other factors to consider before buying a business include the enterpriser's personal motivation and goals, the time the business will require to be managed, the owner's reasons for selling, and whether the enterprise will need to bring in partners.

5. Before buying a business, the enterpriser should know why the current owner is selling. The owner may be ready to retire or be in poor health. Some enterprisers prefer to start businesses and then move on to new ventures once they are up and running. Lack of managerial expertise is another factor that leads to business sales.

6. Enterprisers can find businesses for sale through classified ads in newspapers, magazines, and online or by using a business broker. Brokers will pre-qualify buyers and use this information to match potential buyers and sellers.

7. A business's value is ultimately what a buyer is willing to pay for it and should be based on the firm's ability to generate earnings. Valuing a business begins with considering the value of the opportunity, the enterprise's business model, the future feasibility of the enterprise, and the business plan. Many factors influence the valuation process, including the age and size of the business, quality of physical assets, market considerations, customer base and loyalty, and earning potential. Intangibles, such as the value of the business's reputation and similar factors that come with a going concern, also affect the business value.

8. Asset-based approaches to valuation begin with placing a value on the business's assets. This category has several variations, with some using replacement or market value rather than book (depreciated) value. These methods are relatively easy to calculate. However, they focus on assets

alone and assign no value to the business's ability to use these assets to generate revenues.

9. Market-based valuations are determined by what other people will pay for this business or similar businesses. Industry valuation and multiplier formula valuations are two categories of market-based valuation. Industry valuations begin with sales of comparable businesses. Multiplier formulas use sales, income, or other financial statistics, taking into account business characteristics and the prices paid for similar businesses. Because no two businesses are exactly alike, market-based methods must be applied with care.

10. The primary way to value a business is by exploring the past, current, and future earnings of the business and applying a multiplier of earnings. Multipliers are often based on sales prices of comparable businesses and vary across industry sectors. The riskiness of a business also affects the multiplier.

11. Although they are the most difficult to calculate, valuations based on cash flow can be the most accurate. The value takes into account the present value of future cash flows by applying a discount rate that includes the purchaser's cost of capital, desired return, and future inflation.

12. The purchase terms for a business are as important as the price and require considerable negotiation between buyer and seller. For example, the decision to buy the entire business (assets and liabilities, usually done as a stock sale) rather than buying just the assets has a different tax implication for each party. The buyer may not be able to pay for the business in cash up-front and may want an installment sale. Sellers often provide financing in the form of a note to be repaid over a defined time period. Earn-outs offer another way to pay for the business over time; the seller receives a stated percentage of future profits for a set time period.

13. The purchase agreement may also include a noncompete agreement that prevents the seller from operating a similar business in the same market area for a certain time period. A seller may also agree to take a portion of the sales price in the form of an employment contract, which becomes a tax-deductible expense to the new owner.

14. Before signing a purchase agreement, enterprisers should perform extensive due diligence. This process should include both an accountant and an attorney, who can audit financial records and review legal issues.

Review Questions

1. What are the advantages of buying an existing business compared to starting a new one?

2. What disadvantages might an enterpriser encounter when buying a business?

3. Summarize the key questions an enterpriser should ask when evaluating his or her personal motivation and goals for purchasing a business. What other factors come into play?

4. Why is the owner's reason for selling an important consideration? Describe some of the common reasons for selling a business.

5. How would you search for potential businesses to buy? Would you use business brokers, and why?

6. What factors go into the valuation of a business? Which is the most important, and why?

7. What are the calculations involved in asset-based valuation techniques, and what are their pros and cons?

8. Describe how market-based methods set business valuations and briefly describe the two main types of market-based valuation models.

9. Why are earnings valuations considered the best indicator of a business's worth? How do cash flow techniques incorporate earnings into their models?

10. How does the structure of a business purchase transaction affect the price and the terms? List several possible deal structures and their implications.

11. What sources of financing are available for business purchases? How does an earn-out affect the selling price of a business, and why?

12. Why might a purchase agreement include a noncompete agreement or an employment contract?

13. What other steps should a buyer take before finalizing a business purchase? What legal and accounting issues may arise?

Applying What You've Learned

1. The following *Inc.* article provides a number of insights into the criteria an entrepreneur should consider when purchasing an established business, as well as into the process involved in purchasing and operating it:

   Jay Finegan, "The Insider's Guide: 15 Steps to Owning the Company that's Right for You," *Inc.*, October 1991, http://www.inc.com/magazine/19911001/4874.html

   Now read the following articles, which describe Hendrix Niemann's efforts to buy a business.

   Hendrix F. C. Niemann, "Buying a Business," *Inc.*, February 1990, http://www.inc.com/magazine/19900201/5028.html

   Hendrix F. C. Niemann, "The Rest of the Story," *Inc.*, October 1991, http://www.inc.com/magazine/19911001/4875.html

   After reading Niemann's story, answer the following questions:

   (a) How many of the criteria in the "Insider's Guide" did Mr. Niemann follow in purchasing the business? What did Mr. Niemann do right? What did Mr. Niemann do wrong?

   (b) How well did Mr. Niemann operate the business? What did he do wrong?

   (c) What were the major mistakes that Mr. Niemann made during the search, purchase, and operation of this business? How many of these mistakes could he have avoided?

2. Now consider the Niemann business purchase transaction from the seller's point of view.

   (a) Did Mr. Klosky receive full value for the sale of his business?

   (b) Suggest actions that Mr. Klosky could have performed to achieve a higher price for the business.

   (c) What other alternatives did Mr. Klosky have for "harvesting" his business?

3. Look in the "Businesses for Sale" part of the Classified Ads section of your local newspaper. Note that there are likely to be more advertisements in the Sunday edition of the newspaper than on weekdays. What kinds of businesses are for sale? Who is offering those businesses (e.g., owners, business brokers, accountants, lawyers)? Make some inquires about these advertisements to find out more about these businesses. Why are they being sold? What kinds of prices are they asking, and how are they planning on structuring the deals for these businesses? Prepare a brief summary to share with your classmates.

4. Select a particular kind of business that you would be interested in either starting or buying. Interview business owners to find out whether they started these businesses or purchased them. How might these two types of business owners (start-ups versus purchasers) be different in terms of their backgrounds, skills, and abilities? Why did some of these enterprisers start businesses while others purchased? What advice do both of these groups offer you about being successful as enterprisers?

5. Market-based valuations of different types of businesses vary widely. For example, an accounting practice may sell for 100–125 percent of its annual revenues, but a travel agency may typically sell for 40–60 percent of annual sales. In the retail sector, a bookstore might sell for 15 percent of annual sales plus inventory, whereas a coffee shop price is based on 40–45 percent of annual sales plus inventory.[2] In your opinion, why are these multipliers different, and why would someone be willing to pay more for one kind of business versus another?

Enterprisers on the Web

1. Many sites offer searchable databases of businesses for sale. Explore the following sites and browse the listings.

   (a) International Business Brokers Association, http://www.ibba.org

   (b) Business Broker.net, http://www.businessbroker.net/

   (c) StartupJournal, http://bizbuysell.startupjournal.com

   Now prepare a table that compares the sites in the following areas: Number of listings, how listings are categorized, content of individual listings, ease of navigation, search capabilities, and any other areas you choose.

   Rank the sites based on your findings and explain the rationale for your choices. Why do you prefer your number one site?

2. Pick an industry or business category that appeals to you. Using search engines like Google, Yahoo!, AltaVista, or Lycos, find sites for its trade associations. Visit them to learn more about the industries and summarize your findings. Based on your research, explain why you would or would not continue to look for a business to buy in that industry.

3. Go to the site you liked best from question 1. Search for businesses in at least two different industries located in either your current area or one where you'd like to live. Choose three and compare them in terms of purchase price, reasons for sale, financial information, and other available information. What other information would you need before starting a serious investigation of these businesses?

4. Using any source of business for sale listings, pick one company that interests you. Read the article "What's Your Company Worth Now?" *Inc.,* August 2004, http://www.inc.com/magazine/20040801/valuations_index.html. Then refer to "The Ultimate Valuation Guide" (http://www.inc.com/valuation) and look at prices of comparable businesses. Determine whether the asking price is reasonable. What valuation method seems most appropriate for this company, and why?

5. Use either the International Business Brokers Association (http://www.ibba.org) or Business Broker.net (http://www.businessbroker.net) site to identify business brokers in your area. Select three and interview them to find out more about the kinds of owners who are willing to sell their businesses, as well as the kinds of buyers business brokers are looking for. Based on these interviews, what will you need to do in order for a business broker to want to sell a business to you?

End Notes

1. "The Most, and the Least, Valuable Businesses in America," *Inc.,* January 2007, pp. 102–103.

2. Based on information in *The 2001 Business Reference Guide,* Business Brokerage Press, cited on "Valuing Your Business," http://www.bizhelp24.com/small_business/selling_a_business_5.shtml.

Franchising

KEY CONCEPTS

1. Buying a franchise enables enterprisers to sell brand-name goods and services by entering into a contractual business relationship with a franchisor, the parent business. Franchisees can own one unit or obtain the rights to develop multiple units in a territory. The Federal Trade Commission regulates the offer and sale of franchises, and many states have their own franchise laws.

2. Choosing a franchise requires the same careful due diligence process as other prospective business ventures. Franchising's benefits include training, help and support, system synergies, financing assistance, and economies of scale. However, the franchisee must comply with the franchisor's operating restrictions and contractual obligations and pay the franchisor an initial fee as well as ongoing fees and royalties.

3. Entrepreneurs with an easily replicated business model, a strong brand or trademark, and a unique concept can use franchising to grow their businesses quickly. Other enterprisers become franchisees and provide talent and capital. While becoming a franchisor can be quite profitable, the franchisor loses some profits to the franchisees and also gives up a degree of operating control. Successful franchisors know what it takes to be a good franchisee, have systems in place to recruit and train franchisees, and work closely with system members.

Suppose you and your wife both work and have a new baby to care for. You can no longer go out to dinner whenever you choose. Wouldn't it be great if the restaurants came to you instead?

This was the idea behind Takeout Taxi, a food delivery service started in 1987 by Kevin Abt. He conducted market research to test his idea and learned that other than pizza, there weren't many choices for home delivery. As he refined his business concept, he found that restaurant owners as well as customers liked the idea. The business grew, so Abt decided to franchise his concept in other areas.

As you'll learn in this chapter's case, Takeout Taxi expanded to 15 states. However, it was unable to manage its growth and ran into major problems. The chapter provides information on both how to buy a franchise and how to use franchising to grow your business, to help you avoid the difficulties Abt encountered.

11.0 The Franchise Route to Business Ownership

As you go about your day, you might have breakfast at McDonald's, mail a package from the UPS Store, get your car's brakes repaired at Midas, order a pizza from Domino's, and get a haircut at Supercuts. Meanwhile, you arranged for California Closets to install cabinets in your garage and for Merry Maids to clean your house. At work you contacted Management Recruiters for help finding a sales manager. And a Century 21 realtor found you the house you bought last year. Did you know that in each case you were dealing with a franchised business?

Purchasing a franchise is another way for individuals to become enterprisers. Franchising is a type of business ownership where a parent business (the franchisor) provides an investor (the franchisee) with the rights to sell its products or services and use its trademark and operating procedures. In return, the franchisee pays up-front fees and/or ongoing royalty payments. The term **franchise** refers to the agreement or license between the franchisor and franchisee. A strong and growing franchise has to provide benefits for both franchisors and franchisees. We will see how a franchise system needs to be a win-win for both parties.

The franchising concept has a long history, tracing its origins to the guilds of the Middle Ages. Kings and lords gave certain individuals exclusive rights to engage in such activities as ironwork, stone cutting and masonry work, and barrel making. In the 1840s, German breweries began to offer franchises to tavern owners, giving them exclusive rights to sell their beer. In what would be considered the precursor of many of the activities involved with modern forms of franchising, in 1851 the Singer Sewing Machine Company developed written contracts and sold franchisees exclusive distribution rights to sell its sewing machines from local stores. These early franchise contracts became the model for today's Prospectus or United Offering Circular, which retains much of the same language and format. By the early 1900s, automobile manufacturers followed Singer's lead, and soon oil companies saw franchising as a good way to grow. The first franchised restaurant chain opened in 1924 and was, in fact, a drive-in: A&W Root Beer® drive-in restaurants.[1]

Much of the growth of franchising has occurred since the 1950s, when some of today's major franchisors opened for business. For example, Kentucky Fried Chicken began operations in 1952, followed by Burger King and McDonald's in 1955, Midas Muffler in 1956, and H&R Block in 1958.

Most early franchises centered on the fast food and hotel industries. During the 1960s and 1970s, the franchise concept experienced dynamic growth and expanded into a broader range of business categories. Today, an estimated 765,000 franchised businesses from more than 1,500 franchisors span 75 industries, from restaurants to technology consulting. Exhibit 11.1 shows the distribution of

---

Franchise   The rights to offer specific products or services under explicit guidelines at a certain location for a declared period of time.

---

exhibit
11.1

Franchises by Industry Category

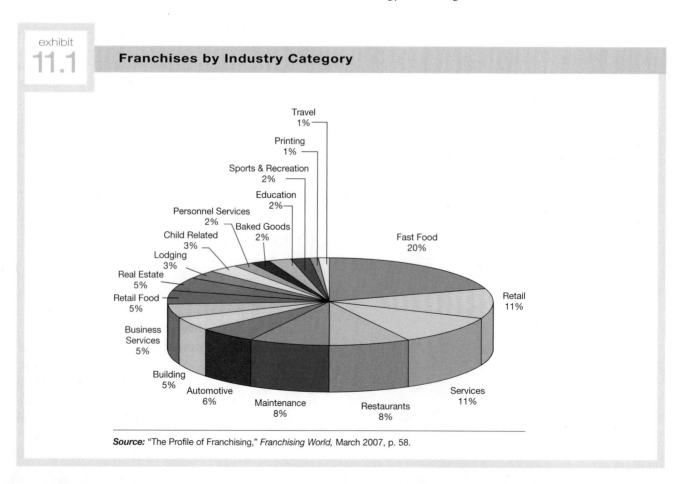

Source: "The Profile of Franchising," *Franchising World,* March 2007, p. 58.

franchises across 18 major industry sectors. Food-related industries—fast food, baked goods, retail food, and restaurants—account for 34 percent of all franchise systems and the highest number of new concepts.

In some industries, franchises are a significant proportion of the number of businesses that compete. For example, nearly 40 percent of all retail sales are made through franchised firms. About 1 of every 12 U.S. businesses is a franchise. In terms of the number of business establishments, franchise units represent over 56 percent of all fast food restaurants, 18 percent of all hotels and motels, 14 percent of retail food stores, and 13 percent of table/full service restaurants.[2]

Franchising has become a major contributor to the world economy. Exhibit 11.2 illustrates the direct impact of franchising on just the U.S. economy. With almost 10 million jobs, the franchising sector represents the second largest category of direct employment, just behind durable goods manufacturing. In addition, franchising indirectly affects these areas of the economy. For example, restaurant franchises require food and other supplies. According to a study commissioned by the International Franchise Association, the indirect and direct impact of franchising accounts for almost 14 percent of the nation's employment and $1.53 trillion in economic output.

Although the big national brands are the first names that come to mind when we think of franchising, most franchisors are in fact small- to medium-sized businesses with 200 units or less. Only about 7 percent of all franchise systems have more than 500 units, while 25 percent have 101 to 500 units, 15 percent have 51 to 100 units, 29 percent have 11 to 50 units, and 25 percent have 10 or fewer units.[3]

Franchising continues to grow as franchisors find new brands to offer and consumers want more specialized services—for example, adult day care, beauty and skin treatments, entertainment, health and home care, and spas. This form of business ownership is gaining popularity among aging baby boomers, who often choose to start new careers rather than retire. Franchisors report that franchisee applicants today present better qualifications than in the past, with more management experience and education.[4]

In this chapter, we will explore this route to business ownership, starting with the basics of franchising and the legal aspects of franchising. We will look at both sides of the franchising equation: becoming either a franchisee or franchisor. We will first discuss how individuals should select a franchise for purchase. Then we will explain how some enterprisers might take their established business and create a franchise system.

11.1 How Franchising Works

Franchising represents a business relationship between the franchisor and franchisee. All franchises share three basic elements: a brand, a business system, and fees. Within that relationship structure, however, franchises have several alternatives from which to choose: the type of franchise (business format or product and trademark) and the number of units the franchisee wishes to own.

Franchise Formats

Franchises fall into two major categories: *business format franchises* and *product and trademark* (also called *product distribution*) *franchises*. About 80 percent of all franchises and jobs fall into the business format category.

---

exhibit
11.2

Direct Contribution of Franchising to the U.S. Economy

Category	In Franchised Businesses	Percent of the Private Sector Economy
Jobs	9,797,117	7.4%
Payroll	$229.1 billion	5.0%
Output	$624.6 billion	3.9%

Source: Economic Impact of Franchised Businesses, a study conducted by PricewaterhouseCoopers for the IFA Educational Foundation, 2004.

In the **business format franchise**, the franchisee purchases a plan, or format, for running the business. In addition to the brand name, the franchisor provides the franchisee with training in how to manage and grow the business, guidelines for operating the business, local and national advertising, and other forms of assistance such as help in locating a site, guidance on building and outfitting the store, and financing. Business format franchisors make their money through fees and royalties. We'll cover the cost elements in greater detail later in the chapter, when we discuss how to evaluate a franchise.

Franchisors offer varying degrees of assistance. Not all franchisors offer financing, for instance. Some have very specific guidelines on how to conduct every aspect of the business. For example, a Subway restaurant will have specific guidelines on how to greet customers, bake the bread for the sandwiches, and place meats, cheeses, and other toppings on each sandwich. Many franchisors require their franchisees to link their cash registers to the franchisor's main computer, so that the franchisor can monitor sales and also help the franchisee order supplies. Other franchisors provide little guidance beyond the operations manual on specific aspects of managing the business.

While fast food restaurants rank first among business format franchises in number of people employed, the business services sector has the most units and generates the highest output of any franchise type.

Affiliation or conversion franchising is a special type of business format franchise. The owner of an operating business joins forces with a franchisor to benefit from the power of the brand and some elements of the operating format. In affiliation franchising, the franchisee may combine the local company's name with the franchisor's brand. This is particularly common in

© David Zalubowski/AP Photo

real estate brokerage franchises, which might use a name such as Coldwell Banker/Lynn Lawrence Realty, and in hotel chains—Best Western Any Town Inn.

Product and trademark (or product distribution) franchises provide franchisees with the right to buy, sell, and advertise the products under the manufacturer's trademarked name. These franchisees create a dealer network for the manufacturer. Unlike business format franchises, which have stringent operating requirements, product and trademark franchisees have considerable latitude in how they run their businesses. The franchisors earn their profits by selling products to the distributors. Because these franchises typically deal with big-ticket purchases, they generate about 30 percent of all franchise payroll and 26 percent of total franchise output.[5]

Automobile and truck dealerships are by far the largest industry group within product and trademark franchises, accounting for 70 percent of the category's output and more than 18 percent of total franchise output.[6] For example, the Ford Motor Company designs

---

Business format franchise   A type of franchise where the franchisee purchases a product and a complete system to operate the business.

Affiliation or conversion franchising   A business format franchise in which an operating business becomes part of a franchise system to take advantage of the brand but has more flexibility with regard to operating format. The unit name may reflect both the franchisor and the local entity.

Product and trademark (or product distribution) franchise   Franchise arrangement under which manufacturers grant franchisees, or dealers, the right to buy, sell, and advertise the products under the manufacturer's trademarked name.

and builds automobiles and sells them to franchised dealerships. These dealerships both sell and service automobiles under the Ford brand. The Ford Motor Company earns its revenues from the sales of automobiles and parts to its dealerships. Ford also advertises its automobiles so that people will buy its cars. The dealerships make money by selling automobiles and parts for a higher price than they paid to Ford and by providing repairs and services.

Other types of product distribution franchises include the sales and distribution of oil and gasoline (Chevron, Shell, ExxonMobil), tire centers (Firestone, Goodyear), soft drink bottlers (Coca-Cola, Pepsi), and heavy equipment manufacturers (John Deere, Caterpillar).

Franchise Purchase Options

Franchisors offer different purchase options to potential franchisees, ranging from the basic single-unit franchise to the multiple-unit area development and master franchise arrangements. The **unit franchise** is the simplest form: the franchisor grants the franchisee the right to open an individual franchise, often in a particular location. Many franchisors prefer to work with *multiple-unit franchisees* that own two or more units of the same franchise. Because those franchisees have more experience operating that particular franchise, the franchisor doesn't have to devote as much time and energy training new franchisees.

Multiple-unit ownership can take one of two forms:

- *Area development franchise:* The franchisor grants the franchisee, or area developer, the rights to open and operate a specific number of franchises within a particular geographic region. The two parties agree on a time schedule for the franchise development. Franchisees sign an area development agreement that defines the region and the timing for the new units and a unit franchise agreement when each individual franchise is developed. Failure to maintain the development timetable may result in termination of the area development agreement. The franchisee usually retains any established units.

- *Master franchise (subfranchising):* A master franchise goes one step further than area development franchising. In addition to granting rights over a particular territory, the franchisor also gives the master franchisee the right to either open franchise units or sell franchises to other unit franchisees, called **subfranchisors,** in that particular

territory. This three-party form of franchising is often used by American franchisors who wish to expand internationally. For example, Jim Bryant holds the master franchise for Subway in China. His agreement with the company allows him to open his own stores, sell to local subfranchisees, and serve as liaison between his subfranchisees and the parent company. In return, he is entitled to 50 percent of the initial fee and one-third of the royalty fees.[7]

Multiple franchise ownership may vary from these traditional forms. Rather than specify a geographic territory, a franchisor may grant the right to sell to a particular customer category—for example, doctors, elementary schools, or an industry sector.

11.2 Legal Aspects of Franchising

Despite the popularity of franchising, the industry is not as heavily regulated as you might expect. Congress passed the first laws in the 1950s to regulate auto and petroleum franchise sales, but other types of franchises remained essentially unregulated. As complaints against fraudulent sales practices rose, California became the first state with a Franchise Investment Law covering disclosure by franchisors to potential investors.

The Federal Trade Commission (FTC) regulates the offer and sale of franchises at the federal level. Laws covering franchise operations vary, however, from state to state. Because franchises commonly fall within the legal definition of a "business opportunity," they are subject to business opportunity laws in about 25 states. Some states have general franchise investment or relationship

Unit franchise   Agreement to open one unit in a particular location.

Area development franchise   Rights to open and operate a specific number of franchises within a particular geographic region.

Master franchise (subfranchising)   A three-party arrangement that grants a master franchisee rights to open franchises in a particular territory, along with the right to sell franchises to other unit franchisees.

Subfranchisor   A franchisee who contracts with a master franchisee to open a franchise within the same territory.

statutes and others may have industry-specific regulations. Franchise relationships also are regulated by antitrust laws and by general business regulations such as contract law.

Is current franchise regulation adequate? Well-known franchise attorney Lewis Rudnick believes it is. "The disclosure laws have gotten rid of fly-by-night, poorly conceived business models," he says. Franchisee advocates such as the American Franchising Association (AFA) disagree, however. According to AFA president Susan Kezios, current laws do not address key issues such as encroachment (opening another franchised- or company-owned store in close proximity of an existing franchise); product sourcing (requiring franchisees to buy products only from approved suppliers regardless of price); and restrictions on selling a franchise to another franchisee. Since 1995, Congress has attempted without success to amend franchise regulations (Rule 436).

Federal Regulation of Franchise Sales

Since 1979, the Federal Trade Commission (FTC) has been responsible for regulating the purchase and sale of franchises under FTC Rule 436, Disclosure Requirements and Prohibitions Concerning Franchising, which mandates minimum pre-sale disclosure requirements. In 2007, the FTC adopted an Amended FTC Franchise Rule designed to streamline the Rule, minimize compliance costs, and reduce inconsistencies between federal and state franchise disclosure laws. The amended Rule updates the original to reflect changes in the marketing of franchises and new technologies, such as the Internet, and addresses franchisee complaints about problems with franchisors. It also amends Rule 436 to cover only the sale of franchises located in the United States and its territories.[8] The North American Securities Administrators Association (NASAA) adopted these disclosure requirements, with some additional requirements, to replace the 1994 Uniform Franchise Offering Circular Guidelines.

The basic provisions of the Rule include the following:

A. *Basic Requirement:* Franchisors must provide potential franchisees with written disclosures of important information about the franchisor, the franchised business, and the franchise relationship, and give them at least 14 calendar days to review it before investing.

Rule 436 Federal Trade Commission regulation that governs disclosure requirements for the offer and sale of franchises in all 50 states.

B. *Disclosure Document:* The Franchise Disclosure Document must be prepared in the format required under the Amended FTC Franchise Rule and in accordance with NASAA requirements. Electronic forms of disclosure documents are permissible.

C. *Coverage:* Rule 436 covers both business format and product and trademark franchises.

D. *No Filing:* Rule 436 does not require the franchisor to register, file, or have reviewed or approved by the FTC any disclosure documents, advertising, or agreements. (State disclosure laws may differ in this regard.)

E. *Remedies:* Rule 436 has the full force and effect of federal law and may only be enforced by the FTC, which may seek injunctions, civil penalties, and consumer redress for violations.

F. *Purpose:* Rule 436 ensures that potential franchisees receive adequate information to evaluate the risks and benefits of a particular franchise prior to investing.[9]

In addition, Rule 436 imposes six requirements related to any "advertising, offering, licensing, contracting, sale, or other promotion" of a franchise that affects commerce:

1. *Basic Disclosures:* Franchisors must give potential investors a basic disclosure document at least 14 calendar days before any money is paid or an agreement is signed in connection with the investment. The franchisor may provide the disclosure document on paper, via email, through a Web page, or on a disc. The cover of the disclosure document should have information about its availability in other formats.

2. *Earnings Claims:* Any historical or forecasted earnings claims a franchisor makes must be based on reasonable assumptions, which must be disclosed along with other required documents.

3. *Advertised Claims:* Ads including an earnings claim must disclose the number and percentage of existing franchisees that have achieved the claimed results, along with cautionary language. These ads are subject to the earnings claims disclosure rules.

4. *Franchise Agreements:* The franchisor must give franchisees a review copy of all standard franchise agreements along with the basic disclosures and execution copies no less than seven calendar days before signing.

5. *Refunds:* Franchisors must make refunds of deposits and initial payments to potential investors in accordance with refund terms stated in the disclosure document.

6. *Contradictory Claims:* No written or oral claims the franchisor makes may contradict information provided in the required disclosure document.[10]

The amended Rule maintains the benefits of the original Rule. However, as of July 1, 2008, all franchisors must comply with the Amended FTC Franchise Rule's disclosure format, the **Uniform Franchise Disclosure Document (UFDD)**. The UFDD replaces the Uniform Franchise Offering Circular (UFOC), which had been used since 1994.

While similar to the original UFOC Guidelines, the UFDD requires more extensive disclosures in some areas, particularly the franchisee-franchisor relationship, and less in others. States may impose additional requirements under state law consistent with the Amended FTC Franchise Rule.[11] Under the amended rule, franchisees will have better information on franchisor litigation against franchisees, protected territories and competition through alternative distribution channels, confidentiality clauses, franchisors' interests in suppliers, renewal terms, and other issues.[12]

All franchisors must provide prospective franchisees with a written UFDD that covers 23 items a franchisor must disclose to a franchisee. Exhibit 11.3 provides a

Uniform Franchise Disclosure Document (UFDD)   Document prepared by franchisor for prospective franchisees that includes 23 sections that disclose background information.

---

exhibit
11.3

Summary of the Uniform Franchise Disclosure Document (UFDD)

Section	Description
Cover Page	Must clearly state FRANCHISE DISCLOSURE DOCUMENT and include: franchisor's name, type of business organization, principal business address and telephone number, a sample of the primary business trademark that the franchisee will use in its business, a brief description of the franchised business, total amounts of Franchisee's Initial Franchisee Fee or Other Payment and Franchisee's Initial Investment, specified disclaimer statements, and the issuance date.
1. The Franchisor, Its Predecessors and Affiliates	Information about the franchisor and its affiliates, addresses, and their prior business experience.
2. Business Experience	A description of the business experience of the franchisor's officers, directors, and management personnel responsible for the franchise system.
3. Litigation	Information on prior or pending lawsuits involving the franchisor, its officers, directors, and management personnel. (Note: Nearly all franchises of a certain age or above a certain size will have had lawsuits with its franchisees.)
4. Bankruptcy	History of any bankruptcies involving the franchisor, its officers, directors, and management personnel.
5. Initial Fees	Information on the initial fees due the franchisor that are required to obtain the franchise and conditions under which these fees are refundable.
6. Other Fees	Other fees involved with the purchase of the franchise besides the initial franchise fee, listed in a specified table format (type of fee, amount, due date, remarks) and including any formulas. (These fees can be very substantial!)
7. Estimated Initial Investment	An indication of the total funds necessary to invest in this franchise, in specified table format, including type of expenditure, amount, payment method, and when and to whom payment is due. Includes initial franchise fee, training expense, real property, equipment and fixtures, inventory, security deposits, etc.
8. Restrictions on Sources of Products and Services	Information on the franchisor's requirements for purchases of goods or services. Many franchisors will require that franchisees purchase all goods and services from the franchisor or a designated supplier.

(continued)

Exhibit 11.3 (*continued*)

9. Franchisee's Obligations	Information on what the franchisee will be required to do, disclosed in specified tabular form, with cross references to the franchise agreement and other documents.
10. Financing	A description of any direct or indirect financing arrangements the franchisor might offer the franchisee.
11. Franchisor's Assistance, Advertising, Computer Systems, and Training	Information on assistance the franchisor may offer the franchisee, such as help in starting up, training, hiring, marketing, and advertising.
12. Territory	Information on the geographic area (if any) to which a franchisee might have exclusive rights.
13. Trademarks	A description of the franchisor's trademarks and under what conditions the franchisee may use these trademarks.
14. Patents, Copyrights, and Proprietary Information	A description of the franchisor's patents, copyrights, and proprietary information and the conditions under which the franchisee may use them.
15. Obligation to Participate in the Actual Operation of the Franchise Business	Most franchisors will require that franchisees be actively involved in the operations of their franchise units. Most franchisors will want investor/operators, rather than investors as the owners of their franchise units.
16. Restrictions on What the Franchisee May Sell	The agreement specifies what goods and services the franchisee may offer for sale.
17. Renewal, Termination, Transfer, and Dispute Resolution	Critical information on how a franchisee license can be renewed (most franchise agreements have a limited life, such as 20 years); the criteria for terminating a franchise agreement; the conditions for transferring a franchise agreement to either the franchisor or another party; the process for resolving disagreements between the franchisor and franchisee. Must be disclosed in a specified table format (provision, section in documentation, summary).
18. Public Figures	Information on whether any public figures are involved in the franchise, either through advertising or other activities.
19. Earnings Claims	Information about the financial performance of franchise units. This information may include data indicating the percentage of franchises that have achieved these projected earnings.
20. Outlets and Franchisee Information	A comprehensive listing summarizing franchise system statistics for the last three fiscal years, provided in several tables. Information includes Systemwide Outlet Summary company-owned units, franchised units, state-by-state transfers from franchisees to new owners, status of franchised and company-owned outlets and changes, estimates of number of units to be sold in the next year by state, names and addresses of all current franchisees, names and addresses of franchises who have dropped out of the franchise system in the past years, disclosure of confidentiality clauses, and more.
21. Financial Statements	A minimum of two fiscal years of the franchisor's audited financial statements.
22. Contracts	Copies of all the contracts the franchisee will sign to purchase the franchise.
23. Receipt	A form the franchisee will sign and return to the franchisor indicating the UFDD has been received.
Exhibits	A. Franchise Agreement B. Equipment Lease C. Lease for Premises D. Loan Agreement

Source: *North American Securities Administrators Association, Inc. 2008 Franchise Registration and Disclosure Guidelines,* North American Securities Administrators Association, http://www.nasaa.org (June 14, 2008).

brief description of what the UFDD covers. The standardization of the UFDD format allows investors to compare offerings from different franchise companies.

The FTC requires that franchisors comply with the UFDD regulations and grants franchisees certain legal rights if the franchisor fails to comply. The FTC does not review the contents or accuracy of UFDDs. Therefore, potential franchisees must perform their own careful due diligence of the UFDD information. We will discuss how to approach this process later in the chapter.

The FTC's website page on franchises and business opportunities (http://www.ftc.gov/bcp/menus/consumer/invest/business.shtm) has links to valuable information for both franchisees and franchisors.

State Regulation

Many states have their own franchise rules and regulations requiring a higher level of franchisor disclosure. The degree of state regulation of franchises varies. Certain states require that franchisors file and register pre-sale offering circulars, while others require appropriate disclosure documents but no filing with a state agency. The most restrictive states apply the same rules to franchises as to security sales. Exhibit 11.4 lists the states in each category.

As you can see, the amount of control and regulation provided in certain states varies. Michigan, for example, requires only that franchisors tell the state that they are selling franchises in the state, while a state such as California requires franchisors to file a disclosure

similar to the FTC UFDD with the state before selling franchises.

States with franchise regulations protect franchisees through state courts, which may be a less expensive and faster resolution process. Many states have courts that can hear and judge such cases faster than the federal court system.

11.3 Why Buy a Franchise?

Franchising provides a middle ground between starting your own business and purchasing an existing one. Will franchising be right for you? "A true entrepreneur has an idea and takes a risk," says Steve Hockett, president of FranChoice, Inc., a consulting firm that works with potential franchisees. "But not all of us wake up in the morning with a great idea and know how to make it into a business. Franchisers know they need people who have motivation and a dream. [Franchisees] have time, talent, skills, energy, and desire. But they don't want to spend years building an idea."[13]

In many respects, the decision criteria for choosing the franchising path to entrepreneurship are similar to those you would consider when either buying or starting an independent business. You would first reflect on your personal and financial goals, how much money you have to invest, your abilities, and your interests. Then you would investigate the operating characteristics, size, growth, profitability, and complexity of the businesses you are considering. In addition, you must add to these

---

exhibit 11.4

State Regulation of Franchises

Regulation	States
Must file disclosure statement with a state agency	California, Hawaii, Illinois, Indiana, Maryland, Minnesota, New York, North Dakota, Rhode Island, South Dakota, Virginia, Washington, Wisconsin
No filing	Oregon
Notice only	Michigan
Business Opportunity Law applies	Connecticut, Florida, Nebraska, Texas, Utah

Source: "State Offices Administering Franchise Disclosure Laws," Federal Trade Commission, http://www.ftc.gov/bcp/franchise/netdiscl.htm (February 15, 2007).

a thorough investigation of the franchisor. Let's review some of the key questions you should ask yourself as you begin to research the franchise option.

- *What are your personal goals?* How important is leisure time, involvement with family, personal growth, financial success, involvement with friends, and social contribution? What do you envision in each of these areas over the next 2, 5, 10, and 25 years?

- *What are your family goals?* What do you envision in each of these goals over the next 2, 5, 10, and 25 years?

- *What are your business goals?* What field do you want to pursue? Which would you rather sell: goods or services? What kind of work do you enjoy most? Would you rather work with people or things? How much annual income do you need? Will you rely solely on the franchise for your income or have other sources? Can you see your-self running this business for 10, 15, or 20 years? Do you want to become an area developer or stick with a single unit?

- *What abilities do you bring to this business venture?* Do you have the education or business experience the franchise requires? How well does the industry fit your prior skills and knowledge? What other skills do you need to successfully run the business, and do you have them (computer literacy, accounting, human relations, management)? Strong interpersonal skills will contribute to your success as a franchisee, helping you to work effectively with your employees and create loyal customers. Can you develop the skills you lack?

- *How much money can you invest in a business?* What percentage of your assets are you willing to put at risk? Will you need or want partners?

- *How much involvement do you want in oper-ating the business?* Do you want to operate the business yourself or hire a manager? This is a particularly important issue when considering a franchise. Some franchisors require that franchisee owners themselves work full time in the franchises they purchase. Other companies are looking for enterprisers who can own and manage a number of franchise locations.

- *Can you take direction from the franchisor?* A fran-chise involves a very specific way of doing busi-ness. Many franchises have operating manuals that provide detailed directions about how the franchise will operate (e.g., how food will be prepared, what items will be on the menu, how customers will be greeted, how the store location will look, the kinds of fixtures that each location will have). Do you like having a proven method of operating your business, and are you willing to learn best practices from others? Then you have the potential to be a successful franchisee. On the other hand, if you prefer to "do your own thing" and can't imagine owning a business that looks and operates exactly like many other franchise locations, then purchasing a franchise is probably not the best form of enterprise for you.

- *Can you be a member rather than the leader?* A franchisee belongs to a system along with many other franchisees. As such, you will likely be required to contribute to marketing efforts that support the franchise system overall, not just your specific unit. Consider the advertising campaign for Subway. TV advertisements are paid for by fees collected from all franchisees, and decisions about when ads will run and the look of these advertisements, as well as the kinds of "deals" that are offered (i.e., sandwich, chips, and a drink combos for a certain price) are determined by the franchisor. You will have to go along with decisions made by all of the franchisees and the franchisor.

Benefits of Franchising

As with any form of business enterprise, franchising offers several distinct advantages for the enterpriser.

- *Proven business model.* A franchise offers a product/service (benefits), and a way of providing those benefits (channel) to a specific market (customers). An enterpriser can evaluate the performance of existing franchisees to learn how well the system's business concept works.

- *Brand name and recognition.* An important value in belonging to a franchise system is the aware-ness that comes with an organization that engages in joint advertising and marketing. Wherever their franchise is located, such brands as McDonald's, Subway, Kentucky Fried Chicken, and H&R Block have instant recognition for the value of their prod-ucts and services.

- *Training and support.* A franchisor provides training and operational, marketing, financial, and manage-rial expertise to help franchisees successfully start and operate their franchise units. A franchisee does not have to invent the entire start-up process alone. Some franchisors, for example, provide help in selecting a location for the franchise, as well as require that prospective franchisees work at other franchise locations to learn how to effectively manage the business, deal with employees, and sell to customers.

- *Financing.* Some franchisors provide help in purchasing one of their franchises. Often financial institutions and investors become familiar with certain franchise systems and are willing to loan money or make equity investments to assist franchisees.

- *System synergies.* Membership in a franchise system creates a supportive network where franchisees can learn from each other. You are in business for yourself, but not by yourself. Most franchise systems have ways for franchisees to meet and share their experiences as well as offer ways for each franchise to compete more efficiently and effectively. Many product and service innovations are first initiated by an individual franchisee, who then shares this with other franchisees in the franchise system. A good example of this is the Egg McMuffin, created by a franchisee who wanted to serve breakfast items.

- *Economies of scale.* As one of many other franchisees in a franchise system, franchisees benefit from the system's ability to make volume purchases of supplies, standardize specific kinds of equipment and building materials, purchase medical and dental insurance, and offer other system discounts. Operating costs will therefore be lower than if an enterprise were to operate the same business as an independent startup.

The Downside to Franchising

Although these benefits contribute to franchising success, franchising has its negative aspects.

- *Operating restrictions.* A franchise is a particular way of doing business. When you purchase a franchise, you are agreeing to operate the business according to the franchisor's guidelines. While this can be an advantage, it can also be a disadvantage if competitive and market conditions change and the franchise system's way of doing business does not meet the current needs of your customers.

- *Costs.* Purchasing a franchise can be quite expensive. In addition to the initial purchase price, the investment in facilities and equipment may add up to a significant financial outlay. The franchisee also pays ongoing fees and royalties to the franchisor and may have to contribute to national advertising. These mandatory expenses reduce the enterpriser's profits—and must be paid whether or not the individual franchise unit is profitable. With an independent business, the owner has greater control over the expense outlay and retains all the profits.

- *Interdependence.* Being a member of the franchise system is not without risks. The actions of the other franchisees will have a significant impact on each member's success. If a number of franchisees provide poor service and products, it will reflect on other members of the franchise system. Suppose a franchisee in California prepares food items incorrectly and many customers become sick. This mistake will affect the sales of all franchisees across the country. In addition, some franchisors have failed, leaving the franchisees in the difficult position of being in a franchise without the support and help they promised.

- *Contractual obligations.* Most franchise agreements are likely to restrict a franchisee's ability to terminate the franchise agreement or sell the franchise to others without the approval of the franchisor. Many franchisors require that franchisees agree to a "noncompete" clause that prevents a franchisee from starting or purchasing a similar business (or franchise). Also, many franchise agreements have a limited life. The franchise rights might be only 20 years long, after which the franchisor may have rights to repurchase the franchise for a specified amount.

- *Business risks.* As with any business, franchises carry risks. A proven business concept does not guarantee success. Recent research shows that franchising may not lead to higher success and growth rates than individual businesses. According to Scott Shane, who conducted a study of franchise systems that started offering franchises for sales in 1983, new franchise systems fail at roughly the same rate as all new businesses. After 10 years, less than 25 percent of the initial group of franchisors he studied was still franchising. "If you buy a new franchise from a new franchisor, there is a 75 percent chance the person who sold it to you won't be around to support you in 10 years," Shane explains. "So, it's very important that people thinking of buying a franchise outlet differentiate from long-standing franchisors and those that just started this year or last year."[14]

Particularly with new franchises, the franchisor may misrepresent the franchise's potential or be overly optimistic in the financial projections.

- *Missed expectations.* Many promises are made between the franchisor and the franchisee (both verbally and in writing) that the franchisor may not meet, such as expected levels of support and help, advertising, and system growth. For example, the franchisor may tell a franchisee that the system will grow by 1,000 units in the next three years, and these expectations might not be fulfilled. If the franchisee was hoping that the growth in extra units would generate synergies in purchasing, advertising, and branding, the franchisee may be very disappointed (and, may also seek damages through a lawsuit).

Situations like these can lead to franchisee discontent and lawsuits against the franchisor. This was the case with Quiznos, a fast food franchisor whose problems are described in the Enterprising Ethics box.

As a franchisee, you are an independent business owner but must pay franchise fees and operate within the franchisor's system. "You have to have the entrepreneurial spirit to quit your job, and you get a check only after you make money," notes Sam Chamberlain, vice president of sales with franchise consultant Fransmart LLC. "However, franchising is about being in a system, and once you are in a system, you cannot change it."[15] Enterprisers who like to do things their own way may find the franchise path restricts their creativity and choose to pursue an independent business venture instead.

ENTERPRISING
ETHICS

Quiznos' Franchisees Lose their Appetites

Starting with recipes developed in the kitchen of an Italian restaurant, Denver-based Quiznos Subs opened its first sandwich shop in 1981. Two years later it began franchising new locations to expand the chain. By 1994, Quiznos Toasted Subs was named a "Hot Concept" by *Nation's Restaurant News.* The chain grew quickly, working its way up in *Entrepreneur*'s Franchise 500 rankings, reaching the top ten in 2001 and the number two spot in 2006. Quiznos was also one of the top ten fastest growing franchises for many years and the number two global franchise in 2006. Today the chain has almost 5,000 restaurants, including 500 international locations in 21 countries.

However, the rosy scene these numbers paint does not portray the whole picture. The franchisor is the defendant in numerous lawsuits from franchisees who claim that Quiznos made many promises that it didn't meet.

A New Jersey case claims that the growth statistics are a sham. Although Quiznos sold about 350 licenses from 2003 to 2005 and collected $7 million in fees, none of the franchisees ever opened a restaurant. "They duped these people into thinking they were getting site assistance, but after they plunked down their $25,000, Quiznos would disappear," said Justin M. Klein, lawyer for the New Jersey plaintiffs.

High operating costs are at the center of other lawsuits. The licensing agreement requires franchisees to

© Ed Andrieski/AP Photo

buy supplies and services only from Quiznos-designated suppliers, at inflated prices. These vendors, some of whom are owned by the parent, then pay "rebates" to the corporation. Franchisees were squeezed because they were unable to set retail prices high enough to make up for the inflated supply prices. "My food cost has gone up 10 percent in a year," says Melody Cox, who operated a Quiznos in Evansville, Indiana. She and her husband owned two units which closed in January 2007.

Encroachment, or opening units in close proximity, is another major complaint. Quiznos' franchise agreement does not offer franchisees exclusive rights to a specific territory or restrict the company from opening franchises within the proximity of existing locations.

Former CEO Rick Schaden defended Quiznos' actions. "We're a convenience item and we're putting restaurants where consumers can grab a quick lunch," he explained. "In the country, that may be four miles apart, but in the city, it may be every five blocks."

Franchisee Glenn Keane, who owns a Quiznos shop in Derby, Connecticut, is one of the dissatisfied franchisees. "When Quiznos allowed a second franchisee to open here last summer, my sales dropped from $15,000 a week to $8,000," he says. "Instead of taking money out of the franchise, I'm now putting my own money in, just to keep going."

In California, Bhupinder and Ratt Baber formed a franchisee organization to advocate for franchisee rights and filed a breach of contract suit against Quiznos in 2004 because the franchisor opened new units within two miles of their restaurants. Quiznos attempted to close the Babers' locations while the case was pending, but a California judge found for the Babers. "There is an implied covenant of good faith and fair dealing that says you don't dump competition on top of your existing franchisees," said Fred Pardes, attorney for the Babers. The problems between the Babers and Quiznos did not end there, however. Sales at the Babers' locations declined 30 percent as new Quiznos stores cannibalized revenues. The Babers refinanced their house to make ends meet. In January 2007, Baber was so distraught over his precarious financial situation that he committed suicide.

Discussion Questions

1. The Quiznos franchise agreement does not include any prohibitions against encroachment, so the franchisor believes it has the right to open new locations where it chooses. Don Boroian, a franchise consultant with Francorp, disagrees, saying that franchisors have an obligation to prevent locations from encroaching on each other's territory. With whom do you agree, and why?

2. Why do most franchise systems require that franchisees buy supplies and services only from approved sources? Where did Quiznos cross the line with its vendor situation? Suggest ways a franchisor can keep franchisees happy with regard to supplier sources.

3. Review the International Franchise Association's Code of Ethics at the IFA site, http://www.franchise.org. Based on information in the box and from your own research, discuss Quiznos' compliance with the code.

4. Quiznos is not the only franchisor facing lawsuits from its franchisees. Using search tools find examples of other cases. What can franchisees do to protect themselves from ethical breaches?

Sources: Based on Julie Bennett, "Pitfalls People May Face When Buying a Franchise," *StartupJournal.com*, March 6, 2006; Amanda Bronstad, "Quiznos Finds Fast Growth Has Its Costs as It Battles Franchisees in Court," *Los Angeles Business Journal*, September 19, 2005, p. 5; Julie Creswell, "Some Quiznos Franchisees Take Chain to Court," *New York Times*, February 24, 2007, p. C1; Bill Medley, "Loss of Quiznos Store Irks Owner," *Evansville Courier & Press* (Indiana), January 27, 2007, p. B6; Carol Tice, "Find Your Franchise Match," *Entrepreneur*, January 2007, http://www.entrepreneur.com; and Toasted Subs Franchise Association, http://www.toastedsubs.info/ (February 23, 2007).

This was the case for Betsy Ludlow, a former Fortune 500 marketing executive, who loved working out at Curves, one of the fastest growing fitness franchises. When corporate life became too stressful, she decided to investigate owning a Curves franchise. As she evaluated the system's disclosure statement and other materials, she thought carefully about how she would like to run her own Curves facility. "I didn't like feeling boxed in with someone else's concept," she said. Instead she chose to open an independent exercise studio. Working with exercise experts to develop her own format, she opened the first Slim and Tone in 2002, advertising it as "A Better 30 Minute Workout." Her concept caught on, and she soon had a chain of four exercise clubs.[16]

11.4 Selecting the Right Franchise

With more than 1,200 franchise concepts covering 75 industries, enterprisers who have decided to go the franchising route have a wealth of options from which to choose. You may want to consider a franchise that you visit frequently and already know and like. Exploring the listings for franchise opportunities in newspapers, magazines such as *Entrepreneur* and *Inc.*, and on the Web is a good way for an enterpriser to narrow the field. Most websites have search features to help you find franchises in a particular industry or price range. Business brokers are another source of franchise offerings.

Take time to research a variety of franchises. You will discover different conceptual approaches and operating methods, even within the same industry. Educating yourself before you buy will help you choose a franchise that meets your personal and business goals. Most Web-based franchise directories provide company background, costs and fees, financing options, training and support, and contact information, along with educational articles and other resources. Be aware that featured franchisors often pay for sponsored listings. Some of the more popular sites include:

- *Entrepreneur*'s FranchiseZone (http://www. entrepreneur.com/franchise/): Publishes the Franchise 500 and special lists for top home-based, low cost, new, fastest growing, and global franchises. You can browse by category, and it has links to *FranchiseZone* magazine and how-to articles.

- *StartupJournal.com* (http://www.startupjournal. com/franchising/): Part of *The Wall Street Journal* center for entrepreneurs, it has articles profiling franchisors, franchise-for-sale listings, and general articles about franchising.

- International Franchise Association (IFA) (http:// www.franchise.org): Search for more than 1,000 different franchises by industry and subcategories, with information on company background and costs; extensive franchising resources.

- *FranchiseHandbook.com* (http://www. franchisehandbook.com): Publishes the *Franchise Handbook* and offers a searchable Web directory.

- *Franchise.com* (http://www.franchise.com): Includes *Franchise Matchmaker* search feature and several directories.

- *FranchiseWorks.com* (http://www.franchiseworks. com): Lists franchises by category; offers help from franchise consultants.

Attending a franchise trade show or exposition is another excellent way to learn about many different franchising opportunities. For example, each year the IFA cosponsors the International Franchise Expo, a three-day event held in Washington, D.C. The IFA also sponsors regional franchise shows. To make the most of these events, have a general idea of how much you can invest and the industry categories that interest you. You can then focus your efforts on specific franchisors and compare what they offer.

Franchise Costs

As with any business start-up or purchase, an enterpriser who buys a franchise wants to develop a profitable business. The total cost to buy a franchise unit depends on many factors such as the industry, products sold, type of physical facilities, and location, and can be less than $20,000 to more than $1 million for lodging franchises. The enterpriser must weigh the extra costs against the benefits gained by becoming a franchisee. Exhibit 11.5 shows the costs involved in starting a franchise in a representative sample of franchise systems. In addition to the initial capital investment, franchisees must also consider the ongoing cost obligations, such as fees and royalties, when calculating the overall return from this investment. Even within the same industry, the total investment and special conditions may vary considerably, as comparisons between Subway and Quiznos and Curves and Jazzercise demonstrate.

Let's take a closer look at seven different cost categories for business format franchises:

1. *Initial franchise fee:* May be nonrefundable and range from a few thousand to several hundred thousand dollars. Most franchise fees—70 percent of systems—are less than $40,000.

2. *Capital costs:* May include costs for real estate, construction or rental of facilities, equipment, and inventory.

3. *Other start-up costs:* Business permits and operating licenses; insurance; some franchisors charge a special promotional fee for a "grand opening."

4. *Royalty payments:* Most franchisors collect royalties for the ongoing use of the brand name and trademark for the period covered by the franchise contract. These are based on a percentage of the unit's weekly or monthly gross income. Royalty payments are due regardless of the level of net income (income after expenses). In other words, the franchisee could be operating at a loss and still owe royalties. Royalties typically range from 5 to 8 percent of gross sales.

5. *Advertising fees:* Many franchise systems require franchisees to pay 3 percent of gross sales for local advertising, as well as a minimum of 1 percent for publications, promotional materials, and national and regional advertising.

6. *Other fees:* May include continuing education and training.

7. *Purchase of supplies:* Franchisees may be required to purchase supplies from the franchisor.

exhibit
11.5

Costs to Buy a Franchise

Franchisor	Industry	Total investment	Initial franchise fee	Royalty payments	Term in years	Comments
Subway	Submarine sandwiches & salads	$76,000–$228,000	$15,000	8%	20	Net worth requirement $30,000–$90,000; 65% of franchisees own multiple units; no absentee ownership
Curves	Women's fitness and weight loss	$31.4K–53.5K	$24.9K–44.9K	5%–6%	5	$75,000 net worth requirement; half of all franchisees own multiple units; absentee ownership allowed; no financial assistance offered
Quizno's	Submarine sandwiches, soups, salads	$29.1K–323.9K	$10K–25K	7%	15	Express/kiosk option available; few franchisees own multiple units; net worth requirement: $125K; absentee ownership allowed
Jani-King	Commercial cleaning services	$11.3K–34.1K	$8.6K–16.3K+	10%	20	No absentee ownership; can be run from home
Jazzercise	Exercise	$3K–33.1K	$500/$1K	To 20%	5	No absentee ownership, can be run from home
Liberty Tax Service	Tax preparation	$33.8K–63.9K	$17K–34K	Varies	Perpetual	50% of all franchisees own more than one unit; absentee ownership allowed
Kumon Math & Reading Centers	Educational services	$30.4K–110.3K	$1K	$30+/student/month	2 years	Cash liquidity requirement: $50K–100K; no absentee ownership

Source: Adapted from the "2008 Franchise 500," *Entrepreneur.com*, http://www.entrepreneur.com/franchise500/index.html (June 16, 2008).

Evaluating a Potential Franchise Opportunity

You've assessed your personal characteristics and skills, researched the universe of franchise opportunities, and decided that a franchise in the lawn care industry/category appeals to you most. After reading the basics on all five franchisors (Lawn Doctor, Scotts Lawn Service, U.S. Lawns, Spring-Green Lawn, and Truly Nolen), you've selected the two that sound best. How do you choose the one that best suits your needs?

Dick Rennick, chairman of the board of the IFA and chief executive officer of the American Leak Detection franchise system, advises franchisees to be thorough in researching a potential franchisor. He compares the franchisor–franchisee relationship to being part of a sports team. "The franchiser is like the team owner or coach, and you have to stay within the rules of the game, or go find another game to play," he says.[17]

As noted earlier, the due diligence involved in purchasing a franchise is similar to the process for other types of business enterprises. Appendix D, Before You Purchase a Franchise, offers many questions that apply to franchising, especially the sections covering economic and industry trends. The following guidelines, which cover the market environment and move on to franchise-specific issues, will help you get started.[18]

- *Demand:* How great is the demand for the franchisor's goods or services in your area? Are the franchise's products technologically current and competitive? Is the current level of demand likely to continue, or is it a passing fad? Is the business year-round or seasonal?

- *Competition:* How much competition is there locally and nationally for the franchisor's products, and how do these products compare to the competition's in terms of quality and price? How well known are the competing companies? Does the franchisor already have many units in your community and where are they located?

- *Brand equity:* How strong is the franchisor's name recognition? How long has it been operating? What is the general reputation associated with this brand—for quality or service, for example? Does the brand attract customers?

- *Franchisor's background:* How long has the franchisor been running this franchise system? What is its track record in its industry and in managing franchisees? How solid is the system's financial condition? Are you confident that the franchisor's management team can provide a high level of assistance and support to its franchisees? How fast is it growing, and does it have adequate financial strength to support this growth?

- *Training and support:* How much training and ongoing support services does the franchisor provide, and at what levels? Is it sufficient to prepare you to compete effectively in your industry? How does your background compare to that of existing franchise owners? If you lack any of the technical or other skills required or suggested to operate a successful franchise, can you acquire them?

- *Operating restrictions:* How extensive are the franchisor's operating restrictions as defined by the license agreement? Are you comfortable complying with these limitations?

- *Other questions:* Does the franchise require professional licenses or other special business experience? What is the process for terminating the franchise relationship?

Don't overlook the economics of operating a specific franchise unit. Look for objective measures to provide clues to the overall operating health of a franchise system. "The numbers don't lie," says Dan Rowe, president and CEO of Fransmart. "Get out the ruler, and make a chart. [See] what the per-unit sales volume has been for the last five years. Then extend that line out a couple more inches, and get a sense of where it's going. Is the food cost going up or going down? Is the check average going up or going down?" Other statistics to check include the number of units opened and closed in the past three to five years. The number of multiunit franchisees is another good indicator of a franchise's success. "To get rich in the franchise business, you never do it on one store; you always do it on multiples. You're building a franchise company," explains Rowe.[19]

Site Visits

Once you have finished your background research, you are ready to see for yourself how well the franchisor lives up to its UFDD claims. When you visit the franchisor's headquarters to meet with the franchisor's management team, ask detailed questions about the company and its background, financial condition, management, and what it offers its franchisees for training and support.

Perhaps the most important part of the due diligence process is visiting actual franchise units and talking to franchisees. This reality check is essential to understanding how the franchise system operates. For example, you may be counting on the franchisor's training programs to fill in your knowledge gaps. "Many franchisees think they will get a lot of training, but find out it's a one-week crash course," says Marko Grunhagen, a franchising specialist at Southern Illinois University–Edwardsville. "One day it's marketing, and one day it's accounting."[20]

When you visit franchise units, look at them from both the owner/manager's and the customer's perspective. Imagine yourself running the unit. Would you enjoy this type of business? Does the physical store appeal to you? Are the employees happy and providing good customer service? Would you want to buy what the company offers? Asking questions about the actual operation of the franchise provides insights into the nuts and bolts of managing the franchise. For example, you can learn whether your financial projections are realistic, the extent and adequacy of the training programs, and how well the franchisor lives up to its promises and supports the system's franchisees.

11.5 Acquiring a Franchise

You have finished your due diligence and chosen the franchise system you wish to join. The next step in the process involves meeting with a franchise attorney to insure that you understand all of the legal details involved with the franchise license agreement and the UFDD.

The Franchise License Agreement

The franchise license agreement is the document that gives the franchisee the right to use the franchisor's registered brands and trademarks together with a specific business operating system. The license is granted for a specified time period—typically eight to ten years—and requires payments that are explicitly set forth in the agreement along with the operating restrictions that apply to the franchisee's use of the brand and the running of the franchise unit.

It's important for a potential franchisee to understand that executing a franchise agreement is not the same as buying a business entity. In fact, the agreement will clearly state that the franchise company retains all ownership rights to the brand, trademarks, and proprietary business operating systems. The franchisee who invests in personal or real property required to operate the franchised business will have an ownership interest based on the proportional share of the investment. However, many franchise agreements require the franchisee to sell such property, often at its depreciated value, back to the franchise company when the franchise agreement terminates.

The Purchase Process

If you understand what you are buying when you sign the franchise agreement, and your franchise attorney is comfortable with the legal issues involved with the franchise agreement and the UFDD, then you are ready to sign the franchise agreement. Once you have signed the franchise agreement and paid the franchisor all of the applicable fees, you will attend training sessions as well as begin the process of opening your franchise.

Other Considerations

As you narrow your choices to a particular industry and then down to a few franchisors within that industry, there are other issues to consider. For example, should you choose the older, more established national franchise or the up-and-coming regionally focused franchise? The answer may not be obvious. According to Kevin Hogan, president of Liberty Development Consulting LLC, who works with the Whattaburger franchise, "It's a matter of individual location, brand awareness, marketing power, and media efficiency."

Smaller franchise systems with local appeal can be a good choice. Sam Fangary opted to buy a California-based hamburger franchise called Farmer Boys instead of a McDonald's or Burger King. Although the franchisor was young and only had seven franchise units, his research showed that local customers loved the chain's hamburgers. "I'd rather invest in a company that's growing—not a company that's already huge—so I have a chance to grow with them," he says. "When Farmer Boys gets as big as some of the big franchisors out there, I can have 20 stores—that's my goal."[21]

You may also find that the opportunity you seek involves working not with the franchisor but with a master franchisee. Some franchisors see the master franchise route as a faster way to grow than contracting directly with numerous individual franchisees. In that case, the master franchisee becomes the major contact point for the franchisee and provides the training and support. When this is the case, a prospective franchisee should investigate not only the franchise system but also the master franchisee's organization. In addition to the ability to recruit additional franchisees, the master franchisee must also be able to provide the requisite training and operating support for its franchisees.

Franchise experts advise visiting franchise units in the general system and also those in the region of the master franchisee you are considering. By doing both, a prospective franchisee will be able to assess the overall quality of the franchise system as a whole and also how well the master franchisee manages its territory. If the franchisor is sound but the problems lie with a specific master franchisee, you would be better off choosing a different master franchisee with whom to work.[22]

11.6 Starting a Franchise System

It is worth considering how and why enterprisers might pursue the development of a franchise system as a way to expand their businesses. Developing a franchise system can be a way to quickly expand a successful business model by attracting both capital investment from potential franchisees and their managerial and operational talents in running their own units. Developing a franchise system requires a significant investment of time and resources by a prospective franchisor. In nearly all instances where enterprisers seek to develop a particular business into a franchise, they will need to involve both a franchise lawyer and a franchise development consultant to help them work through the creation of the UFDD and develop other aspects of the franchise system.

Why would an enterpriser consider becoming a franchisor? Franchising offers a way to

- Expand the business through the use of other people's capital and talents.

- Shorten the time to bring the business concept to a larger market.

- Generate income through fees and royalties from franchisees.

- Harness the effort and creativity of motivated owner/managers.

- Share costs of advertising and other expenses.

- Increase buying power.

By building a network of motivated franchisees who have a personal stake in the success of the franchise system, an enterpriser can often use franchising to create a high-growth business enterprise more easily than opening multiple company-owned locations.

Franchising can be a profitable venture. As we explained earlier, franchisees must pay the franchisor initial fees averaging $20,000 to $30,000 and royalties ranging from 5 to 8 percent. Studies by the International Franchise Association show that the typical new franchisor will sell six to eight units the first year of operation, increasing to as many as 20 a year going forward. If each unit has gross sales of $500,000 and the franchisor sells seven units, the minimum revenue for the first year, assuming a $20,000 fee and 5 percent royalties, will be $315,000 ($140,000 in fees and $175,000 in royalties). By the time a franchisor has 17 units, it will have earned $340,000 from fees and received ongoing royalties of $425,000. In addition, franchisors often earn profits from a mark-up of 10 to 20 percent on sales of proprietary goods to franchisees.[23]

As tempting as these numbers sound, franchising has its downside for the franchisor who will

- Lose a portion of profits to franchisees.

- Lose some control over operations to franchisees.

- Face the difficulty of keeping franchisees happy as the franchise grows and changes over time.

- Expend significant time and energy to grow the franchise system.

- Incur significant legal costs to develop the franchise system.

When to Franchise

Some business situations are better suited to franchising than others. An enterpriser should consider growing a business through the development of a franchise system where the enterpriser has

- A business model that can be replicated in other areas.

- A business that will have a strong brand or trademark.

- A unique concept.

- A business that can be taught easily to others who may not have experience in the industry.

- A business that others can manage.

A franchise offers others an opportunity to both own and manage a business that will be similar to the business a prospective franchisor already operates. An enterpriser who already successfully operates a minimum of three to four other stores (units) might consider creating a franchise. Many enterprisers can often effectively manage two stores through direct supervision—dividing time between each of the two stores. Once the chain reaches three or four locations, most enterprisers can no longer directly manage all of these units. They must therefore hire managers as well as develop operations guides and procedures to insure that each location operates similarly.

Before embarking on the franchise route, enterprisers have to thoughtfully explore the reasons for their business success as well as identify specifically how these businesses operate. The challenge in building a franchise system is developing the operating manuals and procedures that make the business system obvious to others. Creating a franchise requires the enterpriser to specify all of those successful "tricks of the trade" and activities that contributed to the enterpriser's success. If the enterpriser cannot identify the unique formula for success, then, it will be difficult to create a franchise system where others can replicate the enterpriser's success.

Remember Betsy Ludlow, the marketing executive who opened her own exercise studio rather than buying a Curves franchise? The success of her small chain led her to follow the franchise route to growth and develop a website to market franchises online. "I sold 68 clubs working out of my bedroom," she reports. The Slim and Tone franchise now has over 140 units and operates as a division of Nutri-Systems Inc., which acquired the system in 2004. The initial investment of about $32,000, including the franchise fee, includes the exercise machines required to set up the exercise club.[24]

Steps to Franchising a Business

Enterprisers who determine that they have an established business that can be expanded into a franchise system should follow these eight steps:

1. *Develop a business plan for the franchise system.* A franchise system business plan envisions how the franchise system will expand and grow over time. It explains why growth through franchising is more appropriate than other ways of expansion.

2. *Hire a franchise attorney and a franchise development consultant.* Creating the UFDD and all the materials necessary to insure that potential franchisees can successfully develop and operate your prospective franchises is a very complicated process. It is fraught with many legal consequences if you do things incorrectly. As we indicated earlier in this chapter, the FTC and state agencies regulate franchising, but they do not approve or review franchising documents. In other words, the FTC will become involved after the fact—when something goes wrong and the franchisor violates the franchising regulations. It is better to involve franchising experts at the outset to make sure that your franchising system meets all legal requirements than to be sued by disappointed franchisees or have to pay penalties to the FTC or state agencies.

3. *Identify the intellectual property that serves as the basis for the franchise system.* Such intellectual property would include the business's name, trade names, trademarks, trade secrets, operating manuals, training manuals, operating processes and procedures, or any other information that is critical to the success of your business.

4. *Develop the UFDD and the franchise agreement.* It is necessary to have your franchise attorney and franchise development consultant review these documents for omissions and mistakes so that you avoid very costly legal problems later on.

5. *Develop all operating manuals and procedures necessary for a potential franchisee to successfully run a franchise unit.* You should develop a process for training franchisees to execute the franchise operating plans and procedures as specified. In addition, the material on the development of the franchise system will include information on how the franchise will grow through marketing, advertising, and unit expansion.

6. *Identify your franchise development team.* This executive group will identify potential franchisees, train them, and work with them to start and grow their franchise units. If a franchisor is serious about expanding a franchise system, the franchise development team should consist of individuals who are solely devoted to the franchise development effort. A franchisor cannot expect the manager of a store to both manage a store and also help potential franchisees start and grow their franchise units. Most franchisees will require help and guidance to learn the franchise system and effectively run their franchises. Not providing ongoing training, help, and guidance to franchisees often leads to disaster, as franchisees will then not follow franchise system guidelines, or complain (and file lawsuits) if they feel they are not getting the help they expected.

7. *Create a process for attracting prospective franchisees.* Consider how individuals might learn that your business provides a franchise opportunity. Develop an advertising campaign, attend franchise trade fairs, place newspaper advertisements, and make full use of your website and other Internet resources.

8. *Work closely with franchisees.* Help them find locations for franchise units and build units that meet the franchise system specifications. Train them to start and expand their businesses.

This list of activities requires a significant commitment by a franchisor to help the system's franchisees become successful. As we indicated at the beginning of the chapter, a good franchise opportunity is a win-win situation for both the franchisor and the franchisee. A franchisor will be successful if franchisees grow and are profitable. The franchisor benefits because the franchisees are paying royalties on sales from these successful units.

One of the most critical decisions that a franchisor will make is selecting potential franchisees. Ideally, franchisees will be willing to implement the vision and processes of the franchisor as well as provide the necessary capital to grow the number of franchise units. Franchisees are partners in the franchise system and, in some respects, "co-owners" in the success and growth of the franchise overall. A franchisor should look for franchisees who are willing to be partners in the business, as well as individuals who are willing to take direction.

Clearly, franchising isn't a simple process. Nor does operating a successful business—a restaurant, for example—guarantee success in franchising. In addition to issues related to the suitability of the business concept to franchising, an enterpriser must consider the significant regulatory burden of preparing and living up to the UFDD. Relationships with franchisees can be even more complex than other types of business partnerships.

11.7 ENTERPRISERS

Takeout Taxi Breaks Down

Too busy to cook dinner, but don't want to go out? You are not alone, and one entrepreneur trusted his instincts to build a thriving business that is now an industry leader.

The birth of Kevin Abt's daughter in 1987 was a precipitating factor behind the Takeout Taxi concept. He and his wife both worked and often went out to dinner after work. But with a baby, that was no longer practical. Abt, a former marketing executive at Sprint Corp. says, "When I left my corporate career, I was on the fast track, and my peer network looked at me and said, 'Kevin, you know, have you fallen on the ice? What are you doing? You're gonna leave to go schlep pizzas in Herndon, Virginia?' And I said, 'No, no, no, no, no, no.'"

He recognized that many people have to run their lives around their meal schedule, rather than being able to fit their meal into their life schedule. Takeout Taxi, whose slogan was "we bring the restaurants to you," was a business idea that could be national in scope. His timing was right, because off-premise dining is one of the biggest segments of the $160 billion-a-year food-service industry.

Kevin didn't simply assume that everyone else felt the same way that he did. While he thought that was a good starting place, he tested his idea by going back into his corporate network and talked to his friends and affiliates about the idea. "This time famine—is this me or is this us? Is everybody else having home-cooked meals at 5:30, seven days a week or not?" he wondered. "And lo and behold, I heard a resounding mimic of my own life from my entire network. Everybody was saying, 'Look, the only thing we can get delivered to our house is a pizza.' I listened to that and I said they're telling me there's massive demand for real food delivered to the home."

Want something other than pizza? Takeout Taxi can satisfy those cravings. Customers order from 20 to 50 restaurant menus, from local eateries to national chains such as Bennigan's, Fuddruckers, TGI Friday's, Chili's, and Steak and Ale. The orders go into Takeout Taxi's computers and are faxed to the restaurant. The sophisticated computer system not only tracks orders but also helps dispatchers arrange deliveries efficiently. Customers pay the regular menu price plus a delivery charge, and Takeout Taxi receives a commission, typically 30 percent, from the restaurant.

Takeout Taxi developed a targeted marketing strategy that focused on territories covering a 10- to 15-minute driving time and about 30,000–40,000 people. It used direct mail to tell customers about the service, sending restaurant menus, discount coupons for new customers, and contact information for Takeout Taxi. When a customer placed an order, the company fed the information into a database that became the basis of future marketing efforts. Restaurants could work with Takeout Taxi on special promotions.

Takeout Taxi marketed to both restaurants and patrons. "It's been a huge side benefit for us, because it has helped us develop a sense of who our customers are," said Chuck Curcio, owner of a Tortilla Factory restaurant in Herndon, Virginia. "We've been able to use the information for all sorts of direct marketing: birthday clubs, Christmas cards, and direct-mailing pieces about summer specials." Curcio also realized that sales from Takeout Taxi were incremental to onsite revenues and added significantly to his bottom line.

Abt chose to expand his company by selling franchises for an initial fee of $25,000 for rights to serve a guaranteed territory, plus ongoing royalties. In addition to training and one week's help from a corporate specialist to learn how to negotiate with restaurants, franchisees received the hardware and software for the company's computerized ordering system.

The idea proved popular and the company grew rapidly. In 1992, Takeout Taxi had 41 units in 15 states. In 1994, Abt raised $3 million in equity from a venture capital firm to finance an aggressive expansion program. By 1995, company revenues topped $70 million as 101 franchisees delivered meals in 200 locations across 30 states and Canada, for 4,000 restaurants. *Fortune* featured Takeout Taxi in an article about problems in the franchise industry as a company that did franchising the right way.

Why was Takeout Taxi's multirestaurant delivery service a success? Not only did Kevin Abt have a concept for a service with broad market appeal, but he knew how to turn that plan into reality. "Concepts are cheap," he says. "It's really the execution of the details. In new concepts and new ventures, there is a minefield of details between the concept and the bottom line of profits. We spent four long, hard years debugging the concept before we started franchising."

Kevin Abt's basic idea was sound. People liked the idea of calling a meal delivery service to get lunch or dinner brought directly to their homes or offices. Today over 120 restaurant delivery businesses operate in the United States. However, rapid expansion took its toll on the company. Franchisees became dissatisfied about the services they received from corporate headquarters. In 1996, Abt was replaced as CEO by William Howe, who promised to improve the company's systems and overall service to its three types of customers: franchisees, restaurants, and consumers.

Flash forward to 2003. Takeout Taxi filed for Chapter 7 bankruptcy (liquidation of assets). The following year, 15 of the system's franchisees formed a limited liability company called Brand Solutions, LLC, and purchased the trademarks and other key assets from the former franchisor. Brand Solutions then licensed its members to operate their individually owned territories in 18 major markets under the Takeout Taxi trademark.

Discussion Questions

1. Using the five criteria in "When to Franchise" in Section 11.6 (p. 363), evaluate the suitability of the Takeout Taxi concept for growth through franchising.

Was Takeout Taxi a good candidate for this method of growth, and why or why not?

2. Kevin Abt has hired you as his director of franchisee recruitment. Develop a list of criteria you would look for in prospective franchisees. Include personal characteristics as well as business background.

3. What should the training program for Takeout Taxi franchisees cover? Prepare an outline for the one-week curriculum for new franchisees and one for a one-day refresher course for experienced franchisees.

4. As a prospective franchisee, what would you want to know about Takeout Taxi before buying a franchise? Describe your due diligence plan in detail.

5. Meal delivery services have become a popular service business. However, Takeout Taxi was unable to survive as a large-scale franchisor. What factors might have contributed to its demise? Suggest some steps Abt and his management team could have taken to avoid filing for bankruptcy.

6. If you were considering starting an independent business based on the Takeout Taxi concept, estimate the costs and the time to develop a system similar to the Takeout Taxi franchise system. How much do you estimate it would cost you in resources and time to develop your own system versus purchasing the franchise system from Takeout Taxi?

Source: Adapted with permission from Small Business School, the series on PBS, and at http://SmallBusinessSchool.com. "Services That Deliver— Home Meal Replacement," *Nation's Restaurant News,* March 16, 1998, http://www.findarticles.com; "Takeout Taxi: Howe Jumps into Driver's Seat," *Restaurants & Institutions,* March 15, 1996, p. 26; and "Takeout Taxi Speeds up Delivery Sales for Operators," *Nation's Restaurant News,* November 23, 1992, http://www.findarticles.com.

11.8 International Franchising

If you have done any foreign travel, you realize that franchising is now an international form of business. Fast food franchises like McDonald's and Pizza Hut are quickly becoming as common in Moscow and Madrid as in Minneapolis. Not only have U.S. franchise systems expanded into other countries, but overseas franchisors have also brought their concepts to the U.S. Cartridge World, which refills printer ink cartridges, originated in Australia, while Shred-It, a mobile document shredding

franchise, is Toronto-based. Japan's Kumon Math and Reading Centers is the largest foreign-based franchise in the United States. In either situation, crossing national borders increases the complexity, because franchisors must now consider the franchising laws of both countries. Franchising may not be a familiar concept in other countries such as China, where franchisees may not understand the need to adhere to the franchisor's operating system. China recently passed its first franchise laws, which should help overseas franchisors in their quest to tap this huge market.

Many U.S. franchisors who venture abroad discover the benefits of partnering with local business people who can smooth the path through the local business customs. In certain countries, a local partner is a requirement for foreign-based businesses.

Some franchise concepts must be adapted to suit local customs. Bark Busters, a dog-training method from Australia, had to take into account the differences in the way pet owners in each country treat their dogs. In Australia, most dogs are outdoor animals, whereas in the United States, people bring dogs inside and treat them more like children. Others, like Computer Troubleshooters U.S.A., the U.S. arm of an Australian franchisor with units in over 200 countries, find that few adjustments are necessary. The Enterprising World box discusses the franchising strategy of Wagamama, a chain of Japanese noodle restaurants that started in London.

Food franchises, of course, must take into account native tastes. McDonald's added a spicy chicken burger to its Chinese menus, and KFC replaced coleslaw with local vegetable side dishes. When Jim Bryant, master franchisee for Subway in China, opened the first unit in Beijing, he had to print instructions cards to explain to Chinese customers how to order sandwiches, a foreign concept. Overall the sandwich concept has been slow to catch on, and local franchisees criticized the franchisor for not finding ways to adapt the menu. "Subway should have at least one item tailored to Chinese tastes to show that they are respecting the local culture," says franchisee Luo Bing Ling. Time is helping, as a uniquely American item, tuna salad, is now the most popular item.[25]

AN ENTERPRISING WORLD

Wagamama Uses Its Noodle

To the surprise of the editors of *Zagat's 2006 London Restaurant Guides*, the most popular restaurant in the city was not the upscale Gordon Ramsay or Ivy, but a chain of Japanese noodle restaurants called Wagamama. Modeled on the ramen shops popular in Japan for over 200 years, Wagamama's menu features Oriental-style thin noodles with toppings, served either in soups or fried on a grill. Rounding out the menu are rice dishes, fresh juices, and side dishes such as dumplings, chicken skewers, fried shrimp, and salads.

Wagamama prides itself on using the freshest ingredients and preparing all food onsite. The restaurant décor is sleek yet simple, and service is friendly and fast. Patrons sit at communal tables and at most locations can also order food to take out. Good food, affordable prices, and the consistently high level of service bring customers back. In addition to the accolades from *Zagat*'s readers, Wagamama was named *Time Out* guide's best family restaurant.

Restaurateur Alan Yau opened the first Wagamama restaurant in London in 1992. Customers liked its concept, and soon the noodle bars appeared in most major UK cities. Yau sold the business to Ian Neil, Wagamama's current chief executive, in 1997 and moved on to other restaurant ventures.

As Wagamama's popularity grew, its owners raised venture capital funding from Graphite Capital for the chain's initial expansion efforts. The investment was a good one for Graphite, which earned a 500 percent

return when it sold a portion of its interest to Hutton Collins, an investment bank. In 2005, Graphite sold its majority interest to Lion Capital, another private equity firm. "Lion Capital has a big international brand perspective," says Neil. "They also own Jimmy Choo shoes and Weetabix Cereals. I think this experience will help us develop our overseas business." With Lion's backing, Wagamama began its next expansion phase.

By mid-2008, the chain had about 90 restaurants worldwide, with 60 in the UK and international locations in Europe, Australia, New Zealand, the Middle East, and the United States.

In 2007, Wagamama opened the first of its U.S. locations in Boston. "We chose Boston because we know the area and because of the interesting mix of communities in the region, including universities, finance, and business," explained Neil. "It's also easy to access from the UK." Unlike its other overseas units, the U.S. operations will be company-owned. "The U.S. market, should it be successful, is enormous. We believe we'll get better value for our shareholders by controlling the business directly," said Neil.

Discussion Questions

1. Why has Wagamama chosen to franchise its international restaurant operations? What are some of the reasons that Wagamama wants to own and operate its U.S. restaurant sites?

2. How could Wagamama insure that a franchisee in Auckland, New Zealand, is operating a restaurant to the company's standards?

3. Why would a private equity firm be interested in an investment in Wagamama? How might Lion Capital get a return on its investment in the future?

4. What are the advantages and disadvantages of getting private equity money from investors versus using a franchise system to grow Wagamama?

Sources: Based on "Clocking on . . . Luke Fryer of Wagamama," *Hospitality*, March 1, 2006, p. 16; Amanda Mosle Friedman, "Having Words with Ian Neill, Chief Executive, Wagamama," *Nation's Restaurant News*, October 10, 2005, p. 114; "Graphite Makes Partial Exit from Wagamama," *European Venture Capital Journal*, October 2004, p. 13; "Noodle Migration," *Restaurants & Institutions*, February 15, 2006, p. 13; "Wagamama Changes Hands and Sets Out to Conquer the USA," *Caterer & Hotelkeeper*, June 23, 2005, p. 8; "Wagamama Gets £13m to Fund Its Expansion Drive," *Caterer & Hotelkeeper*, September 9, 2004, p. 9; "Wagamama Set to Take On U.S. Market," *Caterer & Hotelkeeper*, January 19, 2006, p. 8; and Wagamama website, http://www.wagamama.com (June 16, 2008).

Summary

1. Franchising is a popular form of business ownership that makes a significant contribution to the national economy. It spans 75 industry groups, from fast food to health care services to pet stores. In a franchise relationship, a parent business (the *franchisor*) provides an investor (the *franchisee*) with the rights to sell its products or services and use its trademark and operating procedures. In return, the franchisee pays up-front fees and/or ongoing royalty payments. About one-third of all franchise outlets are in food-related industries.

2. Business format franchises account for 80 percent of all franchises. The franchisor provides the franchisee a defined format under which to operate the franchise unit, as well as training and other types of support, such as help in locating a site, guidance on building and outfitting the store, and financing. The franchisee also acquires the rights to use the brand name and related trademarks. Franchisees pay fees and royalties to the franchisor. They must adhere to the franchisor's operating guidelines in managing their units.

3. With a product and trademark (or product distribution) franchise, franchisees have the right to buy, sell, and advertise trademarked products and serve as a dealer network for the manufacturer. Product and trademark franchisees have greater operating freedom than business format franchisees. Vehicle dealerships are the most common type of franchise, followed by oil and gas distributorships.

4. The Federal Trade Commission (FTC) under Rule 436 regulates disclosures related to the offer and sale of franchises at the federal level. The law sets forth the minimum disclosure requirements but does not require franchisors to register their filings. Franchisors must provide prospective franchisees with a Uniform Franchise Disclosure Document (UFDD) that covers 23 items in a standard format. Because the FTC does not review the contents or accuracy of UFDDs, prospective franchisees are responsible for their own review. State laws vary in the degree of regulation, with some states requiring that franchisors register their UFDDs.

5. Deciding whether to buy a franchise or another type of business requires the same type of review process as any new business venture, including personal goals, interests, skills, investment requirements, type of business opportunity, industry characteristics, and market environment. A prospective franchisee must also investigate the franchisor to make sure that it can deliver on its promises. The benefits of franchising include a proven business model, brand name and trademarks, training and support from the franchisor, financing assistance, system synergies, and economies of scale. Disadvantages include the need to follow the franchisor's operating systems, costs such as franchise fees and ongoing royalties, inability to act independently of the system, limitations on the sale or termination of the franchise contract, business risks, and unfulfilled expectations on the part of the franchisor.

6. Choosing a franchise opportunity requires substantial research into different franchise concepts. Costs vary considerably, even within the same industry, and depend on the type of unit and required equipment, franchise fee, ongoing royalty

payments, and other fees such as contributions to a systemwide advertising fund. Other areas of comparison include demand for the products, competition, brand equity, amount of training and support, and degree of operating restrictions. Site visits, to both the franchisor's headquarters and to individual franchise units, are an essential part of the due diligence process.

7.   The *franchise license agreement* gives the franchisee the right to use the franchisor's registered brands and trademarks and business operating system. It specifies the contract term, franchisee payments, and operating restrictions.

8.   Franchising also offers a way for an enterpriser to grow a business more quickly by using the talent and capital of other enterprisers, who become franchisees. While becoming a franchisor can be quite profitable, the franchisor loses some profits to the franchisees and also gives up a degree of operating control. Businesses that are well suited to grow by franchising should have an easily replicated business model, a strong brand or trademark, and a unique concept. In addition, the business should be easy for others to learn and manage. The franchisor must be able to identify the qualities that make the business successful and prepare detailed operating manuals to guide the system's franchisees in duplicating them.

9.   Developing a franchise system calls for a significant commitment on the part of the franchisor and starts with a business plan. Working with a franchise attorney and development consultant, the franchisor must prepare the UFDD and supporting materials in accordance with federal and state regulations, identify the system's intellectual property (brand, trademarks, and procedures), write operating manuals and procedures, hire a franchise development team to recruit and train franchisees, create a marketing strategy, and work closely with franchisees on a continuing basis.

10.   The franchise concept has become global in scope, with U.S. franchisors opening units overseas and foreign-based franchises coming to the United States to build their systems. Some types of franchises translate easily to new countries, while others—food-related franchises in particular—require adaptation to local tastes and customs.

Review Questions

1.   What makes a franchise different from other paths to entrepreneurship?

2.   What is the relationship between the franchisor and the franchisee? Name the three basic elements in a franchise.

3.   Differentiate between business format and product and trademark franchises.

4.   Describe the two types of multiple-unit ownership options.

5.   To what extent are franchises regulated at the federal and state level? How do federal and state regulations differ?

6.   What is the Uniform Franchise Disclosure Document (UFDD), and what must it contain to conform to FTC disclosure requirements?

7.   What advantages does franchising offer to the franchisee? What are the negatives in choosing the franchise route?

8.   Describe the process for selecting a franchise opportunity. What areas should an enterpriser take into account with regard to personal characteristics and the business itself before buying a franchise?

9.   What costs are involved in the purchase and operation of a franchise unit?

10.   Why are site visits to the franchisor's headquarters and to existing franchisees integral to the due diligence process? List the questions a prospective franchisee would ask at each type of meeting.

11.   What is a franchise license agreement? How does it treat the franchisee's investments in property?

12.   Why would an entrepreneur decide to use franchising as a way to grow a business? What characteristics should a business have to be suitable for franchising?

13.   Briefly describe the process involved in becoming a franchisor.

14.   Discuss the issues facing U.S. franchisors who wish to expand abroad. What additional concerns might a U.S. enterpriser have in buying a franchise from a foreign-based franchisor?

Applying What You've Learned

1. Your friend has just been laid off from her job as a software support specialist. She has heard about a franchise opportunity that provides computer training to individuals and small businesses. However, she is unsure whether to buy a franchise or to set up her own company and asks for your advice. Describe the pros and cons of each alternative for her. Explain what she can expect in the way of assistance from the franchisor and suggest a game plan for her to follow to evaluate the franchise. What questions should she ask the franchisor? Current franchisees?

2. The International Franchise Association (IFA) is the trade association that works to promote and regulate franchising in ways that benefit all franchisors and franchisees. Visit its website, http://www.franchise.org, and click on the Government Relations section. What are the top regulatory issues currently facing the franchise industry? Summarize the types of legislation that are under consideration at both the state and federal levels.

3. Select five franchises in at least three different industries that have outlets in your community. (Refer to *Entrepreneur's* Franchise 500 lists, http://www.entrepreneur.com/franchise/, if you are not sure whether a business is franchised or independent.) After visiting the stores, choose two you like best and explain why you prefer these franchises. Arrange interviews with the owners and speak to employees. What impressed you about these franchises? Could you see yourself owning a similar franchise? Summarize your findings.

4. Not all kinds of businesses and industries are well suited to establishing a franchise. What kind of business could not be expanded by developing a franchise system and selling it to others? Look through the many listings of different franchises and consider what businesses and industries do not appear to be represented. How do these industries and businesses seem to be different from industries and businesses with a high percentage of franchise systems?

5. Six years ago you opened Scoop Shop, an ice cream parlor patterned after a 1950s soda fountain. The concept was so popular that you opened five more stores in nearby towns. Soon people were approaching you about expanding Scoop Shop to their area, so you decided to become a franchisor. Today you have 33 stores in a three-state region. The Center for Entrepreneurship at your state university has asked you to speak to its students about your success. Prepare a presentation that includes the key factors you considered before deciding to franchise Scoop Shops and how you developed your franchise system. What were the most difficult aspects you faced, and what advice can you give students from the franchisor's perspective about buying a franchise?

6. Some enterprises have focused on purchasing franchises as a way to grow. A good example of this is AutoNation (http://www.autonation.com), which was founded by Wayne Huizenga, who had previously started Waste Management and Blockbuster Video. AutoNation is the largest car dealer in the United States, with over 350 new vehicle franchises in more than 15 states and offers no-haggle sales policies and online sales through http://www.autonation.com and individual dealer websites. How could a company that owns many different automobile franchise systems (e.g., Ford, General Motors, Toyota, Nissan, and Honda) become successful in the marketplace? Are there other industries with a high percentage of franchises where the AutoNation strategy might also work?

Enterprisers on the Web

1. Is franchising the right business venture for you? Take the first section (Questions 1–33) of the quiz you'll find in the article "Are You Suited to Be a Franchisee?" *Entrepreneur's* FranchiseZone, April 19, 2004, http://www.entrepreneur.com/franzone/article/0,5847,315261,00.html. What did you discover about yourself? Were you surprised at the results?

2. Another site that can help you evaluate the franchising option for yourself is the International Franchise Association (http://www.franchise.org) resource site. There are seven readings that provide a good overview of franchising issues. Please be sure to cover the last two readings: "Most Frequently Asked Questions About Franchising" and "Self-Evaluation: Is Franchising for You?"

3. The Federal Trade Commission is the government agency responsible for monitoring and regulating franchises. The FTC site (http://www.ftc.gov) provides links to many resources on franchising, including details on the legal responsibilities of franchisors and franchisees. What kinds of problems should a prospective franchisee look out for when considering a franchise? What kinds of scams are typical in the franchise industry?

4. *Entrepreneur* conducts a number of surveys of the franchise industry and reports on new franchising trends and issues. At the *Entrepreneur* magazine's FranchiseZone site (http://www.entrepreneur.com/franzone/), browse the Franchise 500, as well as the special lists of Top New Franchises, Fast-Growing Franchises, Low-Cost Franchises, and so on. Find three franchise opportunities that are of interest to you. Read their profiles and visit the franchisor websites. Compare these three franchise opportunities in either chart or narrative format. Include the following information for each franchise opportunity:

    Resources necessary to participate

    Up-front costs

    Ongoing costs

    Capabilities of the entrepreneurs these franchises seek

    Advantages that each franchise promotes

    Type of help and support offered

    Of the franchises you analyzed, which franchise seems to be better than the others? Does it meet your needs and suit your background and personality? Explain your rationale in detail.

5. Revisit the three franchisor websites from the previous question, plus any others that interest you. Which websites seemed to be the most appealing to you? What features and information in these websites were more likely to convince you to become a franchisee? Which websites seemed to do a poor job of convincing you to become a franchisee? What are the critical features and information that a franchisor needs to provide to prospective franchisees on their websites?

6. *Inc.* magazine (http://www.inc.com/guides/buy_biz/20674.html) offers insights into how franchisors and franchisees can better manage their businesses. Using the site's resources, discuss ways the owner of a franchise can help motivate employees. What specific expenses and revenue items should you monitor daily in a franchise restaurant business to insure that you are profitable?

End Notes

1. Julie Bennett, "Franchise Regulation: Past, Present and Future," *StartupJournal.com*, January 9, 2002, http:www.startupjournal.com; "Important Facts about Franchising," Franchise Opportunities.com, http://www.franchiseopportunities.com (July 3, 2005).

2. "Answers to the 20 Most Frequently Asked Questions about Franchising," International Franchising Association, 2005, downloaded from http://www.franchise.org.

3. "The Profile of Franchising," *Franchising World*, March 2007, p. 59.

4. Jerry Wilkerson, "2005 Franchise Business Development Forecast and Industry Trends Analysis: 14th Annual Franchise Study," Franchise Recruiters Ltd., March 6, 2005, http://franchiserecruiters.com.

5. *Economic Impact of Franchised Businesses—Policymakers* Digest, IFA Educational Foundation, 2005, p. 3.

6. Ibid.

7. Carlye Adler, "How China Eats a Sandwich," *Fortune*, March 21, 2005, p. F210[B].

8. "FTC Issues Updated Franchise Rule," Federal Trade Commission, January 23, 2007, http://www.ftc.gov/opa/2007/01/franchiserule.shtm.

9. "16 CFR Parts 436 and 437: Disclosure Requirements and Prohibitions Concerning Franchising and Business Opportunities; Final Rule," *Federal Register*, March 30, 2007;

Buying a Franchise: A Consumer Guide, Federal Trade Commission, February 2008, http://www.ftc.gov/bcp/edu/pubs/consumer/invest/inv05.shtm#5; and "Rule Overview," *Guide to the FTC Franchise Rule*, Federal Trade Commission, downloaded from http://www.ftc.gov/bcp/franchise/netrule.htm, accessed July 12, 2005.

10. "16 CFR Parts 436 and 437: Disclosure Requirements and Prohibitions Concerning Franchising and Business Opportunities; Final Rule," *Federal Register*, March 30, 2007; *Buying a Franchise: A Consumer Guide*, Federal Trade Commission, February 2008, http://www.ftc.gov/bcp/edu/pubs/consumer/invest/inv05.shtm#5; and "Rule Requirements," *Guide to the FTC Franchise Rule*, Federal Trade Commission, downloaded from http://www.ftc.gov/bcp/franchise/netrule.htm, accessed July 12, 2005.

11. "FTC Issues Updated Franchise Rule," Federal Trade Commission, January 23, 2007, http://www.ftc.gov/opa/2007/01/franchiserule.shtm.

12. Jim Coen, "The Amended FTC Franchise Rule, from the Prospects' Perspective," *Let's Talk Franchising!*, April 12, 2008, http://www.franchiseperfectino.com.

13. Gene J. Koprowski, "Successful Franchisees Embrace 'The System'," *StartupJournal Online,* March 8, 2004, http://www.startupjournal.com/franchising/.

14. Lea McLees, "Flourishing New Franchises," *Research Horizons* 13, no. 3 (Winter 1996), pp. 14–16.

15. Koprowski, "Successful Franchisees Embrace 'The System'," *StartupJournal Online,* March 8, 2004, http://www. startupjournal.com/franchising/.

16. Paulette Thomas, "Franchise Sparks Idea to Create a New Firm," *Wall Street Journal*, May 31, 2005, p. B12.

17. Koprowski, "Successful Franchisees Embrace 'The System'," *StartupJournal Online*, March 8, 2004, http://www. startupjournal.com/franchising/.

18. Adapted from *A Consumer Guide to Buying a Franchise*, Federal Trade Commission, http://www.ftc.gov/bcp/conline/ pubs/invest/buyfran.htm (July 15, 2005).

19. April Y. Pennington, "Would You Like a Franchise with That?" *Entrepreneur*, January 2005, http://www.entrepreneur.com.

20. Richard Gibson, "Franchise Fever Jumps to Overseas Markets," *Wall Street Journal Online*, February 24, 2004, http://www.startupjournal.com/franchising/.

21. Pennington, "Would You Like a Franchise with That?" *Entrepreneur*, January 2005, http://www.entrepreneur.com.

22. Jeff Elgin, "What is a Master Franchisee?" *Entrepreneur*, September 7, 2004, http://www.entrepreneur.com.

23. "Becoming a Franchisor," Franchise Consulting, http://www. franchiseconsulting.net/intro.html (July 3, 2005).

24. Thomas, "Franchise Sparks Idea to Create a New Firm," *Wall Street Journal*, May 31, 2005, p. B12.

25. Carlye Adler, "How China Eats a Sandwich," *Fortune*, March 21, 2005, p. F210[B].

ENTERPRISE

PART FOUR

The Enterprising Mind

The Enterprising Mind

KEY CONCEPTS

1. After exploring business opportunities, it is time to make the transition from dreams to realities, which requires a shift in focus—from how and why to goals and values. Enterprisers must determine what's important and make sure their actions and commitments correlate with their goals.

2. The way we tell our life stories—where we came from and where we are going—defines our self-perceptions. Telling a more positive story can transform how we think about ourselves and how others think about us, leading to a more successful outcome. A good story uses past experiences to demonstrate how an enterpriser will meet new challenges. It's normal to have many fears as you embark on your enterprising journey, which has many unknowns.

3. Focusing more on the limitations of a particular situation than on the possibilities it presents is a restrictive mind-set that can hinder future success. Ways to improve our mind-set include assuming that everyone wants to do "A" work, believing that we can contribute, not taking ourselves so seriously, and being passionate about what we do.

4. One of the challenges of being an enterpriser is trying to satisfy four different goals: achievement, significance, legacy, and happiness. It's impossible to maximize all four, and we should set priorities and seek success in many arenas: work, family, self, and community.

Suppose you are an action-oriented person who has overcome many difficulties in your life. After a string of 30 jobs in a variety of fields, you are working for a computer sales company. Because you do not agree with management's values and ethics, you decide to leave yet another job—this time to start your own company. Raising financing for your used computer sales business was tough, but you didn't give up. You believed in yourself and your business model.

© Bananastock/Jupiter Images

In this chapter's case, we'll meet Tom Pace, who built PaceButler Corporation into a leading reseller of used computer equipment. He later refocused the company's resales expertise to become a broker for used cellular phones. A factor in his success is the company's "atmosphere statement," developed in 1990 to establish a values orientation that emphasizes an employee-centric, positive, working environment. In 2003, Pace took full responsibility for a major computer problem that almost put the company out of business. His story shows how setting goals, knowing your values, focusing on possibilities, and taking action lead to success.

12.0 Taking Stock

In the preceding 11 chapters, you have learned a lot about business opportunities and the steps required to turn them into actual businesses. You have the tools to execute your dreams—but what, exactly, are your dreams? As you have looked at various opportunities, you have probably reconsidered your goals based on this new information about what might be possible for your life as an enterpriser. The many possibilities that are now available to you can be overwhelming. This chapter is designed to help you take stock of your situation so you can move forward to realize your dreams.

Most enterprisers experience a transition point when they move from the activities involved in starting a business to the actual process of operating and managing an ongoing business. Even from conversations with enterprisers, it is difficult to know when, specifically, they move from starting the business to actually being in business. In many retail establishments and restaurants, you'll notice a dollar bill pasted on the wall next to the cash register. When you ask the business owner about it, you are likely to hear a story related to how he or she earned that dollar, which represents the company's first sale. Often, that marks the enterprise's first day of business.

A good description of this transition period from start-up to ongoing business appears in one of the first studies of the enterprising process undertaken by Orvis Collins and David Moore in the 1960s. They studied individuals who started small manufacturing businesses—basically, machine shops that made parts for the automobile and furniture industries in the Michigan area. In what is a pretty dry study of these enterprisers, they point to this period of transition with these words:

> *In this period of fear and doubt, however, these men found creativity. At a time when it became necessary for them to reorganize their lives and to re-establish their futures, they had the capacity not only to dream but to transmute their dreams into action. They created the business of which they were dreaming. Between the idea and the act falls the shadow. This shadow, which these men had to explore, and out of which they had to hammer a reality, lay immediately ahead. They had now to organize the universe around them in such a way that they could progress in establishing their new business. The first act in this direction is what we will call the act of creation.*[1]

That is a somewhat moody soliloquy, yet it speaks to what nearly all enterprisers go through during the process of turning their dreams into reality. There is a gap—what Collins and Moore call "the shadow"—that lies between our present situation and a vision of our future. In our mind's eye, we might be able to actually see where we want to be in the future. But the specific process of getting there is likely to be less clear. We can see ourselves owning a 100-room hotel, we can imagine what each of the rooms look like, we can see the lobby and the front desk, and we can walk around the hotel in our imagination. The actual process of moving from dreaming about owning a hotel to actually owning a hotel is the "shadow" that we must walk through to make our vision come into existence. Taking your dreams

and turning them into reality takes more than action. While you now have tools for spotting opportunities, evaluating them, and developing the plans to make those opportunities into enterprises, you must also consider your values: What do you really want? The challenge is to transform *your thinking* so you can take in all of the possibilities available to you.

Some aspects of this chapter are similar to the issues we raised in Chapter 3, Enterprising Fundamentals. However, in the earlier chapter we focused more on the *how*. Now we ask you to concentrate on your values and goals—the *why*—and begin to act in ways that support them. For example, in Chapter 3 the focus on time management was *how* to manage your time. In this chapter, we approach time management from a different perspective, on *why* we really want to pursue a particular opportunity. Our actions and commitments should reflect our values and goals. Shifting our focus to values takes some effort. We tend to take action, which sets us on a particular course. We find ourselves on autopilot and may not make the necessary course corrections as we proceed on our journey. Often we realize that our destination is changing: our course is set for London, but we really want to go to Paris. This chapter is about being conscious of our goals and values as we move toward our dreams. As we have identified the opportunities we want to pursue in our lives (through our efforts in Chapters 6 through 8), we will need to make these mid-course corrections in our lives. We need to insure that the direction of our opportunities matches the direction of our goals and values.

12.1　What Are Your Commitments?

Commitments are choices that bind you to some future course of action.[2] Often, we think about a commitment as a big or important choice that has future implications. For example, if you take out a loan to purchase a car, you've made a commitment to make monthly payments to the bank for the next five years to pay off that loan. Buying the car and taking out the loan are choices that constrain your actions, because you'll need to earn income to make the loan payments. The action also opens up opportunities for you: you now have a car that gives you mobility. You can drive where you want, when you want, and you might even use your car to make money—delivering pizzas, driving to a job—to pay for the car.

Larger commitments tend to require other obligations of time, money, and energy as well. For example, if you purchase the car, you are also making a commitment to keep it maintained, which means tune-ups and new tires and parts; the car will require gasoline when you drive it; it will have to be washed and cleaned; and it will need a parking place and insurance. We often underestimate these other minor commitments.

Remember your goals? In Chapter 3 we provided exercises to help you discover your goals and priorities. Now let's see whether your actions and activities are well correlated to these goals. To do this, ask yourself the following questions: What is important to you? What do you really care about (what are your goals and values)?

List these on a piece of paper using the format in Exhibit 12.1. As we suggested in the goal setting section of Chapter 3, try to be as specific as possible about what matters to you. For example, if you write down "family," then begin to identify what goals you have with your family, such as "having fun" with your family, versus "making sure kids in the family get an education." For each goal, then ask yourself what your commitment in money, time, and energy is to accomplish that. Include what you are doing about that goal now. For example, if one of your goals is to be physically fit, you would note how much time, money, and energy you currently devote to keeping fit. Maybe you pay for a gym membership fee as your financial commitment, but you only go to the gym once a month.

In going through this exercise to identify what you find important and where you've been spending money, time, and energy, you can begin to see whether your commitments correspond to your goals and values. Using Exhibit 12.1 as an example, if you really value your health and you are not taking time to exercise and eat well, your commitments clearly don't match your values.

As you develop the opportunities in your life, it is easy to get caught up in activities that, over time, do not bring you closer to the values and goals that matter most to you. Just like in Chapter 3, we encourage you to work smarter rather than work harder. Working harder may not bring you any closer to achieving your goals. For example, we all have a desire to be better off financially, and so we set financial goals. Yet, how much time and energy do we really devote to meeting our financial goals? If we are spending only ten minutes a month balancing our checkbook, then our actions do not reflect much time or energy spent to improve our financial situation.

Once we've identified mismatches between our values and goals and our commitments in money, time, and energy, how do we begin to change them? Just being aware of the mismatches is an important first step. Next, consider your current commitments and how they influence your investment of that time, money, and energy. Suppose you find that you are spending most of your time at work but need to spend more time with your family. Before you cut back your hours, you'll have to talk with your boss and coworkers about your plans. If you suddenly decide to cut back on your work effort without telling anyone, you are likely to be perceived as slacking off—when in fact you've made a conscious

---

exhibit 12.1

What Is Important to Me?

Goal	Money	Time	Energy
Good health	$100 a month for gym	Go twice a week after work	Research most convenient gyms
	Buy more fresh fruits and vegetables	Trips to grocery store	Find best sources, scout out farmer's markets
Learn new skills required to start own business	Tuition for additional courses	3–5 hours a week in class per semester plus studying	Determine which courses will help most
		Enrich current job, take advantage of training opportunities	Find a mentor, seminars, etc.

choice to emphasize other priorities in your life. Realize that others might not always share your excitement about devoting less time and energy to things you've been involved with in the past. Another benefit of sharing your plans: you create a path for yourself (as we will see in the next section).

Second, clear your clutter. Basically, as you review your activities, the money you spend, and the places you put your energy, you should begin to cull things from your list. As we indicated in Chapter 3's section on time management, you can't take on new things unless you get rid of old activities. If one of the things you value in your life is spending time painting and want an hour a day to paint, you have to take that hour from something else on your schedule. A good rule of thumb in evaluating your commitments and making new commitments is to take on a new commitment only when you've ended another.

By looking at your commitments, then, you'll see how your actions match your values and goals. If your goal is to start and own a business, are you putting time, money, and energy into accomplishing this? To be a business owner, you need to act like a business owner. This means you will have to make a commitment to

- devote x number of hours a week to the development and (eventual) operation of your business.

- invest a certain amount of your resources into creating the business.

- put some of your best efforts into making the business a reality.

For example, if your day is devoted entirely to completing school work and being with friends and family, and your only free time to develop your business is late at night (between midnight and 2 AM), you might not be able to devote your best energy to your business. Nor will most customers, suppliers, or others be available at those hours. To do your best on a commitment, then, you will have to rearrange your schedule so you can spend your best time, the time when you have the most energy, to starting a business, so that the circumstances are also best for insuring your success.

In this section, we've helped you identify the gaps between what you want and what you need to do. Yet while we know that we need to take action to move closer to our goals, we get stuck doing the same things we have always done. For example, to create an enterprise we need to build a network of supportive people to help us firm up our business plans. We need to do the cold-calling necessary to identify "strangers" who can eventually become supportive advisors. But we spend the day with our friends and family—people we already know. Inertia keeps us stuck in our old patterns. Part of the reason for being stuck is that we are held back by how we see ourselves and our ideas, as well as the way that others view us. It's easier to keep thinking and acting the same way we have done until now.

12.2 What Is Your Story?

As Zig Ziglar, a well-known business and sales training consultant and author, reminds us, "You cannot consistently perform in a manner which is inconsistent with the way you see yourself." Not only do we need to begin acting like enterprisers and engaging in activities to start and grow businesses, we also need to change how we think and talk about being enterprisers. The way we tell our life stories—where we came from and where we are going—serves as a lever for creating the changes necessary to achieve our goals and dreams.

The stories we relate to others create an overview of where we've been in the past and how those events and experiences of the past will propel us forward into the future.[3] Our personal stories define our self-perceptions. If I tell the story about my life as a series of struggles, about how I overcame many obstacles and difficulties to finally triumph, I'm telling others—and myself—that I'm persistent, hardworking, and will get things done. If instead I tell a story about my life that says that I don't complete tasks, that I don't like to work, and that I'm lazy, that story tells other people how I behaved in the past and am likely to behave in the future. So changing the way you tell that story can help you transform your view of yourself and how others think about you.

A Model for Your Story

The task at hand, then, is to develop the story about how your current opportunities will become real through your efforts and the help of others. Creating your story will not only help you think through issues for yourself but also convey to others where you are in the process of transforming your dreams into realities.

Where do you begin your story about your life? Good stories have drama, an element of suspense. They describe how the main character of the story is confronted with challenges and then solves them. Many enterprisers often suggest using the David and Goliath story as the template for their business start-up struggles. We, too, will use this model to outline the basic aspects of what a story should contain.

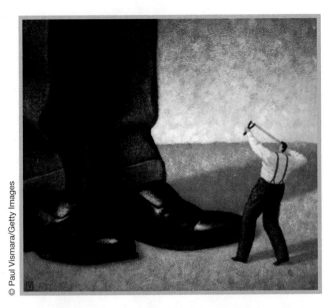

© Paul Vismara/Getty Images

As you'll recall, this story begins with David, the youngest of eight sons of Jesse and a shepherd. David spends most of his days and nights outside the city where his family lives, guarding the sheep from lions and wolves. With these responsibilities, David learns many skills to protect his sheep from harm. One day his father asks David to take food to his brothers, who are soldiers in the army of King Saul that is fighting the Philistines. The Philistines are led by Goliath, a giant who challenges King Saul to send one man to fight him. The outcome of this fight will determine who will win the war. When he arrives at the army camp and hears Goliath making this challenge, David volunteers to fight. Everyone in Saul's army is surprised by the young boy's offer, but no one else volunteers to fight, so David is chosen. Rather than using the heavy armor that most of the soldiers use for fighting, David approaches the giant only with a sling-shot and five stones. The giant is surprised that he will fight a young boy with no armor or weapons and mocks his opponents "Am I a dog that you would come at me with sticks?" In response to Goliath's taunt, David puts a stone in his sling-shot and swings it at Goliath, hits him in the head, and kills him. Goliath's death routs the Philistine army.

The story begins with a protagonist, or main character, and is told in such a way that we can relate to the issues the main character faces. Here we see how a boy can overcome great odds by doing things differently. If David had put on armor and used the kinds of weapons that Goliath was using, David would have surely been killed. By using a sling-shot, something that Goliath did not expect, David won the contest.

Our stories often have similar elements. The main character will face a problem that needs to be solved. In great stories, the main character will solve this problem in an innovative way. Your challenge, then, is to tell your story about developing your business opportunity and the new kinds of problems that you face as you embark on your journey to become an enterpriser.

Developing Your Story

Telling a story about your new path to entrepreneurship is particularly challenging, because you aren't currently at the end of the story. In some respects, you are at the beginning or the middle of the story. You are David, who has just arrived at the camp of Saul's army and realizes that the challenge will be to fight Goliath. Your story will not have an outcome yet, and your challenges may not be specific enough to identify. Yet, you still must talk about your new journey—and how the challenges you've met successfully in the past have prepared you for this undertaking.

For example, Albert Jennings had been a poor student during high school and college, and he had then worked at numerous jobs in various industries. What kind of story could Albert tell that would engage others in his journey to become an enterpriser? First, Albert could talk about his struggles to learn new skills and to explore different jobs and businesses that he thought he might enjoy. He can then talk about what he learned and how these previous struggles have helped him better understand what he wants as an enterpriser. His story can tell of his journey of discovery to realize what he wants to do—rather than focusing on his inability to do well in school and hold a job for any length of time.

Here are five suggestions to develop a story that will help you to become the enterpriser you imagine yourself to be:

1. *Be coherent.* Explain the events and the experiences in your past so that they support your view of what you will become. For example, David could describe how his life as a shepherd taught him how to defend his sheep from lions and wolves. These past incidents would support his view that he could also fight a giant. David has learned fighting skills that he can use now, to meet the current challenges he faces.

2. *Explain your motivations for change and be sure they are consistent with your values and beliefs.* Most stories of enterprisers center on their discovery of what they love and enjoy doing and how they pursued this discovery. Offer consistent reasons to illustrate why these new changes are occurring in your life. For example, you could say, "I discovered in my previous jobs and in my school work that I'm really good at...."

3. *Use your past to help explain what you now want to do.* The more we can point to incidents in our past, the more plausible our story becomes to others. As David can explain, "I may have been a shepherd, but I have had practice fighting lions and wolves, which prepared me to meet the challenge of fighting a giant." We probably will never have the skills and experiences to be fully prepared for many of the challenges confronting us, but we can look to find incidents in our past that have provided some of the requisite capabilities.

4. *Reframe your past experiences to demonstrate how you can meet the new challenges.* While David could tell a story about how skilled he is at tending sheep and guiding them to new areas to graze, he should tell stories that focus on his fighting abilities to convince others of his fighting skills. Look into your past and think about which incidents in your life support your story of becoming an enterpriser.

5. *Begin telling the story of your journey as an enterpriser and get feedback.* The more you tell your story, the more you will learn from others whether your story makes sense to them, and how they, too, might become a part of your journey. We all like to hear stories of success and how people have overcome difficult odds to triumph. Most people would like to help others become successful. As you tell your story, you will learn what additional information others need to know about your past events and experiences and how they support achieving your goals. You'll also discover the skills and abilities you still need to acquire to convince others that you will succeed.

Telling your story is a way to help you to believe in yourself, and for helping others believe in you as well. It goes back to the quote from the beginning of Charles Dickens' *David Copperfield:* "Whether I shall turn out to be the hero of my own life, or whether that station will be held by anybody else, these pages must show." A key challenge, then, in becoming an enterpriser is to tell a story about your life where you are the main character, and that your life is unfolding in a way that you can meet the challenges and problems that are now facing you.

12.3 Facing Your Fears

Frankly, any transition is difficult. When we embark on a new journey, a new effort, we can't be prepared for all of the challenges that might confront us. This is particularly true in the enterprising process. Opportunity recognition,

developing a business model, generating a feasibility study and a business plan—there are so many unknowns that will cause anxiety. We have a vision of where we want to go, we've made plans about how we think we might get there—but we aren't there yet, are we?

Being in "fear and doubt," as Collins and Moore suggest, is really very normal. There are a number of reasons why, at this stage of implementing our dreams, we may have fears and doubts. But we must face those fears and overcome them.

Suppose you fear that you don't have the talents, skills, and abilities to actually achieve your goals and dreams. For example, you might see yourself as the owner of a tour company that offers adventure tours throughout the world, but right now, you may have only been a tour guide, or maybe haven't even gone on a tour! At this early stage, it's hard to know whether you can gain the necessary experience to develop your business. It's one thing to be an expert in the field you've chosen for your enterprise, but in fact most beginning enterprisers are not experts or the best in their fields when they develop their business opportunities. So, you are not alone when you wonder, "Do I have the talent to start this enterprise? Am I good enough?"

A common story about how individuals choose the types of opportunities for their new venture investments goes something like this. If given the choice between investing in an "A" opportunity with a "B" team, or an "A" team with a "B" opportunity, most investors are likely to pick the "A" team with the "B" opportunity. The theory is that investors believe that "A" level enterprisers are more likely to make "B" level opportunities successful. "B" level enterprisers, even with "A" level opportunities, won't have the talents and skills to make their new enterprises work. This story is likely to cause fledgling enterprisers to wonder whether they are "A" level enterprisers. It would be great if before starting out they had ten years of experience in their selected industries, along with all of the connections to investors, suppliers, customers, employees, and advisors. It would be great if they had already started an enterprise in those fields—and even better if those business start-ups succeeded and were exactly like the ones they plan to start.

That is the irony. If you are doing something new, you won't have the experience and knowledge you need to begin your effort. So, it is important to realize that *you begin your journey where you are.* You start with what you have. Whatever talents and skills and knowledge you have, right now, is sufficient for you to begin.

This goes back to Chapter 2, when we talked about "effectual" thinking. The critical task for an enterpriser is *to begin,* to take actions and steps toward enterprising. No situation that you are in is likely to be optimal for developing your opportunity, and you simply will never have all the skills and knowledge you need to pursue your goals and dreams. You may be involved in situations where you are "way over your head" in terms of what you need to be successful. Yet in the reality of enterprising, it's better to take action, to engage in enterprising—even when you might know that you are in over your head—than to not engage in the process at all.

Using a sports analogy: You can't learn to hit the ball in baseball unless you are willing to go to the plate and try. You can practice hitting and simulate the process, but at some point, to play the game you have to go to the plate, face a pitcher, and see whether you can hit the ball. There is no substitute for actually playing the game, and that is how you improve your ability to play. We know that in baseball, not every trip to home plate results in getting a hit. Many times we strike out. But we can't let our fears of whether we are good enough to get a hit prevent us from stepping up to the plate and trying.

We get better at the things we need to do by trying, by practicing. You might not be "good enough" to achieve what you would like, but, if you use your fear that you aren't "good enough" to keep you from trying, then you will never get better.

Many people assume that entrepreneurs have the "right stuff"—and that is what differentiates entrepreneurs from others. Often this belief gets in the way and seems to be an excuse for people to avoid taking action. But is there ever enough "right stuff" for enterprising? We don't think so. There isn't any magic to becoming an enterpriser. We don't need to be more than we are to engage in the activities that enable us to succeed. We all have the "right stuff" necessary for success.

The Great Imposter

Let's say that you are looking to start a business that modifies cars into high performance automobiles. When you spend time with many successful enterprisers in this field, you might fear that you are just pretending that you could be a successful enterpriser in this area. You see what others are doing in your field, and you begin to doubt that you are one of them. Or you want to start a restaurant and you meet a successful restaurateur who has a highly visible restaurant with many favorable reviews in national gourmet and travel magazines. It is humbling to consider that your initial effort at starting a restaurant could put you in the same class. As a result, you might feel like an imposter in the role of an enterpriser.

This feeling arises because you are developing the skills and knowledge necessary to create your enterprise. At the same time, there is much uncertainty about how the process of enterprise creation is going to turn out. Am I really an enterpriser if, at this stage, I'm really a fledgling enterpriser? If I haven't really started a restaurant, am I really a restaurateur?

If you are working at developing an enterprise, you *are* an enterpriser. If you are working to start a restaurant, then you *are* a restaurateur. By doing the work, you become what you are. Going back to our baseball analogy: If you are playing baseball, you are hitting, pitching, and catching. When you are performing those tasks, you aren't pretending—you are playing baseball. So to begin feeling like you are an enterpriser, do the work of an enterpriser. You can't pretend when you are talking with customers, meeting with suppliers, and asking investors for money. Those actions mean that you are an enterpriser.

Expecting Perfection

As an enterpriser, you should have vision of where you want to go and goals for what you want to achieve. Expecting perfection from your efforts can quickly derail your hard work and make you experience the "fear and doubt" we mentioned at the start of this section. Your efforts are probably never going to be perfect in the way you imagine.

Let's say that your enterprise is an event management firm and you will be planning a wedding with 100 guests. While you can imagine the perfect wedding event—perfect cake, perfect flower arrangements, perfectly served food, great tables and chairs, and everything being just right—the odds of that happening are slim to none. Something in the wedding event is likely to go wrong, or turn our differently than expected or planned. For some individuals, the fact that things don't turn out exactly as planned or imagined can be devastating. It can be so disheartening when what you so clearly see in your mind isn't what actually occurs. Some people just give up when they don't achieve what they imagined. They somehow want to have that perfect restaurant, or the perfect bed and breakfast, or the perfect retail store, and they continually disappoint themselves when what they do have doesn't match their vision.

The challenge is to continue to do your work and expect that as you work at being an enterpriser, you will improve over time. If you are doing events, the more events you plan, the better each event is likely to become—even though there may be events along the way that are complete disasters. In many fields, what you might consider a flaw isn't even noticed by the customer. Your expectations might be so much higher than your customer's. While it would be great if our goal was to achieve a "wow" experience for all of our customers, and each time we did something for a customer, they said, "Wow!", but we can still meet our customers' needs without the "wow."

If we seek perfection in everything we do, then, frankly, we probably won't do anything. Most of what we do often won't meet the standards we imagine. Operate using the premise "Anything worth doing is worth doing"—not "Anything worth doing is worth doing well." We strive to do the best we can, but it may not always be "the best."

To combat your fear that your efforts aren't good enough and the outcome of the process isn't perfect, the best thing to do is try. We don't get better at anything unless we undertake the activity. Fearing that your enterprise is not worth doing unless it is perfect is just a recipe for not doing it at all.

How can you identify and defuse your fears, negative beliefs, and self-doubts as you move forward as an enterpriser? Imagine the worst fears and the biggest doubts you have about enterprising. Write them down in the left column of a two-column chart. Then in the right column, answer each with a possible solution or another way of looking at the situation. Exhibit 12.2 shows a sample chart for a hypothetical enterpriser. This exercise is a valuable method to gain insights about what specifically is holding you back and to develop ways to counter these negatives.

Need for Approval

Wouldn't it be great if, before you start, someone who was really knowledgeable about your business gave you a "seal of approval"? Wouldn't it be terrific to have experts in your area tell you that your proposed venture will be a success? On the other hand, how would you feel if that really knowledgeable person told you that your idea was stupid and that you should not do your venture, at all?

While it is nice to get advice from others about the future success or failure of your venture, such input is not always correct or insightful. This is not to say that you should ignore the advice of others, or that you can't gain valuable insights into your business's potential. What you learn from others can be helpful, but it should not be the determining factor of whether or not you pursue your opportunity.

A story about how an actual entrepreneur got into business will help drive this point home. Many years ago, John Morse, an MBA student, approached one of his professors about an idea to start an ice-cream company similar to Ben and Jerry's in the Pacific Northwest. John asked the professor for his advice about whether to pursue this idea or not. The professor recommended looking for another opportunity for the following reason: If a company like Hagen-Das, which makes ice cream in New Jersey, can sell it successfully in the Pacific Northwest, why would there be any competitive advantage to starting an ice-cream company locally?

Based on this advice, John began researching many different business opportunities. After a year, he realized that he had spent 12 months *not* pursuing his dream of starting an ice-cream company. Upon graduating from the MBA program, he took a job as a bartender (so his days would be free), teamed up with his brother, and began looking for dairies in the Pacific Northwest to produce their ice cream. At the same time, they developed

exhibit
12.2

Analyzing Your Fears

Fear/Doubt/Negative Belief	Response
I will be alone a lot as an enterpriser.	I will be involved with many people, including customers, suppliers, friends, and other supportive people.
	I can join a business networking association to make new contacts.
I don't have enough industry knowledge to succeed.	I'm a fast learner.
	I can do research online to acquire more information.
	I can subscribe to a trade journal for my industry.
I have no accounting skills.	I can buy books that will teach me the basics or take a class at the community college.
My business idea is not that good.	I can do a feasibility study that analyzes the market for my idea. With that information I can make an informed decision about how to improve my idea.

recipes for ice creams, contacted local grocery stores to carry their ice creams, and held many in-store samplings to get prospective customers to buy. After 12 dairies turned them down, the 13th said "yes." Their ice-cream company, Fratelli's, became a big success in the Pacific Northwest, and it eventually led to John becoming a frozen desert distributor and a major specialty food distributor. Although his professor had some insights into whether an ice-cream company might or might not work, he couldn't predict whether John could be successful as an ice-cream enterpriser.

The moral of this story is that even highly respected professors of entrepreneurship won't always be right. You will never know whether a particular opportunity will be successful unless you take the effort to find out whether customers will buy your product or service. All opinions, even from experts, are just opinions, not necessarily facts. Perhaps we are less likely to believe in ourselves as we start out, or because our own ideas are not yet as clear or developed as they will be in the end. Rather than give up too easily, we need to be persistent and focus our efforts on discovering, through trial and error, whether our vision for the enterprise is accurate or not.

Don't let advice from others about whether you should go forward with your idea discourage you. No one is likely to be as excited about your idea as you are. You'll always encounter people along the way who will "rain on your parade" and tell you that what you are thinking of doing isn't worth pursuing. Sometimes it is worth taking the next steps to test the advice. Even if the advice is true, the knowledge you've gained can help you modify or change your ideas so that you might be more successful with the revised opportunity.

Be persistent and pursue your ideas. Work at getting beyond other people's opinions. Probe for the specific reasons they believe your idea won't work. Like John Morse, seek evidence to test these opinions. If an advisor says that your opportunity won't work, ask "Why?" Suppose your consultant doesn't think customers would pay the price you have set for your service. Go out and talk to people to learn whether they will become customers and if they are willing to pay for the service at your price point. Treat opinions that people give you about your opportunities as hypotheses: think of other people's judgments about your opportunity as issues that you can test to determine if they are true or not. Opinions are not necessarily facts. Your goal is always to generate evidence. (This is the purpose of doing the feasibility study.)

Exhibit 12.3 provides suggestions for overcoming your fears.

exhibit
12.3

Overcoming Your Fears

- Look for experiences in your life where you have had encouragement. Who offered you compliments along the way? When, and what did people say that you were affirmed for?

- If you think you might be a "great imposter," study how others "play" their roles as enterprisers. As you watch and interview other entrepreneurs, how do they "play" out their role? What kinds of "performances" have you seen other enterprisers play?

- Do you have to be "perfect" in all that you do? Identify what you consider perfection to be for the kind of enterprise that you want. What will it take for you to accomplish this? Can perfection, at this point, be achieved? Probably not. Then, take each part of your perfect enterprise, and ask yourself what you might settle for, today, in terms of what you could achieve. Much as in the strategy of "small wins" in Chapter 3, identify what small achievements you can accomplish now that would move you further down the road to achieving your goals.

- Identify all of the people from whom you seek approval: parents, other family members, friends, teachers, etc. Explore how these individuals support your progress toward achieving your goals. Do they offer positive and supportive insights that help you move forward with your goals, or do some give you negative and critical feedback that makes you feel that you can't move forward at all? While every plan may have problems, the solution to most plans is not inaction or negativity. If you have friends and others around you who are not providing you with support and help, consider whether the time and energy you devote to maintaining these relationships will help you achieve your goals. Instead, find people who want to help you be successful and are supportive when you pursue your dreams.

12.4 The Mind-set for Change

Now let's turn our attention to changing our thinking and our actions. The insights we'll provide in this section will help you take full advantage of the new possibilities that you'll encounter on your journey as enterprisers.[4]

First, it is important to realize that our current situations are "invented." We take for granted the facts of the situation we are in and often don't think very consciously about what those facts are—and whether they are actually true. To underscore this concept, ask yourself this question, which comes from *The Art of Possibility* by Zander and Zander:[5]

What assumption am I making,
That I'm not aware I'm making,
That gives me what I see?

When you have an answer to that question, think about this one:

What might I now invent,
That I haven't yet invented,
That would give me other choices?

What this exercise does is shift the framework of assumptions about your situation and challenge you to speculate about other choices for yourself. For example, what assumptions have you made about the people you've contacted regarding the creation of your enterprise? When you meet people with businesses that might be similar to the one you would like to own, do you think of them as competitors—or as people who might also be colleagues and friends who want you to succeed in developing your dreams?

In the restaurant industry, research shows that many of the founders and owners of restaurants know each other, often have worked for other restaurants, and help each other out. Restaurant owners define their dining business in terms of getting customers to eat more meals out. As the number of restaurants increases, patrons have more choices to eat out rather than at home. Rather than considering that new restaurants mean *less* business for existing restaurants, restaurateurs see them as *expanding* the overall market. What assumptions, then, are you making about your competition? Do you view them as helpful? If you think about your competition in this way, how will you act toward them? Will your behaviors be different than if you thought of your competition in only negative terms?

Not everyone agrees with this approach. In his book *Only the Paranoid Survive,* Andy Grove, former chairman of Intel Corp., suggests that to be competitive we must assume that there is always a competitor out there who is seeking to destroy your business. If you can't identify this competitor, it just means that the competitor is so crafty that you'll be even more surprised and unprepared when this competitor surfaces. Consider the differences between these two views of competition and the way each affects how you would deal with your competitors. Our perceptions color our worldview. What we look for, we find. For example, if we think that the world is full of cheaters, then we tend to see a lot of cheaters—and we are more likely to feel cheated. Awareness of the kind of world we invent, then, can prevent negativism from derailing our efforts.

Next, we can begin to "invent the possible." We tend to think about the limitations of a particular situation as the "givens" of that situation. If we assume that we have a limit on the number of customers, ideas, and resources, then we won't be as open to seeing the many additional options available to us.

During the feasibility and business planning process, we often get stuck analyzing what we see as "already there"—how our customers currently buy products and services, and how our competitors currently meet these customer needs. When we think about the givens and apply the metrics that others use for their success, we often restrict ourselves and fail to consider other ways of being successful.

For example, let's look at the retail industry. For many years, enterprisers focused on selling goods and services to customers in a store. Then they thought of different ways to connect with customers: mail-order catalogues, direct mail, websites, telephone orders, television shopping networks. New businesses arose from these new methods of reaching customers, many of which are now quite large. The bottom line is basic: Things may be one way now—but they don't have to stay that way!

Making Changes

Numerous strategies can help change your mind-set. We'll get you started by describing several approaches, from doing "A" work to living your passion. You can choose the methods that suit you best. Doing these activities can "jumpstart" your thinking about how to pursue your dreams in a new way and give you new ways to think about a situation. When we pursue new opportunities, it's very easy to get stuck in our old ways of thinking, because they are our only frame of reference. These creative approaches will encourage you to think outside the box and prevent falling back on old patterns.

Doing "A" Work

Assume that everyone around you wants to do "A" work. By giving an "A" to people at the outset of your interactions with them, you send a very positive message about your expectations. Doing so enables them to aspire higher and accomplish more. As Zander and Zander explain, "This A is not an expectation to live up to, but a possibility to live into."[6] They suggest performing a simple exercise to reinforce the "A"-work mind-set: Tell yourself and others that you/they will get "A"s for *future* work—but you/they must write a letter *now*, and date it *after* completing the work. The letter begins, "I received an A because…"

Karl Weick describes this kind of writing as the "future perfect" tense.[7] We are writing about a future moment, something that has already been accomplished. If we can project ourselves into the future and then look back on the events of the "past," the actual future, in some respects, is less uncertain or frightening. Because we've already lived it in our imagination, we have less anxiety about acting to create the future. We have some idea of what can happen. Giving one's self and others "A"s helps relax us about whether we have the ability to achieve an "A." We won't have as much anxiety because we can project ourselves into the future and see that we've been able to accomplish what we believed we could. Basically, if you can't see yourself as a winner, it's unlikely that you will become a winner.

You Are the Solution

As we indicated in earlier chapters, opportunities exist because there are individuals (customers) who have problems that need to be solved. Opportunities specify the benefits of solving these problems. When we think of ourselves as part of the solution, we put ourselves in a position to create benefits for others: If I believe that I can make a contribution, I'll think and act in ways to make that contribution. With this strategy, we create a mind-set to take action. If we don't think we will make a difference, we won't take any actions to make a difference, and this negative mind-set becomes a self-fulfilling prophecy.

Lighten Up

An important way to change your mind-set is Zander and Zander's rule number 6: "Don't take yourself so…

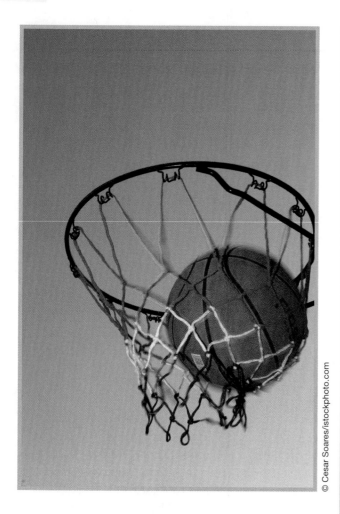

by thinking too much about "what should be," because the "should" is filled with expectations and judgments about our situation. Here are several ways to be in the present:

- Clearing "shoulds"
- Closing the exits: escape, denial, and blame
- Clearing judgments
- Distinguishing physical from conceptual reality

Often our expectations of what we think *should* happen get in the way of actually seeing what *has* happened and what *is* happening. To be open to new possibilities, we need to be aware of the present. One of the things that most people fear is failure. We don't like to admit that things are not working out the way we planned. We don't like it when we make a wrong turn, get lost, are late, make mistakes, or lose money.

Think about a situation where you found it difficult to admit that you were lost even though you didn't have a clue where you were. Because you didn't want to admit that you were lost, you continued in the same direction, and got even more lost! You would only ask for directions if you were lost. People who aren't lost don't ask for directions because they know where they are.

But the first step to finding your way is admitting that you are lost. Once you do that, you stop blaming yourself (well, I got lost because I wasn't paying attention, I didn't get a map beforehand, and so on), and can move ahead to make changes. Basically, we can't change directions in our lives if we don't admit that we might not be on the right path to begin with.

By actually paying attention to what is occurring in the situation, we increase our awareness of the possibilities that might come our way. Suppose you are unhappy that no one you have contacted has been willing to invest in the business. That might be a clue that the business model is incorrect or that others can't see clearly how this business will make money. Perhaps you need to rethink what you are going to do, and why. Or maybe the lesson is that you can develop the enterprise in another way, without investors, and that the business itself might be better operated without outside funding. So rather than blaming the investors who turned you down for not seeing the potential of your opportunity, consider *why* they didn't invest. Pay attention! We can learn to be more mindful and in doing so, open ourselves up to new and different ideas.

seriously."[8] This viewpoint is somewhat similar to the "give yourself an A" lesson. Taking ourselves too seriously increases our anxiety about whether we can control the situation and gets in the way of accomplishing our goals. Once again, a sports example makes this very clear. When you think too much about whether you will make a particular basketball shot, if you get overly anxious about it, you are more likely to miss the basket. When you relax and don't worry as much about the situation, you will probably make the shot.

Being Present

Another way to improve your mind-set is to be in the present. This does not mean resigning yourself to the "things are as they are" mind-set, ignoring negative feelings, or pretending to like something you can't stand. Rather, it means "being present without resistance; being present to what is happening and present to your reactions, no matter how intense." We start from what is, not from what should be.[9] We get stuck

Passion Lights Sparks

Do you believe in what you are doing? When you do, you bring a sense of passion to your tasks. If you don't believe in your future, in your opportunities, you are unlikely to convince others to believe in you, and it becomes very difficult to accomplish what you need to do.

To become passionate, you must first notice where you are holding back—and let go. Then you can participate more fully in the activity you want to do. Suppose the business that you want to start involves consulting with retailers about how to provide their sales staff with a more customer-focused orientation. As we discussed earlier in the chapter, your fears might be stopping you from pitching this idea passionately to retail store owners: "Maybe store owners won't think I have the experience necessary to pay me to improve their customer service. Maybe I'm an imposter and not really a consultant." But in fact, nothing stops you from being passionate about providing this consulting service and having clients pay you for these services. When we authentically communicate to others what we love, other people can see that passion, and they respond to it. When you believe in yourself, others will believe in you, too. If you don't believe in yourself, others can see that hesitancy as well, and they won't get involved, say "yes," or become your customers.

Passion is infectious. When you are passionate about your enterprising activities, you generate sparks so that others see the possibilities and become eager to join you. Passion and excitement breed more of the same, so light a spark within yourself and among your friends and colleagues.

Frameworks for Possibility

New thinking creates frameworks for possibility. As we have mentioned many times throughout this book, the first step in making your dreams real is expressing a vision, which in turn provides real power to achieving that dream. To have a vision is to see something special that is not bounded by time, place, audience, or product. It is not about the right or wrong way to do things but is rather a "long line of possibility."[10] The process of enterprising, then, is more like a journey rather than the actual destination. As you work to see the future of your dreams and to make them real, you become an adventurer taking steps along the way, day to day.

What do you see in your vision of your future enterprise? Can you describe it so that others can see your vision as well? Framing your vision involves several steps, such as seeing your vision in the realm of possibility, distinguishing what is on track from what is off track, and staying focused on what moves you toward your goals.[11] What you can see of your vision now can help you and others move forward. Your vision provides direction, but it is not necessarily the end goal of the process. As you move forward, you see new things on the horizon, and new possibilities will likely be open to you—if you are open to them.

One final note: The fundamental process of enterprising, of identifying and pursuing opportunities, involves other people. The most basic ideas require enterprisers to pay attention to customers (others) to recognize and meet their needs. Enterprising, then, is not just about oneself; it requires that you accomplish something that is of value to someone else. In a broad sense, successful enterprising is more about *we* than about *me*. The story of Muhammad Yunus and Grameen Bank, "Making a World of Difference," offers an excellent example of an enterprise that focuses on the *we* and making a change.

12.5 The Balanced Life

Thinking about actually pursuing your possibilities can be energizing. On the other hand, the scope and depth of all these possibilities can be overwhelming. How can you be successful at filling many roles: enterpriser, spouse, parent, citizen? Can you really have it all when your dreams seem to be bigger than life?

What you are trying to do is to satisfy four different goals: achievement, significance, legacy, and happiness. But you cannot maximize all four. You could probably get what you want—but do you really want what you get? Yes, you could achieve great things in your enterprise, but at what cost? Perhaps your business success would come only at the expense of your personal happiness. For example, many enterprisers run into marital difficulties as they devote more and more hours to growing their businesses. To lead a personally successful life, you must first determine your own priorities.[12] Start by asking some basic questions about your efforts:

- *Achievement: Is this challenging?* Will the goals you intend to accomplish engage all your capabilities? Are you challenged to learn new things,

ENTERPRISING ETHICS

Making a World of Difference

When he began making very small loans for income-generating activities to individuals or groups in his native Bangladesh, Muhammad Yunus did not expect to revolutionize traditional financial norms. His efforts to break the cycle of poverty in rural Bangladesh, however, have had a major impact on the world. In 2006, he and Grameen Bank, which he founded to provide these loans, shared the 2006 Nobel Peace Prize.

After studying in the United States, Yunus returned to Bangladesh to chair the economics department at the University of Chittagong. As he explained in his Nobel Peace Prize acceptance speech, he "found it difficult to teach elegant theories of economics in the university classroom, in the backdrop of a terrible famine in Bangladesh. Suddenly, I felt the emptiness of those theories in the face of crushing hunger and poverty." Observing that unscrupulous lenders took advantage of the poor and charged such exorbitant interest that borrowers couldn't pay off their debts, he saw a way to help.

In 1976, he personally loaned $27 to 42 villagers to pay off their debts. Their joy at his gesture convinced him that these small loans could be good business—and also provide a way to make the villagers self-reliant. He continued making small loans to other villagers for activities such as making crafts or buying farm animals. He required no collateral and charged no interest but instead based the loans on personal trust. All the villagers repaid their loans on time, so Yunus began lending in other villages and then took his program to more districts. Unable to find regular banks that agreed with his belief in the creditworthiness of the poor, he established Grameen Bank in 1983 to expand the program throughout Bangladesh.

Since then Grameen Bank has developed into a profitable and self-financing institution. The largest bank serving the poor, it lends about $800 million each year, in amounts averaging $100 per loan, to 7 million borrowers. By 2006, it had lent close to $6 billion in total, and an astounding 99 percent had been repaid. The depositors own 94 percent of the bank, and the Government of Bangladesh owns the remaining 6 percent. In addition to micro-loans for enterprise, Grameen Bank also provides no-collateral loans for housing and education, along with savings, pension funds, and insurance products. It charges interest of up to 20 percent to cover the high costs of administration for so many small loans.

The principles on which Yunus founded Grameen Bank run counter to traditional banking concepts. It lends funds to poor Bangladeshis based only on "mutual trust, accountability, participation, and creativity." As Yunus explains, "Lend the poor money in amounts which suit them, teach them a few sound financial principles, and they manage on their own."

At the heart of his groundbreaking idea is the idea that micro-credit can break the cycle of poverty and raise living standards by promoting entrepreneurship and recognizing potential. "Poverty is a denial of human rights, and this is not natural," says Yunus. "The current institutional and societal set ups fail to enable people to discover creativity, which remains buried in them. Poverty needs to be addressed by providing bank credit. The poor are denied access to credit and this is a global phenomenon. Two-thirds of the world population is being rejected access to credit by conventional bankers. They are often cited as not creditworthy. It's now time for bankers to turn the wheel and position themselves as people-worthy." With micro-credit, people gain control of their lives and future well-being. Grameen's high repayment rates prove that Yunus' trust was not misplaced.

Yunus also broke with tradition by focusing his attention on women, who account for about 97 percent of Grameen's borrowers. Most banks in developing countries lend only to men. "We found giving loans to women always brought more benefits to the family," he says. Women spend on food and clothes for their families, while men are more likely to spend on themselves. Grameen's loans to women have had a dramatic impact on Bangladesh society. Once they can feed their families, the women send the children to school, creating a better-educated

© Spencer Platt/Getty Images

next generation. Grameen-encouraged this by establishing a scholarship program.

Other bank programs creatively expand the micro-credit concept. For example, Grameen's telephone lady project gave women funds to buy cell phones to sell in their villages. The women gained both a business opportunity and a desirable occupation, and the villagers received access to phone service that was previously not available. Today 300,000 women sell Grameen's phone services to 10 million subscribers. Grameen's Struggling Beggars program provides loans to the poorest Bangladeshis and arranges credit to buy items for resale. The goal is to move them from begging to business activities.

As word of Yunus' success with micro-credit spread, other countries began to follow his lead. Today about 100 nations have micro-credit programs modeled on Grameen. Individuals have also been inspired by Yunus' example to support programs such as Yunus' Grameen Foundation, which provides guarantees to banks for micro-loans. The Michael and Susan Dell Foundation, Google.org, and the Bill and Melinda Gates Foundation are among the charitable organizations to set up microfinance programs.

Others have chosen a different route for their efforts to help the poor. They believe they can fund social impact businesses and also make a profit. Acción International, a network of Latin-American institutions, was one of the first for-profit ventures. Formed in the 1990s, its goal was to commercialize microfinance and gain access to capital markets to raise funds. Today Acción's partners cover the globe and include Bolivia's BancoSol, Mexico's Financiera Compartamos, and Ghana's Ecobank.

Pierre Omidyar, founder of eBay, also believes in microfinance. "It's a self-sustaining, profitable model, which opens the door to reaching large numbers of people who need to be reached by this tool of access to capital," he says. He established the Omidyar Network to foster "individual self-empowerment on a global scale" by commercializing microfinance—a term he prefers over *micro-credit.* (This contrasts with Yunus' primary mission of eliminating poverty.) The network makes for-profit investments and charitable donations. In 2005, he gave $100 million to Tufts University to create the Omidyar-Tufts Microfinance Fund (for international microfinance initiatives). Omidyar's intent is to show other institutional investors that microfinance is a viable investment. As loans are repaid with interest, the funds can be lent to new borrowers. In ten years, he estimates that the $100 million could grow to reach $1 billion. Citigroup also set up a microfinance business division in 2005.

Yunus takes issue with the for-profit model. While he recognizes that these programs also help the poor, he maintains that profit maximization is an inappropriate goal for organizations that make micro-credit loans.

Discussion Questions

1. How did Muhammad Yunus get the idea to start a bank that would lend money to the extremely poor? Do you believe in Yunus' view that poverty can be eliminated through social business initiatives? Why, or why not?

2. What entrepreneurial characteristics does it take to start and grow an enterprise that can affect so many millions of people?

3. What are the kinds of business models that are used to create a sustainable enterprise that loans money to the extremely poor?

4. How does Muhammad Yunus "face his fears" in the creation of Grameen Bank? What could have gone wrong and how might Yunus have dealt with these fears? How does Muhammad Yunus demonstrate a "mind-set for change?"

5. What are the advantages of a "for-profit" business that would make money from lending to the extremely poor? What are the disadvantages? Is making money from lending to the extremely poor as a for-profit business morally right?

6. Robert Annibale, head of Citigroup's microfinance unit, believes that this sector is large enough to support multiple approaches such as for profit initiatives, sustainable programs, and subsidies. Do you agree and why? Why was Citigroup interested in entering the microfinance sphere?

7. Visit the websites of Grameen Bank, http://www.grameen-info.org, and Citigroup's Microfinance unit, http://www.citigroup.com/citigroup/citizen/microfinance/index.htm. Using the sites' resources, including articles by Muhammad Yunus on Grameen's site, summarize the similarities and differences between the banks. Which approach do you support and why?

Sources: Based on Connie Bruck, "Millions for Millions," *New Yorker*, October 30, 2006, pp. 62–73; Riva Froymovich, "Maximizing Microfinance's Cachet," *Investment News*, January 15, 2007, p. 6; Grameen Bank website, http://www.grameen-info.org (February 24, 2007); Professor Ole Danbolt Mjøs, Presentation Speech, Nobel Peace Prize, December 10, 2006, http://www.nobelprize.org; "The Nobel Peace Prize for 2006," press release, October 13, 2006, http://www.nobelprize.org; Michelle Yvonne Szpara, Iftikhar Ahmad, and Patricia Velde Pederson, "Nobel Peace Laureate Muhammad Yunus: A Banker Who Believes Credit Is a Human Right," *Social Education*, January–February 2007, p. 9+; and Muhammad Yunus, Nobel Lecture, Nobel Peace Prize, December 10, 2006, http://www.nobelprize.org.

for example? Success often includes stretching our knowledge, skills, and abilities in new ways. We need to set challenging goals (as we discussed in Chapter 3), and we need to achieve them.

- *Significance: Will this make a difference in the world?* We view our actions as successful when they make a difference to other people. It is important to consider what others care about and to engage in activities that meet others' needs and wants.

- *Legacy: Will this be enduring?* We all want to engage in activities that will have a lasting effect in the world. We want to know that our efforts will have an impact beyond the present moment.

- *Happiness: Is this enjoyable to you?* Many tasks may be valuable to others, challenging to you, and endure into the future. But will engaging in those activities actually make you happy or satisfied? What you are doing may not be enjoyable to you. If not, then you need to ask yourself: Why am I doing this activity if it really doesn't give me much personal satisfaction?

Given that we can't maximize all four goals simultaneously, how can we address all four issues to some degree of satisfaction? Begin by looking at how activities involved with work, family, self, and community might satisfy aspects of those four broad measures of success. For achievement, what challenges have you mastered at work, with your family, for yourself, and for your community? Using a chart like the one in Exhibit 12.4, list activities that made a difference in each of these areas. When you engage in this exercise, you typically discover that you have placed more emphasis on certain areas. This helps you identify what you would like to achieve in each of the four areas of success and in each of the four areas of work, family, self, and community. What would you like to see in each of these areas next week, next month, next year, and in your life? Exhibit 12.4 shows what the charts might look like for a 29-year-old married sales representative at a sporting equipment manufacturer who wants to start a retail sporting goods business. What did your charts reveal?

As you focus on your achievements, you will begin to see overlaps in activities that meet several of these goals. For example, coaching the soccer team fills most of our sales representative's family-related goals. We often get stuck because we look only at one category with one measure of success. We may look for achievement only from our work, rather than seek it in other areas as well, for example in our family time and leisure pursuits. A legacy does not only come from big accomplishments.

A balanced life includes variety and involves many different measures of success across a range of categories. There is no one measure of success, and no one particular area where success can or must be achieved. This broad sense of success offers us a wider sense of who we are and what we can become.

The following lines by German author Johann Wolfgang von Goethe provide an excellent summary of this chapter's concepts. It describes the need to adopt an orientation toward action and realizing our dreams. Such action helps us to shape our environment into a reality that actually supports the development of those dreams. Will you accept its challenge and begin now?

Until one is committed, there is hesitancy,
the chance to draw back, always ineffectiveness.
Concerning all acts of initiative (and creation),
there is one elementary truth the ignorance of which
kills countless ideas and splendid plans:
That the moment one definitely commits oneself,
then providence moves too.
All sorts of things occur to help one that would
never otherwise have occurred.
A whole stream of events issues from the decision,
raising in one's favor all manner of unforeseen
incidents and meetings and material assistance,
which no man could have dreamed would have
come his way.
Whatever you do or dream you can,
Begin,
Boldness has genius, power, and magic in it.
Begin it now.

exhibit
12.4

Achieving Your Goals

Current Activities

Goal	Work	Family	Self	Community
Achievement	Brought in three new customers	Coaching daughter's soccer team		One of the founders of youth soccer program
Significance	Contributed to department's quarterly sales goals	Spend additional time in fun activity		
Legacy		Teaching kids teamwork will help them develop skills		
Happiness	Like meeting new people	Enjoy working with kids		

Commitments to Reach Goals/Timeframe

Goal	Work	Family	Self	Community
Achievement	Attend any classes and workshops offered that add to knowledge of sporting goods industry		Take business classes at university extension program/ start next semester	Join Rotary, Chamber of Commerce, or other organizations to help build contact base/now
Significance			Gain knowledge to use in opening own business	
Legacy				
Happiness	Travel less	Spend more time at home		Make new friends

12.6 ENTERPRISERS

Leading through Values

In 1987, Tom Pace started PaceButler Corporation to buy, refurbish, and resell computers—even though he knew nothing about computers. He had just left a short stint at a similar company because he disagreed with management's ethical practices, or lack thereof. "I don't always have to reinvent the wheel," he explains. "Someone else has already invented the wheel. I just took it under my own wing and took action from there.... I saw a business model that I thought would really work. I got a legal pad and I wrote out a business plan. That was it."

With $62.53 in his bank account, courage, and integrity, he set out to build his company. Banks would not loan him money, so he scraped together $11,000 in seed capital from private sources to fund his start-up.

The first few years were tough. "In 1990, the atmosphere at our company was terrible," Pace says.

"We were on the edge of bankruptcy. That's what happens when you create a company with no knowledge and no capital and the business is changing fast. Nobody wanted to work there. Everybody was dissatisfied. I was dissatisfied. I wanted to give up."

Pace brought in Louis Gandra, a business consultant, to help refocus his efforts. They worked together to make sure that people and their skills matched their positions. Many were in the wrong jobs. "We reorganized from top to bottom," says Pace. "Secretaries became sales people. Some people left."

Gandra encouraged Pace to ask his employees to write an "atmosphere statement" that describes what people experience when they come into the company. The statement his employees prepared in 1990 is still in place today and emphasizes providing "a positive, successful, and healthy atmosphere" that motivates "by enthusiasm, knowledge, and skill" in "an atmosphere that nurtures confidence, love, and power—a climate that produces creative ideas and plans that allow us to easily reach our objectives, goals, and values." Through this value system, employees can accomplish and achieve "excellence in all areas of our lives.... We have an abundance of finances, health, relationships, and family life. We speak the language of faith."

With that values orientation in place, Pace wrote a mission statement, company values, and company goals. The mission statement focuses on quality and customer service: "PaceButler Corporation contributes to the local and worldwide community by providing top quality products and service. We are dedicated to customer satisfaction through constant improvement of systems and procedures. When our customers profit, we profit, resulting in a win/win situation."

With these employee-centric foundations in place, Pace was ready to move forward. By 1992, PaceButler had grown to 30 employees and had sales of $3.5 million. In 1999, the company received the Oklahoma Quality Award and Tom Pace won the model CEO award from the Council of Growing Companies. The company's growth continued, and by 2002 Pace/Butler had 65 employees, a national client base, and sales of $22 million.

Not bad for a kid who got lousy grades and who didn't graduate from college. What Pace had, however, was a belief in himself that came after many difficult years. "I've had over 30 jobs. A friend of mine said, 'No wonder you had to start your own business.' I said, 'Why?' He said, 'No one would hire you with that kind of background.'"

Pace has a commitment to his employees and nurturing their success. "We're all capable of success if we choose to be successful and if we have the right knowledge," Pace says. "The more we use our resources, the stronger the resources get."

Today Pace asks any job applicant who considers coming to work at PaceButler to review the atmosphere statement, mission statement, values, and goals. The idea is to see how close the alignment is between the person and the company principles. If the alignment isn't there, PaceButler is probably not going to be a good fit for that person.

Encouraging positive attitudes, being receptive to new ideas, and remaining passionate about his business has helped PaceButler survive. Pace also recognizes the relationship between success and taking action. In 2002, Pace added a new line of business, purchasing and refurbishing old cell phones, to his major one of selling used business technology systems worldwide. Because Pace expects the best from his employees, he often gets it. "In a corporate society, we need to raise the level of mutual trust and respect. Success breeds success.... It's very, very important to be around other people who share the same values and the same goals and that we can reinforce one another.... It's very easy to say, 'It's not going to work out,' and to give up."

Early in 2003, however, he came close to giving up. Pace had to lay off 55 workers—85 percent of his staff—because of a major computer problem. Pace took full responsibility for the technical glitches, citing "bad business decisions that Tom Pace made in regards to accounting software, which led to the problem of inventory control and cash management," he explained. Instead of welcoming employees to work, he helped them find new jobs. He sold the company's office building and cut back operations to focus on cell phones. Today the company is still in business, with its values intact.

Discussion Questions

1. How did values drive the building and structuring of Tom Pace's business?

2. What values were important to Tom Pace in turning the company around in 1990? Were they congruent with his actions then and in later years? Explain your answer.

3. Tom Pace has asked for your help in telling his story. Make suggestions of how he should frame his life and business experiences.

4. What characteristics of entrepreneurial success does Pace exhibit? Cite examples from the case that relate to the chapter material.

Sources: Adapted with permission from the video "Leading through Values," Small Business School, the series on PBS, and at http://SmallBusinessSchool.com; Elizabeth Camacho, "Edmond, Okla., Computer Resale Firm Forced to Lay Off 55 Due to Software Error," *Daily Oklahoman*, January 29, 2003, http://www.dailyoklahoman.com; Sonya Colberg, "Bottomed-Out Businessman Nearer Top—Owner's Successful Present Imitates No Past Lessons," *Daily Oklahoman*, October 14, 2001, http://www.pacebutler.com (November 25, 2005); Jon Denton, "Used Computer Dealer Thrives," *Daily Oklahoman*, October 3, 1996, http://www.pacebutler.com (November 25, 2005); and Paula Burkes Erickson, "Oklahoma City-Area Companies Escape Perils of Hard Times," *Daily Oklahoman*, November 28, 2003, http://www.dailyoklahoman.com.

Summary

1. After identifying many different business opportunities, enterprisers must reevaluate their goals. Making the transition from dreams to reality can be difficult. It requires a shift in focus. Not only must enterprisers take action, they must also take into account their values: not just the *how,* but also the *why.* Their actions and commitments—choices that bind them to a future course of action—should be congruent with these goals and values. It's important not to underestimate the many commitments enterprisers make when developing a new venture.

2. To pinpoint your goals and values, take the time to make written lists and charts of what is important to you. Once you have a picture of what is important to you, look at the commitments that relate to each item. You'll quickly see whether your commitments are congruent with your goals and values. If not, analyze the gaps and make changes that bring the two closer together and eliminate mismatches. Before taking on new commitments, cut back on others that are not in line with your goals and values.

3. A critical step in becoming a successful enterpriser is picturing yourself in such a role. Your personal story and how you tell it play an important role in how you perceive yourself. Recasting your story to focus on how you will develop your business opportunity and the steps you'll take to overcome any obstacles will highlight the characteristics that contribute to your future success.

4. Telling the story of your entrepreneurial success is difficult because you are still in the middle of the plot. Imagine yourself having succeeded and tell a story that supports your accomplishments. The story should be a coherent description of how and why you will create your business that emphasizes how your past experiences contribute to your ability to reach your business goals.

5. Tell your entrepreneurial story to others and ask for feedback. This will help you revise and fine-tune it—and at the same time build your network of contacts. The story development process will also help you believe in yourself more strongly and enhance your confidence.

6. It's normal to wonder whether you have the ability to develop your business opportunity and to fear that you lack the requisite skills to make it happen. No one ever has all the skills and knowledge at hand when they start a business. Don't let your fears stop you from acting like an enterpriser. Unless you take the first steps and try, you will never be able to improve.

7. By working at developing an enterprise, you become an enterpriser. Accept that you will have to overcome your fears and doubts, and avoid placing unrealistic expectations on yourself. Rather than seeking perfection, focus on meeting customers' needs and look for signs of improvement as you work at being an enterpriser.

8. Advice from others, especially if they have experience in your field, can be helpful. But even the experts can be wrong, so take the time to ask questions, evaluate the advice, and do your own research and feasibility analysis. Your persistence in generating evidence will pay off.

9. Shift your focus from the limitations of a particular situation to the possibilities it presents. Don't let a restrictive mind-set and assumptions that may no longer hold true hinder your future success. Instead of getting bogged down in old ways of thinking, look for ways to "invent the possible." Change can be good! When you expect the best from those around you, they are likely to accomplish more. Believing in your ability to solve problems and not worrying about a situation will help you take actions

with positive results. Don't get stuck in the "what should be" mentality, which just gets in the way of being receptive to new possibilities. Finally, believe in what you are doing and let your passion show. Use your vision of a successful enterprise as a framework for moving forward.

10. One of the challenges of being an enterpriser is trying to satisfy four different goals: achievement, significance, legacy, and happiness. It's impossible to maximize all four at the same time. You should set priorities and seek success in many arenas: work, family, self, and community.

Review Questions

1. What are some of the barriers that make it difficult for enterprisers to turn dreams into reality?

2. Why should enterprisers focus on goals and values as they prepare to start their new ventures?

3. Discuss the importance of achieving congruence between actions and goals. Choose one of your goals and give examples of actions that reflect the goal and some that are out of step with the goal.

4. What are commitments, and why should commitments also match your goals and priorities in life? How can you take steps to eliminate mismatches?

5. What elements in the David and Goliath story make it a good model to use in developing your own story? How can a well-scripted story help you reframe how you see yourself?

6. Describe five ways to develop a strong story that will contribute to your entrepreneurial success.

7. How do fears hold us back from taking action? What can you do to change your thinking so that you overcome fears and doubts?

8. What are the advantages and disadvantages of seeking the opinions of experts in your chosen field? How should you use the information you gather?

9. Compare Zander and Zander's approach to assumptions with Grove's. With which do you agree and why?

10. Describe several ways to develop a positive mind-set. Give a specific example of how you would apply one of these methods.

11. Define the four principal goals that contribute to living a personally successful life. Which are most important to you now, and how are you satisfying them? What changes can you make in your life to achieve more satisfaction in one area?

Applying What You've Learned

1. How much personal time and energy does it take to start and manage your own enterprise? Develop a chart that lists your current activities including school, work, family, and personal interests, and how much time you allocate to them. Review your chart and determine how much time will you have each week to devote to enterprising.

2. Now create a similar chart that identifies the specific tasks you'll need to undertake to take the first steps toward developing your enterprise. Include time estimates for these tasks that show how much time you'll need to spend each week and also the overall time frame. For example, you may wish to dedicate three to five hours a week to interviewing enterprisers and spend two months on this phase of the project.

3. Using the charts you created in Exercises 1 and 2, compare the free time you identified in Exercise 1

with the time you'll need for your enterprising activities. Do you have enough time to begin? If not, what changes can you make to free up time for business development?

4. Identify enterprisers that have the kind of life that you would like to emulate. Ask if you can spend a day "shadowing" two of these people to identify what activities they engage in throughout the day. How much of their time is devoted to aspects of their enterprise? What activities fill the day—for example, meetings with employees, suppliers, customers; administrative and operational matters; solving enterprise problems; talking on the phone; answering e-mails? How much time do these individuals have for their families, friends, and other activities? What are the major commitments that you see these enterprisers have made?

5. Interview the same two enterprisers you chose in Exercise 4 or different ones to learn experiences leading up to and during the development of their enterprises. Prepare summaries of their stories that include the five elements listed on pages 303–304 to help refine their stories. Are there common elements among these stories? What lessons do you see from these stories that can help you write your own?

6. Write a hypothetical story about a successful enterpriser who started the type of business you are most interested in developing. How closely can you match your story to your ideal?

7. Which of the different types of fears mentioned in the chapter—being a great imposter, expecting perfection, needing approval—apply to you? Create a chart like the sample in Exhibit 12.2, being as specific as possible about your self-doubts as they relate to your chosen business venture. Consider why and where these fears came from. Review it often to remind yourself of your talents to take action.

8. An important part of working on your fears is having the imagination to see yourself in a different way. Affirmations that describe who you will be can help you change your mind-set. For example, if your goal is to be a successful restaurateur, write out ten times: "I am a successful restaurateur!" and say this to yourself several times a day. Write out five affirmations that support your business goals that you will say to yourself each day for the next month.

9. Identify all of the areas in your life where you feel stuck, where you think you can't make any changes. What do you believe about these situations that makes you feel you are stuck? Imagine what it would be like if you were "unstuck." What about each of these situations has changed in your "unstuck" world? What would you now have to do to live in the "unstuck" world?

10. Imagine yourself five years from today. Now, look back and write out the story of the achievement of your goals and accomplishments during that time. What happened to you along the way? Write out your story as specifically as possible. Now consider using this story as your game plan for the next five years. You might also consider writing out your life story. Think of yourself 20 years from today. Now, look back and write out that story!

11. Write down all of the ways that you might be the solution to someone else's problems and issues. Consider whether your being the solution to any of these situations might be the genesis for the development of your enterprise.

12. Identify all of the "shoulds" that you believe must happen in your life. Where do these "shoulds" come from? Are these "shoulds" that you believe are important, or are these "shoulds" other people have told you are important? Now, identify what "is" happening in your life. What aspects of your life are you happy with? What aspects of your life are you not? Compare the "shoulds" to the "is." How different are they?

Enterprisers on the Web

1. Need help setting goals? Go to TopAchievement. com, http://www.topachievement.com, and click on "7 Steps to Powerful Goals." Read the article and use it to create personal goals in the six areas listed in point 3. While still at TopAchievement.com, click on "Goal Setting Articles" and select three to read. How did they expand your knowledge of goal setting?

2. The Life Work Transitions website, http://lifeworktransitions.com, is another site with good exercises that will help you identify and refine your goals. Start at the Exercises page, http://lifeworktransitions.com/exercises/exercs.html, and do the three exercises for Chapter 4, Goal Setting. Did you come up with different goals than you did in Exercise 1?

3. The Life Work Transitions website, http://lifeworktransitions.com, also has activities that will help you tell your story. From the Exercises page, http://lifeworktransitions.com/exercises/exercs.html, do the Accomplishments Inventory to help you summarize your achievements and Guidelines for Your Spiritual Autobiography, which deals with values. What did these exercises reveal?

4. How committed are you to achieving your goals? Find out by taking the Perseverance Quotient quiz at TopAchievement.com, http://www.topachievement.com/persevere.html. What did you learn about yourself?

5. What are your values? Using a search engine like Google, Dogpile, Yahoo!, or Lycos, find two sites

with questionnaires you can fill out. Then list your three top values. Break up into small groups to discuss your findings with classmates.

6. How satisfied are you with your life, and what would it take to make yourself happier? Explore the resources and questionnaires at the Authentic Happiness site, http://www.authentichappiness. com, to learn how to take a more positive approach to life. (You'll have to register to use the questionnaires; it's free.) What suggestions would be most useful to you?

End Notes

1. O. F. Collins and D. G. Moore. *The Enterprising Man* (East Lansing, MI: MSU Business Studies, Michigan State University, 1964), p. 160.

2. This section is based on material in Donal N. Sull and Dominic Houlder, "Do Your Commitments Match Your Convictions?" *Harvard Business Review,* January 2005, pp. 82–91.

3. This section is adapted from Herminia Ibarra and Kent Lineback, "What's Your Story?" *Harvard Business Review,* January 2005, pp. 65–71.

4. This section is based on R. S. Zander and B. Zander, *The Art of Possibility* (Boston, MA: Harvard Business School Press, 2000).

5. Ibid., p. 15.

6. Ibid., p. 26.

7. Karl E. Weick. *The Social Psychology of Organizing,* 2nd ed. (New York: Random House, 1979).

8. Zander and Zander, *The Art of Possibility,* p. 79.

9. Ibid., pp. 100, 103.

10. Ibid., p. 170.

11. Ibid., p. 163.

12. Adapted from material in Laura Nash and Howard Stevenson, "Success that Lasts," *Harvard Business Review,* February 2004, pp. 102–109.

Progress, Growth, and Transformation

chapters

Branding and Marketing: Refining and Telling the Enterprise's Story

KEY CONCEPTS

1. The best way to differentiate your enterprise from others is to be authentic and original, focusing on what you do best. Branding is a way to establish your firm's uniqueness and shape the way other people view the enterprise. Your personal identity is the foundation on which you will build your brand. Developing and telling your enterprise's story is an effective way to explore the many facets of the organization's identity and what makes it unique. This story tells others what your company stands for, conveys its values, and demonstrates your passion for it.

2. Four key components of the branding process are brand identity, brand meaning, brand responses, and brand relationships. By creating your enterprise's brand, you engage others' senses, feelings, and thoughts. Once you have created a brand, positioning it through selection of target markets will help you further define its uniqueness. An enterpriser's personal brand serves as the foundation for the company's brand. Emphasizing the personal characteristics of the brand will help you build strong bonds with your customers.

3. Promotion provides a way to inform people about your enterprise. Through promotion, you can change consumer perceptions and encourage them to buy your products and services. Promotion also builds customer loyalty by increasing awareness of your business. The four major avenues to promote your enterprise are public relations, advertising, sales promotion, and personal selling.

Suppose you believe that clothes define who we are, representing personal expression and individuality. You translate that vision into a clothing line that is sophisticated yet ageless and also easy to wear. You are committed to American business and produce all your garments in New York, rather than outsourcing to overseas manufacturers.

American fashion designer Nicole Miller created the company that bears her name around these concepts. As you'll learn in this chapter's case, she is intimately involved in all phases of her company, designing her retail boutiques as well as the clothes, accessories, home furnishings, and cosmetics lines. Everything she does reflects her personal aesthetic and original flair. As you read the chapter, you'll discover how you, like Miller, can use branding to differentiate your enterprise.

13.0 Creating a Unique Enterprise

With this chapter, we shift away from issues of how the enterpriser creates an enterprise to issues about the enterprise itself. The next six chapters will focus on the progress and growth of an ongoing business.

In this chapter, we will begin to answer a very important question: How can your enterprise be unique in a way that it provides value, both for the customer (satisfying needs) and you (operating profitably)? One of the key issues in newer and smaller firms is *differentiation*. Creating a firm that will be different or unique from rival companies is the primary way a small firm can compete against other enterprisers. These differences are what will attract customers to purchase your goods and services.

The idea that customers perceive your enterprise as unique is what we will call the **strategy of authenticity**. As we have seen in earlier chapters on developing your enterprise, every business has a strategy—a way of doing business that enhances its chances of success. We believe that the most fundamental way to identify an enterprise's strategy is by focusing on the core values of the enterpriser and the business. Authenticity means being original, not a counterfeit, not a copy or duplicate of something or someone else. The best way to be original, as an enterpriser, is to be yourself: focus on what you do best and what expresses who you are.

Stories about you and your enterprise are the primary way to express the authenticity of your enterprise. These stories tell others why you and your business are unique and different from others.

The Marketing Concept

Throughout this book, we have discussed the importance of creating an enterprise that identifies customer needs, produces the goods or services that satisfy those needs, and in doing so makes a profit. This basic premise—focusing on customers, not products—is called the **marketing concept** and is at the heart of most successful businesses. Recently, companies have taken the marketing concept even further and focused even more strongly on customer satisfaction through

relationship marketing, or building long-term relationships with their customers.

When people talk about the process of marketing, they typically talk about the **marketing mix,** the unique combination of product, promotion, price, and place (distribution) strategies that create value for your customers. These four Ps of marketing help to determine how and why people are willing to be involved in exchanges with your enterprise:

- *Products* can be goods (physical objects)—a toaster, computer, house, or airplane—or services such as tax advice, career counseling, a stay at a hotel, a baseball game, or watching a movie.

- *Promotion* deals with all the ways that your enterprise will communicate to prospective and actual buyers about your enterprise and how you will engage them in exchanges. Promotion's purpose in marketing is to "tell." You want people to be aware of your enterprise so that they will buy your products and services.

- *Place* refers to the distribution of your enterprise's products/services. By distribution, we refer to the various ways that your customers will have access to your enterprise's products/services through marketing channels. In a subsequent chapter, we will cover the specifics of the supply chain, which is a way to think about the various links between those entities that supply you with the raw materials for your products/services and the final user. We will also look at various places that you can engage in exchanges with your customers, such as retail stores, through the Internet, by phone, through the mail, or at their homes.

- *Price* involves considering what both parties, you and your customers, will give up in order to be involved in an exchange. Typically, we think about the amount of money that a customer will give a business to purchase goods or services. You can also consider the amount of time that a customer must invest to complete a purchase as a part of the price of the product as well. For example, some people will consider the time and cost of driving to a retail store as part of the price of purchasing a product compared to buying that product on the Web, where this transaction might be faster and where the product might be delivered to one's door. However, they will have to wait for the product to be delivered. Determining a price involves all costs to you, as an enterpriser, to provide a product or service, as well as all

---

Strategy of authenticity   The idea that your enterprise is perceived as unique from other businesses.

Marketing concept   Identifying customer needs, producing goods or services to meet those needs, and making a profit while doing so.

Relationship marketing   Building long-term relationships with your customers.

Marketing mix   Unique combination of product, price, promotion, and place (distribution) strategies that results in value for customers.

the benefits that a customer might receive from acquiring this product or service. We will cover more about pricing in the next chapter.

The next two chapters examine marketing issues enterprisers face. This chapter looks at two important aspects of the marketing process:

- Discovering and identifying your story and the characteristics of your enterprise that differentiate it from other businesses.

- Telling your story to grab the attention of potential customers and increasing their willingness to purchase products or services from your enterprise.

The first stage of this effort is called branding. A **brand** comprises all of the ways that others see that you and your business are unique, different, and above all, special. As we mentioned earlier, the primary way your enterprise is likely to be successful is through differentiation. If customers don't perceive your enterprise as unique, you will find yourself competing on price alone—a very difficult way for most enterprises to succeed. Invariably, there will be a competitor who can offer a lower price. With lower prices come lower—or no—profits. We will show you how to not get into the lower-price trap.

The second stage of marketing, telling, is about **promotion**: communicating with others about your enterprise. You want people to be aware of your enterprise so that they will buy your products and services. Promotion involves four major areas: public relations, advertising, sales promotion, and personal selling. We'll cover the first three in this chapter and discuss the selling process in Chapter 14. Chapter 14 focuses on the third and fourth stages in the marketing process:

- Acquiring customers

- Keeping customers loyal to your company

Acquiring customers involves selling, place (distribution), and pricing. Once customers have indicated a willingness to purchase, we can look at how to engage them in completing the purchase process, or selling. We must have a way to deliver the products, at a fair price. The fourth stage of the marketing process focuses on service, which looks at how to build and maintain relationships with your customers over time—your **customer management system (CMS)**. In general, it is easier, cheaper, and more profitable to continue to sell to existing customers than to devote time and energy to finding new customers. A customer management system can help

your enterprise determine which customers you can serve better by selling them more products and services, as well as identifying those customers with whom you might not want to continue having a relationship.

It is important to note that the marketing strategies you will learn in these chapters will not help an enterprise that offers products or services that customers don't want to buy. Strategies for branding and marketing can't overcome poorly made products, shoddy service, poor quality, or other deficiencies. This section's chapters assume that you have done your homework and created an enterprise that exploits an opportunity to provide real value to customers. The challenge for your new enterprise is to establish a solid customer base and work through the operational aspects of your enterprise. The result will be a growing, profitable, and sustainable enterprise.

13.1 What Is a Brand and Why Is It Useful?

One of the key issues facing the progress and growth of any enterprise is the development of the enterprise's brand. By brand, we mean how other people—customers, suppliers, investors, and other stakeholders—perceive the enterprise. From our perspective, the enterprise's brand is the enterprise's identity. Branding refers to how an enterprise displays its identity and differentiates itself from other companies.

This chapter will explore how enterprises identify and develop their distinct identities and then create brand elements that represent those identities. You can think about the branding process much like the identity of people in certain occupations. When you think of a chef, policeman, doctor, or lawyer, you have a sense of how people in these occupations look and behave. For example, when we think of a policeman, we are likely to

---

Brand   The enterprise's identity; how customers, suppliers, investors, and other stakeholders perceive the enterprise.

Promotion   Communicating with others about your enterprise.

Customer management system (CMS)   Building and maintaining relationships with your customers over time.

picture someone who wears a uniform that is probably blue, black shoes, a badge, and a belt with all kinds of equipment on it, such as a gun, radio, and handcuffs. Saying the word "policeman" brings to mind an image of what this person looks like and what this person will do. What might happen if a policeman didn't look that way? How would we respond, and how would we know that this person is in fact a policeman, without the look and behaviors of a policeman?

Branding operates the same way. A brand conveys what your enterprise is about and helps others make sense of what you are and what you do. For example, a brand can help a customer identify you as the source of a particular product or service, articulate your promises as to what a product/service will do, provide a way to reduce the risk of purchase, and indicate quality.

For example, consider these well-known slogans and their brands:

- "Think Blue": IBM uses the color blue on nearly all its advertising, as part of its brand image.

- Golden Arches: They symbolize McDonalds, worldwide.

- "Nothing runs like a Deere": The equipment manufacturer John Deere uses the slogan to suggest to customers that John Deere products will be reliable and not break down.

- "Good to the last drop": Proctor & Gamble's Maxwell House coffee brand suggests that this coffee will always taste great.

- "Tastes great, less filling": This phrase brings to mind Miller Lite.

Branding also conveys quality. We may purchase certain branded items because we believe we will reduce the risk of making a bad purchase. We believe Sunkist oranges will taste sweeter and have more juice than unbranded oranges, and we may buy products like Bayer aspirin because we believe that the quality of this aspirin is better than that of a generic brand. Exhibit 13.1 summarizes the reasons that having a brand is useful for an enterprise.

What Can You Brand?

Basically, nearly anything can be branded so that it has an identity that is distinct from others. Certain types of meat and produce have brands, as do services and organizations. Brands can even be created around people. Here are some examples of well-known brands:

---

exhibit
13.1

Why Have a Brand?

Distinguishes company and products

Improves perceptions of product performance

Facilitates new product sales

Encourages repeat sales and creates loyalty

Makes company less vulnerable to competitive marketing actions

Results in larger margins

Creates more inelastic consumer response to price increases

Provides more elastic consumer response to price decreases

Enhances trade cooperation and support

Increases marketing communication effectiveness

Offers possible licensing opportunities

Generates additional brand extension opportunities

Source: Adapted from Kevin Lane Keller, *Strategic Brand Management*, 2nd ed. (Englewood Cliffs, NJ: Prentice-Hall, 2003), p. 60. Reprinted by permission of Pearson Education, Inc., Upper Saddle River, NJ.

- *Products:* chicken—Perdue, Tyson; bananas—Chiquita, Dole; aspirin—Bayer; soap—Ivory, Dial; flour—Gold Medal, Pillsbury; beer—Budweiser; computer chips—Intel; earth-moving equipment—Caterpillar

- *Services:* banking—Bank of America, Wells Fargo; accounting—PriceWaterhouseCoopers; package delivery—UPS, Federal Express; credit cards—MasterCard, VISA; insurance—Prudential, State Farm

- *Retailing:* Wal-Mart, Target, Best Buy, Sears, Amazon.com

- *People:* Martha Stewart, Donald Trump, Oprah Winfrey, Ralph Lauren, Calvin Kline

- *Organizations:* American Red Cross, Sierra Club, UNICEF, World Wildlife Fund

- *Companies:* American Express, Disney, Ford, General Electric, Hewlett-Packard, Microsoft, Nokia

13.2 Your Story Is Your Identity

Creating an identity for an enterprise is very similar to exploring your own identity as an enterpriser, which we did in Chapter 12. Once again, we can use storytelling to develop and promote an enterprise's brand.

Basically, storytelling serves as the means for creating a brand. Part of what a brand communicates is a set of values about the enterprise. Brands also make an emotional connection to the customer. This emotional connection is critical because many of the choices we make as customers are often based on emotions rather than on purely rational or economic reasons. For example, we may shop at a local hardware store because we know the owner, who greets us by name and knows about our family. We buy from this hardware store because we have an emotional connection and a feeling of loyalty to the local hardware store owner—not because it's cheaper or the quality of the products is any better than the big box hardware store.

The Story's Elements

A story has four elements: the message, the conflict, the characters, and the plot. Every story has a message, an idea that is conveyed. Think about some popular children's fables. In the tortoise and the hare, the message is "slow but sure wins the race." In the ant and the grasshopper, "work hard and save to face hard times ahead." Likewise, one of the key issues in developing a brand's story is to stick with one message.

Each chapter in this book has a case that tells a story about the founders of a business and how they built an enterprise. These stories reflect the development of a brand for each enterprise. For example, Chapter 1's story of Wahoo's Fish Tacos is about three brothers who are surfers, grew up in the restaurant business, and wanted to maintain the same kind of surfing lifestyle in the restaurant they started. Wahoo's Fish Tacos is about developing a surfing brand, a surfing lifestyle and surfing food—and it all begins with the story of Wahoo's founders and their values. Wahoo's has a simple message: surfing food. You can see similar story lines in all the cases.

All great stories have some kind of *conflict*. In stories about enterprises, there is usually some struggle to maintain or attain the core values of the enterprisers. In the story of Debbie Fields, who created Mrs. Field's baked-in-the-store cookies, the conflict is whether people would pay more money for a freshly baked soft cookie, rather than the packaged hard cookies sold in grocery stores. Could she overcome the odds of doing things differently? Basically, people like stories where the hero is in a situation where the odds look difficult yet the hero is able to triumph—like the story of David and Goliath in Chapter 12. Every start-up story has, embedded in it, a story of overcoming difficult odds.

Stories also have *characters* with whom we need to identify. So we need to develop a story that tells others about our heroes, the owners of the enterprise (typically the founders), and provides details about them that make them likeable. We like to see these heroes face adversaries and overcome them. Let's take the local hardware store owner, whose adversary might be Home Depot, the large big box "faceless" retailer that doesn't know its customers personally and is trying to drive local hardware stores out of business. How can our hero compete against such difficult odds? By providing really personal customer service. At B and B Hardware in Los Angeles, a local hardware store that is less than two miles from a Home Depot, a customer service person usually greets you at the door, and walks with you through the aisles of the store to help you find the products you need to solve your household fix-it problems. You don't have to wander around, looking for help, like you often do at Home Depot. Loyal customers praise its great service and selection: "They have just as many people to help you in about 1/10th the space of the giant big box stores. I don't think I've ever gone there looking for something that they didn't have" and "It attracts a huge, loyal, local crowd, but it's still worth it. The prices are cheap and the staff is knowledgeable and helpful. I have always found what I'm looking for and then some."[1] So as we hear the story of B and B Hardware's struggle (the conflict) against an adversary (the home improvement chain store), we identify with the business owner and cheer for the happy ending.

The *plot* is the progression of events in a story that gives a story its drama and enables a reader to care about how the story is resolved. Many companies have key stories that they tell that involve these key elements of message, conflict, characters, and some sequence of events—the plot. Take, for example, stories that are told at Nordstrom, about how a customer comes into a store who has just had all his luggage lost, and, has a big meeting the next day, and the salesperson marshals all of Nordstrom's help to get a suit purchased, have it fitted and tailored, and then goes to the customer's hotel to deliver the suit, shirts, ties, and shoes in time for the big meeting. The message is that Nordstrom's will go out of its way to meet customer needs. The details of the story are the plot line: There is a big issue to resolve, and our heroes are able to solve the problem in time.

Nearly all of the important brands have a story that conveys a key message about the company. Bill Bowerman, a track coach, founded Nike because he wanted his athletes to have the best track shoes for running. He thought he could make a lighter shoe with better cushioning than what was then on the market. One day, while watching his wife make waffles, he realized he could use the waffle iron to make the soles of a track shoe that could be both strong and flexible. His first shoe was based on his experiments using a waffle iron.

© Keith Bedford/Reuters/Landov Media

It sends us the message that Nike is focused on making innovative equipment for athletes—even if the approach seems somewhat radical.

Every company needs a core story about the company and what it stands for. A core story answers: Why? The classic story of "why" is the bricklayer story. A man saw three men laying bricks. He came to the first one and asked what the bricklayer was doing, and he didn't know. He came to the second one and asked, and the bricklayer said he was building a wall. When the third one, who looked very busy, was asked, he responded, "I'm building a cathedral." Which bricklayer is more likely to care about what he is doing? Whom do we want working for us? The third bricklayer has a story to tell about why he is working. A story about our enterprise can really convey the passion for it—not only for our employees, but also to customers.

Developing Your Core Story

Just as a good story has multiple elements, developing that story is a multistep process:

1. **Pass the obituary test:** What would your company's obituary say? Would your enterprise be missed? What would your customers say? What would your competitors say? If your enterprise closed tomorrow, who would care? Why? What kind of difference has this enterprise made in the world?

2. **Screen the basic data:** This step has two parts: identifying the internal characteristics of the enterprise and identifying the image the enterprise projects to the outside world. What would you collect? For internal data, you would identify the company's vision, mission, and values. You would identify the important milestones the enterprise has achieved. And you would collect stories that you and others around you tell, about how the company was founded, how it has been successful, and how it has overcome difficulties along the way. You would also consider why the enterprise is a special place to work. For external data, you would collect information about where you see the market going. What are others doing? You would collect stories from your customers and competitors about your enterprise. What do they say about you?

3. **Distill the basic data:** Taking both the internal characteristics and the external images, what, essentially, is the enterprise's message? What are its core values? Do people on the inside tell the same kinds of stories and convey the same kinds of value that your customers and competitors see and say? The stories should be congruent.

4. **Formulate the core story:** Develop the message, conflict, characters, and plot. Your message begins by answering this question: How does your company make a difference? What kinds of stories can tell how your enterprise has made a difference to your employees, to your customers, and to your competitors? For example, the message of Volvo is safety. The company tells stories about how its cars keep passengers safe in accidents. For a story to have interest for others, there needs to be conflict. Apple Computer has a conflict with the mindless uniformity of the PC world, so that when you buy Apple products, you make choices to be unique and creative. IKEA struggles to insure that they make well-designed inexpensive furniture, rather than expensive furniture for a few. The characters have a goal that relates to the enterprise's cause. They are the heroes who fight against the adversary. Subway's customers fight against fattening assembly line burgers. What are the characteristics of the heroes of your enterprise? How does the hero go about winning? Remember David and the slingshot. The Subway sandwiches are a weapon in the war to lose weight. The enterprise will often be the benefactor if its customers and employees fulfill their dreams in its core story. In the case of FedEx, the manager benefits when the package is delivered on time. The plot is the final aspect of the story. The events should be told in a way that everyone is engaged in your story. In the next section, we describe several types of company stories.

5. **Taking the acid test—is this story unique?** Think of all of the hamburger restaurants that now tell a similar story—Burger King, Wendy's, McDonald's, etc. How is your story different from your competitors'?

Finding Stories That Reflect Your Enterprise's Identity

As you formulate the story of your enterprise, you will need to ask yourself many questions. These questions fall into several categories, such as personal stories about you, why you formed your company, your successes and failures, and more. The list in Exhibit 13.2 provides questions to help you generate ideas for your story.

Another way to get ideas is to think about classic stories, including fables and fairy tales, as models. For example:

- *David and Goliath:* A small enterprise with limited resources defeats larger companies with more resources. Many companies can trace their beginnings to this story. For example, Microsoft began life as a small software company. It

---

exhibit
13.2

Questions for Story Development

Stories about you, the founder or owner of your enterprise:

- What kinds of struggles have you gone through that represent the enterprise's identity?
- What stories do other people tell about you, the founder and owner?

Stories about the founding of the enterprise:

- Why did you start your enterprise?
- What kinds of issues were faced and how were they solved?

Stories about successes and failures:

- What key events has the enterprise faced?
- How have these crises been solved?

Stories that others tell about you:

- Have there been times you have gone out of your way to help your customers?
- When others think about you, does a particular story about you or your enterprise come to mind?

developed several computer languages and then created the MS-DOS operating system for personal computers for IBM. IBM decided they didn't need an exclusive license for the DOS operating system because Microsoft was so small and IBM was so big. This allowed Microsoft to sell its own version of MS-DOS to other computer makers. Soon, more computer buyers were purchasing non-IBM computers with Microsoft's DOS, and Microsoft moved on to build what became the world's largest software company. Another example is Dell Computer, the pioneer in build-to-order PCs that was started by Michael Dell in his dorm room at the University of Texas at Austin. Even Wal-Mart, a company founded in Bentonville, Arkansas, began life setting up discount stores in the rural South and grew in the shadows of such huge retailers as Sears and Kmart.

- *Hare and the Tortoise:* Slow and steady; by following tried and true ways of doing business the company has been able to survive and prosper. Companies that do things the old-fashioned way fall into this category. In-N-Out Burger, a Western hamburger chain, has operated on the same philosophy since the first drive-through opened in 1948: "Give customers the freshest, highest quality foods you can buy and provide them with friendly service in a sparkling clean environment."[2] It has survived and prospered against competitors that cut corners.

- *Robin Hood:* A spunky company that looks out for the customer and prevents customers from being ripped off by the larger guys. Robert Haft, Jr., started Crown Books and began his ads with, "Books are too expensive." He developed a chain of discount bookstores that were very successful until family issues imploded the business.

- *The Ugly Duckling:* An enterprise that no one thought would do well eventually blossoms into the swan. Harley Davidson, which started life as a small company, floundered when it merged with American Machine and Foundry Company (AMF), a large leisure product manufacturer. In 1981, a group of Harley Davidson executives bought back the company and turned it around. In early April 2007, the company had a market value of almost $16 billion—higher than Ford Motor Company.[3]

Now, with these guidelines, write out your story. This core story is the key to telling people about your identity.

13.3 First Steps in Brand Development

Now let's look at the process of developing your story into a brand that will comprise the enterprise's identity. The process of branding will generate characteristics of your enterprise that will help make your enterprise's identity visible to others. There are four important questions to answer that can help your customers see and connect with your enterprise[4]:

1. Who are you? (brand identity)

2. What are you? (brand meaning)

3. What about you? What do I think or feel about you? (brand responses)

4. What about you and me? What kind of association and how much of a connection would I like to have with you? (brand relationships)

Brand Identity

Your enterprise's brand identity provides a sense of what category the brand is in (my brand is about food, or tailoring, or some other category) and the needs it satisfies. This is where one begins to develop mental maps that illustrate a hierarchy of categories of the product or service that you provide.

As you prepare a mental map of your products and services, look at the many ways customers think about goods and services similar to yours. Ask yourself: What do you do best? Is that where you want to focus your efforts? What product characteristics do you think your customers will want?

Suppose your enterprise is a tennis school. We could create a mental map like the one in Exhibit 13.3 to portray the different ways that learning how to play tennis might be valuable to your customers.

exhibit
13.3
Mind Map for Tennis Coaching Business

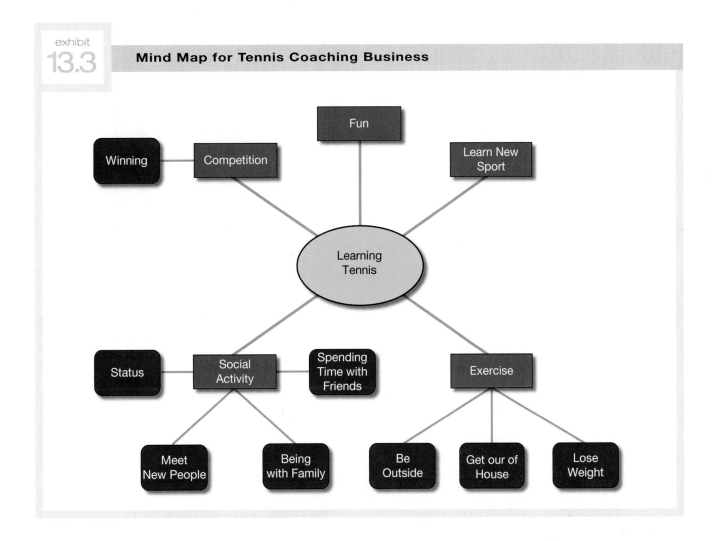

Developing a mental map literally helps you see that there are many different reasons why a customer would purchase a product or service. Our example demonstrates that people have many different reasons for learning to play tennis. In developing the identity of a tennis lesson business, you would consider which reasons might be more relevant to you. For example, you might find that your interest in providing tennis lessons is more authentic if you focus on winning and competition. You might want to attract customers who want to learn how to improve their game and win more competitions. Your program might include a tournament where your students compete against each other to perfect their skills, learn strategy, and gain confidence. Contrast this to an enterprise that provides tennis lessons for customers who are more interested in having fun, socializing, and meeting other people. A two-hour tennis lesson would be very different at each of these businesses.

Brand Meaning

There are two ways that your enterprise will go about answering the question: What are you? The meaning of your brand is determined by two issues: how customers perceive the brand's performance and how customers see the brand through the imagery your brand conveys. **Brand performance** refers to the ways a brand meets a customer's functional needs. We can describe the characteristics of performance as follows:

1. *Primary ingredients and supplementary features:* What are the characteristics of the product or service? For example, what are the characteristics and features of a cell phone? Number pad to enter phone numbers, screen to

Brand performance   How a brand meets a customer's functional needs.

see what is entered, speaker to hear calls, microphone to speak into, plus other features such as call forwarding, voicemail, phone book, custom ring tones, and more.

2. *Product reliability, durability, and serviceability:* Reliability of a product is consistency of performance over time, durability is how long the product will last, and serviceability is how easy it is to repair the product.

3. *Service effectiveness, efficiency, and empathy:* Effectiveness refers to how completely the brand satisfies a customer's service requirements, efficiency is about the speed and responsiveness of the service provided, and empathy is whether the customer sees the product as having the customer's interests in mind.

4. *Style and design:* What the product looks and feels like—issues about size, shape, materials, and color (the Apple iPod is a brand in terms of style and design for MP3 players).

5. *Price:* The price of a product, in relationship to the prices of other products or services, tells a customer about value.

Brand imagery tells us how a brand meets a customer's psychological and social needs. Now we are moving from concrete aspects of the product or service (the brand performance aspects), to intangible characteristics of the brand. Issues to consider in a brand's image include:

1. *User profiles:* Demographic issues, such as gender, age, race, or income. A product, such as shampoo, of one brand might be similar to that of other brands in terms of most of its features and performance characteristics but be different because of gender issues. Some products are oriented to specific consumers—old people, young people, and parents.

2. *Purchase and usage situations:* Sometimes a product or service has more value depending on the type of store at which a customer buys it. The buyer who purchases a tennis shoe at the Nike store may perceive it differently from the same shoe bought at J.C. Penney. The time product or service is provided might make a difference. Starbucks sells coffee to people who are "different" depending on the day. Morning rush-hour purchasers are different than people who buy coffee during the late morning or afternoon times or those who buy on Sunday morning. Buying a Coke from a hotel vending machine is different than buying a Coke at the supermarket. You pay for location and convenience.

Brand imagery   How a brand meets a customer's psychological and social needs.

© Zack Seckler/Getty Images

3. *Personality and values:* There are actually five dimensions of brand personality: sincerity (e.g., honest, wholesome, down-to-earth), excitement (e.g., up-to-date, spirited, daring, imaginative), competence (e.g., successful, reliable, intelligent), sophistication (upper class and charming), and ruggedness (e.g., outdoorsy and tough).

4. *History, heritage, and experiences:* A brand has a history that stays with it, and it is difficult to change it.

Brand Responses

The third major issue that we focus on in developing a brand involves the ways that customers will respond to your enterprise. Individuals respond to brands in both rational and emotional ways. In rational ways, customers make *brand judgments* that concern their evaluation of the products or services. These judgments fall into four broad categories: quality, credibility, consideration, and superiority.

Brand quality is an attitude represented by a perception of the brand's value and how satisfied the customer feels with the product/service. *Brand credibility* refers to the customer's perception of the brand in three areas:

- Expertise—Is the brand competent, innovative, and a market leader?

- Trustworthiness—Is the brand seen as dependable and focused on the customer?

- Likeability—Is the brand seen as fun, interesting, and worth spending time with?

The likelihood a customer would consider purchasing this brand is called *brand consideration.* For example, some people might not even consider purchasing a grocery store brand of an item, let's say, the Safeway brand of tomato sauce but prefer to buy the Hunts or Contadina brands instead. This is related to *brand superiority,* because the consumer who buys the Hunts brand judges that brand as superior to and better than other brands of the same product.

A brand will also evoke an emotional response from customers. In other words, a brand will often call to mind certain feelings that a customer will likely have about an enterprise's products or services. Six types of feelings are associated with building a brand:

- Warmth: feelings that allow a customer to have a sense of calm or peacefulness

- Fun: feelings that the brand is playful, cheerful, amusing, and full of joy

- Excitement: feelings that the brand is energizing, "alive," thrilling

- Security: feelings that the brand provides safety, comfort, and self-assurance

- Social approval: feelings that others would approve of this brand as well

- Self-respect: feelings of a sense of pride, accomplishment, or fulfillment because of the brand

A brand can evoke many different feelings, and part of a brand's uniqueness may be in the way it combines different feelings. Think about how certain adventure tour companies might combine both excitement and security. A company that runs trips down the Grand Canyon in boats may try to evoke the excitement of a white-water rafting trip together with the security of having experienced guides so the raft won't overturn or none of the passengers drown.

Brand Relationships

The final question to be addressed in building a brand is, What about you and me? What kind of association and how much of a connection would I like to have with you? You and your enterprise will develop relationships with your customers. Your brand can help you describe the kinds of relationships that you want to have with customers. Once again, we have four characteristics that describe the ways that people will relate to your brand:

1. *Brand loyalty:* This is typically measured by how often a customer repeats purchases of a business's products or services. A person would be really loyal to McDonald's, for example, if this person ate breakfast, lunch, and dinner there every day. We will discuss the nature and importance of loyalty in the next chapter of the book, when we look at the value of loyalty over the life of a customer's relationship to the enterprise.

2. *Personal attachment:* Researchers have found that, while a customer might be satisfied with a

© Cameron Spencer/Getty Images

particular product or service, the likelihood that the customer remains loyal to that brand has a lot to do with whether they form an attachment to that brand. Products that consumers really love create a sense of attachment. For kids, that might be a Barbie doll, Lego blocks, or a particular video game; for adults, that might be a particular tool, such as an OXO vegetable peeler with a comfort-grip handle, or a type of car, like a sports car, or a piece of clothing.

3. *Sense of community:* Apple has probably done this the best. People who buy Macs are a special community of computer users. The owners of iPods form a special community of MP3-player users. Harley Davidson has a special community of motorcycle users. Some businesses, such as eBay, seem to be primarily about community.

4. *Active engagement:* An enterprise has customers who are so enthusiastic about its products/ services that there are websites, chat rooms, customer-created events to celebrate the enterprise's products, etc. The best examples are, again, companies like Harley Davidson, which has many motorcycle groups that meet to ride together, or any car club, or people who get together to enjoy a company's products, like a wine group that focuses on drinking a particular winery's wines.

In Exhibit 13.4, we've provided a list of questions that might be used to help you evaluate all of the characteristics of your enterprise's brand. These questions can be helpful for identifying aspects of your brand that you've not paid much attention to. The questions enable you to be thorough in your effort to insure that you have a complete "message" to tell others about whom and what your enterprise is. Many of these questions probe issues about the brands of your competitors. To be different from other enterprises, you need to be able to identify how your competitors are different (or similar) to you.

exhibit
13.4

Branding Questions

Brand Identity: Who are you?

What other brands of products or services are similar to your enterprise's brand?

How did you (or your customers) learn about these other brands?

Can you identify the stories that these other brands tell?

In a mental map of the characteristics of brands that you compete against, where is your brand on the map, and where are the other brands?

Brand Meaning: What are you?

Compared to other brands:

How does your brand provide for basic needs?

What special features does your brand exhibit?

How reliable is your brand?

How durable is your brand?

What kinds of service do your competitors provide for their brands?

How effective is the service your enterprise provides?

Is your enterprise more responsive to your customers' service needs?

How fast is the service your enterprise provides?

What differences can your customers identify in the look and feel of your products?

What prices do you charge for products/services compared to your competition?

What are the characteristics of the people who use your brand?

Where would customers be likely to find your products/services for sale?

What do higher or lower prices say to your customers about your brand?

Do your enterprise's products/service look similar to your competitors'?

How would people describe the brand to others?

Brand Responses: What about you?

Compared to your competitors:

Do customers believe your brand is a leader?

Do customers believe your brand provides better value?

Do customers believe your brand is dependable?

Do customers see your brand is more fun and interesting?

Do customers see your brand is superior?

What kinds of feelings (e.g., warmth, fun, excitement, security, approval, and respect) does your brand evoke from customers?

Brand Relationships: What about me and you?

Compared to your competitors:

How loyal are your customers?

Would your customers go out of their way to use your products/services?

Do your customers feel your enterprise is special?

How disappointed would your customers be if they had to use your competitors' products/services?

Would your customers miss your enterprise if you went out of business?

Are there customers who really love your enterprise's products/services?

Can your customers identify with other customers using your enterprise's products/services?

Do your customers feel special that they are your customers?

Do your customers feel that they belong to a special group?

Do your customers talk about your brand to others?

Are your customers proud that they purchase your enterprise's products/services?

Do your customers seek to learn more about your enterprise and want to purchase additional products/services?

13.4 Brand Positioning

Now let's consider the many ways your enterprise's brand is different from other businesses' brands. We will develop dimensions to help you compare your enterprise's uniqueness to others.

The first step is to define your target market. A **market** is all possible customers who might want a particular product or service at a particular price. A **target market** is a subset of those customers, a specific group most likely to purchase a product or service and toward which the enterprise focuses its marketing efforts. Target markets can be based on behaviors: how often they buy (usage), where they buy (occasion), their loyalty, and the kinds of benefits they seek from the product/service. For example, a large beer company might sell beer at supermarkets or liquor stores to a target market that involves high usage, while a micro-brewery might focus on the low-usage buyer who seeks different benefits, such as drinking only expensive, upscale beers found on tap at expensive restaurants. Each company would have a different strategy and promotional message to communicate to these very different target markets.

Other ways to divide a market into target markets include demographic factors such as income, age, sex, race, and family. Car companies try to sell different kinds of cars by brand, based on these demographics. Toyota's Lexus luxury brand targets the older buyer who is willing to spend more for features, while the Toyota line targets mainstream buyers with multiple models to cover many submarkets, from families to young drivers looking for economical models. The mission of its recently introduced Scion brand is, "To satisfy a trend-setting, youthful buyer through distinctive products and an innovative, consumer-driven process." The cars are designed to attract "independent and free thinkers."[5] Even though all three brands come from Toyota, the company recognizes that each has a significantly different target market and promotes the brands separately.

Activities, lifestyle issues, or location can define target markets. Burton Snowboards targets snowboard enthusiasts of all ages with both equipment and apparel for

Market All possible customers who might want a particular product or service at a particular price.

Target market A specific group of customers who are most likely to purchase a product or service and on which the enterprise focuses its marketing efforts.

the sport. Whole Foods grocery stores attract customers who want healthy and organically grown foods and related products.

Exhibit 13.5 provides a list of questions to ask when trying to come up with a target market for your enterprise.

The second activity for developing your uniqueness is exploring how your enterprise compares to your competition. How do others offering similar goods and services talk about themselves, and how do they divide the marketplace into market segments? What are the dimensions that they use for creating their brand? How loyal are their customers to their products and services and how has this loyalty been built up? Will it be easy to persuade customers who buy from your competitors to switch their loyalty to you?

You can learn a lot about yourself from your competition, too. In the automobile industry, for example,

consumers have a vision of what it means to buy a car from a car salesperson. Most disliked the car-buying process, especially dealing with pushy salespeople. General Motors therefore decided to create a brand, Saturn, which features predetermined pricing, so there is no haggling with the salesperson to make a deal. The Saturn brand was based, in part, on how the industry as a whole was being perceived by customers. Many other car dealers and Internet car-buying sites have applied a similar model.

Two other issues are important brand differentiators:

- **Point of Difference (POD):** Something that uniquely characterizes your enterprise's brand—the unique selling proposition, or the compelling reason a customer should buy your product or service. This is also the enterprise's sustainable competitive advantage. Basically, what is special about what your product or service does for customers?

- **Points of Parity (POP):** Dimensions of your brand that are perceived as similar to that of other products/services of your competitors. For example, your enterprise might want to have a point of parity selling top of the line ice cream, so your point of

---

Point of difference (POD)   Something that uniquely characterizes your enterprise's brand.

Points of parity (POP)   Dimensions of your brand that are perceived as similar to other products/services of your competitors.

---

exhibit
13.5

Defining Your Target Market

Identifiability

Can the segment be easily determined?

What are the characteristics of this group of customers?

How and why are they different from other customers in the marketplace, as a whole?

Size

How many customers comprise this target market?

Is this target market large enough to be profitable for the enterprise?

Accessibility

How easy will it be to communicate with these customers?

What are the ways to provide products or services to the target group?

Responsiveness

Will this target market actually respond to your message?

Profitability

How much money can this target market generate?

parity might be that your ice cream is perceived to be as good or better than Häagen Dazs or Ben and Jerry's, rather than having your ice cream's point of parity be the local grocery store's brand.

By now it should be clear that branding is as important for a start-up enterprise as it is for a large corporation like Bank of America, General Electric, Honda, or Gillette. Exhibit 13.6 summarizes our discussions by demonstrating different ways that brands have an impact on consumers.

13.5 More Personal Branding Considerations

Because people would rather deal with other people than with big companies, consider basing your enterprise's brand on your personal brand.[6] Make your enterprise an extension of yourself (see Chapter 12). Some enterprises are more likely to be extensions of your own, personal brand. If your business is based on personal service—for example, a lawn service, a consulting practice, an accounting firm, a printer, or a restaurant—people are more likely to want to do business with you, and your own strengths and abilities become your unique selling proposition. There is only one you.

In addition, a personal brand can show others that you are more accessible than big companies. Since you are an individual, rather than a big company, you can be seen, and you can deal personally with a customer's problems. Customers who call you would get a live voice,

maybe even your voice, rather than a voice-response answering machine. Another key way that enterprisers influence others (see Chapter 3) is by showing them how alike you are to your customers. When a customer shares common interests and values with you, you create a stronger bond between you.

Uniqueness stands out. If your enterprise is based on *you*—your skills, values, and abilities—then you can actually begin to show how you are different from others. Being different will help you get visibility so that others notice you and become aware of your products or services. If you are one of 100 lawn-care companies in the phone book, you probably have less than 1 in 100 of a chance that someone will pick your enterprise for lawn care. If you brand your lawn care business, however, you increase the odds that customers will notice you. Branding achieves this in a way that is authentic to you and the values you bring to your enterprise.

Crafting Your Personal Brand

As we've indicated at the beginning of this chapter, you are the core of your enterprise. Your story is a fundamental part of the story of your enterprise. Basically, without you, there wouldn't be your enterprise. While you are creating your enterprise's brand, you should also consider developing a brand for yourself, your personal brand. Exhibit 13.7 provides some ideas to guide you.

As you gather the information you need to create your brand, keep the following points in mind:

1. *Focus.* The idea of a brand or an identity means that you cannot be "everything to everyone." The process

---

exhibit
13.6

Five Ways Brands Affect Consumer Thinking

1. Benefits and promises: People will buy if they see a compelling benefit. A brand will be perceived as beneficial if it helps fulfill an aspiration or dream, solves a threat or fear, espouses a "spirit" or attitude (passion, ambition, philosophy), or has "magic."

2. Norms and values: People will buy if it resolves an inner conflict with their norms and values.

3. Perceptions and programs: People will buy if your brand is a "logical choice."

4. Identity and self-expression: People will buy if it reflects their desired character and identity.

5. Emotions and love: Some products and services are "loved" by their customers.

Source: Adapted from Andreas Buchholz and Wolfram Wordemann, *What Makes Winning Brands Different?* (New York: John Wiley & Sons, 2000).

exhibit
13.7

First Steps in Branding Yourself

1. Ask other people, such as customers, competitors, and your employees, about your image. How do they see you? What kinds of characteristics do they use to describe you? What do they see as your strengths and weaknesses?

2. Generate a list of your competitors. List their images, characteristics, strengths, and weaknesses.

3. How are you different?

4. Explore the values and interests that you might share with your customers.

5. Meld what your customers want and what you share with them with those characteristics that make you different.

of branding is, by its nature, one of focusing your enterprise to serve a particular group of customers (target market) with specific products and services. A brand stands for a particular approach to doing business. You can't serve all kinds of customers in all kinds of markets if you are developing a brand. During the process of branding, you are deciding to limit your enterprise to serving specific customers with specific needs.

2. *Tell your story, not sell your story.* As we will see later in this chapter, branding is about public relations, not advertising. It is very unlikely that your enterprise will have the financial capital to spend the necessary dollars to advertise your brand. Your brand will need to be developed by telling your story to others, particularly through the process of public relations. You will need to generate publicity (which is free) for your business, rather than spend a lot of money on advertising. Advertising is necessary AFTER your brand has been established.

3. *Be authentic.* Authenticity is about being genuine and trustworthy. It's like the Coca-Cola line, "It's the real thing." Your brand represents you; as your identity, as your story, the brand needs to be authentic. Another way of saying this is that the brand can't be built on lies. You can't say that your brand is about "speedy service"—and then not deliver on that promise. Your brand can't promise that you are available 24/7, when you are not.

4. *Be first.* This might sound hard to do, because there are likely to be many businesses very similar to the one you want to start. Yet, you should discover some

aspect of your enterprise where you can claim to be the first: to offer a particular kind of food at your restaurant or being the first to provide service to a specific group of customers. Being first provides you with a way for your brand to become that category in the business, and automatically makes you the leader in that category. It also helps you define the category and the target market for the products, services, and customers. People like being associated with winners, those who are first.

In summary, a good way to think about a brand is to consider all of the different ways that people will perceive your enterprise. By creating your enterprise's brand, you engage in more than just the five senses of experience (touch, sight, taste, hearing, and smell). You engage others' senses, feelings, and thoughts. As you develop your enterprise's brand, you think through all of the ways that others will have opportunities to be engaged with you. Your brand is how you represent yourself to others. All of these sections in this chapter might suggest that developing your brand can be really complicated. We believe otherwise. Your brand, and your enterprise's brand, is fundamental to the enterprise. It reflects what you stand for and what you believe in. Your identity is the foundation for how your brand will develop.

In the Enterprising World box, you'll learn how a South African winery used the Internet's interactive capabilities to create a very personal global microbrand.

AN ENTERPRISING WORLD

Taking the World by Storm

How does a small winery in a remote area of South Africa become a worldwide phenomenon? Jason Korman and Hugh MacLeod tapped cutting-edge Web technology, going well beyond the usual websites and banner ads. Through Web logs—blogs—and other social networking sites such as wikis (Web applications that allow multiple users to add, remove, and edit content), Web videos, and online photo albums, they turned Stormhoek Wine into a global microbrand.

Stormhoek makes ten varieties of red and white wine, retailing for $10 to $15 a bottle. "We weren't trying to create a cult wine brand," says MacLeod, a former advertising professional and marketing consultant. "We have wine, we like to sell it, we like to meet people who like to buy it. It's not any more complicated than that. We looked at how do we communicate with the rest of the world, possibly from the most remote wine producing area in the world."

The solution was a blog. Easy and inexpensive to set up, these online diaries feature two-way communication. Enterprisers like MacLeod and Korman can create marketing buzz on a very personal level using blogs. "It's not just about you reading a blog and someone else writing a blog; everyone is reading and writing," explains Korman, CEO of Stormhoek's London-based parent company Orbital Wines. "The old fashioned Web site is a pretty storefront that just sits there. Blogs are not particularly pretty, but they are much more engaging conversationally."

Blogs continually change, so readers return to see what's new. Over time, they build rapport and stronger connections. Unlike traditional hard sell approaches, blogs use a more human, conversational style. MacLeod points out that blogs also help marketers by humanizing consumers and providing feedback.

Instead of spending tens of thousands of dollars on ads, the Stormhoek blog cost about $500 for the user license and design template. It is the main feature of the Stormhoek Wine website (http://www.stormhoek.com) and has evolved into a global community. "It's a discussion about things we find interesting that have to do with wine," says Korman. "We talk about the business and what we have to do to sell the wine. For a lot of people that is just as interesting as how it's made."

The blog promotes the wine in novel ways. For example, they offered free bottles of wine upon request to bloggers in the United Kingdom, Ireland, and France, asking them to report back about their wine-tasting experience. Their "100 Wine Geek Dinners in 100 Days," promoted through the blog, provided a free case of wine to individuals willing to host wine dinners in the United States and Great Britain. More than 4,500 people participated in these parties, and many posted photos of these events on photo site Flickr.com. MacLeod, the winery's marketing consultant, often asks bloggers for input for label and bottle design and taglines.

Overall, Stormhoek spent about $50,000 on these marketing efforts—a relatively small investment. The results well exceeded expectations, as Stormhoek's revenues tripled from 2005 through mid-2007.

Discussion Questions

1. Describe the features of blogs that make them good marketing tools. What drawbacks do they have? How does Stormhoek use blogging to promote its products?

2. What types of companies and products work best for blogging, and why? How do they serve the needs of microbrands that wish to expand globally?

3. Visit the Stormhoek website (http://www.stormhoek.com) and read through the blog entries. What is Stormhoek's story? How important is Stormhoek's story to its brand identity?

4. How does the Stormhoek site express the four key components of the branding process: brand identity, brand meaning, brand responses, and brand relationships?

5. Other microbrands that use blogging include two London firms: English Cut, a custom tailor in London (http://www.englishcut.com), and Hard Diamond, a custom jeweler (http://www.harddiamond.com). Visit their blog sites and discuss their branding approaches. How do they compare to Stormhoek's in terms of the brand attributes of identity, meaning, response, and relationship?

Sources: Elizabeth Bennett, "Winery Blogs to Turn Browsers into Buyers," *Baseline*, June 2007, pp. 61–63; Alice Z. Cuneo, "Stormhoek," *Advertising Age*, November 13, 2006, p. S-11; Hugh MacLeod, "The Global Microbrand Rant," GapingVoid.com, October 11, 2005, http://www.gapingvoid.com/Moveable_Type/archives/001976.html; "Marketing and Selling Stormhoek Wines," *YouTube.com*, http://www.youtube.com/watch?v=ODvfb37nR_4 (June 30, 2007).

13.6 ENTERPRISERS

Nicole Miller Designs a Brand

Customers who walk into a Nicole Miller boutique, such as the one in La Jolla, California, are immediately impressed by Miller's special flair for designing clothes that are elegant and timeless. The variety of customers browsing through the boutique's racks reflect her ability to create original designs with an ageless appeal. Just as our clothes help to define us and extend our personalities, the boutique reflects the personality of Nicole Miller, a leading American fashion designer and the company founder. Miller has built a brand around her vision, and everything she does contributes to her brand's identity. From the unique look of her designs to the pricing strategy to the feel of her boutiques—each adds another dimension to how the brand manifests itself.

Since its launching in 1982 by Miller and her partner Bud Konheim, the Nicole Miller company has grown to a sizable enterprise, with more than 165 employees. Her clothes are popular with celebrities such as Angelina Jolie, Jessica Simpson, Daryl Hannah, Kim Cattrall, and Paris Hilton. At the same time, "regular" people flock to the 20 Nicole Miller Boutiques around the country and admire displays of Nicole Miller designs at high-end retailers like Neiman Marcus, Saks Fifth Avenue, and Nordstrom.

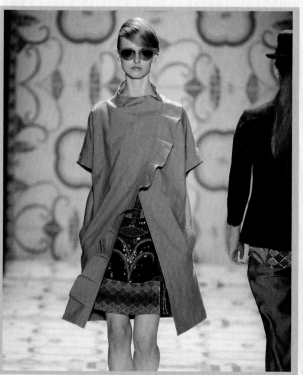

© Karl Prouse/Catwalking/Getty Images

Listen to how Miller describes her fashion line. "My clothes look ageless," she says. "I think a lot of times expensive clothes tend to make women look older and more mature. I've always been against looking older than you are. And I don't think you should be dressing like a teeny-bopper, either, because I think women shouldn't dress so that they look foolish. But I think they should always dress so they look youthful."

This youthful spirit permeates everything Miller does. The company's mission, to quote Konheim, is "about delivering a 'feel good.' We're trying to make a product that makes somebody happy. If it doesn't make them happy, they are not buying it and you're out of business."

The company's pricing strategy also makes customers happy. "The price strategy has to be part of the fun," explains Konheim. If a customer is going to pick up a tag and say "'This is uncomfortable for me,' it's not fun. So it doesn't have to be cheap; it has to be something that she expects it to be. [A customer comes] through a Nicole Miller awning knowing there is no 'designer price punishment.' It's going to be fun clothes, . . . well made, and . . . original design. She expects to pay a certain price in there, and if we break that barrier, it is uncomfortable and she's likely not to buy."

Nicole Miller is a trendsetter in many ways. She opened her first boutique in 1986 as a way to present her entire collection, not just the items a particular store buyer selects. "We found a location on Madison Avenue, we opened a boutique. It was success from day one. It was terrific, it was great!" This started a trend for independent designers who wanted creative freedom from department stores. Miller's 1996 fall runway show featured actresses—for example, Minnie Driver, Gretchen Mol, and Jill Hennessy—rather than models. Other designers soon followed this trend.

The boutiques allow the designer to stay close to her customers, as does limiting her line to selected larger retailers that pride themselves on customer service. "The buyer half the time has no idea who her customer is because department stores deal in traffic," says Konheim. "There is no focus to that and there is no meaning to it. And it is much more difficult when you are buying by some sort of computer profile. A small store deals in trade. [Its manager] knows her customer—she knows Alice, she knows Mary, she knows Sally, she knows Joan—and she buys for them."

Miller's ability to design clothes that are contemporary and trendy yet classic makes it difficult for large stores to categorize. "Nicole Miller . . . absolutely flies in the face of everything," says Konheim. "It is a young looking line at better than young, cheap prices. This is what we do. We are not like anybody else, and we have been very successful doing it."

All of Miller's ideas start with her, on her sketch pad. Here is how she describes planning a season's line: "The first thing I do is plan a color story for the season—and I just do that totally instinctively. And then I look for the fabrics, and I try to find new fabrics and . . . continue some fabrics that have been successful for me in the past. And, then I start to just map out kind of a game plan, sort of like an outline of the direction that the season is going to go in. I'm always sort of trying to find a concept—what 'the girl' is going to be for this season."

Never content to rest on her laurels, Nicole Miller's collection features eclectic designs that convey her individual sense of style. Her label now includes more than fashionable clothes: outerwear, accessories, cosmetics, and a home line sold exclusively at Bed Bath and Beyond. Since 2003, Miller has introduced three other fashion labels. A contemporary sportswear line, millergirl, debuted in 2003, and 2005 marked the arrival of the upscale Signature line and the Nicole by Nicole Miller line of more affordable clothes sold only at JC Penney. "I was most interested in JC Penney because of the importance they placed on the design of the clothes," says Miller. "I'm excited about the opportunity to dress millions of women across America in affordable style." Even kids can wear Nicole Miller clothes. "Sesame Street by Nicole Miller" is a new line combining Miller's designs and the well-known show's characters.

Discussion Questions

1. Create a mental map of all of the reasons that people purchase clothes. Where do you see the kinds of clothes that Nicole Miller sells on your mental map?

2. Go to the Nicole Miller website, http://www.nicolemiller.com. Explore the site, getting a feel for the look and feel of the site and for the clothes. Based on your "experience" of Nicole Miller from the website, describe the Nicole Miller brand.

3. How is Nicole Miller unique? Develop an outline of Nicole Miller's story. How might her story be similar, or different, from the stories of other fashion designers?

4. Using the four key components of brand identity, brand meaning, brand responses, and brand relationships discussed in the chapter, describe the characteristics of the Nicole Miller brand. Include the answers to such questions as:

   - What can Nicole Miller clothes do for a customer that other clothes can't?

   - What are the characteristics of Nicole Miller customers compared to the customers that buy clothes from other fashion designers?

   - Why would Nicole Miller customers be loyal to this brand, and why would they be willing to purchase again?

5. Discuss the brand positioning for Nicole Miller.

6. What are the risks to the very personal Nicole Miller brand of adding product lines such as millergirl and Nicole by Nicole Miller?

Sources: Adapted with permission from Small Business School, the series on PBS, at http://SmallBusinessSchool; Rosemary Feitelberg, "Driving Force," *Women's Wear Daily*, January 31, 2007, downloaded from Business Source Premier database; Nicole Miller website, http://www.niclemiller.com (April 3, 2007); "Penney Rolls Out Nicole Exclusive," *DSN Retailing Today*, March 14, 2005, downloaded from FindArticles.com database.

13.7 Promotion

Promotion involves four major topics: public relations, advertising, sales promotion, and personal selling. **Public relations** refers to ways for your enterprise to be perceived by others, particularly through the media (e.g., TV, newspapers, radio, and the Internet). **Advertising** involves paid communications that your enterprise invests in, typically through such media as newspaper, TV, and radio advertisements; billboards; direct mail; Internet "pop-up" ads; and posters, product displays, etc. **Sales promotion** involves all of those activities such as public relations,

Public relations   Marketing and communications efforts to manage an enterprise's communications with the public.

Advertising   Paid communications that your enterprise invests in, typically through such media as newspaper, TV, and radio advertisements; billboards; direct mail; Internet ads; and posters and product displays.

Sales promotion   Activities such as public relations, advertising, and personal selling that increase the likelihood that people will purchase your enterprise's products/services.

advertising, and personal selling that are necessary to increase the likelihood that people will purchase your enterprise's products/services. **Personal selling** focuses on ways that individuals can better communicate so that they can increase their ability to initiate and complete the process of buying and selling (personal selling is discussed in more detail in Chapter 14). Exhibit 13.8 summarizes the major reasons for promotion.

The basic goals of promotion can be labeled as helping customers undergo the process of AIDA: Attention, Interest, Desire, and Action. We want prospective customers to become *aware* of our enterprise and our products/services. Once we have their attention, we want prospective customers to take an *interest* in these products/services, and that they *desire* to purchase them. Finally, we want to prompt our customers to take *action* to purchase our products/services.

We assume that as an enterpriser, you don't have an unlimited budget for the promotion of your products/services. Our approach is to describe ways to tell your story and sell your enterprise that are not very expensive, substituting your imagination and creativity for cash.

Personal selling   Ways that individuals can increase their ability to initiate and complete the process of buying and selling.

As you think about all of the ways to reach potential customers, consider the many ways other enterprises are trying to reach you now. Which of them work well for you?

It is very difficult to get people to pay attention to your message. For people to pay attention, you'll have to be creative and innovative. You can easily spend a lot of money and effort trying to get your message out—and not get much response. Or, you can use strategies such as those in Exhibit 13.9.

Be careful not to overdo the creativity, however, and know the laws before you proceed. Something as simple as writing menu specials in chalk on the sidewalk outside a restaurant may result in fines if you didn't know that your city requires a permit. Also, a stunt that isn't related to your product won't generate the buzz you want.[7] Handing out lottery tickets attached to flyers about your party planning and catering business won't promote sales. A discount coupon or invitation to a tasting party, on the other hand, will give you a chance to show off your skills to prospective customers.

For more advice on how to promote your business, check out these online resources:

- *Inc.*'s how-to guides for marketing at http://www.inc.com/resources/marketing/

- *Entrepreneur*'s marketing pages, http://www.entrepreneur.com/marketing/index.html

---

exhibit
13.8

The Purpose of Promotion

Inform

Provide an awareness of the enterprise, brand, product/service

Suggest uses of the product/service

Explain how the product/service works

Persuade

Change perceptions of your enterprise, brand, product/service

Push customers to switch to your product/service

Encourage customers to buy now

Cheer customers to engage with you (e.g., call or drop by)

Remind

Alert customers to where they can buy

Remind them of future needs

Keep them aware of your product/service

exhibit
13.9

exhibit 13.9	**Suggestions for More Effective Marketing**

Know your audience and use the right methods to reach them. If your target is senior citizens, Internet-based promotional strategies are unlikely to generate sales. For teens and twenty-somethings, however, they should pay off.

Play up your product's unique qualities. Why will your product attract customers' interest? Then relate its features to the benefits to consumers.

Base benefits on those unique product features—and explain them believably. People buy what is of value to them, so identify a few key benefits to emphasize. Don't exaggerate when you make claims for your product but phrase benefits believably. Include a qualifier such as "almost" or "estimate" rather than citing an exact statistic that may be questioned.

Keep it simple. Giving out samples is one of the most effective ways to promote certain products, such as food. A restaurant that delivered food to radio show hosts received on-air advertising—at no cost.

Relate the promotion to your product. Your ad or promotional tool should have a connection to your business and increase interest in the product.

Grab the consumer's attention. Consumers are bombarded with ads, so yours needs to stand out in some way. Make sure it's not just the ad that they remember, but your product. Your goal is a unique selling proposition.

Seek action from your audience. By asking the viewer to head for the store, call for more information, or clip a discount coupon, you will draw people in and involve them with the product.

Convey your message clearly. Unless viewers understand your key points, your ad pitch is wasted. Be as specific as possible. Vague statements don't sell products.

Make your advertising and your marketing strategy consistent. Develop your overall marketing communications strategy first. Then make your ads congruent with your program and goals.

Source: Adapted from Brooks Barnes, "It Seemed like a Good Idea . . ." *Wall Street Journal*, April 30, 2007, p. R7; and Jay Conrad Levinson, *Guerrilla Marketing Excellence* (New York: Houghton Mifflin Company, 1993).

These and similar sites offer articles on branding, finding customers, public relations, online marketing, and more.

13.8 Public Relations

The purpose of public relations (PR) is to tell the story about your enterprise and the products and services you offer. Most people think about public relations as the process of generating publicity about you and your enterprise. But it is much more than that. A solid public relations campaign is the first step in making your story visible to others.

We define *public relations* as the marketing and communications efforts of your enterprise to manage its communications with the public. Public relations is concerned with how your enterprise is presented to the world at large. Public relations goals include education, correcting a mistruth, or building or improving an image.

Many people may view PR as self-promotion and avoid it. However, public relations should be at the foundation of your marketing effort and is more important than your advertising efforts. To promote your goods or services, you must be able to tell your story in a compelling way. "A company should have a spokesperson—not a celebrity endorser like a Britney Spears—but someone who can be seen as the face of the company," says Laura Ries, president of Atlanta marketing firm Ries & Ries. "A company's founder or CEO needs to represent the company in the eyes of the public."[8]

Public relations strategies get your story into the media—usually for free. According to PR specialists, consumers will react more positively when your product or company is mentioned in a major newspaper, magazine, Web article, or radio or television show than from seeing a television ad. A solid PR campaign can be more successful than a huge ad budget in reaching lots of people and generating positive results.

If you have thoughtfully developed your story and your brand, then you have something to say to everyone about you and your enterprise. "PR comes when people hear a story and they want to know more," says Chip Heath, co-author of *Made to Stick*. Often, enterprisers have especially good human interest stories to tell about finding the idea for the business or getting it started.

The tools of public relations involve press releases, feature stories, company newsletters, interviews and press conferences, sponsored events, and publicity. A **press release** is an announcement to the media about anything involving your enterprise: your grand opening, new products and services, hiring employees, a new location, interesting activities your enterprise undertakes, special activities, and meetings that might interest others. While your enterprise can send out press releases to a wide variety of media outlets (see the Web exercises for media directories), you should identify editors,

writers, and reporters at various media outlets (radio, newspapers, TV, etc.). Cultivate a relationship with those who might be interested in your stories. They want to present interesting and engaging stories to their audiences. Provide newsworthy stories about your company in general or your specific products, and they will share your enterprise's story through their media outlets. Exhibits 13.10 and 13.11 provide pointers on writing an effective press release.

This leads to the next way to gain publicity, through *feature stories*. Writers and reporters at their respective media outlets generate feature stories about you or some aspect of your enterprise. A feature story spotlights a particular individual, enterprise, or event. Most major newspaper or television stories (except for crises like accidents) began with a press release or a story idea that intrigued the reporter enough to develop an article. Many public relations experts devote much of their day-to-day efforts pitching ideas for interesting features to reporters and editors.

Newsletters are a valuable way to provide information about your enterprise and tell your story. Most enterprises generate mailing lists of customers, prospec-

Press release   An announcement to the media about anything involving your enterprise.

---

exhibit
13.10   **Basic Elements of a Press Release**

- FOR IMMEDIATE RELEASE: Place in upper left margin, under company letterhead, in all capital letter.

- Media contacts: List your organization's primary media contacts (your spokespersons) next.

- Headline: Use boldface type.

- Dateline: This includes the city from which you issue the press release and the date you are mailing your release.

- Lead paragraph: Include the five Ws and an H—who, what, when, where, why, and how. Write the opening in a way that it grabs the reader's attention.

- Text: The body of your press release develops your complete message. Write in the style of a news story and include relevant information about your products or services, such as benefits. Quotes from staff members, industry experts, or satisfied customers strengthen your story.

- Summary: Recap key product information.

- Company information: A short section with "boilerplate" information about the company.

- Contact information: Repeat after last paragraph, include website address.

- Other formatting tips: If the press release has multiple pages, place "-more-" at the end of each page. End the press release with "###" or "–30–".

Source: Press-Release-Writing.com, http://www.press-release-writing.com/10_essential_tips.htm (May 1, 2007); "Press Releases," *Wikipedia*, http://en.wikipedia.org/wiki/Public_relations#Press_releases (May 1, 2007).

exhibit
13.11

Tips for Better Press Releases

1. Make sure your news deserves press attention. Wait for the right opportunity rather than flooding the media with routine notices.

2. Focus on what's new or unique about your company or products.

3. For maximum impact, direct your press release to your target segment, rather than the whole market.

4. Let your audience know why this information is newsworthy for them.

5. The first ten words of your release are the most important. Make sure they count.

6. Begin with the attention-grabbing news, then move on to the company telling the story.

7. Understand how people will relate to and connect to the information you present.

8. Keep the language simple and clear.

9. Deal with the facts; avoid hype.

10. Include complete contact information: individual to contact, address, phone, fax, email, and website address.

11. Help media representatives do their jobs by providing newsworthy stories and telling them well.

Source: Press-Release-Writing.com, http://www.press-release-writing.com/10_essential_tips.htm (May 1, 2007); Leslie Taylor, "How to Become a Household Name," *Inc.com*, January 16, 2006, http://www.inc.com.

tive clients, suppliers, and others and send them periodic newsletters about current activities, products, and employees. Posting these newsletters on the company websites increases your audience. As seen in our discussion on branding, an important part of the marketing process is developing a relationship with your customers. Newsletters help you stay connected.

A *press conference* is a staged event that invites members of the media to hear a specific announcement and to ask questions. A company might call press conferences to publicize expansion plans, new products, or management changes. For example, "We've called this press conference to announce that we are expanding into 8 states with 20 locations over the next year and that this expansion will create 250 new jobs and likely generate sales of over $40 million."

Obviously, some announcements will be more newsworthy than others, so attendance depends on whether writers and reporters find your proposed topics interesting to them.

A *sponsored event* can occur in any number of ways. Specific events or community activities can reinforce your brand identity. The events may or may not relate to your products. For example, free "child safety" events where children receive physicals, vaccinations,

and other tests. Such events provide the sponsors with visibility in the media as newspapers and TV stations tell their readers about these free opportunities. Event sponsorship can raise awareness for your enterprise, particularly if these events are for causes and issues that you feel are also a part of the story you want to tell. The Scottsdale, Arizona, branch of P.F. Chang's, a Chinese restaurant, became a sponsor of the area's Rock 'n' Roll Marathon, which features rock bands along the course route. In addition to raising money for charity, the restaurant's connection to the race has enhanced its positive reputation in the community.[9]

Finally, the most important way you can tell your story through public relations is to have a presence on the Web. Every enterprise must have a website: a place where you can be located and where you can tell your story, where people can learn about your company, its products/services, events, and more. Other online avenues to generate PR include:

- **Posting to Internet newsgroups:** These special-interest message boards offer an informal way to tell people about your products or establish your expertise. Posts should offer advice rather than try to sell. Contribute on a regular basis to create name recognition and credibility. By adding value, you'll encourage people to visit your website or email you using the links you provide with every post.

- **Post press releases on free websites:** Gain visibility by sending news to sites such as PRWeb.com, which offer a direct route to the consumer.

- **Get listed in online sources:** For example, you can buy a listing for $500 a year that will put you on Yearbook.com's annual lists of experts in a wide range of industries.[10]

13.9 Advertising

Advertising refers to any paid communication where the enterprise is identified. The distinguishing feature of advertising is that it is paid. You have many options within the advertising category to tell others about you, your enterprise, and your goods or services, Newspapers, yellow pages, magazines, radio, television, outdoor media (billboards, bus stops, taxi-cabs, bus signs), and the Internet are the major ways most businesses advertise.

The critical issue in advertising is your *media mix*: identifying the media outlets where your advertisements are likely to be seen by prospective customers. What you spend on advertising has to generate enough prospective customers, and these customers have to spend enough on your products and services to make the cost of these advertisements profitable. Not easy! If you had a take-out eatery with a few tables in an office building that was only open for lunch, it might not make much sense to advertise your business in the local newspaper or on TV. Instead, you'd reach the most likely customers by sending flyers and other direct mail efforts (like menus) to every business in your building and posting them in the elevators. The key is to spend your advertising dollars on the media that reaches people with a high likelihood of buying from your enterprise.

We will look at this issue in more detail in the next chapter, but the critical issue is the cost to acquire a new customer. Getting new customers to purchase your products and services can be very, very expensive, so, considering how to advertise, effectively, requires that you often use your imagination and creativity to get your message to the right prospective customers.

If you spend $1,000 on newspaper advertising in your community paper, and 20 people who read your advertisement come into your store and buy something from you, then your cost per new customer is $50. The $50 cost to acquire a new customer is not that low for many businesses, however. During the Internet boom of the late 1990s, many Internet companies spent $500 or more to get one customer to make a purchase on their websites. If, for example, the sales generated by that customer totaled $100, and the gross margin for that sale was $25, that initial sale for that customer actually lost the business $475.

To choose the appropriate media for your advertising, you need to measure the results. You can compare various media outlets by cost per contact, or the cost to reach a person in your target market. Suppose, for example, you were interested in selling to parents with babies, you could find a magazine geared to this target group. If it had a 100,000 household subscription base and a full-page advertisement cost $1,000, your cost per contact would be $0.01 per subscriber.

You also should consider the types of people a particular media outlet will attract. **Reach** is defined as the percentage of people in your target markets who are exposed to your advertisement. Some advertising media are more likely to reach your potential customers than others. For example, if your goal was to expose your advertisement to financial analysts and planners, you might find that 60 percent of all financial analysts subscribe to the *Wall Street Journal*, giving you a 60 percent reach to that target market.

While the cost per contact for certain general media outlets like television and newspapers might seem inexpensive, the actual number of people that you reach who might be prospective buyers for your enterprise's products/services could be very small. On television, a morning kids cartoon program will attract a different audience than a police drama on a weekday evening or a football game on Sunday afternoon.

Sometimes a simple approach works well. Placing a circular in newspapers can be an effective way to build traffic, especially for retailers. The cost may be less than a regular ad in the same paper.

Finally, you should consider the frequency of advertising exposure. Viewing an advertisement many times will increase recognition and help customers remember your brand and product. Studies show that it takes three viewings, whether in the same or different media, before people respond to a message.

Another way to advertise to prospective customers is *direct marketing*. Typically we think of direct marketing

Reach The percentage of people in your target markets who are exposed to your advertisement.

as direct mail. A company sends you a letter or a post card that they hope you will open and read, and then, respond. Catalogs are another form of direct marketing.

Enterprisers can purchase mailing lists for customers in their target market groups. For example, if you were selling home repair services, you could purchase a mailing list of all of the people who registered their sales at the county court house (required for deeds and titles for properties). If you had a hobby shop, you could purchase a mailing list of subscribers to hobby magazines. The development of your database of prospective clients is critical to your direct marketing efforts. Besides direct mail, there is also telemarketing, where you call people on the phone. This technique is becoming less useful, however, because people do not like the interruptions. Also, most people sign up to be on "Do not call" lists that make it illegal for you to contact them on the phone to sell them anything.

Finally, you might consider *infomercials* to promote your products and services. You can purchase time on a TV or radio station to talk about your products and services. This form of promotion is particularly valuable for products that need to be demonstrated to show customers how they are used. Infomercials also are a good way to include testimonials of why these products provide value to buyers.

The Digital Marketing Explosion

Today nearly everything can be found, in digital form, on the Internet and its World Wide Web, making digital marketing a key promotional component for companies of all sizes. Online promotion can be especially effective for small businesses because it allows enterprisers to connect with potential customers on a more personal level than traditional marketing avenues. It also has the potential for a very broad and deep reach, at a reasonable cost.

Online marketing takes many forms, including search-engine marketing, email, banner ads, pop-up ads, and webinars (online seminars). More recently, streaming media and podcasting have become popular.

Developing a website and overall Web presence for your enterprise is critical for its establishment and growth. This is a huge topic, well beyond the scope of this book. In this section, we will focus on a few major issues, including how to identify potential customers on the Web and get the word out to them about you and your enterprise.

The first step, obviously, is to get a domain name and to develop Web pages describing your company and products. Even the choice of a domain name should be part of your strategy. If your company name is fairly general or doesn't provide a clue to what you do, choose a domain name that mentions your product. This will help you rank higher in search listings. Because Web surfers typically click through to the top four or five listings, this can be quite important to your success. Suppose your clothing store, Boutique Marbella, sells hand-painted clothing and accessories. Using the store name as your Web domain—http://www.boutiquemarbella.com—will only bring you people who already know your name. Choosing a more customized domain name, such as http://www.marbellahandpaintedapparel.com will help people looking for unique apparel locate you through search engines.

Once someone clicks through to your site, they want to find information with as few clicks as possible, so keep that in mind when designing your site and links. You may want the search engine to link to a specific product site instead of your home page.

Now that most people have email addresses, you can send electronic direct mail messages about you and your enterprise. Such emails could be sale notices, periodic newsletters, and new product announcements. Although often unwanted commercial email messages (spam) end up in a junk mail box or can't get through spam filters, you can give your customers the ability to provide their email addresses and opt in to your mailings. Email provides a relatively inexpensive way to build brand recognition and loyalty. Often, companies ask site visitors to register and provide basic information in a personal profile. This data forms the basis of targeted lists that allow companies to deliver tailored information.

It's critical to use email wisely, however[11]:

- Send relevant and helpful messages to customers who request them.
- Identify your brand and make the subject specific.
- State your point quickly to catch the reader's attention.
- Limit graphics or provide a text-only option.
- Don't flood customer mailboxes.
- Pay attention to the tone of the message.

New software applications are making it easier for smaller firms to use email marketing more effectively. They provide tools to create email campaigns, track results, and monitor Web activity. With enhanced data about how customers respond to email campaigns, companies can focus efforts on the most likely prospects.

For example, ThoughtLava, a Web design and Internet strategy consultant, turned to SalesGenius software for help. Now the consultants know not only if the email reaches prospects or is bounced back, but also whether prospects click on any links in the message and what they view at the company's site. Armed with this knowledge, ThoughtLava's sales team can develop sales presentations that focus on the potential customer's specific interests.[12]

Boosting Search Engine Results

Search engines, such as Yahoo!, Google, or Excite, offer another way to get your message out to potential customers. These websites are generally the first places a customer goes to find product information. In fact, search advertising generates more than 50 percent of online ad revenue.[13]

Most search engines have "spiders" that seek out information on Web pages. Then, through proprietary technology, they rank these pages for customers searching for specific information. Type in "Los Angeles, hot dogs, top ten" and most search engines will return a set of pages that will have some relationship to hot dog stands. With most search engine sites, you can pay to place your website on search results pages by purchasing search words. In this example, if you purchase the words "Los Angeles," "hot dogs," and "top ten," your website would appear as a sponsored website whenever someone puts in those words. You pay the search engine only when a viewer clicks on your ad.

Other ways to increase your ranking are to repeat specific search phrases and key words in product descriptions, avoid overly broad phrases, provide helpful consumer articles and buying guides, and include links to other sites. The more narrowly you can define your search terms, the better your results. Because you pay per click, this reduces your sorts and improves the relevance of the click-throughs.[14] For example, the term "food" will generate more clicks than "hot dogs"—but most will not be relevant to your business.

For more advice on how to use the Web to market your business, from developing a better website to improving search rankings, check out *Inc.*'s how-to guides for marketing at http://www.inc.com/resources/marketing/.

From Banners to Blogs

Banner ads and pop-up advertisements are forms of digital display advertising that also tap the Internet's wide reach. Banners were one of the first forms of digital advertising. Not only do they increase brand awareness, they allow viewers to click through to linked websites.

This provides one measure of the ads' effectiveness, although most clicks don't lead to purchases and fraudulent clicks can unfairly skew results.

Companies buy banner ads, often on sites with similar but non-competing content. Banners need to catch the viewer's attention and get the user to focus not on the Web page they chose but on your ad. Because companies may pay on a per-click basis, click fraud has become a concern for both advertisers and ad placement sites. Pop-up ads appear any time someone searched for certain words in the search engine.

Finally, we should mention the value of blogs. A blog (short for Web log) is defined as a regularly updated online publication with Web links to other sites. Blogs are essentially online journals that allow readers to post comments. Savvy marketers have discovered that blogs provide a forum to tell the story of an enterprise, increasing traffic to their company's website. Blogging has become a dynamic online phenomenon: in May 2007, blog tracking firm Technorati was tracking more than 80 million blogs. About 175,000 new blogs and 1.6 billion updates appear each day, on every imaginable topic.

Through blogs, enterprisers can communicate on a more personal level with existing and prospective customers. Blogs are an effective way to give readers insight to your company's personality and to provide information. Their collaborative features allow you to obtain feedback to improve your products and provide better service. Other benefits of business blogs include networking, building community, enhancing credibility, and ease of creating and updating. Many sites host blogs free of charge, making them an especially attractive marketing tool.[15]

Putting It All Together

The Internet can be a mixed blessing. For many enterprisers it is the primary storefront, expanding their customer base without geographical limits. In addition to promoting their products, they can print mailing labels, track shipments, and research industry trends. Connecting with customers has never been easier. However, the volume of customer inquiries can be overwhelming, and today's shopper wants a quick reply. Susan Gearing, who sells quilted fabrics and accessories from her home-based business at her eBay store SusieCraft, has to answer more than 100 emails each day, as well as write and update item descriptions for her eBay listings. As her business expands, she is considering ways to boost search engine results and whether she should add other online venues and create a blog to enhance her marketing efforts.[16]

ENTERPRISING ETHICS

Where Does the Buck Stop?

Suppose you've recently become interested in making candles as a hobby, but no crafts stores in your area carry the right materials. Or perhaps you are searching for an unusual spice or rare Chinese tea. Knowing that Amazon.com claims to offer the "Earth's Biggest Selection," you search the site (http://www.amazon.com) and find quite an array of products that suit your needs. As you read the product descriptions carefully, however, you notice that these items are not sold by Amazon.com but by a variety of vendors.

For example, a beeswax candle kit comes from the American Homestead Mercantile Company, a small family business located on a farm in San Diego County. The company focuses on providing quality products that represent good value, such as table linens, candles, handmade soaps and bath goods, and fabrics. Amazon also offers a wide assortment of teas and items for personal health from the Far East through Pier Mall, a New York City–based importer and distributor. Both of these companies have their own websites, where customers can place orders—yet each also has a storefront on Amazon.com. By partnering with Amazon, these small businesses have access to Amazon's 60 million customers around the world. Customers gain confidence in buying from these firms because Amazon stands behind them with its "A-to-Z Safe Buying Guarantee," covering delivery and condition of the item.

In these cases, Amazon acts as the reseller, essentially taking orders on behalf of the other merchant and processing the payment through its own checkout process and coordinating the order fulfillment with the seller. Other big online retailers like Buy.com have followed Amazon's lead, offering additional buying options from third-party sellers. Sellers benefit from the reseller's technology and higher site traffic. The reseller site becomes a shopping portal as it expands its product offerings—without having to carry inventory for products desired by relatively few people.

The system also works in reverse. Amazon's Associate program is an affiliate marketing program that lets companies link to Amazon's site and product listings. When someone clicks through to Amazon's site, the host site gets a referral fee for every sale that results. Recently it introduced the aStore program that lets Associates build their own online store to sell Amazon products—as many or as few as they wish.

The eBay Marketplace (http://www.ebay.com) is perhaps the ultimate example of a reseller. Both individuals and businesses list millions of items on its global commerce Internet platform, which facilitates exchanges between buyers and sellers. Although it pioneered the online auction, eBay now offers both auctions and fixed-price trading. eBay has evolved into a major e-commerce force, with quarterly listings often numbering more than 600 million. Active sellers can create their own customizable eBay stores for as little as $16 per month for the basic store. More sophisticated options provide advanced features for higher-volume sellers. eBay also has localized sites for many countries.

Discussion Questions

1. How much should a company reveal about its resources for serving customers on the Web? What other ethical issues arise for both the online reseller and the seller using the online reseller's services?

2. What obligations does an online reseller have to the customers buying from a third party it represents? What are the obligations of the third party? Who stands behind the products offered through a reseller? Which entity should be ultimately responsible for order fulfillment, subsequent service and repairs, and customer satisfaction, and why?

3. How do eBay and Amazon insure that sellers on their websites are legitimate and will provide the goods the sellers are offering? What steps have they taken to insure that both buyers and sellers are treated fairly? Should they monitor sellers, or should buyers using these and other reseller sites just "beware?"

4. How can a business that sells mainly through Amazon, eBay, or another reseller develop its own brand? Explore the Amazon and eBay sites to determine if these resellers have taken any steps to help third party sellers with branding efforts.

5. What advantages does an enterpriser gain from using an online reseller? What are the disadvantages? Should sellers create their own websites to eliminate the fees that resellers charge for transactions?

Source: "Amazon Associates," *Amazon.com*, http://affiliate-program.amazon.com/gp/associates/join (May 20, 2007); "eBay Inc. Announces First Quarter 2007 Financial Results," *eBay.com*, April 18, 2007, http://investor.ebay.com/releases.cfm; "eBay Inc. Announces Fourth Quarter and Full Year 2006 Financial Results," *eBay.com*, January 24, 2007, http://investor.ebay.com/releases.cfm; "Selling at Amazon," *Amazon.com*, http://www.amazon.com (May 26, 2007).

It is easy and quick to set up an online store with a website or through eBay or Amazon. However, just as with a regular store, the behind the scenes operations of an online store must be efficient and responsive. Other issues arise when selling online, especially when you sell through an online reseller such as Amazon or eBay, as the Enterprising Ethics box explains.

In the next chapter, we will discuss how to use the Web to develop an ongoing relationship with your customers.

13.10 Sales Promotion

With advertising, you pay to tell your story so that customers will have reasons to engage in exchanges with your enterprise. The goal of *sales promotions,* activities other than advertising, public relations, or personal selling, is to directly influence people to buy an item or service. Popular sales promotion tools include coupons, rebates, free samples, premiums, contests, loyalty marketing programs, and product placement. Sales promotions can target either the consumer or the trade (the wholesaler, distributor, or retailer).

A *sales coupon* provides a price discount for making a purchase: Buy two, get one free; 20 percent off any item over $50; 15 percent off whatever you can fit in this paper bag. One of the challenges of using coupons is whether customers who redeem your coupons will ever purchase your products or services at the full price. If you offer coupons at your restaurant to buy one entrée and get the second one free, are you attracting more customers who will return and pay full price, or are you preventing other customers from dining and paying full price? Perhaps you want to attract more customers at a different time of day (buy two and get one free if you dine before 5 PM), or, you can make up the price reduction through sales of other items. People who might get two steak dinners for the price of one might spend more on liquor, where there might be a higher margin.

Many products and services offer a *rebate* where, after the purchase is made, the customer receives a payment in the mail. This is an excellent way to build up a mailing list of customers who have purchased your products—particularly if you are not directly selling to them. *Premiums with purchase* are a way to encourage sales without lowering the product's stated price. Many companies provide a premium for customers who make some minimum level of purchase. For example, cosmetics firms may offer a free tote bag for purchases of $35 or

more, and athletic shoe manufacturers may include free sport socks, a water bottle, or duffle bags. The McDonald's Happy Meal toy is another type of premium.

Loyalty marketing programs, such as frequent-buyer awards, reward your best customers and encourage repeat business. Many coffee and sandwich shops have punch tickets where if you buy 10 cups of coffee or sandwiches, the 11th is free. Airlines have frequent-flyer programs where customers who travel a certain number of miles get upgrades to first class, better seating, or free tickets. Customers who belong to a frequent-buyer program could get special alerts through regular mail or email of special sales, receive discount coupons, or have special purchasing days. Nordstrom and other major department stores alert their special customers to sales before they are advertised to the general public.

Product sampling and demonstrations are a great way to introduce new items, particularly foods. Costco features many product demonstrators throughout their stores. Once people taste a product, they may then purchase it at the store, increasing impulse purchases. Some companies send out free samples in the mail or hand them out at events, campuses, and fairs as free samples of their product for people to try.

Point of purchase promotions are special in-store displays. Posters, three-dimensional displays, and machines dispensing coupons in the aisles are some of the ways companies entice you to purchase their products. *Give-aways* are another option for promoting your enterprise. Think of the companies who hand out calendars, pens, bottle openers, or refrigerator magnets with their names on them. If you were a pizza delivery company, wouldn't you want your company's name and phone number on your customer's refrigerator?

Have you seen an actor using an Apple computer or drinking Coca-Cola in a television show or movie? These are examples of *product placement*, which involves paying to have your product used or mentioned in a mass media program or movie. This more subtle promotional technique has become quite popular recently as a way to make consumers aware of products.

The owners of POM Wonderful, Stewart and Lynda Resnick, needed promotional tactics to increase awareness of theirs pomegranate juice and related products. They used sampling at the 2002 Oscar and Emmy award shows to introduce celebrities to its juice. The unique bottle found its way into gift bags at numerous events and appeared in product placements on such shows as *Desperate Housewives*. They created a pomegranate martini, the POMtini, and gave bartenders free juice to feature the cocktail. The Resnicks also funded health research into antioxidant and other benefits of pomegranates and incorporated the positive results into their advertising. Their efforts resulted in a sales increase from just $12 million in 2001 to more than $90 million in 2006.[17]

Summary

1. Creating a firm that will be different from other companies is the primary way for a small firm to compete against other enterprisers. The core values of the enterpriser and the business are at the heart of such a strategy. By knowing who you are, being yourself, and focusing on what you do best, you can build a unique company.

2. A brand reflects how other people perceive the enterprise and serves as the enterprise's identity. Branding refers to how an enterprise displays that identity and differentiates itself from other companies. By building an effective brand, you can distinguish your company and its products from those of competitors and enhance customer loyalty.

3. Storytelling is a good way to explore the enterprise's identity and develop and promote its brand. The story should convey a key message about the company through four elements: the message, the conflict, the characters, and the plot. This story tells others what your company stands for and conveys its values and your passion for it. Steps to story development include thinking about what the company's obituary would say about it, screening basic data to identify internal characteristics of the enterprise and identifying the image the enterprise projects, evaluating that data, and then formulating the core story. The final test is asking yourself if your story is unique. In developing your enterprise's story, you will also look at stories about you (the founder or owner of your enterprise), about the founding of the enterprise, about its successes and failures, and also stories that others tell about you. Classic fairy tales and fables can serve as models, too.

4. The branding process requires you to ask four important questions to generate your enterprise's characteristics: Who are you? (brand identity); What are you? (brand meaning); What do I think or feel about you? (brand responses); and What about you and me? (brand relationships).

5. Your enterprise's brand identity tells others the category of the brand and the needs it satisfies. Drawing a mind map can help you visualize all the categories of the products and services you provide and the different reasons a customer would purchase them from you. Brand meaning is determined by the brand's performance—how it meets a customer's functional needs—and its imagery—how it deals with psychological and social needs. Customers will respond to your enterprise and its brand in rational ways through brand judgments. Brands also evoke feelings, such as warmth, fun, excitement, security, social approval, and self-respect. Your brand can help you describe the kinds of relationships that you want to have with customers. Brand loyalty, personal attachment, sense of community, and active engagement are four characteristics of brand relationships.

6. Once you have developed your brand, brand positioning will help you compare its uniqueness to other companies. Positioning starts with defining the market for your goods or services and selecting target markets, or specific groups of customers. The enterprise can then focus its marketing efforts on those market segments, which can be based on demographics, geography, consumer behavior, activities, or lifestyle issues. Comparing your enterprise to the competition is another way to increase your awareness of your brand's uniqueness. Other brand differentiators include points of difference and points of parity.

7. Your personal brand can form the basis for your enterprise's brand. A brand that emphasizes the personal can be an advantage for smaller businesses, which are then perceived as more accessible than large companies. This personal relationship with customers becomes an important part of the brand's identity. These seemingly subtle differences can make your enterprise more unique to consumers.

8. Promotion deals with all the ways that your enterprise informs, persuades, and reminds prospective and actual buyers about your enterprise and its products. The four elements of an enterprise's promotional mix are public relations, advertising, sales promotions, and personal selling. These should be combined into an integrated

marketing strategy. Four stages in the promotional process are to gain attention, increase interest in your company and product, create the desire to buy, and prompt customers to take action and buy.

9. Public relations (PR) refers to your enterprise's communications efforts that deal with the public. Your PR shapes how the public perceives your business. The principal tools of public relations are press releases, feature stories, company newsletters, interviews and press conferences, sponsored events, and publicity.

10. Paid communication in mass media about a company or product is called advertising. There are many different media in which to advertise your enterprise. Traditional media include newspapers, radio, television, and direct mail. Digital media are expanding the reach of advertisers well beyond local areas. Choosing the right media for your advertisements involves analyzing reach and cost per contact.

11. Online marketing enables enterprisers to reach many customers with a more personal message than traditional mass media. Because the World Wide Web is often the first place consumers go for product information, a company website is a cost-effective way to tell your story and describe your products and services. Search-engine marketing, email, banner ads, pop-up ads, blogs, webinars (online seminars), streaming media, and podcasting are among the many forms of digital marketing.

12. In addition to advertising and public relations, companies use sales promotion techniques to influence purchase decisions. Popular sales promotion tools include coupons, rebates, free samples, premiums, contests, loyalty marketing programs, and product placement.

Review Questions

1. What is the strategy of authenticity, and why is it important for enterprisers?

2. Define the marketing concept and the marketing mix and explain how they contribute to the uniqueness of an enterprise.

3. What is a brand? Discuss the benefits of branding your enterprise and explain the role of storytelling in developing an enterprise's brand. What are the four elements in story development?

4. Summarize the steps in story development. Which of the steps would be most helpful to you in writing the story of your enterprise, and why? What other ideas can help you to develop your story?

5. What are the four key questions to consider when branding your enterprise?

6. Define brand identity. How can a mind map help you create your brand?

7. Compare the two components of brand meaning and their characteristics or issues.

8. In what ways do customers respond to an enterprise? What are the categories of brand judgments and how do they affect brand response? Give several examples of brands that represent these characteristics for you.

9. Name the six feelings a brand can evoke and provide examples of companies that suggest these feelings to you.

10. Discuss the different ways that a brand can build relationships. Which of these have you experienced with a brand? Share your examples with your classmates.

11. How does brand positioning help an enterpriser compare a brand's uniqueness to other companies? What types of questions should you ask when defining the target market for your enterprise?

12. Differentiate between points of difference and points of parity. How do they relate to branding?

13. Why should an enterpriser create a personal brand as well as an enterprise brand? What steps can you take to develop your personal brand?

14. Briefly define the 4 Ps of the marketing mix. What are the three major purposes of promotion?

15. How do public relations and advertising differ? In what ways are they similar? Describe how you might use each to promote your enterprise.

16. List several important areas you must take into account when developing an advertising program.

17. How have digital media revolutionized marketing? What techniques do they offer to promote your enterprise?

18. What is the goal of sales promotion, and how does it accomplish this goal?

Applying What You've Learned

1. Take 5 minutes, look around you, and write down the names of all the brands you notice. Which objects are not branded? Can you think of brands for those objects as well? Is there something that couldn't be branded? If so, why not?

2. Identify three enterprisers whom you would like to emulate. What are their stories, including the message, conflict, characters, and plot? Do their stories fit one of the classic stories, and how are they unique?

3. Chose an enterprise that you would like to develop and write its story. What are the message, conflict, characters, and plot? Does the story of your enterprise fit one of the classic stories? How is the story of your enterprise unique? Describe the marketing mix for your enterprise.

4. Develop a mind map for a product that you use every day (e.g., deodorant, tooth paste, soap, shampoo, or cereal). List the different reasons why people use this product. Does everyone use the product for the same reasons? Identify different groups of customers.

5. Using the enterprise whose story you told in question 3 and the questions in Exhibit 13.4, identify the following for your brand:

    a. Characteristics

    b. Target markets

    c. Point of difference (POD)

    d. Points of parity (POP)

6. Consider how you will brand yourself. What does your look and appearance say about you, as a brand? What do your behaviors say about you, as a brand? How do you see yourself as unique from others? How you might be first in something that others will have to follow?

7. Look at newspaper and magazine articles on different businesses and chose one of particular interest. Using the information provided in Exhibits 13.10 and 13.11, prepare a press release based on the information presented in this feature story.

8. Outline your marketing strategy for your new enterprise, including PR, advertising, and sales promotion. Which media would you use to promote it, and why? Which sales promotion tools would you choose to complement your advertising and public relations efforts?

Enterprisers on the Web

1. Go to http://www.allaboutbranding.com/ to learn more about branding. Also, take the branding exam for you and your enterprise. Take other branding questionnaires at http://www.chadwickcommunications.com/brandiq/, http://www.knocks.com/BrandingQuiz.html, and http://www.workingmatters.com.

    What did you learn from these questionnaires about company and personal brands?

2. Find the websites of three competitors of the business you chose in question 3 of the preceding section. What is the story told by each website about your competitors? What kind of identity does each website convey? What do these websites convey about their brands' performance and imagery? What kinds of responses do these websites evoke? How do these websites go about creating a relationship with you? Summarize your findings in a table.

3. Many people have created their own personal brands. Explore these websites:

    — Tom Peters (http://www.tompeters.com). Tom Peters is a management consultant and has a very interesting website.

    — Malcolm Gladwell (http://www.gladwell.com). Gladwell is a best selling author.

    — Peter Montoya (http://www.petermontoya.com). Montoya is a consultant on personal branding.

    Using the questions in Exhibit 13.4, analyze the personal brands of these three people. How are they the same? How are they different? What is the unique personal brand of these three websites? How does each website communicate the person's identity and values? What differentiates him from other consultants/authors?

4. Use any of the major search engines to enter the "blogosphere"—sites where individuals post their personal blogs about their interests and themselves. Pick out three blogs to study. What does each blog say about this person? How do blogs create a unique brand?

5. Consider creating your own blog at many of the blog sites, e.g., http://www.blogger.com, as a way to talk about you and your enterprise, and to build/create a unique identity. This site also provides insights into how to create a personal brand and talks about the need for "wow" in helping a person stand out from others.

6. Conduct research to learn how much several different search engines would charge for key words, sponsored ads, and similar services. For example, this would be the site for Google, to learn more about buying words and using Google to promote one's enterprise: http://www.google.com/adsense. What techniques could you use to improve your search results?

End Notes

1. "B & B Hardware," Yelp.com, http://www.yelp.com/biz (April 2, 2007).

2. "History," *In-N-Out Burger*, http://www.in-n-out.com (March 30, 2007).

3. "Harley-Davidson Inc.," *Yahoo! Finance*, http://finance.yahoo.com/q?s=HOG (April 5, 2007).

4. Adapted from material in Kevin Lane Keller, *Strategic Brand Management*, 2nd ed. (Englewood Cliffs, NJ: Prentice-Hall, 2003).

5. "About Scion," *Scion*, http://www.scion.com (February 8, 2006).

6. Adapted from material in Peter Montoya and Tim Vandehey, *The Brand Called You* (Santa Ana, CA: Personal Branding Press, 2003).

7. Brooks Barnes, "It Seemed like a Good Idea . . .," *Wall Street Journal*, April 30, 2007, p. R7.

8. Leslie Taylor, "How to Become a Household Name," *Inc.com*, January 16, 2006, http://www.inc.com.

9. Ibid.

10. Ibid.

11. Gail Goodman, "E-Mail Marketing Trends: E-Mail Gets Bigger by Getting Smaller," *Entrepreneur.com*, November 8, 2006, http://www.entrepreneur.com; and Leslie O'Flahavan and Marilynne Rudick, "5 Tips to a Ringing E-mail Tone," *Inc.com*, September 2001, http://www.inc.com.

12. Jeanette Borzo, "Selling Software," *Wall Street Journal*, March 19, 2007, p. R7.

13. Deborah Bonello, "Explore the Online Options," *Marketing*, December 20, 2006, Marketing Manual Supplement, pp. 35–36.

14. Kelly K. Spors, "In Search of Traffic," *Wall Street Journal*, April 30, 2007, p. R1.

15. Peter Alexander, "Should You Start a Business Blog?" *Entrepreneur.com*, February 28, 2007, http://www.entrepreneur.com; and Derek Gehl, "How to Harness the Marketing Power of Blogs," *Entrepreneur.com*, March 27, 2006, http://www.entrepreneur.com.

16. Yuki Noguchi, "Growing Pains for Web Sellers," *San Diego Union-Tribune*, November 25, 2006, p. C3.

17. Andrew Murr, "A Winning Equation," *Newsweek*, August 7, 2006, pp. 42–43.

Sales, Place, Price, and Service: Engaging Your Customers

KEY CONCEPTS

1. After enterprisers develop products, they must identify their target markets. By understanding the needs and desires of these customers and the motivations that cause them to buy, enterprisers can develop appropriate selling strategies for each of the six steps in the selling process: generating leads, qualifying them, approaching customers and assessing needs, developing and proposing solutions, closing the sale, and following up. Paying attention to customers to learn their needs and concerns accurately is an important sales skill to develop.

2. Enterprisers need a cost-effective way to acquire raw materials, make the products, and deliver them to the customer. Place (distribution) strategies are therefore an integral part of the marketing mix. Distribution channels form a network of intermediaries that facilitate the movement of goods from producer to end user. Key distribution decisions include choosing the appropriate channels through which you plan to sell and the supply chain logistics—from acquiring materials to producing, storing, and moving the product to the wholesaler or the end user.

3. Identifying a price for goods and services is a complicated process. The enterpriser seeks to make a profit after covering the costs to produce and provide goods and services to customers, who perceive the products to be fairly priced and of value. Many factors influence pricing decisions, including demand, supply, costs to produce, competition, and pricing objectives and strategies.

4. Creating and maintaining a profitable relationship with customers who value your products and services is a key to enterprise success. In most businesses, the cost of acquiring new customers—promoting and selling them products and services—is very expensive. It is more cost effective to retain existing customers and sell them additional products and services than to acquire a new customer. Customer management systems (CMS) build loyalty.

Suppose your family has a prized recipe for frozen lemonade, and you develop a machine that delivers consistent products every time. Your icy beverage quickly becomes popular on hot summer days in Rhode Island, so you decide to expand your company. Truck-mounted freezer units let you take your treats to your customers. As your brand gains loyal patrons, you recognize that your target market can grow beyond Cranston, Rhode Island. You choose to grow by carefully selecting franchisees who hold the same values as your family: a willingness to work hard and build the brand customer by customer.

© Alexander Nesbitt/Digital Railroad

Today Del's Lemonade, the family business started by Angelo DeLucia in 1948, is still going strong. Not only does Del's have stores throughout New England during the summer months, the company has expanded into warm-weather states such as Florida, California, and Nevada. By listening to their customers, the DeLucias knew what products to add. As you read this chapter, you will learn more about how companies can develop the right selling strategies, distribute their products, price them fairly, and maintain loyal customers.

14.0 Knowing Your Customers

In the previous chapter, we explored the process of developing your brand, your enterprise's identity, and ways to tell your story through the process of promotion. In this chapter, we will look at the specific relationships you will develop with your customers. The chapter is divided into four major sections. The first part focuses on the process of selling, which, from our perspective, involves the process of inviting individuals to become your customers. When enterprises are built on products and services that provide value to customers, the selling process enables individuals to make the choice to purchase from you. Attempting to get people to buy products or services they don't want, or don't believe have value for them, is a waste of both your time and theirs. Selling, then, is primarily about the process of getting to know specific customers so that your enterprise can provide them with products or services that they value.

Once you have developed your products and made the sale, you must get them to your customers. The issues around place, or distribution, include the channels through which you plan to sell, the logistics of the supply chain—from acquiring materials to producing, storing, and moving the product to the wholesaler or the end user.

Another critical aspect of the process of the sales and service relationship focuses on determining the price that your customers will pay you for the goods and services you provide. The determination of price is a challenging balance between the costs to produce and provide goods and services to your customer and the value the customer places on those goods and services. For example, assume it costs you a dollar to grow a small tomato plant from a seedling. If you sell these plants at the farmers market, the customers there might feel that a small tomato plant is worth only 75 cents. Customers at an upscale plant nursery, however, might feel that a small tomato plant is worth $2.50. Clearly, selling plants for 75 cents to customers is not profitable, and the tomato plant–growing enterprise will not succeed. Selling plants for $2.50 may be very profitable for the enterprise. Each person perceives the value of the same product or service differently, based on the place products or services are sold, the individual's needs and desires, and other factors that influence a sense of value.

Identifying a price for goods and services is a complicated process. You want to ensure that your enterprise will be profitable and that customers perceive your products to be fairly priced and of value. We will show you a number of different strategies that enterprises use for determining prices.

Finally, the chapter ends with a look at the process of creating and maintaining a profitable relationship with customers who value your products and services. As you have seen in the previous chapter, it is often very expensive to market, advertise, identify, and sell products and services to individuals who might potentially become your customers. In most businesses, the cost of acquiring new customers is very high. Think about how much money is spent on advertisements on television, the radio, and other media to entice people to purchase automobiles. The cost of this marketing effort might,

for example, run into thousands of dollars for each automobile sold. By focusing on CMS (customer management system), you seek to retain current customers for your products and services. It is more cost effective to retain existing customers and sell them additional products and services than to acquire a new customer. Knowing more about the needs and desires of your existing customers can be extremely valuable to the growth of your business. We will show you ways to pay attention to these customers in order to serve them better.

14.1 Why People Buy

Before you begin approaching prospective customers, you should know their needs and desires so that your enterprise can provide them with goods and services that they will value. A crucial aspect of this process involves learning about the different kinds of customers and the reasons they will appreciate your products and services. Let's examine one way to think about how customers might have different reasons for buying products and services: the product adoption cycle.

The Product Adoption Cycle

The product adoption cycle can be depicted as a bell-shaped curve, as shown in Exhibit 14.1. The number of people who are purchasing the product/service is on the Y axis, and time is on the X axis. As this demonstrates, when a new product is introduced, initially, few people purchase the product, and, over time, more and more people purchase it. Eventually, fewer people purchase the product because everyone has it. The product life cycle curve provides a good approximation for the number of customers who are likely to purchase at each stage of the product life cycle. As you can see in the Exhibit 14.1, the curve is divided into different types of customers: innovators, early adopters, the early majority, the late majority, and the laggards.[1]

Customers purchase a product for different reasons at each of these stages. When a product or service is new, the customer who is likely to try a completely new product or service is called an *innovator*. This group typically represents about 2.5 percent of all of the possible customers who might be willing to buy over the life cycle of this product or service. Innovators like to try new things. These people want the newest cell phone or the newest car model. They flock to the new restaurant and purchase the latest fashions. The challenge

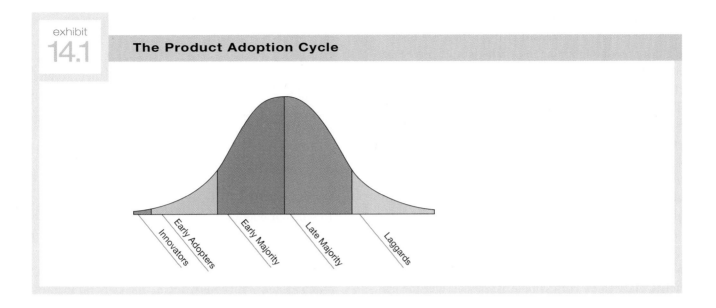

exhibit
14.1

The Product Adoption Cycle

and value provided to the innovator involves offering them important new features and benefits. The risk to innovators is that these new features and benefits might not necessarily be as good as or better than that of established products or services.

For example, are you the kind of person who would go to a new expensive restaurant that has just opened but has not been reviewed in the paper, and you don't know anyone who has tried it yet? What are the risks of going to this new restaurant? Well, you could order an expensive meal that doesn't taste very good, experience poor service, and end up having a horrible evening that costs you a lot of money. On the other hand, you could go to a restaurant that no one else has discovered, have a wonderful meal with great service, and have an experience to talk about with your friends. As one of the first to go to this restaurant, you'd establish some history with the restaurant so that as it gets busier, you find it easier for you to get reservations and great tables, as well as other special privileges.

Innovators play another important role. They are also the customers who are likely to provide either good or bad word of mouth about your enterprise. Others look to innovators to tell them whether something is worth buying or not. Think of your friends and acquaintances and identify which individuals you would go to find out about the latest restaurant, or club, or cell phone. These people are the innovators. Because they have tried new products and services before others, their opinions matter.

The second group, which typically consists of about 13.5 percent of the market, is the *early adopters*. Early

adopters are also willing to try new things and take chances on new products and services without much advice or support from others. However, innovators are more willing to take risks and undergo more hassles to try out new products and services. For example, they are likely to beta test new software. The early adopters tend to wait to try the new software after most of the bugs and problems in the early test versions are worked out. Innovators go to new restaurants on opening night and in the first week, while the restaurant is still working out its operations, whereas early adopters go in the first month, while the restaurant is still new but has smoothed out some of the problems.

The third group, which typically represents 34 percent of the market, is the *early majority*. The early majority is practical. They look to purchase new products and services that they have seen work out for others (the early adopters). They gather more information before buying. Consider the market for cell phones. The innovators are the ones who stood in line for Apple's iPhone, attracted by its unique multimedia features. As these features become more available on cell phones and the price goes down, the early adopters spread the word about how much they like the cell phone's movie features. Then the early majority looks for multimedia capability when purchasing cell phones.

The last two groups, the *late majority* and the *laggards* are those who wait to purchase a product until they see that the majority of buyers in the market now own the new product or have tried the service. For example, once enough of friends have cell phones that send text messages, the remaining members of the group will need to purchase a text messaging cell phone to communicate with the others. The transition from the early to late majority reaches a tipping point where nearly everyone now needs to have the product or service. Think of when the ownership of cell phones, DVD players, flat screen TVs, and iPods reached a tipping point; these electronic products went from novelties to equipment that nearly everyone desired.

Knowing the characteristics of the customer groups who purchase at various points along the product adoption cycle will help market your products more effectively. A complex technology product, for example, will take longer to move along the adoption curve than a new snack food. Your customers' willingness to try a new product or service depends on their interests, needs, and values. For example, if you consider the life cycle of flat screen TVs, the innovators were willing to pay thousands of dollars for the first models, while the late majority and the laggards are only willing to pay hundreds of dollars for the flat screen TV of the same size just a few years later. Newness matters to innovators, it doesn't to laggards.

Selling to Solve Customer Needs

Selling involves listening and paying attention to customers. What people want—why they buy—can vary significantly. As we discussed earlier in this book, customers buy benefits, rather than product features. They may want solutions to their problems, or perhaps status and prestige are more important. They have criteria concerning the reputation of the seller, too, such as honesty, consistency, reliability, and prompt service.[2] Selling involves matching their concerns and desires with what you can provide. Basically, selling is making sure to offer people what they say they want.

As we saw earlier in the product life cycle discussion, most buyers are risk averse. They are more likely to want to buy products or services that solve problems they already have. Selling a solution to potential customers' known problems is much easier, in general, than trying to get them to buy for other reasons, such as to obtain an advantage or exercise an opportunity.

An irony here is that most people want solutions to problems, whereas the goal of the enterprise is to pursue opportunities. Most people see problems. They see what is not working. Part of the aspect of opportunity development, then, is seeing opportunities as ways to find solutions to other people's problems. In other words, be a problem solver, not a problem finder!

14.2 The Selling Process

Selling is a six-step process to develop direct communication with customers that influences them to buy. It begins with lead generation and ends with closing the sale and following up with customers. Exhibit 14.2 summarizes the sales process.

Now let's examine each step in more detail.

Generating Leads

To sell your goods or services, you must first identify a large number of leads, or potential buyers. Another term for this first step is *prospecting*. Through your promotion efforts, customers will know about you and your products and want to buy them. You can also identify potential customers in several other ways:

- *Referrals from other customers:* Many businesses ask (and reward) customers they already have for the names of other people who might be interested in their products/services. For example, if you sell high-end electronics or furniture, you might offer a $50 gift certificate to customers who refer someone who buys a certain price level of your products.

- *Networking:* Joining business associations and other places helps you find possible customers for your products/services.

- *Cold calls:* Random cold calling is rarely effective because you are calling people without knowing about their interests or needs. You may, however, be able to generate lists of people who might have an interest in your product/services and then call them. Suppose you sell in-ground swimming pools. By finding lists of swim club members, you could call to see whether they had ever considered having a pool at home. Another target group might be new home owners who are making other outside improvements to their yard.

Qualifying Leads

Not every lead generated will have the characteristics of a buyer who will actually purchase your goods/service. By qualifying leads, you seek to determine three things about the leads you have generated:

1. *A recognized need:* The prospective customer has reasons for why they want your product/service.

exhibit
14.2

The Sales Process

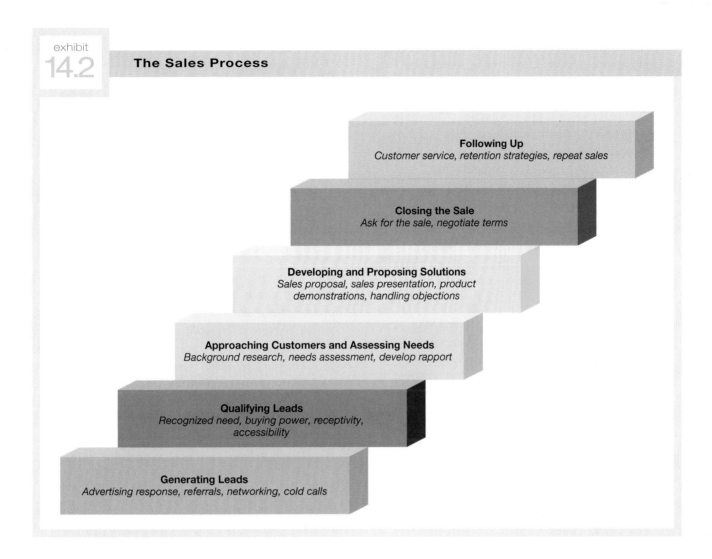

Following Up
Customer service, retention strategies, repeat sales

Closing the Sale
Ask for the sale, negotiate terms

Developing and Proposing Solutions
Sales proposal, sales presentation, product demonstrations, handling objections

Approaching Customers and Assessing Needs
Background research, needs assessment, develop rapport

Qualifying Leads
Recognized need, buying power, receptivity, accessibility

Generating Leads
Advertising response, referrals, networking, cold calls

2. *Buying power:* The prospective customer has the funds and the authority to purchase your product. For example, a person can have a need for a new car, but they don't have the money to buy the car, or, the person isn't the actual decision maker for the purchase.

3. *Receptivity and accessibility:* Obviously, you need to be able to make contact with and sell to customers to complete a sales transaction. Customers may have the needs and the buying power but simply aren't available or accessible.

New features of sales software can help enterprisers contact leads at times when they will be most receptive. At Print Runner, a California online printing company, the sales staff gets alerts from its SalesGenius software when a customer clicks through to the firm's website from a marketing email. Rather than making random calls and not finding the customer in, Print Runner's salespeople know they are available and interested in what the company offers.[3]

Approaching the Customer and Assessing Needs

The process of approaching the customer involves developing trust and competence. Someone who isn't perceived as trustworthy is unlikely to be successful in making the sale. Salespeople develop trust in a number of ways. Good salespeople familiarize themselves with their customers and their needs before the actual meeting. This demonstrates interest and develops rapport when they do meet and can go into greater detail about the customer's needs. Customers also want salespeople who are competent to meet those needs, are knowledgeable about the industry and competition, and understand the product or service. Also, the more the customer feels the salesperson is like himself/herself, the more likely there is some rapport for developing a dialogue between them.

Many subtle signals help create a sense of trustworthiness and connectedness between the salesperson and the customer.

- **Appearance:** Hair, clothes, accessories, and jewelry provide signals about your trustworthiness, competence, and your similarity to your buyers. Many types of jobs have a look or a uniform. An auto mechanic looks a certain way, and, most often, so do lawyers and accountants. There might be an implicit uniform for the kind of job you do. For example, if one is selling computers, is there a need for a certain kind of "computer nerd" look that might help convince buyers of one's qualifications for selling computers?

- **Cars:** Are there certain kinds of cars that your buyers will associate with successful sellers? Think of a real estate agent who takes you around town to look at houses in an old beat-up Toyota Corolla, versus a new Mercedes Benz.

- **Office/Space:** If clients are going to visit your office, what should the office space look like to communicate your enterprise's values and capabilities? What does the office of an architect, product designer, or an advertising agency look like, versus the offices for lawyers or accountants? Does your space need to say that you are creative and fun, or serious and methodical?

An important part of this selling stage is *needs assessment*. This requires the salesperson to evaluate the sales prospect's entire situation: Determining the prospect's needs, matching these needs to your enterprise's products and services, comparing your product/service offerings to your competition's, and realizing how your enterprise fits into the industry as a whole. The goal of needs assessment, then, is to develop a comprehensive grasp of your sales prospect's circumstances so that you can offer solutions that truly meet specific needs. We all have had experiences where sales people offer us solutions without ever asking what we really want. How receptive do we feel in that situation? Not very!

Questions are a critical element in the needs assessment process. Engaging the customer in a meaningful dialogue, asking probing questions, and listening carefully to what your customers tell you will help you identify their objections. Anticipate possible questions and work the answers into your presentation. This creates needs and will put you on the path to making the sale.

Some general questions explore the needs that customers have. The most important question is also a simple one: What do you want?

While the above question is somewhat blunt, the idea is to help customers describe their problems and needs. For example, if you were helping a customer buy a computer,

you would ask, what do you want in a computer? The answers that your customer provides will offer you insights into what the customer's major concerns are—for example, portability, low price, word processing software, Wi-Fi, DVD player, ability to store lots of photos and videos, and ability to talk/see/be seen by others on the Internet. Each of these words means something to the customer, and the goal of the enterprise is to find out what each of these words specifically means and to help the customer deal with trade-offs between these various criteria. For example, what does "low price" mean to the customer: A computer for $500? $1,000? $2,000? What does portability mean to the customer? A computer that weighs 2 lbs? 4 lbs? 6 lbs? Typically, a customer can purchase a low-priced computer, but, such a computer will likely weigh more and have fewer features than a higher-priced computer.

Other questions that help in identifying a customer's needs include:

- What is the problem that you spend the most time and aggravation on?

- What would make your life simpler?

- Can you describe the ideal (product, service, etc.) that would best solve your problem?

- How can I save you money?

- How can I save you time?

Developing and Proposing Solutions

Making a sale involves working jointly with sales prospects to solve their problems. The process of developing and proposing solutions treats the customer as an active participant in this process: "Help me to help you solve your problem."

It is rare that people make decisions right away without voicing concerns they might have about their choices. The process of handling objections involves helping customers identify the reasons they want your enterprise's products or services. Even better, pick up clues of possible objections from your customers and answer the questions *before* they are asked. This may eliminate objections before they arise and avoid a negative attitude on the customer's part.

If you watch any of the home-shopping channels on television, you have seen some of these selling techniques in action. For example, when Maureen Kelly decided to sell items from her Tarte Cosmetics line on QVC network, she first worked with QVC trainers for a day. She was advised not to make a standard sales pitch but rather to show viewers how the products work. Through demonstrations she could explain how her cosmetics are unique and will improve users' appearance—in other words, position the products as problem solvers.[4]

Closing the Sale

The transaction process requires that the sales prospect agree to the sale. Therefore, one of the critical aspects of making a sale involves "asking for the sale." In other words, the salesperson will need to ask the customer to commit. "Are you ready to sign the papers? Can I gift wrap that for you? Will you be using cash, credit card, or personal check?" are all ways that salespeople use to close the sale. Once a customer has agreed to make a purchase, the closing process may also involve negotiating specific aspects of the purchase agreement, such as the price of the product/service, or such features as free installation, free delivery and set up, a discount on the price, payment terms, and trade-in value.

Following Up

The selling process doesn't end when you close the sale. In nearly all enterprises, a sale to a particular customer creates an opportunity for more chances to engage in sales at future dates and times. When you purchase an automobile, for example, the sale doesn't end. There are opportunities for service and to insure that the customer is happy with the purchase. As we will see in later sections, customers who are satisfied with their purchases over time are much more likely to purchase products and services from you again. Unsatisfied customers will not buy from you again, and they are also likely to tell others not to buy from you as well. Keeping your customers satisfied with their purchases after the sale through follow-up builds loyalty that is critical for the future success of your business.

As you can see from the six steps of the selling process, the majority of these steps (steps one to four) involve learning about your customers and finding out what they want.

14.3 Sales Skills and Attitudes

The selling process is a learned behavior. Some people may have inherent capabilities that make it easier for them to sell. For example, people who are good listeners and who are empathetic have an easier time at selling, because those skills and attitudes come naturally for them. However, we all can improve our ability to listen and to be more empathetic.

Fear of Failure and Rejection

As you've developed your enterprise and honed the products and services your enterprise offers, you'll want others to share your confidence that you can meet their needs and solve their problems. It is hard to hear people say "no" to your offer. Indeed, most people would rather not put themselves in a position to hear "no." We tend to take the rejection of our offer personally, taking the "no" to refer to us, rather than about our particular products or services. A "no" might be a misunderstanding. The potential buyer may have misunderstood what you are offering and how it might meet particular buying needs. In fact, most potential customers may not want your products or services! So "no" is likely to be a majority of responses.

The key issue is to realize that you build your enterprise based on the "yeses" you get. Finding customers is a "numbers game." You will need to talk to a lot of customers who will say "no" to reach a sufficient number of customers who say "yes." So be prepared for many more nos than yeses—and remember that those yeses add up!

Paying Attention

Because most people are so fearful that they will receive a "no," they often don't really listen to what their prospective customers say. They are anticipating the "no." As a result, they will miss important information, such as what their customers *do* want and need—even if they are saying "no" at that particular moment.

The following story illustrates this point. A local real estate developer requires that all his salespeople have a real estate license. The developer is selling lakeside homes and condominiums in the $300,000 to $500,000 range. He realizes that most people who will look at his lakeside properties are likely not to buy. However, anyone who does visit is likely in the market for a home or condominium. From his perspective, his salespeople have customers who want to buy a home. If these customers don't want his properties, they might be interested in something else, and his salespeople can work to solve those customer's needs. If salespeople know that they can sell—not only the developer's properties but other properties as well—it enables them to listen more carefully to what each potential customer wants. Surprisingly, some customers who aren't initially interested in the developer's properties eventually do buy, because the sales agents really listen to what these customers want, and, in considering how best to meet these needs, come up with ways to match the customer's needs with what the developer can offer.

The ability to pay attention to what customers are asking for is really helpful. It relates to our discussion of mindfulness in Chapter 6.

One technique that is really helpful for listening is to repeat back to the customer what you think you are hearing. In any restaurant, for example, waiters often repeat the order to make sure they heard it correctly. "You said, 'No onions, with pickles, light mayonnaise, with mustard, no catsup, and tomatoes.'" You can confirm or correct it then, rather than hope that the waiter heard your order correctly and risk getting the wrong food.

In addition to listening and hearing accurately what your customer's concerns are, also watch how your customer is reacting. There are many reasons why a customer might not be focused on the sales task at hand. Maybe your customer is tired, or hungry, or distracted. These or similar issues make it difficult for them to concentrate on the purchase process. Consider, for example, that you are selling automobiles, and a couple with three active children comes into the showroom. The parents will be able to focus on looking at cars and talking to you if their kids can play in a supervised children's play area.

Distribution (or marketing) channel   Network of intermediary organizations that work together to facilitate the movement of goods from producer to end user.

Agent   Professional sales representative for manufacturers and wholesalers but does not take title to goods.

Practice

Most of us get better at a skill as we practice it, and selling is no exception. The more opportunities we have to sell, the better we are likely to get at the selling process. Think of every sales call as a learning experience. Each time you interact with a customer, you increase your ability to diagnose problems and create more effective presentations in the future. Consider why a particular selling presentation was a success, or not. Watch others selling. Learn from their mistakes and successes. And have others watch you and give you feedback on how you engage in the selling process.

14.4   Finding Your Place

Where are you in the web of connections that occur between the products that are created and the customers who actually use them? Enterprisers can be at any one of the many steps along the way, from supplying the raw materials to selling the actual goods or services to the final user. This process of getting goods and services from producer to user is the fourth P in the marketing mix: *place*, also called *distribution*.

Place strategies are an integral part of the marketing mix. We will look at issues involved with the location of your enterprise in Chapter 15, when we explore how your location can be an important resource for insuring the success of your business. This section looks at the process of distribution.

An enterpriser might have the best product to solve a specific customer problem. But to satisfy customer needs, however, an enterpriser must have a cost-effective way to get the raw materials to a manufacturing facility and then deliver the finished goods to customers on time. This process, also called *logistics*, requires an efficient network of organizations that come together in **distribution channels**. Also called *marketing channels*, distribution channels are composed of intermediaries who facilitate the movement of goods from producer to end user. Channel members work together to fulfill customer demands by using resources efficiently. Members have specific roles in the distribution process.[5]

The five major types of distribution intermediaries are:

- Agents: Professional sales representatives of manufacturers and wholesalers; do not take title to goods.

- **Brokers:** Intermediaries who facilitate exchanges of goods by bringing together buyers and sellers; do not take title to goods.

- **Industrial distributors:** Independent wholesalers who specialize in business-to-business markets; buy related product lines from many manufacturers and sell them to industrial users.

- **Wholesalers:** Distributors who buy finished goods from manufacturers and sell them to retailers, other wholesalers, manufacturers, and institutions.

- **Retailers:** Companies that sell goods to end users, both consumers and industrial users.

For example, many companies prefer to outsource their sales function to agents such as independent *manufacturers' representatives*. Manufacturers' reps act as the producer's sales team and work on a commission basis. Because they represent many different product lines, many of which are related, they can give a small company access to many more potential customers than the company would have on its own.

The number and type of intermediary will depend on the type of product. The *direct channel* is the shortest: from producer to customer. *Indirect channels* involve several middlemen. Exhibit 14.3 shows the various channel options for both consumer and industrial products.

The distribution strategy you choose will influence other marketing decisions, including product design and packaging. Exhibit 14.4 lists a few of the many distribution-related questions enterprisers should consider.

Companies aren't limited to just one channel for product distribution. Often they use *multiple channels* to distribute the same product to different target markets. Most retailers today sell in both physical stores and online. Circuit City has physical stores as well as an online store. Customers can even order online and arrange to pick up the item at the nearest store. There are also nontraditional channels that can be used by themselves or in addition to other channels. Examples are Internet stores, infomercials, direct downloads of electronic media, home shopping channels on television, and kiosks in malls and airports.

The Role of the Intermediary

If you have a very small company with a single product sold only locally, you may think you can handle all the distribution yourself. Perhaps you will just sell directly to your customers. However, such a strategy would severely limit your access to potential users. A specialist who knows how to place your products can add value and provide services that facilitate the distribution process. The following are the advantages of selling your products through intermediaries:

- *Reducing the number and cost of transactions.* If every customer purchased directly from every producer, the number of contacts would be enormous and the process would be inefficient and costly. With an intermediary such as a retail store, products from many manufacturers are available for many consumers, all in one place. For example, suppose that you want to buy a new digital camera and are interested in models from six manufacturers: Sony, Olympus, Casio, Kodak, Nikon, and Panasonic. Without an intermediary, you'd have to contact each manufacturer directly—six contacts. Multiply that by just four other consumers who want cameras, too, and you have 24 different transactions. When you have a retailer such as Best Buy or Amazon.com, each producer and each customer makes just one contact, for a total of 11. The six producers sell to one intermediary, and the five customers buy from one retailer.

- *Facilitating transactions.* Intermediaries increase the efficiency of the channel. They contact potential buyers, promote products, provide product information, and seek orders on behalf of the producers they represent.

- *Storing goods.* Often wholesalers maintain product inventory for retailers.

- *Performing logistical functions.* Intermediaries determine how to physically distribute the goods, maintain inventories, and bring together an assortment of goods in one place.

Broker Intermediary that facilitates exchanges of goods by bringing together buyers and sellers, but does not take title to goods.

Industrial distributor Independent wholesaler that buys related product lines from many manufacturers to sell to industrial users.

Wholesaler Distributor who buys finished goods from manufacturers and sells them to retailers, manufacturers, and institutions.

Retailer Company that sells goods to end users, both consumers and industrial users.

exhibit
14.3

Distribution Channels

exhibit
14.4

Distribution Decision Questions

Should I sell directly to the consumer or use a reseller?

Do I need a wholesaler or a reseller network?

How long should the distribution channel be (number of members)?

Should I use multiple channels?

Where should the product or service be available?

When should the product or service be available?

Should distribution be exclusive, selective, or extensive?

Who should control the channel (referred to as the channel captain)?

How formal should channel relationships be?

What are the physical distribution and logistical issues for this product?

Where will I store the products until I sell them?

How can I manage inventory to minimize costs and meet user needs?

How will I transport the product to the end user?

- *Researching markets.* Intermediaries gather valuable market research from other channel participants, such as consumer trends and buying patterns, industry trends, and product development information.

- *Assuming risks.* Some types of intermediaries take title to the goods and therefore assume all risks associated with ownership, from theft and spoilage to obsolescence.

- *Financing assistance.* Channel members may help producers by extending credit, offering loans, and providing other financial services.

Channel Strategy and Relationships

Developing a channel strategy is a complex process. An enterpriser must evaluate channel members in terms of the value they add to the distribution process. Among the key decisions facing enterprisers are market, product, and producer factors and distribution intensity.

Choosing a Channel

Enterprisers have many channel options from which to choose. They must consider market, product, and producer factors—both separately and in relation to each other.

- *Market factors.* Who are the customers? What, when, and how do they buy? Are they non-industrial consumers or industrial customers? How large is the market? Is it geographically concentrated or spread out? These are some of the key market factors enterprisers must analyze when choosing a channel. Each customer group has different characteristics that will affect the channel decision.

- *Product factors.* The characteristics of the product—complexity, cost, perishability/ fragility—may dictate the best channel. High priced and specialized items such as industrial equipment and pharmaceuticals benefit from a direct channel, an in-house sales force, and delivery from the company's factories. High volume, low price items—snacks, cosmetics, batteries, and similar products—can be sold in retail outlets, either physical or online. The manufacturer may ship directly to the retailer or use a wholesaler. Distributors or value-added resellers typically handle the middle price ranges. Perishable goods such as meats and vegetables require a short channel. There are always exceptions, of course. Many retail companies sell directly to the consumer

using mail order and Web stores. Seeing how the products or services in your industry are provided is important for understanding who, then, profits in this system, and how distribution may benefit certain members of the channel more than others.

- *Producer factors.* Some factors, such as size and financial strength, are specific to the producer itself. The more resources it has within the company, the shorter its channels. Smaller companies may not be able to afford their own sales force, warehouses in multiple areas, and credit departments. Instead, they contract with intermediaries to provide some or all of these services.

Channels can change over a product's life. Eisco, Inc., a New Jersey company, makes Clubhouse Kit brand uniform cleaning and sanitizing products for baseball team uniforms. The company began by selling directly to every major league team, who loved the specialty products. Soon minor league teams heard how well the products removed grass and other tough stains and signed on as well. Brad Singer, son of the company founder, knew that many other market segments would

© Jonathan Kirn/MLB Photos/Getty Images

like his cleaners, too. But selling to the large number of youth, high school, and college teams nationally was a very different ball game than contacting about 30 major league teams' managers. How could he spread the word about the cleaning power of Eisco's line? Should he focus on makers of sports equipment or look for sporting goods retailers? How could he convince all the retailers to carry his Clubhouse Kits? Should the product be displayed with uniforms or accessories?

Singer's first move was to add online sales to the company website. Next Singer arranged with several major sporting goods retailers to carry Clubhouse Kits on their websites. One of them, Modell's, now stocks some products in its retail stores. In addition to professional baseball teams, Singer is also adding lacrosse, soccer, and football teams to his customers.[6]

Distribution Intensity

Another channel decision involves how to get the right amount of coverage for the producer's market or degree of intensity. The three options are exclusive, selective, or intensive distribution, and the choice depends on product characteristics.

Exclusive distribution gives the most limited market coverage. It is typically used for very expensive or specialty products and gives one or two intermediaries (wholesalers or retailers) the exclusive right to sell the product within a defined geographic area. Automotive manufacturers use exclusive distribution, as do producers of industrial equipment such as John Deere. Some consumer luxury goods producers use exclusive distribution to enhance the prestige of their products. Choosing exclusive distribution means that products are less widely available. The trade-off is greater selectivity and quality control for the producer, which may increase customer satisfaction.

With *selective distribution*, the producer carefully chooses a limited number of dealers in each area. Consumer shopping goods—computers, televisions, branded consumer goods such as designer clothing and

cosmetics lines—and other specialty items use selective distribution.

Producers use the third type of market coverage, *intensive distribution*, when they want to get their goods on as many retailers' shelves as possible. Low cost, high-frequency consumer convenience purchases such as soft drinks, candy, chips, health and beauty products, and other mass market items are examples of intensely distributed goods. The manufacturers work with most wholesalers who want to carry their products.

Managing the Distribution Function

Once enterprisers determine their companies' distribution strategies, they must develop plans to manage them. This requires establishing a strong supply chain. A firm's **supply chain** is the complete network of businesses that help it create and deliver products to customers. The supply chain includes vendors who supply raw materials, the producers themselves, and the distribution intermediaries. An effective supply chain management system requires coordinating the many activities of the supply chain members to achieve an efficient materials flow and exchange of information across the channel. This process, called **logistics**, has six steps: sourcing and procurement, order processing, production scheduling, choosing a warehouse location and type, setting up an inventory system, and making transportation decisions.

Each of these steps requires finding the most efficient way to accomplish the necessary tasks while minimizing costs. For example, a producer's purchasing agents seek the best prices for raw materials and supplies. They also must coordinate with the production schedulers so that the necessary parts are on site as needed and develop cooperative relationships with vendors. Orders must be processed efficiently and accurately. Today's ordering systems are highly automated, with the Internet and other forms of electronic data interchange streamlining order processing. The locations of warehouses and distribution centers depend on the markets served. Inventory control systems strive to keep a supply of materials or finished goods available to meet producer or customer needs. Cost is a big issue in inventory control. Inventory managers want to have enough on hand to avoid stock-outs—but not so much extra that carrying costs are high.

The cost of transporting goods to the user is a significant component of overall cost, averaging 5–10 percent of the item's price. Transportation managers can ship goods by air, truck, water, train, and pipeline, or a combination of several modes. Each has trade-offs in

Supply chain   The complete network of businesses involved in obtaining inputs, making goods, and delivering products to customers.

Logistics   A system to manage and coordinate the many steps of the supply chain to achieve an efficient materials flow and exchange of information across the channel.

terms of cost, time, reliability, and similar factors. Air is the fastest but costs the most. Water is the least expensive and well suited to bulky commodities such as coal and lumber. But it is slow and not suited to perishables. Shippers are limited by the route of the waterway and will need another carrier such as a truck to get the goods to the customer. Product characteristics are also factors in transportation decisions. Ice cream requires refrigerated trucks or rail cars.

A growing trend is the outsourcing of logistics functions. Many businesses now turn to outside specialists to handle part of all of their supply chain. By relying on logistics experts, producers can focus on product development and manufacturing. Benefits include reduced costs and improved service.

14.5   The Price Is Right

As mentioned at the beginning of this chapter, setting prices is a complex process. Different individuals will value a particular good or service differently. Individuals who place a higher perceived value on a product will pay more for the same product or service than others. Pricing decisions must also take into account a company's pricing objectives (e.g., profit maximization or sales volume) and the demand for and cost to produce the product. Once those are determined, the company can select a pricing strategy that suits its goals and the product.

Pricing is a dynamic process. Over time, changes in the product life cycle stage, demand, costs, and competition call for reevaluation of a company's pricing strategies. There are also price points at which suppliers will want to provide these goods or services. In economics, these are the forces of demand and supply.

Demand

The price a person is willing to pay represents the value that the buyer perceives the item is worth. This is called **demand**, or the quantity of a good or service the customers will buy at different prices. The **demand curve** expresses this in a graph. In general, the higher the price, the fewer the number of people who will buy that good or service. As the price drops, more people are willing to buy it.

Let's say that you own a movie theatre and you are thinking about how to price your tickets. You have the rights to show a first-run movie, and no other movie theatre in a 25-mile radius can show this movie for the next two weeks. Exhibit 14.5 shows the demand schedule and curve for the price people in your area would be willing to pay to see this movie. As you can see, significantly more people are willing to pay only $5.00 for a movie ticket than are willing to pay $25.00.

The demand curve therefore slopes downward: As the price rises, fewer people demand a product. All goods or services have a somewhat similar demand curve. For example, people who want the first model of a new car may be willing to pay a premium over the sticker price. Others won't pay the sticker price for a particular new car. Typically, as prices go down for a good or service, more people are willing to purchase the product or use the service.

The changes in revenue along this demand curve represent customers' **elasticity of demand**. Elasticity is another way to represent change. Given this demand curve, if you calculate the revenue for each of these price points, you see that different prices and numbers of buyers can actually yield similar total revenues. You would receive just as much money by selling tickets at $12.50 as you would by selling tickets at $10. When customers are willing to purchase more or less of a product or service when the price changes, demand is *elastic*. If customers are willing to purchase the same amount of a product or service, no matter what the price, then demand is *inelastic*. When total revenue is the same when prices change, then demand is *unitary*. Exhibit 14.6 lists some simple ways of determining elasticity of demand.

Knowing whether the demand for the business's goods or services is elastic or inelastic can better help an enterpriser decide at what point revenue might be maximized for given numbers of customers. For example, some products, such as milk, might have an elastic price. If the price of milk goes up, demand is likely to go down; people have other options like water, soda, or fruit juice. If the price of milk goes down, more people might switch from the other beverages to milk.

Other products or services are price inelastic. Think of the price of a driver's license. The state posts a price

Demand   The quantity of a good or service the customers will buy at different prices.

Demand curve   Graph that shows the relationship between how much of a good or service that people will buy at various prices.

Elasticity of demand   Responsiveness of quantity demanded to a price change.

exhibit

14.5

Demand Curve and Demand Schedule for Movie Tickets

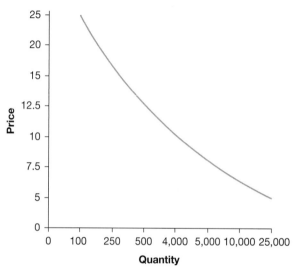

(a) Demand Curve

(b) Demand Schedule

Price of a Movie Ticket	Number of People Who Will Pay This Price	Total Revenue
$25.00	100	$2,500
$20.00	250	$5,000
$15.00	500	$7,500
$12.50	4,000	$50,000
$10.00	5,000	$50,000
$7.50	10,000	$75,000
$5.00	25,000	$125,000

exhibit

14.6

Elasticity of Demand

Demand is elastic when:

Prices go down and revenue goes up.

Prices go up and revenue goes down.

Demand is inelastic when:

Prices go down and revenue goes down.

Prices go up and revenue goes up.

Demand is unitary when:

Prices go up or down, but revenues stay the same.

to obtain a driver's license, and whether a million people purchase driver's licenses or ten million people apply for them, the price will not change. In the short run, certain products are probably price inelastic as well. The price of gasoline could, in a short period of time, double in price. Because most people still need to use their automobiles to commute to work and for errands, gasoline sales won't change substantially. But over the long run, if gasoline stayed at a price double what it now costs, then some people would likely change their behaviors and use less gasoline by combining trips, walking, or purchasing a more gasoline-efficient car.

© Corbis/Jupiter Images

Supply

To fully understand how the market establishes price points, we must also consider **supply**, or the amount of a good or service that a business will make available at different price levels. While the demand curve indicates at what prices customers are willing to purchase a product or service, the **supply curve** indicates at what prices suppliers are willing to offer products or services.

Typically, as the price of a product or service rises, more enterprisers are willing to provide the product or service. For example, if you were in the market to purchase a used mountain bicycle, you might find that only a few people would be willing to sell you their bicycle for $100, while there are likely to be thousands of bicycles offered to you if you offered $10,000 for a bicycle.

A classic example of how rising prices affect supply is the Hunt Family's desire to corner the market on silver in the late 1970s. The Hunts began buying as much silver as they could. They assumed that the supply of silver was inelastic: The amount of silver available was, in the short term, determined by the amount of silver generated from silver mining companies.

As the Hunts purchased more silver, the price of silver rose, bringing more people who owned silver into the market. People with silver table settings were not willing to sell their silver at 10 cents a troy ounce, but when the price rose to nearly 80 cents a troy ounce, they surged into the market. The market for silver was soon flooded with people willing to sell at 80 cents per troy ounce. With so much silver on the market, prices plunged. All of the silver that the Hunts had purchased at 80 cents a troy ounce was worth much less, and they lost much of their fortune.

For our movie theatre example, we could look at supply in terms of the number of movie theatre seats that might be available at a particular price. Typically, the higher the price offered, the more supply of a product or service will be offered. In our case, we can consider a situation where the price of a movie ticket is $1.00. At that price, there would likely be no movie theatres that would consider providing a ticket to see a first-run movie show because the owners couldn't cover their costs. Indeed, we might not find any theatres willing to supply movie tickets for a price less than $5.00. At this price, we might find that some movie theatres will release some of their seats at this price (such as seats for a matinee showing, or any showing of first-run movies that begins before 4 PM on a week day). For a particular area, the number of seats that might be offered at $5.00 is 5,000 seats. At prices of $7.50 or higher, all of the seats that the theatres have to offer are available. In this example, because so many seats are available, supply at $7.50 or higher is *inelastic*.

Let's assume that for a two-week run of a new movie at our 500-seat theater, the theatre could show the film every three hours, for eight shows per day. The maximum number of available seats would be 14 days × 8 showings per day × 500 seats, or 56,000 seats. At $25 per ticket, the theater owner would keep the theatre open 24 hours a day—if there were sufficient demand. At $15.00 per ticket, the owner would probably keep the theatre open 24 hours a day as well. When the price is from $7.50 to $12.50 a ticket, the shows per day drops to four, or 28,000 tickets. At $5.00 per ticket, the owner is willing to show the film only twice a day, for a maximum supply

Supply   The amount of a good or service that a business will make available at different price levels.

Supply curve   Graph that indicates at what prices suppliers are willing to offer products or services.

of 14,000 tickets. Exhibit 14.7 shows the supply schedule and supply curve based on these assumptions.

On the supply side of the price equation, businesses are likely to offer products or services at particular prices based on their cost to supply them. Let's now look at how costs and breakeven affect this situation.

Costs and Breakeven

Price and total revenue are two parts of the profit picture. The other key element is the cost to produce the goods or offer services. Businesses incur two types of costs, fixed and variable. As we learned in Chapter 7, *fixed costs* don't vary, regardless of how many items you sell.

Rent, mortgage, insurance, utilities, and some personnel costs are examples of fixed costs. *Variable costs* are tied to volume. A manufacturer's raw material costs rise with the number of units produced. Wages may also vary based on production volume, particularly in a manufacturing setting.

Let's return to our movie theatre example. You will incur a number of different fixed and variable costs to supply, or show, movies in your theatre, no matter how many people purchase tickets. You must still pay fixed costs for the building, for utilities, and for staff to take tickets, run the projector, and clean the theater. Variable costs may include a per-ticket fee to the movie production company that supplies the film. What you

exhibit 14.7

Supply Curve and Supply Schedule for Movie Tickets

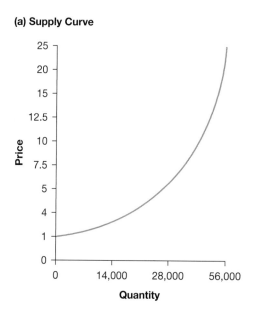

(a) Supply Curve

(b) Supply Schedule

Price of a Movie Ticket	Number of Theatre Seats Available at This Price	Total Revenue
$25.00	56,000	$1,400,000
$20.00	56,000	$1,120,000
$15.00	56,000	$840,000
$12.50	28,000	$350,000
$10.00	28,000	$280,000
$7.50	28,000	$210,000
$5.00	14,000	$70,000
$4.00	0	$0
$1.00	0	$0

pay the production company will vary, depending on how many people purchase tickets. Assume that for the two weeks you show this first-run film, the fixed costs to operate the theatre—those costs that will be paid whether anyone comes to the theatre or not—run $5,000 a week, or $10,000 for the two weeks.

How many tickets would you need to sell to reach a point where the revenue from the tickets you sell equals your variable and fixed costs? This point where your costs equal your revenues is called your **break-even point**. For our movie theatre example, it will depend on the price of the ticket. The general formula would be:

[Variable Cost (VC) $\times$ (Y number of tickets)] + fixed costs (FC) = Price of the ticket $\times$ (number of tickets)

We can simplify this to:

$$[VC \times Y] + FC = Price \times Y$$

Let's assume that the variable cost you owe the movie distributor is $5.00 per ticket and that you set the price of the ticket at $7.50. Substituting these values into our equation and solving it, we get:

$$\$5.00 \times Y + \$10,000 = \$7.50 \times Y$$
$$\$10,000 = \$2.50 \times Y$$
$$4,000 = Y$$

This means that you need to sell 4,000 tickets to cover your fixed and variable costs. If you sell fewer than 4,000 tickets, you will not cover your costs and will have a loss. Exhibit 14.8 shows the break-even point for our movie theatre example. Fixed costs are a constant $10,000, while variable costs (the fee to the movie production company) increase at $5.00 per ticket sold. So for 2,000 tickets, the theater owner incurs $10,000 in fixed costs and $10,000 in variable costs (2,000 tickets $\times$ $5.00), for total costs of $20,000. At this level, we still have a shortfall because revenue is only $15,000.

Now let's assume that your movie theatre seats 500 people, and you will totally fill the house at each showing. It will take you eight showings of the film (4,000 $\div$ 500 $\times$ 8) to break even. Because we saw in our demand schedule (Exhibit 14.5) that there are 10,000 people willing to pay $7.50 for tickets, you could meet all the demand by showing the film 20 times over the two-week period (assuming that you filled the theatre to capacity each time)—and make a profit after the eighth showing.

Suppose, however, you set the price of the ticket at $10.00. Then:

$$\$5.00 \times Y + \$10,000 = \$10.00 \times Y$$
$$\$10,000 = \$5.00 \times Y$$
$$2,000 = Y$$

In this case, you could break even in four showings of the film (2,000 $\div$ 500 = 4), and you could meet all of the demand (5,000 tickets, per Exhibit 14.5) if you showed the film to capacity ten times.

Looking back at the revenue calculations for the demand schedules in Exhibit 14.5, you can see that you will never break even if you price tickets for the entire two weeks at $25.00, $20.00, or $15.00. You will not generate enough total revenues to cover your fixed and variable costs at these levels.

Pricing Strategies

From the demand schedule, we know that people will pay a variety of prices for a particular product or service. Our movie ticket example shows that we have 100 people willing to pay $25.00 for a movie ticket, while thousands are willing to pay lower prices. Are there ways to sell movie tickets at various prices to capture some of this price differential?

We are sure that your own moviegoing experience provides insights into how a theatre owner might charge some customers more for their movie tickets than others, even for the same show and at the same time. For example, you could:

- Charge a premium price for reserved seats, so the movie buyer doesn't have to wait in line to rush into the theatre to find the best seat.

- Promote the first showing of the movie as the local premier and charge moviegoers more to attend this event.

- Fill seats in the theatre during non-peak moviegoing times by charging lower prices, even a price of $5.00 per ticket, which would just cover the variable cost you owe the movie distributor.

- Subsidize movie and fixed costs from substantial earnings from popcorn, candy, drinks, and food sales.

- Offer discounts for the movie to senior citizens, students, and children.

- Charge a lower ticket price for groups of 25 or more who book in advance.

As this example shows, a particular product—in this case, the opportunity to view a brand-new movie

Break-even point   The price level where your costs equal your revenues.

Costs, Revenues, and Break-even Point for Movie Theatre Tickets

(a) Break-even Point

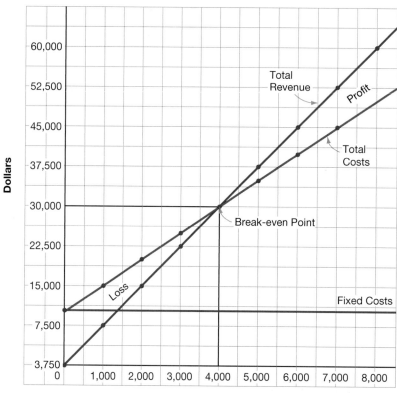

(b) Revenues and Costs

(1) Quantity of Tickets Sold	(2) Total Revenue @ $7.50 per Ticket	(3) Fixed Cost	(4) Total Variable Cost (Quantity × $5)	(5) Total Costs (3) + (4)	(6) Profit or Loss (2)− (5)
1,000	$7,500	$10,000	$5,000	$15,000	($7,500)
2,000	$15,000	$10,000	$10,000	$20,000	($5,000)
3,000	$22,500	$10,000	$15,000	$25,000	($2,500)
4,000	$30,000	$10,000	$20,000	$30,000	$0
5,000	$37,500	$10,000	$25,000	$35,000	$2,500
6,000	$45,000	$10,000	$30,000	$40,000	$5,000
7,000	$52,500	$10,000	$35,000	$45,000	$7,500
8,000	$60,000	$10,000	$40,000	$50,000	$10,000

during a two-week period—has many ways it might be priced. Exhibit 14.9 lists a number of ways to set the price of a product or service. How many of these pricing strategies might be used as ways to price a movie ticket?

The two most commonly used strategies for new products are price skimming and penetration pricing. As a product moves through its life cycle, prices may change to reflect changing demand for the product and market competition.

Of course, enterprisers must comply with government regulations that cover pricing. As we learned in Chapter 5, there are numerous laws that promote fair prices and prohibit unfair pricing. The Enterprising Ethics box takes a closer look at the ethical issues involved in pricing.

exhibit
14.9

Pricing Strategies

Strategy	Description	Example
Price skimming	Charging a high price for new products with a competitive advantage to reach customers who are not price sensitive. Price may later drop to reach other market segments.	Newly introduced products; good for products where demand exceeds supply.
Penetration pricing	Setting initial price low to increase market share and discourage competition.	Mass market products.
Loss leader pricing	Pricing one or more products below cost to attract customers.	Heavily discounting one model of a name brand TV to bring customers into a store so they will buy other items.
Odd-even pricing	Using an odd number, typically 5, 7, or 9, to suggest a bargain price and an even number to suggest quality.	Only $9.99! Plasma TV for $1,995.
Prestige pricing	Setting a high price throughout the product's life because it is unique or has a competitive advantage.	Luxury items: Four Seasons Hotels, Ferraris, designer clothes.
Economy pricing	Setting low prices on basic, no-frills product lines.	Grocery store private label brands, generic brands.
Product line pricing	Offering a range of product options at different price points.	Toyota offers the Yaris and Corolla for budget-minded customers, the Camry and Avalon as more upscale options, and the RAV4 and Highlander for SUV buyers.
Promotional pricing	Temporarily reducing price or offering coupons to promote sales volume.	Buy one, get one free; buy one, second is 50% off; $1.00 off with coupon.
Quantity discount	Offering multiple units for one price; encourages larger purchases.	3 toothbrushes for $4.00 (versus $1.75 each).
Bundling	Selling several products at a package price that is lower than purchasing each separately.	Buy a computer and printer for $750, compared to paying $825 if purchased separately.
Geographical pricing	Setting different prices based on customer's location; may base on demand, cost of living, or distribution costs.	Hotel rooms in New York City cost more than those in Albany, NY, or Sioux Falls, SD. U.S. products typically cost more in international markets.
Time-of-day pricing	Lowering prices at off-peak times.	Discount tickets for weekday movie matinees.
Seasonal pricing	Sale prices at certain peak shopping times.	Back-to-school specials; January white sales; pre- and post-holiday sales.

ENTERPRISING ETHICS

The Laws and Ethics on Pricing

Suppose you are opening a music club in a major city catering to the hip singles crowd. You want to attract lots of young women, so that the men will follow. So you decide to set your cover charges $5 lower for women. On some nights, you may even let them in for free.

Seems reasonable, right? In fact, the National Coalition of Free Men brought a price discrimination suit against the Century Supper Club, a Los Angeles nightclub, for just such pricing tactics. The California Supreme Court upheld the right of four men to sue the club, concurring that such pricing ran afoul of two California laws. According to California state law, businesses must provide equal accommodations regardless of sex, race, religion, and other similar factors. In the court's decision, Chief Justice Ronald George stated that gender discounts represent a denial of equal treatment.

Clearly, enterprisers must be aware of both federal and state regulations that affect pricing. For example, the Sherman Antitrust Act of 1890, the Clayton Act of 1914, the Federal Trade Commission (FTC) Act of 1914, and the Robinson–Patman Act of 1936 have clauses that prohibit one or more of the following:

- *Price fixing:* When two or more firms agree to set the same price for products they both offer.

- *Price discrimination:* Selling the same product to different buyers at about the same time but at different prices.

- *Predatory pricing:* Charging an extremely low price to eliminate competition and then raising prices.

State laws further define what constitutes legal pricing strategies. Many states have unfair trade practice laws that set the lowest level for wholesale and retail prices and require certain markups over cost of the goods and transportation.

The Department of Justice Antitrust Division investigates and prosecutes pricing cases. In 2006, it fined Samsung Electronics and three other memory chip manufacturers for fixing dynamic random access memory prices and sent 18 employees of these firms to prison. It also prosecuted price-fixing cartels in other industries, including chemicals, ready-mix cement, pipelines, and freight-forwarding services.

In another situation, Merck Pharmaceuticals told several large health insurance plans it would match or beat the generic drug price for Zocor, its brand-named cholesterol drug—the day before its patent expired.

Senator Charles Schumer, however, considered this as a form of predatory pricing that would harm generic drug manufacturers and requested that the FTC investigate further. "Merck is taking an end run around the generic drugs laws to make sure there are no generic drugs," Schumer said. Merck responded that the agreement was "nothing more than typical marketplace price competition."

Determining whether your pricing strategies are legal or ethical may not be obvious, as the Century Club and Merck examples demonstrate. Price fixing, for example, must have some aspect of collusion in order for it to be purposeful. Price discrimination is acceptable when the seller can prove that the different price levels result from large order manufacturing or demonstrable quantity discount saving, or when certain market conditions and competitive situations occur.

Discussion Questions

1. Differentiate between price fixing, price discrimination, and predatory pricing. Give some examples of each.

2. Does Merck's decision to allow UnitedHealth to offer its members Zocor at $10 per month, compared to $40 for its generic counterpart, constitute illegal pricing? Or does it put competitive pressure on generic manufacturers to offer low prices? Divide the class into two teams and have each group present their arguments supporting their view.

3. You own a janitorial service company and want to see how your prices compare to similar companies in your area. Posing as a customer, you call the other firms to inquire about the hourly prices for services and what's included. You discover that most companies are charging more, so you raise your prices to meet the highest of the group. Your competitors do the same thing, and each janitorial service company raises its prices to match the highest price. As a result, all the janitorial companies in town charge the same price. Does this constitute price fixing, and why?

4. The local dental association conducts a yearly survey of its members, and, based on this survey, publishes a list of customary charges for dental services such as dental fillings, tooth cleaning, tooth whitening, and other work. One of its members uses this information to determine its prices based

on what other dentists charge. Discuss whether this is a form of price fixing. Does offering a senior citizen's discount on Tuesdays constitute price discrimination, and why?

5. Using the Internet and other resources, find examples of price fixing. What pricing issues arise in these

situations? What led the companies involved to resort to price fixing?

Sources: "Antitrust Division Ends the Year with Second-Highest Level of Criminal Fines, More Merger Challenges," *PR Newswire*, December 21, 2006, retrieved from ProQuest Database; "Court: Nightclub can be sued for price discrimination," Oakland (CA) Tribune, May 31, 2007, p. 1; "Merck's Zocor Deal Stirs Ill Will," *Los Angeles Times*, June 22, 2006, p. C.3.

14.6 Managing Customer Relationships

One of the underlying themes of this chapter is that every customer is unique. Customers buy for different reasons. They pay different prices, at different times, at different places. We've emphasized the importance of knowing why and how customers are different from one another and selling to and servicing each customer's needs. Now we'll use this knowledge to develop strategies for **customer relationship management (CRM)**. CRM looks at how enterprises interact with their customers over the lifetime of their purchases with that enterprise. The more you learn about your customers, the more likely you are to earn their loyalty to your enterprise. A CRM system helps to more accurately identify target customer groups so enterprisers can tailor their marketing strategies to meet customer needs. By gathering and analyzing customer data, enterprises can maximize customer satisfaction. CRM is also likely to result in more sales and higher profitability as you meet these customer needs.

Consider the many businesses from which you purchase products or services. How often have you purchased a product or a service from a particular business only once? In most situations, we prefer to purchase from a familiar business over and over again. Now consider how you would respond if the business knew more about you and what you really wanted, and if using this information, it then actively sought to make your purchases more valuable (productive, efficient, easier, etc.) to you.

For example, suppose you had been shopping at a jewelry store over a number of years. Because the store kept a record of your purchases, its sales staff knew you tended to shop for jewelry for special occasions: Valentine's Day, Christmas, and your spouse's birthday.

Wouldn't it be helpful if the jewelry shop sent you a special note, a month before these special days, inviting you to come into the store? The store might suggest particular items that you might like based on your prior purchases, and could also include a discount coupon. This is what a CRM attempts to do: Gather data and information on customers so that enterprisers can better meet their customers' needs.

One of the fundamental ideas in a CRM system is the *lifetime value of a customer*. In most enterprises, customers purchase products and services more than once. Indeed, customers patronize some businesses—for example, grocery stores, dry cleaners, restaurants, or other retail or service businesses—over many years.

Let's assume that a customer purchased $100 every week at a particular grocery store, generating annual sales of $5,200 for each of the next ten years. This customer has a lifetime value of $52,000 ($5,200 × 10 years) in grocery purchases. Now suppose our customer purchases a bag of apples, finds that most of the apples are rotten, and returns to the store for a refund. Wouldn't it make sense to refund the purchase price of the apples, and maybe even give the customer some kind of discount as well, to keep this customer satisfied? Knowing that this is a regular customer who spends a significant amount each week, the store should keep that customer happy and continuing to shop at that store. Making that customer unhappy could result in losing $5,200 in sales to a competitor this year, and $52,000 in lost sales over the next ten years. That is a sobering realization!

Customer relationship management (CRM)   Enterprise-wide strategy for interacting with customers and managing the relationships for optimal profitability and customer satisfaction.

CRM systems, then, help enterprisers better focus on each of their customers so that they can provide better sales and services to customers. In addition, better service often leads to higher sales from certain customers. Using our movie theatre example, above, what if you knew which of your customers is willing to pay $25.00 to purchase a ticket at your theatre, and why? Perhaps these customers will pay a premium to attend the first showing of a new movie coming to town. If you knew the names and addresses of these customers, you could mail them a postcard with the new movies appearing over the next month and inviting them to reserve seats. If your theatre normally sold tickets at $10.00 each, customers who will buy tickets for $25.00 are very valuable to your business. You'd want to treat them better so that they continue to spend $25.00 per ticket.

Developing and managing your customer relationships is a four step process:

1. Identifying your customers

2. Differentiating your customers

3. Interacting with your customers

4. Customizing your relationship with your customers

Let's now explore how to implement these four steps in an enterprise. We'll also discuss how the customer relationship process can generate significant value to your customers and enhance the ability of your enterprise to be successful.

Identifying Your Customers

Before you can provide more value to your customers, your enterprise will need specific information about each customer. A CRM system, therefore, begins by collecting basic information about each customer: Name, mailing address, email address, and other information about purchasing habits. For example, if you owned a clothing store, you could collect information about each customer's purchases in terms of sizes, colors, and specific types of accessories they have purchased. A bookstore could collect information on the kinds of books each customer purchases. A restaurant could collect information on the meals that each customer orders.

In many enterprises, the owner of the business is the principal employee and often knows exactly what each customer wants based on regular interactions over time. The next step is to make this valuable information available to other members of the enterprise as well, so that they can serve customers better. This requires compiling this specific information about customer preferences and purchasing habits into a customer database.

Enterprisers can gather information about their customers in many ways. A customer loyalty card is one popular method used at grocery stores and many other retail outlets. Customers sign up for a card, providing name and contact information. Each time customers use their cards, point-of-sale computer systems record purchase information at the sales register. Some grocery stores then provide coupons for items similar or complimentary to purchases the customer just made, or the customer may receive discounts after purchasing certain dollar or quantity amounts. By knowing each customer, the store can provide specific value to that customer. The challenge is to provide the right incentives so that customers will want to participate in these programs.

At the same time, companies must protect the privacy of their customers and establish safeguards for the sensitive data they collect. With identity theft on the rise, customers want assurance that data they provide for business transactions will be secure and that they can trust the company to use it only as stated. The FTC encourages companies to create a data security plan that includes the following:

- Knowing the type of personal information the company stores on paper and electronic files.

- Collecting only the information necessary to transact business.

- Keeping information only as long as the business reason continues and deleting it when it is no longer necessary.

- Protecting customer data with physical safeguards such as locked file drawers and restricted access and electronic safeguards to prohibit unauthorized access, including encryption, passwords, virus protection, and more.

- Properly disposing of information that is no longer necessary, making it unreadable to anyone by shredding, burning, or other means.

- Developing a response plan for potential security breaches so that you can take immediate action.[7]

You'll learn in the "Keeping It Private" box that developing a privacy policy is essential for businesses today.

Differentiating Your Customers

The second part of the CRM process is to evaluate the value that each customer generates for your enterprise. This requires linking the sales revenues each customer

KEEPING IT PRIVATE

Congratulations! You've set up your company's CRM system and are ready to use it to build customer loyalty and enhance your interactions with these customers. By knowing such information as how often your customers buy from you, what they buy, and how promptly they pay, you will be able to personalize their shopping experience, send targeted promotions, offer coupons for future purchases, and more.

Because an increasing number of your customers purchase from your website, it's become even easier to develop customer databases from the personal information they fill out electronically. Your company's desire to know as much about your customers as possible comes with a trade-off, however. Before they divulge personal information, customers want to know what steps the company has taken to protect them from identity theft and other privacy-related issues such as selling or misusing personal information.

Creating and publishing an online privacy policy that clearly states how you will collect and use personal information is no longer optional for today's Internet-focused businesses. Legislation such as the Children's Online Privacy Protection Act may apply to your business. (Consult the Better Business Bureau's publication *A Review of Federal and State Privacy Laws*, available online at http://www.bbbonline.org, for more information.)

A carefully crafted privacy policy works to your advantage as well because customers will have greater confidence that you will not abuse their trust when they share personal information. According to the FTC, a good privacy policy addresses five core areas: (1) Notice/Awareness, (2) Choice/Consent, (3) Access/Participation, (4) Integrity/Security, and (5) Enforcement/Redress.

Your policy should list the types of personal data you collect for individual customers, how the company will use—or not use—this information, benefits to the customer of providing information, how a customer can restrict or limit use of personal information (opt-out options), and more. For example, some of the many ways companies can use information include: customizing content for the visitor to the website, sending customers relevant product promotions, using it only for internal purposes, and sharing it with outside organizations who may contact the customer for marketing purposes. The policy should be written in easy to understand language, be easy to locate on your website, reviewed regularly, and updated as necessary to comply with legislative and business changes.

In addition to compliance with U.S. regulations, enterprisers should pay attention to how other countries regulate privacy issues. Rules governing customer data may be quite different in another country. For example, the European Union (EU) Privacy Directive gives its consumers much stronger legal protections than U.S. residents and includes very specific policies about what companies can share and tell others about their customers. Companies that do business with EU countries typically prepare a separate privacy policy.

Several websites offer assistance in developing a comprehensive privacy policy. The Direct Marketing Association site (http://www.the-dma.org) has a Privacy Policy Generator with a questionnaire that creates a policy based on your company's practices. The Organization for Economic Cooperation and Development (OECD) (http://www.oecd.org) offers advice on developing a privacy statement, a policy generator, and links to governmental agencies and privacy resources worldwide.

Discussion Questions

1. Your CRM system collects customer information for the following items: sales volume (units and dollars by year, month, and week), goods or services purchased, purchase frequency, need for service or repairs, and payment and credit history. How could the collection of this information violate a customer's right to privacy?

2. What specific information from the list in question 1 might be very sensitive information that customers wouldn't want others to know about?

3. How should companies protect sensitive customer information?

4. Should customers be compensated if any of their sensitive information were made public? If so, what would be reasonable compensation?

5. Should companies be allowed to sell customer information to others? If so, under what circumstances? Would you, as an enterpriser, ever purchase such information about potential or current customers from others, and why?

Sources: "Create an Online Privacy Policy," *BBBOnline*, http://www.bbbonline.org (August 26, 2007); "How to Construct Your Privacy Policy," Direct Marketing Association, http://www.the-dma.org (November 3, 2007); "How to Write an Online Privacy Policy for Your Website," *Opentracker.net*, http://www.opentracker.net (August 26, 2007); and Don Peppers, Martha Rogers, and Bob Dorf, *The One to One Fieldbook* (New York: Currency/Doubleday, 1999), pp. 59–60.

generates and the costs associated with that customer: the costs of the products or services provided, plus the costs of subsequent service, contacts, etc.

While each company needs to determine what facts are most relevant for that particular type of business, the information to keep track of for each customer might include:

- Sales (by year, month, and week)
- Products purchased
- Services purchased
- Frequency of purchases
- Service/repair frequency
- Payment and credit history

Generating a value for each customer involves thinking about the lifetime value of that customer. How often does a customer purchase from you? How likely is a customer going to purchase from you in the future? How likely is it that the customer will purchase more from you in the future? For example, you might have an enterprise that sells snowboards and snowboarding clothes and equipment. If a customer comes in and purchases a snowboard from you, how likely would this customer be to buy another new snowboard that year? With good service and some interest from your staff, that customer may buy new clothes and other equipment to go along with his board. Perhaps some of your customers might need extra paid services.

It is a challenge to determine the possible lifetime value of a customer. As you gain experience selling to your customer base and tracking sales for each of your customers, you will get a good sense of how much particular customers spend, along with specific data to support this.

Aspects of determining how much value a customer is worth to your enterprise include the following:

- How much did it cost to acquire this customer (overall costs of marketing, selling, etc.)?
- What is the cost to provide services to this customer over time?
- How much does this customer generate in profits from all goods and services sold?
- What might be the lifetime profit from goods and services purchased by this customer in the future?
- Does this customer generate referrals of new profitable customers?

- Will this customer likely purchase more or use more services in the future?
- For those enterprisers selling on credit: How creditworthy is this customer now—and likely to be in the future?

Once you have information on the value of each of your customers, you can begin to rank them into categories that suggest their value to your enterprise. CRM experts such as Don Peppers, Martha Rogers, and Bob Dorf, authors of *The One to One Fieldbook*, suggest dividing customers into three groups:[8]

1. *Most Valuable Customers (MVCs):* As the name suggests, there are customers who are the most important for the success of your business. These most valuable customers spend more, are likely to want to spend even more over time, and should also be the customers who generate the most profits for your enterprise. Obviously, the goal for your enterprise in dealing with MVCs is to keep them.

2. *Most Growable Customers (MGCs):* There are likely to be customers who have potential for purchasing more of the products or services your enterprise provides. The goal for your enterprise is to sell more to these customers. Often this involves thinking through ways to "cross sell" various products and services to them. For example, in the snowboard business, the goal might be to sell more snowboarding clothes, equipment, or snowboarding vacations. Basically, selling beyond one particular good or service to encompass the majority of goods and services your enterprise provides.

3. *Below Zeros (BZs):* There are some customers who will purchase your products or services but will not actually generate any profits for your business, either in the short term or over their lifetime. An example of a BZ customer is one who purchases a lower priced item and then demands the service that goes with a high priced product—which has the cost of the service built into the price. Providing extra service on the low priced product might make the low priced product very unprofitable. If the customer doesn't want to upgrade to a product or service where the sales revenue is higher than the costs associated with it, the challenge for the enterpriser is to think of ways for these customers to consider doing their business with your competitors.

Suppose you own an apartment building. Some renters are likely to be perfect tenants. Their neighbors don't complain, they keep their apartment clean, don't break anything, and pay their rent on time. Other renters don't pay on time, damage the insides and outsides of the apartment, and behave in ways that disturb other tenants and cause them to complain and threaten to leave. The apartment owner is likely to be losing money renting to a problem renter, and these BZs are ones that enterprisers encourage to buy from others.

Note, however, that there are legal issues with refusing to sell goods or services such as housing to others. A decision to not sell to particular customers needs to be based on sound criteria and information that has a legal basis. For example, you could refuse to rent to people who don't have a good credit history, or don't provide a sufficient down payment, or are consistently late with rent payments. So first check with your lawyer to understand the legal issues involved in refusing to sell to customers who don't net your enterprise any profits.

This process of dividing customers into categories actually suggests that no one person or enterprise can make all people always happy. We have a limited amount of time and energy to devote to making our enterprises successes. To do this, we need to focus on those customers to whom we can provide the most value. In return, they can provide us with the highest revenues for the effort and costs we incur.

Interacting with Your Customers

The next step is to take what you've learned about your customers so far and build a closer relationship with them. This involves creating opportunities to interact with your customers, learn about what they want, and then provide them with the goods or services that they value. Sending a postcard to a customer is merely an advertisement, not an interaction. What you are looking for are opportunities to find out what your customers truly value, beyond what you are currently providing, so you can satisfy those needs.

Remember our jewelry store owner who keeps track of what customers buy? Suppose that he or she knows that some customers really like a particular jewelry designer, and this designer is in town. Arranging for the MVCs to meet with the jewelry designer and make purchases before other customers have an opportunity creates a perfect interaction situation. Everyone benefits: The designer makes only a limited amount of jewelry and can present it to the best customers, customers are pleased to be invited to a special event based on what they value, and the store has a strong potential to make additional sales and profits by facilitating the exchange.

Knowing what displeases your customers is just as important. We often think that complainers are just cranks and are likely to be BZ customers: They want a lot but want to pay a little, so they complain and complain until they get that. However, most complaints can provide signals to an enterpriser about the quality of the enterprise's products and services, especially if the same complaint recurs. People with complaints are saying they have problems that they want solved. Complaints are always opportunities to find solutions.

People complain for a number of reasons. First, they don't receive what the enterpriser promised to provide or what they customer expected to get. This could be an issue of differences in expectations between the two parties, or perhaps the customer didn't get what was ordered. A stereo purchased could be defective, the software on the computer might not have been installed properly, the meal order was given to the chef incorrectly. These types of complaints are really helpful because they indicate that something has gone wrong in the enterprise and should be corrected. Paying attention to these complaints allows enterprisers to improve their products and customer service.

Some complaints arise when customers want something beyond the specifications of the products or services currently offered. Often these people are the "innovators," or lead users, described earlier. These customers want better performance or new features that are not yet available and ask for products or services you don't have. Such complaints can signal new opportunities to pursue. Enterprisers who listen and pay attention, rather than ignore the complaint, learn why their customers want particular features or benefits. They can then modify existing products, make new products, or provide new services to meet these complaints.

Often companies who don't hear from their customers assume everything is going well. In fact, customers may be taking their business elsewhere, rather than complain. Finding ways to get customer feedback will help enterprisers continually refine their products and customer service to meet customer needs.

For example, let's return to our $25.00 movie ticket buyer. Suppose you found out that they were complaining about the problems of finding parking when they arrived. They have reservations for a seat, but they had to drive around in the parking lot searching for a space. The lack of parking might be an opportunity to provide another service for these customers: valet parking for an extra fee. Someone willing to pay $25.00 for a movie ticket might also want to pay $10.00 for valet parking to avoid the hassle of finding a parking space.

Again, think about the many different reasons that people buy. Match the reasons people buy to the reasons they complain. You will identify opportunities to solve missed expectations in those areas. When an enterpriser solves a customer's problems, the customer often expresses satisfaction through increasing loyalty and providing referrals.

Customizing Products and Services

The ideal goal in a CRM system is to provide products and services that meet each customer's unique needs. On a simple level, this means that your enterprise has identified and aligned itself with customers to provide goods and services that they find of value. If you are an organic bread bakery, your enterprise has identified and found customers who value—and will pay extra for—organic bread. As you learn about your customers, you may discover that they want other freshly baked organic bread products, such as rolls, cookies, and pastries. Then, you might learn that providing other kinds of fresh organic products—organic milk, eggs, and cheese, for example—would satisfy another need.

One concern with regard to customization is the higher cost of making a product or service for each customer. Instead, focus on learning about your customers so you can identify groups of high value, high profit buyers who are likely to want similar products and services. If one customer wants rolls, other customers may want this product, too. Customization can help you discover market niches—certain groups of buyers with the same needs for certain benefits and features in products and services they purchase.

14.7 ENTERPRISERS

Del's Grown-Up Lemonade Stand

On a hot summer day, customers at Del's Frozen Lemonade stores wait patiently for their frosty lemon ice treats. This family company is based on the recipe Angelo DeLucia's great grandfather prepared in Naples, Italy, in the mid-1800s. In those days, he stored snow in caves until summer, when he mixed it with fresh lemon juice and sugar to make a fruit ice. His son Franco brought the recipe to America, where it stayed in the family until Angelo developed a machine to produce a consistent product. "We started with a little White Mountain ice cream freezer, rock salt and ice," Angelo recalls. "I couldn't stand the fluctuation of the lemon acidity. Some lemons are tart, some lemons are sweet, some don't have enough juice, some of them are too thick." Working with a quality control expert, Angelo standardized the recipe and motorized the freezer. "It made it very easy to make the product. It took about 15, 20 minutes to keep turning and turning," he says.

In 1948, Angelo opened the first Del's Frozen Lemonade stand in Cranston, Rhode Island, next to a bowling galley he owned with his dad. The lack of air conditioning in the bowling alley kept customers away during the summer, which gave Angelo the idea to set up a frozen lemonade stand next to it. The popularity of the drink convinced him to sell the bowling alley in 1955 and focus on the lemonade business. He then modified the freezer so it could be truck mounted and installed it on trucks to become mobile lemonade stands that could bring Del's refreshing beverage to street corners, ball games, festivals, and other events.

Angelo built a second store in 1961. He convinced one of his drivers to become his first franchisee, operating on consignment and running two mobile units. The success of this store led to four more franchised locations, handpicked by Angelo. During the winter months, he would scout possible locations, counting cars with a clicker. Then he'd negotiate for property in desirable spots.

Angelo's son Bruce followed him into the business and grew the company from 5 franchises to 45, mostly in New England, but also in California, Florida, Nevada, Pennsylvania, Texas, Wisconsin, and even the Virgin Islands and Japan. Many retail food markets and restaurants also sell Del's from special freezer units.

Sometimes called "The Taste of Rhode Island," Del's almost became Rhode Island's official drink. Today, the company has about 300 employees and generates revenues of $5 million. In response to customer requests, Del's now offers a lite version of the classic lemonade and other all-natural flavors, such as blueberry, watermelon, cherry, peach-mango, and kiwi. Customers who don't live near a Del's or who crave a Del's in the winter can now make Del's at home using the company's dry mix and a blender.

Despite the traditional nature of the lemonade business, the DeLucias tapped into the power of the Internet to sell their product and expand their franchise base. The company's lively website, http://www.dels.com, offers more than the company history, product information, and a way to find the nearest Del's location. Visitors can also buy logo items and the dry mix, play lemon-themed online games, and try several lemon recipes. Clicking the "Own Del's" button provides potential franchisees details of the franchise opportunity and requirements.

Angelo and Bruce DeLucia are very selective about the franchisees they add to their family's business. They must demonstrate the same characteristics that brought Angelo success. "This is a hard-income business," he says. "You've got to work for it. You've got to want to have it. You've got to be at it as often as possible, even when you're sleeping." He credits his success to his customers, building the brand one customer at a time. "I did nothing in this. I gave a product, and they, in turn, rewarded me. . . . But I gave a lot of product away. I wanted people to know what it was. I would serve 100 people, 5 people would refuse, 95 would take." Once they tasted the lemonade, they wanted more.

Some franchisees are like Bruce Long, who drank Del's as a kid and jumped on the opportunity immediately. "If you're willing to work very, very hard for three or four months and make an annual income,

this is a perfect place for it," he says. "But it's an owner-occupied-type business. It must be owner-run. This is not a business for a lawyer that's gonna hire managers. It doesn't work."

Discussion Questions

1. How would you tell Del's story to others? Why is the Del's story so engaging?

2. Go to the website: http://www.dels.com/. What does the website say about Del's enterprise? In how many different ways does this website involve customers?

3. Describe the channels of distribution and supply chain for a Del's franchisee. What degree of market intensity applies to Del's?

4. How would you go about determining prices for Del's lemonade? Should prices be different during the summer versus the spring and fall? Should prices vary when the prices of lemons and sugar go up or down?

5. Prepare a list of ways that Del's could engage its customers over a lifetime. Pick your two favorites and discuss how to implement them.

6. How could the lessons learned from Del's be applied to the sales of other products? To other food items?

Sources: Adapted with permission from Small Business School, the series on PBS, at http://SmallBusinessSchool.com; "Del's," *Quahog.org*, http://www.quahog.org/cuisine/index.php?id=23 (June 27, 2007); and Del's Lemonade website, http://www.dels.com (July 30, 2007).

Summary

1. After enterprisers develop products, they must identify their target market. By understanding the needs and desires of these customers and the motivations that cause them to buy, enterprisers can develop appropriate selling strategies.

2. The product adoption cycle offers one framework for why people buy goods and services. It classifies them as innovators, early adopters, the early majority, the late majority, and the laggards based on when in a product's life cycle the customer purchases the item. Knowing the characteristics of the customer groups who purchase at various points along the product adoption cycle will help enterprisers market their products more effectively and use selling strategies that solve customer needs.

3. The selling process has six steps: generating leads, qualifying them, approaching customers and assessing needs, developing and proposing solutions, closing the sale, and following up. It starts with prospecting for a large number of potential buyers. Among the many ways to find prospects are promotional strategies such as advertising and public relations, customer referrals, networking, and cold calls to lists of people in the target market.

4. Enterprisers must then evaluate the leads they gather to determine which have the greatest potential to become customers. Qualified buyers have a recognized need, buying power, and receptivity and accessibility.

5. Enterprisers should develop trust and demonstrate competence when they approach customers to assess their needs. The more they know about the prospect before the first meeting, the greater the likelihood of building rapport and engaging in meaningful conversations about customer needs. Customers also expect the seller to have a solid knowledge base about the company's products and industry. By asking probing questions and listening carefully to the answers, enterprisers can identify customer needs, overcome objections, and then move on to the next step, proposing solutions. Once the customer agrees that the product meets his/her needs, the salesperson must ask for the sale and then negotiate the details of the purchase. Good salesmanship doesn't end when the sale is closed and the goods or services delivered. The sale represents the beginning of a relationship that may include service for the product, future opportunities to sell more products to this customer, referrals to other customers, and more.

6. Good selling skills can be learned and increase with practice. Listening to customers and hearing their concerns accurately are among the most important skills to develop. Paying attention to body language also provides clues to the customer's reactions.

7. Because enterprisers need a cost-effective way to acquire raw materials, make the products, and deliver them to the customer, place (distribution) strategies are an integral part of the marketing mix. Distribution channels form a network of intermediaries that facilitate the movement of goods from producer to end user. The major types of intermediaries are agents, brokers, industrial distributors, wholesalers, and retailers. Channels can be direct—from producer to customer—or indirect, involving several middlemen.

8. Distribution intermediaries serve several roles. They can reduce the number and cost of transactions, streamline transactions, maintain product inventory, handle logistics, assume risks, and provide financing assistance. Market, product, and producer factors influence the choice of a channel. Channels often change over the product life cycle. Distribution intensity—exclusive, selective, or intensive—determines the market coverage.

9. Supply chain management systems coordinate the activities of supply chain members to achieve an efficient materials flow and exchange of information across the channel. They cover six steps: sourcing and procurement, order processing, production scheduling, choosing a warehouse location and type, setting up an inventory system, and making transportation decisions.

10. Pricing decisions are complex because people who place a higher perceived value on a product will pay more for the same product or service than others. The forces of demand and supply have a major impact on pricing goods and services. Demand represents the quantity of an item that customers will buy at different price points. In general, as the price rises, fewer people demand a product, and vice versa. Demand is *elastic* when customers are willing to purchase more or less of a product or service when the price changes.

11. Supply refers to the amount of a good or service that a business will make available at different price levels. As the price of a product or service rises, more enterprisers are willing to provide the product or service.

12. Costs also factor into the pricing decision. Fixed costs remain the same, regardless of level of output, whereas variable costs change with different output levels. Calculating the break-even point shows the point where, given a specific price, your costs equal your revenues.

13. Companies can choose from many different pricing strategies. When products are new, the most common strategies are price skimming and penetration pricing. As a product moves through its life cycle, prices may change to reflect different levels of demand for the product and market competition. Other pricing strategies include loss leader, odd-even, prestige, promotional, geographical, and seasonal.

14. CRM builds customer loyalty by finding ways to interact with customers after the first sale. Retaining customers is less expensive than acquiring new ones. CRM systems gather and analyze customer data to maximize customer satisfaction and increase the lifetime value of a customer. CRM is also likely to result in more sales and higher profitability as you meet these customer needs.

15. CRM involves identifying customers, differentiating them based on the value they generate for the enterprise, interacting with them to learn more about their needs, and tailoring the relationship with these customers so that you provide goods and services that meet each customer's unique needs.

Review Questions

1. Define the five categories in the product adoption cycle. How does knowing these customer types help enterprisers market their products?

2. Describe the six steps in the selling process and what they entail.

3. Why are distribution strategies an important part of the marketing mix?

4. What are marketing channels and how do they differ for consumer and industrial products? What functions does each of the five major types of intermediary serve?

5. Describe the reasons why an enterpriser might choose to use marketing intermediaries instead of selling directly to end users.

6. Describe the types of marketing channels Brad Singer uses to distribute Clubhouse Kits (refer to p. 367).

7. How do market, product, and producer factors affect distribution decisions?

8. What is the purpose of supply chain management systems?

9. What are the three degrees of market intensity, and what types of products are best suited to each?

10. How do supply and demand affect pricing decisions?

11. What does it mean to "break even," and why is it important to perform break-even analysis when determining prices?

12. Describe the difference between price skimming and penetration pricing and explain when each strategy applies. Define three other pricing strategies that can be used to refine pricing tactics after a product has been on the market a while.

13. What benefits does CRM bring to a company? Describe the four steps in a successful customer management system.

Applying What You've Learned

1. Make a list of products that you've purchased over the past year. Where would you consider yourself to be in the product adoption cycle of these products? Are you an innovator or early adopter, in the early majority or the late majority, or a laggard for all of your purchases, or are there some product categories where you differ? Prepare a brief summary and compare your findings to your classmates'.

2. How do people sell to you? Go into a number of places where you purchase (clothes, supplies, groceries, etc.) and pay attention to how salespeople treat you. How does the sales interaction work? How do they go through the six-step sales process? Why are there differences in the interactions that you have with salespeople at different kinds of stores?

3. Watch how other people purchase products. Is the selling process the same for each customer or do salespeople vary their sales process?

4. Pick a product from the list you developed in question 1. Trace this product from where you purchased it, all the way back to the raw materials that went into the product. Which companies, distributors, etc. were involved in transforming this product from raw materials all the way through to when you purchased it in a store? Summarize the product's journey.

   Now begin to figure out how much value each company gained for themselves during each step in this process. By value, think of how much money the product was worth before it began a particular step and how much money the product was worth at the next step.

5. Go out to various stores and photograph different types of vegetable peelers (you will find them in grocery stores, drug stores, convenience stores, and specialty stores) and write down the prices you find for these different vegetable peelers. First, what are the common benefits that a person would get by purchasing and using a vegetable peeler? Second, what are the specific features of each vegetable peeler you have identified? Third, why are the prices for these vegetable peelers so different?

6. Using newspapers, magazines, and websites, find examples of any five different pricing strategies listed in Exhibit 14.9. Explain why, in your opinion, the seller choose this strategy, and why it is suitable for the product.

7. Add the services you have purchased in the past year to the products you listed in question 1. Prepare a table to summarize your answers to the following questions. How have the individual sellers of these products and services tried to stay in touch with you? How have these companies kept in contact with you? What kinds of incentives have these companies offered for your further involvement? Which companies have you stayed in contact with and which companies are you not connected to? Based on your experiences, suggest ways that these companies do a better job of developing an ongoing relationship with you as a customer.

Enterprisers on the Web

1. Many software programs help manage customer contact information and provide other sales tools such as contact sharing, networking, lead qualification, company information resources, and more. Read the article "Turning Sales into Science," *Inc.*, December 2006 (http://www.inc.com). From those mentioned in the article, select three categories that you think would be helpful to enterprisers. Research one or two offerings from each and develop a table that compares the products' features. Which would you buy for your enterprise, and why?

2. Using the following websites, summarize the supply chain of a T-shirt, as described in Petra Rivoli's book: *Travel's of a T-Shirt in the Global Economy.* (Search for T-shirt travels.)

   http://www.amazon.com

   http://www.imf.org

   http://www.pbs.org/independentlens

3. Visit the website for Penske Logistics, http://www.penskelogistics.com. Describe the services it provides. What benefits does it bring to enterprisers who chose to outsource some of their distribution functions?

4. It's the beginning of a semester and you have lots of textbooks to purchase. You'd like to save some money so you decide to compare the prices on the Internet with the ones offered by the campus bookstore. Choose three books you needed for this semester and research prices. Who is offering what books, and at what prices? Why are there differences in prices? Summarize your findings in a table.

5. For information on CRM, visit SearchCRM, http://searchcrm.techtarget.com. Look through the many articles it offers. Where is the CRM process headed? How are companies learning more about their customers, and, what are different ways that these companies are engaging and developing relationships with their customers?

6. Consider the kinds of customers who will purchase goods or services from the business you want to start and develop customer profiles for the most valuable customers, most growable customers, and below zeros. Determine the lifetime value of a customer for each group using the online calculator at http://www.imrtn.com/lifetimecalc.asp. Discuss your assumptions and results with your classmates.

End Notes

1. Section based on material in Charles W. Lamb, Jr., Joseph F. Hair, Jr., and Carl McDaniel, *Marketing*, 8th ed. (Mason, OH: Thomson South-Western Publishing, 2006), pp. 348–352; and Geoffrey A. Moore (1991), *Crossing the Chasm.* New York: HarperCollins.

2. Jay Conrad Levinson, *Guerrilla Marketing Excellence* (New York: Houghton Mifflin Company, 1993), pp. 11–12.

3. Jeanette Borzo, "Selling Software," *Wall Street Journal,* March 19, 2007, p. R7.

4. Christina Cheddar Berk, "Retailer Finds a Shortcut on QVC," *Wall Street Journal,* January 17, 2006, p. B8.

5. Section based on information from "Distribution," *Wikipedia. com,* http://en.wikipedia.org/wiki/Distribution_(business)

(June 27, 2007); "Distribution Decisions," *KnowThis.com,* http://www.knowthis.com (June 26, 2007); Lawrence Gitman and Carl McDaniel, "Chapter 14: Distributing Products in a Timely and Efficient Manner," *The Future of Business* (Mason, OH: Thomson South-Western, 2008), pp. 464–489.

6. Gwendolyn Bounds, "Working to Hit a Product Out of the Ballpark," *Wall Street Journal,* October 24, 2006, p. B6.

7. *Protecting Personal Information: A Guide for Business,* Federal Trade Commission, downloaded from http://www.ftc.gov/infosecurity (November 5, 2007).

8. Don Peppers, Martha Rogers, and Bob Dorf, *The One to One Fieldbook* (New York: Currency/Doubleday, 1999), pp. 59–60.

ENTERPRISE

Finding Resources

KEY CONCEPTS

1. By understanding four important rules that apply to resource providers, enterprisers will be in a better position to seek and obtain the funds they require to start and grow their businesses. These rules deal with risk and return, information asymmetry, bricolage, and resources require relationships.

2. Resources to start new enterprises come from many sources and include intangibles such as referrals and advice, assets on hand, and funding. Most enterprisers begin with personal resources such as personal savings, personal credit cards and lines of credit, and loans from friends and family. Angel investors are often the first form of external funding, followed by venture capital investors. Both groups require high rates of return, typically take an equity stake in the company, and want input into strategic decisions. More established businesses can borrow from banks, asset-based lenders such as factors, and leasing companies. Trade credit from suppliers and buyers is another important funding source, as are the many federal, state, and local government programs. Going public is another way to raise capital—but only for larger and strong companies with high growth potential.

3. A company's location is another key resource. When selecting a location, enterprisers must consider the type of business and how customers purchase products or services from them and the points of contact with the customer. Proximity to key markets, labor supply, wage rates, business climate, and competition factor into the choice of location. Most enterprisers start businesses where they live.

4. An enterpriser's personal creativity, imagination, flexibility, and overall resourcefulness are critical assets to harness when starting and building a business. The more resource options an enterpriser can identify, the better. If one falls through, the enterpriser can quickly turn to Plan B as a viable alternative.

Suppose you lose your job as an engineer at a food products company. As you consider your options, a friend asks if you have ever thought of starting your own business. You tell him you are interested but you don't have adequate personal resources. Because he admires your engineering expertise, he offers to provide funding. You recall a comment a visitor to your former employer made about wanting to automate corn dog production, so you meet with him and see how he makes the corn dogs by hand. Quickly you figure out how to design a machine that greatly speeds up the process.

© Steve Goodwin/istockphoto.com

With his new machine and his friend's funding, Glenn Walser leveraged his resources to start Automated Food Systems (AFS), Inc. Today his equipment makes most of the corn dogs in the United States and other countries. As you read this chapter, you'll learn how to identify and use the many different types of available resources, including your own creativity, to turn your business dreams into reality.

15.0 Being Resourceful

In this chapter, we discuss the many different resources that enterprisers might acquire and use for creating and growing their businesses. These essential resources include the enterpriser's personal talents, creativity, flexibility, and contacts, as well as tangible assets such as funding, location in which to operate, supplies, and equipment.

We begin by introducing four rules that apply to resources:

- Risk and Return: Investors make money by not losing it.

- Information Asymmetry: Others can't know what you know.

- Bricolage: Use the resources you have.

- Resources Require Relationships: It is about more than money!

These rules explain how the process of acquiring funds is governed by its own logic—a logic that is not often apparent to enterprisers who are often frustrated that lenders and investors won't provide them with the resources they need.

Enterprisers must also recognize that anyone who provides their enterprise with a resource has very specific reasons for entering into this transaction. Knowing why people chose to provide resources to your venture is a critical step toward obtaining their involvement and developing a successful working relationship.

In the rest of this chapter, we will explore various ways that enterprisers might find and acquire the resources needed to develop and grow their enterprises. This includes the most critical resource for successfully starting and growing your enterprise: You! Your imagination and creativity for identifying and utilizing different kinds of resources, in ways that are innovative and novel, are major contributors to enterprising success. As we have emphasized in previous chapters, the more you know about yourself and your enterprise, the better you will be able to gain insights into your (and the enterprise's) unique capabilities for achieving success. How well you leverage your unique strengths (resources)—and your enterprise's—will ultimately make the difference in whether or not you find success.

15.1 Risk and Return: Investors Make Money by Not Losing It

Why doesn't Lender X (the bank, financing company, supplier, family member, friend, angel investor) lend me money? It's a familiar question that we often hear from enterprisers who are both starting and growing their businesses. Enterprisers must realize that resource providers want to preserve their resources and also generate a return on those resources. These providers of funds set **required returns**, rates of return that will

---

Required return   The rate of return that fully compensates lenders and investors for taking on the risk of a loan or equity investment.

---

compensate them for taking the risk of the loan or equity investment. One of the first rules of resources is that both lenders and investors should not lose money. This is usually the fundamental reason most lenders and investors hesitate to provide funds for new and emerging enterprisers: The return on the loaned or invested funds is not high enough to compensate for the risk of the project.

The Lending Cycle

Investing and lending funds to enterprisers is not as easy or as risk free as many of us would believe, as the following example illustrates. Let's assume that an enterpriser wants to borrow $100 from a bank for one year. The bank is willing to make this loan and will charge 10 percent interest for the loan. A year from the date of the loan, the bank expects to receive the $100 principal plus $10 in interest (10 percent of $100).

Lenders actually borrow money from others to lend this money to enterprisers. The bank may have borrowed the $100 for the enterpriser's loan from one of its customers. That customer expects a 5 percent return on the money it deposited in the bank, and the bank promises to return $105 (the $100 in principal plus $5—5 percent of 100) to the customer one year from the date the money was deposited with the bank.

A bank also has operating costs and expenses, including employee wages and benefits and the costs and expenses for a building. For our $100 loan, assume the bank incurs costs of $4. So, the total costs for the bank to make a $100 loan to an enterpriser are the interest paid to the bank's depositor ($5) plus the costs of operating the bank ($4), or $9 total. The bank, then, would earn $1 on the $100 loan from the enterpriser ($10 in interest from the loan less the $9 in expenses paid to the depositor and for operating the bank = $1 in earnings). This represents a return of just 1 percent.

What happens if the enterpriser does not pay back this loan? What impact does this have on the bank?

If the enterpriser fails to repay the loan principal plus the interest, the bank would lose $109: The $100 principal plus the $5 owed to the depositor plus the $4 operational expenses. Therefore, the bank would need to make 109 more $100 loans to make up for the loss of just one $100 loan. (109 × $1 earned on each $100 loan = $109). Overall, the bank would have to lend $10,900!

When evaluating a borrower, then, the lender looks at the bigger picture—not just at making a $100 loan. The risk goes beyond losing $109 in principal, interest, and expenses. It also involves investing $10,900 to earn back that $109 if the enterpriser cannot repay the loan.

Higher Risks Require Higher Returns

Lenders are very careful to assess the risk of **default**—not repaying the loan—and to look for ways to lessen such risk. The greater the risk of not getting their money back, the higher the return lenders will require.

For example, a bank may charge a fairly risky borrower a high interest rate—let's say 19 percent. Given the same $9 cost for deposits plus expenses described earlier, at the end of the one-year loan term the bank would now earn $10 for this $100 loan ($19 in interest—$5 to the depositor—$4 for bank expenses = $10 income). The bank would only need to invest $1,090 to repay the lost $109. This assumes that the bank loans out funds to other enterprisers at 19 percent as well and all enterprisers repay their loans.

A lender or investor, then, needs a **risk premium**, an additional rate of return, as compensation for taking on a situation with the likelihood that the investment or loan won't be repaid. In such situations, the lender or the investor will want more than, for example, the 1 percent return we originally proposed as the earnings on the $100 loan. A risky loan might carry a 5 percent risk premium. If the usual rate for a loan with "normal" risk is 19 percent, the lender would charge 24 percent for a riskier loan.

Clearly, lenders and investors don't want to lose money when they provide resources. Later in this chapter, we will offer a number of ways that enterprisers can decrease the risk of loss to resource providers who lend to or invest in their enterprises.

15.2 Information Asymmetry: Others Can't Know as Much as You Know

You will, in all circumstances, have more knowledge and insight into your enterprise and your skills and abilities than anyone else. This concept is called **information asymmetry** and occurs when one party in a business transaction has more information than others, thereby creating an information advantage.

With regard to the acquisition and use of resources, an enterpriser will have the greatest knowledge into how those resources might be successfully used in the operation of his or her enterprise. Because lenders or investors have lower levels of knowledge and insights, they perceive higher risk levels in providing you with the necessary resources.

An enterpriser might see that $10,000 invested in the enterprise might generate a yearly return of $2,500, viewing the investment as a "sure thing" that will earn substantial returns and also pay back the principal. On the other hand, an "outsider" to the enterprise, such as a lender or investor, is more likely to see how the loan or investment might be lost and therefore discount the enterpriser's estimates. According to the rule of information asymmetry, others cannot have the amount of knowledge and insights that the enterpriser has. As a result, in most situations, others will have a higher perception of risk than the enterpriser.

Resources provided by outsiders not directly involved in the business will always be seen by enterprisers as expensive and costly. In the example above, the enterpriser is sure that the $10,000 investment will generate a 25 percent return, while lenders and investors will likely want a much higher rate of return than 25 percent for their investment. For them, it is anything but a "sure thing"; they do not see the business as clearly and thoroughly as the enterpriser.

An enterpriser might have to offer a return of 35 or 50 percent to obtain the $10,000. To earn a 50 percent return for an investor, the enterpriser would have to return $5,000 on the $10,000 investment. Where might the enterpriser find the additional $2,500—beyond the "sure thing" of $2,500? Often it comes from earnings on the enterpriser's other resources, making the $10,000 investment very costly to the enterpriser. In most cases, then, enterprisers have to consider other ways to acquire and utilize resources for their enterprises.

As we mentioned in Chapter 8, an important reason for developing a business plan for an enterprise is to provide information for "outsiders" about how the business will make money. When others can see the logic of

Default   The risk that a borrower will fail to repay a loan.

Risk premium   An additional rate of return that reflects the characteristics of the loan and the borrower and compensates lenders or investors for taking greater risk.

Information asymmetry   When one party in a business transaction has more information than others, creating an information advantage.

how the business will succeed and explore the details of how the enterprise will create and develop the enterprise, their information asymmetry decreases. The additional information helps to reduce the perceived risk of the enterprise and decreases the need to generate a higher risk premium. In addition, the more information you provide to others about your business, the more they can suggest ways to better manage your enterprise and compete successfully in the market.

A good way to reduce information asymmetry regarding your enterprise is to find individuals with industry and entrepreneurial experience that matches your business and its industry. Look for people who have had successes and failures in your type of enterprise. Use their insights, resources, and expertise to help you develop your enterprise. Often, advice from the right investors will be more important than the financial resources they provide.

15.3 Bricolage: Use the Resources You Have

"If I only had a million dollars, this enterprise could really get started." Often a constraint or belief about what is missing from a possible opportunity prevents many potential enterprisers from pursuing their goals. We see this in the *Wizard of Oz*: If the scarecrow only had a brain, if the tin man only had a heart, and if the lion only had courage. There is, in any new endeavor, a sense that "if only" something else was provided, then the project could begin. Yet, the "if only" is actually an assumption about what might be required in order to move forward. Did the scarecrow need that brain, the tin man that heart, or the lion that courage in order to move forward in their adventure?

The rule of **bricolage**, or using whatever materials are available, states that enterprisers make do with what is at hand. This idea is somewhat similar to the idea of means and ends that we discussed in Chapter 2. Enterprisers are more likely to leverage the means (resources) they have at hand to pursue a variety of possible ends (outcomes) that might be possible through those means. Ted Baker and Reed Nelson have explored the concept of bricolage in some detail, particularly in looking at how enterprisers

Bricolage   Using whatever materials are available to create something.

are able to create and grow businesses.[1] Their concept of bricolage evolves from ideas offered earlier by Claude Levi-Strauss in his 1967 book *The Savage Mind* in which Strauss describes bricolage as "always to make do with 'whatever is at hand.' "[2] The process of bricolage might seem to limit one's goals and aspirations. In practice, however, bricolage helps enterprisers move forward.

The bricolage perspective suggests that enterprisers will work to expand the limits of what might work as a resource for solving a particular problem. For example, let's assume that an enterpriser has a graphics design business that prepares marketing materials such as advertisements and brochures for others. Our enterpriser needs a very expensive computer with sophisticated page layout and graphics software to operate effectively. If the enterpriser doesn't have the resources to acquire this computer and software, there are other ways she could gain access to these resources. For example, she might know a company that has such a computer and is willing to let the designer use the computer at night and on weekends when the company doesn't need it. The enterpriser could pay a modest fee that benefits the company. She could also lease the computer through a leasing company or team up with other enterprisers who also need such a computer and purchase the equipment jointly. These examples demonstrate how this enterpriser can acquire the use of the required resources without necessarily owning them.

Bricolage also involves combining already available resources in new ways. If the goal of the enterpriser is to design advertisements and brochures for others using a computer, the enterpriser might start by finding an older and less expensive computer, as well as older outdated software. Although the computer and software might not work as fast or as efficiently as the newer versions, they may be adequate to complete the jobs in a satisfactory manner.

Often, these novel combinations of older resources generate innovative solutions. For example, in a study of the Danish wind turbine industry, Garud and Karnoe compared engineers who used pre-existing components, such as turbines, blades, and rotors that were used in other industries, to those who built turbines from scratch. The engineers who took already available components were able to adapt these components more quickly and modify them into a more advanced wind turbine than competitors, who had decided to build the most advanced wind turbine systems with all new parts.[3]

Using bricolage concepts, enterprisers can move quickly into the field to see what resources are actually needed and how they actually will work. For example,

Japanese car manufacturers have been selling hybrid gasoline–electric cars for many years. The Japanese hybrid technology began as an application of off-the-shelf uses of existing gasoline motors and electric power components. These hybrid automobiles do not have any radically innovative technologies. Yet, the combination of existing technologies in the hybrid resulted in the manufacture of automobiles with significantly better gasoline mileage than most other automobiles on the road.

In that process of producing and selling hybrids, these manufacturers have learned how to make them more efficient and less costly. They have also discovered what customers of energy-efficient automobiles want. Compare this to many of the American automobile manufacturers who are investing in hydrogen technologies that, in theory, are far superior to any of the hybrid gasoline–electric technologies. Because the American automobile manufacturers don't have such a car on the market for purchase, they don't make sales, learn from customers, or have an automobile in use to upgrade.

The bricolage process, then, is related to the perspective of "small wins" that we discussed in Chapter 2. Bricolage requires that enterprisers start where they are and do what they can. In the process of making something happen, additional knowledge and skills, as well as contacts and other resources, come into the picture and offer new ways for the enterpriser to be successful. It is

like the *Wizard of Oz*. In the beginning of the journey, the scarecrow doesn't think he has a brain, but he does; the tin man doesn't think he has a heart, but he does; the lion doesn't think he has courage, but he does. All three find out that what they thought they needed to succeed, they actually had in their possession.

Included in the broader bricolage concept is **bootstrapping**, using small amounts of personal funds to start companies. We'll return to this in later sections of the chapter.

Much of the creative process of developing and growing an enterprise requires that enterprisers think in new ways about the resources they think they need. By doing this, they gain a clearer picture of the actual resources they need and how to use them. We will return to this issue in the final section of this chapter, when we focus on *you* as a key resource. Your imagination and creativity are resources that will help you develop the other resources necessary for your enterprise's growth and success.

Is the knowledge to start a business in itself a resource? If so, who owns it? The Enterprising Ethics box describes the lawsuits that arose after Mark Zuckerberg founded the popular social networking site Facebook.com.

Bootstrapping   The use of modest amounts of personal funds to start companies.

ENTERPRISING ETHICS

Facing the Facts

Since its founding in February 2004 by Harvard student Mark Zuckerberg, Facebook.com has changed the way people communicate. What began as a social networking site for college students has expanded into a broader social utility that facilitates communication with friends, family, and coworkers. Facebook pages help member users stay in touch with friends and share information, photos, and videos. The Palo Alto, California-based company continues to develop information-sharing technologies such as the social graph, which digitally maps people's real-world social connections and applications that build on social networks for marketing and other purposes.

As of early 2008, more than 64 million users access the site at least once a month, and an average of 250,000 newcomers register every day. Today, less than half of Facebook users are college students, and the highest growth is from people 25 and older. Facebook is also international in scope: 60 percent of users reside outside of the United States. The value of the privately held company is estimated to be more than $1 billion.

(continued)

Enterprising Ethics (*continued*)

© Paul Sakuma/AP Photo

Zuckerberg was not the only Harvard student working on social networking sites. In December 2002, twin brothers Cameron and Tyler Winklevoss and Divya Narendra came up with the idea of a college social networking site and hired a programmer to develop the technology. In November 2003, they asked Zuckerberg, a computer science major, to work on what later became ConnectU, a single college networking site. Zuckerberg was not paid for his efforts although ConnectU's founders said they'd do so if the site became profitable at a later date.

While still working with them, Zuckerberg registered the domain name thefacebook.com in January 2004. He then went on to launch his own similar site, Facebook.com, which immediately became popular with Harvard students and by April 2004 had expanded to Stanford and Yale. With the help of classmates Dustin Moskovitz and Chris Hughes, Zuckerberg began growing it into a national network. Facebook quickly outpaced ConnectU's site, which never caught hold.

Soon after, ConnectU's founders claimed Zuckerberg violated Harvard's honor code by stealing computer code from them. This attempt to stop Facebook was not successful, and in the following months competition between ConnectU and Facebook was intense. In September 2004, ConnectU's principals sued Zuckerberg for stealing ConnectU's computer code and business plan. This suit was eventually dismissed in March 2007

for lack of documentary evidence. "Dorm-room chitchat does not make a contract," said the judge on the case. ConnectU did not give up, however, and filed a second lawsuit for fraud, copyright infringement, and misappropriation of trade secrets.

Does the suit have merit? Scott Feldmann, an intellectual property lawyer, does not think so. To protect an idea, a person needs to have a trade-secret contract, patents, or copyrights. "It does not appear that ConnectU had Zuckerberg sign a nondisclosure agreement, and disclosing a trade secret to someone without doing so would ordinarily result in loss of any trade secret status," Feldmann explains. He also points out that because Zuckerberg was an unpaid, casual worker at ConnectU, rather than an official employee, he owns the code he developed.

Discussion Questions

1. Is an idea a resource? Explain your reasoning.

2. Did Marc Zuckerberg have any obligations to tell the owners of ConnectU that he was considering starting a similar type of networking site?

3. Should the owners of ConnectU have required Zuckerberg to sign a non-compete agreement before he began building the ConnectU website? In what other ways could have the ConnectU founders protected their idea?

4. How important is the idea of a social networking site to the creation of Facebook? What other kinds of resources are necessary for Facebook to develop and grow?

Sources: Adapted from Kevin Allison, "The Self-assured Geek," *Financial Times*, USA Edition, September 29, 2007, p. 7; Facebook.com website, http://www.facebook.com (February 18, 2008); John Markoff, "Who Found the Bright Idea?" *New York Times*, September 1, 2007, p. C1; Jason Pontin, "Who Owns the Concept if No One Signs the Papers?" *New York Times*, August 12, 2007, p. BU.3; and Owen Thomas, "A Brief History of Mark Zuckerberg's Legal Woes," *Valleywag.com*, July 20, 2007, http://valleywag.com/tech/facebook/a-brief-history-of-mark-zuckerbergs-legal-woes-280901.php.

15.4 Resources Require Relationships: It Is More Than the Money!

It would seem that investors and lenders who have money and resources would always look to put these resources to work in ways that generate the most return. This is typically not the case. Anyone who has control of a resource—a building, some equipment, land, machinery, raw materials, inventory, or money—has different reasons and values for how they or others can use these resources. Many enterprisers assume that offering investors or lenders a really high return on their investment will be enough of an incentive to close the deal. While getting a sufficient rate of return is part of the evaluation process for any lender or investor, there are other concerns that might play an even larger role in the decision process.

Resource owners prefer to offer their resources to people who they trust, like, and admire. It is usually about more than the money. Lenders and investors have many different reasons for why they will provide an enterpriser with resources. An enterpriser, then, is developing a relationship with the lender or investor whenever a resource is about to be exchanged. "A relationship will not guarantee you financing," comments Edward Zimmerman, a New York attorney and founder of AngelVineVC, a network of angel investors and venture funds. "You still have to perform. But there is always some relationship in place before a deal closes."[4]

Successful enterprisers network extensively to cultivate many potential investors, well before they actually ask for funds. They establish credibility by educating their contacts about their business, what it does, and its financial picture—without the pressure to commit funds. At the same time, they learn as much as they can about these potential investors' personal and business interests and preferences to promote closer relationships.

Consider these examples of how lenders and investors use criteria other than return rates as part of their decision process. An accountant had been the auditor and also a financial advisor to a building supply company for many years. The owner of the business suddenly died. The owner's spouse didn't want to manage the business, so he offered to sell the business to the accountant at a price that was significantly below the business' market value and with great payment terms. The widower said to the accountant, "My wife always thought you were a person of great integrity and someone with good business sense, and, I can't think of anyone who might be better for the ownership of this business than you." The accountant was actually very reluctant to become the owner of this business because he already had his accounting business. With much persistence on the part of the widower, the accountant was finally persuaded to make the investment to purchase and operate the building supply company.

A real estate developer wants to develop properties in a new area. He realizes that landowners who eventually sell their land want to sell to people whom they know and trust will develop the property in the best way. He therefore spends the majority of his time getting to know landowners in this area. You might think of this in terms of selling a used car that you have lovingly restored. If you cared about the car, you might—indeed, you would—sell the car to someone who would treat the car well and continue to maintain it, rather than to someone who might pay more for the car but overtax the car and ruin it.

An enterpriser who doesn't know the reasons why, beyond rate of return, an investor might make an investment doesn't have a close-enough relationship with that investor. Often such investments don't occur. Investors and lenders usually need more than high returns to encourage them to provide resources.

15.5 Tapping Your Personal Resources

What is the most popular form of start-up financing for enterprisers? Bank loans? Venture capital? In fact, funds from outside sources comprise a very small percentage of enterprisers' financial resources. In the initial stages of developing an enterprise, nearly all of the resources that will be invested in this endeavor will stem from the enterprisers themselves.

According to the 2007 study *Financing the Emerging Business*, 92.5 percent of all beginning enterprisers used their own money (personal savings and personal lines of credit) to develop their businesses. The remaining 7.5 percent were consultants and others starting service firms. They had the human capital and office resources they required and therefore did not need financial capital to start their firms.[5] Friends and family are another important source of personal funds.

Exhibit 15.1 presents selected statistics from this study, which categorizes capital sources as *unmonitored*, or personal, sources, and *monitored* contributions, sources that require the enterpriser to give the lender regular reports on the company's progress. We'll discuss monitored sources—banks, venture capital, and other more formal sources—in the next section of the chapter.

These findings hold true for more established firms as well. A survey of the 2007 Inc. 500 companies reveals that almost 82 percent of company founders used personal savings to finance their enterprises' initial stages. They also borrowed from family, friends, and business colleagues (22 percent). About 18 percent took bank loans or lines of credit, while venture capital funding was a source for less than 8 percent of these firms.[6]

Before looking at common ways that enterprisers use their own personal financial resources, it is important to note that for many kinds of businesses, the enterpriser may already have the necessary resources. For example, an auto mechanic may already have a garage full of the tools and equipment needed to repair cars, a

exhibit
15.1

Statistics on Financing the Emerging Business

Percentage of enterprisers investing personal funds	92.5%
Median initial unmonitored investment	
Solo enterprisers	$2,000
Enterpriser teams	$3,000
Median unmonitored investment to develop business	
Solo enterprisers	$12,000
Enterpriser teams	$14,000
Percentage of enterprisers seeking monitored funding sources	51%
Median request for monitored funds	$6,500
Median realized amount, monitored funds	$7,250

Source: William B. Gartner, Casey J. Frid, and John Alexander, *Financing the Emerging Business*, paper presented at the 4th Annual Symposium on the Panel Study of Entrepreneurial Dynamics, Charleston, SC, October 2007. Used by permission of William B. Gartner.

woodworker may already have a shop full of the tools and equipment needed to make furniture, cabinets, and other projects, and a consultant may already have a computer, printer, and other equipment needed to complete a consulting project.

Personal Financial Resources

Enterprisers typically look first to immediately available funding sources, such as savings accounts, credit cards, personal lines of credit, home equity lines of credit, and lines of credit based on second or third mortgages on their homes. Personal unmonitored sources are important to enterprisers starting firms they can manage by themselves.[7]

Nearly everyone has access to personal credit that they can use at their discretion. There are many stories of enterprisers who have financed their businesses using credit cards or by mortgaging their houses and using a credit line. Enterprisers should be cautious when using such credit sources, however. Credit cards and other credit lines have very high interest rates, usually around 20 percent or higher. Even most home credit lines have high interest rates (although they have a tax advantage because the interest payments are tax-deductible). Even though an enterpriser can borrow money using credit

cards, he or she is personally liable for repayment if the enterpriser fails to generate sufficient cash.

Wendy Fergerson was able to use her excellent credit rating to provide her company, Integrated Printing Solutions, with working capital in its early years. Taking advantage of credit card offers such as no interest for up to a year on transferred balances, she borrowed as much as $60,000 a month. Because her customers signed contracts for services, she knew when to expect payments and timed her card advances to avoid carrying balances.

Although credit cards worked well for her business, they are not for everyone. "No transaction should be placed on a card without knowing exactly when the payment will come due and having a rock solid plan to meet the obligation," Fergerson cautions. She advises enterprisers to read credit card solicitations very carefully, especially the fine print, to make sure that the deal is as good as it seems. She also documented each card's terms and set up reminders to prevent missed payments that carry late fees and high interest charges.[8]

Credit cards are also helpful for service businesses such as consulting. When Eric Rosenfeld started Adaptive Consulting Partners LLC, no banks would lend him the $50,000 loan he requested. His firm had no tangible assets for them to lend against, only his expertise and drive. Rosenfeld tapped his personal credit cards for $20,000 startup financing. Another benefit for him was the time he saved with this source, compared to the hours required to apply for and negotiate a bank loan. Instead he could use that time to acquire and serve his clients. Like Fergerson, however, he only borrowed what he knew he could repay on time.[9]

Despite the ease of tapping most personal credit sources, they can be expensive (in interest costs and liability) to pay back. Abusing credit cards can ruin an enterpriser's credit score. The bottom line: If you don't think your enterprise will provide earnings that are significantly higher than the cost of the interest rate on your credit card, then be very cautious about using personal credit to fund your enterprise.

Another important consideration is how the money will be provided to the enterprise. If the enterprise is a sole proprietorship, the enterpriser is loaning money to him/herself. When it is either a partnership or a corporation of some form, the legal entity has ownership of the resources once the money is provided. The enterpriser can either make a loan or an equity investment to the enterprise. If the money provided is a loan, the enterpriser should draw up a formal document that specifies the amount of the principal provided, the terms of payment, and the interest rate for the loan. With a loan, the enterpriser has a claim on the enterprise, just as any other lender who has made a loan to the enterprise. If the funds are in the form of an equity investment, the document should specify how many shares of stock or the percentage of the equity ownership of the enterprise the investment represents.

A key advantage of using personal resources is the message it sends to those who provide later rounds of financing, such as angel investors, venture capitalists, and financial institutions (discussed later in this chapter). Enterprisers who invest personal funds show their strong personal commitment to their business ventures. They can focus on product development and building their company, not searching for funding. Once the company is more mature and has proven it can market a product and reach milestones, it will be better positioned to seek outside financing.

The Friends and Family Plan

What groups of people are closest to you? Who knows your strengths and weaknesses and trusts you the most? Your friends and family are most likely to fall in these categories.

Before turning to friends and family, however, enterprisers should consider the issues that influence getting resources from these groups. The most important issue is managing expectations: What are friends and family providing, and what do they expect in return?

First, what kinds of resources can friends and family provide? Besides the obvious resource of money, friends and family can provide:

- Contacts and referrals: Access to people whom they know, such as other investors or lenders; owners of other resources, such as a building or equipment; or suppliers or buyers

- Labor: The help of a spouse or other family members or friends in getting the business started

- Advice: Important insights into how other enterprises might be successful, as well as serving as a sounding board for helping the enterpriser consider how the enterprise might succeed; other people's perspectives on the enterpriser's strengths and weaknesses

In receiving help from family and friends, be it money or any other resource, take the time to list the reasons that each party is involved in this resource exchange and the expectations that each party has for the outcomes of this exchange. This step will avoid problems later.

For example, if one of your friends or family gives you $10,000, is this money a gift, an investment, or a loan? Leaving the outcome undetermined—"Well, let's see how things go"—is a recipe for hurt feelings, lawsuits, and broken relationships. Enterprisers should create a written agreement whenever they receive financial resources—or any resources that are perceived to be of value by others (such as labor, advice, or contacts). If you believe that developing a written understanding or contract about the exchange of resources and the anticipated outcome of this exchange will be difficult to undertake with the resource provider, consider very carefully whether to accept these resources. If you foresee hurt feelings now, consider what might happen without a written contract if the enterprise fails and the resources can't be returned—or if the enterprise is wildly successful and the family member or friend expects to reap a substantial reward for supporting you at the beginning.

Every exchange will have implications. Money that is provided as a gift might be subject to federal tax regulations on gifts. If the money is a loan, the terms of the loan need to be specified (such as the interest rate on the loan and timing of principal repayment). In the case of an equity investment, the enterpriser must determine how much equity he or she is willing to give the investor. Other investor issues include the relationship with the investor: Is the enterprise going to be a partnership or corporation, and as a result will the investor be a partner or shareholder? (See Chapter 4 to review the forms of business organization.) If the money is an investment, what is the expected return from the investment, and how might that be calculated?

One of the primary advantages of getting resources from friends and family is their trust in you, with trust meaning that they expect that you will treat them fairly and that things will turn out okay. To insure that you will meet their expectations, you should state clearly, and preferably in writing, how they will be treated and how their trust will be rewarded. Even if their exchange is in the form of a gift, tell them how that gift will be used and what you expect the outcomes of the gift will be. This builds a relationship between them and your enterprise.

15.6 Informal and Formal Financial Funding Sources

After enterprisers exhaust their personal funding sources, they must seek outside financing. Some of these providers of monitored funds are private and informal—angel investors, for example—whereas others are formal financial institutions such as banks, asset-based lenders, and venture capitalists. Trade credit and government programs are also important funding resources for growing businesses. Many enterprisers who start high growth companies choose to raise equity financing by selling stock in the public security markets when the company reaches an appropriate size and financial condition.

Angels

Many successful enterprisers and wealthy individuals are involved in helping other enterprisers develop and grow their businesses. A common term for individuals who have money to invest in these businesses is **angel investor**. In many instances, an angel investor will have

already been successful in a particular kind of business and not only has money to invest, but also provides insights into how such enterprises can successfully compete and grow.

According to the Small Business Administration, there are more than 250,000 active angels in the United States who have provided funds to about 30,000 small enterprises. Angel investors have many motives for getting involved with other enterprisers. They want to:

- Help others be successful

- Make more money (so getting high rates of return is important)

- Reexperience the rush of growing a business through others

- Enjoy the opportunities to meet with enterprisers and talk business

Angels are often the first outside form of financing enterprisers use after personal sources of funds. The amount of funding can be as low as $50,000 or $100,000 and can go as high as $1 million or more. On average, however, angels invest several hundred thousand dollars. They tend to invest locally and look for high growth companies with a solid management team. About 90 percent of angel investors make personal loans or provide loan guarantees for start-up firms with 20 employees or less. They understand the risks of their investments and expect to be amply rewarded. A study by the University of New Hampshire's Center for Venture Research reports that angels earned 30 to 40 percent rates of return—but they also expect to lose money on about 33 percent of their investments.[10]

In return for their investment, angel investors typically want equity ownership and a seat on the company's board. Many also set other terms and conditions, such as milestones to be met, price protection, and the opportunity to participate in future financing rounds. Many take an active role in the business, although others prefer to be silent partners. They want regular financial and operating reports from the company.

The form an angel investment takes varies. Some angels invest individually. Other groups of angels, such as the Angels' Forum, Palo Alto, CA, create special entities such as LLCs (see Chapter 5) that make the investment. Some establish venture funds to aggregate member contributions.

There are several ways to find angel investors. University entrepreneurship programs, venture capital clubs, the local chamber of commerce, and local angel

Angel investor   A wealthy individual who provides funds for business start-ups.

investor groups are good places to begin. Also ask your attorney, banker, and accountant for referrals. Once you find a potential angel investor, perform your own due diligence. Check with past business associates and other resources to make sure this is the type of person you want to have on your company's team. Then, formally clarify the angel investor's role and the terms of the investment—in a written contract or term sheet. Exhibit 15.2 presents the pros and cons of angel financing.

How do you find your angel? In addition to individual angels, there are more than 250 national, regional, and state networks of angel investors. Sometimes angel groups will come together to form a syndicate to invest jointly in a company. Exhibit 15.3 lists selected national and regional angel networks.

Venture Capital: Professional Equity Investors

The next type of investor a company may approach is the professional investor called a **venture capitalist**. They invest private equity funds called **venture capital** in young businesses that are not ready to seek financing from public securities markets. Venture capitalists (VCs) can be individuals who invest their own money or are organized as corporations or partnerships that also raise funds from other outside investors. Like angel investors, they seek new and growing businesses that have the potential for very high rates of return, often as high as 50 percent per year. Venture capitalists also provide managerial and technical expertise.

A venture capitalist often has a track record building a business that generated high rates of return. This success allows the VC to create venture capital funds that raise money from other wealthy individuals, as well as from pension funds and insurance companies, who want to invest in new high-growth enterprises. Venture funds accumulate substantial funds to invest, typically ranging

Venture capitalists   Individuals or firms that provide venture capital financing.

Venture capital   Early-stage private equity financing from professional investors who specialize in funding small companies with high growth potential.

---

exhibit 15.2

Why Use an Angel?

Angel investors offer:

Willingness to provide start-up funds

Bridge to later, more formal funding

Faster time to arrange financing

Lower level of due diligence

Advice

Referrals to customers, potential employees, and suppliers

But in return they may want:

Enterpriser to give up from 10 to 50 percent of equity in company

Seat on company's board

Additional fees for consulting

Regular financial and operating reports

Rates of return of 25 percent or more

A higher level of involvement in managing business than enterpriser desires

exhibit
15.3

Finding Your Angel

Network/URL	Description	Investment Range
Active Capital (National) http://activecapital.org	Formerly the SBA's Angel Capital Electronic Network (ACE-Net). Not-for-profit listing service to help connect small businesses with private capital sources. Low-cost, Internet-based option to register securities for sale. Regional network operators provide local support.	$250,000–$5,000,000
Gathering of Angels (National) http://www.gatheringofangels.com	Group of private investors who meet monthly in several cities nationwide. Companies pay a flat fee to present their proposals.	$50,000–$1.5 million
Investors' Circle (National) http://www.investorscircle.net	Network of angel investors, venture capitalists, foundations, family offices, and others sources of private capital. Focuses on companies that address social and environmental issues.	$10,000–$6.5 million
Keiretsu Forum (North America) http://www.keiretsuforum.com	Large network with chapters in North America, Europe, and Asia. Includes private equity investors, venture capitalists, and corporate/institutional investors. Entrepreneurs apply online and then make in-person presentations. Diverse portfolio including real estate.	$250,000–$2,000,000
Alliance of Angels (Pacific Northwest) http://www.allianceofangels.com	Regionally focused network that provides early-stage funding to technology companies.	$25,000–$1+ million
Tri-State Investment Group (Virginia, North Carolina, and South Carolina) http://www.tignc.com	Operates as a fund, with focus on technology companies.	$150,000–$600,000
Common Angels (New England) http://www.commonangels.com	Boston-based coinvestment fund of experienced high-tech entrepreneurs; invests in high-growth information technology companies.	$500,000–$2,000,000
Tri-State Private Investors Network (Northeast and Mid-Atlantic) http://www.angelinvestorfunding.com	Based in New York City; invests in early-stage companies in a wide range of industries.	$250,000–$2,000,000
New York Angels http://www.newyorkangels.com	New York City angels with expertise in media businesses; prefer innovative applications for existing technologies.	$100,000–$400,000
Tech Coast Angels (Southern California) http://www.techcoastangels.com	Large angel network serving Los Angeles, Santa Barbara, Orange County, San Diego, and the Inland Empire. Invests in many sectors, including finance, media, life sciences, information technology, consumer products, and biotech.	$250,000–$2,000,000

Band of Angels (Silicon Valley, CA) http://www.bandangels.com	Provides seed financing for high technology companies, mostly in Silicon Valley, California.	$300,000–$750,000 +
Angels Forum (Silicon Valley) http://www.angelsforum.com	Full-time angel investors who are former high-tech executives. Take a very hands-on approach with early-stage technology companies.	$100,000–$1,000,000
Heartland Angels (Midwest) http://www.heartlandangels.com	Prefers innovative technology, real estate, and retail companies within 300 miles of Chicago.	$250,000–$2,000,000
Technology Tree Group http://www.technology-tree.com	Houston-based group specializing in commercializing government-funded technology research.	N/A

Source: Individual angel network websites; FundingPost.com, http://www.fundingpost.com.

from $50 million to $1 billion. These funds are often structured as partnerships, with general partners, who invest the fund's resources in various enterprises, and limited partners, who provide most of the money for the fund. (See Chapter 4 for more information on partnerships.) Once the limited partner's principal is paid back, the other earnings that are generated are usually distributed 20 percent for the general partners and 80 percent for the limited partners.

Assume NextBigThing (NBT) Ventures is a fund that is operated by four general partners and has raised $100 million, which it has invested in a number of start-up companies. After five years, the limited partner's principal investment has been returned, and the fund generated an additional $100 million in returns on its investments. NBT's four general partners would receive 20 percent, or $20 million, and its limited partners would receive $80 million. If the four general partners divided their returns equally, each would receive $5 million. So, during the five years of the fund's operations, each general partner was making $1 million a year.

In nearly all situations where enterprisers receive money from professional equity investors, access to their expertise, insights, advice, and contacts is among the most important benefit. Professional equity investors want a greater degree of involvement in the management of the enterprise than angels. Typically, they don't want input into the day-to-day operations of the business, but they expect to have a say in strategic decisions and the enterprise's direction.

Like angel investors, venture capital investors are looking for a way to get their investment in the enterprise back with a substantial return. Most enterprises will not be able to generate sufficient reserves of cash to pay off these investors, so, typically, angel and professional equity investors get their money back by taking these enterprises public (selling stock in pubic security markets).

The keys point to remember about venture capitalists—and most angel investors, too—are:

- They want their money back at some point—usually in about five years, no later than ten years.

- They require high rates of return on their investments (from 20 percent for the angel investor to upwards of 50 percent for venture capitalists).

Because such high rates of return are unlikely for most enterprises, the number of angel- and venture-funded businesses is extremely low. For example, in any given year, about 6 million new businesses are started. Of those, about 600,000 are corporations, and only about 600 of these new or growing businesses receive venture capital financing. On average, then, the chances of getting venture capital are .01 percent (600/6,000,000 or 1 in 10,000). Venture capital is likely to be offered to businesses that can grow significantly, with the expectation that the VC will generate a substantial return by taking the company public through a stock offering or selling it to a large corporation for a substantial cash or stock payment.

Exhibit 15.4 offers suggestions to help enterprisers make persuasive presentations to private equity investors.

Debt Financing

Banks are a major source of funding for small businesses, providing several forms of credit that can be used for seasonal or longer-term needs.

exhibit
15.4

Tips for Successful Angel and VC Presentations

Prepare thoroughly for your presentation. You only have a short time to make an impression, so make every minute count.

Be mindful of your potential investors' time. Be prompt; know how much time they have for your presentation, and have your presentation well organized.

Know your audience and tailor your presentation to what interests this group of investors.

Anticipate their needs and concerns and address them in your presentation.

Be succinct: Describe your business concept and model in about a minute. Include how the business will make a profit.

Focus on people more than ideas and products. Investors are looking for a strong management team that can execute the business plan, is committed to the company, and has integrity.

Have a time-to-market for your product that shows when you will begin generating sales.

Explain your marketing strategy: target market, competition, and why your company has an advantage that will win market share.

Present realistic sales and financial projections. Pie-in-the-sky forecasts won't help your case.

Describe exactly how you will use the money you are requesting to generate profits.

Include your exit plan in your timeline. Investors want to know when to expect their money back from a sale of the company or public stock offering.

Describe the proposed investment from the investors' perspective, emphasizing both the benefits—the potential return—and the risks of funding your company. Show how you will minimize market, financial, and technological risks.

Bring all supporting documents to the meeting as backup for your presentation.

Don't get overly technical.

Be candid when answering questions. Experienced investors can see through bluffs. Don't be afraid to say you don't know and will get back with an answer.

Respect your prospective investors' business acumen and welcome their advice. They bring more than money to the table.

Sources: Adapted from Paul B. Brown, "Seven Steps to Heaven," *Inc.*, October 2001, http://www.inc.com; Harris Collingwood, "The Private-Capital Survival Guide," *Inc.*, March 2003, http://www.inc.com; and "Do Not Say, 'I Just Want the Money,'" *Inc.*, July 2005, http://www.inc.com.

When evaluating the creditworthiness of a borrower, banks look at the four Cs of credit:

- Capacity: Ability of the enterprise to pay off the loan on time

- Conditions: How the enterprise's industry and environment might affect its capacity

- Collateral: Assets that can be used to secure the loan

- Character: Judgment about the borrower's trustworthiness and competence

Collateral may be the assets for which the borrower needs the loan. For example, your car or house is the collateral for your auto loan or mortgage. It can also be an unrelated asset; the owner of a business might have to put up his or her house as collateral for a business loan.

Commercial bank loans can take several forms, as Exhibit 15.5 shows.

ENTERPRISE

exhibit
15.5

Forms of Bank Credit

Type of Loan	Description	Timeframe	Cost
Commercial loan	A short-term loan; can be secured (something is offered as collateral) or unsecured.	Less than one year	Interest on funds borrowed
Line of credit	A loan with a maximum amount that can be borrowed over a specified time period; can be drawn upon when needed. Balance fluctuates over time. Used to cover seasonal financing needs.	One year or longer; most lines of credit require that the borrower repay them completely over the course of the year	Interest on funds borrowed plus a facility fee for keeping funds available
Intermediate or long-term loans	Loan for a fixed amount and time period. Includes loan covenants (restrictions and financial tests related to company operations).	Up to ten years	Interest on funds borrowed

Asset-Based Lenders and Leasing

An enterprise can use its own assets as a way to generate funds for operating the business. **Asset-based lenders** are finance companies that will take a particular asset of the business as collateral, and then loan the enterprise funds. Assets that a business has that might be used as collateral are: accounts receivable (AR), inventory, equipment, buildings, land—basically, anything on the asset side of the balance sheet.

Companies that make only secured loans to businesses are called commercial finance companies. **Factors** are financial institutions that specialize in purchasing AR. The enterpriser actually sells the AR to the factor at a discount. (For example, $100 worth of AR will be sold to the factor for $80.) The enterpriser receives the $80, and the factor gets $100 in AR, which when collected goes to the factor.

Inventory can also serve as loan collateral. Because inventory can be difficult to sell, lenders typically limit inventory loans to about 50 percent of the inventory's value. Many companies specialize in financing equipment purchases. GE Capital Small Business Finance and other commercial lenders will often finance the purchase of a large piece of equipment or machinery. The equipment is the security for the loan. Interest rates are often high because the value of the machinery could be specific to a particular business and therefore not easily sold to another company. Often the equipment manufacturers finance their own products through a finance subsidiary or assist the enterprise in finding an outside finance company to finance the purchase.

Certain types of assets can be leased rather than owned. The leasing company retains title to the asset. For example, automobiles can be leased for a particular time period, rather than purchased outright with a loan. Machinery, tools, and vehicles are among the most common assets that companies lease. With leasing, the small business can eliminate or minimize the down payment to preserve cash and make a monthly lease payment for the term of the lease. The tax benefits that finance companies receive over the life of the leased equipment can provide advantages to parties in the transaction, often resulting in better terms than a loan to buy the assets.

Asset-based lender   Finance company that lends to businesses based on value of collateral such as accounts receivable, inventory, or other company assets.

Factor   Financial institution that buys a business's accounts receivable at a discount.

Trade Credit: Suppliers and Buyers

One of the most important sources of funding for companies comes in the form of trade credit. Companies typically do not have to pay a supplier of goods immediately for the items shipped and received. Those payment terms become a form of financing for a business, called **vendor financing**. The business has a specified time period, often 30–60 days, to pay the supplier—even though it can sell those goods the first day they arrive. The business can use the money it earns from selling the goods until payment is due. Vendors often provide discounts to buyers who pay more quickly. For example, a business that receives credit terms of 2/10 net 30 will receive a 2 percent discount for paying within 10 days. Otherwise, the full amount is due in 30 days. However, new accounts that don't have a payment history may have to pay vendors cash on delivery (COD) until they have a period of consistent payments.

Enterprisers can often get help from customers as well. A software consultant can request an advance, say 25 percent, when the client signs the contract for the project, a 50 percent progress payment mid-way through the project, and the final 25 percent at the project's completion. The enterpriser can use the up-front and progress payments for ongoing expenses while completing the project. Some equipment manufacturers also require up-front payments. If you were in the business of making specialty computers for clients, you might ask for a 50 percent deposit when the order is placed, to cover the costs of the components, with the remaining amount due when the computer is delivered. In this way, the buyer helps the enterprise finance ongoing costs such as materials and the labor involved in completing a project.

Never underestimate the value of buyer financing. If a buyer is really interested in your product or service, one of the best ways to indicate his or her desire is to make an up-front deposit. Be sure to check with a lawyer regarding the legal requirements for managing deposits in your state. If your state requires that deposits must be put into escrow, they cannot be used for the operations of the business.

Government Programs

Federal, state, and local governments offer financing and advice to enterprisers who want to start and grow their companies. A number of federal agencies offer programs to assist small companies. For example:

- The Economic Development Administration (EDA) provides grants for projects that create and retain jobs in distressed areas. It also offers planning and technical assistance.

- The Department of Housing and Urban Development's Office of Economic Development supports business creation in distressed rural and urban communities.

- The Department of Agriculture Rural Business Cooperative Service works with private sector and community partners to support business and job creation in rural America.

- The Small Business Technology Transfer (STTR) Program funds research and development projects that bring together small businesses with university research institutes or federally funded research and development centers.

Let's take a closer look at two areas of special interest to enterprisers: the Small Business Innovation Research (SBIR) Program and the Small Business Administration (SBA).

Small Business Innovation Research (SBIR) Program

Companies with 500 or fewer employees can take advantage of the **Small Business Innovation Research (SBIR) Program**, which provides early-stage funding for technology R&D. The SBIR is the largest source of early-stage technology funding in the United States. In 2007, the total SBIR/STTR funding from government sources was $2.3 billion, about half from the Department of Defense.[11]

The program's goal is to help small firms commercialize their research. The funds come from 11 federal departments and agencies who are required to allocate a percentage of their R&D budgets for small businesses: Departments of Defense, Agriculture, Commerce, Education, Energy, Health and Human Services, and Transportation; and the Environmental Protection

---

Vendor financing   Short-term trade credit extended to a firm by a supplier, usually for 30 days.

Small Business Innovation Research (SBIR) Program   A federal government program that provides early-stage funding for technology research and development to help small firms commercialize their research.

Agency, NASA, National Science Foundation, and the Homeland Security Advanced Research Projects Agency.

The SBIR has a three-phase process for projects. Companies begin by applying for a Phase I award of up to $100,000, submitting a proposal responding to a specific government department or agency solicitation. These funds are used to determine overall project feasibility for commercialization. Projects that succeed in Phase I, which typically lasts six months, can then apply for a Phase II project development award of up to $750,000 to further develop the concept over a two-year period. Phase III funding to commercialize the concept comes from private sector sources and non-SBIR government follow-on contracts.

Cambridge, Massachusetts-based MÄK Technologies used SBIR funding to commercialize the sophisticated simulation networking software founders Warren Katz and John Morrison developed. They applied for and received MÄK's first Phase I award in 1991. Since then the company's R&D efforts have benefited from 50 Phase I and 20 Phase II SBIR grants. As Katz explains, the SBIR program has many advantages. It provides venture capital from the government in the form of grants that do not have to be repaid. Nor does the company have to give up any equity or intellectual property rights. "In effect, we used SBIRs to bootstrap our product line," Katz says. "When the day came to sell the company in late 2006, the current employees still owned 100 percent of the company."[12]

Small Business Administration (SBA)

The SBA provides a wealth of services for enterprisers, including:

- Financial assistance: Loan guarantees and other types of financial assistance programs, including export financing and international trade programs

- Contract opportunities: Programs to help businesses learn how to position themselves to bid on federal contracts

- Management counseling and training: Counseling through programs such as the Service Corps of Retired Executives (SCORE), Small Business Development Centers (SBDCs), and Women's Business Centers (WBCs); online courses through the Small Business Training Network (SBTN); publications on business topics from the Business Development Library

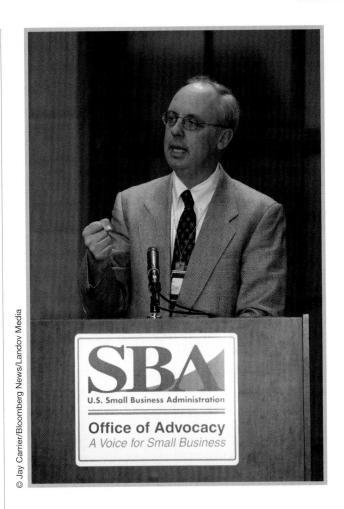

© Jay Carrier/Bloomberg News/Landov Media

The SBA does not provide direct loans but guaranties loans made by private lenders such as commercial lending institutions. Its primary loan program is the 7(A) **Loan Guaranty Program** for qualified small businesses that are unable to secure financing at reasonable rates through normal lending channels. The 7(A) program guarantees can be used for most business purposes, including working capital; purchasing real estate, equipment, and materials; and leasehold improvements.

The SBA's *Section 504 Certified Development Program* supports Certified Development Companies (CDCs), nonprofit corporations formed to contribute to the economic development of their communities. The CDCs work with the SBA and private-sector lenders to provide financing to small businesses.

7(A) Loan Guaranty Program   Primary SBA business loan program; provides loan guaranties for commercial loans to qualified small businesses.

Small businesses and not-for-profit child-care centers can also obtain short-term loans up to $35,000 and management and technical assistance through the SBA's Microloan Program. These guaranteed loans can be used for working capital or to purchase inventory, supplies, furniture, fixtures, machinery, or equipment. The SBA guarantees a loan to an intermediary, who then makes the microloan to the applicant.

In addition, the SBA licenses Small Business Investment Companies (SBICs), private for-profit investment firms that provide venture capital to new and growing businesses.

State and Local Programs

Most states actively promote new business formation to strengthen their economies and create new jobs, offering programs for business financing and assistance. For example, South Carolina's SC Launch (http://www.sclaunch.org) provides financing and advisory services that support new high technology businesses. Michigan's Economic Development Corporation sponsors a variety of programs to stimulate high technology company growth, including an Emerging Technology Challenge Fund, Michigan Entrepreneurship Education Network, and SmartZones, geographical clusters of technology firms. Cities that wish to attract and retain businesses also establish financing programs.

Another form of local help comes from **business incubators**, organizations that provide support services and a wide range of resources to young companies during their start-up and early growth periods. Like CDCs, incubators stimulate economic growth and job creation and retention. Locating within an incubator can be a cost-effective way to launch a company. Among the services an incubator may offer are:

- Rental space with flexible lease terms

- Shared business services and equipment

- Referrals to a network of advisors

- Management guidance

- Technical assistance

Business incubator   Organization that provides support services and a wide range of resources, from physical space to management advice, to emerging companies.

- Mentoring

- Training

- Assistance with business plan preparation

- Supportive entrepreneurial community

Many incubators focus on companies in one industry, while others work with companies in multiple industries. For example, about 40 percent of all incubators specialize in technology companies. Incubators assist their clients in the search for capital resources, providing referrals to angel investors and venture capitalists and helping them prepare funding proposals. Companies that join incubators increase their chances of success. The National Business Incubation Association (NBIA) estimates that the survival rate for firms that graduate from their incubators is 87 percent.[13]

Going Public

Many enterprisers talk about "going public" with their company. In reality, however, most enterprises are simply too small to be part of the public equity markets—and they never will be. Typically, an enterprise would need a minimum of $20 million in revenues to be of sufficient size to issue shares that could be publicly traded. Of the more than 5 million corporations in the United States, about 20,000 corporations are publicly traded on various stock exchanges. Of these, only about 5,000 are large enough to trade actively on the major exchanges, such as the New York Stock Exchange or NASDAQ.

Enterprisers who start companies with a high growth potential often plan to recoup some or all of their initial investment through an issue of common stock. Before they can sell stock to the public, companies should have:

- Several years of significant growth and a high likelihood of continuing growth

- A rapidly growing industry

- Three to five years of audited financial statements

- Solid management team

- Strong board of directors

- Positive references from a known accounting firm and leading investment banker

Exhibit 15.6 summarizes the pros and cons of taking a company public.

15.7   Location, Location, Location

Another important resource for enterprisers is the location of their business. Choosing the appropriate real estate and location to conduct their endeavors raises unique issues for enterprisers.

Every enterpriser will need some type of physical space. In fact, it is possible to build an enterprise with minimal physical presence—only a mailbox to receive invoices, checks, and government forms, for example. An enterpriser who runs a consulting firm or serves as

a computer troubleshooter needs a phone and a mail box but not much more because most of these enterprisers' efforts will occur at their clients' locations. Plumbers or electricians travel from job site to job site and may need only a truck or van for their tools and supplies.

Other enterprisers use their living space as the headquarters for their firms. Michael Dell began Dell Computers in his dorm room at college, and other entrepreneurs have started enterprises in their garages, with Hewlett-Packard as one of the most famous. Many enterprisers sell such products as Tupperware, Avon, and Mary Kay out of their homes or stage jewelry and clothes trunk sales in either their own or friends' homes. An enterpriser who runs a language training program may meet clients at a restaurant for lunch or breakfast to conduct business, and then rent classroom space as needed once clients agree to send their employees for language training. Her place of business is her home, yet she never meets clients there.

The most important question when determining a location for your business is: How will customers purchase products or services from your enterprise? The point of contact between an enterpriser and a potential buyer could be through many different locations. Consider, for example, an enterpriser who has invented a new kind of backscratcher. This device could be sold through the enterpriser's own store, other stores, at kiosks in shopping centers, the enterpriser's website or on eBay, an info-commercial on television, a direct mail

exhibit
15.6

Going Public: Pros and Cons

Pros	Cons
Additional capital for expansion	No guarantee IPO will raise desired funds
Liquidity for owners of the business	Dilution of ownership (more stockholders)
Improved access to capital in the future	Loss of control; now responsible to large group of shareholders
Can use stock for acquisitions	Significant SEC reporting requirements; costly in terms of time and money
Stock options and other forms of stock compensation to attract and retain employees	Increased visibility; must disclose operating and financial data, financing plans, and product information
Higher public profile and image	Substantial fees and expenses to investment bankers, accountants, and attorneys (10–20 percent of amount raised)

campaign at a booth at a county fair or a trade show, or direct door-to-door selling. A review of Section 14.4, "Finding Your Place," will help you evaluate the various issues when making a location decision.

The location of your business can be a strategic resource for your enterprise. Many factors influence an enterpriser's choice of location, such as:

- Closeness to a particular market (or group of customers)

- Closeness to raw materials

- Wage rates

- Labor supply

- Business climate

- Tax rates

- Competition

For example, in terms of labor, someone considering certain kinds of high technology businesses will prefer to locate close to sources of engineers or scientists, such as universities or areas with many high technology companies (Boston, San Diego, Austin, or the Silicon Valley near San Francisco).

However, most enterprisers don't have the luxury of selecting the ideal location for their business. The majority start and operate businesses where they live. In fact, the number of years a person has lived in a particular area can be a predictor of future success. The longer you live in an area, the better you understand its needs. You also have time to build connections to the resources you need for your business.

Exhibit 15.7 lists several websites to use in researching potential locations.

The type of business also affects location issues. A retailer has different needs than a manufacturer or service provider. Questions to ask include:

- How much other competition is there? For certain businesses, having other competitors close by is helpful. For example, restaurants often cluster together because people consider certain areas of the city a place to go and have a good meal.

- What local regulations apply to the business? Zoning laws may restrict businesses from certain locations.

- How large is the trading area for the business? Some stores, such as a dry cleaning store, are likely to draw from a small area surrounding the store, while stores in a regional shopping center will attract customers from 25 to 50 miles away.

- How far will customers travel to patronize your business?

- Is public transportation available?

- Is there enough customer traffic for this type of business? Gas stations, fast food outlets, convenience stores, dry cleaners, and similar businesses depend on a critical mass of customers who walk or drive by.

- Do customers need convenient access, and is it available? How much do utilities and other public services cost?

- Is the area perceived as safe for customers? Does it have a good reputation in general?

exhibit 15.7   Information Resources for Location Research

Website	Data Provided
U.S. Census Bureau http://www.census.gov	Population and income statistics, labor force, economic census by geographic area, industry; survey of business owners
American Factfinder http://factfinder.census.gov	Quick access to population, housing, economic, and geographic data; community fact sheets
http://www.statusa.gov	Site that brings together business, trade, and economic information from across the federal government
Population Reference Bureau http://www.prb.org	International population data and analysis

- Is there adequate parking for customers?

- Is the business visible to customers?

A Web presence changes the standard concept of location, making it possible for enterprisers to attract customers from anywhere in the world. For businesses that sell goods, shipping across borders requires additional considerations such as export and import regulations. Even service businesses can go international, as the Enterprising World box describes.

AN ENTERPRISING WORLD

Music to Go

Most people agree that the Internet has made it easy for enterprisers to expand both nationally and internationally. The actual location of the business becomes less relevant for many types of businesses that sell both goods and services. With a website, businesses can offer their products to customers worldwide. Depending on the item or service, an enterpriser may conduct the entire transaction electronically and never have any face-to-face contact with the customer.

Artists, both visual and performing, are major Internet users as well. Whether newcomers or established stars, they turn to the Internet for many different purposes. According to the Pew Internet & American Life Project report *Artists, Musicians and the Internet*, they are more tech-savvy than average and consider the Internet a valuable tool that helps them create, promote, and sell their works; collaborate with other artists; and communicate with fans.

Musicians are among the heaviest users of the Internet and consider it a very important medium in both creating and distributing their music. Their websites provide ideal locations to connect with audiences worldwide, at any time of the day. Site visitors can learn more about the musicians and their music, listen to audio and watch video clips of performances, look up performance schedules, and buy music at the site or through links to other sites. The benefits to musicians are many: higher CD and concert ticket sales, increasing fan bases, more radio presence, and better communication overall.

Many freelance musicians use the Internet to build audiences and to advertise to potential clients. They can upload song tracks to MySpace and Facebook pages or use a music-focused site like SoundClick.com, where they can set up an artist page with blogs, MP3, and video uploads.

The classified ad pages of Bandname.com, http://www.bandname.com, lists musicians who are looking for work and bands or others who need musicians. The listings are international and cover the full spectrum, from lead and backup singers to performers by instrument and support services for musicians. Artistopia,

http://www.artistopia.com, is a portal for the independent music community that brings together musicians and industry professionals. Musician2Go.com, http://www.musician2go.com, is a site for musicians working in the United States that bills itself as the "website for working musicians." It streamlines the process of hiring freelance musicians of all types, including performers, conductors, composers, arrangers, and more, in all music genres. Musicians who post their résumés broaden their exposure, and contractors can quickly find the musicians they need.

However, performing artists face location constraints different from other service providers. Whereas a freelance writer can work almost anywhere, communicating and sending documents via e-mail, performers usually have to travel to the client's location. Those who provide a very specialized service, such as a soundtrack or backup track, may be able to accept long-distance gigs.

Discussion Questions

1. Is it possible for a musician to have a career through the Internet only? Explain your answer.

2. What are the advantages and disadvantages to musicians of selling to customers living in other countries? To buyers purchasing services from musicians living in other countries?

3. How might a musician develop a customer base on the Internet? Visit several of the sites mentioned above to expand your answer.

4. What other kinds of services could be sold/provided using the Internet? What would be the advantages and disadvantages of purchasing these kinds of services from enterprisers in other companies?

Sources: Bandname.com, http://www.bandname.com (March 25, 2008); *Freelance Musicians*, http://www.freelance-musicians.info (March 14, 2008); Mary Madden, *Artists, Musicians and the Internet* (Washington, DC: Pew Internet & American Life Project, December 5, 2004); Laura Milligan, "Marketing for Musicians: 100 Places to Promote Your Music Online," *Bootstrapper*, September 13, 2007, http://www.businesscreditcards.com/bootstrapper/marketing-for-musicians-100-places-to-promote-your-music-online/; *Musician2Go.com*, http://www.musician2go.com.

15.8 You: Resource Improvisation and Creativity

As we stated at the beginning of the chapter, almost all enterprisers seem to complain that their enterprises don't have enough resources to develop and grow. However, we believe that an enterpriser's resource capabilities are limited only by the enterpriser's own creativity and imagination for developing and acquiring resources. In most of this chapter, we've listed various resources available to enterprisers. What's even more interesting is the many different ways enterprisers can creatively use these resources to develop their businesses.

To act creatively, the enterpriser must understand the business model for success (see Chapter 7, "Feasibility") and know *why* and *how* the enterprise is able to make money. If an enterpriser thoroughly understands the formula for making money, then other opportunities to tweak the variables of this formula can often result in greater profitability and success.

For example, consider an enterpriser who negotiates 90-day payment terms with his or her primary supplier. This gives the enterprise 90 days to pay the invoice for goods it has received. If the enterprise sales staff convinces customers to pay for these goods in 30 days, the company has 60 days extra time to pay for the goods provided by the supplier—even though the money has already been collected. In most situations where such favorable terms are negotiated, an enterprise could basically grow using the 60-day spread between payables and receivables and not use any other source of financing. The supplier to this enterprise is financing this business's growth.

Service businesses often use customer financing to support themselves. As we discussed earlier, a consultant may ask a client for payment terms of 25 percent of the project fee when the contract is signed, 50 percent when the project is turned in, and the last 25 percent when the client agrees the work has been completed to his or her satisfaction. The 25 percent initial payment may be enough for the enterpriser to cover all the project costs. All of the other fees received, then, are profits generated by the project.

Plan B

Another way for enterprisers to use their creativity is to discover as many different ways to generate the resources necessary for their business's creation and growth. As you identify a resource that you need and a specific way to obtain it, also spend time finding other ways to acquire this resource. That is, have a Plan B.

For example, let's say Plan A is to get a loan from your parents for start-up costs. Borrowing money from family and friends has both advantages and disadvantages, which you've taken into consideration before asking them for the loan. You are all set to proceed, and then your father is laid off from his job; the loan falls through. What do you do then? In this situation, your Plan B could be to ask other family members or former business associates for loans.

If the creation and development of your business becomes entirely undone because you only have this one source for financing, then, you need to have a Plan B, that is, an alternative or a series of alternative ways that you can get the resources you need if your Plan A falls through.

The flexibility to look for different ways to get the resources your enterprise needs is critical because rarely will every source for funding eventually come through. A funding source might at the last moment back out of its promises to you. A bank might have agreed to make a loan for your enterprise in February. As it processes the loan documents, the bank discovers a shortfall in other accounts and places a three-month moratorium on new loans. If you don't have alternative funding sources as options, will the enterprise then fail?

Another drawback to having only a Plan A funding source is the issue of control. If this single source realizes the power its funding decision can have over the success or failure of your enterprise, it may use that knowledge to demand a better rate of return or an additional percentage of equity in the business. Will you have options in place in order to say "no" to any demands made by your funding sources, or will you have to take whatever terms that they offer? The more funding options you can identify, the better your bargaining power. If no alternative resources exist, a particular source of funding becomes critical and will require different decisions.

Finding Your Plan B

Enterprisers can turn to many sources for help in generating Plan B alternatives. For example, Bruce Blechman and Jay Conrad Levinson's book *Guerrilla Financing: Alternative Techniques to Finance Any Small Business* (Boston: Houghton Mifflin Company, 1991) offers more than 100 different ways that enterprisers can find the resources to develop and grow their businesses. Another good resource is the Ewing Marion Kauffman

Foundation's eVenturing site (http://www.eVenturing. org), which has a collection of articles on bootstrapping techniques.

Amar Bhide, in his classic article on bootstrapping, points out that enterprisers who are starting businesses on a shoestring require a different mindset and strategies than those who are looking for venture capital. He offers these suggestions from successful entrepreneurs who have learned to do more with less:[14]

1. Get your business up and running quickly. This generates sales, which provides cash to operate the business. It also makes the business visible to potential customers and gives it a track record.

2. Look for quick, break-even, cash-generating projects. Cash flow will keep the business operating. Don't do projects that take a lot of cash, and take a long time to get the cash back.

3. Offer high-value products or services that are suited to direct personal selling. Basically, one looks to sell something that doesn't cost much to sell (except for one's own personal time), and, when the sale is completed, generates a high margin, so that the sale creates cash quickly (related to both the first and second points).

4. Hire for the current position, not the one you need in a year or more, to keep costs down. If you need a bookkeeper to keep the records for the business, hire the bookkeeper, rather than looking for a certified public accountant or the expensive chief financial officer whom the business might need years from now.

5. Manage growth carefully. Businesses that grow too quickly can grow into failure as the cash needs of growth outstrip the abilities of the enterprise to generate enough cash to sustain the growth. (Chapter 16 will offer a return on assets formula for how fast a company can grow without needing outside borrowing.)

6. Focus on cash—not on profits, market share, or anything else. Cash is the lifeblood of the business. If you have cash, you can pay your expenses, your AR, your employees, and taxes. Without cash, you can't pay your bills and the enterprise will fail—even if your enterprise is profitable. It is just that simple: No cash, no survival.

7. Cultivate relationships with banks and other sources of financing before the business becomes creditworthy. Establish relationships with people who have money before you need the money, so that they have some history and understanding of you and your enterprise.

15.9 ENTERPRISERS

Dogging It—Automatically

If you have ever enjoyed a corn dog—a sausage wrapped in cornmeal batter served on a stick—or funnel cake at a mall food court or a county fair, you've probably not thought about how it was made. Odds are it came from equipment developed by Glenn Walser's company, Automated Food Services. Until about 1976, corn dogs were made by hand, a time-consuming process. This changed dramatically when an idea to automate the process came to Glenn Walser, an unemployed engineer looking for a way to make money. "My previous employment was with the Hacienda Mexican Foods in Lubbock making taco shell fryers, which was a revolutionary machine in the early '70s," says Glenn. "A fellow in the corn dog business from Abernathy, Texas, had visited the plant and saw what we'd done with the taco shell machine and he said, 'We really need something like that in the corn dog business.'"

So Walser went to Abernathy to see how they made corn dogs manually. As he drove back to Lubbock, "this vision came through my head of how mechanically I could do this at a much faster rate using fewer employees."

At about the same time, a friend who knew that Walser had lost his job asked if he was interested in starting his own business. He was but didn't have any money. The friend replied, "Well, that's all right. You have engineering expertise, and I'm willing to trust you and back you."

His trust was well placed. With the start-up funding his friend provided, Walser built a prototype machine that turned out 400 dozen corn dogs per hour. That machine became the basis for Automated Food System (AFS). Walser continued to make improvements in his system, which features vertical frying to minimize the amount of oil that soaks into the batter. "Everything on this fryer is almost scientifically developed over the last 20 years, so that it makes it very easy for my customer to make a very consistent, high-quality product," he says. As a result, AFS machinery produces about 95 percent of the more than 2.5 billion corn dogs made in the United States. The company's product line ranges from manual and semi-automated corn dog systems to fully automated machines that produce from 8,000 to 16,000 corn dogs per hour.

However, it was the smaller machines that fueled the company's growth. "We knew that if we were going to really do this, we'd have to make small machines and we would need to sell to small-business people who would, in turn, use this equipment to present this food product to people so that they would know about it," says his wife and partner Wanda. As corn dogs grew in popularity, consumers would want to buy them in supermarkets, which creates demand for the larger machines used by food processors such as State Farm and Jimmy Dean.

The corn dog has even made its way to Europe, Egypt, and Brazil—growth markets for AFS. The company introduced its product by displaying its wares in the Department of Commerce pavilion at trade fairs worldwide. "In the European countries where sausages are so much loved and enjoyed, they've been making corn dogs with a number of different types of sausages that you probably would not recognize over here because they're not the traditional American weiner," says Wanda. "Every country has its own tastes, and that's what makes it so nice and such a good commodity for international markets, because it can adapt itself to the taste of the locale."

Overseas, AFS works primarily with distributors, although it also sells to major corporations. "Our goal is to make the product itself known before we try to sell the big equipment," Wanda says. "We know that most people will like it if it's done right, because they eat sausage and bread every day in some form."

Early on, the Walsers recognized the importance of tight financial controls. "If you do not know your cost, you're going broke," says Glenn. When he creates a design, he first estimates the cost to either purchase or manufacture the components. They also took advantage of buyer financing, which is appropriate for the AFS machinery. "We require a sizable deposit, something like in the order of 40 percent to 45 percent,

because these are very specialized machines," Glenn explains. This covers some of the production costs during the time from placing the order to delivering the machine.

Today, the Walsers have added new product lines that build on their original expertise in automated food production. In addition to the corn dog machines, they have automated manual production systems for kebabs, funnel cakes, batter mixing, and batter pumping. It remains a family business, true to Glenn's business philosophy. He offers this advice to other enterprisers: "Know your costs and to keep accurate records. Don't borrow money that you really don't need. Don't spend money on something that you're not going to use. Make intelligent decisions about what you do purchase and what you commit for. Analyze really what you need. Buy what you need. Don't buy the cheapest. Buy something that's quality, that'll last you for a long time."

Discussion Questions

1. What resources did Wanda and Glen Walser use to start their business? Which of these resources are most important to their success?

2. What alternate sources might they have found for these resources?

3. Could other enterprisers have started this kind of business? If so, what resources would they have needed in order to make this kind of business successful?

4. What resources does AFS use as the foundation for the expansion of their business into other kinds of production systems (such as funnel cakes and kebab systems)?

Sources: Adapted with permission from Small Business School, the series on PBS, at http://SmallBusinessSchool.com; and AFS website, http://www.afstexas.com/ (February 26, 2008).

Summary

1. Enterprisers require resources to begin their businesses. Resources include not just funding but also a wealth of other tangible and intangible assets, such as a location in which to operate, supplies and equipment, personal talents, creativity, contacts, and more.

2. Resource providers want to preserve their resources and also generate a return on those resources. Funds providers require rates of return that will recover any expenses associated with making the loan and compensate them for taking the risk of the loan or equity investment. Investors and lenders require a risk premium for higher-risk projects. One of the first rules of resources is that both lenders and investors should not lose money.

3. The enterpriser has the greatest knowledge about the proposed or existing enterprise. This information asymmetry creates an advantage in acquiring and using resources effectively. At the same time, because they do not possess this knowledge, lenders and investors will perceive the business as more risky than the enterpriser does.

4. The more resourceful an enterpriser is, the better the chances of acquiring necessary resources. Enterprisers who follow the rule of bricolage, using whatever is at hand, leverage the resources they have to pursue desired outcomes and expand the limits of what might work as a resource to solve a particular problem. They also find new ways to combine available resources.

5. Enterprisers who build relationships based on trust are more likely to acquire the resources they need to start and grow their business ventures. Building relationships also gives the enterpriser a more thorough understanding of the lenders' or investors' overall objectives in providing funding. The promise of a high return is not enough by itself to attract lenders or investors, who want to partner with people who demonstrate integrity and business acumen.

6. Most enterprisers use personal, or unmonitored, resources such as savings accounts, credit cards, personal lines of credit, home equity lines of credit, lines of credit based on second or third mortgages on their homes, and loans from family and friends in the early stages of business start-up. The use of personal resources sends a strong message of the enterpriser's personal commitment to the business to later-stage lenders. Friends and family can also provide referrals, labor, and advice to enterprisers.

7. Once an enterprise grows beyond the scope of personal resources, enterprisers will seek monitored resources from outside sources. Angel investors are wealthy private individuals who are often successful entrepreneurs. Venture capitalists also provide private equity and management advice to high-growth businesses. Typically, angels and venture capitalists take equity ownership in the company, get a seat on the board, and require high rates of return for their funds. Many play an active role and offer advice.

8. Banks, asset-based lenders, and leasing companies offer financing for small businesses. Banks provide short-term loans and lines of credit for seasonal needs, as well as longer-term loans. They look at the four Cs of credit—capacity, conditions, collateral, and character—when evaluating borrowers. Asset-based lenders make loans secured by such assets as accounts receivable,

equipment, and inventory. Factors specialize in purchasing accounts receivable. By leasing equipment and vehicles, small businesses can gain the use of the assets without a large down payment.

9. Trade credit from suppliers and buyers is an important funding source. Vendor financing occurs when a business qualifies for credit terms. It can delay payment for goods it receives for a specified time period and use money it generates from the sale of its products in the business. Customers who pay a deposit when placing an order or make progress payments also provide financing help to enterprisers.

10. Many federal, state, and local government agencies offer financing and advice to enterprisers. These include grants and partnerships with private sector lenders. The Small Business Innovation Research (SBIR) Program provides early-stage funding from 11 federal departments and agencies for technology research and development that helps small firms commercialize their research. The Small Business Administration's 7(A) Loan Guaranty Program guaranties loans made by private sector lenders to small businesses. Other loan programs focus on economic development projects and microloans. The SBA also helps small businesses bid for government contracts and has several management counseling and training programs. State programs focus on job creation and economic development. At the local level, business incubators offer support services and resources to fledgling companies.

11. The strongest companies with continuing high growth potential, a minimum of $20 million in revenues, and a top management team may recoup some or all of their initial investment through a public issue of common stock. Once public, the company is accountable to a large group of shareholders and must comply with Securities and Exchange Commission (SEC) reporting requirements.

12. Business location is another major resource for enterprisers. The size and type of physical location will depend on the nature of the business. Choosing a business location involves many factors, including how customers purchase products, proximity to customers and materials, labor supply, competition, and business environment.

13. The enterpriser's own creativity and imagination for developing and acquiring resources is the most significant factor in his or her success. The more options an enterpriser has to acquire the necessary resources, the higher the probability of success. Enterprisers should always have a Plan B ready if the first source does not work.

Review Questions

1. Name the different types of resources enterprisers require to start businesses.

2. What are the primary objectives of resource providers? How do they determine the returns they require for the assets they provide?

3. What is information asymmetry? Why is it important for an enterpriser to reduce it for those outside the business, and how can the enterpriser do this?

4. Define the rule of bricolage and how enterprisers can use it to their advantage.

5. Why are relationships with resource providers more important than the resources themselves? What steps can an enterpriser take to build trust?

6. Differentiate between unmonitored and monitored financial resources. What are the primary sources of unmonitored resources for enterprisers?

7. Compare the similarities and differences between angel investors and venture capital investors.

8. Which financial institutions provide debt financing to enterprisers, and what forms do these loans take?

9. Explain the role of trade credit as a funding resource.

10. Describe four different programs the federal government offers to assist small businesses.

11. What is a business incubator and how does it help a young company?

12. Why do companies decide to sell stock in the public markets, and what are the pros and cons of going public?

13. What major factors should an enterpriser consider when choosing a business location?

14. Explain the importance of Plan B.

Applying What You've Learned

1. Choose a specific type of enterprise that you wish to create, or use one from a feasibility study or business plan you generated earlier in the course. For this business:

   a) List all of the specific resources (human, financial, and social) that you believe it needs.

   b) Identify when, exactly, in the initial stages of development, you will need these resources.

   c) Specify at least three different ways that you might obtain two of your highest priority resources.

   d) List the personal resources that you have (or are certain that you can obtain) to meet the various resource needs of your enterprise.

2. Consider the family members and friends you would ask for resources to help start your enterprise.

   a) Ask these individuals whether they would invest in the creation of an enterprise and why.

   b) If they would invest, inquire about their desired rate of return for this investment.

   c) How would you document these transactions to protect both you and the investor?

   d) How would they feel if the enterprise failed and they lost all of their investment?

3. Identify five individuals who might be able to provide funding and relevant advice to you about the creation and growth of your enterprise. Are these people in your close personal network, acquaintances, or strangers? Write out a one-paragraph targeted "pitch" to each of them that explains why you need their specific financial help and advice.

4. Identify five potential buyers of products or services that your enterprise would provide. Ask them under what conditions would they purchase from a new enterprise, and whether they would also extend payments *before* the goods were supplied or the services provided. Summarize your findings.

5. For those enterprisers involved in businesses that have inventory, contact potential suppliers and ask them under what conditions they extend credit to emerging enterprises. If so, what are their payment terms?

6. Identify at least five locations for your business. For each location, answer the following questions:

    a) Why did you choose this location? (close to customers, costs to operate, transportation access, etc.)

    b) What are the costs related to these locations: rental fees or purchase price? How long are leases for these locations?

    c) Estimate the total costs for putting your enterprise at each particular location. What are the resources necessary, and who will provide them? What will a landlord provide for changes to the location?

Enterprisers on the Web

1. Search the Web to collect information on at least five banks and other lenders that are willing to provide individuals with loans. Prepare a table for these five sources of personal capital that shows:

    a) The interest rates to borrow money, for example, from a credit card, a line of credit, or from a second mortgage

    b) The interest rates to make purchases of goods or services using a credit card

    c) The minimum payment due for taking out any of these types of loans

    d) Other terms and conditions

    e) How likely you would be to use this source, and why

2. Search the Web and collect information on five angel investor groups. Prepare a summary that describes which angel investor groups are closest to your area, the kinds of businesses these investors are willing to evaluate, the criteria they use to make evaluations, and, the amount of money they are likely to invest in any one particular deal.

3. Search the Web and collect information on asset-based lenders who will finance emerging enterprises in your specific industry. If there are no asset-based lenders that you can identify, explain why this is true for this industry.

4. Search the U.S. Small Business Administration's website (http://www.sba.gov/) to explore the various federal programs that assist enterprises. Do any of these programs have criteria that match the characteristics of your enterprise? If so, what circumstances do you believe would enable your enterprise to receive assistance?

5. Search the Web to identify various state and local organizations in your area that provide assistance to emerging enterprises. What criteria do these programs suggest for loaning funds to specific kinds of enterprises? If so, what circumstances do you believe would enable your enterprise to receive assistance?

6. Go to http://www.hoovers.com and go to the IPO Central section of their website (left-hand side, under "Business Intelligence"). Identify the kinds of enterprises that will "go public" or have recently "gone public." What kinds of industries are these enterprises competing in? What appears to be their financial characteristics (such as sales, income, and growth rates)?

7. Search the Web using sites such as the National Business Incubation Association (http://www.nbia.org) to identify any business incubators that focus on enterprises in your chosen industry. Describe the criteria these business incubators use to evaluate an emerging enterprise. What kinds of services do these enterprises provide, and what appears to be their success rate at "hatching" successful growing enterprises?

8. Another way to obtain start-up financing is through people-to-people loan sites such as Prosper. com. How do these work? List the advantages and disadvantages of using this form of financing. Would you use it for your business?

End Notes

1. Ted Baker and Reed E. Nelson, "Creating Something from Nothing: Resource Construction Through Entrepreneurial Bricolage," *Administrative Science Quarterly*, September 2005, pp. 329–366.

2. Claude Levi-Strauss, *The Savage Mind* (Chicago: University of Chicago Press, 1967), p. 17.

3. Raghu Garud and Peter Karnoe, "Bricolage versus Break-Through: Distributed and Embedded Agency in Technology Entrepreneurship," *Research Policy*, February 2003, pp. 277–300.

4. Amy S. Choi, "The Art of the Ask," *Business Week*, October 29, 2007, http://www.businessweek.com.

5. William B. Gartner, Casey J. Frid, and John Alexander, *Financing the Emerging Business*, paper presented at the 4th Annual Symposium on the Panel Study of Entrepreneurial Dynamics, Charleston, SC, October 2007.

6. "The Companies," *Inc. 500*, October 2007, p. 189.

7. William B. Gartner, Casey J. Frid, and John Alexander, *Financing the Emerging Business.*

8. Wendy Fergerson, "Using Credit Cards: Watch the Fine Print," *Kauffman eVenturing*, March 1, 2007, http://www.eventuring.org.

9. Eric Rosenfeld, "Credit Cards: A Small-Business Financing Tool," *Kauffman eVenturing*, March 1, 2007, http://www.eventuring.org.

10. Angus Loten, "As Angel Investor Ranks Swell, Focus Shifts to Later-Stage Companies," *Inc.com*, September 25, 2007, http://www.inc.com.

11. "SBIR and STTR Programs," Department of Defense: SBIR/STTR/Fast Track, http://www.acq.osd.mil/osbp/sbir (October 18, 2007).

12. Warren Katz, "Using SBIR to Bootstrap Your Company," *Kauffman eVenturing*, March 1, 2007, http://www.eventuring.org.

13. "Business Incubation FAQ," *National Business Incubation Association*, http://www.nbia.org (October 27, 2007).

14. Amar Bhide, "Bootstrap Finance: The Art of Start-ups," *Harvard Business Review*, November–December 1992, pp. 109–117.

ENTERPRISE

Monitoring Financial Resources (Accounting)

KEY CONCEPTS

1. Once a business acquires resources, the enterpriser must track how they are used in the enterprise over time. Enterprisers also want to know how well their companies are performing. Accounting is the business function that is responsible for collecting, recording, reporting, and analyzing the enterprise's financial activities. The three basic financial reports managers use to monitor financial performance are the income statement, balance sheet, and cash flow statement.

2. The income statement shows the revenues the enterprise has generated during a certain period of time, the costs and expenses incurred to produce the firm's goods or services, and the profit or loss from its operations. The balance sheet provides a snapshot of the firm's condition at a specific point in time and shows the company's assets, liabilities, and owner's equity. The statement of cash flows shows the sources and uses of cash for a specific time period.

3. Ratio analysis uses data from the financial statements to monitor a firm's performance over time and can warn managers of possible problems. Ratios provide insight into the firm's financial condition, including operations and profitability. They focus on four key areas: liquidity, activity, profitability, and debt. Enterprisers can track their firms' results year to year and also compare ratios to other firms in the same industry.

Suppose you owned a store that sold a wide variety of items, from kitchenware and gourmet foods to toys, home décor, and jewelry. Over time you've developed a flair for choosing unique merchandise and creating a fun atmosphere that brings shoppers back.

© Eliza Snow/istockphoto.com

At Orange Tree Imports, a specialty retailer in Madison, Wisconsin, owners Carol and Den Schroeder know that in addition to choosing products that customers like and buy, they must pay attention to details. This includes pricing products at appropriate levels, analyzing sales and inventory figures, and running the financial side of the business efficiently. By learning about accounting and financial statement analysis, they gained an understanding of what the numbers on the financial statements mean and how they can use them to make better business decisions. This chapter will introduce you to accounting basics so that you will have the tools to monitor the progress of your business.

16.0 Tracking Resources

In Chapter 15, we learned about the many different types of resources an enterpriser will gather to start and operate a business. Once these resources are acquired, the enterpriser must track how they are used in the enterprise over time. This chapter focuses on the specific mechanics of how to account for these valuable assets.

It's certainly possible to run a business with only a shoebox full of cash, receipts, and bills to pay. As long as there is enough money in the box to pay expenses, the enterprise seems to be doing well. But how do you know if the business is really doing well? The process of accounting gives you the tools to know whether or not the business is doing well. It's similar to flying an airplane with instruments. Reading the instruments tells you, regardless of conditions, whether the business is flying high or taking a nosedive.

An enterprise can, in fact, be flying blind. The enterprisers may think the business is doing well because it is generating lots of sales. Growing sales volume is not enough by itself to guarantee success. How is this possible? Many businesses sell to others and receive the buyers' promises to pay, called *accounts receivable.* If the buyer doesn't have to pay for 30 days, the enterprise could run out of the cash it needs to purchase more supplies and equipment and to pay its employees. A company that can't pay its bills is in serious trouble and heading for failure—no matter how fast its sales are growing.

The Accounting Function

Accounting is the business function that is responsible for collecting, recording, reporting, and analyzing the enterprise's financial activities. A single chapter on accounting can only provide a brief and broad introduction to this important topic and cannot cover it in detail. We hope that the chapter encourages you to learn more about accounting so that you can understand how your enterprise makes money. We also encourage you to find an accountant who can provide you with advice and insights to manage your enterprise's resources more efficiently. A knowledgeable accountant can alert you to the many tax and legal implications that affect how you operate your enterprise.

Many enterprisers think that they can save money by not hiring an accountant and a lawyer at the initial stages of their businesses. Yet, the advice and insights these professional advisors provide during the crucial start-up phase will prevent costly mistakes later. Exhibit 16.1 offers suggestions for what to look for when choosing an accountant.

Accounting Methods: Cash versus Accrual

An enterprise can choose to account for revenues and expenses in one of two ways: cash or accrual. The main difference between the two is when sales and purchase transactions are recorded. **Cash basis accounting** is the simplest and recognizes revenues and expenses when cash is actually received or paid out. **Accrual**

© Alessio Ponti/Used under license from Shutterstock

accounting recognizes revenues at the time they are earned, even though no cash may have changed hands yet. This may be when the customer places the order or receives the goods or services. **Liabilities** are recognized when they are incurred, even though they are not yet paid.

A simple example will demonstrate how these methods work. Assume that you purchase a new computer for your business using a credit card. A seller who uses cash basis accounting will not record the sale until it receives the cash from the credit card company. A seller who uses accrual accounting, however, will recognize the sale (as an account receivable) when you take possession of the computer, even though it might not get the cash for a month or more.

The two key tests for deciding whether revenue can be recognized are completion of the earnings process and assurance of payment:

- *Completion of the earnings process:* The seller has completed all significant obligations to the customer. For example, if a customer orders 300 tote bags and the seller delivers 150, the transaction is not complete. When a company sells a product with a 60-day unconditional return policy, it cannot record the sale until after the 60 days has passed.

- *Assurance of payment:* The seller has a high probability of receiving payment for an order.

In addition, companies can choose either the sales basis or percentage of completion to decide when to book the revenue. Under the sales basis, the revenue is recognized when the buyer takes title to the goods or services. It doesn't matter if the sale is for cash or credit. If the buyer receives only a portion of the product, the

---

Accounting   The process of collecting, recording, reporting, and analyzing a firm's financial activities.

Cash basis accounting   Accounting method that recognizes revenues and expenses when cash is actually received or paid out.

Accrual accounting   Accounting method that recognizes revenues at the time they are earned and liabilities when they are incurred, even though no cash may have changed hands.

Liabilities   Financial obligations arising from past transactions or events; creditors' claims on a firm.

exhibit
16.1

Tips for Choosing the Right Accountant

- Look for an accountant who has experience with firms of your size and in your industry. Familiarity with your type of business saves time and is essential to a successful partnership.

- Be sure you feel comfortable with and confident about the person and his or her style because you will be giving them confidential information and want to be able to ask questions.

- Choose a firm whose size is appropriate for your business. A small start-up business may not get the attention it needs from a large CPA firm.

- Ask for referrals from your attorney, banker, or others in your industry.

- Figure out the type of work you want the accountant to do: bookkeeping, monthly reporting, annual audit, advice, etc.

- Determine whether you need a Certified Public Accountant (CPA). Routine bookkeeping and simple tax return preparation may not require a CPA, whereas you will need a CPA for an audit.

- Ask about qualifications such as education and how long the accountant has been in business.

- Conduct in-depth interviews with at least three potential candidates.

- Ask about other services the accountant can provide. Many accountants can provide helpful business advice in addition to financial statement preparation.

- Ask about other clients the accountant serves and check references.

- Find out how the accountant charges. Is there a fixed annual fee, monthly retainer, hourly rate, or a combination of fees? How are expense charges billed?

- Ask how often the accountant expects to interact with you. Regular contact during the year, and not just at tax time, increases the accountant's understanding of your business and its needs.

seller can only book the portion delivered. Suppose a customer pays $600 for a year of monthly pest control services. The exterminator can only book $50 of revenue each month, not the whole amount.

Under the percentage of completion method, a company can book a portion of the revenue from a large project if it has a valid long-term contract and can estimate the percentage of the project completed, using either milestones (such as number of miles of a highway completed) or cost incurred as a percent of total estimated cost. However, buying raw materials for use in a product is not considered an incurred cost until the materials have been used.[1]

Accrual accounting is the preferred method for most companies, except very small ones (annual sales of less than $5 million). It represents the company's financial condition more precisely because it matches revenues and expenses at the time when the *transaction* occurs, not when payment is made or received. The

Internal Revenue System (IRS) requires firms that stock inventory to use accrual accounting.

Basic Financial Statements

The process of accounting gathers the different kinds of accounts that represent business transactions into reports that depict the financial condition of the enterprise. These reports provide the information managers need to know how well the enterprise is doing and to make decisions about future activities.

We will review three basic types of financial statements in this chapter: the income statement, balance sheet, and cash flow statement. These are the primary reports that summarize the firm's financial picture. A number of other financial statements offer additional details to use for managing an enterprise, such as the Aging of Receivables Statement, List of Capital Assets, and Statement of Depreciation.

The basic instruments for operating nearly every business are these three major statements. The **income statement** describes the revenues generated, the costs associated with those revenues, and the resulting **net profit or loss**—the difference between the firm's revenues and its expenses—during a specific time period (week, month, quarter, or year). The **balance sheet** describes what the enterprise owns and owes at a specific moment in time—for example, December 31, 2009. The **statement of cash flows** traces how cash is generated and spent over a span of time, usually one year. In the following sections, we will introduce you to the terminology, the words and labels, used in accounting. Understanding the financial language that accountants and business people use is the first step to sound financial management of an enterprise.

To illustrate each type of financial statement, we will refer to Beau-Ties, Inc., the company whose business plan we discussed in Chapter 8 and is on our website. For this chapter, we will assume that the Beau-Ties, Inc., enterprise has successfully accomplished the first year of enterprise operations, ending on April 30, 2009. The pro forma numbers on the website are the predictions the enterprisers made when they were developing their business plan during the creation of Beau-Ties, Inc. (**Pro forma financial statements** involve making predictions about the future operation of the enterprise. These statements suggest what the enterpriser believes will occur in the future.) The figures that are presented in this chapter describe what actually occurred between May 1, 2008, and April 30, 2009.

If you carefully look at the differences between the pro forma financial statements on the website and the financial statements presented in this chapter, you will see that the major difference in these numbers involves the expenses the enterprise incurred for promotion and advertising. During the first three months of the enterprise's operation, the founders realized that one of the better ways to gain visibility for their business was to invest in public relations efforts rather than to spend resources on advertising. The founders realized they could gain more attention in various media (e.g., radio, newspapers, and television) by having a public relations agency develop. The income statement, then, captures this change in expenses, with more money used to pay a public relations agency (a retainer of $2,000 a month) and no money allocated to advertising.

We can't overemphasize the importance of understanding accounting basics and knowing how to read and analyze your firm's financial statements. Otherwise, you may find yourself making one or more of the accounting mistakes discussed in the Enterprising Ethics box.

16.1 The Income Statement

The income statement shown in Exhibit 16.2 shows the revenues the enterprise has generated during a certain period of time—in this case, for the year ending April 30, 2009, and the expenses it incurred to produce the goods it sold during that annual time period. The income statement will indicate whether the enterprise earns a profit or loss during that time period. For this reason, the income statement is sometimes called the *profit and loss statement*, or *P & L*.

Income statement Financial statement that summarizes the revenues generated, the costs associated with those revenues, and the profit or loss during a specific time period.

Net profit/loss The difference between the firm's revenues and its expenses.

Balance sheet Financial statement that shows what the enterprise owns and owes at a specific moment in time.

Statement of cash flows Financial statement that traces the firm's cash inflows and outflows over a specific time period, typically one year.

Pro forma financial statements Financial statements that predict the future, rather than historical, financial condition and represent management's educated estimates of future financial performance.

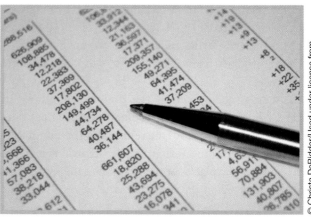

ENTERPRISING ETHICS

Avoiding the Slippery Slope to Financial Ruin

With all the tasks required to launch an enterprise, small business owners may overlook one of the most important steps: setting up an efficient accounting system to track revenues and expenses. It might be quite simple if you are a sole proprietor in a service business with just a few clients. Its complexity increases when you sell products, as you have to track inventory, sales, receivables and collections, expenses and payments, and more. Once you hire employees, you must deal with payroll and related benefits and taxes. And of course, all businesses must carefully track cash flow to prevent shortfalls. The enterpriser should be familiar enough with the business's accounts and have a system of checks and balances to oversee employees who deal with money, to prevent in-house accounting fraud.

Having a basic accounting system in place will help you avoid some of the most common accounting mistakes that new enterprisers make. These mistakes include not setting aside money to pay estimated taxes, poor record keeping with regard to sources of deposits and tracking expenses, and inadequate billing systems and collection processes.

More serious problems arise when enterprisers fail to put away money for social security and other payroll taxes for the employee and employer's portions. Often this occurs if the company runs into cash flow problems. Not paying these taxes when due will quickly bring the IRS to your door. Enterprisers who have set aside funds for these federal tax payments but run into problems making payroll or paying suppliers may be tempted to borrow from those accounts to cover the shortages. This is a major mistake, however, and is considered stealing from the IRS. Find another way to get the funds or the IRS could close your business down!

Determining when to recognize revenues is another area where enterprisers often get into trouble. With accrual accounting, the business recognizes revenues at the time they are earned, rather than when cash changes hands. Even though the two key tests for deciding whether revenue can be recognized—completion of the earnings process and assurance of payment—seem straightforward, the method an enterpriser selects for revenue recognition can change the way an income statement looks.

Suppose an enterpriser is applying for a bank line of credit or term loan for his company. Although sales

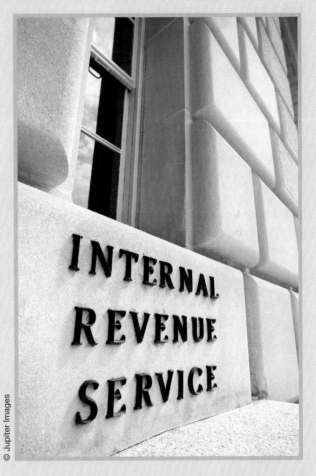

© Jupiter Images

have been steadily increasing, they dipped in the last two quarters. Feeling the pressure as the end of the current quarter approaches, the enterpriser urges his sales team to close all the transactions possible so that the income statement shows an upward trend. On the last day, one very large order is still pending, and the sales representative assures our enterpriser that the sale will close within the next two days. Because previous history with this customer indicates that the order will proceed without a hitch, the enterpriser decides to keep the books open until the sale goes through, so that the company's revenues are higher. After all, it's just a day or two and it will increase your chances of getting the loan. What's the big deal?

This creative accounting approach is, in fact, a serious misrepresentation of the company's financial condition. If the bank approves the loan based on the inflated revenue picture, the company has committed a

(continued)

Enterprising Ethics (*continued*)

felony by fraudulently reporting revenues. The loan could become immediately due. And what if the order goes through but the buyer returns the order, or the company is audited by the IRS?

Clearly, it pays to stay up to date with current rulings for revenue recognition. The IRS and the SEC are cracking down on companies who interpret the rules too loosely. For example, Overstock.com had to restate its revenues and earnings because the SEC took issue with its booking revenue when orders shipped rather than when they were delivered. Another conpany's executives were ordered to make restitution for asking companies that were being acquired to defer booking revenues until the acquisition goes through but to prepay expenses prior to closing to boost the new entity's profit picture.

Discussion Questions

1. Describe situations where enterprisers could tap into cash that has been allocated for payroll taxes, sales taxes, or other state or federal taxes to help meet cash flow problems.

2. How much leeway does an enterpriser have to allocate certain expenses or revenues to other years?

3. How much leeway does an enterpriser have to allocate depreciation expenses to the current year?

4. Identify a number of ways that enterprisers could legally reduce their tax expenses.

5. Identify a number of ways that enterprisers could illegally reduce their tax expenses.

Sources: Adapted from Joe Basile, "Recognizing the Unrecognizable," *Revenue Recognition.com*, March 31, 2008, http://www.revenuerecognition.com/content/experts/8958.asp (April 2, 2008); Ronald L. Clark, "Revenue-Recognition Decisions: A Slippery Slope?" *The CPA Journal*, October 2006, http://www.nysscpa.org/cpajournal/2006/1006/perspectives/p6.htm; "Five Common Accounting Mistakes of Home-based Businesses," *National Federation of Independent Business*, http://www.nfib.com/object/1611505.html (March 27, 2008); Joshua Kennon, "Revenue Recognition," *About.com: Investing for Beginners*, http://beginnersinvest.about.com/od/gaap/a/aa0605.htm (April 2, 2008); Stephen Nelson, "Two Accounting Mistakes Business Owners Should Never Make," *Ezinearticles.com*, http://ezinearticles.com (March 27, 2008); "Overstock Changes Revenue Recognition Policy," *Revenue Recognition.com*, March 31, 2008, http://www.revenuerecognition.com/news; and Stephen Taub, "'Tailwind' Brings Down Ex-CFO, Controller," *CFO.com*, March 14, 2008, http://www.cfo.com.

The first critical component of the income statement is sales, also labeled as **revenue**. Sales are often shown as total or **gross sales**, which include all the revenue generated in this time period. From total sales we then deduct any discounts, such as price reductions for customers who pay early and product returns to calculate the **net sales** (or revenue) for the enterprise.

Cost of goods sold involves all of the costs involved in directly providing the product or service. For Beau-Ties, Inc., costs of goods sold would be all of the costs involved with manufacturing the ties during a specific time period that would be allocated to the sales generated during that time period. If we look at the figures for the year ending April 30, 2009, we see that Beau-Ties, Inc., had total sales of $201,593, less discounts and returns of $1,411, for net sales of $200,182. Deducting the cost of goods sold of $62,822, we get in a **gross profit** of $137,360.

The expense section of the income statement lists all of the **operating expenses** required to run the business during the time period. Like many start-up businesses, the owners decided to operate out of their apartment, eliminating additional rent and utilities expenses. They are doing their own designing for now and have outsourced manufacturing. For its first year, Beau-Ties reduced its marketing expenses compared to the pro-forma estimates, so the enterprise was able to generate a profit of $33,136.

Revenue   The dollar amount of a firm's sales plus any other income it received from sources such as interest, dividends, and rents.

Gross sales   The total dollar amount of a company's sales.

Net sales   The amount left after deducting sales discounts and returns from gross sales.

Cost of goods sold   The total direct costs of buying or producing a firm's goods or services.

Gross profit   The amount a company earns after paying to produce or buy its products but before deducting operating expenses.

Operating expenses   The expenses of running a business that are not directly related to producing or buying its products.

exhibit

16.2

Income Statement for Beau-Ties

Beau-Ties, Inc.
Income Statement for the Year Ending April 30, 2009

Revenues	2009	
Total Sales (Revenue)	$201,593	
Less: Discounts and sales returns	1,411	
Net sales		$200,182
Cost of goods sold		62,822
Gross Profit		$137,360
Expenses		
Selling, general, and administrative expenses	$24,409	
Depreciation and amortization	3,160	
Distribution	1,122	
Promotion	24,000	
Advertising	0	
Designer salary	0	
Salaries	16,500	
Office salary	10,000	
Business and payroll taxes	2,500	
Telephone	2,400	
Legal and audit	7,000	
Rent	0	
Insurance	1,800	
Utilities	0	
Employee benefits	2,250	
Total expenses		$95,141
Net income before interest and taxes		$42,219
Less: Interest expense		5,000
Income taxes		4,083
Net Income (Loss)		$33,136

16.2 The Balance Sheet

While the income statement describes what is occurring to the enterprise during a period of time, the balance sheet describes where the enterprise is at a particular moment in time. Exhibit 16.3, the Beau-Ties, Inc., balance sheet, describes its financial condition at April 30, 2009. It reports the resources of a company (assets), the company's obligations (liabilities), and owners' equity. The balance sheet is so named because the assets are always equal to the liabilities plus owners' equity. For Beau-Ties, total assets in 2009 are $118,136, which is the same as the sum of liabilities and owners' equity.

Assets are what the enterprise owns. They are shown on the balance sheet in order of liquidity, starting with the most liquid. Current assets include cash and other assets that can be turned into cash or consumed within a year, such as marketable securities (short-term investments that can be easily converted to cash), accounts receivables, and inventory. Fixed assets are those assets that are used in the business that have a life span longer than a year, such as equipment, automobiles, buildings, and land. The value of most fixed assets decreases over time, called depreciation. To account for this declining value, a portion of the asset's cost is allocated to it each year. For example, if you purchase a piece of equipment for $20,000 and it has a useful life of five years, it will decrease in value $4,000 each year. The accumulated depreciation increases as the asset value decreases. As shown in Exhibit 16.3, as of April 30, 2009, Beau-Ties has $111,496 in current assets and $6,640 of fixed assets after deducting depreciation.

The second part of the balance sheet describes the liabilities of the enterprise (obligations arising from past transactions or events), as well as the value of the equity provided by the enterprise's owners. Current liabilities are obligations that come due within a year of the date of the balance sheet. They include accounts payable to vendors, the current portion of any long-term debt that must be paid within the year, and accrued expenses (expenses that will come due within a year but for which the firm has not yet been billed, such as wages, taxes, and insurance premiums). Long-term liabilities are obligations due more than one year beyond the date of the balance sheet. Shareholders' equity represents the owners' residual investment in the business, plus any net earnings, or less any new losses the business generates. The net earnings beyond the owner's equity are retained earnings.

As we can see from Exhibit 16.3, Beau-Ties has accounts payables of $10,000, and the current liabilities of the first year's portion of the long-term debt is $10,000. The long-term debt balance is $40,000. The equity investment by the enterprisers totals $25,000 in common stock. At April 30, 2009, it had net profits of $33,136, which is added to the common stock equity.

As we indicated earlier, a balance sheet must balance. The business started with $75,000 in assets—the loan and the enterpriser's initial investment—and added $10,000 in accounts payable, plus it had a gain for the year, increasing the value of the business to $118,136 ($10,000 + $75,000 + $33,136). The increase in assets must be offset by an increase in owner's equity. Adding the retained earnings from owners' equity balances the equation so that assets = liabilities + owner's equity:

$$\$118,136 = \$60,000 + (\$25,000 + \$33,136)$$

Assets   Items of value an enterprise owns.

Current assets   Assets that can or will be converted to cash within the next 12 months.

Fixed assets   Long-term assets used by a firm for more than a year such as land, buildings, and equipment.

Depreciation   The allocation of an asset's original cost to the years in which it is expected to produce revenues.

Current liabilities   Obligations of the enterprise that are due within a year of the date of the balance sheet.

Accrued expenses   Expenses that will come due within a year but for which the firm has not yet been billed, such as wages and taxes.

Long-term liabilities   Obligations of the enterprise that come due more than one year after the date of the balance sheet.

Shareholders' equity   The owners' investment in the business, plus any net earnings, or less any new losses the business generates.

Retained earnings   The amounts left over from profitable operations since the firm's beginning; equal to total profits minus all dividends paid to stockholders.

16.3 The Statement of Cash Flows

The *statement of cash flows* describes how cash is generated and how cash is used during a specific period of time (in our case, by year). It uses data from the income

exhibit
16.3

Balance Sheet for Beau-Ties

Beau-Ties, Inc.
Balance Sheet as of April 30, 2009

Assets	2009	
Current Assets:		
Cash	$58,771	
Marketable securities	15,000	
Accounts receivable	25,960	
Inventory	11,765	
Total Current Assets		$111,496
Fixed Assets	$9,800	
Less: Depreciation	3,160	
Total Fixed Assets		6,640
Total Assets		$118,136
Liabilities and Stockholders' Equity		
Current Liabilities:		
Accounts payable	$10,000	
Accrued expenses	0	
Current portion of long-term debt	$10,000	
Total current liabilities		$20,000
Long-term debt		40,000
Total liabilities		$60,000
Owners' equity:		
Common stock	$25,000	
Retained earnings	33,136	
Less dividends	0	
Total Owners' Equity		$58,136
Total Liabilities and Owners' Equity		$118,136

statement and balance sheet to track the firm's cash receipts and cash payments through the business so that managers can identify cash flow problems and assess the firm's financial viability. Exhibit 16.4 summarizes the sources and uses of cash. For example, an increase in the firm's inventory is an increase in an asset and represents a *use* of cash. Receiving a bank loan, an increase of a liability, is a *source* of cash.

Cash is generated when sales are actually turned into cash. In most businesses, sales for the enterprise result in the creation of accounts receivable, that is, when sales are made on credit terms. When the customer actually

exhibit
16.4

Sources and Uses of Cash

Sources	Uses
Decrease in an asset	Increase in an asset
Increase in a liability	Decrease in a liability
Net profits after taxes	Net loss
Depreciation and other noncash charges	Dividends paid
Sale of stock	Repurchase or retirement of stock

pays for the goods or services, these accounts receivable are converted to cash. As we mentioned at the beginning of the chapter, it is possible for a business to generate increasing sales and subsequently go bankrupt because the sales are made on credit, not cash. Until these accounts receivables become cash, the enterprise cannot pay other expenses.

The Statement of Cash Flows has three categories:

1. Cash flow from operations: Related to the production of goods or services.

2. Cash flow from investments: From the sale or acquisition of fixed assets (e.g., plant, property, and equipment).

3. Cash flow from financing: From the issuance or repayment of bonds, common stock, and dividends.

Exhibit 16.5 shows the Statement of Cash Flows for Beau-Ties' first year of operations, which began May 1, 2008. We compare the account balances at this year-end to those of the prior year-end. In this case, we can assume that the balances in accounts as of April 30, 2008, were $0. The initial $75,000 in cash flow from financing (from the loan and the equity investment) is used for a variety of purposes, such as the purchase of fixed assets and increases in accounts receivables and inventories. The enterprise generates cash through turning accounts

receivables into cash, and creating liabilities, such as accounts payables. By increasing accounts payables, the enterprise is using other people's money in their business. It is similar to taking out a loan from your vendors to grow the business.

16.4 Ratio Analysis and Performance Metrics

In looking over the figures in the income statement and balance sheet, would you say that Beau-Ties is doing well as an enterprise? We can look at the numbers and see whether they increased or decreased compared to the pro forma estimates in the original business plan. This will not tell us enough, however. We must also analyze the figures on the financial statements in relationship to each other and over time. This process, called **ratio analysis**, is a valuable tool that allows enterprisers to monitor whether their enterprise is heading in the right direction and is operating in a successful manner. Ratios can identify areas where the company is doing well or warn of potential problems, so that managers can investigate further. The year-to-year trends the ratios show provide important information to the firms' investors as well as its managers. A firm's ratios can also be compared to other firms in its industry and industry averages. Because ratios are based on historical information, they may not predict future performance.

An enterpriser can use many different ratios and performance metrics to evaluate the health of the

Ratio analysis Calculating and interpreting financial data from financial statements to evaluate a firm's condition and performance.

exhibit
16.5

Statement of Cash Flows for Beau-Ties

Beau-Ties, Inc.
Statement of Cash Flows for the Year Ended April 30, 2009

Cash Flow from Operations		
Net profits after taxes	$33,136	
Depreciation	3,160	
Increase in accounts receivable	(25,960)	
Increase in inventories	(11,765)	
Increase in accounts payable	10,000	
Cash provided by operations		$8,571
Cash Flow from Investments		
Increase in gross fixed assets	($9,800)	
Cash used by investments		(9,800)
Cash Flow from Financing		
Increase in long-term debt	50,000	
Sale of common stock	25,000	
Cash provided by financing		75,000
Net increase in cash and marketable securities		$58,771

company. Ratios can be classified by what they measure: liquidity, profitability, activity, and financing.

Liquidity Ratios

A firm's ability to pay its short-term debts as they come due is an important measure of financial health. The current ratio and the acid-test (quick) ratio are two measures of liquidity and are of special interest to the firm's creditors. For each ratio, we show the formula and the calculation for Beau-Ties.

Current Ratio

The **current ratio** provides a measure of the enterprise's ability to pay current liabilities. It is calculated as follows:

$$\text{Current ratio} = \frac{\text{Current assets}}{\text{Current liabilities}}$$

$$= \frac{\$111,496}{\$20,000} = 5.57$$

A current ratio of 5.57 means that Beau-Ties has $5.57 of current assets to pay for every $1.00 of current liabilities. A general rule of thumb for most enterprises is to have a minimum current ratio 2:1.

Quick Ratio

Since the ability to pay expenses and invoices from debtors and supplies is so critical to the ability of the enterprise to operate, many enterprisers use a more stringent metric for evaluating whether the enterprise can pay its obligations. The **quick ratio** includes all

Current ratio   The ratio of current assets to current liabilities; provides a measure of the enterprise's liquidity.

Quick ratio   The ratio of current assets except inventory to total current liabilities; provides a more conservative liquidity measure because inventory is the least liquid current asset and may not be readily converted into cash.

current assets except inventory, which is the least liquid and may not be readily converted into cash. The calculation of the quick ratio is:

$$\text{Quick ratio} = \frac{\text{Current assets} - \text{inventory}}{\text{Current liabilities}}$$

$$= \frac{\$99,731}{\$20,000} = 4.99$$

The quick ratio of almost 5 is good. Most enterprises seek to operate their firms so that they have a quick ratio of at least 1, the minimum amount they need to meet current liabilities.

Activity Ratios

Activity ratios measure how well a firm uses its assets. They reflect the speed with which resources are converted to cash or sales. Frequently used activity ratios include inventory turnover, accounts receivable turnover, the average collection period, payables turnover, and average payment period.

Inventory Turnover

Inventory turnover indicates the liquidity of a company's inventory by showing number of times that the enterprise sells its inventory (turns its inventory over) during a certain time period, usually a year. Enterprisers would like their businesses to utilize inventory as efficiently as possible. A higher ratio indicates better utilization. For Beau-Ties, the average inventory turnover ratio for the first year of operations is:

$$\text{Average inventory turnover} = \frac{\text{Cost of goods sold}}{\text{Average inventory}}$$

$$= \frac{\$62,822}{\$5,882.50} = 10.68$$

Average inventory is calculated by taking the inventory at the beginning of the period and adding it to the inventory at the end of the period, and dividing that number by 2. In our example, there would be no inventory when the business began, so the calculation

Inventory turnover The ratio of cost of goods sold to average inventory; shows the number of times that the enterprise sells its inventory (turns its inventory over) during a certain time period.

Average collection period The ratio of accounts receivable to average sales per day; provides insight into the average time needed to turn a firm's accounts receivable into cash.

is $0 + \$11,765/2 = \$5,882.50$. The average inventory turnover ratio is $\$62,822/\$5,882.50 = 10.68$ times.

For the Beau-Ties, an inventory turnover of almost 11 is high. Indeed, in many enterprises, an inventory turnover ratio of 2–4 times a year would be considered good. For example, a supermarket might turn its store inventory over 15–20 times a year, while a jewelry store might turn over its inventory twice a year. Therefore, we should compare the Beau-Ties turnover to other apparel accessory manufacturers and, as the company continues operating, to turnover in prior periods.

When this ratio is very high, as in our example, it would be a clue that the enterprise might not have enough inventory on hand to cover any immediate orders that might occur. This enterprise might suffer from stock-outs, which are situations where there is no inventory to sell. A high average inventory turnover ratio can also show that the enterprise has figured out a way to generate sales to customers and satisfy these orders without having much inventory on hand, which might be possible if the enterprise had suppliers willing to provide inventory on demand. This would indicate a very efficient business that is utilizing its inventory wisely.

The average inventory turnover ratio also indicates whether the enterprise needs more inventory to generate sales. The higher the ratio, the lower the inventory level. This means the firm needs lower asset levels to generate sales and profits. Note that many enterprises have important reasons to keep higher or lower levels of inventory on hand during a particular sales cycle. For example, an enterprise that makes the majority of its sales during the Christmas holiday season might stock up on its inventory before these months in order to avoid stock-outs. An enterprise might significantly decrease its inventory if it resides in a location that places a tax on inventory, to minimize the tax it would owe.

Average Collection Period

A firm's average collection period provides insight into how quickly it collects its accounts receivable and turns them into cash. It shows the average age of accounts receivables, or days to collection. For Beau-Ties, this ratio is calculated as:

$$\text{Average collection period} = \frac{\text{Accounts receivable}}{\text{Annual credit sales}/365}$$

$$\text{Average sales per day} = \frac{\text{Annual sales}}{365}$$

$$= \frac{\$201,593}{365} = \$552.51$$

$$\text{Average collection period} = \frac{\$25,960}{\$552.31} = 46.98 \text{ days}$$

For our example, we will assume that all sales are credit sales. For the first year of operations, Beau-Ties takes an average of 47 days to collect accounts receivable from customers.

In most manufacturing firms, a collection period less than 30 days would be extremely rare. Many enterprisers provide credit to their customers, such as terms of 2/10, net 30. Customers who pay within 10 days will receive a 2 percent discount; otherwise, the invoice must be paid in full within 30 days. Many customers, particularly those customers who order frequently, will find the discount particularly rewarding and pay within the 10-day period. For the enterpriser offering credit, the 2 percent discount is a good incentive to insure that customers provide the enterprise with cash.

A collection period of 47 days indicates that Beau-Ties, Inc., has some retailers who do not pay on time or take advantage of the early payment discounts. This measure, then, would suggest that the managers of the business should look very carefully at its credit and collection policies to take steps to shorten the collection period.

As we have indicated repeatedly in this chapter, the most important asset an enterprise has during its creation and development is cash. If the enterprise runs out of cash, it will not be able to pay its bills to other creditors, and the enterprise might fail. Providing incentives to get customers to pay cash is very important.

Finally, consider what happens when customers don't pay their invoices within the 30-day period. As these accounts receivables age (remain outstanding), they become less likely to be collected. If a customer does not pay an invoice within 60 days, it may have problems operating its business and this account receivable might never be collected. Enterprisers monitor the average collection period ratio to discern whether their customers are tending to pay late or early. A rising average collection period ratio shows that customers are taking longer to pay. The enterpriser may want to institute collection procedures to convert these overdue receivables into cash.

Also note that many customers often make it a policy to pay their vendors late. As we will see in the next section, your accounts receivable become your vendors' accounts payable. Accounts payable are basically short-term loans from the vendor to the customer to finance the sales of a product or service. By extending the payment dates from 30 days to 60 days, the customer has 30 days more use of your assets.

In many respects, an enterprise's accounts receivables become a nonperforming asset after 30 days; they are not earning the enterprise any money. Because of this, many enterprises charge an interest rate on payments made by customers after the 30-day span, such as an additional 2 percent a month for late payments. This would imply that an accounts payable that was outstanding for longer than a year would have generated an interest rate of 24 percent for that year.

Average Payment Period

Just as your enterprise is likely to provide your customers with credit terms of 30 days on the purchase of goods or services, your enterprise is likely to receive credit terms of 30 days on purchases or goods or services from your suppliers. We can calculate the **average payment period** to measure how long Beau-Ties takes to pay its bills. This is calculated in a manner similar to the average collection period:

$$\text{Average payment period} = \frac{\text{Accounts payable}}{\text{Average purchases per day}}$$

$$\text{Average purchases per day} = \frac{\text{Annual purchases}}{365}$$

$$= \frac{\$74,587}{365} = \$204.35$$

$$\text{Average payment period} = \frac{\$10,000}{\$204.35} = 48.94 \text{ days}$$

For Beau-Ties, Inc., during the first year of business, average payment period would be calculated in the following manner: Purchases would be determined by taking the ending inventory number, adding the costs of goods sold, and then subtracting beginning inventory, to determine purchases for the period. Since Beau-Ties, Inc., began with no inventory, purchases would be cost of goods sold plus ending inventory or $62,822 + $11,765 = $74,587.

The average payment period of about 49 days becomes meaningful when we compare it to Beau-Ties and its industry's credit terms. If the standard is 30 days, Beau-Ties is not paying its purchase invoices on time.

Average payment period   The ratio of accounts payable to average purchases per day, showing the average amount of time needed to pay a firm's accounts payable.

Asset Turnover

A firm's **asset turnover** compares sales to total assets and shows how well management uses the firm's assets to produce sales. This ratio is calculated as:

$$\text{Nets sales to total assets ratio} = \frac{\text{Net sales}}{\text{Total assets}}$$

$$= \frac{\$200,182}{\$118,136} = 1.69$$

This means that Beau-Ties is generating $1.69 in sales for every dollar of assets. This ratio can help enterprisers figure out whether their assets are being used productively. If this ratio is too low, the assets may be underutilized. If it is too high, it might mean that the enterprise is stretched too thin with not enough resources (e.g., accounts receivables, inventory, plant, and equipment) to support this level of sales. As we will see in another section of this chapter, enterprisers can review comparable ratios for other companies in the same industry to see whether their business is doing better or worse than average.

Profitability

Profitability ratios measure how well the firm is using its resources to generate earnings and how efficiently it is being managed. They are calculated by comparing the firm's profits to its sales, equity, or stock value. The main profitability ratios are net profit margin, return on equity, and earnings per share.

Net Profit Margin

The **net profit margin** provides one measure of the enterprise's ability to generate profits. It is determined as follows:

$$\text{Net profit margin} = \frac{\text{Net profit}}{\text{Net sales}} = \frac{\$33,136}{\$200,182} = 16.6\%$$

Asset turnover   The ratio of sales to total assets; indicates how well management uses the firm's assets to produce sales.

Net profit margin   The ratio of net profit to net sales, which shows what portion of every sales dollar the firm has left after all costs and expenses.

Return on assets (ROA)   The ratio of net profit to total assets; measures how well the enterprise generates profits with its assets (invested capital).

Return on equity (ROE)   The ratio of net profit to equity; measures the return on investors' funds.

This ratio shows that for every dollar of sales, Beau-Ties had 16.6 cents left after all costs and expenses. As with activity ratios, the net profit margin should be viewed in the context of a firm's industry and in comparison to its peers. Different kinds of businesses have different profit margins on sales. Some enterprises have very low net profit on sales ratios. Supermarkets, for example, only earn about 2 percent on every dollar of sales, while the industry average for the textile footwear and accessories category is 10.4 percent and for electronic equipment manufacturers, 4.4 percent.

Return on Assets (ROA) Ratio

The **return on assets (ROA)** ratio provides the enterpriser with a measure of how well the enterprise generates profits with its assets (invested capital). The ratio is determined as follows:

$$\text{Return on assets} = \frac{\text{Net profit}}{\text{Total assets}} = \frac{\$33,136}{\$118,136} = 28.0\%$$

This indicates that the enterprisers who are managing Beau-Ties, Inc., are able to generate high margins for the assets they have in this enterprise. This ratio is also labeled as return on assets or ROA. Like the net profit margin, ROA should be viewed in the context of a firm's industry and the company's previous ROA figures.

The return on assets percentage also provides an approximation of how fast an enterprise can grow using its own internal assets. Beau-Ties, Inc., should be able to grow at 28 percent a year without needing any other outside resources. Any growth rate higher than 28 percent would require the enterprise to either borrow funds from outside sources, or seek additional equity investment from its owners. We should also note that the enterprise has a significant amount of its assets—$73,771—in cash and marketable securities. If it used $50,000 of cash to pay off the loan, total assets would be $68,136 at end of the fiscal year. This would push the ROA to almost 49 percent: $33,136/$68,136 = 48.6 percent.

Return on Equity (ROE) Ratio

Return on equity (ROE), one of the most important ratios we can calculate, measures the ratio of net profit to equity. It is a major indicator of how well the enterpriser uses investors' funds to generate profits and indicates the rate at which the firm's value is growing. This ratio is determined as follows:

$$\text{Return on equity (ROE)} = \frac{\text{Net profit}}{\text{Owner's equity (net worth)}}$$

$$= \frac{\$33,136}{\$58,136} = 57.0\%$$

This is a very good return on the equity the owners of Beau-Ties, Inc., have invested in this enterprise! Of course, it represents only one year, and this first year may not be typical. Beau-Ties' managers and investors will want to track this ratio over time and also compare it to industry norms.

Financing Ratios

We should also look at the mix of debt and equity an enterprise uses to finance its operations. A high level of debt can increase the risk of the firm in making interest payments and repaying loans. Two important financing measures are the debt ratio and the ability of the firm to cover interest payments.

Debt Ratio

The **debt ratio** is a fairly broad measure of the enterprise's ability to pay its debts. It measures the percentage of the enterprise's assets financed by debt. This ratio is calculated as:

$$\text{Debt ratio} = \frac{\text{Total liabilities}}{\text{Total assets}} = \frac{\$60,000}{\$118,136} = 50.8\%$$

For the first year of business for Beau-Ties, this ratio indicates that Beau-Ties has about 51 cents in debt for every $1 of assets. The closer this ratio gets toward 1, the more debt the enterprise has for the assets in the business. In general, the creditors of the enterprise would prefer that the enterprise have less debt per each dollar of assets, so that the firm has adequate assets to pay off its debts.

Times Interest Earned Ratio

The **times interest earned ratio**, also called the *interest coverage ratio*, measure indicates the enterprise's ability to pay the interest on its debts. A higher ratio suggests a better ability to cover its interest payments. For purposes of illustration, let us assume that the founders made a $50,000 long-term loan with a term of five years, repayable in equal installments of $10,000, and a 10 percent annual interest rate. In the first year of operation, Beau-Ties would owe $5,000 in interest. The times interest earned ratio would be calculated as:

Times interest earned ratio

$$= \frac{\text{Earnings before interest and taxes}}{\text{Total interest expense}}$$

$$= \frac{\$42,219}{\$5,000} = 8.44$$

Earnings before interest and taxes is often labeled EBIT in financial statements. For the first year of business, the times interest earned ratio would be 8.44. Most creditors like to see a times interest earned ratio of at least 4 or 6 to 1. Even though the owners of the enterprise are making a loan to themselves for the development of the business, their creditworthiness is within acceptable lender parameters.

Debt-to-Equity Ratio

The **debt-to-equity ratio** offers an insight into what percentage of the enterprise is "owned" by creditors versus that "owned" by the investors. This ratio provides an evaluation of how leveraged the enterprise is, or how much debt the enterprise is using to finance its business. For Beau-Ties, the debt-to-equity ratio for the first year of business would be:

$$\text{Debt-to-equity} = \frac{\text{Total debt (liabilities)}}{\text{Stockholders' equity}}$$

$$= \frac{\$60,000}{\$58,136} = 1.03$$

For 2009, this ratio is 1.03, which indicates that Beau-Ties has $1.03 in debt for every $1 of equity invested in the business. The higher the debt-to-equity ratio, the greater amount of debt the enterprise is using to finance its operations. If the enterprise had a debt-to-equity ratio of 1, then, the creditors would have an equal claim with the investors to the enterprise's assets. With a debt-to-equity ratio greater than one, the creditors have a larger claim to the assets of the enterprise than do the investors. Many businesses are able to succeed with high debt to net worth ratios—as long as these enterprises can pay the interest and current principal owed on their debts.

Debt ratio   The ratio of total liabilities to total assets, which measures the percentage of the enterprise's assets financed by debt.

Times interest earned ratio (*interest coverage ratio*)   The ratio of earnings before interest and taxes to interest expense; measures the enterprise's ability to pay the interest on its debts.

Debt-to-equity ratio   The ratio of total liabilities to stockholders' equity, which provides an evaluation of how leveraged the enterprise is.

16.5 Comparing Enterprise Performance

How would one know whether the ratios that have been calculated for an enterprise are pointing toward a business that is successful, or one that might be headed for failure? Every business will likely have different measures of success. Many organizations publish business performance statistics and ratios for various types of businesses and industry groups. These comparative ratios are very useful for determining how well an enterprise is doing compared to others in its industry. Most major libraries have subscriptions to these reports. Enterprisers may also be able to access this information through their bankers.

The two major services providing this information are the Risk Management Association (RMA) and Dun and Bradstreet, Inc. (D & B). RMA (http://www.rmahq. org/RMA/) provides a number of services for comparing the performance of similar types of businesses. One of the more important services they offer is the Annual Statement Studies, which provides financial benchmarks for a wide variety of businesses and industries.

Whereas D & B (http://www.dnb.com/us/) is primarily known for the credit reports it provides on most businesses, this organization also offers comprehensive insight reports that compare specific types of businesses by their operating ratios and other business statistics.

Comparative financial information is also available from most trade associations, which typically collect business information from all of their members and then report summary information. These reports provide valuable insights into how other enterprises in a specific industry are performing each year. Several government agencies—the Small Business Administration (SBA), the Census Bureau, and the Department of Commerce—collect information on various types of businesses. Financial portal sites such as Yahoo! Finance (http://finance.yahoo.com) include industry statistics as well.

As we suggested earlier, using comparative financial information would likely be the most helpful when used in tandem with an accountant who is working with your enterprise to insure that the financial aspects of the enterprise are being done properly and accurately.

Another place to get financial data about companies in your industry is the SEC's EDGAR (Electronic Data Gathering, Analysis, and Retrieval) database, where you will find all of the financial documents that public companies must file. These include audited financial statements, along with a host of related documents that disclose information about the business, its operations, officers and their compensation, and more. Reviewing these documents also provides insight into the reporting requirements that apply to public companies. The box below discusses in greater detail what "going public" means for a company.

AN ENTERPRISING WORLD

Are You Sure You Want to Be a Public Company?

Going public has definite attractions—the excitement and prestige of joining the "big boys" as a publicly traded corporation, a higher profile for your firm, access to capital markets for future funding, having common stock to reward employees, and a way for owners to cash out, to name a few. However, it's not all fame and glory. Going public is a stressful and challenging process that will consume at least four months of your life, with no guarantees of success. Once you are a public company, you must comply with many government requirements and disclose previously confidential information about the business, from executive salaries to quarterly and annual audited financial statements. Your financial and other business information will be readily available to anyone who

knows how to perform a Web search. An initial public offering (IPO) is an expensive undertaking, with fees and expenses that can cost as much as 25 percent of the total raised.

To successfully sell stock to the public, a company needs a solid track record of past growth, potential future growth of about 20 percent a year, and a minimum market valuation of $100 million (shares outstanding times estimated price). If your company meets these criteria, you will need to find an investment banker to manage and underwrite your IPO—preferably one with experience with similar companies—as well as attorneys and accountants. You must file a registration statement with the SEC before the offering, and the SEC staff reviews it for compliance with disclosure requirements and must declare the registration statement effective before you sell shares.

The basic registration statement, Form S-1, has two parts:

- Part I, the prospectus, is the legal offering document. In the prospectus, your company provides details about its business operations (e.g., business, properties, market, competition, management, financial condition, risks, and other specified information). All potential buyers must have access to the prospectus.

- Part II has supplemental information. You are not required to provide it to investors. However, it is available to anyone through the SEC's public reference rooms or the SEC website.

Issuers using Form S-1 must provide audited financial statements, prepared according to detailed SEC regulations, for three fiscal years.

Before getting to that point, however, stop and imagine yourself as a public company. Are you comfortable disclosing details about your company? For many entrepreneurs, the answer is no, and they choose to stay private and look for alternate ways to raise capital. Also, your company's practices and performance will be subject to public scrutiny. Having a relative who isn't an active employee on the payroll may be fine when you are private, but once you go public, this and other situations could be questioned. You will have to give up some managerial autonomy and flexibility once you are public. Your financial statements will also be examined closely, and you will need an audit committee to oversee your accounting and financial practices. If your independent auditor does not have experience with public companies, you will need to change to another firm, which takes time and may cost more.

Another critical question: Do you have employees with the necessary skills, such as a chief financial officer and support staff, to handle a public company's ongoing regulatory and reporting requirements? You must file information with the SEC and inform shareholders about:

- Business operations;

- Officers, directors, and certain shareholders, including salary, various fringe benefits, and transactions between the company and management;

- Financial condition (independently audited financial statements); and

- Its competitive position and material terms of contracts or lease agreements.

In addition, you must familiarize yourself with the more than 60 different types of forms that you may have to file at some point, as well as separate forms covering international business. The complete list of forms by category is available at the SEC's EDGAR site, http://www.sec.gov/about/forms/secforms.htm. Some of the most commonly filed forms are:

424b1: The company's prospectus

10-K: Company's annual report to the SEC

10-Q: Company's quarterly earnings report

8-K: Current Report used to report the occurrence of any new material events or corporate changes of importance to investors

3: Statement of initial ownership of securities by a director, officer, or owner owning more than 10 percent of the company's stock

4: Changes in ownership by a director, officer, or owner

S-8: Registration of securities to be offered to employees

SC-13D: Disclosure of organizations or persons purchasing more than 5 percent of the company's stock

Discussion Questions

Use a search engine to find IPOs for companies that have gone public within the past three years, preferably in an industry that you are considering for your enterprise (e.g., entering "2007 IPOs" brings up a list of sites with the desired information). Then visit the SEC's EDGAR site, http://www.sec.gov/edgar.shtml, to access the referenced documents and answer the following questions:

1. Locate the prospectus for this company. What kinds of financial estimates is the company making about its future? What does the company say about its chances for success and why it plans to be successful? What percentage of the company will the founders of the company have, once the company has "gone public?"

2. Locate a 10-K for the company two to five years after the company went public. Was the company accurate in the financial estimates it offered in the prospectus? What does the company now say about its chances for success and why it plans to be successful? How has management changed? What percentage of the company do the founders and others now own of the business?

3. Locate the last 10-K annual report or 10-Q quarterly report for the company. How is the company doing? What has changed for this company over the past year? What do they estimate will occur in the future?

(continued)

An Enterprising World (*continued*)

4. For the financial reports you explored, what was the cost this company paid for accountants to audit their financial statements for these reports?

5. How can you use the information provided in these reports to better manage and operate your enterprise? What is this company doing better than your enterprise? What can your enterprise do better than this company? Will your enterprise be able to

generate the same kinds of financial margins for sales that this company is able to do?

Sources: "Going Public," *Entrepreneur.com*, December 7, 2005, http://www.entrepreneur.com/growyourbusiness/howtoguides/article81394.html; "Q&A: Small Business and the SEC," Securities and Exchange Commission, http://www.sec.gov/info/smallbus/qasbsec.htm (April 17, 2008); Theodore F. di Stefano, "Is Going Public the Right Move for Your Company?", *E-Commerce Times*, July 14, 2005, http://www.ecommercetimes.com.

16.6 ENTERPRISERS

Branching Out at Orange Tree Imports

Walking into Orange Tree Imports in Madison, Wisconsin, is a delightful experience. "It's just a fun place to be," says one shopper. "You could spend a whole day here," adds another. Creating such a unique retail atmosphere takes a special touch, and one that Carol and Dean Schroeder clearly have. They started Orange Tree Imports in 1975 and have built it into a thriving gift and kitchenware store that features gourmet products, toys, seasonal decor, foods, jewelry, stationery, soaps, and more.

"Retail is detail," says Carol. "There are many, many details every day, and you have to keep your energy level up and keep excited about what you're doing in order to attend to all those details and make your store as successful as possible." The result of the Schroeders' attention to details, from product selection to promotion and finances, is a store recognized both locally and nationally for its excellence.

After graduating from college in three years and receiving a master's degree in Scandinavian Studies from the University of Wisconsin-Madison, Carol worked at a branch of a Scandinavian import store near the campus. A year later, she and her husband Dean bought the business, which was not doing well, and renamed it Orange Tree Imports. "It was always my dream of owning my own store, and it just came true a little faster than I expected," says Carol, whose nickname is Orange. To fund the purchase, she convinced her parents to give her the money they would have spent on her fourth year of college. "Actually, what we did was we pledged that money as collateral and borrowed money against it, so that when we needed money later and were done using it as collateral, we had a little bit more cash," says Carol.

Neither Carol nor Dean had prior retail or business experience. They made up for their initial shortcomings

with hard work, enthusiasm, and a willingness to learn. Their first major decisions were to stop selling furniture, which was cumbersome to store, display, and sell and to shift the Scandinavian focus to a broader mix of items for home and garden. Today, Orange Tree carries kitchenware, cutlery, candy, gifts, specialty foods, toys, jewelry, cards, soaps, glassware, and more. As kitchenware and gourmet foods became a larger share of their business, the Schroeders added a cooking school to complement and promote those products. To accommodate the store's growth, in 1986 they expanded into an adjacent store when it became available.

A key factor in Orange Tree's success is the Schroeders' knack for choosing and displaying merchandise. As Carol writes in her book *Specialty Shop Retailing*, now in its third edition, "You cannot be all things to all people. The ability to find out what customers want and get it for them quickly is one of the strengths that sets a good specialty shop apart from its mass market competitors." She has a clear focus about what she thinks her store can sell and what her customers will buy. "You really have to discipline yourself not to just buy what you like, but to think about what your customers have told you they like," she says. "They vote with their dollars."

Managing the dollars is another important aspect of any retail business. Carol and Dean turned to the Small Business Development Center at UW-Madison to learn how to operate profitably. Their advisors showed them new pricing techniques and explained how to analyze inventory categories. As business owners, Carol and Dean had to learn accounting and finance basics so that they understand how the numbers are generated and what they mean. Armed with that knowledge they used their income statements and balance sheets to make better decisions about many areas of the business, from inventory levels to advertising budgets and other expense levels.

Carol recommends tracking sales for each major product line separately. When a category's sales are growing, she can increase inventory accordingly. Monitoring expenses is critical as well. While it is useful to develop monthly income statements, retailers should also look at annual statements because expenses don't always come in evenly throughout the year. For example, Orange Tree's inventory purchases will be high in the early fall as it gears up for the holiday shopping season. November and December will have lower purchase levels and higher sales. She also points out that a net profit and a solid balance sheet are not enough to operate successfully. The business also needs cash to buy inventory and pay its employees.

Discussion Questions

1. What lines of businesses is Orange Tree Imports in? How does each line make money?

2. What steps would you take to monitor each business in Orange Tree Imports and determine whether it is successful?

3. How would you evaluate the contribution of each business segment to Orange Tree's overall success?

4. What strategies would you use to price items in the store? How long would you keep particular items before you marked them down?

Sources: Adapted with permission from Small Business School, the series on PBS, at http://SmallBusinessSchool.com; Genie Campbell, "Retail Success: The Story of Orange Tree," *Wisconsin State Journal,* February 2, 1997, retrieved from Business Source Premier database; Orange Tree Imports website, http://www.orangetreeimports.com (January 9, 2008); and Carol Schroeder, "Basic Bookkeeping," *Gifts & Decorative Accessories,* November 2004, pp. 22–23.

Summary

1. Enterprisers must account for the resources they use in their businesses. Using accounting techniques, they can track and monitor the business's assets and liabilities. The accounting function is responsible for collecting, recording, reporting, and analyzing the enterprise's financial activities.

2. There are two ways to account for revenues and expenses. Cash basis accounting recognizes revenues and expenses when cash is actually received or paid out. Accrual accounting recognizes revenues at the time they are earned, even though no cash may have changed hands yet. Most businesses use the accrual method.

3. Businesses use three basic financial reports to monitor their financial condition. The income statement describes the revenues generated, the costs associated with those revenues, and the resulting profit or loss during a specific time period (week, month, quarter, or year). The balance sheet describes what the enterprise owns and owes at a specific moment in time. A statement of cash flows traces how cash is generated and spent over a span of time, usually one year.

4. The income statement, also called the *profit and loss statement,* summarizes the firm's operations during a certain period of time. It shows the sales revenue an enterprise has generated, the costs and expenses it incurred to produce the goods it sold, and whether the enterprise earns a profit or loss during that time period.

5. The balance sheet depicts the financial condition of an enterprise at a specific moment in time. It shows the company's assets, liabilities, and owners' equity. Total assets always equal the liabilities plus owners' equity. Assets are listed in order of liquidity, with current assets first, followed by fixed assets. Liabilities include current and long-term obligations. Owners' equity represents the owners' residual investment in the business, plus any net earnings, or less any new losses the business generates. The net earnings beyond the owner's equity are retained earnings.

6. The statement of cash flows provides a summary of the enterprise's sources and uses of cash during a specific time period. It shows three cash flow streams: from operations, from investments, and from financing.

7. Ratio analysis uses the information on financial statements to provide information on how well a firm is doing and to monitor its progress. Ratios measure liquidity, activity, profitability, and financing. They identify potential trouble spots so managers

can correct them. Investors and managers use ratios to compare a firm's performance over time and to other firms in the industry.

8. Liquidity ratios such as the current and quick ratios indicate the firm's ability to pay current obligations. Activity ratios measure how well a firm uses its assets. They include inventory turnover, average collection period, average payment period, and asset turnover. Profitability ratios—net profit margin, return on assets, and return on equity—provide a measure of how well the firm is managed by showing how it generates profits. Financing ratios indicate the mix of debt and equity used to finance the firm. They include the debt ratio and debt-to-equity ratio. Times interest earned ratio shows the ability of the firm to pay its interest expense on debt.

9. Comparative industry ratios are valuable tools for enterprisers, who use them to benchmark their firm's performance against similar firms. The Risk Management Association and Dun and Bradstreet (D & B) are two services that offer business and industry statistics. Trade associations, government agencies such as the SBA, and financial portal sites on the Internet also provide industry statistics.

Review Questions

1. Why should enterprisers have a basic understanding of accounting procedures?

2. Explain the difference between cash basis and accrual accounting.

3. What is an income statement, and how is it organized? How is net profit or loss calculated?

4. How does the balance sheet differ from the income statement? Name the three major categories in the balance sheet and the accounts in each.

5. What does the statement of cash flows show, and why is it so important for the firm's managers?

6. How can enterprisers use ratio analysis to evaluate the firm's financial performance?

7. What are the two key liquidity ratios and what do they measure?

8. What information do activity ratios provide managers, and which ratios measure activity?

9. Explain how the three profitability ratios indicate how a firm uses its resources to generate profits.

10. What do financing ratios tell an enterpriser? Why are investors interested in these ratios?

11. Why are industry comparisons useful to enterprisers, and where can they find these statistics?

Applying What You've Learned

1. Pick a specific type of enterprise that you would like to start and operate or use the enterprise for which you developed a business plan in Chapter 8. Identify the trade association for the enterprise you chose in question 1 and see whether they will provide you with sample current or historical comparative statistics on enterprises similar to yours. Do these comparative figures match closely with your enterprise's figures?

2. Ask enterprisers in the industry most similar to yours the names of accountants whom they use. Develop a list of questions to use when interviewing potential accountants. Identify at least three accountants and interview them in regard to how they work with clients, the fees they likely charge, and the kinds of activities accountants are likely to do for enterprises similar to yours. Summarize your findings in a comparative table.

3. For the enterprise you are starting and operating, determine the kinds of functions and capabilities that your enterprise would need for an accounting system, e.g., payroll and inventory management.

4. Your firm, Bellamara Gourmet Products, has completed its first year of operations. Using the following account balances for revenues and expenses for the year ending December 31, 2009, prepare the store's income statement following the format in Exhibit 16.2.

Rent	$12,000		Inventory	$15,600
Salaries	$25,600		Common shares	$50,000
Depreciation	$6,300		(50,000 shares at $1)	
Cost of goods sold	$101,000		Long-term debt	$25,000
Utilities	$7,500		Accumulated depreciation	$18,500
Supplies	$3,000		on equipment	
Sales	$203,000		Income taxes payable	$7,500
Advertising	$2,700			
Interest	$2,500			
Taxes	$8,100			

5. Based on the following account balances, prepare Bellamara's balance sheet as of December 31, 2009, following the format in Exhibit 16.3.

Cash	$20,850
Accounts payable	$14,500
Equipment	$55,000
Accounts receivable	$24,050

6. Using the income statement and balance sheet you prepared for Bellamara Gourmet Shop, calculate the following ratios: current ratio, quick ratio, inventory turnover ratio, average collection period, asset turnover, net profit margin, return on assets (ROA), return on equity (ROE), debt-to-equity ratio, and times interest earned. Assume that all sales are credit sales. Use these ratios to evaluate the store's performance.

Enterprisers on the Web

1. A number of companies offer computerized accounting systems with varying degrees of sophistication, such as Quickbooks by Intuit. Conduct an Internet search to identify at least three accounting systems for smaller enterprises. Prepare a table comparing the functions, capabilities, and costs of these systems. Include Web-based accounting programs as well. (These programs reside on the Internet, rather than being installed on your own computer.) Which seems the best suited for your enterprise, and why?

2. Identify a number of publicly held companies that are in an industry similar to the type of enterprise you are starting or operating. Using EDGAR, the Security and Exchange Commissions database (http://www.sec.gov/edgar/searchedgar/webusers. htm), download financial reports from these

companies, such as the most recent 10-K report. What kinds of financial information does each financial report contain? Do these reports provide ratios and evaluations of the financial information that might be relevant to the startup and operation of your enterprise?

3. For the enterprise you are starting or operating, search the Internet to find statistics on comparable firms using the RMA, Dun and Bradstreet, or other financial sites. What can you learn from these comparative figures?

4. Many banks and credit card companies will provide some of the accounting services your enterprise will utilize. Conduct an Internet search to identify the kinds of accounting services that banks and credit card companies provide and the costs to use these services.

End Note

1. Joshua Kennon, "Revenue Recognition," *About.com: Investing for Beginners*, http://beginnersinvest.about.com/od/gaap/a/ aa0605.htm (April 2, 2008).

Managing People

1. As a business grows, an enterpriser must look to others to help manage and operate it. This requires a comprehensive strategy to meet the firm's human resources needs through insiders, who are employed by or under contract to the firm, and outsiders, who are not directly employed by the firm. Outsiders include mentors, boards of advisors, boards of directors, consultants, and service providers.

2. Employees and independent contractors are hired by the firm to perform work. The hiring party has the right to control an employee's work and how it is done. With an independent contractor, the hiring party controls only the result of the work. Employment practices are subject to federal, state, and local regulations that cover issues such as discrimination in hiring, safe working conditions, and the hours worked.

3. Human resources (HR) management begins with a strategic HR plan that includes job analysis and job descriptions, employee recruitment and selection, training, performance appraisal, and compensation. The job description drives the rest of the hiring process by defining the selection and performance criteria. Enterprisers can recruit job candidates through various types of advertising and networking. The selection process involves screening, interviewing, evaluating candidates, checking references, and making an offer.

4. Retaining and motivating employees is as important as hiring them. An orientation program for new employees smooths their transition to the firm, and internal and external training opportunities develop their skills and enhance productivity. A well-structured compensation program of wages or salary and benefits will help you attract and keep qualified employees. Noncash incentive programs also increase employee satisfaction. Understanding what motivates your employees leads to higher productivity, greater satisfaction, and lower turnover.

Suppose you have a dream of owning a car dealership, but as a minority and a woman, many doors are closed to you. You decide to learn all you can about the automotive business and take a job at Ford as a financial analyst. After hearing about automobile companies' diversity initiatives, you leave the corporate environment to get experience at a dealership. With the help of a mentor, you make industry contacts and apply for minority dealership programs. Although your first dealership fails, you don't give up. Your persistence pays off, and today you own one of the top-ranked Chevrolet dealerships in your region.

© Brad Remy/Used under license from Shutterstock

Since assuming the ownership of an underperforming dealership in 1996, Pamela Rodgers has proven her ability to make it in a male-dominated industry. Rodgers Chevrolet has been named a General Motors Dealer of the Year, and Pamela received GM's highest honor, the Jack Smith Leadership Award in 2003. She recognizes that you cannot run a dealership alone, and her ability to nurture and motivate employees has been a key element in her success. In this chapter, you will learn how choosing advisors and managing human resources wisely will help your enterprise grow.

17.0 People: Your Most Important Resource

Thus far, we've covered a wide variety of topics—setting personal goals, choosing a pathway to enterprise creation, branding your enterprise, and finding the necessary resources to start and operate your business. By now, it should be clear that you can't do it all yourself. At some point in the growth and development of the enterprise, you will need help.

For example, assume that you own a restaurant. While you could do all of the tasks—greeting patrons, taking orders, cooking the food, serving the food, and cleaning the tables—it is clearly not a good way to provide good customer service. Trying to do everything yourself makes it impossible to grow the business. It is more efficient and productive to enable other people to take on these tasks.

In general, the separation of tasks into different jobs is called the division of labor. In the first chapter of the book, we described Adam Smith's example of the pin factory. When the tasks involved in making pins were divided into different activities, the result was a very large increase in productivity. Similarly, our restaurateur will be significantly more productive by hiring chefs, cooks, waiters, and cleaning personnel. Dividing the work not only improves customer satisfaction but also is a way to grow the business.

In this chapter, we will explore the different ways to delegate work to others, both by using outside experts such as advisors and consultants and by hiring employees. Because employers have many legal and moral responsibilities to employees, the decision to hire an employee is a significant step for any enterprise. We will introduce you to key human resources topics such as job descriptions, hiring practices, and employee retention, and also discuss critical legal issues related to employees, particularly with regard to hiring and firing.

17.1 Leadership and Delegation

Recruiting, managing, and retaining people who can help you and your enterprise is challenging. Before you can find people who can help you start and run your enterprise, you should answer several key questions:

- What types of assistance do you want?

- Why do you need this help?

- What skills and abilities should the helper have?

It is extremely important to be clear as to what you expect and want from other people. We have found that enterprisers often assume that other people will know exactly what needs to be done and will accomplish these activities. The more likely scenario is that the other person will not be able to read the enterpriser's mind or know what needs to be done—and why. The challenge for the enterpriser is to describe, precisely and in a supportive way, the type of help and assistance that he or she requires and expects, which is not as easy as it seems and is the reason why there are so many books on leadership and delegation.

We view leadership as the expression of what you hope to see occur in your enterprise. As a leader, your role is to point out to others the direction in which you see the enterprise going. Good leaders are also able to manage aspirations and expectations.

Enterprisers often see future goals more clearly than others might. We often can see, in our "mind's eye," the specific aspects of the future of our business: the desk where we will sit, the customers we will serve, and the goods and services we will provide. Others will often have more difficulty seeing these same things. A critical task for leaders, then, is shifting the vision of their helpers so that everyone sees the same vision.

Leadership and delegation require *an ability to act.* What you *do* as a manager and leader is more important than what you *say.* As a manager, your job is to delegate some parts of your work effort to other people. To delegate effectively, you must provide specific expectations of what you want to be accomplished. Also, we tend to delegate when we trust other people. It is hard to trust others to fulfill our expectations if we aren't really sure what needs to happen!

For example, if your aspiration is to "Please the customer," what steps will you take to achieve this goal? Does that mean that an employee might give your product away for free? That would certainly please the customer—but how would it affect your profitability? How will you handle unreasonable service demands? Who will determine if a demand is unreasonable, and how?

The desired outcome of the leadership and delegation process is that *someone else will make decisions and do work,* rather than you having to do it all yourself. If you must monitor and observe every decision and every action, then you have only a helper, or maybe an extension of your hands and body, to get work done—not someone whose expertise will contribute to the success of the enterprise.

The Family and Friends Plan, Part 2

Many enterprises and enterprisers are supported in significant ways through the help of family and friends. As we discussed in Chapter 15, our family and friends are people who know us really well. We've shared our innermost thoughts and aspirations with them and can trust them. It's not too surprising, then, to learn from the academic literature that the first hires in new firms are likely to be family members or friends. Most entrepreneurs first hire people whom they find trustworthy, rather than hiring individuals who might be more qualified or have the skills and abilities for a particular job. Hiring your family members or friends is not always a good idea, however, and gets many enterprisers into trouble because they do not manage their expectations well.

Before you involve family members and friends in your business, ask yourself a series of questions:

- Why are you asking these people for help?

- What do you expect them to do for you?

- Do they have the skills for the tasks?

- What do they expect from you in return?

The first step is to list out, clearly, what you are asking family members to do—and what you are providing to these family members in return. Don't assume anything. Assumptions can lead to very disastrous results and misunderstandings between you and your family members and friends.

If the history of relationships in your family has been a spirit of "all for one, and one for all," the willingness of family members to help out might also imply that any rewards and benefits from the enterprise's growth and success will also be shared. It is important, then, to discuss not only the specifics of what you expect from the efforts of your family and friends, but also what you and they expect to be provided, in return. We suggest that you write down these expectations and that both parties sign them. Indeed, you should consult with an attorney about the legal implications of involving family and friends in your business with regard to what each party expects in return for his or her respective efforts.

Outsiders and Insiders

We can divide the kinds of people who can help you manage and grow your enterprise into two types: outsiders and insiders. *Outsiders* are those individuals who are not directly employed by your enterprise but often have significant roles in guiding and operating the business. Outsiders may include partners who invest in the business in return for an equity stake in the enterprise, mentors you use for advice and counsel, your board of directors, members of a board of advisors, consultants, attorneys, accountants, and special service providers (such as bookkeeping, payroll, and janitorial service companies that provide ongoing services for your business).

Your firm's *insiders* are individuals who work under your guidance or the supervision of other individuals whom you employ. We typically label these individuals as employees, but in some situations, these individuals could be independent contractors or your agents. We will explore later in this chapter what differentiates an employee from an independent contractor and describe the legal and tax obligations specific to each type.

17.2   The Role of Outsiders

Let's now take a closer look at the outsiders who play a role in your enterprise. We've listed them by the type of help they provide, from more general to more specific help: mentors, board of advisors, board of directors, consultants, and service providers.

Mentors

Basically, a *mentor* is someone who can provide you with wisdom and connections.[1] A mentor has knowledge and insight about how to operate your type of enterprise, or enterprises in general. Mentors are well-connected individuals and can share advice about what has worked for them—and what has not. With a mentor's guidance, you can learn more successful ways to move through the day-to-day hassles of enterprise management.

A good mentor serves as an interactive reference guide as you encounter difficult situations for which you don't have ready answers. When you are starting and growing a business, such issues will occur daily. Your mentor should be someone who will take an active interest in your life and business and is willing to devote the time needed to really grow and develop a relationship. Many enterprisers indicate that their mentors are often their parents or close family friends. A mentor might also be a person who can provide you with important industry and business contacts. If you are managing a Web-development company, a mentor might have experience in that field and provide contacts with Web designers, other enterprisers in the Web-development industry, and possible clients.

Before you look for a mentor, think about the type of assistance you need

- What is your personality style, and what type of person would work best with you?

- What goals do you want to accomplish by having a mentor?

- How long would you like the relationship to last?

- What skills do you want to acquire by working with the mentor?

If you are looking for help in a very specific area, you may want a short-term mentor. For broader goals, longer-term mentors will nurture you and your business. Another important consideration is the mentor's personality. You won't benefit from working with a person who is controlling or has a negative attitude. A good mentor acts as a facilitator who motivates you and helps you make decisions, rather than simply giving advice. You want to feel comfortable with your mentor and be able to talk openly about your ideas and dreams. It may take several meetings with a person to determine if his or her mentoring style works for you.

Where can you find mentors? Here are some suggestions:

- A current or past employer: The company may have a formal mentoring program, or you can seek out someone you respect.

- Your college alumni association or career office: Many colleges and universities have career networks of alumni who have offered to serve as mentors or will provide advice on careers.

- Professional organizations and trade associations: These may have formal mentoring programs or you can network to find potential mentors.

- Community and social groups: Hobby groups, religious congregations, volunteer organizations, and similar groups to which you belong are other good resources.

Take a proactive approach to finding a mentor. Use the networking skills you developed in Chapter 3 to get referrals for prospective mentors. The more specific you are about your needs, the better your leads will be.

Once you find a person you would like to have as your mentor, you should discuss what each of you wants from the relationship and how it will proceed. The best mentoring relationships are mutually beneficial.

Mentors are critical advisors in our lives. Developing relationships with people who can provide you with direction to help build your enterprise will be time well spent. Don't overlook potential mentors in your desired field. Many industries have a history of strong mentor relationships. For example, the restaurant industry is full of restaurateurs who have helped their employees and others start other restaurants.

Board of Advisors

In addition to turning to mentors for advice and insights, many enterprisers develop outside boards of advisors.[2] This group of individuals meets with the enterpriser on a reoccurring basis to offer insights into issues the enterpriser faces. A board of advisors is distinct from a board of directors and has an informal advisory role, without any legal responsibilities for the direction and functions of the enterprise. A board of directors has legal obligations as set forth by the corporation's charter and bylaws. We will delve into the legal and fiduciary obligations of boards of directors in the next section.

The expertise of a board of advisors brings many benefits to an enterprise. It can

- provide both operational and strategic advice.

- help the firm develop and implement strategic plans.

- provide a big-picture view of the firm.

- monitor progress toward goals.

- bring new ideas to the management.

- motivate the company to achieve more.

- serve as a forum to explore new ideas.

- help settle disputes and solve problems.

- prevent problems from arising.

- offer independent opinions.

- provide another source of business expertise.

- confirm and support management's decisions.

- enhance the firm's community presence.

Clearly, the time an enterpriser devotes to building a board of advisors is well spent. Choosing the members of this board is challenging. The size of the board depends on your company and may range from three to eight members. Selecting people with business expertise and some with experience in a related industry is important. Those with success in your market can help you reach your goals. You should also look for diversity to get a wide range of insights. Independent thinkers who will be honest with you will provide a more valuable sounding board than those who agree with you all the time. Don't hesitate to ask the best people you know. The higher the quality of your board, the better the advice you will get. Your attorney and accountant can provide referrals to potential candidates.

Before asking people to serve on your board, you should have a clear idea of what you seek from an advisory board. Here are some questions to help determine its role and scope:

1. What types of issues do you want to bring to the advisory board?

2. Do you want second opinions on management decisions or broader advice about strategy, company direction, etc.?

3. Are you willing to listen to diverse opinions that may differ from yours?

You should compensate your board members for their time and reimburse them for expenses. Your board of advisors should meet regularly. Quarterly meetings work well to keep members up to date about company operations without placing too great a demand on their time. Meetings should be structured for maximum effectiveness. Because of the informal nature of an advisory board, you may want to use the consensus approach rather than have formal votes. Consensus decisions are a group process that is participatory. The members discuss issues and work cooperatively to reach a solution. The goal is to reach the best possible decision for the group, not to let the majority decide. This encourages the participants to voice their opinions and contribute to the decision.

Board of Directors

All corporations must have a board of directors that has legal responsibility for its actions and those of its employees, officers, and directors.[3] The board of directors governs and manages the corporation, and its structure is specified in the corporation's bylaws. Because of the board's legal obligations, you should work with a lawyer to establish and manage the company's board.

Businesses that are not incorporated are not required to have a board of directors. However, having a formal board of directors can be an asset to the company and its owners. The board can provide advice and expertise to help the company achieve its goals.

Although we normally think of a board as a group, a board can be one person or 30 or more. For example, in a corporation that is primarily owned by the founder of the business, the founder may be the only board member, or appoint only one or two others to the board. This arrangement satisfies the legal requirement to have a board. However, we do not recommend such a practice because it runs counter to the purpose of having a board, which is to provide oversight and offer guidance.

© Comstock/Jupiter Images

Purpose, Structure, and Responsibility of the Board of Directors

A company's board of directors helps management develop business plans and strategies and establish policy objectives. Directors also monitor the company's business operations and financial performance. Typically the board appoints the corporate officers to oversee the daily operations of a company, with departmental and functional responsibilities, whereas the board of directors takes a broader view.

The structure of the board is defined by the corporate bylaws. Enterprisers should consider the following in setting up a board of directors:

- *How many members will the board have?* Think about the best size to help the company achieve its mission and the roles board members need to fill. Having an odd number of directors is good to avoid tie votes. Big is not necessarily better; smaller boards can be more cohesive and productive. Most newly public companies have from 5 to 12 directors on their board.

- *How and when will board members be elected? What is the term they will serve?* A typical board term is two to four years. It's advisable to have terms expiring on a staggered basis so that there are always experienced members continuing.

- *What officers and committee structure will your board have?* Committees help boards operate more efficiently and capitalize on your directors' specialized expertise. The basic committees that all boards should have are the audit, nominating, and compensation committees.

- *How many members will the board have?* Think about the best size to fill the necessary roles and bring the skills the company requires to achieve its mission.

Board members are expected to attend and prepare for meetings. They have numerous responsibilities with regard to the corporation, as described in Exhibit 17.1.

Selecting Board Members

A well-chosen board of directors is viewed as an asset by potential lenders and investors. It can help you make the transition from a privately held company to a public one.

In selecting board members, you should seek breadth, depth, and diversity of experience. Together your board of directors should bring the corporation business skills, knowledge, and expertise. Before approaching anyone, however, you should know what you expect from your board members in addition to the standard responsibilities. For example, you may want a director who can help you raise capital or promote the company. Your board should reflect the demographics of your main constituencies. If you are filling vacancies

on an existing board, first assess which areas need to be strengthened. Exhibit 17.2 summarizes the experience and personal qualities to consider in recruiting and evaluating potential directors.

Your board should include a sizable percentage of directors who are independent—with no direct relationship to the company—and can be more objective than those with vested interests. Public companies must comply with the corporate governance requirements of the stock exchange where their securities trade. NASDAQ requires a company to have at least two independent directors, for example.

Where can you find candidates for your board of directors? You will find a large talent pool by tapping networks of personal and industry contacts, academics, and prominent management executives, both active and retired. You should compensate your directors for contributing their time and expertise. Most companies

---

exhibit

17.1

Responsibilities of Directors

1. Define the organization's mission and purpose.

2. Select the chief executive officer, determine compensation, evaluate performance, and support the executive; dismiss if required.

3. Implement effective organizational planning procedures, including evaluation of strategic and operational business plans. Provide support to management for plan implementation.

4. Oversee the firm's finances and ensure that adequate financial resources are available by approving the budget and monitoring performance against budget, hiring an independent auditor, and overseeing investment policies and capital expenditures, etc.

5. Approve certain types of corporate activities and transactions, such as contracts and similar agreements, election of new corporate officers, major asset purchases and sales, approval of new corporate policies, and amendments to the corporation's bylaws or articles of incorporation.

6. Ensure that the corporation's resources, both financial and human, are managed effectively.

7. Determine and monitor the organization's programs and services.

8. Respond to shareholder needs.

9. Be knowledgeable about company operations and issues that affect its business.

10. Evaluate how well the board performs; make necessary changes to improve how well it functions.

11. Follow the company's ethics policies, such as those covering confidentiality and conflicts of interest.

12. Promote and support the success of the company.

Sources: Adapted from information in "Board of Directors," *Small Business Notes*, http://www.smallbusinessnotes.com/operating/leadership/board.html (April 28, 2008); Carter McNamara, "Overview of Roles and Responsibilities of Corporate Board of Directors," *Free Management Library*, http://www.managementhelp.org/boards/brdrspon.htm (April 28, 2008); and "Ten Basic Responsibilities of Nonprofit Boards," *BoardSource*, http://www.boardsource.org/Knowledge.asp?ID=3.368 (March 26, 2008).

exhibit
17.2

Qualities to Seek in Board Members

Business and professional experience: What type of business experience does the candidate bring to the board? In addition to those working in the same or a similar industry, board members from educational institutions, the professions, nonprofit organizations, and government bring valuable insights.

Participation on other boards: People who have served on boards of for-profit and nonprofit organizations should understand what it takes to make a board work effectively.

Responsibilities: Prospective directors should be knowledgeable about the legal and other responsibilities they will be undertaking.

Ethics: Candidates should have the highest moral standards and integrity and uphold the company's code of ethics.

Personal characteristics: Board members should exhibit the personal traits to participate fully and contribute to board discussions and decisions. They should be honest, intelligent, self-confident, enthusiastic, open minded, and cooperative. A sense of humor, good judgment, and excellent communication skills are also essential.

Strength of their convictions: Directors must be able to analyze proposals and ask difficult questions as they grapple with complex business problems and issues. They should be able to support their positions, even when these positions run counter to management's views.

Commitment and dependability: Potential directors should be committed to your company's goals and plans. This includes having sufficient time to prepare for and attend meetings, participate actively, and serve on committees.

Teamwork: Board members should be team players who can cooperate and work effectively with their fellow directors and company officers.

Skills: Directors should contribute skills to help the board carry out its duties and legal obligations. The expertise most companies need includes accounting and finance, business law, operational and strategic planning, human resources, information technology, marketing and promotion, operations and production, sales, and corporate governance.

Sources: Adapted from "Board of Directors," *Small Business Notes,* http://www.smallbusinessnotes.com/operating/leadership/board.html (April 28, 2008); Glenn Faulkner, "Selecting a Board of Directors for the Emerging Company," John Pappajohn Entrepreneurial Center of the University of Northern Iowa, http://www.jpec.org/handouts/jpec63.pdf (March 26, 2008); and "Finding a Director," *Directors Source,* http://www.directorssource.com (April 29, 2008).

pay an annual retainer plus a per meeting fee and reimburse out-of-pocket expense such as travel to and lodging for the meetings.

Consultants

Often, an enterpriser will simply not have the expertise and insights necessary to create or grow the enterprise and advice from others will not be enough of a solution. Such situations call for hiring a consultant to provide specialized knowledge and also to engage actively in specific projects.[4] For example, while there are many tools for building and developing a website that are free and simple enough for some enterprisers to use themselves, other enterprisers prefer to put their time and energy toward other tasks. They will hire someone else

to design and build their company's website. Similarly, an enterpriser may retain a public relations expert to devise a publicity campaign to publicize the enterprise, write press releases, and write and place stories with various media outlets.

A consultant is different from a service provider. A *consultant* is an expert you hire sporadically to solve a specific problem or for a one-time project. A *service provider* is someone you will use on a regular basis to provide an ongoing service, such as an attorney, bookkeeper, payroll service, accountant, billing service, or janitorial service. We'll cover service providers in the following section.

Before looking for outside consultants, determine whether you need one. Review the talents of your staff. Do any of your employees have the skills to handle the assignment? If you do need to look outside the company, carefully consider the goals you want the consultant to achieve. The more specific you can be, the better your results. Specific goals will help you control costs by focusing the consultant's work.

In addition to knowing the expertise you require, you should consider a consultant's personality and style. Does it mesh with yours? A consultant who is dictatorial will not be effective in a company with a collegial corporate culture.

Where can you find consultants?

- Contact other enterprisers who are in similar or related industries for referrals to consultants they have used in the past. Ask questions: How helpful have they been? What do they charge? What do you get in return? Would you hire them again?

- Contact your industry or trade association. While these associations might not offer you specific advice on specific consultants, they often have lists of consultants that focus on your kind of enterprise and the issues facing your enterprise.

- Attend trade shows and trade association meetings. In addition to general networking, visit the exhibitors' booths and listen to consultants who specialize in your industry describe their services.

- Search online, in trade publications and journals, and in regional newspapers for articles written by consultants that describe their experiences and their theories. They can help you understand how the consultant sees markets and business factors that may affect you.

- Review management or technical literature.

After identifying potential consultants, interview them. Ask probing questions about the consultant's prior professional experience before becoming a consultant as well as prior consulting assignments. How well do they match your needs? A consultant who was a top executive at a company similar to yours will have a better grasp of the issues you face and be able to recommend better strategies to resolve them. Find out how they charge for their services: hourly rate, flat project fee, fee plus performance bonus, fee based on specific metrics such as increased sales, reduced expenses, or other measures.

If possible, request that the consultant teach you to handle many of these tasks yourself afterward, rather than having to depend on him or her. Training should be a critical part of the assignment.

When you've narrowed the field to two or three consultants, ask for a written proposal. This step will show you how well each candidate understands the problem you want to resolve and provides an opportunity to describe how he or she will approach it. The proposal should include a proposed budget. Exhibit 17.3 offers additional suggestions to help you hire effective consultants.

Once you've hired a consultant, introduce the consultant to your staff so that they know why the consultant is on site and what types of information they may be asked to provide.

Service Providers

As noted above, service providers are outside companies or sole practitioners whom you will use on an ongoing basis. They are an important source of help for young enterprisers who cannot justify hiring full-time employees to handle specific responsibilities. For example, suppose your enterprise requires about ten hours a week to record its financial transactions. Outsourcing this service to a bookkeeper is the most cost-effective way to get qualified help. Even though enterprisers might know how to use a computer package such as QuickBooks as their firms' accounting system, doing the accounting themselves may not be the best use of time. Hiring a specialized service provider to design and operate the accounting system can save money, while bringing expertise and additional knowledge to the company. It also allows enterprisers to focus on the bigger picture—operating and growing their businesses—rather than spending time on tasks that can be delegated to others.

In fact, accounting and bookkeeping services are among the most frequently used service providers, along with payroll services and janitorial services. The benefits of using service providers include the following:[5]

- **Efficiency:** The service provider is a specialist in a particular area and knows the best methods to get the job done quickly and properly.

- **Lower employee and other costs:** With a service provider, you pay only for the time it takes to do the agreed-upon task. You don't have to pay an employee or the associated costs such as payroll taxes, workers' compensation, and employee benefits. Janitorial services bring their own equipment, saving you the cost of purchasing your own.

- **Expertise:** The service provider brings skills that can enhance your business productivity.

<table>
<tr><td>exhibit
17.3</td><td>**Tips to Hire the Right Consultant**</td></tr>
</table>

1. **Know what services you need.** Don't let yourself be talked into extra services until you are sure they are necessary. It's better to add to the contract than to overpay in the beginning.

2. **Look for consultants who have served similar clients and handled comparable projects.**

3. **Interview several prospective consultants to find the best match.** Talk to several consultants to get valuable insights that will help you refine your needs and define the issues you want to resolve. Conduct a thorough interview, just as you would for an employee. Prepare a comprehensive list of questions ahead of time.

4. **Perform due diligence on the consultant.** Check out the consultant's professional experience before hiring a consultant as well as prior consulting assignments to make sure that it matches your needs. Request references from former clients and contact them.

5. **Know who will be doing the work.** Some consultants are sole practitioners, while others have a larger firm and may assign a team to the project.

6. **Have a contractual agreement signed by both parties.** This should define the relationship between the parties and the scope of the work assignment, including deadlines, and be signed by both parties.

7. **Know the going rate before agreeing to compensation.** Researching the fee ranges for consultants in the industry will save you money.

8. **Specify which expenses are included in the contract and which are reimbursed separately.** This prevents surprises and disagreements later.

9. **Confirm that the consultant is available for the desired time period.** Consultants may take on several assignments simultaneously. Be sure that the consultant will have enough time for your project.

10. **Insist on a letter of confidentiality.** You are giving the consultant access to company information that may be sensitive. Consultants may later work for a competitor, and you don't want company secrets shared. You and your employees should feel confident that you can trust the consultant's discretion.

11. **Describe the project accurately.** Lack of clear communication is a common mistake. Too often contractors and employers are not on the same page from the start, which leads to numerous complications later on.

Sources: From "Guidelines for Hiring Consultants," *The Consulting Exchange*, http://www.cx.com/guidelines.htm (May 7, 2008); "Hiring a Consultant: Ten Questions to Ask," *Sideroad.com*, http://www.sideroad.com/Consulting/hiring-a-consultant.html (May 7, 2008); and "Top 10 Mistakes Made When Hiring Consultants," *AllBusiness.com*, http://www.allbusiness.com/human-resources/workforce-management-hiring-consulting/3996-1.html (May 7, 2008).

The list of people who are likely to support your enterprise in some form can be substantial! Other areas in which companies may use service providers include human resources, security, merchandise delivery, information technology, computer maintenance, landscaping and grounds upkeep, window washing, waste management, and repair services for specialized equipment.

Many of the issues involved in choosing service providers are similar to the ones we described in the section on hiring and evaluating consultants. The first step is to assess your needs:

- What do you need the service provider to do?
- How often do you need the services performed?
- Do you have any special requirements?
- How much can you spend on these services?

Ask for referrals from other enterprisers, and plan to interview two or three candidates.

Prepare your questions in advance and be as specific as possible about what you need done and any special services you may require. If you own a restaurant, your cleaning needs are very different from a retail store. You must comply with government regulations for food service establishments, which set much higher standards for health and safety reasons. Pressure washing and cleaning exhaust fans, stove hoods, ducts and filters, and grease traps are among the special janitorial services you'd need.[6] Exhibit 17.4 provides guidelines to help you choose service providers.

---

exhibit 17.4

Choosing Service Providers

1. *Find out how long the company has been in business.* You want to be sure the company is financially stable and will be around to provide the services you need.

2. *Ask about insurance coverage and bonding.* These will protect you from damage and theft.

3. *Know what the firm's hiring practices are.* Will it be sending long-time, trusted employees to service your account, or will it be hiring new staff for your job? Make sure the company performs background checks on its employees.

4. *Determine what services the company offers and describe in detail what you need.* Ask specific questions to find out if the company has experience in the areas you need.

5. *Make sure the company's availability matches your requirements.* You don't want to find out that the janitorial services company you hired can only fit you in during your regular office hours.

6. *Ask how the company charges for its services and what are included in those charges.* Does it fall within your budget? You don't want any surprises when you receive your invoice.

7. *How does the company provide customer service and support, and when is support coverage available?* Offering 24-hour phone service, a support email address, and a dedicated account rep to service your account is no guarantee that the company will respond promptly to your requests. Ask for a copy of its documented procedure for handling customer problems and look for response time standards. What recourse do you have if a matter is not resolved within a reasonable time period?

8. *Review a sample contract.* Be prepared to add clauses if any areas are missing. Does it include performance guarantees and response times for customer support? What are the termination policies? Is there an automatic renewal clause? Are there automatic pricing adjustments over time?

9. *Request references who have used this service, including companies who are similar to yours.* Contact them and ask detailed questions about the quality of work performed, dependability, honesty, customer service when problems arise, and actual cost versus estimated cost.

10. *Investigate the company's reputation with national organizations.* Check the Better Business Bureau and industry organizations to see if the company has any complaints against it.

11. *Carefully review your contract.* Everything should be spelled out in writing: services provided, when they will be performed, costs, etc. The greater the detail, the less chance of subsequent misunderstanding.

12. *Can the provider grow with your company?* Does the range of service it currently provides meet your estimated future needs? You don't want to have to keep changing and training new providers as your needs expand.

Sources: Adapted from information in "Choosing a Service Provider Requires Careful Research," *Change Tech Solutions Inc.*, January 29, 2003, http://articles.techrepublic.com.com/5100-10878_11-1060263.html; and "Selecting the Right Cleaning Companies," *Cleaning Service Comparison*, http://www.cleaningservicecomparison.com/selecting-cleaning-companies.jsp? (April 24, 2008).

17.3 Employees

Now that we have covered the roles outside help plays in operating your business, let's turn to the insiders who work for you: employees (full- and part-time) and independent contractors. Many of the issues we discuss in this section of the chapter involve legal issues. With so many federal, state, and local laws about how to treat employees, it is very easy to violate a regulation without being aware of it. We will alert you to many of the issues that may arise. We also recommend that you consult a labor lawyer for advice about these employment issues as they arise.

Who Is an Employee?

The first issue to consider is whether someone is an employee or an independent contractor. To determine a person's employment status, you will need to answer questions about the kind of relationship you have with that person, such as who directs and controls the worker?

People who perform work for you can be employees or independent contractors. People who follow an independent trade, business, or profession in which they offer their services to the public, such as lawyers, consultants, contractors, and subcontractors, are called **independent contractors.** The Internal Revenue System (IRS) considers someone an independent contractor if the hiring party controls only the result of the work and not how the contractor accomplishes the work. Consultants and service providers fall into the independent contractor category, as do others who perform specific work assignments for the company on a temporary or limited basis such as electricians and plumbers. In most cases, the hiring entity does not have to withhold income taxes, withhold and pay Social Security and Medicare taxes, or pay unemployment tax on payments to independent contractors. Typically, those payments are required for wages paid to an employee.[7]

If you have the right to control the work a person does and how it is done, that person is an **employee.** For example, a salesperson who has assigned hours to be at your store each week and reports to the sales manager is an employee. A freelance graphics designer whom you engage to prepare marketing brochures for three product lines at $750 per brochure is an independent contractor. Both parties have signed a written agreement, such as a letter of agreement or a work-for-hire contract, that sets forth the terms of the assignment: scope of work, deadlines, fees,

timing of payment, and other relevant factors. You do not care if the writer works on your project at 9 AM or 11 PM, for 10 hours or 25 hours, as long as she meets your deadlines and the results of her work are satisfactory. She uses her own office space, computer, phone, and printer. (IRS Publication 15-A, *Employer's Supplemental Tax Guide*, has more information on IRS regulations for these categories of workers, as well as two other categories—statutory employees and statutory nonemployees.)

The box "Independent Contractor or Employee?" provides additional information on how the IRS decides whether someone is an employee or an independent contractor, as well as the pros and cons of using independent contractors.

Regulation of Employment Practices

As discussed in Chapter 5, employment practices are also subject to federal, state, and local regulation. Numerous regulations apply to employment issues such as discrimination in hiring, safe working conditions, and the hours worked. Exhibit 5.3 on page 110 summarizes the most important employment and labor laws.

Discrimination laws are among the most important for employers to understand. Various equal employment opportunity (EEO) laws prohibit specific types of employment discrimination in hiring and termination: race, color, religion, sex, age, national origin, and status as an individual with a disability or protected veteran. The 1964 Civil Rights Act is the major law that covers discrimination and applies to firms with 15 or more employees. In 1967, the Age Discrimination Act was passed to protect workers age 40 and older. It was followed in 1990 by the Americans with Disabilities Act, which prohibits discrimination based on mental or physical disabilities. The Equal Employment Opportunity Commission (EEOC) is the federal agency that enforces anti-discrimination laws.

Independent contractor   A person who follows an independent trade, business, or profession and offers services to the public, such as lawyers, consultants, contractors, and subcontractors. The IRS considers someone an independent contractor if the hiring party controls only the result of the work and not how the contractor accomplishes the work.

Employee   A worker who falls under the control of the hiring party with regard to the work that person does and how it is done.

INDEPENDENT CONTRACTOR OR EMPLOYEE?

Your business is growing and you need a more sophisticated marketing program. However, you aren't sure whether the business is ready to hire a full-time marketing person, so you decide to hire a marketing specialist to help. Before moving ahead, however, you should familiarize yourself with the rules to properly classify workers.

To qualify as an independent contractor, the person performing the work must meet the requirements set by the IRS regarding who has the right to control or direct the worker. This includes the work procedures as well as the results. The IRS monitors compliance and may challenge a company's decision to treat a worker as an independent contractor. If the IRS finds that the classification is incorrect, the company is liable for back withholding and payroll taxes and may have to pay penalties and interest on the amount due.

The IRS category rules consider the amount of control or independence in three areas of the worker–employer relationship: behavioral, financial, and type of relationship. The facts that provide evidence of the degree of control and independence fall into three categories:

1. **Behavioral:** Who controls or has the right to control what the worker does, when the work is done, and how the worker does his or her job? Does the business train the worker?

2. **Financial:** Who controls the business aspects of the worker's job, such as how the worker is paid, whether expenses are reimbursed, or who provides tools/supplies? Are the worker's services available to the public or just the hiring company?

3. **Type of Relationship:** Do written contracts govern the relationship? Are there employee-type benefits (i.e., pension plan, insurance, vacation pay, etc.)? How long will the relationship between the company and the worker continue? Is the work performed a key aspect of the business?

For the marketing consultant to qualify as an independent contractor, then, you should have a written work-for-hire contract that focuses on the project, the desired results, deadlines, and payment. It should not specify where or how the work should be done.

Why would you want to hire the marketing pro as an independent contractor rather than an employee? Several advantages come to mind:

- The hiring company is not required to withhold federal, state, and local taxes for independent contractors or to pay employee benefits to the independent contractor.

- Overall cost is generally lower because the hiring company may not have to provide workspace, computer and related equipment, or cover other expenses.

- The company does not have to pay employee benefits such as health insurance, vacation, and sick days, which can add 30 percent or more to an employee's salary expense.

- The contractor works on demand, for a specific task, and the relationship ends when the task is completed. This avoids having to hire employees and then lay them off when their services are no longer required.

- The contractor is already trained for the tasks you want performed.

On the other hand, employees offer many benefits:

- Employees are typically more loyal to the company and feel a greater sense of responsibility, which can lead to higher productivity.

- Staffing flexibility is greater with employees, who can take on a wide variety of tasks as the need arises.

- Employees are available during their assigned work hours whereas independent contractors may have other clients.

- Workflow can improve as employees move up the learning curve.

- You know how much you are paying the employee; independent contractors can change their rates with each project.

Using independent contractors is an excellent way to get the help you need—without taking on the major responsibilities that come with employees, both financial and managerial. Even well-established firms with many employees can benefit from the availability of these specialists on an as-needed basis.

Discussion Questions

1. Describe the differences between an employee and an independent contractor. How are they similar?

2. How does the IRS determine whether someone is an employee or an independent contractor? Briefly describe the three categories it applies and steps to take to qualify a person as an independent contractor.

3. What are the advantages and disadvantages of independent contractors? Name several situations where an enterpriser might prefer to hire an independent contractor instead of an employee.

4. Your six-month-old business wants to hire the following people. Discuss whether you would hire them as employees or independent contractors, and why:

   a. Receptionist

   b. Computer technician

   c. Sales representative

   d. Proposal writer

Sources: *Employer's Supplemental Tax Guide, Publication 15-A* (Washington, DC: Internal Revenue Service, 2008), pp. 6–7; "Independent Contractor (Self-Employed) or Employee?", *Internal Revenue Service,* http://www.irs.gov/businesses/small/article/0, id=99921,00.html (May 29, 2008); and Darrell Zahorsky, "The Great Debate: Employee vs. Independent Contractor," *About.com: Small Business Information,* http://sbinformation.about.com/cs/laborlaws/a/contractor.htm (May 29, 2008).

Other key federal laws include the following:

- *Fair Labor Standards Act:* Passed in 1938, this act applies to firms with two or more employees who engage in interstate commerce. It sets the standards for the basic minimum wage level and also governs the number of hours an employee can work before receiving overtime pay. Typically, once an employee works 40 hours in one week, the pay rate increases to time and a half for additional hours.

- *Equal Pay Act:* This 1963 law prohibits pay differentials based on gender.

- *Occupational Safety and Health Act:* In 1971, this act established the Occupational Safety and Health Administration (OSHA) to set and enforce guidelines for workplace safety and employee health. Since its inception, the number of employee injuries and deaths has declined.

- *Family and Medical Leave Act:* Since 1993, firms of 50 or more employees are required to allow workers who have been with the company for 12 months or worked a minimum of 1,250 hours to take up to 12 weeks of unpaid leave for childbirth or adoption or special family needs. In 2008, the law was amended to include leave during a family member's active military duty and injured service member family leave.

Clearly, an enterpriser who plans to hire employees should research these and other laws. The U.S. Department of Labor website (http://www.dol.gov) has a section devoted specifically to employers.

Each state has its own labor and employment laws that prohibit discriminatory practices. These laws may go further than federal laws. Be sure to research your state's regulations to be aware of any additional restrictions.

Labor Unions

Although we generally think of labor unions as part of the large corporate business environment, small business owners may have dealings with unions as well. For example, certain trades and professions, such as electricians and plumbers, are likely to be unionized. Service workers may also belong to unions. A general contractor or a transportation company will probably employ union workers.

A **labor union** is an organization of workers formed to serve its members' collective interests with regard to wages and working conditions. Labor unions represent their members by negotiating contracts and working arrangements through the collective bargaining process that involves representatives from the employer and the union. Then, the union administers the agreements and resolves any problems that arise.

Labor union   An organization of workers formed to serve its members' collective interests with regard to wages and working conditions. Labor unions represent their members through the collective bargaining process that involves representatives from the employer and the union and also administer the negotiated agreements.

The extent of unionization depends on industry, geography, and type of work. Some industries—the building trades and transportation—are heavily unionized, as are certain regions of the country, such as the Midwest. The Southeast, on the other hand, tends to be nonunion. The United Food and Commercial Workers union covers employees of some supermarkets and other retailers.

Any enterpriser who employs union workers should understand the laws pertaining to collective bargaining. The National Labor Relations Act (NLRA) is the primary law that governs relationships between labor unions and employers in the private sector. It protects employees' rights to form, join, or support unions and for workers who are union members to bargain collectively with their employers. The NLRA also extends rights to a group of two or more employees without a union, who join together to ask for changes in wages or working conditions. The law also protects employers against unfair actions of labor organizations.

If employees in your enterprise decide to form or join a union, you should familiarize yourself with regulations that cover the unionizing process and what kinds of activities you, as an employer, can engage in during the unionization process. A good place to learn about the rights of employees and employers is the National Labor Relations Board website (http://www.nlrb.gov).

17.4 Human Resources Planning

The decision to hire employees is a major one in the life of an enterprise. Knowing when it's time to hire additional help and whom to hire—independent contractor, full-time employee, part-time employee—is critical to the future success of the enterprise. No longer will the enterprise be flying solo but will add a new role—employer—to the many he or she already plays. As discussed earlier, becoming an employer subjects the firm to additional governmental regulation. It is a huge undertaking that involves recruiting and selecting employees, negotiating compensation, training them, and evaluating performance.

Many enterprisers wait too long to hire their first employee and miss opportunities. Caught up in day-to-day matters, they lose sight of the bigger picture and don't have time to develop a strategic plan to grow the firm. Another risk is finding yourself in a crunch and

rushing the hiring process, increasing the likelihood of hiring the wrong person.

Before you can begin to look for qualified candidates to join your firm, however, you should develop a human resources plan. This starts with a needs assessment: What jobs do you wish to delegate, what skills do they require, and what is the best way to fill them? You may need administrative help to take on mundane tasks or specialized help in sales, marketing, or finance to provide expertise you lack or can't handle yourself as the business grows. You should also look into the future and forecast your needs for one, three, and five years.

The next steps are to prepare job descriptions to guide the search process and then recruit candidates. The employee selection process involves screening prospects, interviewing them, evaluating their skills and experience for the job you wish to fill, checking references, deciding which applicant to hire, and making and negotiating the offer of employment.

The employee planning and management process doesn't end once an applicant accepts your offer, however. New employees require guidance to be effective. You should have an orientation session to introduce new employees to the way you operate your enterprise. In a small company this can be quite informal. You will also need to devote time to training and development of your employees. Again, the level and formality of these activities depends on the size and type of firm.

Employees want to know how they are doing on the job, so it's essential to set up a schedule for performance evaluations. Compensation and benefit reviews and adjustments are another aspect of human resources management. You will also want to find ways to motivate your employees and increase job satisfaction so that you retain them. Exhibit 17.5 summarizes the steps in the human resources management process.

Job Analysis and Descriptions

After working too many late nights and weekends, you've decided to hire your first employee. Or perhaps your company is growing and you need to add staff. In either case, before you can advertise to fill the job, you should perform an in-depth job analysis to determine the tasks and responsibilities of the position, as well as the knowledge and skills the job requires. Then you can prepare a formal job description that will guide not only the hiring process, but also be the basis for compensation and performance reviews.[8]

exhibit

17.5

The Human Resources Management Process

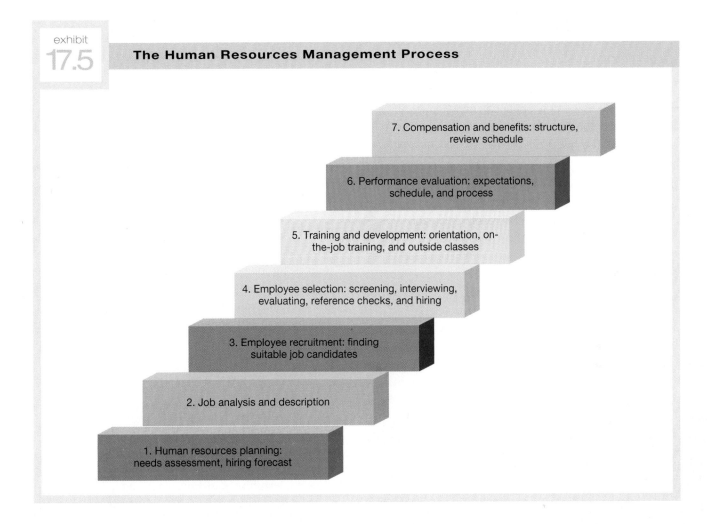

7. Compensation and benefits: structure, review schedule

6. Performance evaluation: expectations, schedule, and process

5. Training and development: orientation, on-the-job training, and outside classes

4. Employee selection: screening, interviewing, evaluating, reference checks, and hiring

3. Employee recruitment: finding suitable job candidates

2. Job analysis and description

1. Human resources planning: needs assessment, hiring forecast

A job description includes the title, pay range, duties, responsibilities, required qualifications (knowledge, skills, and abilities), and reporting relationships of a particular job. It should communicate clearly and concisely the job's responsibilities and tasks, as well as the qualities that contribute to excellent performance. Physical demands, if relevant to the job, should also be stated. Every job should have a formal job description on file, and these should be reviewed and updated on a regular schedule.

Well-crafted job descriptions can be a valuable tool for your firm's success. They show potential and existing employees how they will fit into your firm, help them understand your mission and goals, provide direction, and establish clear expectations of performance. Resources such as the *Occupational Outlook Handbook* and *Dictionary of Occupational Titles* provide helpful information to prepare job descriptions.

Job descriptions must also be in compliance with legal requirements. This point is extremely important. A job description is considered a legal document and must therefore not discriminate in terms of race, color, religion, age, sex, national origin or nationality, or physical or mental disability. The hiring standards must relate to job performance. For example:

- Use gender-neutral language—salesperson, not salesman; repair person, not handyman.

- Avoid age discrimination by stating the minimum experience level, without an upper limit; rather than young, say dynamic or energetic.

- State the minimum requirements for education. If you specify a degree, be prepared to show that it is necessary for the job. A safer way to word this qualification is "Associate's degree or equivalent experience."

- Base the description on job-related skills and responsibilities.

Other more general suggestions for writing good job descriptions include the following:

- Go beyond the current or past job description to include how the job can contribute to the company's future needs.

- Begin with clearly stated tasks and responsibilities before defining the qualifications and attributes to perform the job.

- Take a big-picture view that includes priorities.

- Make sure that any educational, experience, or physical credentials for the job are directly related to the employee's ability to perform the job well.

- State responsibilities as specifically as possible. Rather than "good computer skills," specify the software in which proficiency is required for the job: "Proficiency with Microsoft Office and QuickBooks." Provide details of administrative tasks such as filing, typing, answering phones, and sending invoices.

- Keep job descriptions flexible, especially in a small company, so that employees will pitch in and help, not just stick to what's on the list of duties.

Exhibit 17.6 shows the main categories for a job description.

Job analysis can be challenging for the enterpriser hiring his or her first employee. However, it is well worth the time to think about your most pressing needs. Take notes about the tasks you now perform yourself and wish to delegate. Then you can determine the credentials someone needs to perform these duties well. Once you have employees, seek their input into the job description process. Have them keep logs of what they do and use these as the basis for the description of the position.

The job description drives the rest of the hiring process. Without it, you will not be able to create effective advertisements to attract applicants with the appropriate qualifications for your needs.

17.5 Recruiting and Selecting Employees

With job description in hand, you are now ready to recruit and evaluate applicants to fill your position. Recruitment techniques vary from word of mouth to Internet job board postings. As noted earlier, the selection process involves screening, interviewing, evaluating, checking references, and making an offer.

Finding Job Candidates

Where should you look for prospective employees? The sources are many, and you should select the ones that are most applicable to the type of job, your company, its location, and your budget. For example, if you have a retail location you can post a sign in the window so that passers-by and customers can inquire about the job. Your website is another good place to post an announcement.

Tap into your many networks. Let friends and business colleagues know about the job you wish to fill. Employees are a good resource for referrals of friends. Many enterprises offer small bonuses, such as $50 or $100 for referrals of friends. The placement offices and campus recruiting centers of colleges and universities welcome listings for student internships, part-time work, and full-time jobs.

As you receive responses to ads or general employment inquiries, you should acknowledge receipt of the job seeker's resume using postcards or email. If the applicant has the qualifications you seek, say that you will be in touch to schedule an interview. Otherwise, say that you will keep the application/resume on file for a year in case other opportunities arise.

exhibit

17.6

Outline for a Job Description

- Facts about the position: title, department, and pay range

- Reports to (to whom the person directly reports)

- Summary of overall responsibilities

- Key areas of responsibility

- Consults with (those who the person works with on a regular basis)

- Knowledge, skills, and abilities

- Qualifications (education, experience required)

- Special requirements (overtime, language proficiency)

Advertising

Help-wanted advertising is another recruiting tool. Today, there are numerous places to place advertisements: Web job boards, radio, television, local and regional newspapers and their print and online classified sections, and trade publications. Online ads have become one of the leading resources and can provide a cost-effective way to reach a wider pool of applicants, who can search by location and type of job. Recent studies show that almost three-quarters of job applicants search online ads.

The type of job will affect where you advertise. For example, local newspapers would be a good source for a general administrative position. A position that calls for specialized skills may require you to not only look locally but also use Web job boards such as Monster.com and CareerBuilder.com, industry-focused job boards, and trade journals. These websites also allow employers to search resumes posted by job seekers to find candidates who match their qualifications. Job fairs and trade shows also provide recruiting opportunities.

Your employment ad should clearly state the following information:

- The position: the job title should be the headline of the ad

- Job requirements: selection criteria such as professional experience, education, skills, and background

- Other related information: location, hours, and travel

- Benefits of working for your firm: Market yourself by including a brief description of your organization (the employer), the positive aspects of the work environment, insurance benefits, and other selling points (relocation allowance, flexible hours). Highlight benefits that differentiate you from other employers.

- Rewards: competitive salaries, bonus potential, training, tuition reimbursement, and career advancement

- How to apply: Provide a deadline to receive applications, the information you require (resume, cover letter, salary requirements, etc.), and how to submit: email, fax, in person, via mail.

- Contact information

- Other information: equal-opportunity employer, any restrictions, etc.

Ads for online job boards are structured differently from print ads. They feature a summary that allows interested parties to click through to the full description

© Rob Belknap/istockphoto.com

of the position. This summary should make your ad stand out and attract the reader's attention by emphasizing the benefits of the job to the employee. The full ad should include the same information as a print ad.[9]

The legal cautions we discussed in the job description section also apply to employment ads. Choose your wording carefully so that you do not discriminate in terms of race, color, religion, age, sex, national origin or nationality, or physical or mental disability. Be sure that the stated job requirements are in fact necessary. For example, does a sales position really call for a degree, or are experience and a proven record of success more important? Using the phrase "degree or equivalent experience" will help you attract qualified applicants. Make sure the skills, experience, and other factors relate to a valid business purpose. If you have a physical requirement, it must be directly tied to the ability to perform the job. You can state that a warehouse supervisor be able to lift 50 pounds. Setting height or weight restrictions for an office position, however, is illegal.

Executive Search Firms and Employment Agencies

Executive search firms and employment agencies are service firms you can hire to find employees to fill specific jobs. Their fees are paid by either the hiring company or the applicant, depending on the type of agency:

- *Executive search/executive recruiters:* These firms focus on higher-level positions. The employer pays a per assignment fee or a retainer. They usually work on an exclusive basis. Some firms specialize in industries or fields such as finance or marketing.

- *Employment agencies:* Agencies work on a contingency basis and earn their fee—either from the employer or the applicant—when they fill a job.

The fee is usually a percentage of the first year's salary and can range from 10 to 25 percent. These firms handle a variety of positions, from clerical to management. Employers can place a job assignment with more than one agency if they wish. Agencies may specialize in certain fields.

- *Temporary staffing agencies:* No longer just for clerical jobs, temporary agencies now handle technical and professional positions as well. The employer pays the agency a percentage markup above the employee's rate (25–100 percent or more). Placements may be as short as one day, to fill in for an absent employee, or a year for specialized skills. Employers can hire a temporary employee permanently by paying the agency a placement fee.

Why would an enterpriser use an agency rather than conduct the job search in-house? Recruiting is a very time-consuming activity. The enterpriser may not have the staff or the expertise to devote to the hiring process. Sorting through the stacks of responses that come in from a print or online ad takes time away from business operations.

Search firms are especially helpful for high-level positions and those in a particular field or requiring specialized experience that may be harder to find. Search firms generally have a greater network of contacts from which to choose. Confidentiality is another benefit of using a search firm or employment agency, which keeps the job search private.

Temporary employment agencies fill several needs. Perhaps you have seasonal spikes in sales and need additional staff for just a few months. Rather than hire employees for whom you will have to pay taxes and benefits and then lay them off, you can obtain help through a temporary staffing agency, which handles the payroll taxes. A temporary placement offers you the chance to try out an employee before making a permanent commitment.

Note that search firms and employment agencies must follow the same anti-discrimination regulations as employers. If you use one of these firms, make sure that its practices conform to legal requirements.

Evaluating Potential Employees

The next step in the hiring process is to evaluate job applicants and select the one that best matches your job needs. Having the right people on your staff is critical to your future success, and understanding how to screen, interview, and assess job candidates will serve you well.

Screening

Applicant screening is the first step in evaluating prospects. Review the cover letters, resumes and/or applications you've received against the qualifications and criteria you established in your job description and ad.

Many firms use an application form to make a preliminary assessment of a candidate's qualifications. These forms provide a consistent way to gather information about the job seeker's education and work experience. The way the form is filled out also offers important clues, such as the applicant's ability to spell, write neatly, and provide complete information. Your online ads can include a link to an online application.

If you choose to develop an application form, follow the same legal guidelines we've mentioned earlier. You cannot ask about race, color, gender, religious beliefs, national origin, physical disability, or age if the person is at least 40 years old. You should ask whether an applicant is eligible to work in the United States. Include only questions that provide information related to the job. The EEOC requires employers to keep unsolicited job applications for at least one year.

Often employers conduct brief screening interviews by phone. These focused chats are a very efficient way to narrow the field of potential applicants and focus on the most qualified candidates, who are then invited to come in for a personal interview. To make the best use of screening interviews:

- Prepare before you call and know what you want to achieve during the call.

- Develop a list of questions to ask each candidate so that you can assess their qualifications, cultural fit, and salary expectations.

- Use the same questions for all applicants; this makes it easier to compare them.

- Take notes and listen carefully as you engage the candidate in conversation.

- At the end of the interview, tell the applicant what to expect next: that you want to bring the person to the firm for an in-person interview, you need to complete your other interviews before making a decision and will get back to the person within a certain time frame, or that the person's qualifications do not match your criteria but that you will keep them in mind for other positions.

- Follow up with applicants to leave a positive impression about your company.

Interviewing Applicants

Conducting effective job interviews is central to an enterpriser's ability to hire the right people for the business. Interviewing takes time and requires skills; it's not just a conversation about the company and the job. Develop a process for interviews, know how to structure and direct the interview to obtain the information you need, and be aware of what questions you can and cannot legally ask. The following are the steps to a successful interview:

- **Preparation:** As with screening interviews, preparation is the first step. In addition to reviewing the job description, developing questions to ask, and setting up an agenda that structures the interview, familiarize yourself with the applicant's qualifications before the interview begins.

- **Introduction:** The interview should begin with an introductory conversation that sets a pleasant tone. Be welcoming and friendly, chat for a few minutes to put the interviewee at ease. Then guide the transition into the main content of the interview by describing your agenda for the interview. For example, tell the applicant your role in the process, the title of the position you will be discussing, and how the interview will proceed. You might explain that you'd like to begin by discussing the applicant's background, and then talk about the company and the specific position.

- **Ask questions:** While you might be tempted to begin with the description of the company and the job, it's preferable to focus on the applicant first. You will get a more accurate view of the person's qualifications. If you talk about the job first, the candidate is likely to tailor the responses to your questions to fit the position. Structure the questions carefully to determine how well suited the applicant is for the job and

have a list of questions to make it easier to get revealing answers from a job candidate. Through the screening process, you decided that the basics were there; now dig deeper to get more information about professional experience, skills, education, strengths, weaknesses, and personality. Look for clues to the person's style and attitude. Don't hesitate to bring up any issues you may have.

- **Position and company:** Describe the opportunity, working from the job description. If this is a first interview, you may want to keep this part general and get more specific in subsequent interviews. Provide information about the company and the opportunities it provides. Be enthusiastic, but at the same time be realistic and do not oversell.

- **Answer questions:** Allow time for the interviewee to ask questions.

- **Close:** End the interview with some positive comments, and thank the applicant for his or her interest. Give the applicant some indication as to your timing and when to expect to hear from you. You may just be starting to interview or be ready to move to the next step.

- **Evaluate:** After the interview, summarize your impressions in writing while they are still fresh in your mind.

- **Follow up:** Send a letter of thanks, regardless of whether the applicant is hired.

If you already have other employees working for your enterprise, it is a good idea to involve them in the interview process as well. The more perspective and viewpoints you can get on a potential candidate, the better your decision will be. This perspective is particularly important when an interviewee, if selected, will be working with your other employees.

Interview questions range from the general to job-specific. The questions should give you information about the candidate's experience, job performance strengths and weaknesses, ambitions, attitudes, and other personal qualities. Using open-ended interview questions—ones that require more than a "yes" or "no" answer—will give you considerably more information about the person's style and abilities.

Begin with general questions to break the ice and set a congenial tone before you get into the job itself and the skills and characteristics you seek. You may

© Rmarmion/Dreamstime LLC

also choose to pose behavioral questions that give the applicant a realistic job situation and ask how he or she would handle it, or ask about a job-related situation. For example:

- Tell me about an important goal that you set for yourself and how you reached it.

- Please describe a situation in which you had to arrive at a compromise or guide others to a compromise.

- Tell me about a time when you had to go above and beyond the call of duty in order to get a job done.

- As a supervisor, how do you motivate your employees?

Many resources are available to help you develop suitable questions for your interviews, such as the websites listed below:

- Job-Interview.net (http://www.job-interview.net): Has a question bank with questions by job skills for different functional areas as well as more general questions and mock interviews. An Interviewer's Guide provides advice on conducting effective interviews.

- Job Interview Questions (http://www. jobinterviewquestions.org): Has a section for interviewers that includes questions to avoid as well as ones to ask.

- Quint Careers' Job Interview Questions Database (http://www.quintcareers.com/interview_question_database/): While this site is geared toward job seekers, it provides 150 questions with sample answers.

- Nolo.com (http://www.nolo.com): The Hiring section's article on Conducting Job Interviews covers the pitfalls that an unprepared interviewer might encounter.

Legal Issues

As with employment advertising, it's easy to inadvertently violate anti-discrimination laws. Take the time to learn about the types of questions you can and cannot ask during a job interview. Check the Job Interview Questions and Nolo.com websites, referenced above, for examples of illegal questions and possible alternatives. Avoid asking questions about topics that you cannot consider in making an employment decision, such as race, religion, age, marital status, plans to have children, etc. Instead, focus on topics that are relevant to the job: education,

prior experience, and job successes. Be cautious about the promises you make regarding the company's future prospects and the job's potential. Otherwise you might be sued for fraudulent claims or breach of contract.

Reference and Background Checks

Once you've identified your top candidates for the job, it's time to carefully and diligently check references. In your haste to make an offer to your favorite applicant, don't be tempted to skip this critical step! Reference checks help you discover how the person performed in prior work situations and can prevent you from hiring the wrong person. Also, by checking references and verifying a person's resume, you will find out how trustworthy and honest the potential employee is. Fabrications or inconsistencies on the resume or application (indicating they went to a school or worked at accompany that they didn't, dates that don't match with other records), are a good indication of potential trustworthiness problems.

You should also conduct a background check to rule out criminal offenses. If you do not conduct the appropriate reference and background checks, you could find yourself with more issues than hiring someone who does not have the skills you need. Hiring someone with a history of problems on the job could result in legal liability.

Many previous employers are reluctant to release more than the basics of employment dates and job title. Some companies ask applicants to sign a waiver and release of liability form that authorizes prior employers to release any requested information.

Checking references by phone is a good way to quickly get the information you require. You can also tell a lot from how it is said and also by what is *not* said. Neutral comments can be very telling. Verify facts such as dates of employment/school attendance, job title and responsibilities, salary, and reason for leaving. If references are not willing to provide the information, you may be able to verify that information the applicant has provided you is consistent with their records. Any discrepancies are red flags that require further investigation.

Develop specific rather than vague questions. For example, you might say, "Mr./Ms. Applicant told me about working on Project X. How did he/she contribute to that project?" You can also ask about ability to work on a team, examples of performance success or failure, suitability for the job you are filling, and similar questions. Be sure to ask if the reference would rehire the person and why or why not.

Documenting your reference and background checks will protect you from claims of negligent hiring.

Testing and Physical Exams

Performance-related tests may apply in certain job situations. For example, you may wish to test an applicant's proficiency with word processing or spreadsheet preparation. To be legal, such tests must relate to the specific job criteria, be valid determinants of job performance, and be nondiscriminatory.

Likewise, physical exams can be required to determine whether the applicant can fulfill the physical tasks related to a job. The law requires that these exams must take place *after* the applicant receives a job offer that is contingent on passing the exam. Drug screening is legal for all applicants and can be a part of a physical exam or a separate test.

Making the Offer

Once an applicant has successfully completed the steps in the selection process, it's time to make an offer. Here, too, there are possible future legal concerns. To protect yourself, make the offer in writing and state the compensation very clearly. It is preferable to express it on a weekly, biweekly, or monthly basis, rather than annual. This strategy avoids any implied promise that you will keep the employee at least a year.

Have a written and signed employment agreement or offer letter with each employee. This document should include the terms of employment and state that the employee understands the hiring terms and the "at-will" nature of employment. This means that either the employer can terminate employment at any time for any nondiscriminatory reason or the employee can leave at any time. (An employee who is under contract is not considered an at-will employee.) You can find samples of offer letters and other hiring-related forms online at websites such as About.com's Human Resources pages (http://humanresources.about.com).

17.6 Retaining Employees

Now that you have recruited and hired an employee, you want to make sure he or she performs well on the job and is satisfied working for you. This calls for orientation, training, and future development and motivation. You should also develop an employee handbook that summarizes your policies and guidelines for conduct and also establishes compensation and evaluation procedures.

Orientation and Training

Orientation and subsequent training are essential elements of the overall hiring and retention program. Orientation programs get employees off to a good start at your firm. By providing ongoing training opportunities, you will help your employees develop their skills and managerial abilities so that they can advance professionally.

All new employees should receive some orientation to introduce them to the workplace and to the requirements that their job entails. This step is important and goes a long way to creating a positive introduction to your firm and making the employee feel welcomed and valued. Taking the time to conduct an organized orientation program, even if it is informal, will bring the new employee up to speed more quickly, ease new-job jitters, and increase job satisfaction.

In designing an orientation program, ask yourself what new employees should know to make them comfortable in your work environment. The orientation might include an overview of your enterprise; why and how you do business; key policies and procedures; introductions to other employees; what your expectations are for treating other employees, suppliers, and customers; how to complete certain forms; how people are paid and when they are paid; who reports to whom; who is responsible for what; and how to resolve disputes and issues that come up at work.

Ongoing training to enhance an employee's technical and other skills is an important part of managing and motivating your employees. You want your employees to improve their abilities to perform their current jobs more accurately and efficiently. In addition, training programs will help them to acquire skills to keep up with the latest technology, develop strategies relating to their particular functional areas (sales, marketing, and financial management), and advance to other positions. Training in management techniques is particularly valuable as well. Provide a variety of opportunities for training and create a work environment that promotes learning.

Your employees can receive training in several ways:

- **On-the-job (internal) training:** Offer specific training related to job performance; on-site seminars, coaching, apprenticeship and mentoring programs; informal training by peers and supervisors; and cross-training and job rotations to familiarize workers with several different jobs to increase their flexibility.

- **External programs:** Off-site programs are readily available for almost every topic imaginable and range from short workshops to multi-day classes and seminars. Adult education and continuing education programs at local colleges are another way to train employees.

- **Professional and trade associations:** They offer training sessions through seminars, meetings, and conferences.

- **E-training:** E-learning is fast becoming a cost-effective and efficient way to deliver training programs. It involves computerized instructional modules on CDs and DVDs, classes by email, and Web-based training, with instructional modules, virtual classrooms, computer games, and more. Employees can take these at their convenience and can move at their own pace. The availability of e-learning options is increasing as interactive technology becomes widely accessible.

Employee Handbooks

As you add employees, you will find it beneficial to develop an employee handbook or manual that describes your company's policies and procedures for the conduct of business. An employee handbook tells employees what you expect from them and documents what they can expect from your firm. Having all your policies in one place and in writing can help your business to run more smoothly, save time, and prevent disputes. Developing the handbook helps you become a better manager by deciding what the company policies should be. Having clearly defined policies provides guidelines not just for employees but for your managers. Exhibit 17.7 summarizes the key elements to include in your employee handbook.

For more details on developing policies and writing an employee handbook, consult websites such as Small

exhibit
17.7

Contents of an Employee Handbook

Introduction

Company overview: history, growth, goals, ethics, and management philosophy

Equal opportunity/nondiscrimination statement

Standards of conduct: attendance, dress code, and policies on sexual harassment and substance abuse

General information: parking, lunch, etc.

Work hours and overtime policies

Paid holidays

Vacation and policies for sick, military, funeral, personal, family, medical, and jury duty leaves

Other employee policies

Payroll issues: pay periods and methods of payment

Employment classification categories

Performance reviews

Fringe benefits: health and other insurance coverage and other benefits such as tuition reimbursement

Pension or profit-sharing plans

Complaint procedures

Termination: causes for which you will fire an employee, such as criminal activity, poor performance, dishonesty, security breaches, insubordination, and company policy violations

Employee acknowledgment: a form for the employee to sign that says the employee has received and read the handbook; protects your liability

Disclaimer: state that the handbook is not a contract, its policies can be changed at any time, and all employment is "at will"

Business Notes (http://www.smallbusinessnotes.com/) and About.com's Human Resources pages (http://humanresources.about.com). You can also purchase templates to use as a starting point, customizing them to fit your company's needs.

Evaluating Employees

A formal employee evaluation process is an important part of human resources management. It covers a wide range of issues, including job expectations, career path, compensation, and advancement. Effective employee evaluations, performed on a regular basis, help employees understand the company's goals and their role in helping to reach them.[10]

The evaluation process begins with the establishment of performance standards for the position. The employee's job performance can then be measured against these standards, which include quality of work, level of output, and job knowledge. Other criteria also come into play, such as work habits, attitude, punctuality, interpersonal skills, and initiative. The logistics of the review process should also be considered: who will conduct reviews and how often. It's critical to apply the same standards to all employees and to inform employees of the evaluation process.

Developing an evaluation form gives managers a guideline to follow in evaluating and discussing performance. The performance evaluation form should include a list of the position's major functions and responsibilities and a definition of the rating standards or scale. Ratings sections can be tailored for the specific job or list more general categories such as the following:

- Technical skills: categories relating to application of job knowledge and skills, etc.

- Work quantity: volume of work completed, meeting deadlines, setting priorities, etc.

- Work quality: accuracy, completeness, reliability, follow-through, judgment, etc.

- Interpersonal skills: interactions with colleagues, supervisors, customers, project groups, etc.

- Communication skills: oral, written, communication style, etc.

- Work attitudes: efficiency, planning, initiative, attendance/punctuality, etc.

- Managerial/supervisory/leadership skills: training of staff, delegating, motivating staff, goal setting, process improvement, cost control, etc.

The supervisor may wish to note specifics for some of the general categories.

The evaluation form should then have an overall performance rating, a place for the evaluator to provide additional comments in narrative form, an action plan that includes future goals, performance expectations, and training for the next review period, a section where the employee can record his or her comments relating to the evaluation, and places for the supervisor and employee to sign and date the form.

Many managers are uncomfortable with giving evaluations, also called performance appraisals, to their employees. However, evaluations should not be given short shrift. They are a valuable management tool that will motivate employees and enhance productivity. They also provide a way to select employees for promotions and incentive bonuses and form the legal basis to terminate an employee by documenting a history of poor performance.

Planning ahead and preparing an agenda for the review can lessen the stress and lead to more meaningful review sessions. Employees deserve to know how the manager sees their strengths and weaknesses, where they can improve, and how to advance in the company. Exhibit 17.8 offers suggestions to improve the evaluation interview.

Compensation and Benefits

Employee compensation is one of the most important and difficult topics an enterpriser faces.[11] The right compensation plan keeps your employees motivated to do their best work for your company. It will help you attract qualified employees to your company, motivate and reward current employees, retain employees, and create loyalty to your company.

Compensation includes not only salary but also the benefits, employee perks, and stock options you offer your workers. As with other areas of human resources management, you must comply with government regulations. You may not discriminate in some types of compensation as required by law. For example, if you pay wages, then you also must pay social security for each employee and deduct social security taxes from their paychecks and pay unemployment insurance and workers' compensation insurance. Workers' compensation insurance is based on the type of workers you have. For more dangerous jobs with a greater likelihood of worker injuries, the rates can be very high.

In developing your compensation plan, you should strive to balance the company's financial goals with

exhibit
17.8

Tips for Better Evaluation Reviews

- Focus on performance, rather than the person.

- Take a positive approach. Provide as much encouraging feedback as possible, and avoid assigning blame.

- Look for specific examples to support the evaluation, such as not meeting sales quotas or other established goals. Also include positives—what the employee is doing well.

- Set priorities so that the employee knows where to focus his or her efforts.

- Make the review a two-way communication. For example, ask the employee to evaluate his or her own performance. An employee who has a chance to participate and offer suggestions feels valued. Encourage employees to offer their own solutions to problems that arise.

- Cover the whole review period, not just the most recent month or two. Don't let only recent performance determine the overall tone of the review. An employee who is doing well now may have had a rough start; recognizing the improvement is motivating. Conversely, acknowledge the good work done earlier in the year by a worker who is having a poor month.

- Don't wait until a formal review to provide feedback. Ongoing informal evaluations, particularly after completion of a task or project, give employees feedback to correct performance issues right away.

Sources: "Conducting Employee Reviews" and "Employee Performance Reviews," *Gaebler Ventures Resources for Entrepreneurs*, http://www.gaebler.com/resources-for-entrepreneurs.htm (July 1, 2008); and Margaret Steen, "Managers' Tips for Evaluating Employees," *Yahoo! HotJobs*, http://hotjobs.yahoo.com (July 1, 2008).

employee expectations. Your job descriptions and employee evaluation procedures are key inputs for your compensation plan.

As your enterprise grows, it will become critical for you to either develop in-house expertise in employment issues or to outsource this division to one or more firms that can provide you with the necessary human resources services. You may wish to hire a payroll specialist to process your payroll and pay your payroll taxes. Benefits consultants can help make choices about which insurance and retirement plans to provide and then administer your programs.

Wages and Salary

How do you decide what to pay your first employee? A good starting place is publicly available wage and salary information to learn what the going rates are in your area for the jobs you have to fill. There are many compensation surveys available online. For example, the California JobStar site, http://jobstar.org, offers links to more than 300 free California and national online salary surveys for many professions and industries. Monster.com, CareerBuiilders.com, and other online job sites have links to salary surveys. HR consulting

firms such as William Mercer and the Hay Group offer some free information online. The U.S. government's Bureau of Labor Statistics (BLS) is also a good resource. The BLS *Occupational Outlook Handbook* provides general information including earnings levels for most occupations. Once you have this information, you can set pay ranges for each type of position that are competitive with similar firms in your area and industry.

When setting your firm's pay structure, you should consider the level and importance of each job as well as the type of business and how pay is structured in your industry. The base pay for equivalent jobs should be the same. Wages and salaries are usually based on the amount of time employees work (*base pay*; per hour, month, or year), the amount they produce (*incentive pay*), or a combination of base and incentive pay. If you offer incentive pay, your base pay will be lower than if you don't offer incentives. For example, you may pay an office manager $3,250 a month. Your production workers may receive base pay of $18 per hour and a per-item incentive tied to some measure of output. Sales compensation tied to performance benefits both the company and the employee. Sales positions' compensation may include salary and commissions or be all commission.

Jobs are classified as exempt or nonexempt. **Exempt employees** receive a fixed salary per time interval, regardless of hours worked. The exempt category is usually assigned to professional, management, technical, and highly skilled jobs. **Nonexempt employees** are usually in less-skilled jobs. They are paid on an hourly basis and are eligible for overtime if they work more than 40 hours per week or on holidays.

Another aspect of your firm's compensation plan is when to give raises. Pay increases should take into account the length of time an employee has worked for you and the employee's job performance and special contributions to the company.

Incentive Programs

Incentive programs motivate employees and reward them for above-average performance. Incentive-based compensation can take different forms. It can be tied to performance of a specific individual or group or be based on the firm's financial performance and take the form of quarterly or annual bonuses or profit sharing. Incentives can be cash or noncash (trips, special event outings, extra vacation days, etc.).

Stock ownership in the company is another type of incentive program. Many privately held corporations set up stock option programs to motivate and reward employees. These can take one of several forms, such as incentive stock options and employee stock ownership plans (ESOPs). (We will discuss ESOPs in Chapter 19.)

Benefits

In addition to direct pay in the form of salary and wages, companies can offer a wide array of indirect compensation in the form of benefits. Some benefits are mandatory, such as state and federal unemployment insurance, workers' compensation, social security, and Medicare. Other benefits include paid vacations and holidays, sick days, insurance plans (health, disability, dental, vision, and life), retirement plans, and tuition reimbursement.

Benefits are a major cost for a small firm. According to the Employee Benefit Research Institute (EBRI), benefit costs as a percentage of total compensation costs were 30.2 percent at the end of 2007.[12] As expensive as they are, voluntary benefit plans are an important consideration in attracting and retaining employees, who view benefits as a part of their overall compensation. Developing a suitable benefits package for your company—and one it can afford—is a challenging task. Insurance brokers and other specialists can help you tailor a benefits plan to your company's needs.

As with salary planning, you should research what benefits are standard at other companies in your industry and area. Know how much benefits will cost you before offering them—today and for the long term. Begin with a basic benefits plan, adding on as the company grows. When budgeting for payroll, include mandatory benefits as well as voluntary ones.

Today many companies offer flexible benefit plans, also called cafeteria plans. Employees get a certain amount of money to spend and can select the benefits that they need from a menu of offerings.

Lifestyle benefits are also popular with small companies, who can use them to improve working conditions for their employees. These include flexible schedules, the opportunity to work from home one or more days a week, casual dress days, childcare, on-site classes and seminars, staff parties, and similar creative benefits.

Employee Leasing

Because of the complexities involved in managing human resources, some companies turn to employee leasing using **professional employer organizations (PEOs)**. PEOs take over many of the employee services for small or mid-size business.[13] The PEO becomes the legal employer, and for a fee, typically between 1 and 5 percent of total payroll costs, provides your enterprise with administrative services for payroll, taxes, insurance, retirement plans, and more. The client company continues to handle hiring, salary, and promotion decisions.

The benefit of such an arrangement is that the PEO handles the considerable amount of paperwork. Another advantage is the ability to offer a wider range of benefits. Because they employ many more people than their individual client companies, PEOs can often negotiate discounts from health care providers and insurers that can be passed along to your enterprise. You also avoid the costs of staffing a human resources department.

Exempt employee   An employee who receives a fixed salary per time interval, regardless of hours worked.

Nonexempt employee   Employee paid on an hourly basis who is eligible for overtime for working more than 40 hours per week or on holidays.

Professional employer organization (PEO)   An outside firm that, for a fee, becomes the legal employer of a company's employees and provides administrative services for payroll, taxes, insurance, retirement plans, and more.

There are disadvantages as well. You are no longer the employer of record; your employees must be terminated and rehired by the PEO. You may lose flexibility because you are limited to the PEO's benefit offerings.

Legal Issues

Many of the same laws that relate to hiring practices also apply once you have hired an employee. As noted in the section on regulation of employment practices (p. 451), employers must comply with the Civil Rights, Age Discrimination, Americans with Disabilities, Fair Labor Standards, Equal Pay, Occupational Safety and Health Administration (OSHA), and Family and Medical Leave Acts.

Some types of compensation, beyond direct salary, are required by law. For example, if you pay wages, then you must also pay social security for each employee as well as deduct social security taxes from their paychecks. The federal government and the states require unemployment insurance, and each state requires workers' compensation insurance. The rates for workers' compensation are based on the type of job. Companies with dangerous jobs that have a greater likelihood of injury will pay higher rates.

One of the most difficult issues for employers is firing employees for unsatisfactory performance or inappropriate conduct. The Enterprising Ethics box discusses how to handle the termination process properly.

ENTERPRISING ETHICS

How to Fire an Employee

No matter how well you recruit, interview, and evaluate employees, some will not work out. Before you terminate anyone's employment, however, you should be aware of the legal and ethical issues involved. You should also have in place written policies and procedures that cover employee terminations.

It's a good idea to consult an attorney who specializes in employment issues before beginning the termination process. The laws governing termination vary by state. It is also important to know what kinds of rights employees have.

Even though an employee may work "at will," the law says that you may not fire an employee for reasons that may be judged discriminatory. State laws may be even broader than federal ones. It is illegal to fire employees in retaliation for standing up for their employee rights. Even though in many states you can fire someone without a reason, you should have a valid job-related reason. Otherwise, you may be sued for discrimination.

Before making the decision to fire an employee, the manager should notify the employee of the problem or inappropriate behavior and give him or her the chance to correct it. This process may start with a verbal warning, but repeated infractions should be documented with written and dated warnings that clearly state the problem, how it should be corrected, the assistance that will be given, and in what time frame the improvement should occur. Subsequent documentation should indicate that the situation has not improved or declined further.

Make sure that the employee understands what the deficiencies are and has acknowledged them by means of a signed performance evaluation. Such warnings can be given at any time and do not have to wait for a formal evaluation. It's critical to document an employee's poor performance or incidents where he or she does not follow company policies—for example, with regard to harassment or substance abuse. Such documentation will be necessary if the terminated employee sues the company.

Managers should be aware of the financial and other impacts of firing an employee. Although the firm no longer has to pay the discharged employee's salary, its unemployment insurance premiums may rise. The work the person did must be transferred to someone else, either existing employees or a replacement. Other workers may be uneasy after a fellow employee is fired.

The way in which you fire employees says a lot about how you and your company treat employees. Don't resort to impersonal means to deliver the bad news—even if the reason for letting someone go is economic rather than poor performance. No matter how much you dread facing the employee, tell him or her in person. Consider how you would feel if you received an email or voicemail telling you your job was being eliminated. Poor firing practices send a negative message about your firm, lower the morale of remaining employees, and make it harder to recruit new personnel.

When conducting the termination interview, the manager should clearly state the reasons for letting the employee go. They should not come as a surprise to the employee, who has received several warnings. Here are some other suggestions for managers faced with this difficult task:

- *Prepare in advance for the exit interview.* Develop an agenda, prepare the paperwork, include a written letter of termination that documents the reasons for letting the person go, and have a clear idea of what you plan to say. You may want to have a written script and rehearse it. Refer to the company's formal policies to support your case. Deliver a check for any vacation or other pay due the employee. Familiarize yourself with state and federal regulations so you can answer questions about unemployment insurance and similar topics.

- *Don't fire in haste but terminate a person soon after deciding to take action.* After deciding to fire an employee, give yourself a short time to reflect. Then act promptly. There is no "right" time to fire someone. Letting the employee continue to work can affect the morale of other employees. Be discreet so that the employee's dignity is maintained.

- *Keep the discussion focused and brief.* Be careful not to say too much or to hesitate. Be direct, honest, and clear that this is a final decision. Stick to your prepared script, don't assign blame and don't be drawn into an argument. Try to be positive and helpful. Inform the employee of severance benefits, if any. Let the employee express his or her anger or frustrations. You can acknowledge them but don't try to counter them. Express regret that the situation did not work out but be careful not to make promises.

- *Have the employee return company property, provide passwords, and leave the premises.* Be sure to get any keys to the premises, company equipment, and system passwords. Then give the person a set amount of time to clean out his or her desk, perhaps under observation.

- *Follow up.* Prepare a memo documenting the termination session. Arrange to have the fired employee's work covered. Change locks and computer and phone passwords. Inform your other employees.

- *Decide how to handle reference checks.* Be careful not to make statements that could lead to litigation. Consult your lawyer to determine how to be truthful and what information you can provide.

- *Be sensitive to the dismissed employee.* Show respect for his or her dignity. Conduct the interview in private and at the end of a day. Give reasons for the firing, and if possible allow the employee to leave the premises without having to face other employees.

Discussion Questions

1. What are some of the legal and ethical issues to consider before terminating an employee?

2. Describe the preliminary steps a manager should take before making the decision to fire an employee.

3. How can a manager conduct an effective termination interview? What follow-up actions may be required?

Sources: Based on Latosha Craig, "How to Fire an Employee," *University of South Carolina School of Library and Information Science*, April 26, 2004, http://www.libsci.sc.edu/bob/class/clis724/SpecialLibrariesHandbook/Firing.htm; "Illegal Reasons for Firing Employees," *Nolo.com*, http://www.nolo.com (July 3, 2008); Carter McNamara, "Basics of Firing an Employee," adapted from the *Field Guide to Leadership and Supervision*, downloaded from Free Management Library, http://www.managementhelp.org (July 3, 2008); Sarah E. Needleman, "Bad Firings Can Hurt Firm's Reputation," *Wall Street Journal*, July 8, 2008, p. D4; and "Top 10 Employee Firing Mistakes," *AllBusiness.com*, http://www.allbusiness.com/human-resources/workforce-management-termination/4010-1.html (May 7, 2008).

Motivating Employees

Because an enterprise's employees are its most valuable assets, the ability to motivate them is a key element in the firm's success. Numerous research studies have shown that motivated employees are more productive, more creative, more satisfied, and more committed to the firm.[14]

Motivation, or the desire to engage in a certain behavior to reach a goal, is a complex topic. It is an essential component of performance that requires both ability and motivation. For example, a person may want to be a website designer and be highly motivated to apply for that position with your firm. If the applicant

---

Motivation   The desire to engage in a certain behavior to reach a goal.

does not know HTML, a necessary computer language for designing websites, he or she does not have the ability and skill to perform the job. On the other hand, you may have an employee who is a Web designer with superb technical skills—but is bored with and unenthusiastic about the job so that he or she does not produce work of the high quality you seek.

Improving an employee's abilities requires training and education, which can take considerable time. Increasing motivation can be achieved more quickly through such strategies as positive reinforcement, meeting employee needs, job design, rewards tied to job performance, and more.

People are unique, and their individual characteristics, values, beliefs, and abilities affect what motivates them. For example, some employees may be motivated by higher pay, whereas others place a higher value on insurance benefits, more flexible work hours, status, recognition, advancement, challenge, learning new skills, or job security. In addition, an organization's goals may differ from those of its employees. Thus, managers must understand what motivates the employees who report to them and also find ways to help use those motivations to reach the organization's goals.

In developing appropriate strategies to motivate employees, enterprisers should ask themselves:

- *Why* is someone willing to work for them?

- *What* will encourage their employees to put in the time and effort to undertake tasks that lead to the enterprise's success?

- *How* can they implement effective motivational programs?

Theories of Motivation

There are many theories of motivation, and they focus on motivating through either intrinsic or extrinsic rewards. *Intrinsic* rewards derive from a person's inner needs, such as happiness, contentment, satisfaction, pride, and self-esteem. *Extrinsic* rewards come from outside sources and include promotions, bonuses and other incentive programs, pay raises, recognition, and awards.

Let's now take a look at several motivational theories that have had a significant influence on current management thought:

- **McGregor's Theory X and Theory Y:** These theories focus on managerial attitudes. Theory X is a negative one that assumes that people are lazy, do not like to work, and will avoid work if possible. Theory X managers motivate through threats and coercion. In contrast, Theory Y assumes a generally positive view of people: that they want to learn, enjoy taking responsibility, and will do work that allows self-direction.

- **Maslow's Hierarchy of Needs:** Abraham Maslow believed that we have five levels of needs that we wish to satisfy. The most basic needs are physiological: food, water, clothing, and shelter. Once we satisfy those, we move to the next levels, safety and security, followed by social needs (friendship, belonging) and self-esteem. The highest level is self-actualization, where we realize our full potential. Maslow's emphasis on self-esteem has influenced managers to look beyond pay and benefits to motivate employees through appreciation, respect, advancement, recognition, and more challenging work.

- **Herzberg's Two-Factor Theory:** Frederick Herzberg's theory describes two types of factors that contribute to satisfaction. Motivating, or job satisfying, factors are intrinsic to the job, and hygiene, or job dissatisfying, factors are external. Herzberg's six motivators are achievement, advancement, growth, recognition, responsibility, and the work itself. (These are similar to Maslow's higher needs of self-esteem and self-actualization.) The six hygiene factors are compensation, supervision, working conditions, company policy, status, and interpersonal relationships at work. According to Herzberg's theory, motivators can increase satisfaction but do not create dissatisfaction. Hygiene factors can reduce dissatisfaction if they are not present. However, these extrinsic factors do not create satisfaction.

- **McClelland's Achievement Motivation Theory:** Employee needs can be grouped into three categories: affiliation (friendly interpersonal relationships), achievement, and power (control). Mangers who identify how these needs apply to their workers can develop suitable motivators.

- **Job Characteristics Model:** Hackman and Oldham's model focuses on the characteristics of the job as motivators, which include skill variety, task identity, task significance, autonomy, and task feedback. Before applying the model, however, a manager should consider the worker's needs and match the job to the worker. Not everyone is looking for challenging work that they perform independently, for example.

The theories described above are but a few of the many available. To read more about current studies and theories of motivation, use a search engine to locate relevant websites.

From Theory to Practice

The theoretical underpinnings of motivation can help enterprisers understand the many different needs that motivate today's employees. Money is no longer the primary motivator for most workers. Surveys reveal that interesting and meaningful work, career opportunities, empowerment/responsibility, a good work environment, and visible achievement are important factors to consider when developing appropriate motivational strategies.

The first step in determining the right motivational techniques for your employees is to ask them about their needs and opinions. What types of perks do your employees value? What needs do they have that, if met, would make them happier, more productive employees? How could their jobs be enhanced to increase their satisfaction?

Some of the best nonmonetary strategies to apply are the most obvious:

- Give your employees praise and recognition at the time it is earned.

- Show your appreciation and respect by saying thank you often.

- Communicate effectively and often.

- Be a coach for your employees.

- Offer many training opportunities to develop employee skills.

- Create a positive work environment.

- Provide flexible work schedules where possible.

- Allow employees to work from home one day a week.

- Some positions may lend themselves to job sharing.

- Schedule social gatherings.

- Host informal pizza parties, ice cream socials, or similar casual events.

We've mentioned several types of monetary incentives in the compensation section (bonuses, profit sharing, and stock options). Contests, trips, and other expensive reward programs are usually not viable options for many businesses. However, small rewards can go a long way in motivating employees. Even the smallest business can surprise employees with gift cards to a local restaurant or discount store, movie tickets, and similar gifts.

The way you design your firm's jobs can increase employee satisfaction. Job enhancement can motivate employees by making work more meaningful and increasing the sense of responsibility an employee feels. You can use three principal methods to develop, modify, or restructure jobs:

1. **Job enrichment:** Expanding a job vertically to increase its complexity and depth gives employees more autonomy and decision-making authority, a chance to use more skills, and greater control over the work. This enrichment increases the sense of achievement and overall satisfaction.

2. **Job enlargement**: Enlarging a job expands it horizontally by adding more types of tasks. It differs from enrichment because the tasks are at the same levels of skill and responsibility. This enlargement provides greater variety and can increase satisfaction by reducing boredom in certain types of jobs. Don't add too much to any one job, however, or employees may feel overburdened.

3. **Job rotation:** Moving workers through a series of jobs can raise interest and motivation. Also called *cross-training*, rotation allows employees to use more of their skills and learn new ones, and add challenge to jobs that have become routine. It benefits the firm as well, because employees become familiar with other areas of the organization and can cover other jobs if the need arises.

You will find numerous resources in books and online that provide many more ideas to motivate employees. For example, *1001 Ways to Reward Employees* by Bob Nelson offers real-world, proven ideas that companies use to show their appreciation. The resources section of his website, http://www.nelson-motivation.com/, also provides practical tips.

Or, simply enter "ways to motivate employees" into your favorite search engine to locate articles about motivational strategies.

17.7 ENTERPRISERS

Pamela Rodger's Neighborhood Is a Good Place to Work

Entering the waiting area of Rodgers Chevrolet's service department, customers know at once that it is no ordinary car dealership. Instead of bland, beige walls, customers are treated to brightly painted walls with a speedway theme.

Just as the waiting room is unusual, so is the dealership. Its owner is Pamela Rodgers, one of the few women to buy a car dealership directly. Her path to enterprising success took persistence and a willingness to learn the business from the ground up. While working at Ford Motor Company as a financial analyst, she learned about the Minority Dealer Program. Recognizing that as an African American woman, the time was right to pursue her dream of owning a dealership, she left Ford to get hands-on operations experience at a Buick dealership. Soon after, she met General Motors dealer Charles Harrell, who became her mentor and gave her a job at his Flat Rock dealership. "I shared my goals and ambitions with him, and he took me under his wing," says Rodgers. She credits Harrell with helping her gain acceptance into what was a men's club, introducing her to the right people and teaching her the jargon and other essentials.

It took four applications for Pamela to be accepted by Ford's and GM's minority dealer programs. In 1990, after completing Ford's training program, she and a partner received a dealership in Flint, Michigan—a town with nine GM plants. Selling Fords in GM's backyard was tough enough, but the economy in 1990 was weak as well. "It was impossible to make that boat float," she says. Soon after, her male partner died. "Women still weren't accepted into that business, and they didn't think a woman could do it. So we liquidated the store."

Harrell, who had bought a second dealership in Detroit, hired Rodgers to manage the Flat Rock location. When he decided to sell the Flat Rock store, whose performance lagged his new dealership, Rodgers bought it in 1993—even though it was cash poor and didn't have a huge customer base. "I wasn't ready to give up. I was still determined to become a dealer."

Her hard work and determination paid off as Rodgers built sales to $19 million and received the top "service satisfaction" designation in the Detroit area. When GM consolidated dealerships in 1996, they closed Flat Rock and rewarded her with a larger location in suburban Woodhaven, renaming it Rodgers Chevrolet. Since taking over the dealership, she and her team of 85 employees increased annual revenues from $37 million to an average of more than $75 million, as sales rose from 40 to 210 cars, and 1,200 vehicles a month visited the service department.

Providing superb service in every aspect of the car purchase process—from the phone initial contact with the receptionist or sales person to the showroom visit, arranging the purchase and financing, and servicing the car afterwards—is what drives sales at a car dealership. "The client is the reason we come to work every day. For your client to be happy, you have to have satisfied employees. You can teach ability, but there is no substitute for attitude," she says.

Serving customers well requires a motivated and loyal team of employees, and to do that Pamela provides good service *for* her employees. "It might not translate to the bottom line as quickly as negative reinforcement, but when it does . . . you build a strong foundation. Something that can grow and nurture, that has roots."

Just as Charles Harrell gave Pamela increasing responsibility as she proved herself, Pamela does the same for her employees. A supportive environment for them to work and grow and a willingness to delegate builds loyalty. Because she uses positive reinforcement to motivate them, her employees enjoy working for her and praise her direction, leadership, and motivation: "Pam demands excellence in a way where people want to give her the best that they have." "I have my own latitude." "She's really good to her employees." Maureen Monroe adds, "She's great to work for. I'm glad she gave me the opportunity to be the Parts Manager." Other women also hold key positions at the dealership, unusual in this industry.

Pamela Rodgers understands that you cannot build a business alone. "You need an ecosystem of customers, employees, suppliers, and vendors. If you are running a solid business and you pay people properly and you have in place your industry's best-practices, being nice will take you to the top. Everyone wants to do business with a nice person. Period."

Discussion Questions

1. What role did her mentor play in Pamela Rodgers' success?

2. How does Pamela Rodgers manage her key employees? Why are her employees loyal?

3. Pamela Rodgers has just learned that her business manager, who is responsible for handling the documentation for new and used car purchases and arranging financing for car buyers, is relocating out of state. Develop a plan to recruit and select a new business manager. What should Rodgers do to retain and motivate the person she chooses?

4. What strategies would you recommend to Pamela Rodgers to reward people for carrying out their jobs successfully? Should the service department have different measures of success than the sales department or the parts department?

Sources: Adapted with permission from Small Business School, the series on PBS, at http://smallbusinessschool.com; and "Pamela E. Rodgers Chevrolet Dealer Owner to be Honored by the Women's Automotive Association International," *PR Web*, September 13, 2006, http://www.prweb.com.

Summary

1. Enterprisers who want to grow their businesses must exhibit leadership characteristics and recruit other people to help manage and operate the firm. To be leaders, they must have a clear vision of the firm's future, share it with others, and take action. When delegating work, leaders must have a clear expectation of what is required and be able to describe it to others. Before asking anyone for help, including family and friends, know why you are asking this particular person, what you expect them to do, whether they have the skills for the work, and what they expect in return.

2. You can receive help from outsiders who are not directly employed by the firm and insiders who are employed by or under contract to the firm. Outsiders include mentors, board of advisors, board of directors, consultants, and service providers. Mentors are advisors with knowledge and insight about how to operate your type of enterprise, or enterprises in general. A board of advisors that meets regularly is another way to get informal guidance on issues facing the firm. These advisors should be people with business expertise and some with experience in a related industry.

3. A corporation's board of directors has legal responsibility for its actions and those of its employees, officers, and directors. Its structure is mandated in the corporate bylaws. The board helps management develop business plans and strategies, establishes policy objectives, monitors the company's business operations and financial performance. The board takes a big-picture view and usually appoints the corporate officers who oversee the company's daily operations. The board should include independent directors who can be objective as well as officers of the company.

4. Enterprisers often choose to hire consultants to handle projects that require specialized knowledge. Service providers offer ongoing services such as bookkeeping, accounting, maintenance and janitorial, waste management, landscaping, and other specialized areas where it is not cost-effective to hire a permanent employee.

5. Employees and independent contractors are hired by the firm to perform work. The hiring party has the right to control an employee's work and how it is done. It must withhold income taxes, withhold and pay social security and Medicare taxes, and pay unemployment tax for employees. In the case of an independent contractor, the hiring party controls only the result of the work and not how the contractor accomplishes the work. It does not have to withhold or pay any taxes for independent contractors.

6. Numerous federal and state regulations apply to employment issues such as discrimination in hiring, safe working conditions, and the hours worked. Discrimination laws are among the most important for employers to understand. Various equal-employment opportunity (EEO) laws prohibit specific types of employment discrimination in hiring and termination: race, color, religion, sex, age, national origin, and status as an individual with a disability or protected veteran.

7. A labor union is an organization of workers formed to represent its members by negotiating contracts and working arrangements through the collective bargaining process that involves representatives from the employer and the union. It then administers the agreements and resolves any problems that arise. Often the independent contractors in certain trades belong to unions.

8. The human resources (HR) management process begins with the development of an HR plan. The first step is a needs assessment and forecast of the jobs required to grow the firm, followed by job analysis and preparation of job descriptions that guide the hiring process, compensation, and performance reviews. All aspects of HR management require compliance with anti-discrimination and other laws. The job analysis determines the tasks and responsibilities of the position as well as the knowledge and skills the job requires. The analysis is the basis for the formal job description, which drives the rest of the hiring process. It includes the title, pay range, duties, responsibilities, required qualifications (knowledge, skills, and abilities), and reporting relationships.

9. Firms can use a variety of resources to find qualified job candidates. These resources include employee referrals, networking, and advertising on Web job boards, radio, television, local and regional newspapers and their print and online classified sections, and trade publications. Employment ads should clearly describe the position and its requirements and how to respond. Executive search firms and employment agencies are also sources of job candidates.

10. The selection process involves screening, interviewing, evaluating, checking references, and making an offer. Screening can be done by reviewing resumes and conducting brief phone interviews to identify the most qualified applicants, who are then invited to come for a personal interview. A successful interview requires preparation to set an agenda and develop questions. Before making an offer, perform reference and background checks.

11. The HR process doesn't end when an employee is hired. It also includes strategies to retain and motivate employees. Orientation programs help a new employee make a smooth transition to the firm. Training, both on the job and through external programs, enhances an employee's skills and improves job performance. Developing an employee handbook gathers all your policies in one place and in writing and can help your business to run more smoothly, save time, and prevent disputes. An employee handbook tells employees what you expect from them and documents what they can expect from your firm. A formal employee evaluation process helps employees understand the company's goals and their role in helping to reach them. It should include job expectations, career path, compensation, and advancement. A well-structured compensation program of wages or salary and benefits will help you attract and keep qualified employees.

12. Some small companies use professional employer organizations (PEOs) for many of their human resources functions. The firm continues to handle recruitment, hiring, promotion, and compensation decisions, while the PEO focuses on administration of payroll and benefits.

13. Motivated employees are more productive, more creative, more satisfied, and more committed to the firm. Understanding key theories of motivation helps managers to develop appropriate strategies for their employees. In addition to economic incentives, strategies such as positive reinforcement, meeting employee needs, job design, and rewards tied to job performance increase employee motivation.

Review Questions

1. What questions should an enterpriser consider before asking others for help?

2. How can mentors and boards of advisors help enterprisers to be more successful? How should you find and chose mentors and advisors?

3. What are the major differences between a board of advisors and board of directors? What are the responsibilities of directors?

4. Compare and contrast the role of consultants and service providers in the enterprise.

5. What factors determine whether a person is an employee or an independent contractor?

6. Briefly describe the major federal laws covering employment issues.

7. What is a labor union, and how does it achieve its objectives?

8. Summarize the steps in the human resources management process.

9. How does job analysis drive the hiring process? What should a job description contain?

10. Outline the steps you would use to recruit qualified candidates and to select an employee to hire.

11. Why are orientation and training, employee evaluation, and compensation programs important strategies for employee retention?

12. Discuss the reasons a firm should have an employee handbook and list what it should include.

13. What are the benefits of knowing how to motivate employees? Describe several important motivational theories and strategies that apply them.

Applying What You've Learned

1. Identify several people who would be valuable mentors for you and your enterprise. Why did you choose these people, and what advice do you want them to provide? Contact one or two and ask that person to become your mentor. Find out how they think they can best help you. Summarize your findings and share them with the class.

2. Make a list of the duties and time commitments you want your board of advisors to fulfill. Then identify people who are willing to serve on your enterprise's board of advisors. Ask them whether these criteria are reasonable and how they think they can best help you. Share your results with the class.

3. Identify the first three jobs you plan to hire for in your new enterprise. Select one position and develop:

   a. Its job description

   b. A job advertisement for the local newspaper and one for an online posting

   c. An interview guide to help you match the job's requirements with their skills and experience.

4. You have hired the most qualified person to fill the position you chose in question 3. What would you do to help the new employee make a smooth transition to your company and to further his or her professional development?

5. How would you structure your firm's employee evaluation program?

6. Prepare a brief description of the compensation and benefits plan for your enterprise. Include the types of incentive programs, if any, you will offer. Why did you choose this structure?

7. Based on the type of firm you plan to start and your answers to the prior questions in this section, what types of intrinsic and extrinsic motivational methods would you use to increase employee satisfaction? List several specific ideas you would implement.

Enterprisers on the Web

1. Use search engines to discover the many types of consultants who could assist your enterprise and their areas of expertise. Examples include graphic design consultants to prepare logos for the enterprise, website designers, marketing consultants, and consultants who could set up a purchasing or an accounting system. Develop a list of the most important and identify several you would consider hiring. Summarize key information for each, such as the services they offer, how much each consultant charges, and how they structure a work agreement.

2. Perform an online search for companies in an industry in which you would like to start your business. Select two of these companies and, using the company website, find a list of the board of directors. Using the Annual Report, Form 10-K, or website management biographies, examine their backgrounds and experiences. For each director, determine why the company has asked them to be on the board. What expertise do these people provide to that company?

3. Identify various ways to advertise for jobs online. Prepare a list of websites you might use, such as monster.com, careerbuilders.com, craigslist.com, and local and regional newspapers. Also look for specialized job sites that focus on a particular industry or job field (e.g., human resources and purchasing). Make a table and compare them in terms of cost, size, ease of use, and other criteria that you need.

4. Use an Internet search engine to find two or three employment manuals from enterprises similar to yours or that operate in a way that you admire. Divide the class into small groups. Choosing one set of manuals as a guideline, assign each person in the group several sections and prepare an employment manual for the enterprise. Have each group present and discuss their manuals.

5. Would leasing your employees from a professional employee organization (PEO) make sense for your company? Learn more about how PEOs operate and the benefits they offer at the site for the National Association of PEOs, http://www.napeo.org. Use the site's "find a member" service to locate providers who serve your area. Choose three and compare them in terms of services, quality of website, and other criteria. Summarize your findings in a report that includes your rationale for using a PEO or keeping your HR management in-house.

6. What types of employee benefits should you offer? Refer to the latest Bureau of Labor Statistics National Compensation Survey—Benefits, http://www.bls.gov/ncs/ebs/home.htm, and prepare a summary of benefits offered by private industries and the percentage of employers offering them. Which benefits would be the most important for your company, and why?

7. The Internet can help you create a meaningful rewards program for your company. Search for advice on employee recognition strategies at sites such as *Incentive* magazine, http://www.incentivemag.com, the U.S. Office of Personnel Management, http://www.opm.gov/perform/reward.html, About.com's human resources and employee recognition pages, http://humanresources.about.com, and others. Using the material you find there, outline the plan you would recommend for your company.

End Notes

1. Section adapted from Katherine Hansen, "Finding a Mentor," *QuintCareers.com*, http://www.quintcareers.com/mentor_value.htm (March 14, 2008); F. John Reh, "Mentors and Mentoring," *About.com: Management*, http://management.about.com (March 14, 2008); and "Seven Tips for Finding a Great Mentor," *Inc.*, April 2001, http://www.inc.com.

2. Section adapted from Laddie Blaskowski, "Developing a Board of Advisors," *EasyPeasy*, February 18, 2006, http://www.easypeasy.com/guides/article.php?article=184; Bruce Camber, "Create a Board of Advisors," *Small Business School*, http://smallbusiness school.org (March 15, 2008); and Alan Shulman, "Establish an Outside Board of Advisors," *Insurance Journal*, South Central Edition, July 18, 2005, http://www.insurancejournal.com/magazines/southcentral/2005/07/18/features/58458.htm.

3. Section based on "Board of Directors," *Small Business Notes*, http://www.smallbusinessnotes.com/operating/leadership/board.html (April 28, 2008); "Corporate Structure: Directors to Shareholders," *FindLaw for Small Business*, http://smallbusiness.findlaw.com/business-structures/corporations/corporations-structure.html (April 28, 2008); Glenn Faulkner, "Selecting a Board of Directors for the Emerging Company," John Pappajohn Entrepreneurial Center of the University of Northern Iowa, http://www.jpec.org/handouts/jpec63.pdf (March 26, 2008); "Finding a Director," *Directors Source*, http://www.directorssource.com (April 29, 2008); and Carter McNamara, "Overview of Roles and Responsibilities of Corporate Board of Directors," *Free Management Library*, http://www.managementhelp.org/boards/brdrspon.htm (April 28, 2008).

4. Section based on "Guidelines for Hiring Consultants," *The Consulting Exchange*, http://www.cx.com/guidelines.htm (May 7, 2008); "Hiring a Consultant: Ten Questions to Ask," *Sideroad.com*, http://www.sideroad.com/Consulting/hiring-a-consultant.html (May 7, 2008); and "Top 10 Mistakes Made

When Hiring Consultants," *AllBusiness.com*, http://www.allbusiness.com/human-resources/workforce-management-hiring-consulting/3996-1.html (May 7, 2008).

5. "Outsource My Bookkeeping?", *Samarak Business Services*, http://www.samarak.com/bookkeeping-center/outsource-your-bookkeeping.html (April 24, 2008).

6 "Industry-Specific Cleaning," *Cleaning Service Comparison*, http://www.cleaningservicecomparison.com/industry-specific-cleaning.jsp?id (April 24, 2008).

7. *Employer's Supplemental Tax Guide, Publication 15-A* (Washington, DC: Internal Revenue Service, 2008), pp. 4–9.

8. Adapted from Susan M. Heathfield, "Job Descriptions: Why Effective Job Descriptions Make Good Business Sense," *About.com*, http://humanresources.about.com (June 5, 2008); and Judith Lindenberger, "How to Write a Job Description," *Business Know-How.com*, http://www.businessknowhow.com/manage/jobdesc.htm (June 5, 2008).

9. Section adapted from Tracey Bowyer, "How to Write an Effective Online Employment Advertisement," *EzineArticles*, September 13, 2006, http://EzineArticles.com/?expert=Tracey_Bowyer; "How Do I Write an Employment Ad?" *Learnthat.com*, November 24, 2004, http://www.learnthat.com; Courtney Flaherty, "How to Write a Great Employment Advertisement," E-How.com, http://www.ehow.com/how_2150794_write-great-employment-advertisment.html (June 4, 2008); Patricia Van Zandt, "Writing Employment Ads—Times Are a Changing," Recruiters Network, http://www.recruitersnetwork.com/articles/printer.cfm?ID=136 (June 4, 2008); and "Writing Good Employment Advertising Copy," *Jobs in Planning*, http://www.jobsinplanning.com/employment-advertising-tips/writing-good-employment-advertising-copy/ (June 4, 2008).

10. Section based on "Conducting Employee Reviews" and "Employee Performance Reviews," *Gaebler Ventures*

Resources for Entrepreneurs, http://www.gaebler.com/resources-for-entrepreneurs.htm (July 1, 2008); and Margaret Steen, "Managers' Tips for Evaluating Employees," *Yahoo! HotJobs*, http://hotjobs.yahoo.com (July 1, 2008).

11. Section based on Carter McNamara, "Employee Compensation (in the U.S.A.)," adapted from the *Field Guide to Leadership and Supervision*, downloaded from Free Management Library, http://www.managementhelp.org (July 2, 2008); Pam Newman, "Determining Employee Compensation," *Entrepreneur.com*, August 31, 2007, http://www.entrepreneur.com; Lee Ann Obringer, "How Employee Compensation Works," *How Stuff Works*, http://money.howstuffworks.com/benefits.htm (July 2, 2008); and F. John Reh, "Compensation Planning for Your Employees," *About.com*, http://management.about.com/cs/people/a/CompPlanning.htm (July 2, 2008).

12. "FAQs About Benefits—General Overview," *Employee Benefit Research Institute*, http://www.ebri.com/publications/benfaq/index.cfm?fa=ovfaq1 (July 2, 2008).

13. "Using PEOs," *Gaebler Ventures Resources for Entrepreneurs*, http://www.gaebler.com/resources-for-entrepreneurs.htm (July 1, 2008).

14. Section based on Cary Dessler and Jean Philips, "Motivating Employees," *Managing Now* (Houghton Mifflin Company, 2008), pp. 404–431; and "Employee Motivation: Theory and Practice," *Accel-Team*, http://www.accel-team.com/motivation/ (July 11, 2008).

Managing the Enterprise

KEY CONCEPTS

1. Enterprisers should pay attention to, measure, and monitor themselves, their enterprise, and the environment in which their business operates. This attention requires thorough analysis of products, pricing, and people, using the information they gather to develop appropriate metrics. Emulating the strategies of highly reliable organizations and expecting and planning for the unexpected will help enterprisers identify, respond to, and resolve problems quickly. Studying the characteristics of excellent companies and the strategies companies use to transform themselves from good to great provides guidance on how to evaluate progress and success.

2. Enterprisers who are satisfied with their lives and look for ways to enhance their personal well-being are more productive. They recognize the signs of burnout and take steps to prevent and manage it.

3. Each company must determine the appropriate metrics to measure its progress, taking into account the type of business and its industry. Collecting relevant data and evaluating the metrics provides insights into enterprise performance and efficiency and helps managers improve operations.

Suppose you loved to fish but couldn't get enough live crickets for bait. Assuming that you are not the only one with this problem, you take the unusual step of starting a cricket farm. As it grows, you tire of the business and turn it over to your children, who grow the business into one of the world's largest suppliers of insect feedstock and related products and of reptiles for pet stores.

In this chapter's case, we'll meet the Fluker family, three siblings who took over Fluker Farms from their father. The business has flourished for more than 50 years as the second generation found new products and customers for their unique product line by paying attention to themselves, their company, and the environment.

18.0 Your Attention, Please

Now we'll turn our focus to ways to pay attention to, measure, and monitor the three most important aspects of your life: you, your enterprise, and your situation (the environment). In Chapter 16, we described how to monitor the financial aspects of your business to insure that your enterprise has enough cash to sustain its operations, as well as monitor whether the enterprise is earning a profit. The challenge in operating your enterprise, however, is finding the right measures to indicate whether your enterprise is successful or heading in the right direction. Often financial measures appear a bit too late to be useful. Because they are based on historical information, looking at financial measures is like looking in the rear view mirror to figure out what is up ahead. You are depending on the past while driving into the future.

For example, suppose you are measuring current sales levels compared to sales last month or last year. Today's decline in sales may reflect lost sales from customers who had unsatisfactory interactions with your employees several months ago. Rather than observing that sales are declining, measurements of customer satisfaction would provide more valuable information. This measurement will help you take action *before* customers take their business to a competitor.

Thomas H. Davenport, a professor at Babson College, suggests that one of the major ways that enterprises can compete successfully with other firms is through *analytics*, quantitative, fact-based decision making.[1]

Analytics involves the use of sophisticated information systems and rigorous analysis to measure how the enterprise is doing. Davenport labels companies that focus on analytics as having "information based strategies." They use the information they can gain from their enterprises, their customers, and the environment to identify better ways to operate more profitably. Firms can compete by using information they have in their enterprises about:

- *Products and inventory:* Companies like Dell make computers to order for their customers. They must monitor what components are needed to make computers that customers want and have a supply of the right components at the right time to fill these orders. Both Wal-Mart and Amazon also monitor their inventories to insure that the right products are available, there are no stock-outs, and that they do not carry too much inventory that may require marking down in price if demand is low.

- *Pricing:* The Marriott Hotel Company tracks the various price points for hotel rooms for particular days at particular places. It uses this information to insure that each hotel maximizes the number of rooms rented each day at the optimal price per room, maximizing the total revenue per day for rooms as well as for other services such as meals and convention space rentals.

- *Human capital:* A number of sports teams, particularly the Boston Red Sox in baseball and the New England Patriots in football, use analytics extensively to select the best players for certain positions. They analyze statistics to determine the success of particular positions on the team and to develop measures of how good particular players are as well as to determine their "value" and compensation. These championship-winning teams attribute part of their success to their ability to measure and identify star players and acquire them for reasonable salaries.

As these examples demonstrate, paying attention to the right information can drive the success of your enterprise.

This chapter offers you tools to stay more current in the management of your enterprise, so you can take

Highly reliable organizations (HROs)
Organizations that have fewer failures and make fewer mistakes.

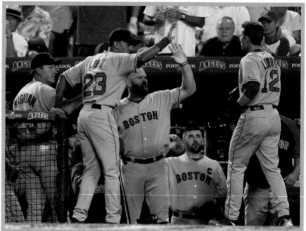
© Danny Moloshok/Reuters/Landov Media

action to correct problems as they arise. In addition to considering how your enterprise is doing, you should also pay attention to yourself and what is happening around you and your enterprise. As we have suggested throughout this book, creating and operating a successful enterprise does not necessarily insure that *you* will be successful. Your enterprise has its own path, irrespective of your own needs and interests. Balancing the interests and goals of you, your enterprise, and those involved with your enterprise (the environment) is difficult—but extremely important.

18.1 Paying Attention

In Chapter 6, "Discovering Opportunities," we described how to pay attention to new opportunities by increasing your "mindfulness," which is one way to see what is going on around you. In this chapter, we will look at a more thorough process for insuring that you notice critical issues in your life and in your surroundings: the "unexpected." In Chapter 6, we approached unexpected events as opportunities. By noticing them, we then developed ways to exploit them into viable enterprises. At this stage in the enterprising process, when the enterprise is established and growing, the "unexpected" is more likely to involve issues that might lead to problems in operating the business or in meeting new competitive threats. We want to identify potential pitfalls and avoid or change them before they become problems that become too big to handle.

In their book *Managing the Unexpected*, Karl Weick and Kathleen Sutcliffe discuss how we can learn from **highly reliable organizations (HROs)**—organizations that have fewer accidents or failures and make fewer mistakes. They studied organizations such as nuclear power plants and aircraft carriers, which have many opportunities for disasters (a nuclear reactor blows up, airplanes attempting to land or take off fall into the ocean). Surprisingly, both nuclear power plants and aircraft carriers have few accidents. How can this be the case?

Basically, all organizations encounter problems and errors in their operations. In some organizations these errors stay small, while in others these problems escalate into disasters. It is like the old nursery rhyme:

> For want of a nail the shoe was lost.
> For want of a shoe the horse was lost.
> For want of a horse the rider was lost.
> For want of a rider the battle was lost.
> For want of a battle the kingdom was lost.
> And all for the want of a horseshoe nail.[2]

The challenge is to pay attention to small problems that crop up in your life, your enterprise, and your surroundings and to deal with those problems before they become catastrophes. To become an HRO you need to do the following:

- Pay attention to and notice problems and errors before they become too big.

- Respond promptly so these problems stay small.

- Solve problems and adapt as necessary.

HROs have five primary strategies that help them manage their unexpected issues:

1. They are preoccupied with failure.

2. They don't simplify the reasons that things go wrong.

3. They are sensitive to their situations.

4. They are resilient when things go wrong.

5. They are willing to listen to people who have expertise and use their insights.

Let's take a closer look at each of these tactics.[3]

Signals from Failure

How can you be preoccupied with failure? First, you set up systems that encourage reporting of errors. For example, many businesses have suggestion boxes for employees to submit complaints about problems in their companies. HROs view these complaints and suggestions as signals about what is happening in the enterprise—what the front line employees see as problems to be solved.

Suppose you run a shoe store and one of your employees came to you complaining that customers were asking for red shoes. Your store only carries those styles in black. You could respond that you only sell black or take the complaint as a signal that color preferences in certain shoe styles are changing. You may decide to order some red shoes to meet the needs of your customers. Would you view a customer's complaint that your bathrooms aren't clean enough as something positive? Is the complaint an opportunity to solve a problem quickly, or do you see a complaining customer?

Encourage your employees to report when things are going wrong, such as when a sale isn't made, when a customer isn't happy, when the product you are manufacturing has a defect. You can't fix a problem if you don't know it is there. Make sure that your employees and customers are willing to give you bad news about the business. "Complainers" are an important source of knowledge about how your enterprise is doing. Listen to them.

It's Not That Simple

HROs don't simplify the reasons that things go wrong. They do not stop with the obvious, easy reason but challenge themselves to look for many different reasons why things might be going wrong.

What if you are running a restaurant and a number of the dishes coming out of the kitchen were overcooked? You might want to simplify this mistake by saying that the chef had a bad night or wasn't paying attention. However, there could be other reasons why dishes coming out of the kitchen are not up to par. The wait staff is submitting too many orders to the kitchen at the same time and overloading the kitchen crew. Perhaps the wait staff is not picking up orders on time and plates sit too long under the heat lamps. Or the timing of certain dishes is off, so that some of a table's orders sit too long before serving.

The source of the problems could be the kitchen crew, the wait staff, or the time that diners arrive. If too many patrons are seated at the same time, too many orders come into the kitchen at once, overwhelming both the wait staff and the kitchen crew. Maybe the kitchen or service areas are understaffed.

The reluctance to simplify asks us to look at all facets of the process, rather than just the most immediate. By looking for multiple sources of problems, the enterpriser will discover many more options to determine what actually causes the problems. We tend to put the blame on the people or processes immediately connected to the problem when we become aware of it. In the overcooked food example, our first instinct is to blame the chef—rather than other operational processes occurring before or after the food is prepared.

Sensitivity Counts

HROs are sensitive to their situations. Basically, problems and errors occur in the details of the situation. Noticing problems, therefore, is often less about the big picture and more about the specific situations where problems might occur.

For example, customer service begins with specific employees dealing with specific customers. If a customer is unhappy about a certain product or a particular sales encounter, the enterpriser needs to pay attention to what specifically is occurring. Is it the employee's attitude toward the customer? Are the right products available? Is there enough sales staff to serve customers promptly and efficiently? Is the store layout and space comfortable for customers?

HROs promote a culture where employees can talk about problems, and these problems are seen as opportunities rather than as complaints. In many HROs, managers and supervisors spend a lot of time working with front line employees to understand the problems and issues that employees face when solving customer problems. Managers ask employees about the kinds of problems they face.

Another way HROs show sensitivity is through flexibility. They have the ability to shift employees and resources to adapt to changes in the day-to-day situations. For example, an airline might have one employee assigned to take tickets and check passengers in at the boarding gate. If the plane needs to be boarded quickly, the airline can move employees from other positions over to the gate to take tickets as well to speed up the boarding process.

Resiliency and Humility Solve Problems

HROs are resilient when things go wrong. Organizations that make fewer mistakes, or who deal with mistakes sooner, are more likely to devote a considerable amount of time thinking about how things can go wrong. Then they devise ways to deal with these problems if they do go wrong. These resilient organizations focus on prevention and learn from mistakes after they occur. It is like having a fire drill at your home or at your place of work. While the chances of a fire are typically very low, the consequences of having a fire are very high. Fire drills therefore make sense because people know what to do if a fire occurs.

Organizations that pay attention have "fire drills" for all kinds of potential problems. If the organization has a fire, can critical records be saved? Will there be product available for customers that need it? In the case of a power outage, can critical machinery be started again quickly? If certain components for your products are not available from your supplier, do you have alternative sources of supply? How would the loss of a critical customer affect your organization? What if a key employee is sick? What if you are sick and can't work?

HROs assume that unexpected events will occur. They simulate these worst case scenarios to develop a response strategy to use if the situations actually happen. HROs have back-up systems in place to keep problems small and deal with them promptly. They cross-train employees to have several people, not just one, with the skills to accomplish critical tasks. The enterprise develops options for solving problems: It has not only Plan A and Plan B—but also a Plan C.

Finally, HROs are humble. They realize that mistakes and errors are likely, that success is never a sure thing. They continuously assume that problems will occur and never rest on their laurels.

Ask the Experts

HROs defer to and listen to people who have expertise. Typically, the person who has the actual experience is often the best person to tell others about the problem or error. Unfortunately, many individuals who become managers think that they should only talk to their direct subordinates: A manager only talks to a supervisor, who then must talk to the front line employee to find out what the problem or mistake was. Successful enterprisers and managers go right to the source and talk to the person most directly involved. That person has the most details about and insights into the situation. It is similar to the adage, "having boots on the ground" in a conflict. It is difficult to know what the combat situation is without having information from the people actually in the situation. Getting insights second-hand often means getting no insights at all into what is actually occurring.

Exhibit 18.1 provides suggestions to help you pay more attention. The gist of these strategies for paying attention is the recognition that things change. It is easy to become complacent about how and why we and our enterprise have been successful in the past. When we fail to pay attention, when we fail to have some humility about whether we and our enterprise continue to serve our customers well, mistakes and problems are likely to occur. Unless we pay attention to these problems while

they are small and manageable, we can quickly find that these issues grow into much larger problems that might overwhelm our capabilities to solve them.

18.2 Measuring What Is Important to You

An important idea that runs through many chapters in this book is that you need to pay attention to yourself, as an enterpriser. It is very easy to get lost in the

---

exhibit 18.1

Tips to Help You Increase Your Attention

Seek out and track down bad news.

Clarify how and what needs to be proved.

Pursue what seems to be inconsistent or out of the ordinary.

Take nothing for granted.

Define the near miss—what almost went wrong?

Investigate when and why the firm's constituents feel dissatisfied.

Examine how you deal with feedback so that you encourage employees to speak up.

Manage unexpected events and figure out why they occurred.

Restate your goals to incorporate mistakes that must not occur.

Increase your efforts at mindfulness.

Become aware of your weaknesses.

Develop humility and acknowledge your mistakes.

Learn from bad days by discovering why things went wrong and how things work.

Create a supportive environment for people to tell you when things are going wrong.

Encourage different viewpoints.

Encourage managers and employees to speak up.

Emphasize interpersonal skills so people know how to listen and interact effectively.

Cross-train employees to understand operations outside their own jobs and notice when things go wrong.

Encourage skepticism.

Be suspicious of good news.

Test your expectations.

Welcome uncertainty.

Source: Adapted from Karl Weick and Kathleen Sutcliffe, *Managing the Unexpected* (San Francisco: Jossey-Bass, 2001), pp. 159–171.

management of the day-to-day activities of the enterprise. Indeed, it is often very easy to get so focused on insuring that the enterprise succeeds that you fail to pay attention to whether you are successful. Part of the focus of Chapter 12, "The Enterprising Mind," was helping you determine how to develop a balanced life in regards to your commitments to self, work, family, and community as you created your enterprise. In this section, we will revisit some of these issues as well as provide some additional tools for helping you pay attention to your needs and aspirations as you live in the day-to-day realities of enterprising.

There are two sides to measuring how you are doing, as an enterpriser. On one side, the positive side, are signs that business is going well for you. You feel energized; you feel purpose and passion. On the other side, the negative side, there are the signs that business is not going well for you. Typically, these signs are signs of burnout.

It is well worth visiting the Values in Action website, http://viacharacter.org/, to take the "Inventory of Signature Strengths" test to determine what your five signature strengths are. The challenge for you is to evaluate whether your current situation supports your strengths. What we know from the literature and research on success is that our day-to-day lives need to engage our core strengths. Otherwise, we lose a sense of well-being and happiness.

Are You Happy?

How do you know if you are happy? Professor Ed Diener, a psychologist from the University of Illinois, has designed a quick, five-question test to help you find out. Go online and search for: Diener's Happiness test (it's available on several sites). Take the test and submit your answers to get a life satisfaction score and Professor Diener's analysis of what it means.

According to Professor Diener, it is possible to measure your happiness. A single key to happiness, however, does not exist. In Diener's findings, satisfaction with one's life is typically due to a combination of factors. Diener asserts that social relationships figure greatly into most people's perceptions of happiness. His research indicates that those who rate themselves as having a high level of "life satisfaction" tend to have "close and supportive family and friends." Conversely, people who lack such family and friends tend to rate themselves as "dissatisfied" with their lives. Diener's findings further indicate that "performance in an important role" at work, school, or in the home is a leading determinant in the individual's satisfaction with his or her life, as is a variable personal factor—such as "satisfaction with the self, religious or spiritual life, learning and growth, and leisure."

Additional sources of satisfaction can include health, one's general temperament, setting and seeking to achieve goals that stem from one's values, and a sense of "connection to something larger than oneself." Diener explains that when the sources of one's happiness are hindered, "they can become powerful sources of dissatisfaction," but he also points out that those who strive consistently to improve their situations, by making key changes in their lives or by allowing themselves time to recover from loss, tend to increase their satisfaction with their lives. Developing "more positive attitudes toward life and the world" can aid those who are dissatisfied in achieving greater happiness.[4]

Actually, we can measure happiness with one question: Do you feel happy, in general? A recent study examined the accuracy of using this question to measure happiness, based on a scale of 0–10. The study reported high positive correlations between this test and the Oxford Happiness Inventory and Professor Diener's Satisfaction with Life Scale.[5]

Based on these studies, we see that the amount of money one makes is not the total determinant of one's happiness. Social aspects of our lives are critical to how happy we feel. The goal is personal excellence: Being the best you believe you can be. As you pay attention to yourself, first ask yourself, "Am I happy?" Then dig further. Why are you happy or not happy? What activities do you think you are doing well? What energizes you? What are you not doing well? By comparing yourself at your best and at your worst, you engage in an ongoing self-discovery process.

Recognizing and Avoiding Burnout

Do you feel emotionally exhausted? Irritable? Frustrated and hopeless? You may be experiencing burnout. Signs of burnout are typically more mental than physical. Other feelings that indicate burnout include powerlessness, isolation, despair, cynicism, and apathy. You feel overwhelmed, sad, and empty. All your problems seem too big to overcome, and you are not motivated to take action to change the situation. You begin to pull away from family and friends.

Burnout is not the same as stress, although it may be seen as the result of too much stress. Exhibit 18.2 summarizes the differences between stress and burnout. Where stress creates feelings of too much pressure and too many demands, burnout leads to feelings of emptiness, of not caring, of pulling away and tuning out.

exhibit
18.2

Stress or Burnout?

Stress	Burnout
Characterized by overengagement	Characterized by disengagement
Emotions are overreactive	Emotions are blunted
Produces urgency and hyperactivity	Produces helplessness and hopelessness
Loss of energy	Loss of motivation, ideals, and hope
Leads to anxiety disorders	Leads to detachment and depression
Primary damage is physical	Primary damage is emotional
May kill you prematurely	

Source: Melinda Smith, M.A., Ellen Jaffe-Gill, M.A., Jeanne Segal, Ph.D., and Robert Segal, M.A., "Preventing Burnout," *Helpguide,* October 26, 2007, http://www.helpguide.org/mental/burnout_signs_symptoms.htm (July 2, 2008).

People who are under a lot of stress may still be able to function and regain control. Those who are burned out, on the other hand, see their situation as hopeless.

It's important to understand the differences between stress and burnout. Remedies for stress do not work for burnout. For example, an overly stressed enterpriser may be recharged by spending a relaxing long weekend away from work pressures, whereas the burnt out enterpriser might feel even more alone and empty from "enforced" relaxation.

How can you tell if you are experiencing stress or burnout? Take the 36-item quiz offered by Coping.org, found at http://www.coping.org/growth/burnout.htm. The list of feelings provides a comprehensive description of burnout.

When you experience job-related burnout, you are likely to respond in one of seven ways. According to the American Institute for Preventive Medicine, if you think you may be burnt out, ask yourself which of the following traits applies to you and why:[6]

1. **Perfectionism** (Everything must be perfect.)

2. **Overly unselfish** (My own needs aren't important.)

3. **Too passive** (I won't make waves.)

4. **Ostrich** (Ignore the problem.)

5. **Workaholic** (Over-compensates.)

6. **Scapegoat** (It's someone else's fault.)

7. **Guilt trip** (I should be Superman or Superwoman.)

Burnout can occur at any stage of the business. Often it strikes when the business is successful! The start-up and growth stages are highly stressful, but the stress tends to be more positive and energizing. It may abate as the enterprise passes through the other stages. Burnout, on the other hand, may set in when the thrill of creating the business is gone. Many entrepreneurs thrive on the challenge and feel let down and bored when they reach success and the novelty is gone.[7]

One of the ironies for enterprisers is that the job of enterpriser is, in the end, self-chosen. And as an enterpriser, you make choices and accept responsibilities that may lead to burnout. A critical part in dealing with burnout, then, is setting priorities and realistic goals and reevaluating them on a regular basis.

There are other ways to manage burnout:[8]

- Recognize your body's physical and emotional signals of burnout.

- Make time for exercise, which reduces stress levels before they get out of control. They also promote positive feelings that push away the negativity that comes with burnout.

- Reduce the number of hours you work. Too much overtime can lead to burnout.

- Set realistic goals and expectations. Keep your priorities in focus when you set goals. Don't expect so much of yourself that you set yourself up for failure.

- Know your limitations in all areas: family, job, and self.

- Learn to delegate.
- Simplify your life as much as you can.
- Use time management techniques so you have time to do things that satisfy you.
- Use relaxation techniques to unwind. Give yourself breaks during the work day to relax.
- Find ways to add variety to your job.
- Know what you can control or change and what you cannot change. Change what you can and let go of what you can't change.

How can you prevent burnout from taking over your life? First, identify the causes of your frustration so that you can develop appropriate strategies to deal with your personal sources of burnout. Then you will know what works best when you need to decompress. Don't be afraid to ask for help before your problems get out of hand. A support system of friends and colleagues gives you a sounding board to talk about issues and resolve them. Look for activities that contribute to your personal growth and pleasure, both professionally and personally. Multiple sources of self-esteem will make you feel better about yourself when one area is getting you down. Don't overschedule your life and learn when to say no to new projects or activities.

For more advice on coping with and preventing burnout, on the job or in general, check out these Web resources:

- "Preventing Burnout," *Coping.org*, http://www.coping.org/growth/burnout.htm.
- "Ten Tips for Preventing Burnout," American Institute for Preventive Medicine, http://aipm.wellnesscheckpoint.com.
- "Preventing Burnout," *Helpguide*, October 26, 2007, http://www.helpguide.org/mental/burnout_signs_symptoms.htm.

18.3 What Is Important to the Enterprise?

Along with paying attention to yourself, of course you must pay attention to the health of your enterprise and its progress toward goals. As with self-evaluation, you should look at both the positive and negative signals. Let's start with a big-picture view of the characteristics of successful enterprises and then look at more specific measures of achievement.

Measuring Excellence

What signs indicate whether an enterprise is operating in a successful way? What do successful enterprises look like? Many, many different books and articles have been written on the characteristics of successful businesses. Here we will offer a few major ways that thoughtful scholars and practitioners have attempted to address this issue.

Probably the first book to stimulate interest in the characteristics of successful organizations was *In Search of Excellence*, Thomas J. Peters and Robert H. Waterman, Jr.'s 1982 book. They selected successful American companies such as McDonald's, General Electric, Hewlett-Packard, and Procter & Gamble and examined them closely to discover the successful operational methods they had in common. *Search* promoted a new style of management that focuses on people, not numbers. Peters and Waterman identified eight characteristics of excellent organizations:

1. **A bias for action:** Use active decision making.
2. **Close to the customer:** Learn from the people served by the business.
3. **Autonomy and entrepreneurship:** Foster innovation and nurture "champions."
4. **Productivity through people:** Treat rank-and-file employees as a source of quality.
5. **Hands-on, value-driven:** Management philosophy that guides everyday practice; management showing its commitment.
6. **Stick to the knitting:** Stay with the business that you know.
7. **Simple form, lean staff:** Some of the best companies have minimal headquarters staff.
8. **Simultaneous loose–tight properties:** Give autonomy in shop-floor activities with centralized values.

These eight characteristics have been criticized over the years, and it has been pointed out that about one-third of the companies that Peters and Waterman used as exemplars of excellence were in serious financial difficulties five years after the book was published. We don't believe that this fact negates the insights the book provides or that these eight characteristics aren't issues that enterprises might strive to emulate. These ideas are still valid underpinnings of excellence, although they have changed with the times.

In an article commemorating the 20th anniversary of the book's publication, Peters writes, "*Search* was about people, customers, and action. Twenty years later, it's about ideas, liberation, and speed." He explains that we've gone beyond putting people first to paying close attention to people and the "good ideas that passionate, motivated, fully engaged people can generate." Because today's customers have more choices, companies must innovate and try new things, "To escape from the straitjacket of 'That's the way we do things around here.'" Customers don't care about how you do it; they want "the newest, fastest, best way." Action was a novel idea when *Search* was published, "because the norm was analysis-paralysis. So action—any action—was better than 'Ready, aim, aim, aim …' Today, it's all about speed. It's 'Fire, fire, fire.'"[9]

Peters' comments about why he and Waterman searched for excellence rather than growth or profits describe what enterprising is all about:

> Business isn't some disembodied bloodless enterprise. Profit is fine—a sign that the customer honors the value of what we do. But "enterprise" (a lovely word) is about heart. … About people throwing themselves on the line. It's about passion and the selfless pursuit of an ideal. … *In Search of Excellence*—even the title—is a reminder that business isn't dry, dreary, boring, or by the numbers. Life at work can be cool—and work that's cool isn't confined to Tiger Woods, Yo-Yo Ma, or Tom Hanks. It's available to all of us and any of us.[10]

Another important book on the characteristics of successful organizations is *Good to Great* by Jim Collins (New York: HarperBusiness, 2001). Collins identified 11 companies who underwent a major transition from underperforming in the stock market to a sustained improvement (15 years of performing three times better than the market and above their industries and peers). He then looked at the strategies these good companies used to become great companies. They include:

- **Level 5 Leaders:** Leaders with both "personal humility" and "professional will." Diligent and hard working, they have a strong desire to succeed and the commitment to make their organizations better. They define success in terms of the organization's achievements rather than their own.

- **Focus on Who before What:** Great companies start with getting the right team of people in place and don't depend on one person. Then they can look at products, operations, and strategies. They place a premium on quality work.

- **Confront the Brutal Facts:** Face reality, even when it is difficult. Don't lose sight of your goals, but temper them with the practicalities of the situation. This contributes to better decision making. Create an atmosphere where people feel free to be honest with managers about what works and what doesn't.

- **The Hedgehog Concept:** Look at the big picture and identify the unique thing that gives you a competitive advantage. To find this, look for something you are passionate about, can make money doing it, and are best at. Have a simple but clear concept of the business. Know what you can't be good at and avoid it.

- **Create a Culture of Discipline:** Find a balance between an entrepreneurial mindset and a sense of discipline. Encourage people to try new things and give them some independence but also have a well-defined workplace system. Hire people who are self-disciplined rather than enforcing it from above.

- **Use Technology Wisely:** View technology as a tool to enhance the company's competitive advantage and to promote and accelerate change, not as an end in itself.

- **The Flywheel and Doom Loop:** The Flywheel refers to positive momentum. Hard, steady work gets it in motion. As you keep it going, momentum builds, the company is able to overcome obstacles, and success comes more quickly. Change is gradual rather than dramatic. The Doom Loop is the attempt to find the magic bullet for success. Companies get into a downward cycle by scattered efforts to make a revolutionary discovery or change direction: an acquisition, a new CEO, or similar strategy. Such abrupt changes rarely lead to success.

Collins characterizes great companies as those with distinctive characteristics, unique operating methods, and strong core values that go beyond making money. They pay attention to their environment and revise their strategies to adapt to changing conditions.

Measuring and Monitoring Your Enterprise

Every enterprise will have different metrics that it will need to collect and evaluate. For example, an upscale gourmet restaurant is likely to monitor the number of reservations for tables for each night as well as the number of people who were unable to make reservations because the reservation list was already full. Other key items to track include what menu items sell the most, the size of the average check per guest, the time each table turns over, and the size and percentage of the tip per table. In addition, the restaurant might monitor its supplies of food and beverages ordered and served, along with other issues that it considers critical to its success.

Your own enterprise will have some critical areas that call for close attention and measurement, usually on a daily basis. In some cases, you may want to check certain items on an hourly basis. A **metric** is a measure of a key performance characteristic. These metrics offer insights into how the enterprise is doing. With some experience, enterprisers can look at these metrics and gain insights into how to manage the business in a more effective way. For example, a retailer's metrics may include the number of people who enter the store every hour compared to the number of people who purchase items during that hour and the average amount of a customer's purchase during the day. The owner of a fast food franchise may need to measure hourly demand for certain menu items to maximize efficiency and minimize wasted food.

In Chapter 16, we described how to perform ratio analysis using data from the firm's financial statements. By calculating these liquidity, activity, profitability, and debt ratios over time, enterprisers can monitor the firm's operations and profitability. Ratios serve as an early warning system of potential problem areas and can warn managers of possible problems. We'll refer back to this discussion as we recommend ways to manage assets, liabilities, and operations.

Let's now look at how to monitor your enterprise's operations through financial metrics covering assets, liabilities, income, and expenses.

Asset Control Systems

Look at the balance sheet for your enterprise. Every one of those asset categories can be monitored and often managed in a way to insure that your enterprise is more profitable and effective. Let's go down the list of assets and discuss how to monitor and manage them.

Cash. Every business needs cash, typically held in a checking account, to pay invoices from your suppliers, pay expenses, and meet payroll. As we suggested in Chapter 16, an enterprise typically needs a minimum of $1 cash for every $1 of current liabilities. Is that enough of a cushion for your enterprise? You may need to have more. By monitoring your cash levels, you will make sure you have enough to meet current and future needs.

What happens if your enterprise generates significantly more cash each month than it needs to operate? Many enterprisers deposit any excess cash in a money

market account that earns interest. If you are certain that you won't need this cash soon, you can invest it in certificate of deposit or other short-term securities that earn a higher interest rate. This way, the cash is earning money rather than sitting idle.

Accounts Receivable. As we discussed in Chapter 16, *accounts receivable* are funds owed to the enterprise from customers. Ideally, an enterprise would collect cash from a customer upon receipt of the goods or services provided. In many businesses, such as restaurants and retail stores, most customers pay right away. In other industries, credit terms allowing customers to pay weeks or months after the sale are standard and necessary to attract customers and increase sales. If most other businesses in your industry offer credit terms, you should, too.

The first step in collecting receivables promptly is to know how to determine whether a customer is credit worthy. You will need to educate yourself about credit and then develop a disciplined system that includes credit standards, credit applications, and a review process:

- **Credit policies and standards:** Decide on your policies for extending credit. Will you offer credit to all customers? What terms do you wish to offer, and how do they compare to industry standards? Do you want to offer discounts for early payment? What is the maximum debt ratio level at which you will offer credit?

- **Application procedures:** Create an application to collect necessary information, such as income amount and sources and other debt outstanding. You can search online for sample applications to use in preparing your own. Have your lawyer review your application to make sure it complies with federal and state laws. Get a written application from the customer.

- **Review of applications:** Review the information a customer provides to make sure that it meets your credit standards. Validate the information through a credit bureau or independent agency such as Dun & Bradstreet. Stick to your credit policies. If a customer doesn't meet your credit tests, do not extend credit. Giving credit to a payment risk will cost you in time and money later. (By law, you must notify a customer in writing of the reasons you are denying credit.)

Be sure you follow federal credit regulations such as the Fair Credit Reporting Act (FCRA), Equal Credit Opportunity Act (ECOA), the Fair Credit and Charge

Metric   Measure of a key performance characteristic.

Card Disclosure Act, and Fair Debt Collections Practices Act (FDCPA).

The next step is to evaluate your firm's accounts receivable by monitoring your average collection period, using the formula on page 430. This evaluation offers a big-picture view of your collections period. If you offer terms such as 2/10, net 30 (customers who pay within 10 days receive a 2 percent discount; otherwise the invoice is to be paid in full in 30 days), also track how many customers are taking the 2 percent discount and paying in 10 days and how many take the full 30 days. You should prepare an **accounts receivable aging schedule**, a list that shows each customer, how much the customer owes, the current amount due, and the amount that is 30, 60, or more days past due. Exhibit 18.3 shows a sample of a receivables aging schedule for a restaurant supplies distributor.

Most businesses update this schedule monthly. By analyzing your receivables aging you will spot possible cash flow problems before they occur and identify which customers are taking longer than the 30 days to pay. You should also investigate the causes behind month-to-month changes. Do they result from a change in your credit policy? A billing problem? Will this change in accounts receivable affect next month's cash inflows?

When customers pay late, your cash flow suffers. At what point should you contact a customer to find out when the invoice will be paid? Many enterprisers contact customers when their payment is seven days past due. Even a week may be too long, however. From experience, we know that as the days overdue increase, the likelihood of payment diminishes. Therefore, monitoring accounts receivables and following up with late payers are critical actions for any enterprise that wants to receive payment. The sooner you begin the collection process, the better your chances of getting paid.

You will probably want to stop offering credit terms to customers whose accounts become more than 60 days past due or who habitually pay late.

Exhibit 18.4 summarizes common strategies to improve receivables collections.

Accounts receivable aging schedule   A list that shows each customer, how much the customer owes, the current amount due, and the amount that is 30, 60, or more days past due.

exhibit
18.3

Accounts Receivable Aging Schedule

Accounts Receivable Aging Report
The Kitchen Table Company
September 30, 2009

Customer Name	Total Accts. Rec.	Current	1–30 Days Past Due	31–60 Days Past Due	Over 60 Days Past Due
Quick Burger	$2,610	$1,300	$500	$505	$305
Shayne's BBQ	2,735	1,800	935	—	—
Tessa's Treats	2,450	2,450	—	—	—
Brew Pub	1,328	—	1,328	—	—
Dine 'n' Wine	2,243	1,137	604	502	—
Enzo's Eats	809	405	404	—	—
Asian Delight Cooking School	650	650	—	—	—
Gourmet to Go	1,345	1,345	—	—	—
Total	$14,170	$9,087	$3,771	$1,007	$305

exhibit
18.4

Techniques to Improve Receivables Collections

Establish policies for extending credit and review credit reports before granting credit terms.

Have a systematic collection plan that includes automatic trigger dates to send overdue payment notices.

Have your sales people explain credit terms to customers.

State payment terms clearly on the invoice or in the contract, along with penalties for late payment.

Invoice promptly, with order shipment if possible.

Apply payment rules consistently.

Send a reminder to pay several days before the due date.

Don't procrastinate; call or email the customer as soon as the invoice becomes late.

Have a standard set of letters or emails ready to send.

Use sales people to help with collections, as they know your customers best.

Follow up letters or emails with phone calls or personal visits.

Be firm: Ask for a commitment on when a customer will send payment and follow up.

Find out why the payment is late and work toward a mutual solution.

Be flexible and work out a repayment schedule to accommodate extenuating circumstances.

Remind debtors that late payments harm their credit ratings.

If all else fails and the amount overdue is sizable, turn the account over to a collection agency.

Inventory. If your enterprise sells or provides goods to customers or you manufacture goods to be sold, you must establish systems to account for and monitor inventory. Unless you make sure that you have the right products, raw materials, and work in process available at the right time, you will not be able to supply the right product when your customer wants it. If you have the wrong product or don't have the product to sell (a stock out), you've lost a sale—and often a customer as well.

How do you know whether you have enough inventory on hand? You must pay attention to and monitor it. Many retail stores purchase inventory control systems that link the cash register to a database that keeps track of every item you sell. When the sale is made, you know how many more of that particular product you have on hand. Some systems will automatically order more of a particular product when you drop below a specified level.

We suggest that you look for systems that can manage your inventory in real time to show you at what you have in stock at any moment. Otherwise you will end up having to do manual counts frequently. Real-time systems are especially important for enterprises where inventory is the primary asset.

You will have to perform a manual inventory count at least once a year to know whether your actual physical inventory matches what your inventory control system says. This count will identify goods and items lost due to theft or damage. Eventually, your inventory turns into sales and profits. Without knowing the true state of your inventory, you don't have a good sense of whether the firm will be profitable.

Equipment. A list of all of your capital equipment and the associated depreciation schedule for each piece of equipment is required to monitor these assets. All equipment depreciates, and you are entitled to deduct the decrease in value of your assets from your income. Many legal issues are involved with the amount of depreciation you can take for particular asset categories, such as automobiles, trucks, heavy machinery, computers, and so on.

Liability and Payables Management

As noted in Chapter 15, trade credit is an important source of funding for companies. Maximizing trade credit requires managing your accounts payable wisely. The key is to extend your average payment period as far as you can—without jeopardizing your creditworthiness—by strategic timing of cash outlays.

Payables management is often overlooked as enterprisers focus on receivables collection. However, payables have an advantage: you control when the payments occur, rather than having to wait for customers to pay you. Here are some suggestions to help you manage payables:

- Prioritize bills. Not all should be paid right away, or even on time. Use the full credit period to preserve cash. The highest priority vendors are ones with critical supplies or services. Know which vendors have no penalties for late payment.

- Compare the benefit of taking discounts for early payment to the advantage of holding cash longer. Don't assume that discounts are worthwhile. Consider the effect of early payment on the firm's monthly cash flow.

- Consider credit terms as well as the price of goods when selecting a vendor. A slightly higher price and more payment flexibility may be a better choice than the lowest price.

- Develop a good relationship and open lines of communication with your suppliers, which will serve you well if you need to negotiate special payment terms.

- Have more than one supplier where possible, so you aren't tied to one particular vendor.

- Don't be afraid to negotiate for better payment terms, lower prices, and quantity discounts.[11]

Expense Controls

Operating ratios are particularly helpful in controlling expenses. In addition to the net profit margin ratio described in Chapter 16, you should take a more detailed look at the ratio of expenses to sales. A **common-size income statement** provides a quick way to track expenses. Rather than dollar amounts, it expresses each expense category as a percent of sales. Exhibit 18.5 shows this statement for Acme, Inc., a manufacturing company. By comparing the percentages over several time periods,

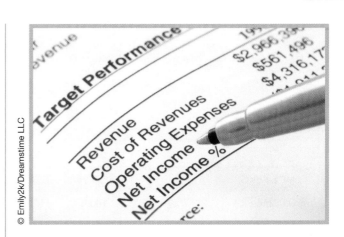

© Emily2k/Dreamstime LLC

you can see how expenses move in relationship to sales. For example, if Acme's general and administrative expenses had typically been about 5 percent of sales and over the past two years rose to 5.8 percent, managers would investigate the reasons by looking at the expenses that make up this category. If the gross profit margin were rising instead of falling, they would look into the costs of raw materials and direct labor. If this trend continues, they might want to reevaluate product prices.

Measuring Productivity and Conduct

Financial metrics offer a quantitative method to evaluate the firm's progress. On a more subjective level, how do you measure a firm's success in terms of work productivity? This measurement is much harder, of course. An employee may be working, but is he or she making progress toward a goal? Some tasks are easy to measure because you can see when they are completed or have a tangible finished product—for example, an assembled item ready for sale or a marketing brochure. Multi-step tasks or projects are more difficult to measure because the intermediate progress is not readily apparent.

Determining how to measure productivity at a particular firm calls for creativity on the enterpriser's part.[12] In this case, one set of metrics does not fit all. While it's easy to measure such things as hours worked, sales calls made, emails sent, and reports written/presented, these metrics tell us nothing about progress toward a goal or quality of the work, only activities that were completed.

Common-size income statement   An income statement that shows each expense category as a percentage of sales rather than as a dollar figure.

exhibit
18.5

Common-Size Income Statement

Acme, Inc.
Common-Size Income Statement

	2009	2008	Analysis	Comments
Net Sales $	$256,950	$223,400	better	Additional sales staff increased unit sales
Net Sales	100.0%	100.0%		
Cost of Goods Sold	61.2	63.3	better	Found lower cost materials supplier
Gross Profit	38.8%	36.7%	better	
Less: Operating Expenses				
Selling expense	9.4%	8.3%	worse	Hired another salesperson
General and administrative expenses	5.8	5.4	worse	Salary increases
Depreciation and amortization	6.7	7.1	better	
Rent	2.1	2.4	better	
Total Operating Expenses	24.0%	23.2%	worse	
Operating Profit Margin	14.8%	13.5%	better	
Less: Interest expense	1.9	2.6	better	Floating rate debt interest rate dropped
Net profits before taxes	12.9%	10.9%	worse	
Less: Income taxes	2.3	2.9	better	
Net Profit Margin	10.6%	8.0%	better	Increase in operating expenses offset by lower cost of goods sold and nonoperating expenses

Measuring progress requires first defining the tasks and setting goals that the work accomplishes. Then you can evaluate how the task contributes to reaching specific goals. Possible categories to consider, for both individuals and teams, include:

- Progress toward stated goal
- Whether quality levels are acceptable
- Challenges overcome/problems resolved
- Barriers to further progress
- Employee morale
- How to improve future efforts

These qualitative measures require that managers talk to their employees and ask the right questions. Quantitative measures may not apply to creative endeavors. It may take twice as long to find a high quality solution as an average one.

Another difficult area to evaluate is effectiveness of the company's code of conduct. In Chapter 8, we described the importance of having an ethics plan, or code of conduct, and how to develop one for your company. Once you have a code and implement it, how do you evaluate it? Does it meet accepted standards not only in the United States but also worldwide? The Enterprising Ethics box suggests an approach to this issue.

ENTERPRISING ETHICS

Does Your Code Measure Up?

As we discussed in Chapter 8's ethics box, a formal code of conduct states a company's values and standards clearly to all stakeholders. Whether your company is public or private, a code of conduct is a valuable document to guide your business practices. A code is mandatory for public companies in the United States, and numerous international organizations and regulatory bodies recommend that companies develop comprehensive codes that foster corporate responsibility. As a result, widespread support exists throughout the global business community for a corporate social contract based on a universal set of ethical principles and standards.

We provided basic guidelines for writing a code of conduct in the earlier box and revising it as situations change. The better the code, the more likely it is to be an effective tool. However, most companies that create a code do not have adequate metrics to monitor its implementation. A recent survey revealed that most companies track only a few metrics, such as the number of employees completing training. Fewer than 10 percent of companies have any metrics that relate to best practices, making it difficult to evaluate the code's effectiveness and how to improve it.

If you have a code, how can you determine whether it includes the right provisions to achieve its purposes? How can you make a good code better?

One useful tool is the Global Business Standards Codex, which is derived from close analysis of five internationally respected sets of broadly based code guidelines, the codes of 14 major multinational corporations and nine companies in emerging markets, and U.S. regulatory and legal sources. Developed at the Harvard Business School, the Codex brings together into one comprehensive format the basic ethical principles that give a code legitimacy as well as the standards for conduct. These principles and standards have a broad base of support worldwide and provide a starting point to help companies develop their own codes, which they can customize for their own situation. The Codex also serves as a benchmark against which to evaluate an existing code of conduct.

The survey authors grouped the standards into eight categories of ethical principles, summarized below:

1. *Fiduciary principle:* Act as a fiduciary for the company and its investors. Conduct the company's business with diligence and loyalty. Avoid conflicts of interest.

2. *Property principle:* Respect and protect the property and the rights of company assets, including intellectual property, and those of competitors. Do not steal or misappropriate company resources.

3. *Reliability principle:* Honor your commitments, including promises, agreements, and other voluntary undertakings, whether implicit obligations or in formal contracts.

4. *Transparency principle:* Conduct business truthfully and openly. Avoid deceptive acts and practices and disclose material information in a timely manner while respecting obligations of confidentiality and privacy.

5. *Dignity principle:* Respect the dignity of all people. Protect the health, safety, privacy, and human rights of others; refrain from coercion; and adopt practices that enhance human development in the workplace, the marketplace, and the community.

6. *Fairness principle:* Engage in free and fair competition, deal with all parties fairly and equitably, and practice nondiscrimination in employment and contracting.

7. *Citizenship principle:* Act responsibly, obey the law, and actively work to improve the community.

8. *Responsiveness principle:* Respond to those with claims and concerns relating to the company's activities. Support community efforts and policies for economic and social development.

Within each principle, the Codex lists the standards that support each principle, grouped by key concepts and the constituency the standard affects. The table below presents a representative list of concepts, constituencies, and standards.

We recommend that you read the complete article in the December 2005 *Harvard Business Review* for a more complete review of code of conduct best practices.

(continued)

Enterprising Ethics (*continued*)

Principle	Concept	Constituency	Standard
Fiduciary	Loyalty	Company Investors	Do not accept excessive gifts and entertainment. Do not use insider information to trade in the company's stock.
Property	Theft	Company	Protect company assets, including confidential and proprietary information, funds, and equipment.
		Competitors	Respect rivals' personal and intellectual property rights.
Reliability	Contracts	Suppliers and Partners	Pay suppliers and partners on time and in accordance with agreed-on terms.
	Commitments	All	Fulfill implicit and explicit obligations to all constituencies.
Transparency	Disclosure	Customers	Provide accurate information about the content, use, and maintenance of products.
	Objectivity	All	Adhere to independent auditing and financial-reporting standards.
Dignity	Respect for the Individual	Employees	Adopt work practices that respect employees' dignity and human rights.
	Privacy and Confidentiality	Customers	Protect confidential customer information.
Fairness	Fair dealing	Investors	Deal fairly with minority share owners.
	Fair competition	Competitors	Do not engage in any form of collusion with rivals.
Citizenship	Law and Regulation	Public	Obey environmental laws and standards.
	Civic Contribution	Public	Support employee involvement in civic affairs.
Responsiveness	Addressing Concerns	Customers	Provide timely service and remedies for customer complaints.
		Employees	Respond to employees' suggestions, requests, and complaints.

Discussion Questions

1. Take the principles in the Global Business Standards Codex and develop specific metrics for measuring how well an enterprise meets these conduct guidelines.

2. Identify a publicly held company in your enterprise's industry. Go to its website and find its code of conduct. Evaluate the code of conduct using the metrics you developed in question 1. How well does it rate?

3. Identify which of these metrics are the most important to monitor the performance of your planned or established enterprise. Why would you use these particular metrics?

4. Would these conduct principles and metrics differ for other kinds of companies? Why?

5. Do you think these code of conduct principles would be different for companies operating in different countries? Why?

Sources: "Companies Show Major Weaknesses in Setting Corporate Codes of Conduct," *Corporate Board,* March–April 2008, p. 27; and Lynn Paine, Rohit Deshpande, Joshua D. Margolis, and Kim Eric Bettcher, "Up to Code: Does Your Company's Conduct Meet World-Class Standards?", *Harvard Business Review,* December 2005, pp. 122–133.

18.4 Monitoring the Environment

How do we insure that we are paying attention to our surroundings so that new events and situations don't blind-side us with problems and crises? For example, was it possible for enterprises involved in building houses in 2007 to see that the mortgage lending industry might have provided financing to many unqualified buyers? Was it possible for home builders to brace themselves for a decline in housing sales? Was it possible for American automobile manufacturers to have seen and then prepared for rising gas prices in 2008?

As we began this chapter with techniques about paying attention, we end the chapter with some additional suggestions for how enterprisers might improve their ability to see what might be coming up ahead.

In their article "Scanning the Periphery," George Day and Paul Schoemaker suggest that the organizations that are best at seeing what will occur next first learn from the past.[13] They seek to understand where they have been blind before. They look back a few decades and consider how the major social, technological, economic, environmental, and political changes currently affect their organization.

If you look at all of the changes that have occurred, particularly the ones that affect your enterprise, which changes in the environment did you correctly identify? Which changes did you miss completely? Why do you think you missed these changes? For example, if your business involves providing Web design services, have you been affected by competition from India or other non-American organizations? Will the increasing popularity of free interactive services such as Skype, which enable people to converse and see each other on video for free, change the dynamics of your business model? How important was face-to-face contact in selling and providing services in the past? Will face-to-face contact continue to be an important selling point, or not?

Look to emulate enterprises that do a great job of responding to changes in the environment. How do these enterprises keep themselves sensitive to environmental changes? Who are the exemplars in your industry that seem to always know what is about to happen and take advantage of the new opportunities that these changes bring? In Chapter 6, we identified a number of changes that are likely to occur in the environment over the next 10 years. How will these trends affect your enterprise, now, and in the future? Are you prepared for these changes?

As we mentioned earlier in this chapter, one of the best ways to pay attention to changes that are occurring in

© Konstantin Sutyagin/Used under license from Shutterstock

your environment is to pay attention to the complainers. People who complain, be they customers or employees or suppliers can offer you insights into what might be important upcoming changes in the environment. A complainer can be seen as a "leading indicator" that something might be changing and that it might be valuable to pay attention to these complaints and work to respond to them.

Do you and your enterprise have the capabilities for peripheral vision? Here are a few key questions to ask:

- How important is it for you to know what is going on around you?

- How far into the future do you look? Are you thinking more than five years out?

- Are you willing to test basic assumptions about how success in your industry occurs?

- What do you measure as an "early warning" system that things are changing?

- Is your enterprise able to make mistakes and learn from them?

18.5 ENTERPRISERS

If It's Bugging You, Contact Fluker Farms

Richard Fluker's unique family business arose to fill a personal need. "I've always been an avid fisherman, but a lot of times you'd go to the bait shop and they didn't have the bait on hand," he says. In 1953, he started a cricket farm to supply bait shops and made it a full-time venture in 1958 after losing his job with a large corporation. He then expanded his cricket sales to zoos and educational and research institutions that used crickets as food for reptiles, birds, and other animals. Soon annual cricket sales reached about $500,000.

As the business grew, however, Richard Fluker's interest waned. Rather than continue and experience burnout, he retired and turned over the business to his three children, David, Howard, and Diane. David Fluker, the company's president, saw a larger target market beyond regional bait shops and a few pet shops. "If I have one pet shop, why can't I get them all?" he asked himself. Purchasing a list of the 4,000 pet shops in the United States, he designed a simple postcard about the crickets and sent out a bulk mailing. "We got a phenomenal response," David says. "It wasn't very expensive, and for the cost it was probably the most bang for the buck." After using mailings for two years, he wanted to add a telemarketing campaign but didn't have funds for a sales staff. He took a creative approach and advertised for part-time college students from nearby Louisiana State University. This approach proved to be the ideal way to find articulate and energetic salespeople whom he could hire on an as-needed basis.

Next, the Flukers considered other feeder insects their current customers might use. "If they buy crickets, well, chances are they also buy mealworms," says David. "We were right." At Howard's suggestion, they added reptiles: "Why don't we do iguanas, because they're a bread-and-butter item within the pet industry?" Raising reptiles has become a second major product line for Fluker, with Howard in charge of Fluker Farms International (FFI) in El Salvador, one of the world's largest captive reptile breeding facilities.

While the Flukers found success in breeding insects and reptiles and in selling related products, not every idea they tried worked as well. For two years, they tried raising mice but couldn't fill their orders because of difficulty raising the mice, perhaps due to climate issues. The estimated cost of items they could not use when that venture failed, along with labor and time, was close to $100,000. David acknowledges, however, that you have to be willing to take chances and try new things—and to know when to call it quits.

Since its early days, "Serving Satisfied Customers" has been the Fluker Farms motto. "A satisfied customer always gives you future business," Richard says. Fluker Farms guarantees live delivery on overnight shipments. Employees monitor the weather, and the company offers its customers shipping options. Unless otherwise specified, the order ships regardless of weather. If the insects are dead on arrival, Fluker will replace them but the customer pays freight charges. In the winter, the customer can ask Fluker to hold the shipment for up to one week until the customer's night temperature reaches acceptable levels.

Keeping customers satisfied requires loyal and productive employees. "Unfortunately this is a hot, dirty job, so basically we try to pay a little better than the average hot, dirty job," David says. "And that's how we've managed to keep a lot of our workers. It's not easy to find people. We do have a turnover rate because of the job. It's just not a real clean, you know, office-type job." Fluker also offers a better employee benefits package than other farms—year-end bonuses, partial payment of health insurance for employees and their families, paid vacation and sick time, and paid holidays—many of which are unusual in this type of industry.

Working together, the siblings have grown Fluker Farms into one of the world's largest producers of insect feedstock and related products and manufacturers of bird, ferret, and reptile products. Today, the Port Allen, Louisiana, company ships 2.5 million live crickets and hundreds of thousands of mealworms and super worms each week to bait shops, pet stores, zoos, and educational institutions. Under Howard's direction, FFI's 150 employees produce 500,000 iguanas, 40,000 bearded dragons, and many other reptiles and specialty animals.

Running a family business can stress the sibling relationship, but the Flukers have made it work. "We've never really disagreed on the big ideas," says Howard. "We just disagreed on how to implement them." Living in different countries helps, because neither Howard nor David is involved in the day-to-day activities of the other company unit. "If it's a big decision, my family and I all get together and we discuss it, but I know that my suggestions and what I want to say carry a lot of weight," adds David. "They'll typically go with what I want to do, provided it's not totally ludicrous. But at the same time, that's a lot of motivation in itself, knowing that you're the guy that's got the ball, and if you drop the ball, well, then you've totally hurt the lives of your father, your sister, your brother, my wife, and all their families."

Discussion Questions

1. Identify five metrics to measure how the enterprise is doing. For each metric, indicate why this metric is important to measure and monitor.

2. For each of the following categories, identify three metrics that could serve as an "early warning" for Fluker that changes are occurring: (a) internally (in the enterprise's operations), (b) with the enterprise's customers, and (c) in the enterprise's environment.

3. How would you measure success for Fluker Farms as an enterprise, using the criteria in the chapter's sections on excellence?

4. How would you measure success for the Fluker family, as a family, and for each member of the family? How well do they pay attention to themselves, the company, and their environment?

5. Evaluate Fluker Farms on the "Code of Conduct" criteria listed in the ethics box.

Sources: Adapted with permission from Small Business School, the series on PBS, at http://smallbusinessschool.com; and Fluker Farms website, http://www.flukerfarms.com.

Summary

1. Enterprisers should pay attention to, measure, and monitor themselves, their enterprise, and the environment in which their business operates. This attention requires thorough analysis of products, pricing, and people, using the information they gather to develop appropriate metrics.

2. Highly reliable organizations (HROs) have fewer accidents or failures and make fewer mistakes. They identify, respond to, and resolve problems quickly, thereby keeping them small and more manageable. The five strategies they use—preoccupation with failure, not simplifying reasons for things going wrong, sensitivity to situations, resiliency, and willingness to listen—provide a good game plan for enterprisers to implement.

3. HROs encourage their employees to speak up, whether to report errors or offer suggestions to improve operations. Complaints are another sign that changes may need to occur. Listening to bad news is a good way to head off problems in their early stages. HROs don't stop at the obvious reason something goes wrong. They dig deeper to truly understand why things go wrong, identifying many possible causes to find the one at the root of the problem. This sensitivity to details pays off, as does flexibility in adapting to changing situations.

4. HROs assume that unexpected events will occur and plan ahead for them with response plans and backup systems. This makes an organization resilient and often prevents difficult situations from arising in the first place. They continue to be alert for possible mistakes in the future rather than being content with the status quo. They don't assume that they know all the answers and seek out those with expertise.

5. Enterprisers who are happy are more productive. They are satisfied with their lives and look for ways to enhance their personal well-being. They recognize the signs of burnout, such as emotional exhaustion, irritability, a sense of hopelessness, despair, cynicism, and emptiness. People respond to job-related burnout in different ways, from perfectionism to passivity or being a workaholic. Knowing how to manage burnout is critical for enterprisers, who should develop a supportive network and satisfying activities outside of work.

6. Measuring the progress of your enterprise begins with understanding the characteristics and best practices of excellent companies, which include Peters and Waterman's eight characteristics: decisiveness, paying attention to customer needs, fostering innovation, focusing on people and treating them well, using a hands-on, value-driven management style, sticking to the core business, keeping the organization lean, and giving autonomy where appropriate. Collins defines great companies as those with distinctive characteristics, unique operating methods, and strong core values that go beyond making money. They pay attention to their environment and revise their strategies to adapt to changing conditions. Collins' strategies for making good companies great include humble yet diligently hardworking leaders, focusing on people before products, willingness to face reality, seeing the big picture, creating a culture of discipline, using technology as a tool, and creating positive momentum.

7. Every enterprise will have different metrics that it will need to collect and evaluate. These metrics are based on the type of business and its industry. Identifying and tracking critical areas will provide insights into how the enterprise is doing and also help managers improve operations. Tracking financial statement ratios over time is one way to monitor the firm's operations and profitability and also serves as an early warning system of potential problems. Managing accounts receivable calls for establishing disciplined policies for extending credit and collecting receivables and monitoring the firm's average collection period. An aging schedule is helpful in analyzing the pattern of customer payments. Inventory management systems and equipment lists are equally important tools for asset management.

8. On the expense side of the balance sheet, knowing how to extend accounts payable without jeopardizing the company's creditworthiness helps companies maximize trade credit and manage cash flow. A common-size income statement provides a detailed look at expenses in relation to sales.

9. Measuring productivity calls for both quantitative and qualitative measure. Quantitative measures such as hours worked or sales volume are easy to track. It's important to look at subjective factors as well: quality of work, employee morale, and progress toward goals. These metrics are more difficult to define.

10. By paying attention to the environment in which the business operates, enterprisers are able to respond and adapt to new events and situations. Companies that are sensitive to environmental changes are positioned to take advantage of new opportunities and more able to prevent problems and crises.

Review Questions

1. How can analytics and information-based strategies help companies to pay closer attention to their environment?

2. What strategies do HROs use to manage the unexpected? Provide an example of a way to apply each strategy.

3. Differentiate between stress and burnout. What are the symptoms of burnout, and how can enterprisers prevent burnout from occurring?

4. Summarize the eight characteristics of excellent companies that Peters and Waterman identify.

5. Briefly describe each of Collins' seven strategies to make good companies great. Which have the most applicability for your planned or existing enterprise, and why?

6. Why should managers develop metrics to track and monitor the firm's performance? What role do financial ratios play?

7. Describe the parts of a receivables management system. How does an aging schedule help to improve collections? List five strategies to improve collections.

8. What are the benefits of an inventory control system?

9. How should a firm manage its accounts payable, and what strategies can it use to do this effectively?

10. What can you learn by creating and analyzing a common-size income statement?

11. Why are qualitative measures of productivity important to measure, and what makes them difficult to create?

Applying What You've Learned

1. Find out what your competitors are doing to measure their progress and success. What kinds of analytics are they using in order to be successful? In your opinion, are they measuring the right things? Note: The best way to accomplish this task is to meet with your competitors, or call them on the telephone, and ask.

2. For your planned or already established enterprise, what "early warning systems" will you use to insure that your enterprise will make fewer mistakes, or you can find these mistakes early and correct them?

3. For your planned or already established enterprise, take the list in Exhibit 18.1 and come up with activities that would make the list concrete for you. For example, how would you go about developing a skeptic in your enterprise? What would that role entail and who would be responsible for being the skeptic? How would one go about seeking out bad news in your enterprise?

What would you do in the day-to-day business operations to insure that bad news came to you?

4. For your planned or already established enterprise, restate your goals and the goals of your enterprise in the form of "mistakes that must not occur." What cannot go wrong?

5. Review the list of possible responses to burnout. Which are most likely to apply to you? What strategies would you use to overcome burnout?

6. Look at organizations that you would like your enterprise to emulate. How and why are these companies "excellent?" What are the characteristics of excellent enterprises in your industry?

7. How do your competitors, particularly those competitors you admire, go about scanning the environment?

Enterprisers on the Web

1. Tom Peters (http://www.tompeters.com/) continues to stay at the edge of management thought and practice. Go to his website and explore what he currently thinks about "excellence" as well as look at other management resources the site provides. Look through his slide shows and identify at least five ideas that might help you better manage your enterprise.

2. Where is your planned or already established enterprise in the process of going from "good to great"? Download the diagnostic tool at Jim Collins' website (http://www.jimcollins.com), and use it to evaluate the status of your enterprise. What ideas from the site are most helpful to you in achieving greatness? How can you use this tool while your enterprise is still in the planning stages?

3. Peter Drucker (http://www.druckerinstitute.com/) (July 31, 2008) is considered by many executives and management scholars as one of the leading thinkers about the nature of management and leadership. Go to his website to explore his writings and thoughts. Identify five of Peter Drucker's ideas that you found helpful for managing enterprises and for managing yourself. Why did you choose these ideas?

4. Search the Web for businesses that sell inventory and stock management systems. How much is a system likely to cost for your type of enterprise? What will this system be able to do for your enterprise? Develop a table comparing at least three systems. Which would you choose, and why?

5. Are you credit worthy? Visit sites about credit scoring, such as the ones suggested below. Develop a brief presentation for the class that explains how credit scores work. Include suggestions to boost your score.

    http://money.howstuffworks.com/credit-score.htm

    http://www.bankrate.com/brm/news/credit-scoring/20031104a1.asp

    http://www.myfico.com/CreditEducation/CreditScores.aspx

    http://articles.moneycentral.msn.com/Banking/YourCreditRating/4creditScoringMyths.aspx

End Notes

1. Thomas H. Davenport, "Competing on Analytics," *Harvard Business Review,* January 2006, pp. 98–107.

2. The earliest known written version of the rhyme is in John Gower's "Confesio Amantis," dated approximately 1390.

3. This section and what follows is based on Karl Weick and Kathleen Sutcliffe, *Managing the Unexpected* (San Francisco: Jossey-Bass, 2001).

4. Ed Diener, "Test Your Happiness," *BBC online,* March 8, 2006, http://news.bbc.co.uk/1/hi/programmes/happiness_formula/4785402.stm (August 21, 2008).

5. Ahmed M. Abdel-Khalek, "Measuring Happiness with a Single-Item Scale," *Social Behavior and Personality,* 2006, http://findarticles.com/p/articles/mi_qa3852/is_200601/ai_n17170164.

6. "Identify Your Burnout Traits," © copyright 2001 American Institute for Preventive Medicine Systematic Stress Management, http://aipm.wellnesscheckpoint.com/library/banner_main.asp?P=34899CASMCD&zsection=Identify%20Your%20Burnout%20Traits&lang=E&title=N (July 2, 2008).

7. Steven Berglas, "The Big Lie," *Inc.*, March 1996, http://www.inc.com.

8. Based on information in "Preventing Burnout," *Coping.org,* http://www.coping.org/growth/burnout.htm (July 2, 2008); and "Ten Tips for Preventing Burnout," *American Institute for Preventive Medicine,* http://aipm.wellnesscheckpoint.com (July 2, 2008).

9. Tom Peters, "Tom Peters's True Confessions," *Fast Company,* November 2001, http://www.fastcompany.com.

10. Ibid.

11. "Cash Flow Improvement: Managing Payables," *The Forte Newsletter,* http://www.inconcertfinancialgroup.com/forte-consulting/managing-payables.shtml (July 7, 2008); Marcy Fisher, "Are You Down with Your APP (Average Payables Period)?" *eTECHnews.* January 9, 2007, http://www.rainmakerlegal.com/articles.htm and "How to Better Manage Your Cash Flow," *Entrepreneur.com,* December 11, 2003, http://www.entrepreneur.com/money/moneymanagement/managingcashflow/article66008.html.

12. Based on Scott Berkun, "Work vs. Progress," *Scottberkun.com,* http://www.scottberkun.com/essays/45-work-vs-progress/ (July 3, 2008).

13. George S. Day and Paul J. H. Schoemaker, "Scanning the Periphery," *Harvard Business Review,* November 2005, pp. 135–148.

Personal and Business Transition

KEY CONCEPTS

1. Successful enterprisers respond to changes in the business, the environment, and themselves. Enterprisers face many tradeoffs, such as the one between financial gain and maintaining control. Growing an enterprise usually requires outside financing, which means giving up control to a larger group of equity holders. Enterprisers should expect to make many transitions over their lifetimes and develop a strategy to prepare for life after the enterprise.

2. Enterprisers also need to plan how they will leave their businesses to move on to other endeavors. Exit strategies differ and include passing on a family business to the next generation, employee stock ownership plans (ESOPs), selling the business, and bankruptcy and dissolution. Each has its pros and cons, and enterprisers should consider issues of ownership, management, and taxes. Succession planning should begin early so the enterpriser has an exit strategy in place when the time comes to move on.

3. Going public is an exit strategy for enterprisers whose companies need at least $50 million of new equity investment to expand and show high potential for growth and profitability. A public company has diversified ownership and an established value for its equity. Once a company goes public, however, it is subject to stringent disclosure and reporting regulations. Managing a public company is considerably more difficult than managing a private one, and enterprisers must be prepared to deal with the loss of independence.

Suppose you took up golf and soon became a pretty good player—but then hit a plateau and couldn't improve your game. Frustrated by your inability to putt well, you applied your engineering savvy to the dynamics of club design. The putter that resulted looked strange but sent your ball straight toward the hole. The sound the ball made when the club hit it—"ping"—inspired you to start a company named Ping Golf to manufacture the clubs. Your son followed you into the business, and Ping became a leader in innovative golf equipment.

© Toshio Hoshi/Jupiter Images

In this chapter's case, we'll meet Karsten Solheim, founder of Karsten Manufacturing and Ping Golf, and his son John, the current chairman of the companies. Responding to the changes in their business and in them was challenging as they transferred the business to the next generation. We'll now describe how to develop strategies to prepare for the personal and business transitions that enterprisers face as their organizations grow.

19.0 Changing Needs and Circumstances: Personal, Business, Environment

What changes as a business develops? Everything! First, there are the inherent tradeoffs that any enterpriser will face in starting and growing a business. Noam Wasserman, in his article "The Founder's Dilemma" in the *Harvard Business Review*, suggests that founders of businesses will likely face the tradeoff between financial gains in developing the enterprise and having control.[1] His research found that very few enterprisers are able to continue to control their enterprises while also making a lot of money. Those who do are the exceptions rather than the rule. Most enterprisers must choose either to have control over their enterprises—and keep them small to maintain control—or to give up control by issuing stock and selling it to investors so that their enterprise has the funding to expand.

You will have to address this issue as the enterprise moves forward: Do you want to continue to control what happens, or are you willing to let others be in charge so that your enterprise might provide higher financial returns? Think of design firms such as fashion, architecture, product and graphic, where the founders of the business provide the creative inspiration for all decisions in their enterprises. Will founders of these businesses let others make design choices? Can they let others play creative roles in these firms? Unless they can give up some of the design responsibilities and allow others to be involved in important decisions in the business, the likelihood that the business can grow is minimal. One person can only do so much. Yet, many owners of businesses don't want to let others have power to make choices. As we saw in Chapter 17, it can be very difficult for enterprisers to delegate to employees or outsource to others.

Change in all aspects of your life is inevitable. You will change as a person because you will be older and may have family obligations and concerns. Your friends will be older, and they will have families. As your parents age, their issues will be different from today. You need to think ahead.

The enterprise itself will change over time. It ages, just as you age. The way you operated an enterprise ten years ago is probably not the way you operate an enterprise today, and it will certainly not be the way to manage and operate the business ten years from now. New technologies will transform how enterprises operate. Consider how rapidly the use of computers for managing sales and inventory control in retail enterprises has changed how sales are made, how and when new items are ordered, and when mark-downs occur. Think of how these processes will change when new technologies using radio frequency devices (RFDs) allow placing sensors on all products so that any item can be identified, in real time. Think of how RFDs might transform restaurants if all plates have RFDs embedded in them, for example. New people will come into the enterprise as well. As we described in Chapter 17, all enterprises face a turnover in employees over time. With a change in employees, enterprisers must integrate the interests, values, and capabilities of the new personnel into their enterprise's operations.

And finally, the environment will change. As we described in Chapter 6, significant trends and forces occurring in the world change how particular kinds of enterprises and industries will fare in the future. These trends and forces don't stabilize once you have taken advantage of them when you create your enterprise. Indeed, they continue to change. It is somewhat like surfing. While you can decide to choose the waves to ride and work to stay on top of the wave, eventually the wave crashes, and you have to find others to ride. What today is a given is likely to be different tomorrow. Even if you know, with some certainty, how broad trends will play out in the future, the specifics of when and how are likely to be different from what we may imagine today.

19.1 Letting Go: You are Not Your Enterprise

It might seem odd that we would have a chapter on issues about ending your involvement in an enterprise after devoting the rest of the book to exploring how to start and grow enterprises. Yet, as we indicated in Exhibit 1.4, most enterprises do not last very long. The likelihood that the enterprise that you will start will be in existence ten years from now is only about 20 percent. Given the odds that enterprisers who start firms have an 80 percent chance of being involved in something else besides the enterprise they founded ten years earlier, we believe it is worth considering the options enterprisers face after the start-up and growth process.

Let's begin with this observation made by Chaucer in 1374: "There is an end to everything, to good things as well." Realizing that the efforts and resources enterprisers invest in their enterprises have a finite life can actually help in thinking through how to start and grow the enterprise. Because most of us are likely to be alive for 70 or more years and most enterprises last fewer than 10 years, most enterprisers will be involved in many different enterprising activities over their lifetimes. Knowing when to quit is an important part of the enterprising process, too. Quite frankly, it is difficult to start and grow something else if you are still involved in whatever you are doing now. As we learned in the section on time management in Chapter 3, it is very difficult to begin new projects without ending others. Know how and when the time is right to move on.

Moving Through Halftime and Finishing Well

Bob Buford, who started and grew a successful network of cable systems across the United States and then sold that enterprise, has explored the transitions that successful individuals make in their lives.[2] He suggests that once successful individuals have achieved their goals, they reach "halftime" and begin to desire significance. In Chapter 12, we looked at how we struggle with balancing four major goals in our lives: achievement (Is this challenging?), significance (Will this make a difference in the world?), legacy (Will this be enduring?), and happiness (Is this enjoyable to you?). In Buford's research, he finds that individuals tend to strive for achievement first in their careers and that once they have met their achievement goals they then strive for significance and legacy.

The issue for successful enterprisers, then, is the following: Once you have achieved your goals, what do you do now? Buford calls the next stage of one's life the "second half" and offers advice from his research about how successful individuals complete the second part of their lives by "finishing well." We suggest that enterprisers will not only have a "second half" in their lives, but also a "third half," "fourth half," and more!

Buford offers these ten insights gleaned from Peter Drucker (1909–2005; writer and management consultant) for how to think about making a transition from what you are doing now to doing something else:[3]

1. *Work to "know yourself."* Change makes sense only when we know who we are and where we belong. It is easier to make changes when we are successful; therefore, don't think of change as a failure.

2. *Reposition yourself for the long term.* People who are successful in their careers plan well into the

future—beyond 10, 20, 30 years. It is never too early in your career to do this kind of planning.

3. *Identify your core beliefs.* Drucker saw a correlation between people who identify strong core beliefs and success.

4. *Make your life meaningful.* To have a meaningful life and to make a difference in the world, we should seek achievements that really matter to others. "Make your life your endgame," Drucker said.

5. *Planning sets the stage for opportunity, but the plan isn't the opportunity.* We need to be flexible and ready to recognize opportunities—even when they're not part of the plan.

6. *Value what you do.* The more you value and respect your job, the better you will be at it—and success will follow.

7. *Define what success means to you.* Your definition of success will likely change throughout the course of your career and life, so be sure to stay in touch with what it means to you at these different stages.

8. *Know when to stop planting and begin harvesting.* "For many years, I measured my work by my output—mainly in terms of books and other writing that I was doing," Drucker said. "I was very productive for many years. I am not so productive today, because these are years of harvesting rather than years of planting."

9. *Move beyond intentions to results.* Stay focused on the results you want to achieve and ask questions. Then work with others who have the ability and means to help you achieve these results.

10. *Grow or die.* Drucker grouped successful people who make it to their mid-forties or beyond, into three groups. The first one is those who retire. "They

usually don't live very long," he said. "The second group keeps on doing what they've been doing, but they're losing their enthusiasm, feeling less alive. The third group keeps doing what they've been doing, but they're looking for ways to make a contribution. They feel they've been given a lot and they're looking for a chance to give back. They're not satisfied with just writing checks; they want to be involved, to help other people in a more positive way." And those in the third group are the ones, Drucker said, who finish well.

Preparing for the Rest of Your Life

Besides Buford's view of Drucker's ideas about developing the second half of one's life, Drucker's own writings on this topic are enlightening, particularly his article "Managing Oneself" in the March/April 1999 *Harvard Business Review*. For example, Drucker discusses the problem of boredom, which often occurs if we have been doing something for 20 years. We already know how to do our jobs well, and there simply isn't much more to learn or to challenge us. At this point, we should consider a second career. He suggests three ways to make this happen:

- Do the same thing in a new context or do something new in a new context. If you are an accountant whose firm focuses on manufacturing firms, switch to doing accounting for service firms or health care providers. A doctor might become a lawyer.

- Have a parallel career, such as a part-time job doing something else. You could work for a nonprofit organization or do part-time consulting.

- Become a social enterpriser who creates and develops enterprises that are more focused on significance than achievement. (We will discuss social enterprises in Chapter 20.)

Drucker suggests that few individuals are conscious about the need to develop a strategy for the second half of their lives. He believes that the process for developing a second half takes 10 to 20 years to really work, in part because we need time to develop the skills to do other things. So we need to prepare for transitions or else we face burnout.

Another good reason to have a second career or a second life is to help us deal with the setbacks that will invariably occur in our first career. Not everything we start and develop will turn out as the success we imagine it to be. Drucker thinks that for many people at times the goal in life becomes an absence of failure. He points out that wherever there is success, there has to be failure. The second career, pursuing opportunities in other fields, provides us with other ways to achieve success and significance.

What is ahead for most of the readers of this book is midlife, when you enter your 40s and 50s. Remember, if 40–50 is about halfway through your life, you could have another 40 years left—and that is a long time.

Many other consultants recognize the need for individuals to prepare for midlife and for making changes at the midpoint in their lives. The key word is preparation. According to Carlo Strenger and Arie Ruttenberg, many people have a number of misperceptions of what will occur during this time of change.[4] The first myth is that of decline. The only decline that people face as they get older involves certain physical limitations. Most people won't have the same strength and stamina they had in their 20s and 30s, but there is little evidence of a decline in mental or emotional capabilities. What does change is a sense that there is a belief in endless possibilities in one's life. The reality though is that the successes and failures of one's life become the foundation to engage in other kinds of opportunities—opportunities that would not have been available in one's youth. Those previous successes and failures are, in fact, the experiences that make these midlife opportunities available. The key, as Strenger and Ruttenberg see it, is the need to prepare for personal transformation. Another myth they identify is that individuals have "magical" midlife transformations, where they suddenly take on new beliefs and values and then engage in new and radically different careers and interests. Rather, what stops people from changing is that they simply don't plan for change.

Finally, the research of Steward D. Friedman indicates there are nine domains of your life where you can make changes:[5]

- *Tracking and reflecting*: keeping a record of what you do and how you feel about your activities and accomplishment

- *Planning and organizing*: preparing and organizing your future activities

- *Rejuvenating and restoring*: taking care of your body and mind

- *Appreciating and caring*: being with others—having fun, taking care, respecting and bonding with others

- *Focusing and concentrating*: being physically and psychologically present (mindfulness)

- *Revealing and engaging*: being able to share yourself with others and being able to listen

- *Time-shifting and "replacing"*: doing things at a different time and place, and doing different things

- *Delegating and developing*: being able to give tasks and responsibilities to others, and to help them succeed at those tasks

- *Exploring and venturing*: doing something new—job, career, or other activity

He suggests that enterprisers "experiment" with these nine categories of tasks to enrich their lives and to win in four areas: at work, home, community, and self. We don't have to do big things to make changes occur. Take some steps, in any of these nine categories over time to begin to enrich ourselves now and in anticipation of the changes that await us.

19.2   Transition Pathways

Now we turn our attention to ways to leave your enterprise—or ways that your enterprise can leave you—and move on. We'll consider four pathways: succession in the family business, employee stock ownership plans (ESOPs), selling the business, and bankruptcy and dissolution. Our purpose is to help you see where your enterprise might be in the future and to consider how the enterprise might grow if you utilize any of these pathways. Note that we covered ways to value your enterprise in Chapter 10. In that chapter, we covered many different ways you can determine the financial value of the enterprise. Please review this chapter, as it offers many insights and tools into making judgments as to what your business is worth as well as some of the tax and legal issues involved with leaving your enterprise and moving on to pursue other opportunities.

Succession in Family Businesses

In many respects, nearly all enterprises are family businesses. In the Panel Study of Entrepreneurial Dynamics (Reynolds, 2007; see Chapter 2), we found that the majority of businesses that were started as teams were primarily started with spouses. Other team start-ups involved partnerships between parents and children, sibling partnerships, and other relatives. Most enterprisers will have some connections to family members. As we saw in Chapter 18's Fluker Farms case, the businesses these individuals operate will influence how everyone acts toward each other.

Typically, we think of family businesses as those businesses where equity ownership is shared among family members. In many family businesses, one family member is the sole owner, and other family members work for the business. In Chapter 17, we covered some of the issues that might arise when enterprisers employ members of their family in their enterprises. In this section, we will explore some of the issues involved with succession planning among family members, when ownership and control of the business is transferred from some family members to others. Often, transfer of ownership and control of the enterprise occurs between the parents and their children, but there are many instances where transfer of ownership and control of the enterprise occurs from parents to their children, from one spouse to another, from siblings to siblings, and among relatives (both blood and relatives by marriage).

There are three main transfer strategies for owners of a family business:

1. Retain family ownership and management control.

2. Retain family ownership but not management control.

3. Sell to an outside party.

When considering the transfer of an enterprise from one family member to another (or others), the family has to take into account management, ownership, and taxes.[6] Issues about management involve determining who will be operating and running the day-to-day operations of the enterprise. Issues of ownership involve determining who will actually have equity ownership in the business as well as how income and profits from the enterprise will be provided to family members, either through stock sales, dividends, or through salaries. Selling an enterprise and transferring wealth among family members involves significant tax issues. Finally, intergenerational conflicts must be considered. Since many enterprisers do not think ahead and consider that they will eventually die (sometimes unexpectedly), it is actually very wise for family members to consider how to deal with estate taxes if the principal owner of the family business dies and the bulk of the value of the estate is transferred to members of the family.

Succession planning is a difficult endeavor, but one that enterprisers should not postpone. Studies indicate that only 30 percent of family businesses survive the transition from first- to second-generation ownership, and only 15 percent make it to the third generation. The most common reason for this high failure rate is the lack of a succession plan. Exhibit 19.1 offers suggestions to help you get started on this important activity.

exhibit
19.1

Suggestions for Succession Planning

1. **Start early.** The general rule for succession planning is to think ahead five to ten years and to begin when the owner is in good health and active. In fact, it makes sense to develop a succession plan as part of the business startup process. Unexpected events such as serious illness, accidents, or disabilities can put the firm's survival in peril. A succession plan will improve the firm's likelihood of continuing to operate.

2. **Involve all family members in business succession planning discussions.** As we learned in previous sections of the book on how to manage people, the best way to insure that everyone will reach consensus on a solution to a problem is to involve them in identifying the problem and coming up with solutions. Enterprisers who don't involve others in the process are likely to generate hurt feelings and many misunderstandings among family members.

3. **Look at each family member realistically and plan accordingly.** It is very important to consider the goals and objectives of the business (the enterprise imperative—Chapter 1) and whether the strengths and capabilities of your family members match what the enterprise needs to grow and prosper. You may find no family members have an interest in running and growing the enterprise—or they may not have the skills and capabilities.

4. **Consider what "fairness" means among family members.** Many parents think that the most equitable way to divide a family business is equally among family members. For an enterprise to function, however, it needs strong leadership and direction. When ownership is divided among many individuals, it is often hard for decisions to be made about the enterprise's direction and growth. It would be better to consider other ways to transfer wealth among family members than to give each person an equal share of the enterprise. Ownership of the enterprise should likely be given to those individuals who will be involved in operating and growing the business, so that they have the ability to make decisions and control the business.

5. **Develop a timeline.** This timeline should show when you begin transferring some of the control, how that transferring will continue until the successor has assumed all of your responsibilities, and when you will formally retire.

6. **Share your knowledge and insights with your successor(s).** Because many enterprisers have made all the decisions about how to operate and grow their enterprises themselves, they may feel that they can just leave the business to their successors and assume that their successors will make the right decisions in the future: "It is your business now, good luck!" Successful transition requires that enterprisers share their business knowledge and insights with their successors. A one- to two-year training period will make this transition period a smooth one and provides time to test whether the chosen successors can operate the business.

7. **Involve "outsiders" in the business succession process.** With so many tax, legal, and interpersonal issues involved in developing a successful family business transition plan, it is important to involve experts such as lawyers, accountants, financial advisors, and family business consultants in the process. Just as we suggest that enterprisers involve outsiders in the growth and development of their enterprises, it makes sense to involve them to help transfer the enterprise to family members or others when you are ready to move on to other projects.

Sources: Adapted from "Succession Planning" and "Choosing Your Successor," *Small Business Notes,* http://www.smallbusinessnotes. com/operating/leadership/succession.html (August 25, 2008); and Susan Ward, "Family Business Succession Planning, Part 2: Six Business Succession Planning Tips," *About.com,* http://sbinfocanada.about.com (July 21, 2008).

We suggest that the most important tool to use for succession planning is life insurance. Estate taxes are due nine months after death, so the heirs of an estate have little time to raise the funds that are often necessary to pay taxes on an enterprise whose assets are tied up in plant, equipment, real estate, or other kinds of noncash assets. A life insurance policy is critical for paying any amount due for state and federal taxes. Don't wait to investigate how large an insurance policy you would need. For more information on the value of life insurance in estate planning and choosing a policy, see the article "Using Life Insurance as an Estate Planning Tool" in the October 2007 *Inc.* (http://www.inc.com/magazine/). Another good resource is the Business Owner's Toolkit guide *Planning for Succession* at http://www.toolkit.com/small_business_guide/. It covers such key topics as transferring power, transfer of assets, selecting a successor, intergenerational conflict, different agendas, goals of first and second generations, training, and timing.

While this discussion has focused on family businesses, it applies to closely held businesses as well. Enterprisers in these firms also need to have a succession plan in place so that they can move on when the time comes and leave the business in good hands.

ESOPS

Another way to transfer ownership of an enterprise to others is through an **employee stock ownership plan,** or **ESOP,** a tax-qualified employee benefit plan that invests primarily in stock of the sponsoring employer.[7] ESOPs must meet governmental regulations issued by the U.S. Department of Labor (DOL) and the Internal Revenue Service (IRS). An ESOP is a variation of a traditional profit-sharing plan. Contributions made to the ESOP are tax deductible and earnings by the ESOP are tax deferred. Since the ESOP is a benefit plan, employees are not taxed until money from their accounts is withdrawn.

There are two key distinctions between an ESOP and a profit-sharing plan or a pension plan:

- An ESOP is the only qualified employee benefit plan that can borrow money.

- An ESOP invests primarily in employer stock and may own anywhere from a fraction of 1 percent to 100 percent of a company's stock, whereas traditional pension plans are subject to stricter diversification requirements.

Similar to other pension plans, ESOP stock is held in a trust that is a separate legal entity. Separate accounts are maintained for individual stockholders within this trust.

The number of ESOPs in the United States has increased from approximately 200 ESOPs employing 250,000 workers in 1974 to over 11,000 ESOPs in 2005, covering an estimated 11.5 million employees. The growth of employee ownership over the past three decades is due to the legal recognition of ESOPs in the Employee Retirement Income Security Act of 1974 (ERISA). This act made into a reality the concepts introduced by Louis Kelso and Patricia Hetter in *How to Turn Eighty Million Workers into Capitalists on Borrowed Money* (1967). Kelso and Hetter believed that economic growth could be achieved by turning more workers into capitalists. They suggested that the accumulation of capital is the primary way that individuals become wealthy, so allowing more workers to become stockholders would be likely to increase their wealth and then benefit the economy. Kelso and Hetter suggested that corporations be offered tax incentives and financing. Less than a decade later their suggestions were made part of U.S. economic policy as Congress awarded ESOPs tax-favored status under ERISA.

The tax incentives to encourage corporations to set up ESOPs are:

1. Individuals who sell 30 percent or more of their stock in a closely held corporation to an ESOP may defer capital gains tax. If the replacement securities from the ESOP sale pass into an estate, the transfer to any beneficiaries is treated as a stepped-up basis (the cost at the time of owner's death), and no capital gains taxes are paid.

2. If a corporation uses an ESOP to obtain a loan, it may deduct the principal and the interest payments on the loan. This may cut borrowing costs by one-third.

3. Dividends paid in cash on shares held by an ESOP are tax deductible by the corporation if they are passed through to the participants in the plan or they are used to pay off a loan taken out to finance the purchase of company stock.

4. Participants in an ESOP have tax-sheltered accounts until their benefits are withdrawn, typically at retirement.

In addition to the tax incentives and financing opportunities that ESOPs provide, research on the performance of ESOP corporations has found that these companies have more involved workers and higher levels of production and performance. Enterprisers who want to explore the process of forming an ESOP should first find other enterprisers who have taken this path and discuss this transition option with family and employees to determine whether this is appropriate. For more information about ESOPs, begin at the ESOP Association website, http://www.esopassociation.org.

Employee stock ownership plan (ESOP) A tax-qualified employee benefit plan that invests primarily in stock of the sponsoring employer.

Selling the Business

We covered the process of purchasing an enterprise in Chapter 10 of this book. In that chapter, we took the perspective of a potential buyer and explored the issues involved in the due diligence process. We also covered how one would go about structuring the purchase transaction. In this section, we will emphasize some of the issues that you, as the seller of a business, should take into consideration.

First, we assume that you've undertaken a valuation of your enterprise and that multiple pricing formulas have given you a good sense of the value of the business. You have also taken some time to check the range of prices with experts to be sure that the price range for your business is not too high or too low. Second, you have considered the many tax implications of selling your business and structuring how the sale might take place. As we mentioned in Chapter 10, the parties to the transaction will want to keep their tax liabilities as low as possible. Sellers typically want to sell in a way that involves paying taxes on capital gains, whose tax rates are typically lower than taxes on current income. Third, consider how any legal liabilities might be handled. Ideally, the seller of an enterprise wants to assign any liabilities (past, present, and future) to the buyer of the business, while the buyer of the enterprise wants any liabilities past and present to remain with the seller. Consider who will be liable for any future warranty or service work, or who would be liable for any damages from products or services that occurred while you, as the seller, operated the enterprise.

Finally, consider the "quality" of the buyer. Rarely are businesses sold for cash only. Many buyers will ask sellers to take a note for some portion of the value of the enterprise to be paid over time with interest. It is therefore wise to consider whether the buyer can pay back this note on schedule. You also need to be comfortable with how the buyer is likely to operate the business once you leave. Some sellers, as a part of the sales contract, specify how employees are to be treated in such areas as severance packages if employees are terminated. An enterprise can become, for many enterprisers, much like a family member. So consider how a particular buyer will treat your "child" once you've sold it. Just as buyers need to do due diligence on the value of the enterprise, the seller needs to do substantial due diligence on the buyer and the buyer's capabilities to operate and grow the enterprise in a successful and ethical manner.

Bankruptcy and Dissolution

In Chapter 5, we outlined the legal issues involved with bankruptcy laws in the United States Bankruptcy Courts through Chapter 7 (liquidation), Chapter 11 (reorganization), and Chapter 13 (adjustment) of the Bankruptcy Reform Act. Now we will look at the issues involved with making the decision either to file for bankruptcy or to work toward dissolution of the enterprise in ways that do not result in debts or obligations to others.

How do you know that your enterprise is in serious trouble? Exhibit 19.2 offers signals that can alert you.

Altman's Z Score

The most famous model for predicting whether a business will eventually end up in bankruptcy is Edward Altman's Z Score.[8] Our intention in offering this formula, which is based on five financial ratios, is not that you will use it to calculate whether your enterprise is headed toward bankruptcy. Rather, it will help you understand what aspects of your enterprise's operations you should monitor to determine whether your enterprise is having trouble.

The formula for calculating Altman's Z Score is:

$$Z = 1.2\,(A) + 1.4\,(B) + 3.3\,(C) + 0.6\,(D) + 1.0\,(E)$$

Where (A) = Working Capital/Total Assets. This variable measures liquid assets in relation to the firm's size. Ideally, one would want to have a higher percentage of working capital to total assets.

Where (B) = Retained Earnings/Total Assets. This is a measure of cumulative profitability that reflects, in some respects, both the firm's age as well as its earning power. Ideally, one would want to have a higher percentage of retained earnings to total assets.

Where (C) = Earnings before Income Taxes/Total Assets. This is a measure of operating efficiency separated from any of the effects of leverage (debt) on the enterprise. This measure recognizes that operating earnings is the key to the long-run viability of an enterprise.

Where (D) = Market Value of Equity/Book Value of Debt. This ratio adds a market dimension. Academic studies of stock markets suggest that security price changes may foreshadow upcoming problems. Since most enterprises will not be public companies, this measure will likely not be an indicator.

Z Score   A formula to predict bankruptcy based on five financial ratios.

exhibit
19.2

Warning Signs of Impending Business Failure

1. You have difficulty paying bills.

2. The market for your product is decreasing.

3. More customers are complaining, indicating that you are not meeting their needs.

4. You are losing customers.

5. Inventory levels are building up at a rate faster than sales.

6. Your company has a high debt ratio.

7. Your company depends too much on one person to manage it.

8. Management does not communicate well with employees.

9. You are behind on bookkeeping and financial reporting is always late.

10. Sales are growing but net income is not.

11. Expenses are out of control and you are bouncing checks.

12. You are using personal credit cards to prop up a struggling business.

13. You are borrowing from the government by not paying your taxes.

14. You are not paying trade creditors so that business debt increases.

15. You are working longer hours and still not showing a profit.

Sources: Jill Michaux, "When to Pull the Plug on Your Failing Business?", *Bankruptcy Law Network*, October 8, 2007, http://www.bankruptcylawnetwork.com/2007/10/08/when-to-pull-the-plug-on-your-failing-business/; and Tonia Shakespeare, "Warning Signs that Your Business Is Failing," *Black Enterprise*, November 1996, http://findarticles.com/p/articles/mi_m1365/is_n4_v27/ai_18818282/pg_4?tag=artBody;col1.

Where (E) = Sales/Total Assets. This is the standard measure for turnover. As we discussed in Chapter 16, this turnover ratio will differ depending on the industry the enterprise is in.

This formula was first developed for publicly held manufacturing companies. Altman then adapted his Z Score for privately held manufacturing and general companies as follows:

$$Z = .717 \,(A) + .847 \,(B) + 3.107 \,(C) + 0.42 \,(D) + .998 \,(E)$$

Exhibit 19.3 shows how to interpret Altman's Z Scores for the three categories of companies. Note that the scores only represent the company's status as of the date of the financial data used. Companies that stayed in businesses had significantly different Z Scores than companies that failed. What the Z Score measures point toward is: CASH. Enterprises generate cash from operations to stay in business. Once the company generates enough cash to build retained earnings, it has a cushion to handle any problems it encounters.

Reorganize or Liquidate?

If your company exhibits many of the warning signs in Exhibit 19.2 or has a dangerously low Z Score, what's the next step? Here are some decision rules for dealing with enterprise failure and deciding whether to file for bankruptcy under the Bankruptcy Reform Act (Chapter 7 or Chapter 13) or reorganization (Chapter 11).[9]

Under Chapter 11 reorganization, the owners can continue to operate their company and have some control of the bankruptcy process. Although Chapter 11 provides a way—and time—to repair the company's failing business, it isn't an instant solution. It doesn't improve the business's operations, attract new customers, fix other deficiencies, or redeem poor management skills. Reorganization can, however, free up cash used to pay

exhibit
19.3

Interpreting Altman's Z Score

Type of Firm	Safe from Bankruptcy	Bankruptcy Highly Likely in 2 Years	Bankruptcy Is Likely
Public manufacturer	3.0 or higher	2.7–1.8	1.8 or below
Private manufacturer	2.9 or higher	2.9–1.23	1.23 or below
Private general firm	2.6 or higher	2.60–1.1	1.1 or below

debts and continue current operations, cancel leases and contracts, and prevent loss of assets or cash to creditors. Some companies are able to develop a plan that leads to profitable operations. Others may decide that the reorganization won't succeed and eventually liquidate. The issue of whether to reorganize or to liquidate depends primarily on whether the enterpriser has the desire, skills, and resources to go through the reorganization process.

Bankruptcy reorganization through Chapter 11 requires a substantial commitment on the part of the owners and managers of the enterprise. It's a time-consuming process to fulfill the requirements of the bankruptcy system and develop a reorganization plan, deal with lawyers, and negotiate with creditors. The bankruptcy court must sign off on all major business decisions. The "bankruptcy bargain" is that in exchange for Chapter 11 protection, the debtor provides full disclosure of its financial condition to creditors and the court, both at the beginning of the case and on a monthly basis thereafter, and the court operates as a fiduciary agent for the enterprise's creditors while the bankruptcy is ongoing. The reorganization plan includes a classification of claims against the company and specifies how each class of claims will be treated under the plan. If the plan proposes modifying any creditors' contractual rights or paying less than the full value of their claims under the plan, they vote on the plan. A Chapter 11 reorganization takes a significant amount of time to manage, and the money involved to pay legal fees can be substantial. Most reorganizations fail because they lack

a plan to solve the problems that got the enterprise into trouble in the first place.

Is liquidation a better option? If the enterprise requires little capital to start and has few assets, it might make more sense to liquidate a failing enterprise and start again. Under Chapter 7 bankruptcy (liquidation), the company stops all operations and goes completely out of business.

It is usually the best course of action when the enterpriser determines that:

- The enterprise does not have a viable business model.

- The debts of the enterprise are so substantial that restructuring them is unlikely.

- The few assets or capabilities in the enterprise are duplicated easily after a bankruptcy.

If the enterprise is a sole proprietorship, then individuals can get a discharge of debts and a chance to start over. A **discharge** is the legal elimination of debt in a bankruptcy case. When a debt is discharged, it is no longer

Discharge   The legal elimination of debt in a bankruptcy case.

legally enforceable against the debtor, though any lien (an interest in personal or real property that secures a debt) that secures the debt may survive the bankruptcy case.

Corporations are not eligible for discharges of debt, however. The benefit to corporations of Chapter 7 is that a court-appointed trustee oversees the methodical liquidation process, which is carried out at no cost to shareholders. Chapter 7 offers assurance that all claims will be paid according to priority and the extent of

available assets and that assets remaining after paying the expenses of Chapter 7 go to pay taxes these individuals may owe.

Bankruptcy laws govern the debtor's ability to discharge debts and the speed with which he or she can emerge from bankruptcy. As we'll learn in the Enterprising World box, these laws differ from country to country and affect the rate of entrepreneurial activity in the country.

AN ENTERPRISING WORLD

Bankruptcy Laws Make a Difference

Does the legal environment in a country, especially with regard to bankruptcies, influence its level of entrepreneurship? A study of self-employment data from 15 European Union (EU) countries and the United States for the period 1990–2005 indicates that bankruptcy laws have the most statistically and economically significant effect on levels of self-employment across countries. In fact, they are more important than economic determinants such as real GDP growth and stock market returns.

The study compared bankruptcy laws in these countries, especially with regard to the time to discharge of debts and to the rate of entrepreneurial activity and growth in the economy. It found that countries with harsher bankruptcy laws (that mandate a long time period before a person can emerge from bankruptcy) also have lower rates of entrepreneurship. Some European countries required enterprisers to wait a decade or longer before obtaining a "fresh start" and discharging their debts. This is in direct contrast to the United States, where under Chapter 7 a fresh start is immediate. As one European Commission official commented in 2005, "We punish entrepreneurs when they fail as if they are crooks. The Commission will find out how we can change the culture so it's more acceptable to honestly fail."

As a result of pressure from senior EU officials, many countries have revised their bankruptcy laws to introduce a "fresh start" or to shorten the time until it is available. A more forgiving bankruptcy law reduces the stigma of failure and thus makes it less risky to start a business. In 2004, the UK has reduced the waiting period from three years to one year. Germany first introduced a discharge period of seven years in 1999 and reduced it to six years in 2001. The Netherlands' three-year discharge period was introduced in 1998.

Another difference between the United States and EU countries is in the area of exemptions. Under U.S. bankruptcy law, a person who files for bankruptcy can protect a certain amount of assets, such as a portion of the value of one's house or automobile. In Europe, there are few if any exemptions. Bankruptcy in Europe may also carry civic penalties such as losing one's right to vote and there can be restrictions on travel. Finally, there are issues about the complexity of dealing with creditors in the bankruptcy process. In general, the greater complexity of European bankruptcy laws lengthens the time it takes to emerge from bankruptcy. Overall, the bankruptcy process in the United States carries less of a stigma than in Europe and makes it easier and faster to emerge from bankruptcy. Our rates of entrepreneurial activity are indeed higher, in part because of our more forgiving bankruptcy laws.

Discussion Questions

1. What do a country's bankruptcy laws say about how that society views failure?

2. How do a country's bankruptcy laws affect the rate of new business formation?

3. Why is it easier to make a fresh start in the United States than in many other countries?

4. Should individuals be given a second (third, fourth, etc.) chance to succeed? How might failure teach lessons about how to be successful?

Sources: John Armour and Douglas Cumming, "Bankruptcy Law and Entrepreneurship," *European Corporate Governance Institute*, February 2008, downloaded from http://ssrn.com; and Richard Tyler, "Bankruptcy Laws Are 'Too Strict in EU'", *The Daily Telegraph* (London), November 15, 2005.

19.3 The Publicly Held Company

Going public is one of the biggest business and personal transitions an enterpriser can make. While many individuals dream about the riches they might receive if they are able to take their businesses public, significant risks and challenges come with managing and operating a publicly held corporation. We briefly discussed going public in Chapter 15, including the criteria for readiness. Now let's take a closer look at what it means to be a public company.[10]

Companies go public through an **initial public offering (IPO)**, the sale of shares of stock to the public for the first time. These shares will be listed on a public securities exchange, such as the New York Stock Exchange, Nasdaq, or a regional stock exchange, where investors can buy and sell the shares. Each major exchange has its own listing requirements for a company's financial size, performance, and trading activity. For example, to list on the Nasdaq National Market, all companies must have at least 400 shareholders with more than 100 shares, a minimum of 1.1 million publicly-traded shares, and a minimum bid price of $5. Companies must comply with Nasdaq's corporate governance rules and meet one of three financial requirement rules with regard to minimums for shareholder equity, operating income, and market value. The Nasdaq Small Cap Market has less stringent listing requirements.

Going Public: Pros and Cons

Going public allows owners to raise equity capital for growth and to diversify their personal assets beyond the ownership of their enterprise, rather than have their worth dependent on one source. By selling stock to others, they spread the risk of the business. Going public also establishes a value for the company's equity and signals to others—customers, suppliers, lenders, and investors—that the company has reached certain levels of achievement. Having a known market value for its stock makes it easier to acquire other companies or be acquired. It's worth noting that owners typically do not sell their own stock in an IPO, so they are not receiving cash. In fact, there is a restriction period during which they may not sell their stock. However, they can more easily sell their holdings later because of the stock's enhanced marketability.

A publicly held company can use stock and stock options as incentives to hire, retain, and motivate employees. Enterprises that are publicly held typically raise more equity in their public offerings. Raising more equity lowers the debt to equity ratio, then, for these businesses, which then tends to lower the costs to borrow money. Public companies tend to be valued more highly than privately held companies because the shares of publicly held companies are more liquid (easily bought and sold). A publicly held company can use this extra value as a way to purchase other privately held companies.

The difficulties and problems of operating a publicly held corporation involve the legal requirements for reporting the financial and business aspects of the enterprise to the Securities and Exchange Commission (SEC) every quarter. These requirements cannot be underestimated in terms of the time and expenses required to comply with all of the legal regulations. Corporations that are publicly held must have audited financial statements from a certified public accountant (CPA). These audits are expensive and also require significant commitments from employees to provide the necessary data.

In addition, many aspects of enterprise operations will now be public knowledge, such as the compensation of the directors and officers of the company, information about stock options, payments for other kinds of compensation to officers and employees, significant consulting contracts to others, and important financial information such as total sales, gross profits, net income, debt, and plans for the future. Much of this information must be published quarterly with more details provided in an annual report. Officers of the company must also provide information to the public, such as answering questions from stock analysts about the company and future plans or any upcoming material changes to the company's operations. Corporations that have not been forthcoming with important information about the company's operations have been sued, and many of these companies have had to pay millions of dollars to lawyers and shareholders because of this lack of candor.

Publicly held corporations are now owned by the shareholders, all of whom have a voice in the management of the corporation through the board of directors. The board of directors has a fiduciary responsibility to insure that all stockholders are treated properly. Therefore, the board of directors ultimately makes the decisions about how the company will be operated, and the CEO, COO, and others must comply with these

Initial public offering (IPO)   The sale of shares of stock to the public for the first time.

directions. Finally, the cost of preparing for an IPO is expensive, typically costing a minimum of $100,000 in audit fees, complying with legal regulations, and paying for an underwriter to sell the stock. The IPO itself is expensive: the issuing company typically receives about 90 percent of the proceeds, with the remainder going to other participants in the IPO process, such as the investment banker who sells the shares.

The primary difficulty, though, with taking a corporation public will be loss of the independence that the owner/managers of the privately held company have enjoyed. Every decision made will now be second-guessed by outsiders who expect the publicly held company to grow its earnings and increase the value of its shares. Publicly held corporations who do not meet their earnings projections often lose significant share value, and many CEOs of these organizations lose their jobs because of it.

With the additional burden of disclosure and a very different operating environment from a private company, why would an enterpriser choose to go public? We suggest that the primary reason for taking a company public should be that the enterprise needs significantly more equity investment from others in order to grow. For example, when Google went public with an IPO in 2004, it sold about 20 million shares of stock for $85 a share: $1.7 billion. This money was used to significantly expand the enterprise by hiring more people, investing in more computer equipment, and purchasing other firms that could help build its core business of Internet search and sales of targeted advertising through these searches. If an enterprise can grow without acquiring outside investment, then it should think twice about going public. Companies don't have to be public to grow. From the ratios offered in Chapter 16, we know that, as a rule of thumb, companies can typically grow at the rate of their return on assets (ROA)—without needing outside investment. Many professional service enterprises and consulting firms have very high ROAs, so a significant amount of growth can occur using internally generated funds.

There are two reasons a corporation's IPO will be successful. The primary reason depends on the fundamentals of the corporation itself. First, the enterprises must be of sufficient size to warrant an equity investment of about $50 million in size at the outset. These enterprises must have a high potential for growth and profitability. Second, the underwriter (investment banker) needs to have a strong track record selling the stock of companies in the corporation's industry. It should have the resources to support analysts to track and follow the

© Jerzy Dabrowski/DPA/Landov Media

stock over time so that investors can gain insights into the relative strengths and weaknesses of the corporation. Underwriters should also have a strong base of clients willing to invest in new corporations.

Today's IPO market is considerably different from a decade ago, when Internet companies were going public well before they were ready. The story of the dot-com bubble and its aftermath, described in the Enterprising Ethics box, holds lessons for enterprisers who are considering an IPO.

The IPO Process

Corporations can raise public equity from investors in a number of ways. It is possible to sell equity only within a state. Each state has its own security laws (called "Blue Sky Laws") that govern security sales within its borders. We suggest that you contact the state's corporate commission office to learn about the specific rules for your state. What will be of particular interest to these state regulators will be the offering's size and that you only sell to investors who are residents of the state. Corporations that have securities outstanding in a particular state through a state's blue sky laws will have some difficulty and expense reregistering these shares for a public offering at the federal level.

For most corporations, the best way to go public is to register with the SEC and gain its approval. The approval process involves completing an S-1 document, which describes many details about the corporation's operations and financial status. The SEC reads the S-1 document and then goes back and forth with the company to adjust it. Then the SEC either approves the document or denies it.

The next step involves shareholder approval. The company is a private company prior to the IPO. Its private investors must vote on whether to approve the IPO. If

ENTERPRISING ETHICS

Lessons from the Bubble

Until the mid-1990s, the typical company that went public had been around for at least seven years, had a product or service on the market, and had a track record of profitable operations. This pattern changed in 1995 when Netscape, an Internet browser company less than 18 months old and with little revenue and no profits, went public. The IPO caught everyone by surprise. The stock debuted at $28 per share, twice the original offering price, and closed at $75 the first day. The company's revenues doubled every quarter in 1995 as investors watched their shares increase in value.

The Netscape IPO was the first of many from start-up companies looking to make it big in the Internet economy. The venture capital (VC) companies backing them became more aggressive in pushing companies to go public, whether or not they were profitable. "If you were growing fast enough, at some point in the future, you would grow into profitability," said Jay Hoag, partner at venture firm Technology Crossover Ventures. Soon everyone wanted to get in on the action. Investment bankers hunted for new clients and encouraged them to consider going public instead of looking for additional venture capital funding. From 1995 to 2000, the IPO market was flush with new offerings. New issue prices "popped," shooting up two and three times on the first day of trading.

Fueled by the belief that the Internet revolution would change every area of the business world, investors scrambled to buy the stocks of early-stage Internet companies in expectation of huge future profits. They saw the first-day pops as indications of future success and high stock prices. In fact, those first-day gains were often the biggest the company had. When the Internet bubble burst in 2000, many of the dot-com companies failed, and shareholders lost considerable amounts. For example, Pets.com raised $66 million from its IPO—and failed a mere ten months later.

By spring 2001, 316 of the 367 Internet companies that had done IPOs since 1997 and were still trading posted stock prices lower than their offering prices, according to Thomson Financial. In just one year, the market capitalization of Internet companies fell by $2.5 trillion.

In the aftermath of the tech market's collapse, many market observers questioned whether Wall Street and the VC firms violated the public's trust by inappropriately pushing companies into the public arena. Instead of nurturing these young firms until they were sustainable, greedy VCs and investment bankers transferred the risk they had assumed in the past to naïve investors. "Public investors were effectively making venture-stage investments," said Henry Blodgett, then a top Merrill Lynch stock analyst covering Internet companies. "VCs understand the risks of those investments, but I don't think everybody understood." Investment bankers pulled in huge up-front fees from taking companies public: $2.1 billion from 1997 to early 2001. The VCs and investment bankers claimed that the excessive speculation of frenzied investors seeking riches was to blame and did not see a need to curtail the upward trend in IPO pops. "Investors wanted these stocks," said Blodgett. "It's tough to tell a CEO, 'We won't take you public' when investors are shouting, 'Bring it on!'" After all, who didn't want to buy a company at $15 or $20 a share and flip it for $100 or more the same day or shortly thereafter?

As Joe Nocera, former executive editor of *Fortune* and now a *New York Times* business columnist, points out, companies go public to raise capital for expansion, and their proceeds are based on the offering price. "When you have a situation where [the stock price is] going up 300 percent on the first day, that's 300 percent that the company is not getting," he says. "If the investment banks ... really had the best interests of their companies at heart, you would have never seen the situation where IPOs go up 200, 300, 400 percent on the first day," he says. "I mean, that is a crime."

Another area of concern was market manipulation and allocation of new issues. Federal investigators delved into whether investment bankers allocated hot IPO shares in exchange for kickbacks from institutional investors and to executives who were in a position to choose their company's underwriters. The general public was not able to buy the stock until it hit the aftermarket and had popped. The executives were then able to "spin"—sell—the shares to make a quick, and often huge, profit. In one such example, Robertson Stephens gave the CEO of a videogame company the chance to buy 100,000 IPO shares of Pixar Animation Studios. The executive spun the shares for a $2 million profit and later chose Robertson Stephens to underwrite its own IPO and to help with subsequent acquisitions.

Regulators also investigated possible conflicts of interest between the research and investment banking operations of the Wall Street firms. After the shares were sold, the analysts issued periodic stock reports for the investing public and also hyped the stocks on television shows and in magazines. They did not reveal, however, that their firms had business relationships with the companies they are covering, that they had a vested interest in keeping the stock prices up, or that their bonuses were tied to how well their employer did overall. One analyst admitted that she was pressured to keep the news of the companies she followed positive. The public heard sound bites, and few read the written reports where the disclosures appeared. Rarely did analysts, who were supposed to issue objective opinions, recommend selling a stock.

Stronger security regulations and codes of conduct were put into place to correct these and other transgressions. At the same time, money managers cautioned investors that relying on the so-called experts is no guarantee of profits. As the Internet bubble proved, there is no substitute for personal due diligence before investing.

Discussion Questions

1. As an investment banker at Goldman Sachs commented after the Internet bubble burst, "We want to be responsible, but at the end of the day investors are going to make their own decisions." Do you agree with this statement, and why? Divide the class into two teams to debate the issue of whether investment bankers abdicated their responsibility.

2. Should it be illegal to allocate IPO shares to the investment bank's top customers? Is this bribery, or is it the underwriter's right to distribute the offering as it sees fit? Defend your answer.

3. Who in the IPO process should have an ethical responsibility to the investors buying the stock of these companies?

4. What steps should a company that is considering an IPO take to insure that the offering is handled ethically?

***

Sources: "Boosting the Bubble," *Frontline*, http://www.pbs.org/wgbh/pages/frontline/shows/dotcon/crying/analysts.html (August 30, 2008); "Dot Con," *Frontline*, January 24, 2002, http://www.pbs.org/wgbh/pages/frontline/shows/dotcon/etc/script.html (August 30, 2008); "The Great Internet Money Game," *Business Week*, April 16, 2001, p. EB16, http://www.businessweek.com; "Inside the Dot.com IPO Game," *Frontline*, http://www.pbs.org/wgbh/pages/frontline/shows/dotcon/thinking/game.html (August 30, 2008); Mark Lewis, "Pop Goes the IPO," *Forbes*, February 16, 2001, http://www.forbes.com; and Michael Siconolfi, "'Spinning' of Hot IPOs Is Probed—U.S. Attorney Begins Criminal Investigation," *Wall Street Journal*, April 16, 1998, p. C1.

***

these shareholders approve the IPO, the company can continue with the IPO process. The specific process of taking an enterprise public takes between 14 weeks and a year to complete. Here are some of the steps involved.[11]

Preparing for the IPO

All of the individuals involved with the IPO process (members of the corporation, auditors, lawyers, and investment bankers) meet to determine the size of the initial offering and share price, as well as what each member will be responsible for accomplishing. During this time, the S-1 registration statement is created and the audited quarterly financial statements will be completed. The S-1 requires three years of audited financial information. This process typically takes between five weeks and two months.

Filing and Review with the SEC and a Stock Exchange

Once the S-1 registration statement has been completed, it is filed with the SEC, where it is reviewed and revised until approved. This information is also filed with the stock exchange where the corporation plans to list. For most new publicly held corporations, this exchange is likely to be the Nasdaq. The turnaround time for comments from the SEC is typically about a month, and each response from the SEC requires revisions and amendments to the registration statement. This process is likely to take from one month (if no revisions are required, which is unlikely) to four months or longer. Finally, once the registration statement has been approved, a prospectus is printed for distribution to prospective investors.

The "Road Show"

Once the S-1 has been approved, the goal will be to sell shares to prospective investors. This sale is typically done through a "road show," in which the primary leaders of the new corporation (the CEO, COO, and CFO), their key advisors (accountants and lawyers), and the underwriting team travel to various locations to meet with potential investors. They demonstrate for these institutional investors, stockbrokers, and other possible investors (such as other corporations) the new corporation's potential and managerial talent. During this time, the underwriters will collect orders for shares from these investors. A "road show" typically lasts about a month or less, but during that time, the presenters will face a grueling ordeal of pointed questions that have to be answered carefully as to comply with what has been stated in the registration documents.

Closing

Finally, once the SEC has declared the registration statement effective and the road show is over, the underwriters and issuer can make a determination about the level of interest in the IPO. Then they determine the share price and the underwriter awards share allocations to various investors. Once trading begins, the corporation prepares a press release about the offering and publishes a "tombstone" advertisement in many major newspapers. Once shares are sold, the corporation receives proceeds from the sale, less commissions and underwriting fees.

The cost of undergoing the IPO process is substantial, typically about 10 percent of the total value of the offering. If the size of the offering is $50 million, the costs are likely to be about $5 million, consisting of underwriting costs of 7 percent of the offering ($3.5 million), $450,000 for legal and accounting fees, and $150,000 for document printing.

19.4 ENTERPRISERS

Ping Golf

Not only high technology companies start in the founder's garage. Karsten Solheim began making golf clubs in his Redwood City, California, garage in 1959. Today, Karsten Manufacturing is a privately held, 900-employee company that manufactures Ping golf clubs, one of the most popular brands in golf today. This innovative line of golf clubs grew out of Karsten Solheim's frustration with his own golf game. A latecomer to the sport, Solheim was 42 and an engineer at General Electric (GE) when he started to play. He loved the game and was good at it—but frustrated that he couldn't improve his performance more. Disappointed with the putting portion of his game, he realized that improving the dynamics of the club would help him putt straighter.

Applying his knowledge of physics and engineering, Solheim designed a putter with additional weights on the ends of the club to stabilize it, which prevents twisting and keeps the ball from bouncing and skipping on the green—for better control. The sound the club made when it hit the ball—"ping"—inspired the club name. Sales took off in the early 1960s, and in 1967 Solheim left GE to manufacture his golf clubs and sell them through pro shops. He subsequently developed a full line of golf clubs under the Ping brand. His innovative golf club designs weren't accepted at first but were later adapted as industry standards. The only golf club manufacturer inducted into the World Golf Hall of Fame, Karsten, who died in 2000 at the age of 88, turned the company over in 1995 to his youngest son John, who had worked with Karsten for 40 years. His other sons, Allan and Karsten Louis, also work for Ping, and his daughter Sandra is a Ping sales representative. The third generation is there, too! John's son John Karsten Solheim is currently vice president of engineering.

"When we started, I was in junior high, drilling putters in our garage," says John. "It took us a long time to get out of our garage—seven years—and my dad really questioned leaving General Electric at the time." The distinctive new putter design wasn't well accepted by the public until golf matches began to be televised and viewers saw pros like Jack Nicklaus and Gary Player successfully putting with Ping's funny-looking clubs. Karsten also ran into problems when the United States Golf Association (USGA) banned all but one Ping putter design and again in 1987 when the USGA claimed the Ping Eye2 iron design gave players an unfair advantage. "Fortunately, we came to a settlement with the USGA. The golfers were the winners, because they got to continue using the clubs, and we made some changes and minor adjustments to the clubs," says John.

Another way the Solheims and Ping revolutionized golf was with the custom fitting of clubs designed specifically for the player. The company trains golf shop pros to take customer measurements, including golf swing, and with this information either select the right club from existing models or order a customized set of clubs, complete with serial number. And the time to get a set of custom clubs—once as long as three months—is short, too. "We deliver custom-built, custom-fit golf clubs within 48 hours," says Ping president and COO Doug Hawken. Because of the serial number, a customer who loses a club can get an exact replacement for it.

Ping clubs adhere to the highest quality standards, and most club heads are cast in the company's own foundry. Each color-coded club has its own specifications, which are checked and adjusted as necessary. "The interesting thing here is we don't have inspectors as such," says John. "Everybody is considered an inspector. In other words, anybody can reject a club throughout the system at any time."

Despite their long-term working relationship, father and son did not always agree on how to run Karsten/Ping—especially as Karsten aged. Karsten was displeased with John's design concessions to the USGA, for example. "If I had an idea and brought it up to my dad, that guaranteed it wouldn't happen," says John. "So I had other people bring my ideas to him. And that worked very well." Management differences between Karsten and John hindered decision-making and product development. "I got fired a few times, and I left for a couple of days on my own one time, too," John Solheim says. The company's market share declined in the early 1990s as it lost touch with its marketplace.

Once John assumed the chairmanship, he made significant changes. He returned Karsten/Ping's focus to golf manufacturing, selling off unrelated ventures. Delegating authority was perhaps the most important change. John brought in non-family employees to strengthen management. "It used to be Karsten and me," said John. "It was too individualized. What I enjoy most is doing design and leaving the business details to Doug Hawken because I have a lot of confidence in him." According to Hawken, John is more open to feedback and advice than Karsten. "I think that leads to better decisions, especially in a competitive environment," he says. "It was 'Karsten's way' before John took over. Now, it's a team. It took a different management style to remain competitive."

Unlike his father, John tests competitor's clubs and is receptive to changing trends. Recognizing the increasing popularity of blade irons, which Karsten resisted in favor of his own design, John authorized their development and subsequent 2003 introduction. The company brings retailers to Ping's Phoenix headquarters for training in how to fit clubs and gives them the opportunity to share their ideas with management. Committed to continuous improvement, Ping recently implemented 3-D product development software that shortens product development cycles from two years to nine months.

Ping employees enjoy working for a company that is committed to achieving the best. "John [Solheim] has set an edict that we're going to strive to be the number one in irons, putters and metal woods, not so much in volume but in high-performance, high-quality products," says John Bliss, a director of engineering who has been at Ping for more than 20 years. "And everybody has a passion for that precision, for that quality, to strive to achieve the best."

The Solheim family treats its employees like family and helps them develop into their skills. "You make sure that you pay them well, that you have a bonus plan for them, you have retirement plans and medical insurance," says Solheim. "But then, you give them a challenge, and that's much more important. You give them a job that they're responsible for."

Despite reaching more than $200 million in sales, Karsten/Ping has stayed private and is the largest family-owned golf equipment company. "We always were and always will remain a family-owned company," states John. "It's my goal and my brother Allan's goal to hand the company down like it was handed down to us." Staying private gives the company flexibility.

"We don't have to answer to stockholders to meet a quarterly [earnings number]. That causes big industry to do things that really can hurt the brand and hurt you long term. And we're not going to do that. We're going to take our time and then put it on the marketplace, give it a little bit of time to mature."

Today Karsten/Ping continues to reflect Karsten Solheim's philosophy of loving golf and the people who play it. "The way my dad would have put it was, if you build a better product, the dollars will take care of themselves, and we've never really worried about the dollars," John says. "If you're just a 'me, too,' then you're not leading."

Discussion Questions

1. What kind of succession plan should John Solheim have in place? How should he involve his family in the operations of the business?

2. What should John Solheim do to keep Ping a family business?

3. Given that Ping is a very employee-oriented business, how might Ping become an ESOP? Would this be good for the family and the employees?

4. What are the advantages and disadvantages for taking Ping public—for the Solheim family and for the employees?

5. How would you monitor how Ping is doing as an enterprise? What metrics would be most important?

Sources: Adapted with permission from Small Business School, the series on PBS, at http://SmallBusinessSchool.com; Brian Hook, "Faster Product Launches Keep Ping Swinging," *The Financial Times*, February 28, 2007, retrieved from General OneFile database, http://find.galegroup.com/itx/start.do?prodId=ITOF; E. Michael Johnson, "Q&A with Doug Hawken: Ping President and Chief Operating Officer," *Golf World Business*, January 2002, retrieved from General OneFile database, http://find.galegroup.com/itx/start.do?prodId=SPJ.SP06; Mark S. Murphy, "Reason to Smile: CEO John Solheim and Ping Execs Faced a Challenge," *Golf World*, January 28, 2005, retrieved from General OneFile database, http://find.galegroup.com/itx/start.do?prodId=ITOF; and Edward F. Pazdur, "The Chairman's Page: An Interview with John A. Solheim, CEO of Ping," *Executive Golfer*, http://www.executivegolfermagazine.com/articles/solheim.htm (August 30, 2008).

Summary

1. As a business develops and grows, it changes. Enterprisers face many tradeoffs, such as the one between financial gain and maintaining control. To grow an enterprise usually requires outside financing, which means giving up control to a larger group of equity holders. Enterprisers and their businesses change over time, as does the environment in which they operate. The ability to respond to such changes is an important characteristic of successful enterprisers.

2. Because most enterprises last for less than ten years, enterprisers face many transitions and will be involved in many different activities over their lifetimes. Once they satisfy their achievement goals, they focus in the second half of their lives on significance and leaving a lasting legacy. Enterprisers should seek to know themselves and what defines success for them, have a long-term vision, look for achievements that are meaningful personally, and keep growing and learning. Planning for the inevitable changes to come by developing a strategy for a second—or third—career will smooth these transitions. Preparation is the key to a satisfying second half.

3. Another planning process for enterprisers involves exit strategies to leave their businesses. These include succession in the family business, employee stock ownership plans (ESOPs), selling the business, and bankruptcy and dissolution.

4. Family businesses have three primary transfer strategies: retaining family ownership and control by transferring the business to the next generation, retaining family ownership and shifting management control to others, or selling to a third party. Issues to consider in designing a succession plan are management of the enterprise, ownership, and tax considerations. Succession planning is an important activity that should begin early, while the current enterpriser is active in the business and can train his or her successors. Life insurance is another key element of a succession plan and helps to pay taxes while cash is tied up in the business's assets.

5. An employee stock ownership plan (ESOP) is a tax-qualified employee benefit plan that invests primarily in stock of the sponsoring employer. It is a variation on a profit sharing plan that offers another exit strategy for enterprisers. Employees of companies with ESOPs tend to be more involved than workers who exhibit higher levels of production and performance.

6. Enterprisers who wish to leave their businesses may choose to sell to an outside party. The steps involved include establishing a value using several valuation methods, taking tax issues into consideration, and deciding how to handle legal liabilities. It's critical to consider the quality and integrity of the buyer.

7. Enterprises that are in serious financial trouble may have to file bankruptcy and either reorganize or liquidate. Altman's Z Score provides one way to determine if your company is heading toward bankruptcy. With Chapter 11 of the Bankruptcy Reform Act (reorganization), the owners continue to operate the business but the bankruptcy court must approve all major business decisions. The reorganization plan sets forth how the company's debts will be repaid. Reorganizations are time consuming, take a major commitment from the owners, and are expensive to complete. There is no guarantee that reorganization will succeed; many companies who file Chapter 11 end up in Chapter 7, liquidation. Liquidation is the preferred solution if the enterprise's business model is not viable, the company has too much debt to restructure, or it is easy to duplicate the company after liquidation. A court-appointed trustee handles the process, selling the assets and paying creditors and taxes.

8. Taking a company public is another exit strategy for enterprisers. Companies that wish to go public should have reached certain levels of financial performance prior to beginning the process. They should need at least $50 million of new equity investment and have a potential for high growth and profitability. Financial strength and operating fundamentals are the keys to success. The primary reason to take a company public through an IPO is to raise equity capital for growth now and in the future. It also diversifies the company's ownership among many shareholders and establishes a market value for the company, raising its profile. Stock options are an attractive incentive for employees. At the same time, operating a public company brings with it substantial disclosure and reporting requirements. IPOs are costly; about 10 percent of the proceeds

go to expenses and the underwriters. The main drawback for the enterpriser is the loss of independence.

9.   The IPO process is lengthy and complex, taking from 14 weeks to a year. It begins with preparation of the S-1 document, filing it with the SEC for review and revision, and getting approval from existing shareholders. The company must have three years of audited financial statements to include with the S-1. The marketing of the shares is handled through "road show" presentations by the company management and its underwriters to prospective groups of major shareholders. After the road show, the level of interest in the offering is used to determine the size and price of the offering. The shares are then sold to the public and the company receives the proceeds.

Review Questions

1.   Discuss the types of changes that occur during a business's life cycle. How do these changes affect the founding enterpriser?

2.   Why should enterprisers plan now for the time when they decide to leave their company? How will their goals change, and what steps can they take to prepare for their "second half?"

3.   What are the three primary strategies to transfer family businesses? Briefly discuss the key issues an enterpriser should consider in developing a succession plan.

4.   What is an employee stock ownership plan (ESOP), and how does it differ from a profit-sharing plan? What are the advantages of transferring ownership of the company to its employees?

5.   Summarize the steps an enterpriser should take to sell the business to an outside party.

6.   List the six warning signs of impending bankruptcy that you consider the most important for an enterprise to notice.

7.   What is Altman's Z Score, and how does it predict bankruptcy?

8.   What is Chapter 11 and why would a company choose this type of bankruptcy? What considerations should the enterpriser take into account before deciding to proceed with Chapter 11?

9.   List the reasons a company should consider Chapter 7 liquidation instead of Chapter 11 reorganization.

10.   What are the advantages and disadvantages of becoming a public company?

11.   Describe the steps in the IPO process.

Applying What You've Learned

1.   What do you want your legacy to be? Your enterprise's legacy? How do you define success for yourself? Write these down, along with your reasons for choosing them. Divide the class into small groups to share and discuss your responses.

2.   Identify three family-owned businesses that have successfully made a transition between generations, and three family-owned businesses that apparently failed in a transition between generations. What are the similarities and differences between the successes and failures?

3.   Consider ways that enterprisers can protect themselves from the failure of their enterprises. For your enterprise, how can you insure that you will not fail if your enterprise fails? Summarize your ideas and share them with the class.

4.   Identify the key "red flags" that would signal to you that your enterprise is failing. What corrective action could you take?

5.   Write out a possible story for each of the transition pathways for your enterprise: family business, ESOP, sale, liquidation, and going public. What will it take to fulfill each of these pathways?

Enterprisers on the Web

1. Download the SBA's document "Transferring Management in the Family-Owned Business" from http://www.sba.gov/idc/groups/public/documents/sba_homepage/serv_sbp_exit.pdf. Use Appendix A to conduct a "Family Business Assessment Inventory" of your enterprise.

2. Read the *Inc.* case study of the Rosen family and the succession process for Sam's Wines (http://www.inc.com/magazine/20070801/splitting-heirs.html). Why did things go wrong? What steps would you have taken if you were Fred Rosen to insure the succession of this enterprise was successful? Now describe the steps you would take as one of the sons. How would you determine what success means for each of the family members involved?

3. "Family Planning: A Rough Guide to Business Succession," http://www.inc.com/magazine/20070801/family-planning-a-rough-guide-to-business-succession.html offers a variety of Web sources on succession planning for family businesses. Using these resources, develop your own steps to talk, write, hire, and ask.

4. You can find information on the blue sky laws of all 50 states at sites such as Securities Links, http://www.seclinks.com/id16.html, and "Introduction to Blue Sky Laws" at Sec Law.com, http://www.seclaw.com/bluesky.htm. Use these sites to explore the differences and similarities in the IPO processes among the state you reside in and three other states that you might consider doing business in. Summarize your findings.

5. Go to the website for SEC filings and forms, EDGAR (http://www.sec.gov/edgar.shtml), and select a company in the same industry as your planned or existing enterprise. Follow the history of the documents and forms filed by the company over time. What was the size of the IPO? Has the company sold other shares of stock over time?

End Notes

1. Noam Wasserman, "The Founder's Dilemma," *Harvard Business Review*, February 2008, pp. 103–109.

2. Bob Buford, *Finishing Well* (Brentwood, TN: Integrity Publishers, 2004); and Bob Buford and Terry Whalin, *Halftime* (Grand Rapids, MI: Zondervan Publishing, 1995).

3. Peter Drucker, "Ten Principles for Finding Meaning in the Second Half of Life," adapted from Bob Buford, *Finishing Well* (Brentwood, TN: Integrity Publishers, 2004) and downloaded from *ACTIVEenergy.net*, http://www.activeenergy.net (July 21, 2008).

4. Carlo Strenger and Arie Ruttenberg, "The Existential Necessity of Midlife Change," *Harvard Business Review*, February 2008, pp. 82–90.

5. Steward D. Friedman, "Be a Better Leader, Have a Richer Life," *Harvard Business Review*, April 2008, pp. 112–118.

6. Paul D. Reynolds, *Entrepreneurship in the US: The Future is Now* (New York: Springer, 2007).

7. Section based on information from the National Center for Employee Ownership, http://www.nceo.org/esops/esop_articles.html (August 26, 2008); and "When Employee Ownership Makes Sense," *Ohio Employee Ownership Center*, Kent State University, http://dept.kent.edu/oeoc/BuyoutAssistance/WhenEOMakesSense.htm (July 21, 2008).

8. "Measuring the 'Fiscal-Fitness' of a Company: The Altman Z-Score," *CreditGuru.com,* http://www.creditguru.com/CalcAltZ.shtml (August 26, 2008); and "Z-Score," *Value Based Management*, http://www.valuebasedmanagement.net/methods_altman_z-score.html (August 26, 2008).

9. "Bankruptcy in Brief," *Moran Law Group*, http://www.moranlaw.net/struggling.htm (July 22, 2008); "Bankruptcy Law—Business Bankruptcy Center," *FreeAdvice*, http://bankruptcy-law.freeadvice.com/business_bankruptcy/ (August 26, 2008); and "Reorganization Under the Bankruptcy Code," *U.S. Courts.com*, http://www.uscourts.gov/bankruptcycourts/bankruptcybasics/chapter11.html#work.

10. Section based on Michael Davis, "Thinking of Doing an IPO?" *Graziado Business Report*, Spring 2000, http://gbr.pepperdine.edu/002/ipo.html; Michael Davis, "Still Thinking of Doing an IPO?", *Graziado Business Report*, Summer 2000, http://gbr.pepperdine.edu/003/ipo.html; and "Going Public: The Pros and Cons," *J.H. Chapman Group*, http://www.jhchapman.com/lib_goingpublic.htm (July 25, 2008).

11. Based on Marshall Brain, "How NASDAQ IPOs Work," *How Stuff Works.com*, http://money.howstuffworks.com/nasdaq-ipo.htm (August 27, 2008); Davis, "Still Thinking of Doing an IPO?"; and Matt H. Evans, "The IPO Process," http://www.exinfm.com/board/ipo_process.htm (July 25, 2008), http://www.sharebuilder.com/about_us/articles/ipo/article2.htm.

PART SIX

Creating the Social Enterprise

Creating and Growing the Social Enterprise

1. Social enterprises focus on creating systemic and sustainable change while solving the needs of others—irrespective of whether meeting these needs is financially feasible. Much of the social enterpriser's challenge comes from closing the funding gap between the cost to provide important services and goods and the funds available from individuals to pay for the services and goods they need. Social enterprises offer multiple opportunities for individuals to provide the resources, whether cash, time, or expertise, to help social enterprises fulfill their missions.

2. The mission statement of a social enterprise clearly defines its purpose by answering the four Cs of the business concept: customers, consideration, connection, and commitment. Social enterprise customers include not only individuals served by the social enterprise but also those who contribute funding and volunteer their time. These organizations must balance the interests of their different stakeholder groups. The social enterpriser sets the tone by demonstrating a high level of commitment to the mission. The social enterpriser should develop metrics to evaluate how efficiently the social enterprise has used its inputs to deliver its outputs and make an impact on society.

3. Although social enterprises can take any legal form, only tax-exempt 501(c)(3) status allows the organization to accept donations that are tax-exempt for the donors. Other legal considerations include registering with the appropriate governmental agencies and tax status for local and state taxes. Ethical issues of concern include conflicts of interest, salaries and benefits, outside remuneration to employees, nepotism, transparency, and IRS compliance.

Suppose you enjoy your work at an insurance services firm and want to advance further in your career by moving on to sales. However, your boss won't promote you because he feels that women should stay in administrative roles. You decide to forge ahead and start your own company to offer independent truckers insurance and other benefits through a trade association. You hire mostly women and create a supportive workplace environment with excellent benefits, where they can grow personally and achieve their potential. As your business thrives, you become involved with your community, contributing time and money to various causes.

This chapter's case introduces us to Cheryl Womack, a social enterpriser who believes in giving back to the community. After selling her successful insurance and benefits company, she focused on helping other women and founded a not-for-profit advocacy organization for women entrepreneurs. Read on to learn more about the way social enterprises create systemic and sustainable change while solving the needs of others.

20.0 Social Enterprises

This last chapter of *Enterprise* explores how individuals create enterprises for a social purpose—that is, to solve a social problem or to address a market failure. **Social enterprises** also generate value for others while operating in a financially efficient and effective manner, with many of the innovative capabilities of a privately owned business. Social enterprises, then, have:

- *An enterprise orientation:* A focus on "customers" (but more broadly defined than "customers"

Social enterprise   Enterprise created to solve a social problem or address a market failure, while operating in a financially sound manner.

521

in Chapters 13 and 14, to include donors and volunteers).

- *Social aims:* The values of the organization focus on the community and the environment.

- *Social ownership:* These enterprises are typically overseen by members of the community accountable to a wider group of stakeholders who are concerned with making an impact that may have a social, environmental, or economic impact on others.

Our purpose in describing social enterprises is to offer insights into a variety of ways to create enterprises in situations beyond the traditional for-profit model (although a social enterprise can also be a for-profit enterprise as well). One of the fundamental assumptions guiding this book until this point has been the importance of the "discipline of the marketplace" in determining whether enterprisers should pursue and exploit opportunities. The "discipline of the marketplace" refers to evaluating opportunities and their feasibility (Chapter 7) based on whether the business concept will make money. As we have learned, business models are feasible when they identify customers who will pay a price for the enterprise's goods or services that is higher than the costs to provide these goods or services.

Now let's explore ways that enterprisers can pursue and exploit opportunities where the direct users of the enterprise's goods and services *cannot* pay the market price for providing these products to them. Instead, other individuals step in to provide the resources necessary to keep the enterprise operating. It is the involvement of these other groups in sustaining the enterprise's mission that significantly differentiates a social enterprise from other enterprises. We will describe the different types of social enterprises that exist, the variety of business models used in social enterprises, and strategies for effectively operating social enterprises.

20.1 What Makes an Enterprise "Social"?

There are many definitions for social enterprises that describe how they are different from other kinds of enterprises. A common thread in all of them, however, is the distinct sense that social enterprises involve a social mission. They focus on creating systemic and sustainable change while solving the needs of others—irrespective of whether meeting these needs is financially feasible.

For example, many individuals need housing but cannot afford to pay for it. While it is an important social good that all individuals have adequate housing, our current economic system (the "marketplace") doesn't necessarily insure that all individuals have decent housing. In some respects, then, we have a failure of the market system. The mechanisms of the marketplace have not ensured that everyone's needs are met at some basic level (such as insuring that everyone has food, shelter, security, an education, and a job). We tend to assume that there will be government agencies and programs that will meet social needs such as housing, education, and employment. In practice, however, government programs are not flexible enough to meet many social needs as our society changes. Social enterprises fill these changing needs.

Social enterprisers also have a bigger sense of purpose that goes beyond filling in the gaps between private enterprises and the government. As Bill Drayton, founder of Ashoka (a social enterprise funding organization), suggests,

> Social entrepreneurs are not happy until their ideas have changed the whole society. That's very different from almost everyone else. Scholars and artists come to rest when they've expressed an idea. Managers, when they solve a problem for their company, complete their goal… None of this satisfies a social entrepreneur. The entrepreneur simply knows in a very deep way that, "I have got to change the whole society."[1]

While we might think that this way of approaching the world might only be for enterprisers who want to address large world problems, such as insuring that everyone has clean drinking water or that everyone lives in an environmentally sustainable way, an enterpriser might have a vision to change society by staging Mozart operas in high schools, teaching playwriting in prisons, or through other activities that improve the lives of others.

The focus of social enterprises, then, is on the "social"—on others. Social enterprisers pursue opportunities that provide value to others, whether or not these enterprises generate financial value. As we will explore in this chapter, much of the social enterpriser's challenge comes from closing the funding gap between the cost to provide important services and goods and the funds available from individuals to pay for the services and goods they need. Many of the innovative ways that social enterprisers generate resources to meet their social missions involve recruiting others to take *social ownership.* Social ownership means that individuals are willing to volunteer their time and resources to meet the goals of the social enterprise and is a critical part of social enterprising.

Types of Social Enterprise

Social enterprises operate on a spectrum between purely philanthropic and purely commercial.[2] Purely philanthropic enterprises typically ask for gifts and grants from donors and then provide free services and goods to beneficiaries. These enterprises are more likely to depend on volunteers and are mission driven toward providing social goods. Purely commercial enterprises are market driven. These enterprises provide economic value by supplying goods and services to customers who pay market prices. They pay market rate wages, purchase market rate materials, and use resources that are priced at the market rate.

Many voluntary organizations, particularly religious organizations, tend to be on the purely philanthropic side of the spectrum. Most religious organizations depend on donations. Individuals who attend church services do not pay an admission fee. Members of the church expect to receive the benefits of membership, whether they donate money to the church or not. Yet even religious organizations charge their members and others for certain services. Most weddings are performed for a fee. Religious organizations often rent out their meeting rooms to others. Some religious organizations sponsor schools and charge tuition to attend. Thus, the ability of an enterprise to be purely philanthropic in nature is often rather limited in practice, unless the social enterprise is a foundation with an endowment.

Most social enterprises, then, operate somewhere between the ends of the philanthropic-commercial spectrum in terms of how they raise income for their social missions. There are three broad ways that they generate the income to run their operations:

- *Those who receive services pay.* For example, the YMCA operates hundreds of gyms and exercise facilities in the United States and sells memberships for use of these facilities. The Y typically charges members additional fees for lessons and training, sports classes, trips, and child care and camp programs. The entire cost of providing these services may not be covered completely by user fees. Organizations such as the Y solicit contributions from those who receive services, as well as from other donors. Examples of social enterprises where member fees cover the costs of services include trade associations

and unions. Members of both of these kinds of organizations pay dues to receive insurance and other benefits that the group might provide.

- *Third parties with a vested interest pay.* If the beneficiary of the services or goods provided by the social enterprise cannot pay, other organizations that see the value of these services will contribute to these organizations to pay for its beneficiaries. Often, the third party with a vested interest is a government agency who needs services to be provided to certain clients. For example, a government agency may fund a social enterprise to operate a health care clinic in a poor neighborhood to give children access to health services before they become too sick and require hospitalization. Other third parties might also have a vested interest in a health clinic in a poor neighborhood. A commercial enterprise that employs members of the neighborhood may find that paying for a community health care clinic reduces absenteeism among its employees.

- *Others pay.* There are two ways to think about "others paying." Some social enterprises produce products and services that can be sold in the marketplace. These goods and services may not directly have a relationship to the mission of the social enterprise. Their sale raises funds that support the enterprise's mission. For example, Goodwill Industries takes marginally skilled individuals and trains and employs them to make products for other companies. The mission of Goodwill Industries involves training, but the products the employees of Goodwill produce can be anything of value, such as computers or housewares. The Haley House Bakery in Roxbury, Massachusetts, maintains a café and bakery that provides training for ten underemployed individuals over a six-month period as a part of a larger mission to provide housing, employment, and sustainable agriculture opportunities for individuals in the South Boston area. The Girl Scout Cookie Program generates revenues for scouting programs through the sale of cookies. These sales not only provide funding for each Girl Scout Troop, but also provide skills and training for girls in marketing, management, and self-reliance.

Others also pay for goods and services through donations of time, money, and other resources to the organization. Many social enterprises depend on monetary, time, and other kinds of donations from its members.

Habitat for Humanity International (HFHI) describes itself as "a nonprofit, ecumenical Christian housing ministry. HFHI seeks to eliminate poverty housing and homelessness from the world and to make decent shelter a matter of conscience and action."[3] It provides opportunities for individuals to donate houses, provide funds to build and rebuild houses, participate in eight different volunteer programs that engage people in projects throughout the world, purchase products from the Habitat for Humanity store, or work for HFHI for pay. The Nature Conservancy, which describes itself as "the leading conservation organization working around the world to protect ecologically important lands and waters for nature and people,"[4] also provides multiple opportunities for individuals to support the organization. They can make cash donations, provide funds through a will or trust, purchase merchandise, attend seminars and tours sponsored by the organization, stay at Nature Conservancy owned lodges, and volunteer for hundreds of activities directed by local and international chapters of the organization.

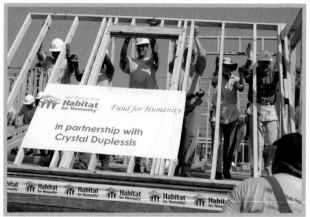

© Chris Graythen/Getty Images

Social enterprises, then, are likely to offer multiple opportunities for individuals to involve themselves in their operations to provide the resources necessary for the social enterprise to fulfill their missions.

How do you become a social enterpriser? One way is to become a KaosPilot, as the Enterprising World box explains.

AN ENTERPRISING WORLD

Piloting Social Entrepreneurship

Can you teach social entrepreneurship? KaosPilot International believes that you can. The Danish organization specializes in new business design and social innovation, offering a three-year entrepreneurial education program featuring "intense training and real world projects encompassing the issues of sustainability, social innovation, and cultural diversity."

As stated on its website, KaosPilot International believes that it offers "much more than an education. It's a mindset. A competency environment for young, creative and socially responsible people and change agents who wish to make a positive difference in society and shape the society of tomorrow." The school, located in Aarhus, Denmark, has a clearly defined set of six core values and attitudes that it integrates into all of its programs, projects, and decisions:

- *Playful:* Curriculum content has to be motivational, creative, and constructive to be part of the Kaos-Pilots' educational program.

- *Real world:* Students and staff have to work with real problems, real people, and real conflicts.

- *Streetwise:* The school must never be out of touch with what is happening at street level in our society.

- *Risk taking:* The program and the staff must possess the will to be brave and take risks.

- *Balanced:* The school must strive for the right dynamic and balance between body and soul, between form and content and, last but not least, between human, time, and economic resources.

- *Compassionate*: Human compassion and social responsibility must be the hallmarks of the school.

In addition, the school focuses on three key areas of curriculum content: sustainability, cultural diversity, and social innovation. Its staff members serve as role models for students, embodying the key values and other KaosPilot principles.

Founded in 1991, the school has developed into an internationally respected institution known for its

(continued)

An Enterprising World (*continued*)

creativity and action-oriented learning environment. While some academics criticize KaosPilots for a lack of academic depth, the results speak for themselves. More than 50 percent of KaosPilots' graduates have started their own businesses, and many others are working in established organizations as change agents or creative staff members.

The three-year academic program is structured around three core disciplines:

1. *Project design:* Project-based learning framework, including project management, finances, intrapreneurship, and event design.

2. *Process design:* Knowledge and competencies, learning processes, creative processes, personal leadership, team building, and process consultation.

3. *Business design:* Reading the cultural, social, and economic trends and using them to identify new socially responsible business concepts; training in entrepreneurship, business economy, social awareness and sustainability, arts and business, corporate identity and branding, and PR and marketing.

It accomplishes its objectives through learning tools that immerse students in an entrepreneurial environment. For example, Praxis-oriented learning means that students tackle real projects for actual clients, not hypothetical ones. Students also get hands-on experience through internships. Teaching techniques balance theoretical concepts with practical projects, individual and team assignments, and local and global issues. Another key concept of KaosPilots is its philosophy of "win-win-win" and social responsibility: Any business between two parties is about more than what each of the two parties gains. It is also about how the deal/collaboration/project/solution benefits a third party—society or the environment. Proactive thinking, personal leadership, and high expectations of student performance are among the other tools that support the educational program. After completing the KaosPilots' program, students have learned to deal with ambiguity, be curious, and communicate positively.

In their first year at KaosPilots, students get a foundation for the future by learning methods and theory and undertaking practical project work. Process design and process management, including the design and facilitation of processes for external customers, are the focus of the second year, during which students are also part of a team that does a three-month "outpost" to implement a project for an external customer. The final year deals with business design (entrepreneurship and building the business plan), and students do an individual world practicum and an individual project leading to the final exam.

What does the admissions committee look for in selecting new team members for KaosPilots? Students must be at least 21 and have experience working in a project environment. The characteristics of potential KaosPilots, according to the website, include:

- The ability to have ideas constantly bubbling and pushing up inside.

- The desire to bring your innovative and creative ability one step further.

- The will and passion to develop socially responsible leadership in organizational and business contexts.

They also seek students who are not afraid of making mistakes or of conflicts, are self-starters, see opportunities rather than limits, have high morals and work ethics, are excellent storytellers, perform well under stress, don't give up, and are generally optimistic.

Discussion Questions

1. What kinds of skills, knowledge, and attitudes does the KaosPilot training program provide? How do KaosPilots go about demonstrating their skills?

2. Explore the KaosPilot website, and look at some of the projects they have undertaken. Which projects seem to be "for profit driven," which appear to be "nonprofit" driven, and which appear to be a blend of both?

3. What kinds of enterprises would be interested in hiring a KaosPilot as an employee? What skills, knowledge, and attitudes would a KaosPilot bring to the organization?

4. What would you measure to indicate whether the KaosPilot program has been successful?

5. If you could design the ideal "enterprise creation and growth" training program, what would it look like, how would it operate, what skills and knowledge would it impart, and how, specifically, would this training occur, and what would be the outcomes of this program?

Sources: Adapted from Poul Rind Christesen and Anne Kirketerp, "Entrepreneurial Action in Shaping Education for Entrepreneurship," working paper presented December 2006 at the National Council for Graduate Entrepreneurship, http://www.ncge.org.uk/communities/index.php; and material on the KaosPilot website, http://www.kaospilot.dk (September 9, 2008).

20.2 The Business Concept: What Is Your Mission?

Like all enterprises, social enterprises need a clear definition of their business concept: their story about the opportunity they will pursue and develop. Typically, the organization's mission statement describes the business concept for a social enterprise. Mission statements provide answers to the four Cs of the business concept (covered in Chapters 6 and 7):

1. Who is the *customer*?

2. What does the customer want? (*consideration*)

3. How will the enterprise provide this consideration? (*connection*)

4. Are you *committed* to the idea and willing to create an ongoing enterprise?

In the social enterprise, the fifth question in the business model—Can you make money doing this?—is broadened to include revenue sources beyond the specific customers who will use the enterprise's goods or services. In this section of the chapter, we will explore how social enterprise business concepts and business models differ from other enterprise business models.

A mission statement for a social enterprise can be summed up simply as a description of the reasons that the organization exists, that is, a description of the enterprise's purpose. Ideally, the mission statement will describe how and why the organization will make a difference for others, what specific kinds of individuals it will serve, and how it will provide these services. For example, the International Council of Museums describes the mission of a museum as:

> A museum is a non-profit making, permanent institution in the service of society and of its development, and open to the public, which acquires, conserves, researches, communicates and exhibits, for purposes of study, education and enjoyment, material evidence of people and their environment.[5]

This mission statement provides a broad sense of the general focus of museums. It describes the four Cs of the business concept: customers—society; consideration—purposes of study, education, and enjoyment; connection—permanent institution...open to the public which acquires, conserves, researchers, communicates, and exhibits; and commitment—service.

Exhibit 20.1 provides the mission statements for three different art museums. These examples demonstrate how each museum interprets this broader mission in a more specific manner. The Museum of Modern Art focuses on modern art, while the Parrish Museum specializes in American art with a particular interest in the eastern part of Long Island, where it is located. As a university art museum, the Anderson Gallery at the University of Buffalo supports the university's cultural life and academic programs, including its museum studies program.

Who Are Your Customers?

A key challenge in creating and growing a social enterprise is insuring that the mission of the organization stays focused. This is often very difficult because the social enterprise is likely to serve a very large number of customers.

In Chapter 1, we introduced the concept of stakeholders, those individuals and entities that have a legitimate interest in the processes and activities of the enterprise. As we indicate throughout the book, the critical stakeholders are the customers the enterprise serves. In the social enterprise, the definition of customer expands to include more groups of stakeholders. The "social" in social enterprise comes to the forefront.

Customers include not only the individuals who are served by the social enterprise but also those who contribute funding for, volunteer their efforts to, and assist in the support of the social enterprise. Though including more stakeholders in the definition of a customer may make it appear that we are suggesting that "everyone" is a customer, we are not. The critical key to success as a social enterprise is carefully considering who these different stakeholder groups are, why they have a legitimate relationship to the social enterprise,

Exhibit
20.1

Art Museum Mission Statements

The Museum of Modern Art (New York)

Founded in 1929 as an educational institution, The Museum of Modern Art is dedicated to being the foremost museum of modern art in the world.

Through the leadership of its trustees and staff, The Museum of Modern Art manifests this commitment by establishing, preserving, and documenting a permanent collection of the highest order that reflects the vitality, complexity, and unfolding patterns of modern and contemporary art; by presenting exhibitions and educational programs of unparalleled significance; by sustaining a library, archives, and conservation laboratory that are recognized as international centers of research; and by supporting scholarship and publications of preeminent intellectual merit.

Central to The Museum of Modern Art's mission is the encouragement of an ever-deeper understanding and enjoyment of modern and contemporary art by the diverse local, national, and international audiences that it serves.

Source: Museum of Modern Art, http://www.moma.org/about_moma/ (August 25, 2008).

The Parrish Art Museum (Southampton, New York)

The Parrish Art Museum is devoted to the collection, preservation, interpretation, and dissemination of American art with particular focus on the art of the East End of Long Island. The Museum is committed to bringing art and people together in its education and outreach programs.

While the Museum's programs, its exhibitions, collections, educational activities, and publications are related specifically to American culture, its past and present, each is related broadly to other cultures, to artifacts, to all visual forms, and to aesthetic and humanist concerns.

Through its programs, the Museum pursues innovative and experimental approaches, and stimulates dialogue and inquiry. It also encourages scholarship of its professional staff and initiates collaboration with related institutions.

The Parrish seeks to be a vital cultural resource for the region and neighboring communities, and to serve beyond the region with its traveling exhibitions and publications.

Overall, the Museum seeks to provide information and inspiration for its current audiences, to actively attract new audiences, and to be an accessible presence for future generations.

Source: Parrish Art Museum, http://www.parrishart.org/parrish.asp?id=162 (August 25, 2008).

The University of Buffalo Museum of Art

The mission of the University of Buffalo Museum of Art Anderson Gallery, the University at Buffalo's museum and home to its museum studies program, is education, research, and maintenance of the university's permanent collection. It provides an adventuresome and accessible environment, therefore offering a rich cultural resource to the campus, scholars, regional communities, and the public.

The museum fulfills its educational mission by presenting exhibitions and programs in support of the curriculum, and by providing study and research opportunities.

The gallery is dedicated to collaboration between the university, cultural institutions, and the community in order to enrich our educational programs.

Source: UB Art Galleries, http://ubartgalleries.buffalo.edu/pages/UBAndersonGallery/andmission.shtml (August 25, 2008).

and how to provide answers to the three Cs for these stakeholder groups.

Let us use a local art museum as an example and explore the different customers, considerations, and connections each group might have. The museum will have customers who come to the museum to view the

art exhibitions. These individuals would be interested in the aesthetic experience they enjoy from visiting the museum. They are likely to pay an admission fee to attend exhibitions or events. Other individuals will participate in museum events because of the social value they receive from these events. Many art museums involve wealthy individuals, for whom attending such art events provides opportunities to meet and develop relationships with other wealthy and powerful people in the community. The art museum might also have an onsite café that individuals may use to meet friends or enjoy a meal in beautiful surroundings. The museum's store offers a variety of art-related products, from posters to jewelry and books.

The art museum is likely to involve students in local schools, who may visit the museum to learn more about art. The museum has an educational program for these students that also involves their teachers and the administrators of the schools, who make arrangements between the museum and these schools. Some visitors will come to the museum to learn art skills and techniques through the art classes the museum might offer evenings and weekends. These classes may be taught for a fee.

Some patrons of the art museum may also be involved as members of the museum's board of directors. These individuals provide funds to maintain and grow the museum and to meet the mission of the museum. Often, board members come from the upper classes of the community, and they use these service opportunities to meet with other wealthy individuals in more relaxed, nonbusiness settings to develop stronger bonds and relationships. Patrons of the art museum are also likely to see the value of the museum's aesthetic mission to the community.

As the preceding discussion indicates, there are many different customers whom the local art museum serves: attendees, patrons, schoolchildren, high school and college students, art students, purchasers of art, and café and gift store customers. Each group of customers will have different reasons for its involvement with the art museum. The challenge in managing such diverse groups is in determining the common mission that joins these individuals together. In addition, the social enterprise will need to insure that each group of customers receives specific benefits from their involvement to keep it engaged in the enterprise's success.

Enterprises, and particularly social enterprises with a broad range of customers, often find themselves in what is called "mission drift" or "mission shift." The primary mission of the social enterprise begins to change or lose focus as it deals with different customer groups. For example, if the art museum experiences a significant demand for the art classes it sponsors, it may add more courses. At some point, the museum may decide to develop a full-time art program where students could earn a college degree. Is a college-level art school within the mission of the art museum? Would an art school distract the members of the art museum from the museum's mission? If the art museum has a gift shop, should the museum focus its sales on local artists? If so, do sales at the art museum compete with local galleries, or does an art museum gift shop enhance local gallery efforts?

In Exhibit 20.2, we have listed a few of the museum's customer categories and identified specific considerations (benefits) and ways to connect with these customers.

For an art museum to be successful as a social enterprise, it must effectively manage all of these customer groups and involve them in ways that provide them with benefits, as well as support the mission of the enterprise. Balancing these different stakeholder interests can be difficult. The mission statement provides a way to give the organization some direction and meaning for all those "customers" involved in its activities by describing: who benefits from the enterprise's efforts (customers); how their well-being will be enhanced (consideration); and how services are provided to these customers (connection).

Volunteers

For most social enterprises, volunteers are an important resource for achieving their missions. The word *volunteer* comes from a Latin word that means willing. The essence of volunteering involves a willingness to engage. Much like the word *enterprise*, which means "to undertake," the volunteer has freedom to undertake the mission of a social enterprise. Because a social enterprise's volunteers form one of its primary groups of customers, encouraging individuals to volunteer for a social enterprise is a very important task for the social enterpriser. Besides the intrinsic benefits that a volunteer will enjoy through helping others—a significant benefit, to say the least—there are numerous other reasons why someone might volunteer their time and effort in a social enterprise. They may want to

- Learn new skills.

- Build confidence through achievements.

- Meet new and different people.

- Build a network.

- Have fun.

- Improve their health; studies indicate that volunteering provides a sense of well-being, helps people sleep better, and builds their immune system.

exhibit
20.2

Consideration and Connections for Museum Customers

Customers	Considerations	Connections
Art museum attendees	Viewing art in a beautiful setting Learning about art	Visiting the art museum
Art museum members	Social connections	Newsletter Special events
Patrons	Name on building Meet other wealthy people Enhance community	Board of Directors Patrons Ball Other special events
Schoolchildren	Learn about art Get out of school	Visiting the art museum
Art students	Learn to make art	Attending art classes
Docents (volunteer tour guides)	Teaching others about the art in the museum's collection Meeting new people	Spending time in the art museum
Volunteers (other functions, such as ticket sales, information desk, and gift store sales)	Helping visitors enjoy the museum Meeting new people Networking with other volunteers	Forming friendships with other art lovers

- Improve career options by enhancing and increasing skills through a voluntary position.

- Gain information about and exposure to different jobs.

- Learn or develop strengths (communication, teamwork, time management, positive attitude, and initiative).

- Acquire meaningful work experience that also provides additional positive work references.[6]

A training manual is an important tool for insuring that volunteers are able to learn new skills and make a contribution to the social enterprise. In Chapter 17, we briefly discussed what you would include in an employee manual. These same considerations apply in the social enterprise, where volunteers may comprise a large portion of your workforce. Selecting and training the right volunteers for your social enterprise is similar to hiring and training employees. All volunteers want their efforts to provide value to others. By developing a training manual for volunteers, social enterprises can

ensure that volunteers have the skills and knowledge to make an impact. Listed below are several organizations with volunteer training manuals on their websites (you can find the manuals by going to the site and searching for "volunteer training manual"). These manuals and similar examples available on the Web provide insights into the kinds of skills and knowledge a volunteer will gain through involvement:

- The National Court Appointed Special Advocate Association, http://www.casanet.org

- USDA Forest Service Volunteer Manual for Counting Trees, http://www.umass.edu/urbantree/volmanual.pdf

- Po-Ha-Ba Native Healing Center, http://www.poohabah.com

- Youth Volunteer Corps, http://www.nationalserviceresources.org

Finally, as we indicated in Chapter 17, the ability to grow an enterprise depends on the enterpriser involving others, particularly individuals who can serve as mentors, directors, and advisors to the enterprise. A social enterprise will grow only if it has a strong board of directors or advisors committed to the organization's mission. The characteristics of board members for social enterprises are somewhat different than for other kinds of enterprises. For a social enterprise, one would look for board members who:

- Are committed to the social enterprise's mission, values, and goals.

- Are willing to devote their time and energy to growing the social enterprise.

- Will either provide resources or work to raise funds to support the social enterprise.

- Are connected and have access to individuals in the community who can also provide support and assistance.

- Have expertise in social enterprises (e.g., legal, fund raising, and managerial).

- Bring diverse backgrounds and viewpoints, so that the board represents the community, the organizations, and the people it serves.

Commitment

Volunteers, donors, board members and advisors, or anyone else will be more likely to participate in a social enterprise when they see that the enterpriser is committed to its mission. It is critical that the enterpriser demonstrates and articulates a vision about the value of the social enterprise's mission to others. As we suggested in Chapter 6 (Discovering Opportunities), the enterpriser should tell a story about why it is important to start and grow the enterprise. This story will help convince others of your commitment to the social enterprise if it answers the following questions:

- Why do you believe this social enterprise should be supported?

- How has (or will) this social enterprise make a difference in other people's lives?

- What led you to the realization that this social enterprise is necessary?

- What will this social enterprise do that other organizations can't?

- What personal investment (your time, effort, and funds) have you made to create and grow this enterprise?

- Why should others get involved?

The answers to these questions lie in the business concept and the four Cs: *customers, consideration, connection, and commitment.* If you can succinctly cover all of these questions in your story in less than two minutes, you will have a powerful message that will engage others to join you in your efforts.

20.3 Social Enterprise Feasibility and Business Plans

The insights offered in Chapters 7 (Feasibility) and 8 (Business Plans and Planning) are also applicable to evaluating and developing a social enterprise opportunity. Be sure to review those chapters as the foundation for conducting a feasibility study or a business plan for a social enterprise. This section will offer a few additional suggestions about how feasibility studies and business plans may differ from the studies and plans of other kinds of enterprises. Exhibit 20.3 provides six categories of questions to ask as you develop your plans.

Examples of different feasibility studies and business plans for nonprofit organizations are available on the Web and can assist you in formulating your own. All of these plans attempt to identify ways that these social enterprises make valuable, important, and specific social impacts. Here are a few sites to consult:

- Write Boston, http://www.socialinnovationforum. org/finalists/WriteBostonProspectus.pdf

- Circle Catering (formerly Tacos Unidos), http:// www.socialinnovationforum.org/finalists/ TacosUnidosProspectus.pdf

- Connecticut Motorsports Business Association (Trade Association), http://www.bplans.com/ sample_business_plans/Nonprofit_Business_Plans/

- Npower Capital City, http://www.si.umich. edu/~presnick/courses/winter01/575/docs/ Sample%20bizplan.pdf

- Helping Hand, a Nonprofit Food Bank, http:// www.morebusiness.com/nonprofit-food-business-plan

exhibit
20.3

Questions for a Social Enterprise Feasibility Study

1. *Clarity about the social opportunity your enterprise will pursue*

   - Who are the customers your social enterprise will serve?
   - Why do these individuals need your help?
   - What other enterprises and government organizations are also trying to solve this problem?
   - Why is your social enterprise unique?
   - What do you bring to the table that these other organizations don't?

2. *Solving your customers' needs*

   - What is the process by which your enterprise will involve others to provide specific benefits and services to your customers?
   - What resources are necessary, and when are they required?
   - How do these resources match the specific outcomes that your social enterprise will achieve?

3. *Meeting specific social needs*

   - Why and how will your customers be better off because of the activities of your social enterprise?

4. *Measuring results*

   - How will you identify metrics that demonstrate the value of your social enterprise's activities?
   - What metrics will be most useful to measuring results?
   - What benchmarks should your social enterprise achieve to insure that others see its value over time?

5. *Finding and allocating resources (money, volunteers, donations, etc.)*

   - How will your social enterprise acquire resources, and from whom?
   - How will your organization engage these resource providers in the future?
   - What steps will you take to identify and acquire other sources of funding as the social enterprise grows?

6. *Developing leadership*

   - Why are you involved and committed to this social enterprise, and how can you make a difference?
   - How will you identify the key individuals involved in the social enterprise, their skills, and the reasons for their commitment to the mission of the enterprise?

20.4 Measuring Social Enterprise Success

Success in social enterprises can be measured in many different ways. In the end, the value of a social enterprise to others will depend on whether it provides benefits to others. A for-profit enterprise can demonstrate its value by showing financial profits from operations. In a social enterprise, other measures show that value has been provided to others—effectively and efficiently. In this section, we offer a number of different performance and impact measures that social enterprisers can use.[7]

There are three broad ways to measure the effectiveness and efficiency of social enterprises: input measures, output measures, and impact measures. *Input measures* indicate what resources the social enterprise is utilizing in order to sustain and grow its operations. For example, a social enterprise can measure:

- The dollar amount of donations given to the organization (weekly, monthly, annually, and by each member)

- The number of paid and unpaid volunteers

- The amount of time volunteers provide

- Involvement with other organizations

- Names of prominent individuals involved

Output measures indicate what the social enterprise is specifically doing with its inputs. These could be measures of:

- The number of beneficiaries served by the social enterprise's services

- The types of beneficiaries served and their specific needs

- Descriptions of the programs the enterprise offers

- The specific services each program provides

- Listings of the number of times particular services were provided (by service)

- The number of meetings or events held

- The number of fund raising efforts and awareness efforts

- The number of people involved in all events, by event

Impact measures provide a sense of whether the social enterprise has actually made a difference in the lives of others in the community. An enterprise can be engaged in many different activities, but the most important question is, Are these activities really making a difference? Measures that indicate impact might include:

- For beneficiaries—Changes in skills (skill-based tests; percentage who qualified)

- For beneficiaries—Changes in behaviors (success rates for accomplishing certain activities; number of people who didn't relapse)

- For beneficiaries—Changes in status (number who graduated, number who avoided undesirable behavior, number who got jobs, and number who have reduced health problems)

- The process—How are beneficiaries followed to insure that impacts have been attained?

- Social cost benefits—Can the benefits to society of the social enterprise's activities be measured?

- Social cost savings—Can the savings to society of the social enterprise's activities be measured?

The more ways that people can see that the social enterprise has made a difference in society, the more likely that the social enterprise will be able to continue its efforts and expand through the support of others. Identifying the specific inputs, outputs, and impact provides a tangible way of seeing success.

The social enterpriser should evaluate how efficiently the social enterprise has used its inputs to deliver its outputs and make an impact. Just as investors in for-profit enterprises seek to gain as much return on the funds they provide, donors, volunteers, and others want to know that the social enterprise has used the resources they give to it in the most efficient and effective manner possible.

Finally, a very significant way for describing the success of a social enterprise is through stories that describe how specific lives of individuals have been changed because of the social enterprise's activities. These stories put a "face" on the measures of success. Collecting and disseminating stories can show how specific programs and activities actually work to improve lives and make changes. Stories can evoke the emotions and feelings that come through service to others in ways that make a difference.

20.5 Social Enterprise Legal and Ethical Issues

A social enterprise can take one of several legal forms, from sole proprietorship, partnership, corporation, or nonprofit organization (see Chapter 4 for an overview). If the social enterprise is going to take donations and donors want to claim a tax deduction for these donations, the enterprise will need to form as a 501(c)(3) organization as described by the Internal Revenue Service. The various advantages and disadvantages of a 501(c)(3) organization are listed in Chapter 4.

Like their for-profit colleagues, social enterprisers will need competent legal advice both to develop the social enterprise and to grow it. Below are four legal issues that they will need to address early in the startup process:

- Will the social enterprise have tax-exempt status? (This is important for receiving donations and funds from individuals and other nonprofit organizations. Tax-exempt status does not, however, prevent governments from assessing taxes on income earned that is not directly related to the mission of the enterprise.)

- Will the social enterprise have members who can vote and make decisions?

- Is the social enterprise registered with federal, state, and local authorities to solicit funds from others?

- Is the social enterprise exempt from state and local taxes, such as sales taxes or property taxes?

Ethical Issues

Social enterprisers face ethical issues that are different from those in other kinds of organizations. *Conflict of interest* is one major concern. Can the enterpriser, staff members, volunteers, or board members financially benefit from business relationships with the social enterprise? For example, if the social enterprise needs a public relations campaign, it may be a conflict of interest to pay a board member or a relative of a board member to conduct this work. The IRS has a number of forms and documents outlining types of conflicts of interest that may be unethical or illegal.

In the area of salaries and benefits, social enterprises tend to pay staff less than for-profit enterprises do. However, there are issues about providing excessive compensation to social enterprisers beyond what might be appropriate for the size of the enterprise and the duties involved. Indeed, the Taxpayer Bill of Rights 2, a law that provides punishments to individuals involved in social enterprises that are involved in financial misconduct, includes legal regulations regarding what might be excessive compensation. On the other side, there is the concern that staff members of the social enterprise be paid enough so that they have a life-sustainable wage, have health benefits, and can live at a reasonable standard of living. It should also be noted that it is inappropriate to compensate employees or outside consultants for fundraising activities where compensation is based on a percentage of the amount raised.

A social enterpriser's outside activities can also be called into question. If the social enterprise is the primary activity of the social enterpriser and this individual receives a salary and benefits from the organization, should any income derived from the enterpriser's other efforts be given to the social enterprise? Many social enterprisers are asked to make presentations or write books and give speeches that generate income from fees and royalties. If the enterpriser is employed full time by the social enterprise, should these earnings be the enterpriser's or the enterprises? The social enterprise should establish a stated and written policy regarding how outside remuneration to employees of the social enterprise is handled.

Nepotism is another concern. To keep conflict of interest issues to a minimum, social enterprises should not hire family members. Such a policy would also promote a merit-oriented organization, rather than one based on family advantages or personal contacts.

Transparency and IRS compliance must also be taken into consideration. The U.S. Internal Revenue Service issued new regulations and forms in 2008 that require nonprofit organizations to provide substantial details about: the salaries and compensation of key employees, how the organization is managed and governed, and specifics about the kinds of programs and activities the organization provides. The information is provided to the IRS on the IRS Form 990 and becomes public information once it is filed and processed. The kinds of questions that IRS Form 990 asks include:

- Detailed financial statements of all sources of funding acquired and used. (These forms are similar to income statements and balance sheets.) Information will need to be provided on all donations, as well as any income earned.

- Did any officer, director, trustee, or key employee have a family relationship or a business relationship with any other officer, director, trustee, or key employee?

- Were minutes taken at meetings of the board of directors and committees of the board?

- Does the organization have a written conflict of interest policy, and does the organization regularly and consistently monitor and enforce compliance with the conflict of interest policy?

- Does the organization have a written document retention and destruction policy?

- Describe your three largest programs.

- Provide information on compensation to officers, directors, and employees.

Information on compensation will include information about nontaxable benefits such as retirement plan contributions, health-club dues reimbursement, and first-class travel. Nonprofit organizations are also required to report how compensation is determined and by whom (such as a board of directors), and to provide comparisons to individuals in similar positions at other organizations. Finally, it should be noted that these reporting requirements are being phased in through 2010, and that smaller nonprofit organizations (based on gross receipts) may only need to submit a less complicated form (Form 990-EZ).

As we have suggested in a number of places throughout this book, and particularly in Chapter 18, all enterprises should have a written code of conduct that specifies the ethical standards by which the enterprise will operate. Social enterprises are no exception.

20.6 ENTERPRISERS

Cheryl Womack's Road to Success

Frustrated by roadblocks that prevented her from advancing in her career, Cheryl Womack started her own firm. "In 1980 I was the manager for a department that provided services for owner operators in the trucking industry," she recalls. "I made $17,000 a year and was denied the opportunity to go out on the road and sell because I was a woman. So, I started my own business. My primary goal was to be in charge of my personal and financial destiny." Along the way, she developed multiple businesses that allowed her to achieve her goals—and help others, especially other women, along the way.

Womack founded her first company, VCW Inc., in 1981, and operated it from her basement. The name of the company stands for Very Cute Women—and at first she hired only women because they are very detail-oriented and also very customer service-oriented. Although her company provided similar insurance services as her previous employer, changes in the legal environment called for some creativity in structuring the business. "Things were changing in how you could write policies and who needed to be the policy owner," she explains. "You couldn't be a master policyholder in the name of the trucking company and take care of the independent contractors. It needed to be either in their name or in some master name." So she started an association, the National Association for Independent Truckers (NAIT), to be the named insured. Then she asked herself, "What are the benefits I can offer?"

As she answered that question, she developed an organization that would serve, support, and represent independent trucking entrepreneurs and their businesses over the long term. NAIT partners with independent truckers to reduce costs of providing benefits through the group's purchasing power. Among the benefits it offers are cost-effective insurance coverages, retirement benefit plans, and low-interest credit cards. NAIT also works with truckers to resolve problems common to independent truckers; inform them about current issues;

© ColorBlind Images/Jupiter Images

and facilitate communication between NAIT members and governmental and regulatory bodies, service and product providers, and others in the industry.

This pioneering woman entrepreneur became a success in two male-dominated industries, insurance and trucking. She is an innovative leader, developing numerous groundbreaking insurance products, including an alternative to workers' compensation for independent contractors that has become a model for the industry.

Womack provided excellent benefits not just to her customers in the trucking industry but also for her employees. "Everything I do here cultivates and grows those employees," she says. Because her former employer did not respect her talent, recognize that she was responsible for much of his business's growth, or give her an opportunity to excel, she was determined not to make the same mistake with her own company. She created an environment where people's talents are recognized so they can succeed. The workplace itself supports the employees with a beautiful work setting, low-cost home-cooked lunches, onsite daycare, a company store, and flexible dental and health plans. She asked people to expand their jobs and encouraged and rewarded suggestions, paying as much as $1,000 cash for good ideas.

These benefits paid off in terms of reducing employee turnover, enhancing overall loyalty and fostering a positive attitude. "We maintained benefits that could be measured against Fortune 100 corporations and were named for two consecutive years as one of the Top 100 Companies to Work For in the United States by *Working Woman* magazine," Womack says. "We were staffed 80 percent by women, and management was made up of 80 percent women." Her employees viewed her as a mentor. "I think Cheryl is incredibly able to get all the other people who work here to buy into her vision," said Theresa Bramicome, president of NAIT. "She doesn't want people to just get up and go to work, she wants them to get up and be excited about what they're going to do that day."

"I have believed from the beginning in becoming personally involved in the community," says Womack. NAIT and VCW contributed more than $100,000 a year to Kansas City cultural organizations. She chaired several major local fundraising events; is a founding member of GrassRoots Impact, Inc., an organization that connects corporate America and political leaders to small business owners, including women-owned businesses, minorities, and women in business; and founded Entrepreneur's Exchange. She served on the Small Business Council for the U.S. Chamber of Commerce and the U.S. Chamber's Board of Directors. She also donated $2 million to the University of Kansas for a women's softball stadium.

By 2002, Womack's business had grown to serve more than 12,000 members and generate in excess of $100 million in revenues. Her original intent was to sell 65 percent of the business to her employees when she turned 50. "I never started [the business] with a lifelong dream to own it to my end," she says. "I started it to create the ability for me to make choices in my life. So these businesses really were just stepping-stones for me. ... This company is not my identity. I really have a big influence on this company and how it appears to people, but there are lots of other influences here, and this company is not me." However, instead she sold NAIT and its related companies to a major private equity firm, remaining as executive vice president for two years, and at age 51 formed VCW Holding LLC to partner with and provide consulting and administrative services for a variety of mid-sized growth companies.

She also turned to her special interest in empowering women in business. She founded and currently chairs Leading Women Entrepreneurs of the World (LWEW), a not-for-profit organization that advocates for women business owners. This group of about 300 international women entrepreneurs employs 350,000 people and does over $32 billion in annual gross revenues. The organization provides an exclusive forum for honorees to exchange ideas and network. In addition, she is President and CEO of the Star Group team, which handles program and partnership development for annual events recognizing and honoring The Leading Women Entrepreneurs of the World. Never content with the status quo, in 2006, she started Off the Page Publishing Company, LLC, and began writing columns for the *Kansas City Star* and *Flourish*, a magazine for Kansas City businesswomen.

Discussion Questions

1. Is VCW Inc. a social enterprise even though it is a for-profit business? On what do you base your answer? Is Cheryl Womack a social enterpriser?

2. In what other ways could the NAIT be organized to serve its members? Is the for-profit model the best way, and why?

3. Identify the different customers that VCW Inc. serves. What kinds of benefits does VCW provide each set of customers? How does serving one set of customers benefit the others?

4. How successful was Cheryl Womack in responding to changes in the business environment and personally? What was her legacy, and how has she redefined herself since selling NAIT?

5. Womack's original exit strategy was to sell the company to her employees. What circumstances might have caused her to sell it to an outside firm instead?

6. There are over 35,000 different associations currently operating in the United States. Go to any number of websites offering directories of associations [e.g., http://www.ipl.org/div/aon/ (August 22, 2008) or http://www.directoryofassociations.com/ (August 22, 2008)] to find associations in areas that you would be interested in joining. What kinds of benefits and services do these membership organizations provide? Compare the similarities and differences between these associations to the NAIT.

Sources: Adapted with permission from Small Business School, the series on PBS, at http://SmallBusinessSchool.com; "Cheryl Womack of VCW," *Ziggs.com*, http://www.ziggs.com/apps/profile/bio.aspx?uid=1802 (September 9, 2008); "Keep on Trucking: Cheryl Womack, The Leading Women Entrepreneurs of the World," *O, The Oprah Magazine*, September 2005, http://images.oprah.com/omagazine/200509/omag_200509_million_101.jhtml; "V. Cheryl Womack," *Kansas City Pubic Schools 2004 Alumni Recognition*, http://www.kckps.org/recognition/alumni/2004/womack.html (September 5, 2008); and "Women Creating Wealth," *KC Small Business*, July 2003, http://www.kcsmallbusiness.com.

Summary

1. Social enterprises are enterprises whose mission is to solve a social problem or address a market failure while generating value for others. They focus on creating systemic and sustainable change while solving the needs of others—irrespective of whether meeting these needs is financially feasible. They should, however, operate in a financially efficient and effective manner. These enterprises are typically overseen by members of the community who are in turn accountable to a wider group of stakeholders. Unlike for-profit enterprise customers, who pay for goods and services received, the direct users of social enterprise cannot pay the market price for these goods and services. The necessary resources are provided by other individuals.

2. Social enterprisers pursue opportunities that provide value to others, whether or not these enterprises generate financial value. Closing the funding gap between the cost to provide important services and goods and the funds available from individuals to pay for the services and goods they need is one of the major challenges for social enterprisers.

3. Social enterprises can be purely philanthropic, fully supported by gifts and grants from donors and then providing free services and goods to beneficiaries. Some use a mixed model to generate income from donations and from other sources. They may charge membership dues or fees to those who receive services. Third parties with a vested interest in the service provided may subsidize the operations of a social enterprise. Other social enterprises produce products and services that can be sold in the marketplace. In addition, the time and resource contributions of volunteers are essential to the social enterprise's ability to provide services.

4. The mission statement of a social enterprise clearly defines its purpose by answering the four Cs of the business concept: customers, consideration, connection, and commitment. It describes how and why the organization will make a difference for others; what specific kinds of individuals it will serve; and how it will provide these services.

5. Social enterprisers serve a large and varied group of customers, including the individuals served by the social enterprise, those who contribute funding for the enterprise, volunteers who give time to the enterprise, and others who support the social enterprise. They must understand who these customers are, how best to serve them through the other 3 Cs, and how to balance the interests of different stakeholder groups.

6. Volunteers form one of a social enterprise's primary groups of customers. The benefits volunteers receive include the satisfaction of helping others, learning new personal and career skills, meeting new people, and acquiring meaningful work experience. Social enterprises should select and train their volunteers as carefully as other enterprisers hire employees. A strong board of directors or advisors committed to its mission is necessary to fulfill the organization's goals. The social enterpriser sets the tome by demonstrating a high level of commitment to the mission.

7. The feasibility study for a social enterprise should clearly explain the social opportunity the entity will pursue, how it will solve and fulfill customer needs, and why key leaders are committed to the organization. It should also describe the funding plan to acquire resources and metrics that will measure the value of the enterprise.

8. Three ways to measure the effectiveness and efficiency of social enterprises are input measures, output measures, and impact measures. Inputs focus on the resources—money, numbers of volunteers, hours served—to sustain and grow operations. Output measures such as beneficiaries served and programs and services offered, and people involved in events show how the social enterprise uses its inputs to provide services. The impact of a social enterprise addresses how its activities make a difference for the various customer groups.

9. Social enterprises can take any legal form. They should choose tax-exempt 501(c)(3) status if they want to accept donations that are tax-exempt for the donors. Other legal considerations include registering with the appropriate governmental agencies and tax status for local and state taxes. Ethical issues of concern are conflicts of interest, salaries and benefits, outside remuneration to employees, nepotism, transparency, and IRS compliance.

Review Questions

1. Define social enterprise and differentiate it from other types of enterprises. What is the social ownership concept?

2. From what sources does a social enterprise derive its income?

3. What is the purpose of a social enterprise's mission statement? What questions should it answer?

4. Describe the different types of customers a social enterprise serves.

5. What value does volunteering provide to the social enterprise and to its customers? What kinds of experiences and benefits does a volunteer gain?

6. What does the feasibility study for a social enterprise contain?

7. How does a social enterprise measure its effectiveness?

8. Name the key legal considerations of a social enterprise.

9. Summarize the ethical issues that social enterprises face.

Applying What You've Learned

1. Identify three social enterprisers who have founded and are currently operating social enterprises in your community. As a start, use the interview guideline (Question 2 in "Apply What You've Learned" in Chapter 2) to learn their stories and reasons for becoming a social enterpriser. How are these social enterprisers different/similar from other kinds of enterprisers?

2. Identify a group of individuals who you believe are underserved by current businesses, nonprofits and governmental agencies in your community. What benefits and services are currently being offered by each of these groups? How might they better provide their services? How might a new social enterprise better provide services to this group of individuals?

3. As an exercise, identify other customer types that might be involved in a local art museum, list the reasons they would be involved in the museum, and, the benefits you would think they might receive from their involvement.

4. Identify three social enterprises in your community that you would be interested in volunteering for. What appeals to you about these three organizations? Why would you be interested in participating in their efforts? Include the benefits the organization will receive from your participation and what benefits volunteering will give you personally.

5. What metrics can a social enterprise use to measure its progress and success in meeting its goals? How will this vary with the type of enterprise? Select one of the social enterprises you chose in Question 3 and develop a set of metrics for it.

Enterprisers on the Web

1. How many social enterprises operate in your community? Identify the various kinds of social enterprises in your city (or state), using Google or one or more of the following websites:

   National Council of Nonprofit Associations (NCNA), http://www.ncna.org/

   Corporation for National and Community Service, http://www.nationalserviceresources.org/

   Ashoka, http://www.ashoka.org/home/index.cfm

   Social Venture Network, http://www.svn.org/

   Social Enterprise Alliance, http://www.se-alliance.org/

   International Association of Investors in the Social Economy, http://www.inaise.org/

   Chronicle of Philanthropy, http://philanthropy.com/

2. Go to the websites of five social enterprises in your community and identify: their mission

statements, ways they measure the success of meeting their mission, and ways they involve volunteers. How does each website go about telling their story?

3. Go to MissionStatements.com, http://www.missionstatements.com/index.html, to explore various kinds of mission statements. What mission statements best appeal to you? Why?

4. Each year, the magazine *Fast Company* sponsors the Social Capitalist Awards (http://www.fastcompany.com/social/2008/index.html). First, look at the methodology section (http://www.fastcompany.com/social/2008/articles/methodology.html) that describes the criteria that *Fast Company* uses to select award winners. Using these criteria, browse through the list of award winners and identify why five of these winners meet the evaluation criteria. In addition, explore how these winners tell their story, describe their mission, engage volunteers, and measure success.

5. Several organizations have undertaken detailed analyses of the metrics social enterprises might utilize to evaluate their success, including:

    • REDF, http://www.redf.org. Offers a number of templates and tools to evaluate the feasibility and impact of social enterprises.

    • Schwab Foundation for Social Enterprise, http://www.schwabfound.org. Describes their selection criteria for the social entrepreneurs of the year.

    • The United Way, http://www.liveunited.org. Provides many different resources to evaluate programs they are involved with.

    How do they measure whether a social enterprise should be given funding or not? Revisit the metrics you developed in Question 5 of the previous exercise and compare them to the ones suggested by these organizations.

End Notes

1. Bill Drayton, "15 Minutes with Bill Drayton," *Stanford Social Innovation Review*, Spring 2004, pp. 11–12.

2. J. Gregory Dees, "Enterprising Nonprofits," *Harvard Business Review*, January 1998, pp. 55–67.

3. "Fact Sheet," *Habitat for Humanity International*, http://www.habitat.org/how/factsheet.aspx (August 28, 2008).

4. "About Us," *The Nature Conservancy*, http://www.nature.org/ (August 26, 2008).

5. International Council of Museums, http://icom.museum/definition.html (August 26, 2008).

6. List based on information in "Benefits of Volunteering," *Working.com,* http://working.canada.com/national/resources/jobseekers/story.html?id=0655199d-f747-4787-b05d-fb5eac351a69 (August 26, 2008); "The Benefits of Volunteer Work," *Suite 101.com,* http://careeradvice.suite101.com/article.cfm/the_benefits_of_volunteer_work (August 26, 2008); "Developing and Managing Volunteers," *Free Management Library,* http://www.managementhelp.org/staffing/outsrcng/volnteer/volnteer.htm (August 26, 2008); "What Volunteering Can Do for You," *TimeBank.org,* http://www.timebank.org.uk/aboutgiving/benefits_vol.htm (August 26, 2008); and "The Personal Benefits of Volunteer Work," *HubPages.com,* http://hubpages.com/hub/The-Personal-Benefits-of-Volunteer-Work (August 26, 2008).

7. Section based on Catherine Clark, William Rosenzweig, David Long, and Sara Olsen, *Double Bottom Line Project Report: Assessing Social Impact in Double Bottom Line Ventures*, Research Initiative on Social Entrepreneurship, January 2004, http://www.riseproject.org/dbl_methods_catalog.pdf; J. Cutt, "Performance Measurement in Non-Profit Organizations: Integration and Focus within Comprehensiveness," *Asian Journal of Public Administration*, June 1998, pp. 3–29; Mark R. Kramer, "Measuring Innovation: Evaluation in the Field of Social Entrepreneurship" (Boston: FSG Social Impact Advisors, 2005), http://76.12.250.43/ideas/item/353; Linda M. Lampkin, Mary Kopczynski Winkler, Janelle Kerlin, Harry P. Hatry, Debra Natenshon, Jason Saul, Julia Melkers, and Anna Seshadri, "Building a Common Outcome Framework to Measure Nonprofit Performance," *Urban Institute*, January 5, 2007, http://www.urban.org/publications/411404.html; "Measuring Programmatic Success: Tips for Nonprofit Boards," *Council on Foundations*, http://www.cof.org/files/Documents/Governing_Boards/Board%20Tools/boardtips.pdf (August 28, 2008); Tammy Hobbs Miracky, Amy Lieb, and Mia Kulla, "The SoCap Way," *Fast Company*, December 2007, http://www.fastcompany.com/social/2008/articles/methodology.html; and *"REDF's* Current Approach to SROI," *REDF*, http://www.redf.org/download/sroi/REDFs-Current-Approach-to-SROI.pdf (August 28, 2008).

Time Management

How Do You Manage Your Time?

How well do you manage your time? The quiz in Exhibit A.1 will give you more clues to how well you manage time.

Where Did the Day Go?

Before you determine how to use time better, you have to understand how you currently spend your time. This process starts with recording everything you do on a time log.[1] An easy way to track your time is on a chart that divides your day into 30-minute segments. Keep the log for at least two weeks, and longer if your work follows a monthly cycle. You may want to track your whole day, including personal time, or just focus on work-related activities. Armed with your detailed log, analyze how you spent your time.

- **Set up task categories.** Divide your tasks into relevant categories, such as commuting, staff meetings, client meetings, business phone calls/email, personal phone calls/email, writing proposals, personal errands, family time, and new business development. Add up the time spent for each category and calculate the percentage of time you spend on each task category. You will quickly see where your time went!

- **Classify categories into three or four broader groups.** These can relate to Covey's four quadrants (Exhibit 3.2, p. 56), or you may prefer to divide them into A-B-C groups; for example, A tasks: important and urgent/planning and development; B tasks: either important or urgent/ongoing projects; C tasks: routine tasks. Determine how much time you spend in each group. Studies indicate that most of us devote about 60 percent of our time to routine tasks (Quadrants 3 and 4), 25 percent to ongoing projects (Quadrant 1), and a mere 15 percent to planning and development (Quadrant 2). The

"ideal" distribution is, in fact, the opposite, with 60 percent spent on activities that further your career or business or contribute to your personal growth, and only 15 percent on routine matters.

- **Look for patterns.** Review your time logs in detail to analyze your current time usage compared to your ideal. Also note whether you finish tasks in the allocated time frame and when you do things during the day. If you have slow periods at the same time most days, schedule activities that require concentration and creativity in those periods. Organize your day so that your workflow is relatively consistent.

Time Management Strategies

Now that you've set goals, established priorities, and assessed how you use your time, you're ready to take control of your time. While we can't provide a complete time management course in this book, we can start you on the right path.

A Sharper Focus

Imagine that a genie has granted your wish for more hours in the day. Poof! Your day now has 27 hours and your time management problems are over. Unfortunately, having more hours isn't the answer. Your 27-hour-day time logs will probably show that you have continued to allocate your time to the same tasks, wasting even larger blocks of time.

It's not more time you need, but more effective use of what you already have. Don't confuse being busy with making progress. The key to effective time management is *focus*. To stay focused on what's important:

- *Consult your personal mission statement and goals often.* These should be the foundation of your weekly schedule and will keep you focused on activities that move you closer to your goals.

- *Make and use a weekly plan and a daily "to-do" list.* Label each task with its priority code (more on this in the next section).

How Time-Worthy Are You?

Assessing Your Ability

*T*he key of successful management is the possession of good time-management skills. Think about how well you manage your time by responding to the following statements, then mark the options that are closest to your experience. Be as honest as you can: If your answer is "never," mark Option 1; if your answer is "always," mark Option 4; and so on. Add your scores together, then refer to the Analysis to see how you scored. Use your answers to identify the areas that need the most improvement.

OPTIONS
1 Never
2 Occasionally
3 Frequently
4 Always

1 I arrive on time and prepared for meetings.
1 2 3 4

2 I ensure that a clock is visible in the room where meetings are held.
1 2 3 4

3 The meetings I organize achieve their purpose.
1 2 3 4

4 The meetings I organize finish on time.
1 2 3 4

5 I open my mail as soon as it arrives on my desk.
1 2 3 4

6 I skim any relevant newspaper and magazine articles.
1 2 3 4

7 I cross my name off the circulation list for magazines and jourals I do not read.
1 2 3 4

8 I read my faxes on the day on which I receive them.
1 2 3 4

9 I am able to complete tasks without interruptions from colleagues.
1 2 3 4

10 I decide how many times I can be interrupted in a day.
1 2 3 4

11 I reserve certain hours for visits from colleagues.
1 2 3 4

12 I close my office door when I want to think strategically.
1 2 3 4

13 I tell telephone callers that I will return their calls, and I do so.
1 2 3 4

14 I limit the duration of my telephone calls.
1 2 3 4

15 I allow a colleague or secretary to screen my telephone calls.
1 2 3 4

16 I decide how many telephone calls I can deal with personally in a day.
1 2 3 4

(continued)

Exhibit A.1 (*continued*)

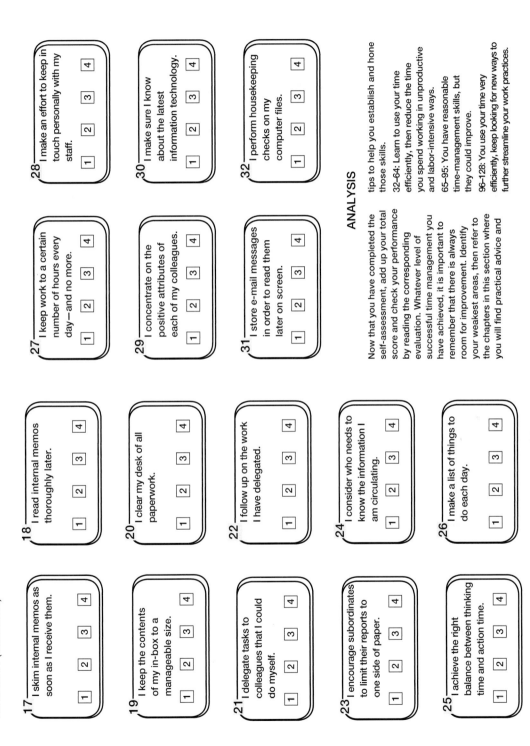

ANALYSIS

Now that you have completed the self-assessment, add up your total score and check your performance by reading the corresponding evaluation. Whatever level of successful time management you have achieved, it is important to remember that there is always room for improvement. Identify your weakest areas, then refer to the chapters in this section where you will find practical advice and tips to help you establish and hone those skills.

32–64: Learn to use your time efficiently, then reduce the time you spend working in unproductive and labor-intensive ways.

65–95: You have reasonable time-management skills, but they could improve.

96–128: You use your time very efficiently, keep looking for new ways to further streamline your work practices.

17 I skim internal memos as soon as I receive them.   1 2 3 4

18 I read internal memos thoroughly later.   1 2 3 4

19 I keep the contents of my in-box to a manageable size.   1 2 3 4

20 I clear my desk of all paperwork.   1 2 3 4

21 I delegate tasks to colleagues that I could do myself.   1 2 3 4

22 I follow up on the work I have delegated.   1 2 3 4

23 I encourage subordinates to limit their reports to one side of paper.   1 2 3 4

24 I consider who needs to know the information I am circulating.   1 2 3 4

25 I achieve the right balance between thinking time and action time.   1 2 3 4

26 I make a list of things to do each day.   1 2 3 4

27 I keep work to a certain number of hours every day—and no more.   1 2 3 4

28 I make an effort to keep in touch personally with my staff.   1 2 3 4

29 I concentrate on the positive attributes of each of my colleagues.   1 2 3 4

30 I make sure I know about the latest information technology.   1 2 3 4

31 I store e-mail messages in order to read them later on screen.   1 2 3 4

32 I perform housekeeping checks on my computer files.   1 2 3 4

Source: From Essential Managers: Managing Change by Robert Heller (Dorling Kindersley 1998). Copyright (c) Dorling Kindersley Ltd., 1998. Text copyright (c) Robert Heller, 1998. Reprinted by permission of Penguin Group (UK).

- *Make appointments with yourself.* Schedule important tasks and *ignore interruptions* when you work on a project.

- *Just say no.* Otherwise you will take on more than you can accomplish. Ask yourself if the new task or responsibility is a better use of your time than what you're already doing.

- *Delegate.* You can't—and shouldn't—do it all yourself. Determine what you do best, and delegate everything else.

- *Set realistic time estimates.* Build in a cushion, because tasks usually take much more time than you expect. Keep track of how long you actually need for specific tasks, so the next time you can allocate an appropriate amount of time and won't get off schedule.

- *Build in time for yourself.* Your health and your productivity will suffer if you try to work 24/7. Breaks during your work day, whether a quick walk around the block or a trip to the gym, will keep you stay fresh. You also need time for family and personal interests, as well as planned vacations.

Your Weekly Plan

A weekly decision-making framework forms the basis of your time management plan.[2] Go back to your mission statement and goals and ask yourself, "What is the most important thing I could do in each role this week to have the greatest positive impact?" Then prepare a weekly schedule with daily to-do lists and time blocks—large, interchangeable chunks of time—for specific and important activities. Leave open time and be flexible. Crises will crop up, and you need time to deal with them. When you focus on your mission statement, roles, and key goals, you put the most important (Quadrant 2) goals first. Remember to *enter the most important tasks first.* Build your calendar around these activities, and *then* fit in the Quadrant 1 and 3 goals. Otherwise you will fritter away time on less important tasks.

Why take a weekly view, instead of going from your mission and goals to a daily view? When you focus on each day as a separate time unit, you tend to do what's most pressing and urgent—the crises become the priorities. This approach doesn't help you reach your goals. The weekly perspective allows you to connect the big picture to your daily activities and achieve a better balance in your life. It retains some immediacy but also places the activities in a larger context so that you do not lose sight of future goals.[3]

Many companies offer time management systems and diaries. Investigate several options to find the one that best serves your needs and style: a simple or a complete system; a page-a-day format or week-at-a-time; a personal digital assistant (PDA); or personal information manager (PIM) software. A $300 PDA is worthless if you haven't updated it for three weeks. Technophobes may find a more traditional paper-based planner easier to maintain. If you enjoy using the latest technology, the PDA is a good way to go. Exhibit A.2 lists several good time management resources.

exhibit
A.2

Time Management Resources

You'll find many good time management resources at your local bookstore. Here are a few websites and books to get you started.

- Day-Timer: http://www.daytimer.com. The Library page of this time management product company has a good selection of time management articles, productivity tips, and other time-related information.

- Franklin Covey: http://www.franklincovey.com. Another leading time management services company, it offers articles, learning tools, courses, and other time management resources.

- "Managing Time" in Robert Heller and Tim Hindle, *Essential Manager's Manual* (New York: DK Publishing, Inc., 1998), pp. 82–149: A comprehensive time management reference, including analyzing time and work patterns, using time planners, and practical tips to be more efficient in all aspects of your life.

- Stephen R. Covey, A. Roger Merrill, and Rebecca R. Merrill, *First Things First* (New York: Simon & Schuster, 1995).

Revisit your weekly schedule each day and update it as you complete tasks and begin new ones. You may want to review a day's activities at the end of the day, or first thing in the morning. Either way, identifying the Quadrant 1 and 2 activities will reinforce your priorities. Then assess your progress at the end of the week and update your progress toward reaching your goals. You may not achieve all your goals by the end of the week, but you will learn from the process where you went off course and can make changes.

The A List

As you prepare your weekly plan, you create your daily to-do lists, the five to ten items you want to accomplish during a particular day. Be realistic about what you can do in a day. Then assign each task a priority using the system you chose when grouping your tasks in your time log, and write this priority on the weekly plan. You may want to create a daily schedule that lists the highest priority tasks first. When assigning priorities, evaluate the task's payoff in terms of meeting your goals. Don't try to do all the high priority tasks first and then move down the list. You will get more done by spreading the tasks out and giving yourself a break from the most demanding tasks.

You should also chart your daily energy levels. Schedule the highest priority and most difficult tasks when you are at your physical and mental best, whether it's first thing in the morning or late afternoon. Work on strategic projects during your first peak period. Not only does that put you in a positive frame of mind, but you will also have accomplished something significant and feel good about moving your life forward. Build in the flexibility to modify your priorities and schedule when the situation changes. For example, the presentation to a new client moves down the list when the meeting is rescheduled for next week instead of tomorrow. Exhibit A.3 offers more tips for better time management.

Your reaction to reading all these suggestions for organizing your time may be, "I'm too busy to do all this planning!" However, the feeling that you are too busy to be productive is a clear indication that it's time to set priorities.

exhibit
A.3

Tips to Organize Your Time

- Schedule thinking and quiet time each day, and make sure you aren't interrupted.

- Follow through on task completion.

- Use different colors for each priority category.

- Estimate how long a task will take and then compare it to the actual time required to develop better estimates in the future.

- Delegate more effectively by defining the task's objectives and setting realistic deadlines.

- Break large projects into smaller tasks.

- Schedule specific times to answer phone calls and emails—and stick to them!

- Do a little each day on big projects—it will add up over time.

- Have a list of tasks to do when time unexpectedly frees up.

- At the end of the day, prioritize and schedule tasks for tomorrow.

- Don't get bogged down in "administrivia," those routine-task time hogs.

- Reduce clutter. An organized work space, a good filing system, and regular attention to maintaining order go a long way in improving time management.

- Before calling a meeting, consider other ways to accomplish the business matters.

- Plan meetings carefully in terms of who needs to attend. Develop an agenda with a time allocated to each topic.

(continued)

Exhibit 11.3 (*continued*)

- Reduce shopping time: Keep a list, combine errands, order online, have things picked up or delivered whenever possible, even if is more expensive. Time is money!

- Reduce drive time. Have appointments at your office rather than away if possible. Schedule off-site meetings at the beginning or end of the day.

- Give yourself time for family and leisure activities.

End Notes

1. Adapted from Robert Heller and Tim Hindle, "Analyzing Use of Time," *Essential Manager's Manual* (New York: DK Publishing, Inc., 1998), pp. 88–91.

2. Lori Ioannou, "Stephen Covey on Time Management," *FSB (Fortune Small Business),* June 1, 2002, p. 73.

3. Stephen R. Covey, A. Roger Merrill, and Rebecca R. Merrill, *First Things First* (New York: Simon & Schuster, 1995), pp. 154–156.

Feasibility Studies

Feasibility Study Format Guidelines

The following outline provides a framework to prepare a feasibility study for your proposed business concept.

Cover Page

Identify the "title" (name of the business) of your feasibility study.

Identify the names of the team members involved in the feasibility study.

Contact information (mailing address, phone number, and e-mail address).

Executive Summary

This is a summary of the entire feasibility study.

A well-written Executive Summary is less than a page.

Table of Contents

1. Feasibility Decision
2. The Business Model
3. Industry/Market Analyses
4. Product/Service Development Plan
5. Management Team and Organization
6. Financial Plan
7. Timeline to Launch/Implementation Risk
8. Sources of Information and Appendixes

Feasibility Decision

Briefly describe the business you are considering.

Describe the conditions under which you are willing to go forward.

Briefly describe the major risks (customers, benefits, channel, and implementation) that are involved and how these risks might be overcome (or not).

Indicate a YES or a NO about your decision to pursue your feasibility project in the future and what major contingencies influence this decision.

The Business Model

What is the business?

Describe the value proposition of the business: the specific benefits/features that you will offer through specific channels to specific customers.

Describe your customers in detail.

Why were these customers chosen versus others?

What are the revenue sources from these customers?

Describe the benefits provided to your customers in detail.

Why were these benefits chosen versus others?

What are the cost drivers for providing these benefits?

Describe the distribution channel in detail.

Why was this channel (or channels) chosen versus others?

What are the cost drivers for using these channels?

How will this business make money?

Briefly provide an overview of investment size (maximum financing needs, and when there will be positive cash flow and cash breakeven)

What are the critical success factors for this business?

Describe, in detail, the major risks in this business and how you plan to address them. Point to other sections of the feasibility study where these risks are identified and dealt with.

Industry/Market Analyses

Describe the industry/competition.

What are the business models that exist in the industry you will be competing in? (Identify business models of specific rivals.)

What are the business models of the substitutes of your business?

If there are no businesses similar to your business, then provide business models of businesses that would be analogous to your business model.

Identify how and why each of these businesses makes money.

Provide a competitive grid highlighting key success attributes and weaknesses among all players (rivals and substitutes).

Describe the market and customers.

What are the various types of customers in this industry?

Provide a customer profile.

Why were these customers chosen versus others?

Provide a customer grid highlighting the key attributes of each of the customer segments.

Describe the distribution channels.

Describe the value chains of competitors, substitutes, and analogues.

Identify specific costs and revenues at each point in the value chain.

Show your value chain and compare and contrast this value chain to the others.

Initial sales plan.

How will the first customers buy your product/service?

Provide a timeline for the selling cycle.

When will cash from your first customers be received?

Product/Service Development Plan

Describe the features of your product/service that meet the benefits provided to your customers.

What is the current status of product/service development?

Identify the specific tasks that will need to be accomplished (and when) in order for your product/service to be ready for sale.

Provide a specific timeline of critical events in product/service development (identify specific resources, people involved, and activities).

Management Team and Organization

Who will be involved in this business and why?

What are the qualifications of the founding team members and how do their skills and abilities match the needs of the business?

What are the critical skills and abilities needed to start and run the proposed business?

Who has these critical skills and abilities on the founding team?

If the founding team does not have these critical skills and abilities, how will other people be involved (employees, professional advisors, board of directors, and independent contracts)?

Financial Plan

What are the key assumptions (based on information provided in other sections of the plan) for how and why this business will make money?

What kinds of resources will be needed for this business (and when will they be needed)?

Provide a pro-forma income statement (one to three years).

Identify critical financial categories of the business only.

Provide footnotes for each financial category and identify the assumptions used to develop the figures in the financial estimates.

Provide a break-even analysis.

When will the business reach positive cash flow?

How much income will this business likely provide (and when) and is this level of income sufficient for the time and resources involved?

Timeline to Launch/Implementation Risk

What needs to be accomplished (and when) in order to get the business up and running?

What tasks incur the most risk of not getting accomplished and how will these risks be managed?

Sources of Information and Appendixes

Provide endnotes and a bibliography of the sources of the information used to support your idea.

Provide support for the earlier sections of the feasibility study (resumes, market surveys, questionnaires, customer lists, quotes, and bids for critical services or equipment needed).

Business Plans

Business Plan Outline

Cover Page

1. Your name
2. Company name
3. Address
4. Phone number
5. Month and year plan issued
6. Copy number
7. Statement of plan's confidentiality

Executive Summary

A one- to two-page summary of the Business Plan. It should provide an overview of the entire business plan and describe the plan's highlights and significant details. Most readers will only read the Executive Summary. A good Executive Summary should be able to serve as a stand-alone document. It should be short, but comprehensive and thorough.

Table of Contents

1. Business Description
2. Market Analysis/Marketing Strategy
3. Management and Organization
4. Operations
5. Execution Plan
6. Financial Plan
7. Appendix (supporting documents)

Business Description

1. Describe the kind of business you are in.
2. Explain the goals and objectives of this business.

3. Describe your products/services in detail (customer need fulfilled, unique features, and industry perception).
4. Discuss competitive products/services on the market (compare quality and features, why customers buy, pricing strategies).
5. Provide a chart that compares your product lines, product categories, and services to other product lines, product categories, and services offered by competitors by price and benefits. Describe the benefits in detail. For example:

Product	Price	Benefit A	Benefit B	Benefit C
Your Product	$$$	Details	Details	Details
Product X	$$	Details	Details	Details
Product Y	$$$$	Details	Details	Details

Service	Price	Benefit A	Benefit B	Benefit C
Your Service	$$$	Details	Details	Details
Service X	$$	Details	Details	Details
Service Y	$$$$	Details	Details	Details

6. Indicate the business' mix of products/services by percent of sales.
7. Summarize the expected costs and profits for product line, product category, and service.
8. Assess the life cycle of each product line, product category, and service.

Market Analysis/Marketing Strategy

1. Describe current and potential types of customers: (a) Who are they (location and demographics)? (b) Why will they purchase? (c) What is their sensitivity to price, quality, service, and features?
2. Describe your market: (a) size, (b) state of growth, (c) history, (d) forecast for future, (e) trends.
3. Describe your competition (list major participants by critical success factors—CSFs).
   a. Provide a chart that compares your company to your competitors. For example:

Company	CSF1	CSF2	CSF3
Your company	Details	Details	Details
Competitor A	Details	Details	Details
Competitor B	Details	Details	Details

b. Discuss the chart and point out strengths and weaknesses of your company and that of your competitors.

c. Describe the barriers to entry and growth in this industry.

d. How will changes in the economy affect the industry?

e. What is the role of innovation and change?

f. What roles does government regulation play?

4. Describe sales goals and their rationale.

a. How will you identify, target, and attract customers?

b. For advertising and promotion, where (media selection) will you spend your dollars? How much will you spend? How often will you spend? What is your message? How will you measure the results?

c. What are your pricing options (price, terms, credit policy, service and warranty policies)?

d. Who will sell the product and what kind of training is needed to enable them to be effective?

e. What is your merchandising strategy?

f. Is there "congruence" among your advertising and promotion strategy, pricing options, selling strategy, and merchandising strategy?

Management and Organization

1. What are the key skills required for this business to succeed?

2. Who are the key managers (and employees) who have these key skills and what are their backgrounds? (Provide resumes in the Appendix.)

3. If you don't have all the key personnel, how will you attract them?

4. What other experts and advisors are important to the company?

Operations

1. How will the business sell its product and deliver its service? (Describe how the sales and service functions are undertaken, the personnel needed to accomplish these tasks and the training necessary for each role.)

2. What kinds of training for sales and service personnel are necessary to attract and retain customers?

3. Describe critical elements, likely bottlenecks, quality, supply, sales, service, delivery, inventory, and cash flow issues.

4. Identify necessary resources and equipment likely to be required.

5. Identify the systems (e.g., sales management, inventory control) necessary to operate the business.

Execution Plan

1. Provide a timeline of important activities that were identified in other parts of the plan. The timeline will show that your activities are internally consistent and coordinated with the financial projections.

Financial Plan

1. Present any past financial statements for the past two to five years.

2. Present prospective financial information for the next two to five years: Income statements, balance sheets, and cash flow statements. Prepare statements showing monthly figures for the first year and quarterly for years two to five.

3. For all financial statements, provide key assumptions, such as your goals for profits and sales. The best way to do this is to footnote all items.

4. Link your financial statements to key industry ratios and standards.

5. Identify your financing needs.

Appendix (Supporting Documents)

1. Include resumes of the management team.

2. Provide documentation for assumptions you make in the body of the plan.

a. market analysis data and market research studies

b. action plans for sales and distribution

c. product specifications and photos

d. action plans for production, operations, and service

e. letters of reference

f. census and demographic data

g. contracts

h. letters of commitment from customers, suppliers, and lenders

i. buy/sell agreements among partners

Before You Purchase a Franchise

A Pre-Purchase Checklist

The following questions provide a useful outline when performing due diligence on a potential business purchase.

The Economy

- What are current national, regional, and local economic trends? If interest rates are rising, for example, this may decrease sales for businesses dependent on customers getting loans such as automobiles and houses.

- What are local and regional economic trends? If your business is dependent on local sales, is the area that your business is in an area that is growing? Are industries in your area poised to grow, or are they declining?

Industry Characteristics

- Channels of Distribution: Are the ways that customers buy products/services in your industry changing? Is the business you plan to buy likely to be competitive in those channels?

- Technology: Are the products/services in your industry changing? Are the ways that these products or services are created rapidly changing? How is the business's technology (both products/services and ability to create) up to date?

- Competition: How is competition changing in your industry? Can new businesses enter into the same industry as your business?

- Regulations: Many businesses need specific licenses to operate. Is your business in compliance? For example, if you are planning on purchasing a bakery, the bakery is likely to need a health permit as well as zoning approvals for the bakery's location. Are these current? Many localities limit the number of liquor permits in their area, so, if you were planning on buying a restaurant in that locality, will the liquor permit be transferable to you? Also, there may be upcoming regulatory changes that may affect the business. For example, you may be considering purchasing a business that restores automobiles. As part of the process, you'll need to spray-paint them. Many localities regulate the use of spray paints. You may find that you will need to install special hoods and filters to capture the paint fumes. The current business might be "grandfathered" into past regulations about spray painting, but, in a transfer of business ownership, you may need to meet new current regulations.

- Products/Services: Are the products or services offered by the business current and competitive? Are competitors likely to offer products/services that are better, faster, and cheaper?

- Intellectual Property: Does the business depend on patents, copyrights, and trademarks for its success? Are these intellectual property rights up to date and defensible?

- Service and Warranty Obligations: What kinds of liabilities might the business incur from sales of products/services that may still be under a service or warranty obligation? If you purchase a business that sold a defective part in the past, you may be obligated to replace all of these defective parts in the future.

Suppliers

- Contracts: Does the business have contracts with suppliers for the purchase of goods or services? These contracts may be a benefit or a liability. You might be required to purchase goods or services from a supplier at prices higher than what you could purchase these products for on the open market.

- Exclusivity: The business you are looking at may have exclusive relationships with certain suppliers. For example, you may be looking at an outdoor kayaking store that sells lines of kayaks that no other stores can sell in your state. Will this exclusive relationship continue if you purchase the store?

Customers

- Continuity: Will the business's current customers continue to purchase products/services from you?

- Growth: Can the number of customers be expanded for your products/services?

- Purchase Criteria: Will customers purchase your enterprise's current products/services given their quality, price, and performance characteristics?

Management and Employees

- Key Employees: Are there certain employees that have critical knowledge about customers, service, product development, and manufacturing? Will these employees continue with the business if it is purchased? If not, do these employees have noncompete agreements? How will this knowledge be transferred to other people in your organization?

- Compensation: Is compensation too high or too low for current employees?

- Number: Is the business overstaffed or understaffed?

- Climate: Are employees happy? Are there conflicts and fighting among them? Do employees work together well? Have many employees recently left the organization?

Plant and Equipment

- Condition: Do buildings and equipment need repair or updating?

- Utilities: Are utilities adequate to operate the business?

- Size: Are plant and equipment large enough to handle any growth the business may have?

- Leases: How long is the business obligated to stay at a particular place? What happens to the lease if the business is purchased? Will the lease expire, or will the rental price rise?

Ownership

- Many businesses are owned by more than one individual. Will you be purchasing the ownership of all of the partners of the business? Will some of the owners be unwilling to sell their shares or percentage of the partnership to you? Will you be purchasing a majority interest in the business or minority interest? If you have a majority interest, you will have more control over making decisions about the business. But even with a majority interest, you will need to take into consideration the interests of your minority partners and shareholders.

A

accounting The process of collecting, recording, reporting, and analyzing a firm's financial activities.

accounts receivable aging schedule A list that shows each customer, how much the customer owes, the current amount due, and the amount that is 30, 60, or more days past due.

accrual accounting Accounting method that recognizes revenues at the time they are earned and liabilities when they are incurred, even though no cash may have changed hands.

accrued expenses Expenses that will come due within a year but for which the firm has not yet been billed, such as wages and taxes.

administrative agencies Organizations created by all levels of government to develop, implement, and enforce regulations pertinent to a specialized area.

advertising Paid communications that your enterprise invests in, typically through such media as newspaper, TV, and radio advertisements; billboards; direct mail; Internet ads; and posters and product displays.

affiliation or conversion franchising A business format franchise in which an operating business becomes part of a franchise system to take advantage of the brand but has more flexibility with regard to operating format. The unit name may reflect both the franchisor and the local entity.

agency Situation where one party, the agent, agrees to represent and act on behalf of another party, the principal.

agent Professional sales representative for manufacturers and wholesalers but does not take title to goods.

alternative dispute resolution (ADR) Nonjudicial method of resolving disputes.

angel investor A wealthy individual who provides funds for business start-ups.

arbitration Out-of-court method of dispute resolution whereby an impartial third party (the arbitrator or arbitration panel) hears the evidence and makes a ruling.

archetype A model or prototype from which similar things can be made.

area development franchise Rights to open and operate a specific number of franchises within a particular geographic region.

asset-based lender Finance company that lends to businesses based on value of collateral such as accounts receivable, inventory, or other company assets.

asset-based valuation Determination of a business's value based on the company's assets.

assets Items of value an enterprise owns.

asset turnover The ratio of sales to total assets; indicates how well management uses the firm's assets to produce sales.

average collection period The ratio of accounts receivable to average sales per day; provides insight into the average time needed to turn a firm's accounts receivable into cash.

average payment period The ratio of accounts payable to average purchases per day, showing the average amount of time needed to pay a firm's accounts payable.

B

balance sheet Financial statement that shows what the enterprise owns and owes at a specific moment in time.

bankruptcy Situation where an individual or business cannot meet financial obligations and seeks legal protection to repay or restructure debts.

BATNA (best alternative to a negotiated agreement) What each party will do if the negotiation process fails to reach an acceptable agreement.

board of directors A group of people elected by the stockholders to handle the overall management of a corporation, such as setting corporate goals and policies, hiring corporate officers, and overseeing the firm's operations and finances.

bootstrapping The use of modest amounts of personal funds to start companies.

brand The enterprise's identity; how customers, suppliers, investors, and other stakeholders perceive the enterprise.

brand imagery How a brand meets a customer's psychological and social needs.

brand performance How a brand meets a customer's functional needs.

breach of contract When one party does not perform as required under the contract terms.

break-even point The price level where your costs equal your revenues.

bricolage Using whatever materials are available to create something.

broker Intermediary that facilitates exchanges of goods by bringing together buyers and sellers, but does not take title to goods.

business An organization that is started and operated for the purposes of its owners.

business ethics Application of moral standards and values to business situations.

business format franchise A type of franchise where the franchisee purchases a product and a complete system to operate the business.

business incubator Organization that provides support services and a wide range of resources, from physical space to management advice, to emerging companies.

business law Regulations that provide a standardized environment to conduct commercial dealings.

business model A plan that shows how all of the different major aspects of a business work together to generate a profit.

business plan A written plan for a business that documents an enterpriser's past, present, and future actions and helps identify the right actions for success. Shows where you are going and where you have been.

buyer cooperatives Consumer-owned or business cooperatives that combine members' purchasing power to buy goods or services in volume, at lower prices.

C

cash basis accounting Accounting method that recognizes revenues and expenses when cash is actually received or paid out.

cash flow Cash generated by the business after subtracting taxes and adding back noncash expenses such as depreciation.

C corporation A conventional or basic corporate form of organization.

cognition Thought process that reveals what and how you think, significantly influencing what you are likely to do.

cognitive characteristics Intellectual rather than physical traits—the ability to think, learn, and remember. Examples include comprehension, reasoning, perception, decision making, planning, and learning.

commitment The enterpriser's dedication to the idea and willingness to implement it.

common-size income statement An income statement that shows each expense category as a percentage of sales rather than as a dollar figure.

community A collection of related industries.

compensatory damages Monetary award to repay the victim for actual loss and suffering.

connection How enterprisers will identify and reach specific customers.

consideration The exchange of something of value; must be present to have a valid contract.

consumerism A social movement that emphasizes strengthening buyer rights and powers with regard to sellers.

contract A legally enforceable agreement between two or more parties with regard to the performance of a specific action.

cooperatives Legal entities typically formed by people with similar interests, such as customers or suppliers, to reduce costs and gain economic power. A cooperative has limited liability, an unlimited life span, an elected board of directors, and an administrative staff; all profits are distributed to the member-owners in proportion to their contributions.

copyright Gives the creator of an original work the exclusive rights to publish, perform, copy, or sell the work.

corporation A legal entity with an existence and life separate from its owners who are not personally liable for the entity's debts. A corporation is chartered by the state in which it is formed and can own

property, enter into contracts, sue and be sued, and engage in business operations under the terms of its charter.

cost of goods sold The total direct costs of buying or producing a firm's goods or services.

critical path The activities required to complete a project and the order in which they must be completed to keep a project on track.

critical success factors (CSFs) Operational functions or competencies that a company requires to be profitable.

current assets Assets that can or will be converted to cash within the next 12 months.

current liabilities Obligations of the enterprise that are due within a year of the date of the balance sheet.

current ratio The ratio of current assets to current liabilities; provides a measure of the enterprise's liquidity.

customer management system (CMS) Building and maintaining relationships with your customers over time.

customer relationship management (CRM) Enterprise-wide strategy for interacting with customers and managing the relationships for optimal profitability and customer satisfaction.

customers Those who buy an enterpriser's goods or services.

D

debt ratio The ratio of total liabilities to total assets, which measures the percentage of the enterprise's assets financed by debt.

debt-to-equity ratio The ratio of total liabilities to stockholders' equity, which provides an evaluation of how leveraged the enterprise is.

deed Written document that transfers ownership of real property from one party to another.

default The risk that a borrower will fail to repay a loan.

demand The quantity of a good or service the customers will buy at different prices.

demand curve Graph that shows the relationship between how much of a good or service that people will buy at various prices.

depreciation The allocation of an asset's original cost to the years in which it is expected to produce revenues.

discharge The legal elimination of debt in a bankruptcy case.

discount rate A rate that represents the buyer's expected cost of capital (the interest rate for a loan to buy the company), as well as the desired return on investment and an adjustment for inflation.

discounted cash flow (DCF) Valuation technique that finds the present value of a future cash flow stream at a specified discount rate.

disposition A set of personality characteristics that generally remains stable in nearly all situations, such as a person's temperament, character, or personality.

dispositional characteristics A person's natural or acquired habits or characteristic tendencies.

distribution (or marketing) channel Network of intermediary organizations that work together to facilitate the movement of goods from producer to end user.

due diligence The process of thoroughly investigating all parties who will be involved in your business, including investors, partners, potential employees, customers, and suppliers.

E

earn-out Payment strategy that gives the seller of a business a certain amount of the future earnings of the business over a specified time period.

elasticity of demand Responsiveness of quantity demanded to a price change.

emergence The first stage of a business's life cycle: New venture formation.

employee A worker who falls under the control of the hiring party with regard to the work that person does and how it is done.

employee stock ownership plan (ESOP) A tax-qualified employee benefit plan that invests primarily in stock of the sponsoring employer.

enterpriser An individual who engages in activities to initiate and then direct an organization to serve his or her purposes.

entrepreneur An individual involved in the start-up of a business.

environment The entire context of activities that surrounds the operation of a business.

ethics A set of moral standards and values that helps individuals choose between right and wrong.

exempt employee An employee who receives a fixed salary per time interval, regardless of hours worked.

express warranties Indications by the seller that the buyer can interpret as fact, such as descriptions of an item, promises of quality and performance, or samples of products; written warranties must indicate whether they are full or limited.

F

factor Financial institution that buys a business's accounts receivable at a discount.

fair market value The price that a business would command from a knowledgeable buyer and a seller with the relevant information about the business and willingness to undertake the transaction.

feasibility Process of revising the business concept to test whether a business is worth pursuing and under which conditions.

fixed assets Long-term assets used by a firm for more than a year such as land, buildings, and equipment.

fixed costs Costs that do not vary with sales volume, such as rent.

franchise The rights to offer specific products or services under explicit guidelines at a certain location for a declared period of time.

franchise license agreement The principal legal document that defines the terms of the relationship between the franchisor and franchisee, including the license to use the franchisor's brand for a specified time period, payment terms, and operating restrictions.

franchisee The individual or company that owns one or more franchises and sells goods or services in accordance with the terms set by the *franchisor*.

franchising A form of business ownership involving a contractual arrangement where a parent business (the *franchisor*) provides an investor (the *franchisee*) with the rights to sell products or services in exchange for fees and/or royalty payments.

franchisor Parent company that owns and controls the rights to offer the franchise's product concept to the *franchisee*.

G

general partnership All individuals share in the profits and the management responsibilities of the business, as well as any liabilities that the business might generate.

gross profit The amount a company earns after paying to produce or buy its products but before deducting operating expenses.

gross sales The total dollar amount of a company's sales.

H

highly reliable organizations (HROs) Organizations that have fewer failures and make fewer mistakes.

I

implied warranties Unwritten warranties specified by law that grant certain protections to the buyer, including warranties of title, merchantability (merchandise will perform as advertised), and fitness for a particular purpose (the item will serve its intended purpose).

income statement Financial statement that summarizes the revenues generated, the costs associated with those revenues, and the profit or loss during a specific time period.

independent contractor A person who follows an independent trade, business, or profession and offers services to the public, such as lawyers, consultants, contractors, and subcontractors. The IRS considers someone an independent contractor if the hiring party controls only the result of the work and not how the contractor accomplishes the work.

industrial distributor Independent wholesaler that buys related product lines from many manufacturers to sell to industrial users.

industry A group of businesses producing similar products and services.

information asymmetry When one party in a business transaction has more information than others, creating an information advantage.

initial public offering (IPO) The sale of shares of stock to the public for the first time.

intellectual property Property arising from a person's creative activities.

intentional tort Deliberate action that could injure another party.

inventory turnover The ratio of cost of goods sold to average inventory; shows the number of times that the enterprise sells its inventory (turns its inventory over) during a certain time period.

J

joint venture An alliance between two or more companies to pursue a specific project for a specified time period.

judiciary Branch of government that interprets and applies the law to resolve disputes for individuals, enterprises, and government. It uses a multilevel court system to accomplish these objectives.

L

labor union An organization of workers formed to serve its members' collective interests with regard to wages and working conditions. Labor unions represent their members through the collective bargaining process that involves representatives from the employer and the union and also administer the negotiated agreements.

law A statute enacted and enforced to establish rules of conduct for a society.

lease Written agreement that temporarily transfers interest in real estate or other tangible assets to the user for a specified time period.

liabilities Financial obligations arising from past transactions or events; creditors' claims on a firm.

life cycle of enterprise The three stages of an enterprise's life: emergence, newness, and transformation.

limited liability company (LLC) A hybrid organization that offers the same liability protection as a corporation but may be taxed as either a partnership or a corporation.

limited partnership There are two types of partners: general partners, who share in profits, management responsibilities, and all liabilities; and limited partners, who do not share in the management of the business.

logistics A system to manage and coordinate the many steps of the supply chain to achieve an efficient materials flow and exchange of information across the channel.

long-term liabilities Obligations of the enterprise that come due more than one year after the date of the balance sheet.

M

market All possible customers who might want a particular product or service at a particular price.

market-based valuation Valuation method that looks at process paid for comparable firms. Industry valuation and multiplier formula valuations are two categories of market-based valuation.

marketing concept Identifying customer needs, producing goods or services to meet those needs, and making a profit while doing so.

marketing mix Unique combination of product, price, promotion, and place (distribution) strategies that results in value for customers.

master franchise (subfranchising) A three-party arrangement that grants a master franchisee rights to open franchises in a particular territory, along with the right to sell franchises to other unit franchisees.

mediation Less formal dispute resolution process that uses a neutral third party (the mediator) to help the parties negotiate a mutually agreeable solution.

metric Measure of a key performance characteristic.

mindfulness As defined by Ellen J. Langer, an awareness of the present moment that includes openness to new information and multiple perspectives.

motivation The desire to engage in a certain behavior to reach a goal.

N

nascent entrepreneurs Individuals who undertake the efforts necessary to initiate and start new businesses.

negligence Failure to use a reasonable amount of care to protect others from injury.

negotiation Back-and-forth communication process by which two parties try to reach a mutually acceptable solution to a problem or to accomplish something that neither party could do on its own.

net profit/loss The difference between the firm's revenues and its expenses.

net profit margin The ratio of net profit to net sales, which shows what portion of every sales dollar the firm has left after all costs and expenses.

net sales The amount left after deducting sales discounts and returns from gross sales.

network The total of a person's relationships and connections with other people.

networking The process of asking people you know (or could get to know through others) for information, advice, ideas, or help, as you plan and pursue your goals.

newness The stage in a business's life cycle that involves developing and managing a fledgling business so that it survives and flourishes.

noncompete agreement Agreement prohibiting the seller from entering into a similar kind of business for a set time period within the geographic area in which the purchased business competes.

nonexempt employee Employee paid on an hourly basis who is eligible for overtime for working more than 40 hours per week or on holidays.

nonrecurring costs Fixed costs that occur only once during the life of a business.

not-for-profit organization An organization that is exempt from most state and federal income taxes and has a purpose that will benefit others.

O

officers In a corporation, these individuals are hired by the board and responsible for achieving corporate goals and policies. They include top management such as the president and chief executive officer (CEO), vice-presidents, treasurer, and secretary.

operating expenses The expenses of running a business that are not directly related to producing or buying its products.

opportunity or business concept Favorable events involving customers, consideration, connection, and commitment (the 4 Cs) that have the potential to become a successful business.

optimist A person who believes that good things will happen.

organization An entity that involves people doing work for a purpose.

organizational behavior The study of people and how they act in organizations.

organizational imperative Concept that a business has its own needs and objectives separate from the needs and objectives of any of the business's other stakeholders.

P

partnership An association of two or more persons who agree to operate a business together for profit.

patent Exclusive right to make, use, or sell the product or process for 20 years from the date the patent application was filed.

personal property All property other than real property.

personal selling Ways that individuals can increase their ability to initiate and complete the process of buying and selling.

persuasion Deliberately seeking attitude change through communication—using your personal influence to get someone to do or believe something.

point of difference (POD) Something that uniquely characterizes your enterprise's brand.

points of parity (POP) Dimensions of your brand that are perceived as similar to other products/services of your competitors.

press release An announcement to the media about anything involving your enterprise.

product and trademark (or product distribution) franchise Franchise arrangement under which manufacturers grant franchisees, or dealers, the right to buy, sell, and advertise the products under the manufacturer's trademarked name.

product liability Concept which holds manufacturers and sellers responsible for injuries caused by defects in their products.

professional employer organization (PEO) An outside firm that, for a fee, becomes the legal employer of a company's employees and provides administrative services for payroll, taxes, insurance, retirement plans, and more.

Pro forma financial statements Financial statements that predict the future, rather than historical, financial condition and represent management's educated estimates of future financial performance.

profit The money left over after all expenses are paid.

promotion Communicating with others about your enterprise.

public relations Marketing and communications efforts to manage an enterprise's communications with the public.

punitive damages Monetary payments that greatly exceed actual losses; intended to punish the wrongdoer.

Q

quick ratio The ratio of current assets except inventory to total current liabilities; provides a more conservative liquidity measure because inventory is the least liquid current asset and may not be readily converted into cash.

R

ratio analysis Calculating and interpreting financial data from financial statements to evaluate a firm's condition and performance.

reach The percentage of people in your target markets who are exposed to your advertisement.

real property Land and anything permanently attached to it.

relationship marketing Building long-term relationships with your customers.

required return The rate of return that fully compensates lenders and investors for taking on the risk of a loan or equity investment.

retailer Company that sells goods to end users, both consumers and industrial users.

retained earnings The amounts left over from profitable operations since the firm's beginning; equal to total profits minus all dividends paid to stockholders.

return on assets (ROA) The ratio of net profit to total assets; measures how well the enterprise generates profits with its assets (invested capital).

return on equity (ROE) The ratio of net profit to equity; measures the return on investors' funds.

revenue The dollar amount of a firm's sales plus any other income it received from sources such as interest, dividends, and rents.

revenue model All the revenue streams a business will generate from sources such as subscriptions/memberships, volume- or unit-based pricing, advertising sales, licensing fees, and transaction fees.

risk A situation that causes concern and/or uncertainty and could therefore result in negative outcomes.

risk premium An additional rate of return that reflects the characteristics of the loan and the borrower and compensates lenders or investors for taking greater risk.

Rule 436 Federal Trade Commission regulation that governs disclosure requirements for the offer and sale of franchises in all 50 states.

S

sales promotion Activities such as public relations, advertising, and personal selling that increase the likelihood that people will purchase your enterprise's products/services.

S corporation A hybrid entity that is organized like a corporation, with stockholders, directors, and officers, but taxed like a partnership, with income and losses flowing through to the stockholders and taxed as their personal income.

seller (producer-owned) cooperatives Individual producers who join together to compete more effectively with large producers. Members jointly support market development, national advertising, and other business activities.

semi-variable costs Costs that change, but not in direct relationship to sales volume.

7(A) Loan Guaranty Program Primary SBA business loan program; provides loan guaranties for commercial loans to qualified small businesses.

seven intelligences The seven different types of intelligences that people may possess, as categorized by Howard Gardner: musical, bodily–kinesthetic, logical–mathematical, linguistic, spatial, interpersonal, and intrapersonal.

shareholders' equity The owners' investment in the business, plus any net earnings, or less any new losses the business generates.

signature strength A strength that you are more likely to use frequently, feel good about using, and want to use more often.

Small Business Innovation Research (SBIR) Program A federal government program that provides early-stage funding for technology research and development to help small firms commercialize their research.

small wins Achievable, tangible accomplishments that are within a person's capabilities and produce visible results.

social enterprise Enterprise created to solve a social problem or address a market failure, while operating in a financially sound manner.

sole-proprietorship A business that is established, owned, operated, and often financed by one person.

stakeholder An entity that has a legitimate interest in the processes and activities of a business.

statement of cash flows Financial statement that traces the firm's cash inflows and outflows over a specific time period, typically one year.

statutory law Law written by legislative bodies (the U.S. Congress, state legislatures, and local governments); incorporation and bankruptcy laws are examples of statutory laws.

stockholders The owners of a corporation who hold shares of stock that provide certain rights; also known as *shareholders*.

strategy of authenticity The idea that your enterprise is perceived as unique from other businesses.

strict liability Type of liability that holds a manufacturer or seller liable for any defects in a product, even if these parties have exercised reasonable care in designing, making, and selling the product.

structural holes Gaps in the connections among people, where opportunities for success occur.

subfranchisor A franchisee who contracts with a master franchisee to open a franchise within the same territory.

supply The amount of a good or service that a business will make available at different price levels.

supply chain The complete network of businesses involved in obtaining inputs, making goods, and delivering products to customers.

supply curve Graph that indicates at what prices suppliers are willing to offer products or services.

systematic innovation As defined by Peter Drucker, a purposeful and organized search for and analysis of changes and the opportunities these changes create.

T

target market A specific group of customers who are most likely to purchase a product or service and on which the enterprise focuses its marketing efforts.

times interest earned ratio (*interest coverage ratio*) The ratio of earnings before interest and taxes to interest expense; measures the enterprise's ability to pay the interest on its debts.

tort Civil (noncriminal) act that injures a person or property and does not arise from a breach of contract.

trademark Words, names, slogans, packaging, colors, or symbols that identify a company and its goods and services.

transformation The transitions a business goes through during its life cycle to adapt to changing circumstances.

U

Uniform Commercial Code (UCC) Set of business laws that provide a standard way for businesses to operate.

Uniform Franchise Disclosure Document (UFDD) Document prepared by franchisor for prospective franchisees that includes 23 sections that disclose background information.

unit franchise Agreement to open one unit in a particular location.

V

value chain The process by which a product or service moves from inputs to the final customer.

variable costs Costs that vary directly and proportionally with sales such as raw materials and shipping costs.

vendor financing Short-term trade credit extended to a firm by a supplier, usually for 30 days.

venture capital Early-stage private equity financing from professional investors who specialize in funding small companies with high growth potential.

venture capitalists Individuals or firms that provide venture capital financing.

W

wholesaler Distributor who buys finished goods from manufacturers and sells them to retailers, manufacturers, and institutions.

worker-owned cooperatives Employee-owned and controlled businesses.

Z

Z score A formula to predict bankruptcy based on five financial ratios.